MONTANA
HANDBOOK

MONTANA HANDBOOK

INCLUDING GLACIER NATIONAL PARK

FOURTH EDITION

W.C. MCRAE & JUDY JEWELL

MOON
TRAVEL
HANDBOOKS

MONTANA HANDBOOK
FOURTH EDITION

Published by
  Moon Publications, Inc.
  P.O. Box 3040
  Chico, California 95927-3040, USA

Printed by
  Colorcraft Ltd.

© Text and photographs copyright W.C. McRae, 1999.
  All rights reserved.

© Illustrations and maps copyright Moon Publications, Inc., 1999.
  All rights reserved.

  Some photos and illustrations are used by permission
  and are the property of the original copyright owners.

ISBN: 1-56691-142-7
ISSN: 1082-2654

Editor: Gregor Johnson Krause
Map Editor: Gina Wilson Birtcil
Production & Design: Rob Warner
Cartography: Brian Bardwell and Bob Race
Index: Sondra Nation

Front cover photo: bear grass blooms above Hidden Lake, by Jon Gnass,
courtesy of Jon Gnass Photo Images

All illustrations by Bob Race unless otherwise noted.

Distributed in the United States and Canada by Publishers Group West

Printed in China

Please send all comments,
corrections, additions,
amendments, and critiques to:

**MONTANA HANDBOOK
MOON TRAVEL HANDBOOKS
P.O. BOX 3040
CHICO, CA 95927-3040, USA
e-mail: travel@moon.com
www.moon.com**

Printing History
  1st edition—1992
  4th edition—April 1999

To our parents,
Frank and Betty,
Charley and Hazel

CONTENTS

MAPS

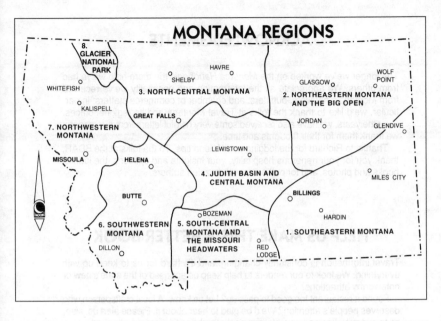

MONTANA REGIONS

8. GLACIER NATIONAL PARK

WHITEFISH

KALISPELL

7. NORTHWESTERN MONTANA

MISSOULA

SHELBY

HAVRE

3. NORTH-CENTRAL MONTANA

GREAT FALLS

GLASGOW

WOLF POINT

2. NORTHEASTERN MONTANA AND THE BIG OPEN

JORDAN

GLENDIVE

LEWISTOWN

HELENA

4. JUDITH BASIN AND CENTRAL MONTANA

MILES CITY

BUTTE

BOZEMAN

6. SOUTHWESTERN MONTANA

5. SOUTH-CENTRAL MONTANA AND THE MISSOURI HEADWATERS

DILLON

RED LODGE

BILLINGS

HARDIN

1. SOUTHEASTERN MONTANA

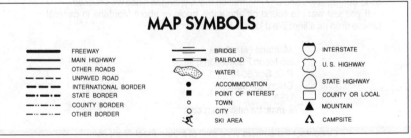

MAP SYMBOLS

FREEWAY
MAIN HIGHWAY
OTHER ROADS
UNPAVED ROAD
INTERNATIONAL BORDER
STATE BORDER
COUNTY BORDER
OTHER BORDER

BRIDGE
RAILROAD
WATER

ACCOMMODATION
POINT OF INTEREST
TOWN
CITY
SKI AREA

INTERSTATE
U. S. HIGHWAY
STATE HIGHWAY
COUNTY OR LOCAL
MOUNTAIN
CAMPSITE

ACKNOWLEDGMENTS

The longer we've worked on the *Montana Handbook,* the more help we've had from others. We appreciate all the information and hospitality we've received from Montana's hoteliers, outfitters, and chamber of commerce staffers. In particular, we'd like to thank the folks at Travel Montana and its regional offices. Over the years, we have also received some very helpful letters from our readers; we thank them for their thoughts and time.

Thanks to Richard for the lodging and Helena tips. To the folks at the BDAR, thank you for your generous hospitality, your insights and opinions, the loan of books and photos, and for putting up with frazzled authors.

HELP US MAKE THIS A BETTER BOOK

Travel information is constantly changing, and it's hard for us to keep up with everything. We look to our readers to help keep us apprised of the state's new or noteworthy attractions.

Found a restaurant too good to pass up? Let us know. A local craftsperson who deserves people's attention? We'd be glad to hear about it. Please alert us, also, as to our mistakes and any information that's changed since we checked.

If you just want to sound off about this book, or about Montana in general, please drop us a line. We'd love to hear from you.

> *Montana Handbook*
> c/o Moon Publications, Inc.
> P.O. Box 3040
> Chico, CA 95927
> USA
> e-mail: travel@moon.com

Or contact the authors via e-mail at mthandbook@aol.com.

Montana seems to me to be what a small boy would think Texas is like from hearing from Texans.

—JOHN STEINBECK

DOVER PUBLICATIONS, INC.

INTRODUCTION

Montana has been a traveler's destination for centuries. During summers, Indian hunting parties journeyed into Montana, returning to their mountain homes with stories of a rich, mysterious land full of buffalo and holy sites. Cattle drovers, following the seasons northward, summered in Montana and returned south with tales of abundant game, endless grasslands, and high adventure. Immigrant farmers and ranchers were drawn to the expanses of Montana, and brought the newcomer's conviction of fresh beginnings and wry aspirations. Nowadays, Montana attracts writers and artists who find in the state a "sense of place" both nurturing and hostile to the people who endure there.

Montana is often described as if it were two states—an eastern prairie and a western mountain range. But more than a common government links these regions. A visitor first notices the space: a sense of monumentality unites Montana, whether it's the glaciered peaks of the west or the corroded badlands of the east. It's called the Big Sky Country; out here nature limbers up, stretches past the horizons, takes up room.

But as much as space, it's the people that define Montana. Today's Montanans derive from many strains: immigrant farmer, sheepherder, Indian, miner, logger, shopkeeper, rancher. They were all people who came to a hard land and stayed, making from Montana a living only of sorts, but always a home. Montanans are self-reliant, quick to see humor, with personalities so expansive that so few really do fill the state.

History is not very old here. Montanans are still experiencing their past, not as western history, but as western ethic. In 1995, Montana eliminated the daytime speed limit as soon as the federal government allowed states to set their own speed laws. The old limit was observed only intermittently by the locals, who have miles to go before they shop, visit, feed, or do much of anything in this huge state. This guidebook, however, recommends that the traveler take it slow. Stop to investigate Montana's towns and cities, its streams and parks. Follow a hunch, dawdle along a side road: the land fairly explodes with small epiphanies of beauty. Take the long way around to a spot where a moment of history can be relived, where a lazy picnic can be shared, or where the obscure and the out of the way can be found for its own sake.

THE LAND

Montana's borders rope in just over 147,000 square miles, making it the fourth-largest state behind Alaska, Texas, and California. The northern edge of the state spans the Canadian province of Alberta and catches two-thirds of Saskatchewan and the eastern part of British Columbia to boot. North and South Dakota lie off to the east, Wyoming flanks much of the south, and the Idaho state line rims the Bitterroot Mountains at the western and southwestern borders.

Western Montana is where the state's name (from the Spanish word for mountainous) rings particularly true: steep pitches and narrow north-south valleys line up from the Idaho border to I-15. Central Montana is particularly varied, with high plateaus and isolated mountain ranges running in no set direction. The Continental Divide enters from Canada in Glacier National Park, twists through the western mountains, and exits on a high, flat stretch of land just west of Yellowstone Park. The eastern part of the state, renowned for its dryness, is coursed by the Missouri and the Yellowstone Rivers and a host of smaller valleys. Contorted badlands, eroded terraces, and steep rimrocks fringe river valleys and dot the plains. Minerals, coal, and oil are concealed throughout the state, giving rise to the nickname "Treasure State."

GEOLOGIC OVERVIEW

Over 570 million years ago, Precambrian sand and mud deposits blanketed the land that would become western Montana, before the supercontinent of Pangaea broke up into Europe, Africa, and the Americas. Traces of blue-green algae are the only fossils found in Precambrian-era rocks, which can still be seen in western and central Montana where later movements forced them to the surface. Glacier National Park is almost entirely Precambrian in origin.

Toward the end of the Mesozoic era, tectonic plates were scudding all over the earth. According to plate-tectonics theory, as the Atlantic Ocean widened, the North American Plate was shoved into the Pacific Ocean Plate, which slipped under

the western edge of the continent. The crust of western Montana crumpled, cracked, and faulted, then lifted way up above sea level. About 70 million years ago, the Rocky Mountains were produced by this upheaval.

Sedimentary layers were scrambled during these crustal movements, and in some places old rocks slipped on top of younger ones. This is especially apparent in Glacier National Park. When the Rockies lifted, layers of rocks skidded eastward from what are now the Flathead and North Fork Valleys, ending up as the Lewis Overthrust on the eastern front of the Rockies. Volcanic intrusions further developed the Rockies and formed separate mountain ranges to the east of them.

As western Montana lifted, ancient seas rolled back off the eastern part of the state for the final time. Swamps and floodplains stretched across eastern Montana by the end of the Mesozoic era. Many plants and animals lived on these sedimentary flats, and their remains, as oil, go into our gas tanks today. Peat swamps were prevalent; eventually they crumbled and rotted into thick veins of coal.

Volcanoes began erupting in present-day Yellowstone Park about 50 million years ago. A monumental eruption 600,000 years ago shot magma over the West, leaving a large crater, or caldera. Recurrent outpourings of lava formed the high plateau that's there now.

Alternating wet and dry periods over the past 40 million years modified terrain all over the state. During dry spells, river valleys filled with sediments, nearly burying many mountain peaks. When the climate dampened, rivers washed away the fill to re-expose underlying structures. This deposit-erosion cycle has made eastern Montana a paleontologist's dream. The largest complete tyrannosaurus skeleton on record was unearthed in remote Garfield County.

Cenozoic glaciers advanced south about 15,000 years ago. Valley glaciers ran down from northwestern Montana mountaintops and scoured out broad U-shaped valleys along their route. East of the divide, glaciers plowed the land flat as far south as the Missouri. The Beartooth Plateau, just north of Yellowstone

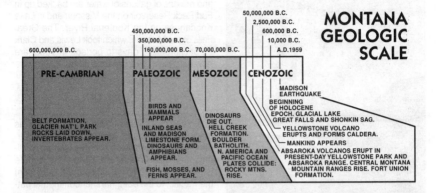

MONTANA GEOLOGIC SCALE

600,000,000 B.C. | 450,000,000 B.C. | 350,000,000 B.C. | 160,000,000 B.C. | 70,000,000 B.C. | 50,000,000 B.C. | 2,500,000 B.C. | 600,000 B.C. | 10,000 B.C. | A.D. 1959

PRE-CAMBRIAN | PALEOZOIC | MESOZOIC | CENOZOIC

BELT FORMATION. GLACIER NAT'L PARK ROCKS LAID DOWN, INVERTEBRATES APPEAR.

BIRDS AND MAMMALS APPEAR

INLAND SEAS AND MADISON LIMESTONE FORM. DINOSAURS AND AMPHIBIANS APPEAR.

FISH, MOSSES, AND FERNS APPEAR.

DINOSAURS DIE OUT. HELL CREEK FORMATION. BOULDER BATHOLITH. N. AMERICA AND PACIFIC OCEAN PLATES COLLIDE: ROCKY MTNS. RISE.

MADISON EARTHQUAKE
BEGINNING OF HOLOCENE EPOCH. GLACIAL LAKE GREAT FALLS AND SHONKIN SAG.
YELLOWSTONE VOLCANO ERUPTS AND FORMS CALDERA.
MANKIND APPEARS
ABSAROKA VOLCANOS ERUPT IN PRESENT-DAY YELLOWSTONE PARK AND ABSAROKA RANGE. CENTRAL MONTANA MOUNTAIN RANGES RISE. FORT UNION FORMATION.

Park, was glacier-covered at much the same time lava was flowing over it. An ice dam in Idaho backed up the Clark Fork River until most of the valleys in western Montana were covered by glacial Lake Missoula. When the ice dam gave way, which it did time and time again, torrents of water barreled across the Northwest, scouring topsoil and carving river gorges all the way to the Pacific coast.

East of the Rockies, glacial Lake Great Falls formed at the southern edge of the glacial sheet and reached from Great Falls to Cut Bank. Glacial ice forced the Missouri River, which originally emptied into Hudson's Bay, to alter its course southward to the Mississippi; the Milk River now flows in a section of the Missouri's original bed.

The Plains
Erosion and uplifts formed the prairie landscape. Water, frost, and wind have cut gullies and gulches into the plains and sculpted benches or terraces along river valleys. Northeastern Montana prairie is broad, flat, and underlain by gravel beds. These high plains were formed 3-15 million years ago in a dry climate. The gravel layer allows efficient surface drainage, avoiding erosion and the channels and gullies of the badlands. Glacial debris has further enriched the soil, making this some of the state's best agricultural land.

Montana's badlands, desolate and vegetation-poor, tend to be found south of the Missouri, where glaciers never deposited thick layers of good soil. Soft bedrock just beneath the surface of bare ground is easily eroded by rain; gullies

form, with sediment outwashes spreading from their mouths. The bare, rain-pounded soil develops a hard crust, which exacerbates the runoff and makes it all the more difficult for any vegetation to take hold. The barrenness of the badlands perpetuates itself.

The Mountains
The ranges of the Rockies have different geologic histories and compositions. The Boulder Batholith, a mass of intrusive granite between Butte and Helena, is filled with mineral veins, especially copper and silver. The Absarokas and the Gallatin Range are blanketed with volcanic rocks from eruptions in and around Yellowstone Park.

In the far northwestern part of the state, glaciers shrouded the mountains, leaving them relatively small and softly shaped. Where glaciers ran down from high cirques into mountain valleys, there is a characteristic straightening of the valley's path and a U-shape to its floor, unlike the V-shaped river valleys. Glaciers also pushed along gravel and soil; these moraines are still visible to the geologically savvy.

The isolated mountain ranges of central Montana are not part of the Rockies. Many of them were formed at the end of the Mesozoic era, about 20 million years after the Rockies rose, when molten granite shot up from the depths of the earth and bowed up the overlying sedimentary formations. Other areas of central Montana were lifted along faults to form high plateaus and buttes.

en route to Grinnell Glacier

JUDY JEWELL

Rivers

The Missouri and the Yellowstone Rivers look on the map like a big crab's pincer, joined to the leg just over the North Dakota border and grasping a big chunk of eastern Montana. Western rivers such as the Clark Fork of the Columbia, the Flathead, and the Kootenai are tucked into mountain valleys. Rivers provided the way into Montana for the first white explorers, who were hoping to sail out on the Columbia. Trappers and traders also used the rivers as thoroughfares. Steamboats made the difficult trip up the Missouri from St. Louis through sandbars, rapids, and fallen trees to Fort Benton—until railroads took over the transportation business. Towns sprang up in the river valleys, and highways were built on their banks.

The dams that now harness water power and create reservoirs across the state have altered Montana's geography. Every large river but the Yellowstone has been dammed at some point,

and millions of gallons of water are backed up in Fort Peck Reservoir on the Missouri and in Lake Koocanusa on the Kootenai River. The Great Falls of the Missouri, which took Lewis and Clark 22 backbreaking days to portage in 1805, are now a series of hydroelectric dams.

CLIMATE

There's as much variety in Montana's weather as there is in the state's topography. The Continental Divide splits Montana into two broad climatic regions. West of the Divide, the climate is influenced strongly by mild marine air from the Pacific; to the east, harsher continental patterns prevail.

Stories of extreme weather abound in Montana. Indeed, it can get *cold;* the lowest temperature in the lower 48 states was recorded at Rogers Pass, northwest of Helena, in 1954: -70° F. Hot summers are common, with temperatures of 117° recorded in both Glendive and Medicine Lake.

During the spring, the winds shift, and moisture comes up from the Gulf of Mexico. These storms sweep through the Midwest and hit the east slopes of the Rockies. May and June are the wettest months over most of the state; the exception is in the northwest, which gets most of its moisture from winter Pacific storms.

July and August are usually the warmest months. It does rain during the summer, but brief thunderstorms are the norm. By September, the weather may start to change for the colder and wetter, but there is frequently a lovely Indian summer in October. Winter storms can begin anytime, but roads are often clear through early November.

Chinooks

Warm, dry winter winds coming off the east slopes of the Rockies and across the plains are called "chinooks." As the Pacific air passes over the mountains, it unloads its moisture and is warmed on its eastern downslope run. Chinook winds carry an almost mythological force. They can bring incredibly rapid relief from frigid weather; in Great Falls, the temperature once rose from -32° to 15° in seven minutes, almost seven degrees a minute.

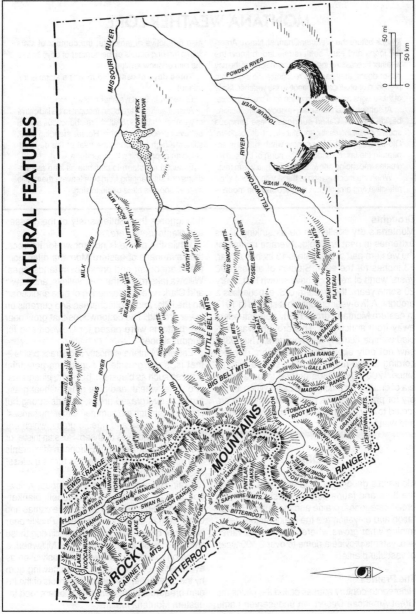

NATURAL FEATURES

© MOON PUBLICATIONS, INC.

MONTANA WEATHER LORE

Back before the Weather Channel, Native Americans and early settlers needed to know the weather forecast. As they spent the majority of the day out-of-doors, they came to recognize the signs that preceded or produced a change in the weather. Many of these signs are still a part of the rural prairie folklore.

At sunset, watch for small, rainbowlike reflections beside the sun. Called **sundogs**, these luminous spots indicate increasing moisture in the atmosphere. Old-timers predict rain or snow when sundogs appear. In the fall, a sundog to the north of the sun indicates impending snow; to the south, a warm rain.

When the moon is high in the sky, look for a wide reflective ring around it. A **ring around the moon** is also predictive of moisture; the number of stars within the ring equals of the number of days before the rain or snow arrives.

Three days of east wind means a storm is imminent.

Expect rain 90 days after a heavy fog.

Animal activities are often thought to be indicative of weather changes. Skittish, rambunctious animal behavior preceeds a storm. Horses standing stock still on a high hill during the heat of the day indicates an approaching thunderstorm.

Expect a rainstorm to continue as long as raindrops are still hanging from tree leaves; the rain is over as soon as birds begin to sing.

Droughts

Montana's dry spells can be as striking as its extremes in heat and cold. Average rainfall for the western part of the state is 18 inches a year, 13 inches for the east. Studies of almost 300 years' worth of tree rings have shown that, every 20-some years, the western U.S. experiences a drought. A five-year drought that started in 1917 in eastern Montana drove many homesteaders away from agriculture. This drought was coupled with particularly harsh winters. The 1930s saw not only economic depression, but (according to tree rings) the most severe drought since 1700. The 1980s proved to be another era of drought for much of the state. When it's too dry for prairie grasses to survive, ranchers are forced to buy expensive feed, or sell their herds and wait for rain.

FLORA

Montana's geography dictates its habitats, and the flora and fauna can be considered in two broad categories: prairie and mountain. Precipitation and elevation are the major factors determining what grows where. The state's varied ecosystems provide a home to over 2,400 types of vascular plants.

The Prairies

Nineteenth-century atlases called the plains the Great American Desert, an undeserved name that ignores the subtle variety of the grasses and plants found here.

While the prairie is not known for its trees, the savannahs of eastern Montana offer more than sagebrush and prickly pear landscapes. Willows take root in the river valleys, and Lewis and Clark noted a "scattering of pine and cedar" on the hills, and chokecherries and currants on lower ground. The cottonwoods that grow near riverbottoms were prized for firewood and for dugout canoes.

Eastern Montana is mostly shortgrass prairie—that is, a dry grassland supporting perennial grasses such as bluestem, bluejoint, bluegrama, and June, wheat, and pine grass. Cheat grass grows in overgrazed areas; it starts strong but can't last through the summer. Other "nuisances" are feather grass and needle grass, which irritate the skin and eyes of sheep. Russian thistle, or tumbleweed, arrived with European immigrants and is almost universally reviled for its uselessness and prolific nature.

Prairie flowers include the buttercup, yellowbell, crocus, shooting star, bluebell, blanketflower, golden aster, and daisy. Blue camas and death camas grow in moist areas. Prickly pear and three other species of cactus still dog those who try to walk across the prairie. Milkweed, a common roadside plant, was variously used as eye medicine, gravy stock, and chewing gum by the Cheyenne. The deep, thick roots of the Indian breadroot plant were an important food for eastern Montana Indians.

Chokecherry bushes are widespread on the northern plains and into the Rockies. Chokecherries were pounded, dried, and stored for the winter by Plains Indians. Indians also brewed a tea from the bark to relieve stomach ailments; unripe chokecherry puree was used by both Indians and white settlers to treat diarrhea.

Prairie sage is a traditional sacred and medicinal plant to many Montana Indians.

Coniferous Forests

Most of western Montana supports lush growth, dominated by coniferous forests. Though there are some western Montana prairies (especially around the Mission Valley and Dillon), timbered hillsides are the rule. This category is usually broken down into at least two separate habitats: lower montane and higher subalpine. The highest peaks of Montana also support small areas of alpine tundra.

Ponderosa pine predominates low on the slopes. A little higher, Douglas fir takes over and, above that, lodgepole pine (a species that depends on fire for its propagation) may form dense stands. Western larch, western red cedar, western white pine, grand fir, aspen, and birch can also be found. Willows and alders sprout up along streambeds, and kinnikinnick, Oregon grape, and serviceberries are common elements of the understory.

Subalpine forests are rooted in subalpine fir and Engelmann spruce. Huckleberries are the best-loved subalpine understory shrub. Alpine larch is another hardy, high-elevation conifer. An autumn hillside of reddish-gold "evergreens" doesn't necessarily mean a lot of dead trees. Rather, it's probably a stand of larch, one of the few conifer species that drops its needles in the winter.

Wildflower meadows of glacier lilies, alpine poppies, columbine, Indian paintbrush, asters, arnica, globeflowers, white dryads, and bear grass color the midsummer hillsides. Dogtooth violets and mariposa lilies grow a little farther down the slopes. In the valleys and low on the hills, the state flower, the bitterroot, blossoms in early June. Serviceberry bushes turn white with flowers early in May and bear pur-

plish berries late in July. This member of the rose family grows on the slopes and canyons of the Rocky Mountains.

Alpine Tundra

Alpine conditions exist in a few places in Montana. Above the timberline (9,000-10,000 feet) the gray-green ground cover includes small, low-lying vegetation: grasses, mosses, lichens, sedges, and krummholz (small, twisted trees pruned by the wind) of whitebark pine.

FAUNA

Montana's wildlife is varied and abundant. Lewis and Clark's journals, the first written account of the region's flora and fauna, are filled with wonder at the vast numbers of animals never encountered in the eastern states.

Today, Montana hosts some 107 species of mammals, 382 kinds of birds, 86 sorts of fish, 17 varieties each of reptiles and amphibians, and 315 different mollusks and crustaceans.

The Prairies

Lewis and Clark found the plains fairly swarming with wildlife, and not just with "musquetoes," either. Just upstream from the confluence of the Missouri and Yellowstone Rivers, Lewis noted:

The whole face of the country was covered with herds of Buffaloe, Elk & Antelopes; deer are also abundant, but keep themselves more concealed in the woodland. the buffaloe Elk and Antelope are so gentle that we pass near them while feeding, without appearing to excite any alarm among them; and when we attract their attention, they frequently approach us more nearly to discover what we are, and in some instances pursue us to a considerable distance apparently with that view.

blue grama

MIKE WELLINS

GETTING ALONG WITH MONTANA'S BEARS

When a bear's spotted in western Montana, there's always the question—grizzly or black? Grizzly bears are huge; adults commonly weigh 600-800 pounds and stand four feet tall at their muscular shoulder humps. A grizzly's dish-shaped profile contrasts with the black bear's straight Roman nose. Black bears are also smaller (about 200 pounds and about three feet tall) and lack a shoulder hump.

Color is not a reliable distinguishing trait—no shade of brown is unusual for either bear. Black bears can be honey-colored and are commonly cinnamon; grizzlies are not always silver-tipped and grizzled looking.

But perhaps the ability to tell bears apart is not the most important thing to know when confronted by any ursine specimen.

Safety Considerations

Find out where bears, especially grizzlies, live, and take precautions. In Montana, grizzlies live in Glacier and Yellowstone National Parks, and in wilderness areas throughout the Rockies. Rangers will usually know if bears have been spotted locally, and trails are sometimes closed due to bear activity.

Try not to surprise a bear. Stay alert and make some noise while hiking—many hikers wear bells. Keep strong odors down. Don't wear a fragrance; don't cook strong-smelling foods (freeze-dried foods are almost odor-free). At night,

keep food and smelly clothing inside a car or strung high in a tree. Sleep well away from the cooking area. Women are frequently cautioned to avoid bear country while menstruating.

If you do see a bear, give it plenty of room. Try to stay upwind of the bear so it can get your scent. If the bear becomes aggressive, drop something that may absorb its attention and climb the nearest tall tree. If this isn't possible, the next best bet is probably to curl up into a ball, clasp your hands behind your neck, and play dead, even if the bear begins to bat you around.

Bears can, and occasionally do, kill people, but most people who enter bear country never have any problem. In fact, it is a special thing to see a grizzly; they are as impressive as they are rare. Precautions and respect for bears will ensure not only your continued survival, but theirs as well.

grizzly bear, Ursus arctos

They also reported encounters with rattlesnakes, wolves, black bears, grizzlies, beaver (one of which gave Lewis's dog a nasty bite), bighorn sheep (whose meat was reportedly a delicacy), a "polecat" (skunk), mule deer, and prairie dogs. On their trip up the Missouri, Lewis provided the first descriptions of the sage grouse, the western meadowlark, and the cutthroat trout.

The buffalo, bears, and wolves may be gone from the prairies, but what Lewis called "our trio of pests"—mosquitoes, gnats, and prickly pear—remain.

Prairie life calls for adaptation, and many animals who live here dig burrows. Witness the **prairie dog.** It can metabolize its own waste

water and survive for years without drinking. The black-tailed prairie dogs of Montana live in "towns" of burrows, which are occasionally sublet by burrowing owls.

Another burrowing animal is the **pocket gopher,** a long-clawed, small-eyed rodent that comes aboveground only for quick passes at mating. Pocket gophers get their nutrition—both food and water—from plants they suck, roots first, into their burrows.

While burrows may provide defense for many rodents and birds, the **pronghorn** relies on fleetness. Individuals have been clocked at 70 mph. Their horn is part of a sheath composed of keratin (a fingernail-like protein) and fused hairs covering a core of bone. Pronghorns (which, despite the common appellation, are not antelopes) shed their horn sheaths annually and pass the winter and spring sporting the bare, bony horn core. They are the only mammals that shed horns (as opposed to antlers, which are, as a rule, dropped annually).

Deer, both white-tailed and the large-eared mule deer, roam the breaks of the big eastern Montana rivers. **Coyotes** still prey on both wild and stock animals.

Rattlesnakes can turn up just about anywhere in eastern Montana, and it pays to watch where you put your hands and feet. Wear sturdy shoes for hiking. Though healthy adults rarely die from a rattlesnake's venom, a bite does warrant prompt medical attention.

There's no dearth of **insect** life on the prairie. Most everyone who's read a Western novel can conjure an image of grasshoppers scouring the grasslands and swarming around cattle, cowboys, and horses.

Though magpies seem to control Montana's airways, the sharp-tailed grouse, mourning dove, killdeer, bobolink, long-billed curlew, horned lark, western meadowlark, goldfinch, Brewer's blackbird, and sparrow hawk are all **birds** to be spotted above the eastern Montana plains.

Warm-water species of fish, such as paddlefish, walleye, northern pike, and channel catfish inhabit the Yellowstone and the Missouri where they cross the plains.

Coniferous Forests

Both **black bears** and **grizzlies** live in and around western Montana's forests. **Elk** live high in the summer, low in the winter. They're sometimes called wapiti, and they grow their antlers fresh every summer and shed them in the winter. **Moose** are common but private. **Mule deer** negotiate rough forest terrain; **white-tailed deer** run across more open areas. Transition areas between two types of habitat (such as the edges of a meadow or clearcut) are usually good places to look for all sorts of wildlife. **Bighorn sheep, mountain goats,** and grizzly bears are all more likely to be seen high on the slopes of the Rockies.

Mountain lions have been showing up in some unlikely places, like the streets of Columbia Falls, the parks of Missoula, and the campgrounds of Glacier National Park. Big people can usually frighten them off with shouting and menacing gestures, but children and small adults have been attacked. Youngsters should hike within sight of adults.

Because of its predatory instincts, the **wolf** has been trapped, hunted, and poisoned to near-extinction. Since receiving protection as an endangered species, wolf populations have made a comeback, mostly near Glacier National Park and in the far reaches of northwestern Montana. Even before wolves were introduced to Yellowstone National Park, some seemed to have slipped in unescorted. The wolf's smaller relative, the **coyote,** has managed not only to survive the abuses given to predator species but to actually thrive in human-inhabited areas.

Birds such as dippers, Clark's nutcrackers, spruce grouse, owls, woodpeckers, jays, chickadees, wrens, sparrows, flycatchers, mountain bluebirds, western tanagers, warblers, rufous hummingbirds, waterfowl, bald eagles, ospreys, and hawks all find niches in the varied habitats provided by western Montana's forests.

Westslope cutthroat trout, the state fish, is native to Montana's streams and lakes. First described by Meriwether Lewis, its Latin name, *Salmo clarki,* remembers William Clark. The name cutthroat is just as revealing: these black-specked fish sport two red slashes under their jaws. Because of their tendency to hybridize with rainbow trout, cutthroat are becoming rarer.

Bull trout live mostly in northwestern Montana, especially in their native Clark Fork and Flathead drainages, though stream degradation from overlogging has severely damaged their habitat and

cutthroat trout,
Salmo clarki

reduced their numbers. They're olive green with orange or yellow spots on their sides, and can run up to 30 pounds.

Brown trout were imported from Europe in the 1880s and their numbers have now surpassed many native species. Browns have a reputation for being wily and tough to hook. Another introduced species, the **brook trout,** comes from the eastern United States. The backs of these fish have light-colored "worm tracks" on their otherwise dark olive backs.

Whitefish are silver-sided with olive-green backs and small mouths. They are usually five pounds or less and live in the western part of the state.

Arctic grayling are trout cousins; they're not common, but they can be caught in southwestern and south-central Montana. These small copper-colored or bluish fish are usually less than a foot long, with large dorsal fins.

Until recently, **kokanee salmon,** landlocked salmon with small dark spots on a blue-tinted body, thrived in Flathead Lake, where they'd been planted in the 1920s. Although changes in the lake's ecology have not favored the Flathead kokanee, they are still abundant in other parts of northwestern Montana.

Alpine Tundra

Plants and animals pack as much as possible into the short, cool summers of the high country. Hoary marmots, ground squirrels, pikas, and mountain goats are commonly spotted around Logan Pass, one of Glacier Park's alpine communities. The white-tailed ptarmigan is the only bird living year-round on the tundra, though other species, such as water pipits and finches, summer here.

ENVIRONMENTAL ISSUES

Timber

The timber industry has not stepped lightly in northwestern Montana in the past 15 years. In the 1980s the region's two timber giants, Plum Creek and Champion International, abandoned sustained-yield forestry and cut heavily for maximum immediate profit. Timber-industry officials and some congresspeople argue that such intensive logging is necessary to keep the regional economy afloat.

These huge clearcuts have affected water quality, wildlife habitats, and aesthetics. The Blackfoot River, site of Norman Maclean's *A River Runs Through It,* now disappoints anglers as silt dribbling down from clearcuts (and pollution from abandoned mines) has destroyed spawning grounds.

Northwestern Montana has been so seriously overcut that the Forest Service has scaled down logging operations on some of its land in an effort to mitigate the damage done nearby by private companies. These attempts to slow excessive logging were dealt a blow in 1991, when Regional Forester John Mumma, who was behind the Forest Service cutbacks, was transferred from the territory. Richard Manning, formerly a reporter for the *Missoulian* who was pulled from the environmental beat after too much investigative reporting, has written *Last Stand,* a book chronicling overcutting in the Swan Valley.

In 1993, when Champion pulled out of Montana, both environmentalists and timber workers decried the "cut and run" policies. Meanwhile, Plum Creek launched a media campaign touting its new, gentler forestry methods.

Mining

Even though copper mining has ceased in Butte, the Berkeley Pit remains a reservoir for toxic water, and the Butte/Anaconda area is the nation's largest Superfund site. (The Environmental Protection Agency's Superfund allows for cleanup of particularly toxic areas.)

In other parts of the state, current and proposed mining has environmentalists concerned, although the state's most notorious mining development has been quashed, and other mining projects seem to be collapsing under their own weight.

Noranda, a Canadian mining conglomerate, sought to mine gold in the high country of the Beartooth range just three miles outside of Yellowstone National Park. The New World Mine would have opened to mining a fragile, high-altitude site surrounded on three sides by wilderness areas straddling three Yellowstone River watersheds, including a creek that flows directly into the national park and another draining into the Clarks Fork of the Yellowstone. A 1996 agreement between Noranda and the Clinton

Administration turns over the lands once scheduled for mining to public ownership. In return, Noranda will receive $65 million in federal assets, of which approximately $22 million will be invested in reclaiming the site. The agreement stops the Canadian conglomerate Noranda from ever developing this area, ensuring that the threats this mine posed to water and wildlife will be eliminated.

In northern Montana's Little Rocky Mountains, the Pegasus gold mine in Landusky is closing. A similarly unhappy fate is befalling the coal generated electric plants near Colstrip, in southeastern Montana. These huge strip mines and coal-fired electrical generators were highly controversial when they were first proposed and implemented in the 1970s. Now, the original financial backers of the generators—major power brokers in the Pacific Northwest and Montana—are backing away from the generators, and it looks as if at least a couple of the four plants will close due to lack of interest.

Land Use

Land-use planning is a major environmental challenge facing Montana. Many of Montana's land use laws were written with few restrictions on the rights of landowners. In the days when family ranchers and famers controlled the majority of the private land in the state, and federal agencies controlled most everything else, these unrestrictive laws provided sufficient stability in land use.

In recent years the situation has changed drastically. The state is in the midst of a real-estate boom and out-of-staters are buying up agricultural land to build their trophy homes and vacation ranchettes. For Montana's famers and ranchers, the results of this land boom have been unsettling and sometimes disastrous; increasingly, the land boom has served to build

bridges between traditional agricultural and environmentalist interests, groups that have historically viewed each other with deep mistrust.

Farmers and ranchers have much to lose in the 1990s land boom. Most small ranches and farms are just breaking even, and small changes in the costs of running the family homestead can have a major impact. When local land values suddenly increase, property taxes correspondingly skyrocket. Also, when a neighboring ranch sells out to developers, dozens of new families move onto the north forty. Some of these new landowners use their mini-farm or ranch as a tax shield, laying claim to agricultural tax breaks designed for family farms and ranches. But while farmers and ranchers may decry the suburbanization of agricultural land and rural communities, they also fear zoning restrictions that would slash the market value of their land.

The Montana government has changed some state laws, making it more difficult for agricultural land to be subdivided. Formerly, a landowner could subdivide land into parcels as small as 20 acres without environmental or community review. Current law demands that any subdivision of fewer than 160 acres go through an environmental assessment.

Another tool that farmers, ranchers, and environmentalists have developed is the conservation easement. Easements are restrictions placed on the land title, which makes it impossible for current farm and ranch land to be developed for subdivision or other unauthorized non-agricultural usage. The conservation easement makes the land less valuable, which reduces the tax on it substantially. Crippling tax loads are therefore averted, and the state reimburses family farmers and ranchers in a one-time payment for the difference between the value of their land as speculative real estate, and as its value as agricultural land.

HISTORY

EARLY INHABITANTS AND EXPLORATION

The First Settlers

Proto-Indians first arrived in Montana from Asia about 10,000-15,000 years ago. After crossing the Bering Sea causeway, they traveled along the Great North Trail, the rift that opened up along the east face of the Rocky Mountains when the ice fields of the last ice age retreated into the mountains. These people hunted big game and used tools made of chipped stone. Between 8000 and 6000 B.C., these early Indians lived principally on the plains and foothills. Around 5000 B.C. a desert climate developed, and game animals and people left.

Buffalo again spread across the region as a more moderate climate developed about A.D. 500. The hunters returned, probably from the south and west, bringing with them new techniques and cultural practices. These early dwellers of Montana were probably the ancestors of the Salish Indians. Prior to the introduction of horses, hunting techniques such as using a buffalo jump, or *pishkun,* were developed. Entire herds of buffalo would be stampeded off precipices and then slaughtered for meat. The use of the tepee, or moveable skin tent, was introduced. Pictographs and petroglyphs, rock paintings and carvings, were first made during this period.

Historic Indian Tribes

When white traders and settlers arrived in the region in the early 1800s, they did not find a land peopled with indigenous native tribes. Instead, the Indians of Montana were themselves only recent immigrants, attempting to establish homelands and work out the cultural changes that their recent uprooting had set loose.

Some of the tribes that migrated to Montana during this period were not traditionally nomadic. Most came from woodlands in the Great Lakes–Mississippi basin region, where they were sedentary, sometimes agricultural people who lived in permanent earthen dwellings. During the process of dislocation to the West, agriculture was lost and a hunting culture developed. The earth lodge was abandoned for the tepee. For these people, the buffalo became more than a food source: it was the central assumption upon which their entire cultural life was predicated. Social organization was structured by warrior societies, and in some cases, by clan. Women were responsible for most of the daily work, save hunting and fighting. The Plains Indians shared an animistic religion.

The first tribe to enter Montana during the historic period was the Shoshone, who began to move into the southwestern corner of the state from the Great Basin area about 1600. They drove the resident Salish tribes (who had migrated from the Pacific Northwest several centuries earlier) farther north into the mountains. The Shoshone were fearsome warriors and the first Montana tribe to ride horses.

The Crow Indians arrived in Montana shortly thereafter and settled along the Yellowstone River drainages, the first tribe to actually settle on the Montana prairies. The Blackfeet entered Montana from the north and east about a century later, around 1730, and brought with them the rifle. The Blackfeet, and their allies the Gros Ventre and the Assiniboine, soon established dominance over the northern Montana plains.

Further pressure from white settlement forced the Sioux and Northern Cheyenne into eastern Montana. The Cree and Chippewa tribes entered Montana in the 1870s as they were displaced from the Canadian prairies. As more and more tribes were squeezed into the area that would later become Montana, intertribal rivalries intensified. The Crow were hated enemies of the Blackfeet. The Blackfeet slaughtered the Salish or Kootenai Indians who dared to leave the safety of the mountains. As the Sioux entered Montana, they too became enemies of the Crow.

The Salish and Kootenai retained some traditions of the Northwest Indian tribes. Although these tribes once traveled over the Rockies to hunt buffalo, the presence of the fierce Blackfeet confederation on the prairies soon made these hunting expeditions too dangerous.

The Corps of Discovery

In 1803 President Thomas Jefferson purchased the Louisiana Territory from France for $11,250,000. The territory was understood to be the land west of the Mississippi to its Missouri headwaters, and north of the Arkansas River to the 49th parallel. Jefferson engaged his personal secretary, Meriwether Lewis, to head an expedition to explore this new American territory, and to search for a passage from the Missouri River to the headwaters of the Columbia River. Lewis in turn chose William Clark to be the co-commander of what Jefferson called the Corps of Discovery.

The two captains, three sergeants, 23 enlisted men, and Clark's black slave, York, left St. Louis in May of 1804. In North Dakota, they were joined by French trader Toussaint Charbonneau. Charbonneau had traveled widely on the upper Missouri, and he spoke several Indian languages. One of his wives, a 15-year-old Shoshone girl named Sacajawea, gave birth during the spring. Lewis and Clark hired Charbonneau as interpreter and allowed the young mother and baby to accompany the Corps, as they later expected to travel through Shoshone territory.

The Corps entered Montana on April 26, 1805, passing the confluence of the Missouri and the Yellowstone rivers. They wound their way up the Missouri, traveling in pirogues, huge French Canadian dugout canoes.

By July 25, they were at the Three Forks of the Missouri and were heartened by Sacajawea's claim that they were near her homeland. Nineteen days later, near Lemhi Pass, Lewis encountered the expedition's first Montana Indian (a Shoshone, who led them to Sacajawea's brother). They beached their pirogues, traded for horses, and proceeded down the Bitterroot Valley. On September 13,

Meriwether Lewis

William Clark

they crossed Lolo Pass out of Montana toward the Pacific Coast.

After a hungry and flea-ridden winter on the Oregon coast, the Corps started back up the Columbia. They backtracked to Lolo Pass and crossed into Montana on June 27, 1806. On July 1, at the point where Lolo Creek meets the Bitterroot River, the expedition divided. Clark took part of the Corps and retraced the previous journey to the Missouri headwaters, but this time followed the Gallatin River over the Bozeman Pass in order to explore the Yellowstone River Valley. Lewis took the rest of the men and followed old Indian trails up the Blackfoot River and thence over the Rockies to the Great Falls in order to scout a more direct passage over the Continental Divide. While Clark had an uneventful journey down the Yellowstone, Lewis had a confrontation with a group of Blackfeet that left two Indian warriors dead.

The two parties met at the confluence of the Yellowstone and the Missouri on August 12. By September 23, 1806, they were in St. Louis. This amazing journey had an almost immediate effect on the history of Montana. Members of the Corps retold stories of vast amounts of wildlife, especially pelt-bearing mammals. Within a year, the first trading fort was built in Montana.

Trading Posts

The first fur-trading post, Fort Ramon, was founded in 1807 by Manuel Lisa, at the confluence of the Bighorn and Yellowstone Rivers, between present-day Billings and Miles City. Beaver, much sought after in European fashions, was the major item of trade. Some Indian tribes, notably the Salish and Crow, maintained friendly relations with the white traders and trappers. The Blackfeet, who controlled the Missouri River area, were hostile to the Salish, Crow, and whites.

John Jacob Astor's American Fur Company built Fort Union at the confluence of the Yellowstone and Missouri in 1829, and finally induced the Blackfeet to trade peacefully by dispatching a Blackfeet-speaking trapper to bring them to the fort for a conference. The Blackfeet complied. In 1838, 4,000 beaver pelts were taken from the heart of the dreaded Blackfeet territory by Astor's trappers.

Fort Union, and the American Fur Company, soon ruled the Montana fur trade. As beaver were increasingly trapped out (and European fashion changed), trade continued in buffalo hides. By 1840, the era of the trapper and mountain man was over; almost three dozen trading forts had been built in Montana before the beaver was trapped to near extinction.

The Black Robes

Iroquois Indians accompanied French trappers to western Montana in the early 1800s. While the Iroquois were to teach the local Flathead and Nez Perce how to trap, they also passed on information about Christianity. The Montana Indians heard of "Black Robes" who possessed a Book of Heaven, whose "medicine" or power was great. The Flathead were greatly intrigued and sent four delegations to St. Louis to ask for a Black Robe to come and visit the tribe.

Finally, in 1840, Father Pierre Jean deSmet, a Belgian-born Jesuit, came west. Although the Indians' spiritual demands had more to do with the search for powerful medicine to protect them from the hostile Blackfeet than with traditional salvation, the Flathead and Nez Perce seemed genuinely friendly and anxious to learn the way of the Catholic fathers.

In 1841, St. Mary's Mission was established in the Bitterroot Valley, near Stevensville. Here, the Jesuits taught the Indians agriculture, music, milling, and, of course, religion. The original mission was abandoned in 1850, after deSmet made the mistake of starting missionary work with the Blackfeet. The Flathead were not anxious to share their "medicine" with their enemies, and lost interest in deSmet's projects. Another influential early church, St. Ignatius Mission, was established in 1854 in the Mission Valley amongst the Pend d'Oreille Indians.

Little attempt was made to bring Christianity to the Plains Indians until they were on reserva-

tions. Most of the early missionary work was done by the Catholic Church. Protestant missionaries entered the state only after white settlement had begun, and gold ore and high living induced the kind of bad doings best corrected by regular churchgoing.

WHITE SETTLEMENT AND INDIAN WARS

Gold

The trappers and traders of the early part of the 19th century left little behind them, except endangered species. There were no roads, no communications networks, and almost no settlements (only Fort Benton still exists as a community).

James and Granville Stuart discovered gold on Gold Creek near Deer Lodge in 1860. In 1862, gold was found on Grasshopper Creek near Bannack, and the next year saw prospecting along Alder Gulch near Virginia City. Last Chance Gulch, which was to become Helena, boomed in 1864.

These large strikes, and many smaller mines, attracted people of varied character to Montana. There were fewer than 100 whites in the state in 1860. By 1870, there were over 20,000. Some men came to Montana to prospect for gold and get rich; others came to get rich by stealing and killing. Travel between the settlements of Virginia City, Bannack, and other mining camps became increasingly dangerous as "road agents" preyed on stagecoaches and miners.

For its protection, Virginia City elected as sheriff Henry Plummer. Plummer, however, doubled as leader of the principal gang of road agents, called the "Innocents." Over 100 people were killed by the Innocents during 1862-63. In response, committees of vigilantes formed, and after reaching summary judgment the Innocents were hanged.

By 1870, approximately $100 million in gold had been extracted from Montana claims. The advent of great wealth and property soon made firm government and community lawfulness imperative. In 1864, Montana became a territory, with Bannack its capital. Schools, churches, and other civic institutions were established in Virginia City. The miners began to bring their families out to the frontier to settle.

Treaties Made and Broken

While the Indians of the western mountains accommodated the arrival of white miners, trappers, and missionaries, the Plains Indians largely maintained their traditional ways during the first years of white ingress.

The first trail across the northern U.S. was the Oregon Trail. To protect travelers along its passage through Wyoming, the U.S. government produced the Fort Laramie Treaty in 1851, which was signed by the Crow, Gros Ventre, and Assiniboine. These tribes were assigned reservations in eastern Montana, along with the Blackfeet, who did not attend the meeting and who did not sign the treaty, but were in absentia assigned a reservation.

The discovery of gold in the western mountains increased the demand for transportation routes across treatied Indian country. The Bozeman Trail, blazed during the 1860s, cut across Sioux tribal land to reach Montana's goldfields. Three military forts were built to protect the trail. Gold was discovered in the Black Hills of South Dakota, country considered sacred by the Sioux, and prospectors flooded in.

These infractions by the whites infuriated the Indians. The American government responded by unilaterally diminishing the size of the original reservations. The Sioux and Cheyenne, among the last of the tribes to be forced into Montana by white western expansion, were especially angry at the ongoing incursions. After the gold rush in the Black Hills, the Sioux quit the reservation completely and resumed their traditional plains lifestyle on the prairies of eastern Montana.

Army vs. Indian

The U.S. government in 1876 ordered the Sioux and the Cheyenne back onto the reservation. The Indians refused, and the Army was dispatched to compel them back. Three columns of infantry set out. The first column to arrive in Indian country divided, sending Gen. George Custer and the Seventh Cavalry on ahead to seek the hostiles. They found the combined Cheyenne and Sioux force (perhaps 3,000 warriors) on June 26, 1876. Custer rashly decided to do battle alone, and his entire command (265 men) was destroyed.

The next year the Nez Perce under Chief Joseph fled from their Oregon reservation across Montana, attempting to reach sanctuary in Canada. After a battle at the Big Hole in western Montana, the Nez Perce struggled south to the Yellowstone Park area and then veered north, hoping to escape into Canada near Havre. Thirty miles from the border, Gen. Nelson Miles overtook the fleeing tribe. The Nez Perce, of Northwest origins, were sent to reservations in Oklahoma.

Custer's annihilation notwithstanding, by 1877 all the Indians in Montana were incarcerated on reservations. In fact, many forces besides the Army had worked to weaken and inevitably subjugate the Indian. Diseases introduced from white settlements devastated Indian populations; an outbreak of smallpox amongst the Blackfeet in 1837 is reckoned to have killed three-quarters of the tribe. Alcohol was illegally traded to the Indians, which corrupted and debilitated the traditional warrior societies.

As trade evolved from peltry to buffalo robes, the Indians were unwittingly involved in exterminating the animal that provided the cornerstone of their entire traditional culture. Before white settlers reached the plains, 60 million buffalo lived in North America. By 1870, that number was down to 10-20 million. By 1883, after railroads crossed the West and settlers were streaming in after the Civil War, there were only 100-200 buffalo left in the U.S.

With the buffalo largely exterminated, Native Americans were reduced to complete dependence on handouts from the government's Indian agent. By the mid-1880s, the federal government spent $7 a year per Indian on a reservation, while it spent $1,000 a year on a soldier stationed in Montana's Indian land.

The Railroad Arrives

Riverboats were the only form of transportation linking Montana and the rest of the nation until the 1880s. Boats could reach as far inland as Fort Benton on the Missouri and to Pompey's Pillar on the Yellowstone. But real economic growth and settlement awaited the coming of the railroad.

The Union Pacific built a spur line north from Utah to Butte in 1881. The Northern Pacific crossed the length of Montana, linking Portland and Chicago in 1883. In return for opening the northern transcontinental line, the Northern Pacific was given a land grant: for every mile of track laid, the railroad received forty sections (40 square miles) of land. In Montana alone, this amounted to 17 million acres.

The Great Northern stretched its service along the Montana-Canada border, joining Minneapolis and Seattle in 1893. The Milwaukee Road crossed central Montana on its way to Seattle in 1909. With access to coastal markets, Montana opened up to further development and immigration.

Cattle Country

Montana had had a cattle trade in the western valleys and foothills since the 1860s as ranches grew up to feed the mining camps, and Texas longhorns had been trailed into Montana as early as 1866. But the era of the cattleman didn't really begin until the 1880s, when longhorn cattle were trailed north from Texas in great numbers.

Typically, the large "outfits" that brought cattle into Montana at this time were owned by a group of investors, who bought shares in herds often numbering in the tens of thousands. Cowboys would herd these longhorns north from Texas, summer them free on the grassy unfenced prairies of Montana, and then round them up, sort them by brand, and sell them to eastern markets. This get-rich-quick scheme worked for many, because with a small investment in the start-up animal, low labor costs with the cowboys, and no feed bills to pay, the profitability was great.

Initially, the fattened steers were trailed south into Wyoming to railheads on the Union Pacific. With the construction of the Northern Pacific along the course of the Yellowstone River in 1881-82, railheads such as Wibaux, Miles City, and Billings became centers for the livestock trade, and turned into full-blooded Old West cattle towns. In 1870, there were 48,000 head of cattle in Montana. By 1886, the height of the open-range period, there were 675,000 head.

Butte

In 1864, two miners staked a claim for gold on a lonely bluff near the Continental Divide at the headwaters of the Clark Fork River. The gold soon played out, but miners discovered something else: silver.

As a source of wealth, silver was as good as gold. But the mining techniques were quite different. Gold can be panned from streams by individuals working alone, and sold as powder or lumps. Silver, however, requires underground mining to extract the ore, which then has to be refined by smelters. As mining at Butte developed in the 1870s, the era of the independent prospector passed and corporate mining began. Then, as silver ran out, copper became the lodestone of Butte mining.

The transcontinental railroads vied for lucrative contracts to take the refined metal to world markets. The railroads also brought in immigrants to work the deep veins. Railroads were built between Butte and Anaconda, and between Butte and Great Falls, to take the ore to smelters.

Butte, soon to be known as the "richest hill on earth," was dominated by smokestacks, peopled by immigrants, and undercut with 10,000 miles of mineshafts. It quickly became Montana's largest and wealthiest city. The city never slept: miners worked the veins 24 hours a day, and bars, restaurants, and other businesses were always open to serve their customers. The huge influx of immigrants that poured into Butte during this period from Central Europe, Italy, Cornwall, Ireland, and China, in particular, gave Butte its cosmopolitan flavor and its ethnic neighborhoods.

Other factors were not so positive. Butte was an environmental disaster. The pollution from the smelters soon killed all the vegetation within a 20-mile radius. The trees that weren't killed by smoke were cut for mine supports or to fuel the smelters. Smelting also used vast amounts of water, which was simply returned to streams laden with toxic chemicals and minerals. The mining process produced mountains of tailings, some of which were radioactive. Entire communities were built on these tailings.

EMPIRES GAINED AND LOST

The End of the Open Range

While Butte was booming during the 1880s and '90s, events conspired to end the Old West cattle days on the eastern prairies. The winter of 1886-87 has been made most famous by the grim drawing of the "Last of the 5,000" by artist Charlie Russell. A very dry summer led to a long, extremely cold winter. The warm-weather longhorn, summered on the drought-stricken plains, died in huge numbers as temperatures remained below zero for weeks. One-half to three-quarters of the cattle in Montana reportedly froze or starved to death. A single winter ended the era of the great cattle drives.

Sheep had played a part in Montana agriculture since the days of deSmet's St. Mary's Mission, but now the number of sheep on the plains increased considerably as ranchers realized that the hardy sheep were a good hedge against losses of the more temperate cattle. In 1870, there were just 2,000 head of sheep in the state, one for every 10 settlers; by 1900, with six million head, sheep outnumbered people 24 to one.

Also, while the railroads opened up the growth of the cattle trade in Montana, they also brought in settlements. The open range was increasingly privately owned. The various homesteading acts of the late 1800s and early 1900s opened public land for settlement. With the hegemony of the big cattle outfits broken after 1886, homesteaders set up along the fertile valley bottoms, fencing some of the best range and water access.

Homesteaders

Rail entrepreneurs like James Hill of the Great Northern quickly realized the benefits of establishing settlements all along his rail lines. Huge advertising campaigns were launched to tempt the homesteader to the plains of Montana. Rural European communities received advice from experts regarding the fertility of the Great Plains, and immigrants were pamphleted as they disembarked onto U.S. soil.

Much of the promotional material presented by the railroads was fanciful, and some of it was flat wrong. It promised, for example, plenty of rain, fertile soil, and opportunities for all. Nonetheless, the advertising worked. The population of Montana grew 60% during the first decade of this century, and the number of farms doubled.

While homesteading acts allotted 320 acres of "free land" per individual (a husband and wife qualified for two allotments), even this quantity of land was insufficient to make a living in Montana. During good years with plenty of rain, the prairies provided adequate grazing. But most new settlers did not come to raise livestock (stockmen were seen as anachronisms). Farmers represented progress and the evolution of the West: they came to turn the soil over and raise grain.

Communities sprang up along the rail lines, particularly along the Great Northern near the Hi-Line and along the Milwaukee Road through central Montana. Towns were established along the rail sidings and usually consisted of a grain elevator, a bank, a hotel, and bar. Farms were "improved on" according to Homestead Act requirements, but were often little more than a tar paper or sod shack with ad hoc outbuildings for livestock. Eastern Montana has never been more populated than it was in 1918, with at least one homestead per square mile of arable land.

The Company

In the first years of this century, the Copper Kings Fritz Augustus Heinze, Marcus Daly, and William Clark, largely to spite each other, each sold out to the buyer least likely to benefit the others. In each case it was Standard Oil. By 1906, Standard Oil, soon to reconfigure its holdings as the Anaconda Company, controlled almost everything in Butte. It became known simply as The Company. Then, in the 1910s, when the Anaconda Company became yoked with the Montana Power Company, these two corporations controlled practically the whole state.

The Copper Kings had been largely beneficent to their workers, and even suffered the unions gladly. Not so The Company. During the 1910s, Butte was a battlefield of labor-management disputes. Conditions in the mines worsened. The presence of Wobblies during WW I led to the Anaconda Company targeting "communist" influences that resulted in lynchings. The Great Depression further darkened conditions in Butte as the world price of copper fell 80%. Production of copper in 1933 was 10% of what it had been in 1929. The Company shifted much of its operations to Chile and Mexico, where copper was mined in open pits, involving fewer labor costs. Butte, once one of the richest towns in the West, now faced unemployment problems.

The Dust Bowl Years

For a time the weather cooperated with the homesteaders in eastern Montana. Then, from the late 1910s to the mid-'20s, nature shifted gears. In 1916, Shelby, on the Hi-Line, received over 15 inches of rain; in 1919, the third year of intense drought, the town received less than seven inches. Drought continued, coupled with

THE KINGS OF COPPER

During the boom years of copper and silver mining in Butte—in the 1870s and '80s—the mines, the city, and, indeed, the whole state were dominated by three men, called the Copper Kings.

William Clark made his first fortune mining and smelting silver, and extended his empire into banking and politics. Marcus Daly cannily bought up depleted silver mines in order to exploit the mines' rich veins of copper (electrical power created a market for copper wire, which turned copper from a junk metal to one of Montana's most precious commodities). Daly also had large business holdings in the lumber industry; his Butte-area mines used 40,000 board feet of timber a day. Fritz Augustus Heinze cleverly manipulated the "Apex Law," which states that if a vein of ore surfaces on one person's claim, then that person has the right to the rest of the vein, no matter where it goes when underground. Because he owned the apex of mines owned by large mining interests, Heinze was able to thumb his nose at big business while becoming very wealthy.

CHRIS PARMENTER/3

William Andrews Clark

Each of these men led an almost raucously public life. Heinze's wealth and reputation had less to do with his mining knowledge than with his control of the courtrooms. He courted public affection by publicly taking on the giant companies, such as Standard Oil, that were swallowing up Butte mining. Daly and Clark engaged in a fiercely contested rivalry involving wealth, political influence, and popular opinion. Each controlled newspapers, bought judges, and paid off legislators. A classic battle was fought in 1889 as Montana became a state. Daly favored Anaconda as state capital, while Clark lobbied for and triumphed with his choice of Helena. Daly got revenge by denying Clark a long-sought-after seat in the U.S. Senate. These and other battles were chronicled in the state press, and were the stuff of public gossip and debate.

Marcus Daly

Butte was not the only area influenced by the era of the Copper Kings. Missoula and Hamilton were largely built by the Daly logging empire. Anaconda was essentially a Daly company town, built around his Washoe smelter, but with great pretensions. The growth of Great Falls was assured when smelters were built on the banks of the Missouri to refine Butte ore.

The political complexion of early Montana was largely established by events centered in Butte. Many of the early miners and prospectors who were attracted to the gold strikes of the 1860s, and the boom of the 1870s, were Southerners dislocated by the Civil War. They brought to Montana a strong hatred of Yankee Republicanism; most Irish immigrants were dependably Democratic. Both Daly and Clark fought their political battles from within the Democratic party. Butte was the largest city in the state by far, and its population of workers, when unionized, voted unswervingly Democratic. To this day, Montana has a stronger Democratic party than many western states.

Fritz Augustus Heinze

high winds and grasshoppers. Range fires ruined crops and destroyed communities. By 1925, 60,000 people had left Montana, representing 11,000 abandoned farms; 214 state banks failed and Montana led the nation in bankruptcies. A few years later, disaster struck again. The stock market crash, combined with a second severe drought during the Dust Bowl years of the 1930s, eliminated many more farmers and ranchers.

Federal Spending

As elsewhere in the U.S., in Montana the 1930s Depression was followed by the spending programs of the New Deal. The works projects had great impact on the state. Not only did programs like the Civilian Conservation Corps (CCC) and the Work Projects Administration give employment and training to people out of jobs, they produced monumental results. One of the largest public works projects in the country was Fort Peck Dam, completed in 1940 to dam the Missouri. Going-to-the-Sun Highway in Glacier Park was a CCC project.

After the end of the New Deal era, government spending in Montana ceased to be a civilian affair and was given over to the military. Malmstrom Air Force Base was built in Great Falls in 1942 as a transit base for war material shipped to the United States' then-ally the Soviet Union. By the 1950s, it became a strategic air base that was assigned fighter jets to defend against then-enemy the Soviet Union. In the 1960s, Malmstrom became the first center for the Minuteman Missile system. By 1970, 200 Minutemen were buried in silos under 23,000 acres of central Montana prairie, pointed at equivalent missiles in Russia. The Glasgow Air Force Base brought population and business to that eastern Montana town until the base was closed in 1969.

Decline of the West

While the 19th century saw the buildup of wealth and influence in western Montana, the 20th century brought decline to the mining and logging industries that had fueled early growth.

Butte struggled on until 1955, when open-pit mining began. Open-pit mining diminished overhead and overburden at the same time. The old Butte communities were ripped apart as steam shovels tore into the soil. The huge Berkeley Pit swallowed up Meaderville, which was once a lively Italian neighborhood sitting on a vein of low-grade copper ore. Although Berkeley Pit revived industry in Butte for about 20 years, by the 1980s Anaconda Company had sold all its holdings in Butte. A mile high and a mile deep, Butte contained just a century's worth of riches.

Likewise, centralized ownership and over-production has crippled the timber-products industry. Huge companies control much of the timber production in Montana and have put local lumber mills and logging companies out of business. Much of the good timber in easily accessible private and state lands has already been harvested. With the old-growth trees gone, local loggers and mills have had to bear the expense of retooling machinery to accommodate smaller trees. Even though the loss of jobs and revenue in logging towns is a result of market forces, environmentalists usually receive the blame.

Coal and Oil

The 20th century saw other mineral development come to the eastern prairies. Coal had been mined in Montana since the early days of settlement, but large-scale exploitation of the incredible reserves of fossil fuels waited until the railroads arrived. The Northern Pacific developed Red Lodge, and later Colstrip, as sources of fuel for its steam trains, and the Milwaukee built up Roundup as its source. After trains were converted to electricity, coal mining ceased for a number of years. However, as machinery and technology more finely developed the techniques of strip-mining, the vast reserves of coal in the Fort Union Formation in southeastern Montana became more attractive.

In the 1970s energy companies proposed building four electric generators in Colstrip, with the power to be sold to markets on the West Coast. Battles erupted in courtrooms and communities as the breadth of the mining and environmental damage became clear. The issues surrounding development sundered many communities as the benefits of conservation and economic opportunity were debated. Despite grassroots opposition from ranchers, Indians, and environmentalists, the generators went in.

Oil and gas exploration also brought wealth to some eastern Montana communities. Refineries helped Billings boom during the 1970s, and towns such as Sidney, Broadus, and Baker escaped the worst of recent agricultural downturns because of the presence of large nearby oil reserves.

Farming and Ranching

Bad years still follow good in Montana agriculture. A series of good years in the 1960s and early '70s brought prosperity and high land prices. The family ranch and farm began to modernize after borrowing against the inflated real estate values of the land. Then drought hit again, and land values fell. Farmers and ranchers found themselves with unsecured loans. The drought, bad markets, and financial breakdown of the 1970s and '80s became known as the Farm-Ranch Crisis, an echo of earlier times and of an ongoing cycle.

Government programs in the 1970s and '80s were designed to help the family farm and ranch, but were too easily manipulated by unscrupulous investors. Huge tracts of cheap drought-stricken grazing land were bought up solely for the government payments available for plowing it. The broken land, plowed but not planted, simply drifted on the wind across the prairies while the investment "farmers" pocketed the payments.

Farms and ranches are large and far between in Montana. Those that remain have long histories and many experiences of lean times. Most are still operated as family businesses, with the work and pleasures shared by several generations living together on one farm or ranch site. While during much of the 20th century agriculture became more specialized and reliant on production of only one commodity (usually cattle or wheat), rural Montana is taking on the 1990s with its eyes cast backward. A ranch that raises cattle, sheep, hay, wheat, and keeps chickens and a milk cow not only has a diversified product to sell but also goes a long way toward being self-sufficient. The repeated cycle of boom and bust, rain and drought, will continue. But after surviving three generations in eastern Montana, farmers and ranchers don't pretend to be in it for the money.

The New and *Really* Wild West

As people have become increasingly disillusioned with urban life, more and more look to the rural West as a place to relocate. Montana, with its spectacular scenery, great fishing, and comparatively low cost of living, has become a mecca for this second wave of homesteaders. Ranchettes and subdivisions are latter-day homesteads, and celebrity ranchers such as Ted Turner and Brooke Shields are pale 1990s versions of copper kings.

Movie stars aren't the only ones to have an impact on rural Montana in the 1990s. Anyone who has followed the news in the last few years knows that Montana is also a haven for wild-eyed anti-social misanthropes and anti-government individuals and groups. In 1995, the nation learned that Montana is so law hating that its citizens can't even endure a speed limit (never mind that now the state has the highest per capita vehicle death rate in the nation). The Unabomber, the Freemen, and others who tote guns for sport and end up shooting up the federal Capitol, make Montana seem like a breeding ground for nutcases. When coverage of these fringe elements coincided with the outbreak in Britain of mad cow disease, enterprising (and characteristically wry) Montanans began boasting on bumper stickers, "At Least Our Cows Are Sane." Finally, in 1998, the state governor actually made an address to the press pleading for people to understand that not everyone in Montana is a scofflaw and lunatic.

Of course, he was right: a visitor to Montana will in all likelihood only meet very gracious, law-abiding and friendly people who are genuinely glad to see people of all makes and models visit their state.

However, it can't be denied that Montana has had a real public relations nightmare in recent years, and that there must be some reason for certifiably crazy and dangerous people to take refuge in the hills. Perhaps the state's long-standing "live and let live" philosophy fits too nicely with fin de siècle currents of violence and disenfranchisement.

Anti-government factions in Montana form two basic groups. One is part of the more general influx of white separatists and Neo Nazis into the Pacific Northwest, where they hope to found an Aryan homeland. These people are generally in extreme western Montana, near the Idaho border. The second group is the equally disturbing Freeman's Movement. These latter-day "patriots" are Second Amendment zealots with massive weapons arsenals who are often, coincidentally, just clinging to economic survival on bankrupt farms and ranches. Freeman members are absolutely contemptuous of what they see as governmental interference in their sovereign individual rights, and have gone as far as to issue dead-or-alive warrants for duly elected county officials that have dared to cross their paths (usually in order to collect on bad debt).

This fringe group became front-page news when Freeman (and women) from across the West came streaming into Jordan, Montana, where they set up a headquarters at the ranch of a notable and vocal sympathizer. The Freemen established their own government and currency, issuing death threats and bounties on people they considered their enemies. After the Freemen shattered the small-town harmony of Jordan, issued millions of dollars in bad checks, and threatened the lives of the sheriff, county attorney, and others who fell afoul of their self-made new laws, the FBI moved in. After Federal agents snatched up the ring-leaders in a helicopter raid, the remaining Freemen settled in for a long siege on their ranch. After 81 days, the Freemen only gave themselves up when the Feds turned off their electricity and phone service. The locals speculate whether it was the lack of hot water or Internet contact that drove the Freemen from their lair.

Jordan is not the only hotbed of Freeman activity. Roundup, Hamilton, Darby, and Noxon are also hot spots for militia cells, though there are sympathizers in rural areas across the state.

And then there was the Unabomber. Ted Kaczynski was apprehended in 1996 at his mini home-made 10-by-12 foot cabin near Lincoln, Montana, and charged with the anti-technology bombing crimes of the Unabomber. In a federal trial in Sacramento, Kaczynski later pleaded guilty to four bombings in 1985, 1993 and 1995 that killed two people and maimed two. But his plea bargain resolves all federal charges against him growing out of a 17-year string of 16 bombings that killed three people and injured 29.

In return for a guarantee that he will not be executed, Kaczynski agreed to accept life in prison or a federal psychiatric facility without the possibility of parole.

Then, in 1998, a part-time Montana resident named Russell Weston Jr. entered the federal Capitol building and fired on a number of people, killing two security guards.

If travelers need any kind of assurance that they'll be safe from anti-establishment zealots while visiting Montana, at least realize that most of the crazy folk from Montana prefer to play out their life of crime outside of the state. Chances are very good that all the people you'll meet in Montana are going to welcoming and mostly sane. Or sane enough.

GOVERNMENT

Montana became a territory in 1864 and a state in 1889. The original state constitution of 1889 reflected the mining and timber interests that dominated the early days of the state. Due in part to that document's datedness, and to the climate of political reform in the late 1960s, Montanans voted to draft a new constitution. The results of the second Constitutional Convention in 1972 were a reformist, populist set of laws that affirms that the state government exists by consent of the people and for their benefit. The privileges of business and industry were diminished accordingly.

Montana granted women's suffrage in 1916, four years before the passage of the 19th Amendment. Jeannette Rankin, the first woman representative in the U.S. Congress, was elected from Montana in the same year.

The Montana Legislature is a bicameral, biennial body. There are 56 counties. Since the 1990 census, there is only one federal House member (down from two). One particularity of the Montana primary system is its open ballot. Voters are not asked to identify party affiliation to receive a primary ballot; instead, they receive a voting form from both the Democratic and Republican parties. In the voting booth, the voter marks only one form, and both are deposited in the ballot box. The system has been both hailed as the truest form of democratic voting and denounced as the most open to political hanky-panky.

Reservation Self-Government
Indian reservations make up nine percent of Montana and, even though a substantial amount

of this land may be owned by non-Indians, tribal law prevails within reservation boundaries. Indian reservations are recognized by the federal government as independent political units. Legal jurisdiction is therefore something of a puzzle on reservations.

Tribes have certain inherent sovereign rights. Tribes can run their own schools, regulate transport and trade, and have their own constitutions, legislative councils, and tribal court and police systems. The state cannot tax reservation land or transactions that occur on reservations. While such legal considerations may not seem crucial to the traveler, Montana has in effect seven independent political entities within its borders. Visitors need to be aware that certain state laws do not apply on reservations.

Those cheap gas stations advertising cheap cigarettes aren't found just inside reservations by accident. State fuel and cigarette taxes aren't levied on those products sold by tribal members within reservations. Some local roads on reservation land are maintained by the tribes. Do not automatically assume that there is public access; sometimes use is reserved for tribal members. For instance, some of the Crow Reservation is off-limits to non-Indians.

Not all areas are open for recreation. The state does not have authority to regulate hunting, fishing, and recreation on reservations. Tribes can issue their own licenses for hunting and fishing, and may levy a user fee for hikers and campers. If you are not a tribe member, always check with tribal authorities before crossing reservation land.

ECONOMY

Montana is a rural state. Agriculture, mining, and the timber industry were among the founding trades of Montana and remain among its most important. Tourism is increasingly lucrative, and service industries like trucking and medical-treatment centers are major employers. Because it is so far from coastal markets or other significant population centers, it is unlikely that Montana will quickly become anything but a source for raw materials. Transport costs make industry unprofitable in so remote a state.

Agriculture
Montanans make strict differentiations between farms and ranches. Farms raise grain; ranches raise livestock. To the purist, any amount of cultivation degrades a ranch to a farm. Even though most people think of Montana as primarily an agricultural state, less than 10% of the population makes a living from farming and ranching. Still, recent census figures indicate that the number of farms and ranches in Montana is increasing slightly (there are more than 15,000); however, their average income has declined over the last decade. Beef cattle production is the most common form of ranching, with sheep production remaining a steady alternative. Spring and winter wheat are by far the most common crops, with barley a significant third. Along the Yellowstone River, corn, soybeans, and sugar beets grow in irrigated fields. In the Flathead Lake re-

gion, sweet cherry orchards augment the local tourist economy.

Mining
The state of Montana was born of prospecting and mining camps. However, the copper, silver, and gold that established the Montana economy are largely depleted. Traditional centers of mining, such as Butte and Anaconda, have fallen on hard times as the world market has moved elsewhere to find cheaper, more easily mined minerals. But it's not that Montana has given up mining; copper, silver, and gold are still produced, but with modern techniques that don't demand an entire city's workforce.

Montana remains rich in other mineral wealth: from the unpronounceable molybdenum to the sublime Yogo sapphire to ordinary talcum powder. Mining in Montana has moved to the rich coal and oil fields of eastern Montana and the palladium mines on the Stillwater River. Thirty-foot-thick veins of bituminous coal lie under much of southeastern Montana and are unearthed by modern strip-mining techniques at places like Colstrip. The Stillwater Mine is the only U.S. source for valuable platinum. Oil and gas wells dot the eastern prairies.

Lumber
About half of Montana is forested. However, early overcutting and slow regrowth have limited the state's competitiveness in the world timber

MONTANA'S LIVESTOCK

Montana is one of the largest livestock producers in the nation, with 65% of its land in agricultural production (although only eight percent of the population is engaged in ranching and farming). Different breeds of livestock have been developed for different needs and different environments, and ranchers put a lot of thought into the types of animals they raise. And for Montanans, livestock breeds are another coded system of meanings that serve to characterize individuals: just as there are Ford or Chevy families, there are Black Angus or Targhee families, and each means something in the system.

Cattle

Black Angus are probably the most prevalent cattle breed in the state. Ranchers prize these all-black beef cattle for their milking ability on the shortgrass prairie and for their hardy disposition. These qualities make Angus cows the preferred mother stock in many herds, especially for ranchers who choose to cross-breed.

Hereford cattle come either horned or polled (that is, naturally unhorned), and are distinguished by their red bodies and white heads and legs. Herefords are as traditional a breed as Angus and share many of the same attributes, but they are somewhat less popular nowadays because of the horns on the larger and more vigorous variety, and because the udders of white-fleshed Herefords can easily sunburn, causing the mothers to reject the hungry advances of newborn calves. Longhorn cattle established Montana cowtowns like Miles City. But these cattle from Texas proved to be too delicate for Montana winters. Longhorn cattle are raised today mostly for rodeo stock.

So-called exotic breeds were brought to the U.S. in the 1960s from Europe to introduce larger bone structures into local Hereford and Angus cattle. Federal livestock laws forbade the direct importation of live breeding stock, but not the importation of semen. Exotic cattle made artificial insemination of cows an everyday occurrence on Montana ranches. Because exotic breeds (most are named for the European region where they originated, like Maine-Anjou or Charolais) are much larger than the Angus or Hereford, they produce larger calves. But larger cattle demand more food and range; the economic benefit of exotic cattle depends largely on the condition of the range.

The number of dairy cattle has fallen as transportation costs and centralization of processing has made Montana herds uncompetitive. It is cheaper to ship in milk from out of state than to ship in the feed to support a dairy cow.

Sheep

The war between sheep raisers and cattlemen was never as fierce in Montana as in other western states, because in harsh and unpredictable climates sheep have proved to be a sensible livestock adjunct to cattle ranching. As a commodity, sheep have two basic values: in wool and meat. Sheep that are best for wool production are not the best for meat production, however. In fact, the qualities exist in inverse proportion to each other. The larger and meatier the sheep, the coarser the wool. While all sheep produce wool, the staples that can be spun into suit wool fetch the highest prices; in a bad year, the cost of shearing the sheep may be greater than the fleece price of poor-quality wool.

Black-face sheep produce the most desirable carcass (the most meat per pound of grain), but the wool is almost worthless. White-faced, polled sheep like Columbias and Targhees are the sheepman's choice for mid-quality fleece and good-quality carcasses. If it's wool you're after, then the Rambouillet, with its large curving horns and fine fleece, is Montana's best wool breed. If the wool market isn't good, however, you can't expect top price for the comparatively small-framed lambs.

Horses

Most jobs on most Montana ranches could be done by various machines or vehicles, but many Montanans persist in using horses for everyday work. It's part of the heritage, and, besides, grain is cheaper than gasoline. Most stock horses are quarter horses, known for their endurance and speed in short distances. Appaloosas are the horses with the spots on their hindquarters. Draft horses appear on farms and ranches occasionally, as fuel prices and whimsy dictate. Driving a team and wagon to feed stock is not common, but certainly not rare.

Hogs

Pigs are the single livestock commodity that has no Old West antecedent. But they are prevalent. Most farmers keep pigs, simply because the ratio of feed to profit is lower than with other livestock: put simply, pigs can utilize food disdained by sheep or cattle. Compare it to a diversified investment portfolio: like sheep, hogs can serve as a hedge against bad grain or cattle markets.

market. Locally owned mills have been forced to close when they can't compete against large corporate "timber-product" conglomerates, whose efficient automated factories have transformed logging from a lifestyle to a job, and which have largely practiced extractive "cut and run" logging, with little concern for the forests' future. The forests still provide a living for enterprising Montanans, though: Christmas tree farms are found in northwestern Montana, and log-home manufacturers have moved Montana into the first ranks of home-kit producers in the nation. More log homes are shipped each year to Japan than remain in Montana.

THE ARTS AND CULTURE

If there is a western culture, a lack of snobbery lies at its heart. Even in the literature it shows: a rancher's memoirs share a bookshelf with poems that don't rhyme. Both writers are from Montana, and natives brag on them both. Rural cafes often sell local arts and crafts, whether it's homemade pottery or country scenes painted on old saws. And locals will buy both. Montanans respect people who are creative; rare is the rural community that doesn't have a resident poet, painter, or musician. L'art naïf or kitsch? In Montana, as often as not, it's the urge to express that's admired; it's not polite to question the quality of the expression.

From pioneers who kept journals and sent letters back east, to fourth-generation ranchers, to established novelists who have found a home in the state, Montana's literary tradition is a source of pride to Montanans, who generally read a lot and who positively devour the work of regional writers. It's not surprising that Montana should harbor such a dynamic writing community. It's a small step to go from respecting the work of a local rhymester to welcoming a nationally known author to the farm next door.

LITERATURE

Any state that can fill a 1,150-page anthology with its literature is impressive. To have that become a regional best-seller points to a phenomenon. *The Last Best Place* chronicles the literary history of Montana, from Native American stories to modern cowboy poetry. Those unfamiliar with Montana's place in the literary firmament will be surprised at the number of writers who have had Montana addresses.

Early Writers
Montana literary history begins with the diaries and memoirs of early settlers and the translitera-

tion of Indian tales. Teddy Blue Abbott trailed cattle up from Texas to Montana during the 1870s and '80s and wrote *We Pointed Them North.* Andrew Garcia was a novice mountain man when he married a Nez Perce woman who just escaped following Chief Joseph's surrender at Bear Paw. In *Tough Trip through Paradise,* Garcia gives his version of the Nez Perce flight in the 1870s and of what it was like for him to be an innocent among mountain men and Indians. Frank Bird Linderman got to know Crow chief Plenty Coups and Pretty Shield, a Crow medicine woman, and recorded their stories. *Indian Why Stories* and *How It Came About Stories* are his versions of Indian fireside tales.

Frontier photographer L.A. Huffman brought his camera to early eastern Montana; *Before Barbed Wire* by Mark Brown and W.R. Felton features his photographs and recounts Huffman's life. Evelyn Cameron was an English immigrant whose passion for photographing the early settlement of remote Terry, Montana, resulted in the book *Photographing Montana: 1894-1928* by Donna Lucey. Charlie Russell, whose greatest fame derives from his paintings of frontier Montana, also wrote books. His life straddled the open range and the homesteading eras; his book, *Trails Plowed Under,* recounts this period. Will James had a ranch south of Billings. Books like *Cow Country* were popular adolescent reading during the '30s.

The Missoula School
The University of Montana at Missoula has had a seminal effect on serious writing in the state. In 1919, a writing program was established by Professor H.G. Merriam at the university, only the second such program in the nation. Merriam, who had left Colorado to attend Oxford, returned west determined to promote regional Montana writing. He began the literary journal *Frontier and Midland.* His writing program flourished,

Andrew Garcia tells of his life among Indians (he was married to a Nez Perce woman) and mountain men in Tough Trip through Paradise, *discovered years after his death.*

soon growing to offer a Master of Fine Arts degree. Students have included A.B. Guthrie Jr., author of *The Big Sky,* and Dorothy Johnson, author of *The Man Who Shot Liberty Valance* and other popular western stories.

The program has attracted many talented students, as well as nationally recognized faculty. Poet Richard Hugo inherited the writing program from Leslie Fielder in 1964 and remained until his death in 1982. Hugo had a tremendous influence on the development of Northwest regional literature. His poems speak of disappointment and abandonment in both life and the physical world, sometimes ending with a wry glimmer of hope. Joining Hugo at the U of M at one time or another were Madeline DeFrees, Patricia Goedicke, William Kittredge (who with Annick Smith edited *The Last Best Place*), William Pitt Root, and Tess Gallagher.

Missoula has also attracted writers whose connections with the writing program are more tenuous. Rick deMarinis *(Under the Wheat)* did a stint

as a mathematician before becoming a full-time writer. James Crumley, whose hard-boiled detective novels are frequently placed in the Northwest, still lives in Missoula. Norman Maclean, who wrote *A River Runs Through It,* an idyll to fly-fishing and the spirit, grew up in Missoula. James Welch, who spent his youth on the Blackfoot and Fort Belknap reservations, studied with Hugo and now lives in Missoula. Welch has written several fine contemporary and historic novels of Indian life, including *Winter in the Blood.* Another Missoulian by way of the Hi-Line is Deirdre McNamer, whose novel *Rima in the Weeds* is set amongst the missile silos of northern Montana. The transcendently witty Ian Frazier (*Great Plains,* articles in the *New Yorker)* has moved back to Montana.

Natives and Newcomers

Although there are writers scattered across the expanse of Montana, a principality of established authors has grown up around the town of Livingston, north of Yellowstone Park. Thomas McGuane's novels, including *Keep the Change,* are westerns filled with modern neuroses. McGuane lives in the area, as has Richard Ford *(Rock Springs).* Ford's *Wildlife* is set in Great Falls, and many of his stories are set in small Montana towns. Richard Brautigan, famous for *Trout Fishing in America,* was also a resident. Jamie Harrison writes Montana-based detective novels (*Going Local, Unfortunate Prairie Occurrence*) from her Livingston home.

In the age of modems and fax machines, writers can live just about anywhere, and Rick Bass's book *Winter: Notes from Montana* chronicles the author's first winter in remote northwestern Montana. Bass has also written *The Ninemile Wolves,* a passionate book about wolves reestablishing themselves in Montana.

Not all Montana authors are imported. Joseph Kinsey Howard, a journalist and lightning rod for progressive politics in the 1940s, wrote a classic Montana history in *Montana: High, Wide and Handsome.* Ivan Doig's memoirs of his Montana boyhood *(This House of Sky)* and his fictional trilogy about Scottish ranchers in Montana *(Dancing at the Rascal Fair, English Creek,* and *Ride with Me Mariah Montana)* have garnered a wide readership.

Wallace Stegner, though not strictly a Montana writer, spent part of his boyhood in Montana and has written western novels and memoirs such as *Big Rock Candy Mountain.* Wally McRae, eastern Montana rancher and conservationist, is admired on the cowboy-poet circuit. Another rancher-writer was Spike Van Cleve, who wrote with wit of the changing West in *A Day Late and a Dollar Short*.

To catch the latest breaking literary movements in Montana, check out these two on-line magazines: *Peaks* at http://aetherserv.com/peaks/ and *Cutbank* at www.umt.edu/cutbank/.

ART

Montana was visited in its earliest days of settlement by noted artists, who left a rich legacy of landscape and wildlife art. Early artist-explorers Karl Bodmer and John James Audubon passed through Fort Union and up the Missouri; their journals and paintings portray Montana before settlement.

Charlie Russell is the quintessential Montana painter. He knew the West from the inside, having lived the life of a cowhand for many years. A native of St. Louis, Russell came west during the days of the great cattle ranches and lived in the Judith Basin area of central Montana. He began by sketching in bars and around campfires; the lives of the Indians and cowboys that he encountered daily became his subject matter. Often he traded his sketches for drinks, and until recently some of the best collections of his works were in bars. His studio in Great Falls is now the Charles M. Russell Memorial Museum. His works are also on display in the Montana Historical Society Museum in Helena.

The regional and western tradition is still strong in Montana art. Ace Powell of Great Falls inherited the mantle of Charlie Russell and painted fine tableaus of the emerging West. A contemporary master of reproducing the light and shade of the Montana landscape is Russell Chatham. His carefully balanced scenes capture the expanse and intimacy of the Montana countryside. Gary Carter paints wildlife and Western scenes, while Clyde Aspevig concentrates on landscapes.

The Montana arts scene doesn't end with western-themed painting and sculpture. The universities and the Montana Arts Council foster more experimental artists. In Missoula, Rudy Autio produces nationally recognized ceramic sculpture. Another former U of M professor was

MONTANA HISTORICAL SOCIETY, HELENA

Hallowed western artist Charles M. Russell spent his youth as a range cowboy.

Walter Hook, a math-professor-turned-painter. Hook developed a wry syntax of images, including buffalo, kites, and Easter eggs, that recur like visitants across his canvases.

John Buck and Debbie Butterfield are Bozeman-area artists whose work flirts with western icons. Butterfield sculpts horses out of old signs or commercial media to achieve a haunting dissonance. Buck confounds western art images, ready-mades, and methods—such as whittling—by incorporating them in aggressively modern constructions.

While the mountains allure writers, the prairies seem to attract—and inspire—visual artists. Far-flung ranches and small towns in eastern Montana harbor conceptual artists. Pat Zentz and Dennis Voss are ranchers who each employ quirky and experimental sculpture and assemblages to convey a sense of Montanan ritual and whimsy. Ted Waddell employs modern expressionistic techniques to paint the cows on his ranch, imbuing them with near-totemic presence. Gary Hornick's installations juxtapose isolation and a rich historicity.

A Missoulian who garnered fame as a poster illustrator is Monte Dolack. His movie and commercial poster paintings are immediately recognizable and avidly collected. Dolack's Missoula gallery markets his stylish and whimsical fine-art prints.

Regional Art Centers

A number of Montana communities, some of them quite small, have community art centers. These host touring shows of regional art, and often feature the works of local artists; the gift shop is often a great place to buy that special souvenir. You may be surprised at the sophistication of work turned out by a ranch wife, or by a retired railroad worker. Look for regional art centers in Glendive, Miles City, Kalispell, Anaconda, Bigfork, Billings, Colstrip, Great Falls, Hardin, Helena, Lewistown, and Missoula.

Additionally, some towns have developed a reputation as a visual arts center, and privately owned galleries proliferate. If you're planning a visual arts tour across Montana, you'll want to check out the private galleries at Bigfork, Livingston, Bozeman, Big Timber, Missoula, Billings, and Red Lodge.

THEATER

While the most vital theaters in Montana are associated with the universities in Missoula and Bozeman, other community theaters are of note. Billings has two theater venues, and the Missoula Children's Theater has an excellent reputation throughout the Northwest.

Summer-stock theater is especially good in Montana. Bigfork's summer theater recruits many of its actors from the University of Montana. The Fort Peck summer theater also draws heavily from the Montana universities; the theater building itself is a lovely relic from the CCC days of the 1930s. Virginia City presents summer melodramas in a frontier opera house; West Yellowstone also has a summer family theater.

Montana State University presents an ambitious Shakespeare in the Parks series. During summers, the troupe tours the entire state, including remote towns in eastern Montana, with its productions.

THE PEOPLE

The first residents of Montana arrived from Asia via the Bering land bridge over 14,000 years ago, after the last ice age. These prehistoric people were the ancestors of the North American Indians. However, the Indians who now live in Montana were not native to the area: they were forced westward after being displaced by other tribes and white settlers from the east (see below).

Montana was one of the last states to be settled by whites. Railroads and the Homestead Act made Montana's free acreage very tempting to the thousands of immigrants who poured into the United States in the early 20th century. Many communities still retain their strong European heritage.

NATIVE AMERICANS

There are approximately 50,000 Native Americans living in Montana today (16% of the state's total population), representing 11 different tribes.

The majority live on reservations, which make up nine percent of Montana's total land area.

Native Americans are often lumped together as "Indians," with the assumption that one culture, language, and history link these people. However, the tribes that now live in Montana come from very different traditions, speak different languages, and have not always been friendly toward each other.

Kootenai

The Kootenai tribe had settled in the Kootenai River area by 1500, and there is evidence that they are descended from the area's prehistoric inhabitants. Their original range included the northwestern corner of Montana and adjacent areas of Alberta and British Columbia. As a people, the Kootenai are closely related to Indians of the Columbia Basin, although they speak a language seemingly unrelated to other languages of the area.

The Kootenai share the Flathead Reservation with the Flathead and Pend d'Oreille Indians. Approximately 1,500 Kootenai Indians presently live on the reservation.

Pend d'Oreille

These Salish-speaking people are closely related to tribes of the Pacific coast, but they moved up the Columbia drainages into Montana many thousands of years ago.

The Salish tribes were the first to welcome white missionaries to Montana, and St. Ignatius Mission was built in 1854 to minister to the Pend d'Oreille tribe's spiritual needs. The Pend d'Oreille largely retained the culture of Northwest coast Indians, although Plains Indians' influence was evident in some aspects.

The Flathead

There is no satisfactory explanation for the term "Flathead," for these Salish-speaking people never practiced head flattening (though other Salish tribes did). The Flathead also differed from Salish kinsmen by leaving the river valleys of the Columbia drainage and moving onto the plains of central Montana. Here they evolved a culture based largely on the buffalo while maintaining the religious and social traditions of the Northwest coast.

Like other Salish tribes, the Flathead were generally friendly to whites as they entered Montana. The tribe was moved from the Bitterroot Valley and settled on the Flathead Reservation in the Mission Valley.

The Crow

The Crow were the first of the contemporary Indian residents to enter Montana from the east, arriving as early as 1600 in response to dislocations farther to the east. The Crow, or the Absarokee, originally lived in the Great Lakes region, where they lived in earthen lodges and practiced agriculture.

Having arrived first onto the Montana plains, the Crow had the most to lose as other tribes crowded into the state. They became sworn enemies of the Blackfeet and later the Sioux.

The Blackfeet

Like other Plains tribes, the Blackfeet originally lived farther east, in the forests north of the Great Lakes. As they drifted westward across the

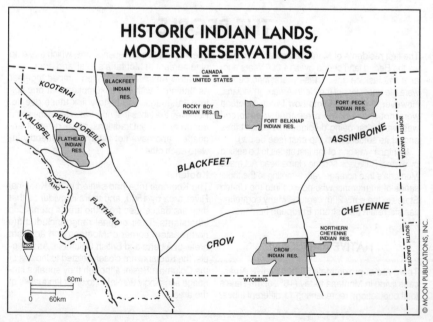

HISTORIC INDIAN LANDS, MODERN RESERVATIONS

Canadian prairies, the various Blackfeet tribes evolved into a loose confederation of entities sharing a common language (an Algonquian dialect) and mutual defense of their hunting lands. These groups, later known as the Piegan, the Blood, and the Northern Blackfeet, combined to form the Blackfeet Nation, one of the largest and most feared of Indian tribes.

The Piegan ventured farthest south, taking control of much of northern Montana by 1800. The Blackfeet were celebrated horsemen and warriors, and their social order was structured by membership in military societies. Men who were not militarily inclined were treated as women; first reported by French trappers, this cultural practice, called the *berdache,* was later found to be common in aboriginal societies. Religious practice centered on the ritual Sun Dance, and shamanistic powers derived from dreams and visions.

Gros Ventre
Meaning literally "Big Belly," Gros Ventre is a misnomer for a tribe more properly known as the Atsina. The Gros Ventre represent the northernmost tribe of the Arapaho, and belong to the Algonquian linguistic family. After moving to the Montana plains from their Minnesota homeland in the late 1700s, they allied themselves with the Blackfeet, sharing in their dominance over the prairies. The Fort Belknap Reservation was established in 1888 for the Gros Ventre and Assiniboine. The Gros Ventre tribe now claims about 2,500 members.

Assiniboine
The Assiniboine are a Siouan-speaking people who historically represented the most northerly of the Yanktonai Sioux in their original homeland north of Lake Superior. They were traditionally allied with the Cree against their common enemy, the Blackfeet. By the 1700s the Assiniboine had crossed into the present-day U.S., where they established a territory in the northeastern corner of Montana where the state meets North Dakota. The 2,000-member tribe is today divided onto two reservations, Fort Belknap and Fort Peck.

Sioux
The Sioux represent one of the largest Indian nations in North America, which divides into three large linguistic groups: the Dakota, the Lakota, and the Nakota. All originally came from Canada and were pushed westward as white settlements dis-

placed other tribes along the eastern seaboard. They arrived on the northern plains comparatively late, around 1800, when they settled in the Dakotas, southern Saskatchewan, and eastern Montana. They were regarded as a noble but fearsome people, skilled in battle and famed hunters of buffalo.

The Yanktonai Sioux settled around Fort Peck and, along with some Assiniboine kinsmen, became residents of that reservation when it was created in 1888. Today, almost 10,000 individuals belong to the tribe.

Northern Cheyenne
The Cheyenne are a tribe of Algonquian linguistic ancestry who lived largely agrarian lives in the Minnesota area. Pressures from other tribes forced the Cheyenne westward, and in about a 25-year period they evolved from a people who cultivated corn and other grains and made pottery to a nomadic Plains culture predicated on buffalo hunting. About 1830, after reaching the Black Hills, the tribe divided, with one group moving south to Colorado and the other moving farther westward into traditional Crow territory. Today, there are about 5,300 members of the Northern Cheyenne tribe.

Chippewa and Cree
The Chippewa and Cree originally lived in northern Michigan and southern Manitoba. On these northern prairies, the tribes lived in close proximity to French trappers and settlers. Intermarriage produced a culture and a people known as Metis. Like so many other native peoples around this time, they moved west in the mid-1700s in response to displacement in the east.

By 1818, when the U.S. border was established, there were estimated to be about 10,000-12,000 Metis people living on the prairies. In 1868 a Metis leader named Louis Riel declared the Metis land a separate province of Canada. His rebellion against English Canadian authorities failed, and the Chippewa under their chief Rocky Boy along with some of the Metis moved south to Spring Creek, near Lewistown, Montana. In the following years, as the U.S. evacuated the Metis to Canada and the Canadians deported them back south, they were part of the "landless Indians" (Indians without a reservation) who wandered the West after the U.S. decided to forego its policy of er gold was discovered in the 1860s did people start to build communities and settle in the state permanently. In addition to the gold diggers from other western states, like California, where gold had already played out, the first towns were peopled by Southerners who had been displaced by the Civil War.

The Immigrants

The establishment of the huge silver and copper mines in western Montana in the 1880s called for a large and stable workforce, supplied mostly by immigrants. As Butte and Anaconda demanded workers, Europe had workers to spare. Irish laborers emigrated in huge numbers, and "Cousin Jack" miners from Cornwall found easy employment. The population of Montana grew 365% from 1880 to 1890, largely due to immigration.

By the 1890s large numbers of Germans, Slavs, Italians, Finns, and Eastern Europeans poured into Butte to work the mines. These foreign workers settled into separate ethnic neighborhoods, where traditional food, customs, and languages prevailed. A number of Jewish immigrants moved to the thriving mining centers and set up retail establishments. In 1910 black settlers in Montana numbered almost 2,000, most of whom lived in mining towns. Only after the establishment of Air Force bases near Glasgow and Great Falls in the 1960s were there more black residents in the state. Chinese immigrants were also attracted to Butte, where they set up laundries and restaurants. Although Butte's preeminence in Montana has dimmed, the early growth of immigrant populations in the mining communities served to establish Roman Catholicism as the state's dominant religion, and Butte set a standard of openness to immigrants still observed by Montanans.

The railroads brought settlers to the plains of eastern Montana. Ambitious campaigns by the Great Northern and the Milwaukee Railroad succeeded in luring thousands of farmers to cultivate the dry prairie. Between 1900 and 1910 the number of farms and ranches in Montana doubled, and while many American-born homesteaders settled in Montana during this time, immigrants had an especially strong influence in eastern

Montana. By 1910, one-quarter of all Montanans were foreign-born. Entire communities of Germans, Russians, and Scandinavians were founded as farms and towns sprung up alongside rail sidings, with a telltale Lutheran church. Scots and Irish continued to settle the plains as ranchers and herdsmen. Today, in northern and central Montana, the names in small-town phone books read like similar directories in Norway, Sweden, or Scotland.

Even though droughts and the Depression worked to depopulate the Montana plains, the foreign character remains in communities founded by immigrant farmers and ranchers. Many eastern Montanans are only first-generation Americans. From 1900 to 1920, 50,000 foreign-born settlers moved to the state, while 120,000 American-born settlers did so. But during the droughts and bad markets of the 1920s, 10 times as many American-born homesteaders as immigrants gave up and moved on. By 1930, people of foreign birth or first-generation Montanans made up 45% of the population.

Some foreign settlers moved to Montana expressly to form communities. Mennonite groups settled in Montana during the homesteading years, but many left after the state Legislature, urged on by an organization called the Montana Council of Defense, drafted laws during WW I forbidding the German language. Hutterites maintain 22 communities in Montana and currently number over 2,000 adherents.

War policies have not always driven Montanans from the state. During WW II, Japanese internees from California were shipped to the state to work in sugar beet fields. Some found Montana to their liking; farming communities along the Yellowstone are still home to Japanese families.

Although not an ethnic minority, Mormons have established communities in Montana whose solidarity rivals that of old European enclaves. The Bitterroot Valley (and southwestern Montana in general) and the Great Falls area each have large Mormon communities. The Mormon Church is now the fourth largest in Montana.

DOVER PUBLICATIONS, INC.

ON THE ROAD

SIGHTSEEING HIGHLIGHTS

Montana is a very big state, and unless you have weeks to spend on the road, you simply won't be able to see and experience all that the state has to offer. If your time is limited, be sure not to miss the following regional highlights.

SOUTHEASTERN MONTANA

One absolute must-see in this part of the state is the **Little Bighorn Battlefield National Monument.** The clash of Custer's troops with the warriors of the Sioux and Cheyenne Nations is one of those defining moments in history, and the visitors center and the battlefield itself are haunted places.

Near Glendive, **Makoshika State Park** is a badlands preserve with hiking trails through a wildly eroded landscape. Miles City's **Range Riders Museum** is one of the state's best community museums, complete with relics and buildings from old Fort Keogh. East of Billings, **Pompey's Pillar** is a sandstone bluff with carvings

made by members of the Lewis and Clark Expedition, almost 200 years ago. It's a mandatory stop for fans of the Corps of Discovery. The **Bighorn River,** just north of the Wyoming state line, in the Crow Reservation, is one of Montana's best trout fishing rivers. You don't have to be an angler to be amazed by the river's mighty **Bighorn Canyon** and the **Yellowtail Dam.**

NORTHEASTERN MONTANA AND THE BIG OPEN

As its name indicates, this part of Montana is full of wide open spaces. If you're looking for unadulterated Western Experience, stop in little towns such as Malta or Jordan for an eyeful of cowboy and cowgirl culture. If you're passing through on a summer weekend, check to see if there's **rodeo** in the area. **Wolf Point's Stampede** is one of the state's most famous. Massive **Fort Peck** is one of the world's largest dams, backing up the

Missouri River for 150 miles. Surrounding it is the **C.M. Russell National Wildlife Refuge,** the largest in the contiguous U.S. and home to most of the prairie species indigenous to the upper Great Plains and to a wealth of **fossils** (these are some of the richest dinosaur digs in the world).

Migratory birds make stop-overs at **Medicine Lake** in extreme northeast Montana, a series of prairie wetlands. **Fort Union Trading Post National Historic Site,** near the confluence of the Missouri and Yellowstone Rivers, is a wonderful re-creation of an 1840s fur trading fort that was once the center of trade and culture in this part of North America.

NORTH-CENTRAL MONTANA

Montana's wheat-growing province, this mostly flat agricultural area brushes up against the front range of the Rocky Mountains. Great Falls is home to the new **Lewis and Clark National Historic Trail Interpretive Center,** which retells the story of the Corps of Discovery's 1805-06 journey from St. Louis to the Pacific and back. The facility overlooks some of the Great Falls of the Missouri, which gave Lewis and Clark and their men such difficulties. Also in Great Falls, the **C.M. Russell Museum** preserves a large collection of this amazing artist's works, as well as a gallery full of work by other Western artists.

Havre's raucous pioneer days are revealed in the **Havre Beneath the Streets** tours, which show the businesses and communities that thrived below the city's streets in the 1890s. Near Choteau, **Egg Mountain** is one of the nation's foremost **dinosaur fossil digs.** Public tours lead to fossil beds that reveal dinosaur egg nests, formations that have revolutionized palaentological theories.

Just west of Choteau, the **Rocky Mountain Front** rears up, a beautiful and remote area where the prairie meets the mountains. Some of Montana's finest guest ranches are located here.

THE JUDITH BASIN
AND CENTRAL MONTANA

Rolling prairies and isolated mountain ranges make this one of Montana's most lovely, low-key destinations. **Lewistown** is a friendly town

with a beautiful old downtown little changed from the 1910s. In mid-August, the state's premier cowboy poetry event is held here. **Harlowton** is another well-preserved railroad town along the Musselshell River and Hwy. 12, one of the most scenic routes across the state. **White Sulphur Springs** offers hot springs cures and mineral baths, and just down the valley the wild **Smith River** entices white-water rafters and anglers to explore a remote river canyon.

SOUTH-CENTRAL
AND THE MISSOURI HEADWATERS

In this mountainous region, all roads lead to **Yellowstone National Park,** the nation's oldest and largest. Three of the park's entrances are in Montana. Be sure to stop and spend time in **Bozeman,** a charming small city filled with art galleries, great restaurants, and student energy (Montana State University is here). **Livingston** is another well-preserved town that's been transformed by the cutting edge community of visual and literary art by the famous artists and writers who have moved here.

Big Sky, the state's most upscale ski resort, and the ski area at **Red Lodge** make this a great winter destination. In summer, hikers take to the mountains in **Absaroka-Beartooth Wilderness,** which boasts Montana's highest peaks and oddities including grasshopper glaciers. Anglers come from around the world to toss a fly in fabled trout waters of the **Madison, Gallatin,** and Yellowstone Rivers.

SOUTHWESTERN MONTANA

This is the region of Montana's first gold rush and its early mining history. Ghost towns such as **Bannack** and **Virginia City** tell the fascinating story of Vigilantes and the early gold-mining frontier.

Helena, the state capital, is a gold camp that managed to evolve into an endearing small city, filled with fantastic architecture. The **Montana Historical Society** contains the state's best museum, and the **Capitol Building** is a magnificent building modeled on the federal capitol.

Butte is one of the state's most fascinating cities. Called the "Richest Hill on Earth," it was the center of vast mining empires, early labor organizing, and incredible environmental devastation. There's more history per square inch in Butte than anywhere else in Montana.

For recreation and beauty, it's hard to beat the **Big Hole Valley.** Fishing is very good in this high and isolated valley, and there's history at the **Big Hole Battlefield,** where Chief Joseph and his Nez Perce defeated the US cavalry.

Dillon is a charming town at the center of a huge ranching valley. Fishing is excellent, and there's marvelous wildlife viewing at **Red Rock Lakes,** home to rare trumpeter swans.

NORTHWESTERN MONTANA

Missoula is a friendly, student-oriented town that's home to the University of Montana, legions of writers, and a dynamic arts community. To the south, the narrow **Bitterroot Valley** is a recreational wonderland, with hiking trails leading to high-country lakes and craggy peaks. The Bitterroot River is renowned for trout fishing. Overlooking the rugged and picturesque **Mission Mountains,** the **National Bison Range** pre-

ANNUAL EVENTS

Here is a selective list of some of the most notable annual events in Montana.

January
last weekend—Montana Winter Fair, Bozeman

February
mid-month—Race to the Sky dogsled race, from Helena to Holland Lake and back

March
early—Rendezvous cross-country ski race and Winter Festival, West Yellowstone
mid-month—C.M. Russell Western Art Auction, Great Falls
March 17—St. Patrick's Day Parade, Butte

April
early—International Wildlife Film Festival, Missoula

May
third weekend—Jaycee Bucking Horse Sale, Miles City

June
second weekend—Virginia City Days
mid-month—College National Finals Rodeo, Bozeman
third weekend—Custer's Last Stand Reenactment, Hardin
late—Lewis and Clark Festival, Great Falls
last Sunday—American Legion Rodeo, Augusta

July
July 4—Northern Cheyenne Powwow, Lame Deer; Terry Rodeo, Terry
July 4 weekend—Arlee Powwow, Arlee
mid-month—International Choral Festival, Missoula; Logger Days, Libby; Yellowstone Boat Float, Livingston to Columbus

third weekend, Crow Fair, Crow Reservation; North American Indian Days, Browning; Standing Arrow Powwow, Elmo
last weekend—Cutting Horse Show, Big Timber

August
first week—Montana State Fair, Great Falls
first weekend—Sweet Pea Festival, Bozeman
second week—Festival of Nations, Red Lodge
midmonth—Montana Cowboy Poetry Gathering, Lewistown
third week—Montana Fair, Billings; Northwestern Montana Fair, Missoula
third weekend, Eastern Montana Fair, Miles City

September
Labor Day—Ashland Powwow, Ashland
first Saturday—big-game bowhunting/game-bird season opens
third Sunday—backcountry big game season opens
third weekend—Nordicfest, Libby

October
first weekend—Fort Belknap Powwow, Fort Belknap
third weekend—Northern International Livestock Exposition, Billings
fourth Sunday—general big-game season opens

November
November 8—Anniversary of Montana's statehood (1889)

December
midmonth—Christmas home tour, Butte
all month—Christmas lights and decorations, Bigfork

serves a wild herd of the American Buffalo, hunted nearly to extinction in other parts of the West.

Flathead Lake is one of the state's most popular destinations. Flanked by mountains, cherry orchards, and luxury homes, this is an ideal place for a quiet vacation of water sports and fishing. **Bigfork,** on the lake's east side, is one of the artiest small towns in Montana, with a good summer theater, tons of galleries, and some of the best restaurants in the state. **Whitefish** sits at the base of the large destination ski resort **Big Mountain.** The two combine to create a lively and youthful recreational scene, both in winter and summer.

GLACIER NATIONAL PARK

The single most scenic destination in Montana, this park protects a wilderness of lakes, towering glacier-scarred peaks, and fragile alpine meadows. **Lake McDonald** glimmers at the base of the fantasically carved peaks, and tour boats wend their way through its sky-blue waters. You'd be hard pressed to find a more scenic drive in North America than **Going-to-the-Sun Road,** which climbs from the lake to cross the Continental Divide beneath regal snow-capped mountains.

On the east side of the park, the Great Plains roll up to meet the Rockies, which rise above them in miles-high cliffs. Consider spending the night at the old log lodge at **East Glacier** or the Swiss chalet-like **Many Glacier Lodge,** located on the shores of a glacial lake, just below glacier-hung crags. **Waterton Lakes National Park,** adjoining Glacier Park in Canada, continues this wonderful mountain and lake scenery, with an even grander old hotel, the **Prince of Wales.**

It's the backcountry that makes Glacier Park so thrilling. Be sure to get out of the car and explore. Trails lead to remote alpine lakes, tundra meadows, and ancient ice fields. In winter, stay at the charming **Izaak Walton Inn,** on the park's south flank, and explore the park on cross-country skis.

RECREATION

PUBLIC LANDS

Public lands (state and national forests and BLM land) constitute roughly 35% of the state, opening much of the state up for recreation and multi-use development.

State Parks
Montana operates about 40 state parks focusing on both recreation and history. Many of the parks include campgrounds, which are open from mid-May to mid-September. Day-use fees are $4 at most state parks, with an additional $7 for overnight campers. State parks are as diverse as For a pamphlet detailing all the state parks, write to the **Parks Division, Montana Dept. of Fish, Wildlife, and Parks,** 1420 E. 6th Ave., Helena, MT 59620, tel. (406) 444-2535.

U.S. Forest Service Lands
Much of the public land in Montana's western and southern mountains is administered by the US Forest Service. Forest Service ranger stations are good places to get information on camping and recreation. All National Forests contain developed hiking trails, and Forest Service roads in winter become de facto cross-country skiing trails. Most National Forests also have developed trail systems for mountain bikers and can provide maps highlighting roads and areas best suited for backcountry cycling. Most National Forest land is also open to hunting in season—usually late September through November. Forest Service maps are good for exploring and for spotting hiking trails and campsites.

Forest Service campgrounds are widespread in western Montana. Fees range from free to $14, depending on the amenities (free campgrounds are those with a pit toilet and no running water—they're usually remote and rarely crowded). The Forest Service also rents out some rustic cabins and fire lookouts, usually for about $25 a night. The Forest Service Regional Office in Missoula can supply a list of currently available cabins and tell you what supplies you'll need to bring along. Reach them at P.O. Box 7669, Missoula, MT 59807, tel. (406) 329-3511.

Wilderness Areas
Montana has 16 federally managed wilderness areas, roadless and closed to mechanized use,

including mountain bikes. Designated wilderness areas are sometimes more heavily used than remote, nonwilderness areas. Stop in at a Forest Service ranger station and ask which local trails they favor. In addition to the wilderness areas that fall under the jurisdiction of the Forest Service, there are several tribal wilderness areas in Montana. Before hiking or fishing on tribal land, be sure that you have the necessary permits.

National Parks

Glacier National Park falls entirely within Montana, and its Canadian counterpart, Waterton Lakes National Park, is directly above the border. Though the bulk of Yellowstone National Park is in Wyoming, three of the park's entrances, as well as its northern edge, are in Montana. Entrance fees are $10 for Glacier and $20 for Yellowstone. This pays for a week's unlimited entrance into the specified park. An extra fee is charged to camp in park campgrounds.

PRIVATE LAND

Even though much of Montana is publicly owned, you sometimes need to cross land that is privately owned to get *to* public land. This is an issue especially for anglers and hunters, as access to the best streams and hunting grounds is often across private land.

Always ask permission to cross private land—especially when it's fenced and *always* if there is a No Trespassing sign. Don't be surprised if you are asked to pay a small fee to cross private lands, especially in popular fishing areas such as the Madison Valley. In parts of Eastern Montana, the state has agreements with private landowners to allow access to private lands for hunting purposes. However, you must have written permission to hunt on these lands, and must report in to the landowner.

Most landowners are tolerant of people who ask permission to their land, but don't be surprised if permission is not granted. If a pasture is filled with cows and young calves, a rancher probably won't want people trooping through to fly fish, and certainly wouldn't allow someone in to start shooting rifles. Be considerate and polite and you'll usually get the permission you want. You may even make a friendly acquaintance with a real Montanan.

Tribal Lands

Each of Montana's seven Indian reservations is self-governing, and the state does not have authority to regulate fishing, hunting, or other recreational activities on tribal land. In fact, most reservation land is off-limits to all but tribe members. Remember that for many tribes, the land contains sacred sites and possesses a deeper significance to them than it may to you—it's perhaps more than just a cool place to race a mountain bike, in other words. Some tribes are more open to multi-use recreation than others; the Flathead reservation is generally open to non-members (as long as they have tribal permits), while the Crow reservation is generally off-limits to the public.

As you would for any privately owned land, always ask permission before trespassing. Tribal permits for hiking or fishing, if necessary, are generally available from most businesses on the reservation. They may be free or they may cost a small fee. When in doubt, call the tribal office to inquire about access and permits.

None of the above is intended to give the impression that reservations are closed to visitors, or that tourism isn't welcome. Respectful visitors are welcome at powwows and other cultural and sporting events (Indian rodeos are especially enjoyable). Ask Travel Montana for a brochure on tourism on the state's reservation.

OUTDOOR PURSUITS

Hiking and Backpacking

In a state that's as big as all outdoors, don't be surprised to find that hiking and backpacking are the preferred outdoor activities. Indeed, long backpacking trips through National Forests and wilderness areas are something of a rite of passage for many Montanans.

The most famous hiking area in the state is **Glacier National Park.** More so than Yellowstone, Glacier only yields up its wonders to those who get out of the car and hike up its trails. However, in high summer, the trails can be very busy and may therefore not deliver the wilderness experience you're looking for. Other areas to consider for longer backpacking trips are the **Bob Marshall Wilderness,** south of Glacier Park, the **Bitterroot Mountains,** south of Missoula, and the **Absaroka-Beartooth Wilderness,** north of Yellowstone.

HOW TO SELECT AN OUTFITTER

Montana is filled with outfitters, guides, trail drive operators, and guest ranches, all of whom promise to get you outdoors and into an Old West adventure. However, all outfitting and recreational services are not created equal. The most important consideration in choosing an outfitter is safety, the second is your comfort. Make sure you feel confident on both counts before signing on.

Here are some points to ponder while you plan your adventure vacation.

All outfitters should be licensed or accredited by the state, and be happy to provide you with proof. This means that they are bonded, carry the necessary insurance, and have money and organizational wherewithal to register with the province. This rules out fly-by-night operations and college students who've decided to set up business for the summer. If you're just starting to plan an excursion, ask Travel Montana for their complete list of licensed outfitters, or contact the Montana Outfitters and Guides Association, Box 1248, Helena, MT 59624, tel. (406) 449-3578.

Often a number of outfitters offer similar trips. When you've narrowed down your choice, call and talk to the outfitters on your short list. Ask lots of questions, and try to get a sense of who these people are; you'll be spending a lot time with them, so make sure you feel comfortable. You may not want to go on a weeklong wagon train trip with the local Montana Militia commander. If you have special interests, like bird or wildlife watching, be sure to mention them to your potential outfitter. A good outfitter will also take your interests into account when planning a trip.

If there's a wide disparity in prices between outfitters for the same trip, find out what makes up the difference. The cheapest trip may not be the best choice for you. Food is one of the most common areas to economize in. If you don't mind having cold cuts each meal for your five day pack trip, then maybe the cheapest outfitter is okay. If you prefer a cooked meal, or alcoholic beverages, or choice of entrees, then be prepared to pay more. On a long trip, it might be worth it to you. Also be sure you know what kind of accommodations are included in multi-day trips. You may pay more to have a tent or cabin to yourself; again, it may be worth it to you.

Ask how many years an outfitter has been in business and how long your particular escort has guided this trip. While a start-up outfitting service can be perfectly fine, you should know what level of experience you are buying. If you have questions, especially for longer or more dangerous trips, ask for referrals.

Most outfitters will demand that you pay a portion (usually half) of your fee well in advance to secure your place, so be sure to ask about your outfitter's cancellation policy. Some lengthy float trips can cost thousands of dollars; if cancellation means the forfeiture of the deposit, then you need to know that. Also, find out what the tipping or gratuity policy is for your outfitter. Sometimes 15 or 20% extra is added to your bill as a tip for the "hands." While this is undoubtedly nice for the help, you should be aware that your gratuities for a week's stay can run into the hundreds of dollars.

The National Forests are all laced with hiking trails, and the staff at any ranger station can help you put together a hiking trip that suits your interests, time limitations, your endurance.

Cycle Touring and Mountain Biking

There are plenty of opportunities for both touring and mountain biking, from Glacier Park to the Pryor Mountains. Missoula is home to **Adventure Cycling Association** (formerly Bikecentennial), a touring organization and advocacy group for cyclists. They lead rides across the state and the nation and can answer questions regarding routes and conditions. Contact the association at P.O. Box 8308, Missoula, MT

59807, tel. (406) 721-1776, or visit their offices in Missoula at 150 E. Pine. Bozeman is another center for biking—especially mountain biking.

Leading local bike shops are usually noted in the text, and heir staffs can offer plenty of good advice and route ideas. Many shops carry route maps showing local trails. Most national forests have developed information and maps for mountain bikers, and ranger stations are another good place to seek advice.

In general, cyclists need to remember two things: Montana is a very big place, and it's a long way between towns—especially in eastern and central Montana. Weather is another consideration. Summer can be a short season, and inclement weather can blow in very quickly. Also, much of Montana is very windy.

The state Department of Transport operates an office that deals with cycling. It can provide information on the suitability of specific roads and on road-repair schedules. Contact Bicycle/Pedestrian Program, Montana Dept. of Transportation, P.O. Box 201001, Helena, MT 59620-1001, tel. (406) 444-9273.

Hunting

Hunters flock to Montana in the fall for elk, pronghorn, pheasants, deer, bear, and the occasional mountain lion or bighorn sheep. A basic hunting license, which includes fishing, is $64 for Montanans, $150-485 for nonresidents. To hunt for certain animals—including moose, mountain sheep, and mountain goat—hunters need to enter special drawings. Nonresidents also need permits to hunt for antelope. For more information, contact **Montana Fish, Wildlife, and Parks,** 1420 E. 6th Ave., Helena, MT 59620, tel. (406) 444-2535, or visit the very thorough website: http://fwp.mt.gov. If you'd like to enlist the aid of a hunting guide, check the text for recommendations on established outfitters, or contact the **Montana Guides and Outfitters Association,** P.O. Box 1248, Helena, MT 59624, tel. (406) 449-3578, for a list of licensed outfitters.

Fishing

Montana's streams and rivers are famous for their plentiful but wily trout. Though it's theoretically possible to fish year-round in lakes and large rivers, late June through October are the most popular months for fishing. The state maintains more than 300 fishing access areas across the state. The basic fee for a fishing license is $13 for Montana residents, $45 for nonresident year-long license (or $10 for a two-day license). A $5 nonresident/$4 resident conservation license is also required.

The list of blue-ribbon fishing streams in Montana is very lengthy, and includes such well-known (and now crowded) rivers as the Yellowstone, Bighorn, Madison, and Big Hole. However, these are just the famous fisheries—many other rivers and streams provide ample sport and fishing pleasure. Lake fishing is also popular, especially in northwestern Montana, with such bodies as Flathead Lake.

Even arid eastern Montana is a fishing destination, with famed walleye fishing in Fort Peck Reservoir and paddlefishing in the Yellowstone River near Glendive.

You don't have to hire a fishing guide or outfitter to fish in Montana, but if you're new to angling or would like to gain more skill as a flyfisher, it's a good idea to enlist the aid of an outfitter. Also, access to fishing holes can be a problem, and a local outfitter can remove potential hassles that could otherwise ruin a quick fishing trip to Montana. Each chapter of this book includes the names of reputable fishing guides and fly shops.

Contact the **Montana Dept. of Fish, Wildlife, and Parks,** 1420 E. 6th Ave., Helena, MT 59620, tel. (406) 444-2535, website: http://fwp.mt.gov, for up-to-date information on licensing and season dates. The agency can also provide a list of licensed outfitters, as can **Fishing Outfitters Association of Montana** (FOAM), P.O. Box 37, Gallatin Gateway, MT 59730.

Falcon Press publishes comprehensive guidebooks on fishing in Montana (see **Booklist**), well worth reading in order to familiarize yourself with local conditions.

Skiing

Big Mountain, just outside of Whitefish, and Big Sky, some 30 miles south of Bozeman, are Montana's two big "destination" ski resorts. If you'd rather avoid the development but still can't resist the thrills of downhill, try one of the smaller ski areas outside Libby, Missoula, Bozeman, Anaconda, Darby, Dillon, Neihart, Red Lodge, or Choteau. The ski season generally runs from Thanksgiving through mid-March.

Once the back roads of national forests are covered with snow, many of them become **cross-country** ski trails. The Forest Service distributes a list of ski trails, and local ranger stations have specific maps for their areas. Trails groomed for both standard cross-country skiing and "freestyle," or "skating," are maintained by lodges, such as the Izaak Walton Inn in Essex, and by individual communities, like the Rendezvous Trails in West Yellowstone. There may be a fee to ski on groomed trails.

For an overview of downhill and cross-country ski areas, contact **Travel Montana,** and request the *Montana Winter Guide*. This brochure also contains information about **snowmobiling.** Most ski resorts and all larger towns have ski, snowboard, and snowshoe rental facilties.

River Rafting and Floating
Montana's many rivers are popular for whitewater rafting and more leisurely float trips. The most famous whitewater rivers are the branches of the Flathead near Glacier National Park and the Gallatin and Yellowstone near Yellowstone Park. These rivers are also popular with kayakers. Other river trips will take you to remote areas of wilderness reached only on multi-day float trips. The Wild and Scenic portion of the Missouri, downstream from Fort Benton, is a favorite for naturalists and devotees of Lewis and Clark. The Smith River takes anglers through limestone canyons to otherwise unreachable fishing holes.

River trips are offered by a number of guide services, and boats can be rented in most river towns. For most multi-day trips, advance reservations are required; in fact, for popular rivers such as the Smith, you'll need reservations many months in advance. Most whitewater guide services offer day and part-day trips that require only a day's advance reservations.

Dependable and experienced guides are listed in the text. For a complete list of guides, contact the **Montana Outfitters and Guides Association,** Box 1248, Helena, MT 59624, tel. (406) 449-3578, or the **Montana Board of Outfitters,** Department of Commerce, 111 N. Jackson, Helena, MT 59620, tel. (406) 444-3738. Travel Montana's handy *Travel Planner* also contains a list of all licensed outfitters.

Curt Thompson's extremely comprehensive book, *Floating and Recreation on Montana Rivers,* is a good investment for anyone who wants to canoe, kayak, or raft their way through Montana.

Windsurfing hasn't been particularly developed in Montana, but occasionally a sail goes up on Flathead Lake. Strong winds on the Blackfeet Reservation and around Livingston have generated talk, if not actual windsurfing sites.

Horseback Riding and Cattle Drives
Outfitters, resorts, and guest ranches all generally offer horseback riding. Guided trail rides are the norm, though longer pack trips into the mountains are also scheduled. **Cattle drives** are becoming increasingly popular, with over 20 Mon-

tana ranches now offering guests the chance to trail cattle from pasture to pasture or ranch to town. These trips usually involve several days of horseback riding, camping out on the prairie, and eating meals from chuckwagons.

Again, the **Montana Outfitters and Guides Association,** Box 1248, Helena, MT 59624, tel. (406) 449-3578, is a good place to start. A list of guest and dude ranches, as well as wagon train and cattle drive outfitters, is included in Travel Montana's **Travel Planner,** or contact the **Montana Ranch Vacation Association,** P.O. Box 492, Ekalaka, MT 59324, tel. (406) 775-6204.

Rockhounding and Prospecting
Explore the Treasure State with a pan or a bucket. Prospect for gold near Libby, or buy a bucket of dirt outside of Helena or Philipsburg and pick through it in search of sapphires. Hunt for garnets in southwestern Montana, agates along the Yellowstone, and petrified wood in the Gallatin National Forest. The *Rockhound's Guide to Montana* contains detailed information on sites and facilities throughout the state.

GAMBLING IN MONTANA

A number of forms of gambling are legal in Montana, as any visitor to the state will instantly notice—many old-time bars, taverns, clubs, and lounges have all become casinos. Gambling is regulated by the state, which takes 10-15% of the proceeds from the various games—and makes about $275 million a year in the process.

While card rooms have always been legal—or at least tolerated—in Montana, electronic gambling has been legalized only recently. Other forms of gambling, such as pari-mutuel and video-link horse racing, calcuttas, and shake-a-day dice games, are legal as well. Montana also participates in three multistate lotteries.

Card Room Games
In the back room of many an old-time bar is a well-burnished green-felt table, usually watched over—with hawklike vigilance—by a number of sharp-eyed denizens. At some cue—perhaps the arrival of a newcomer with fresh money, or the advent of a lucky omen—the game begins, often lasting long into the early hours of the morning.

W.C. McRAE

Enterprising young prospectors examine pans for glints of gold.

All traditional forms of poker are legal; stud and draw are the favored games. There's a $300 pot limit. To play, you need to buy chips from the house; if you're lucky and win, you cash out your chips from the house. The house will keep its—and the state's—share.

Blackjack, pan, pitch, and other card games in which the players bet against the house are *not* legal in Montana. Neither are most dice games—including craps—or "beat-the-house" games, such as roulette.

Keno, a hopped-up version of bingo, is legal, both as an electronic game and in its original form—as a barroom diversion. If you've ever wondered what that large checkered game board on the wall of an old bar is, you're probably looking at a lighted keno display.

While it's permissible to watch strangers play poker in the back rooms of bars, remember that there is frequently a lot of money at risk, tempers can be short, and often liquor has flowed liberally. Keep your mouth shut and act reverential. Don't do anything that might break the concentration of the players or that may be interpreted as interaction.

Electronic Games

Video poker is by far the most popular of the various kinds of electronic gambling in Montana. The whirring, ringing, and beeping of the machines have all but eliminated the gentle buzz of conversation in Montana watering holes.

To play video poker, you put a coin—usually a quarter—in the slot. A random five-card hand ap-

pears on the screen, and you decide which, if any, of the cards you want to keep. Press the corresponding buttons, then press a different button to receive replacement cards. The machine will let you know if you have any combination of winning cards. Should you win, don't expect a cascade of small change. Winning combinations earn points (which usually equal quarters). You decide whether to use your points to play more hands or to cash them out by contacting the bartender or game-room manager.

Other Legal Gambling

Pari-mutuel **horse racing** is popular at summer fairs. Some bars and clubs offer a more cutting-edge method of betting on horseflesh—video broadcasts of live horse races. You get racing forms, track conditions, lines at the betting booth—everything but the dust and the smell of horse sweat.

A more distinctly Montana form of legal betting is the **calcutta.** A calcutta,usually held as a charity event, involves auctioning off the performance of a sportsman, usually a rodeo contestant or golfer. If the cowboy you "buy" wins his event, then you get a share of his prize money, while the majority of the money raised from the auction goes to the charity.

As in other states, Indians on federal reservations have opened casinos that feature games not otherwise allowed by Montana state law. Under the confusing laws that govern activities on reservations, Native Americans can bypass restrictive state laws by invoking federal laws that recognize reservations as sovereign entities. Nevada-style casinos are present in a number of locations on Montana reservations.

SPECTATOR SPORTS

Rodeos

Most communities in Montana have rodeos at least once each summer, often on the Fourth of July, during the county fair, or sometimes just whenever enough interested parties come together in one place. "Little Britches" rodeos are held for grade-school children. High-school rodeo clubs are often the largest extracurricular groups in small towns. Intercollegiate rodeo is also popular—and a source of scholarships for Montana students. Bozeman hosts the national finals for intercollegiate rodeo.

Make every attempt to attend *some* rodeo. Rodeos are quintessentially Western but haven't yet become heavily commercialized. Be prepared to get hot and dusty, and be friendly. Summer rodeos are a community's way to visit with friends and family. Dates of rodeos are available from local chambers of commerce or from publications available from regional tourism bureaus.

Rodeos can be confusing to the first-time spectator. **Saddle-bronc riding** involves a cowboy staying on a saddled bucking horse for eight seconds. Similarly, in **bareback bronc riding,** the rider tries to stay aboard a bucking horse for eight seconds, but he has only a "rigging" (a very small, seatless leather saddle) for assistance. **Bull riding** pitches an enormous bull, usually a Brahma, against a cowboy, who must ride **that** for eight seconds. The bulls and the horses in these events are strapped around their lower abdomen with a "flank cinch," which annoys the animals into greater bucking fits. In all events, the cowboy must make the ride using only one hand to hang on (using two hands, even very briefly, results in disqualification). The cowboys are not judged on the length of their ride. If they make it the necessary eight seconds, the ride is then judged on its particular merits, including amount and quality of spurring (which further annoys the animal, increasing the bucking), the general comportment of the cowboy on the animal, and the fierceness of the animal's bucking.

In **bulldogging,** a steer emerges at full lope from the chute. A cowboy gives chase aboard a galloping horse, jumps from the horse to the steer, and wrestles the steer to the ground. Winners are determined by speed. **Calf roping** begins similarly, but the cowboy must lasso the calf, leap from his horse (while the horse keeps the rope taut), and ties three of the calf's legs to immobilize it for five seconds. Some rodeos also include **team roping,** where one of a pair of cowboys ropes the head and the other the hind legs of a steer.

The sole *cowgirl's* event is barrel racing, in which riders zip in a cloverleaf pattern around three barrels. If the horse knocks over a barrel, five seconds are added to the contestant's time.

Other rodeo events include the **grand entry** at the beginning of the rodeo, wherein two young cowgirls "present the colors" (U.S. and state) while galloping around the arena on horseback. Every entrant who has brought a horse to the event immediately joins the flagbearers in the arena for a horseback national anthem.

Clowns are also a part of the rodeo. During the bull-riding event, irate bulls can turn on thrown, addled riders and gore them. Clowns draw the bull's attention to themselves by teasing or throwing tractor inner tubes at the bull, while the dazed cowboy makes a safe escape.

Some rodeos also include **novelty events** such as wild-cow milking (first team with any milk at all wins), various kinds of racing; or some children's events such as greased pig contests or wild-sheep riding.

Montana Baseball

The only other spectator sport in Montana is AAA baseball. Professional baseball's Pioneer League has been a crowd-pleaser here since 1939. Most of the players are recent draft picks, and the Pioneer League is their first real baseball job.

The Billings Mustangs (a farm team for the Cincinnati Reds), the Butte Copper Kings (associated with the Texas Rangers), the Great Falls Dodgers (Los Angeles Dodgers), and the Helena Brewers (Milwaukee Brewers) make up the northern division of the Pioneer League.

Each team plays 70 games between mid-June and the end of August. Games are taken seriously, and fans often develop a rapport with the young players.

Reach the Pioneer League's Billings office at (406) 248-3401. Staff there can provide schedule information.

ACCOMMODATIONS AND FOOD

ACCOMMODATIONS

Traditional Lodging

The recent tourism boom in Montana has brought a wide variety of lodging options to the state. Generally speaking, rooms in hotels and motels are rather expensive in summer season, and often in short supply. Reserve rooms several days in advance, especially if you want a specific type of room or a special hotel. Especially around the national parks, but anywhere on a summer weekend, expect the lodging situation to be tight.

Prices in this guide reflect summer high season rack rates. These prices are usually for the least expensive standard room. Often room prices will change due to the night of the week (weekends may be more expensive). If you're traveling out of season, expect to find cheaper room rates, especially in tourist areas.

The development of the freeway system has led to clusters of chain motels around the off-ramps on the edges of town. Often, better deals on lodgings are found away from these developments, along the old arterials. Also, don't dismiss staying at old downtown hotels. Some are renovated and reflect the splendor of yore; others, for the more daring, have survived as residential hotels. Chances are you'll have a unique experience.

Guest Ranches and Resorts

High-end resorts have begun to spring up across the state, many with the ambience of a country lodge or guest ranch. More traditional dude and guest ranches and hot springs resorts, many with a lengthy pedigree, abound: there's scarcely a community in Montana now that does not offer some form of guest ranch accommodation. Some of these can be wonderfully rustic and lo-

---

HOT SPRINGS

A traveler could do worse than plan a hot springs tour of Montana. Hot water gurgles up all over the state, and it's exploited to one degree or another by a wide variety of resorts, from the rustic to the chic.

South Central Montana

Bozeman; Bozeman Hot Springs; (406) 586-6492; pool at the local KOA campground

Norris; Beartrap Hot Springs in Yellowstone Park; (406) 685-3303; small pool and RV campground

Pony; Potosi Hot Springs; a recent and remote development

Pray; Chico Hot Springs; (406) 333-4933; huge outdoor pool with lodge

Southwestern Montana

Anaconda; Fairmont Hot Springs; 406) 797-3241; four pools, two Olympic-sized, and full resort facilities

Boulder; Boulder Hot Springs; (406) 225-4339; large old hotel, now partially renovated, with nice outdoor pool and indoor plunges

Jackson; Jackson Hot Springs; (406) 843-3151; large outdoor pool and western lodge right on Jackson's main street

Polaris; Elkhorn Hot Springs; (406) 834-3434; two outdoor pools, a sauna, and a rustic lodge and cabins

Northwestern Montana

Lolo; Lolo Hot Springs; (406) 273-2201; big outdoor pool, indoor soaking pool, motel, and camping

Hot Springs; Camp Aqua Bathhouse; (406) 741-2361; private "plunges" and steam rooms

Hot Springs; Symes Hotel & Mineral Baths; (406) 741-2361; historic hotel with therapeutic treatments, newly renovated and pleasant

Sula; Lost Trail Hot Springs; (406) 821-3574; nice outdoor pool, indoor hot tub and saunas; lodge, cabins, and camprground

Paradise; Quinn's Hot Springs; (406) 826-3150; natural mineral hot springs with motel and camping

Central Montana

White Sulphur Springs; Spa Hot Springs Motel; (406) 547-3366; outdoor swimming pool, indoor soaking pool, and motel

cated in a beautiful rural settings, and most offer unlimited horseback riding in addition to other recreational activities. Some small guest ranches enjoy a quiet fame with a long-standing blue-chip (and even royal!) clientele; hot springs resorts vary from the full-blown convention-sized facilities, such as Fairmont Hot Springs, to modest mom-and-pop affairs. Some ski resorts like Big Sky and Big Mountain have reputations that precede them; they are open year-round for hiking, fishing, and other summer activities.

Other guest ranches and resorts can be much more modest; your rustic farm vacation might call for you to sleep in the sheep wagon. When you're deciding on a guest ranch vacation, ask plenty of questions on the phone before booking, and make sure that you're comfortable with the accommodations and facilities. The guest ranches and resorts recommended in this guide have each been inspected and represent good values; any should guarantee an enjoyable stay.

Another good source for information on guest ranches is the **Montana Ranch Vacation Association,** P.O. Box 492, Ekalaka, MT 59324, tel. (406) 775-6204, which can provide information on its member ranches.

Bed and Breakfasts

Bed and breakfasts have exploded in popularity in Montana in the last few years; in the Flathead Valley alone, there are more than 75 B&B inns. Many of the newer B&Bs are quite luxurious indeed, with swimming pools, trendy New West decor, and hot tubs; others are located in historic homes or buildings, and provide a wonderfully evocative insight into the Old West.

If you are amongst those people leery of B&Bs, or have had bad experiences at homestays where it was too much like staying in the back bedroom under Aunt Lulu's watchful eye, rest assured that all the B&Bs listed in this guide have been personally inspected and are heartily recommended. Another good source for information on quality B&Bs is the **Montana Bed and Breakfast Association,** 2986 Hwy. 93, Stevensville, MT 59870. Call (800) 453-8870 to request a copy of the member directory. Check out the website at www.wtp.net/go/montana.

The MBBA is a self-policing membership organization whose accommodations are inspected and approved according to a rigorous standard of requirements. These standards provide for the highest degree of cleanliness, convenience, and comfort for the traveler and are regulated with regular inspections by the association.

Camping and RV Parks

If you're at all inclined toward camping, bring along your gear and head out to the wilds of Montana. Western Montana is especially well endowed with public campgrounds in national forests and state parks. Tent campers need to plan ahead in other parts of the state if they want formal campsites, as public campgrounds thin out on the prairies. Ask to camp in town parks; the locals will be glad to have their parks appreciated. RV campers will find campgrounds in most towns. Fees in public campgrounds usually range from free to $14; privately owned campgrounds charge $10-22 a night (most have rudimentary facilities for tent campers).

In between a motel and a campground are Forest Service cabins and lookouts, rustic accommodations, generally with outhouses and without bedding or cooking utensils. They normally rent for $25 a night. Write or call the USDA Forest Service, Northern Region Office, 200 E. Broadway, Missoula, MT 59802, tel. (406) 329-3511 for a cabin directory.

FOOD AND DRINK

Here's the stereotype, mostly true: steaks are standard and usually good. Vegetarians manage to make do with the pervasive salad bars. Though the '90s have brought espresso machines to all corners of the state, be prepared for plenty of thin, often bitter coffee laden with sugar and Cremora.

There really isn't anything to justify the label "Montana cuisine." Dishes peculiar to the region usually ring changes on established entrees, which is not to say they're bad. Adding huckleberries to every dish does not a cuisine make. However, local beef and fresh Montana trout give even a teenage fry cook a chance for greatness.

Buffalo burgers are simply hamburgers made with ground buffalo meat; promoters claim buffalo is a leaner, more flavorful alternative to beef. Indian tacos load taco ingredients onto fry bread.

MONTANA MICROBREWERIES

Montana has joined the Pacific Northwest in its revival of small breweries. A number of microbreweries have sprung up across the state, providing thirsty travelers a chance to taste local beers. Ask for locally brewed beer in Montana. Chances are it will come from one of the following established breweries.

A note: Montana state law does not allow for brew pubs. Microbrewed beer must be sold, like any other alcohol product, in a separately owned and licensed facility. However, a tavern next door to a microbrewery can sell anything it likes, as long as walls separate the brewing facility from the drinking area.

Bayern Brewing, Missoula: This microbrewery makes some of the best German-style beer in the state. Brews include a dark lager, an amber ale, and a delicious pilsner. There are up to eight seasonal beers as well. Bayern beer is also available bottled.

Big Sky Brewing Co, Missoula: You know these beers are popular with students—different brews have names including Moose Drool Ale, Scape Goat Stout, and the like.

Whitefish Brewing Company, Whitefish: Available on draft only, this northwestern Montana brewery sells its beer under the "Milikian" label. Ask for Milikian's pale and nut-brown ales, as well as a number of seasonal brews. Tours of the brewery are available, but there is no brewpub.

Kessler Brewing Company, Helena: The oldest microbrewery in the state, Kessler beer is widely distributed, both on tap and in bottles. Kessler produces Dopelbock, Ale No. 7, Centennial, and Lorelei (a wheat beer). Seasonal brews are also available. The brewery is open for tours, but there is no brewpub.

Milestown Brewing Company, Miles City: Another new entry to the brewery scene, Milestown is available in Miles City bars. If you're lucky enough to be in town for the Bucking Horse Sale, then try out the special bock beer brewed in conjunction. There's also Milestown Amber Ale and dark, rich, Coal Porter.

Spanish Peaks Brewing Company, Bozeman: A brewery that has reached almost instant success, Spanish Peaks is available across the state in both bottles and on draft. Watch for their wheat ale, pale ale, amber Black Dog Ale, and Spanish Peaks Porter. Seasonal beers are available on draft.

Yellowstone Valley Brewing, Billings: This eastern Montana brewery has introduced Billings Brown Ale and will be adding to the list soon. Ask for it in Billings bars.

Rocky Mountain oysters are more often threatened than served; served correctly, lamb or calf testicles are the quintessential offal meat, surprisingly palatable.

But even when restaurant fare seems unimaginative compared to cuisine on the coasts, the general quality of the food is quite good. Home cooking sets the standard, and simple, unprepossessing food is often the best.

There are happy exceptions to the rule, however. Chefs have mastered sauces in some pretty out-of-the-way places: where you least expect it—Chico, Willow Creek, Essex—isolated but enterprising cooks have established restaurants with sophisticated dining. The Flathead Valley is accumulating quite a collection of good restaurants; Bigfork can boast of being the culinary capital of the state.

Montanans like to eat out. Cafes and restaurants are social centers, and eating out is a way of combating isolation. The bar is another meeting place, and not just for adults. Entire families meet up at bars, where it's perfectly normal to stick to soft drinks.

SHOPPING

Montana has no sales tax, and you'll begin to like the idea of provisioning for the holidays while on vacation.

Gifts and Souvenirs

There aren't many places that evoke the Wild West as clearly as Montana, and a gift or souvenir that recalls the Western past makes a good keepsake. Most every town will have a clothing store and saddlery featuring western clothes. Pearl snap shirts, tooled leather belts, and other leather goods make nice and functional gifts. If you're wondering why cowboys and cowgirls look so good in their jeans, it's because the pants are Wrangler brand. Look for the Rodeo Cut jeans if you want squeeze into something that's

OUT OF THE WATER CLOSET

Montanans delight in finding alternatives to boring old "men" and "women" on the doors of bathrooms in bars and restaurants throughout the state. Don't be fooled! A sampling:

Bulls and Heifers (the Jersey Lily, Ingomar)
Does and Bucks (Q-Ds, Jordan)
Eski-Mas and Eski-Pas (Wades, Harlowton)
Jackeroos and Jilleroos (the Longbranch, Dillon)
Pistols and Holsters (the Dixon Bar)
Pointers and Setters, with dog portraits (the Buckhorn Bar, Fort Peck)

bound to get attention when you get back home. Likewise, Montana is a good place to buy a pair of cowboy boots. A number of saddleries make boots to order, though be ready to mortgage your house to pay for them.

Although none of Montana's Indian tribes has a long tradition of commericial arts or crafts, a number of gift shops and galleries now feature the works of native artists. Look for silver or beaded jewelry and leather goods, as well as paintings on hide.

Other local artists and artisans show their works in local craftshops and galleries. Most of the larger towns across Montana—including Sidney, Miles City, Lewistown, Kalispell, Billings, and Glendive—have community art centers which feature the works of local people.

Montana is also a major center for Western art, especially for blue-chip bronze statuary and wildlife art. Bozeman, Livingston, Kalispell, Whitefish, Big Fork, and even such unlikely towns as Wisdom and Big Timber all feature world-class galleries.

Another good gift or souvenir idea is Montana food products. Native fruits and berries make up into delicious jams and jellies. Huckleberry and chokecherry products will make nice remembrances. Local honey is also common and easy to find. Local cherries and wild huckleberries find their way into a wide selection of candies and confections. On the other end of the food scale, dried jerkies and smoked fish are produced by small local companies.

Sporting Goods

Montana is a real mecca of recreation and sports, and a number of excellent manufacturers and stores have sprung up to serve the market. Again, without a sales tax, Montana may be a tempting place to buy these items.

Almost every little town in western Montana has a fly fishing shop, complete with hand-tied flies and fancy rods and reels. The R.L Winston fly rod company in Twin Bridges is especially famous, a place many anglers approach almost with the reverence of religious supplicants on a pilgrimage to a holy site.

Many ski shops turn mountain bike shops by summer, and vice versa, and you can often get really good prices on skies or bikes if you visit Montana in the right season. Likewise, canoes and kayaks can get pretty cheap at the end of the season, when proprietors need to make room for snowboards.

While it's not a piece of sporting gear that the average reader will use often, nothing says Montana quite like a handmade saddle. The state is home to a number of famous saddlers, who make saddles to order for professional cowboys, celebrity ranchers, and anyone else capable of paying for them. Expect a handmade saddle to start around $2,500.

TRANSPORTATION

Montana is a long way from just about anywhere, and once you get there, it's a long way between stops. Although Montana has fine airline and bus service, and Amtrak's Empire Builder rolls along Montana's 550-mile border with Canada, the best way to visit the state is with your own vehicle. With so much territory to move around in, you'll want to wander freely.

GETTING THERE

By Air
There are no international airports in Montana with direct service to foreign destinations, except for regional flights to Alberta. The closest international airports are Seattle in the west, Denver and Salt Lake City to the south, Minneapolis to the east, and Calgary to the north. Billings is the major air hub in Montana, and is served by most major western airlines. Missoula, Bozeman, Butte, Helena, Kalispell, and Great Falls are also serviced by major carriers.

By Train
Amtrak's **Empire Builder,** which travels four times weekly between Chicago and Seattle and Portland, provides rail service to extreme northern Montana. Unfortunately, most of Montana's population and many of its popular tourist destinations are farther to the south (with the exception of Glacier National Park). Public transport linking these northern tier cities to the rest of the state is sketchy, partly because Amtrak has trouble keeping its trains close to their schedule. If you are dependent on public transportation or rental cars, then make sure that your Amtrak destination at least offers bus service to other parts of Montana or has vehicles for rent.

Passenger trains pulled out of the southern Montana routes more than 20 years ago, but today you can once again travel this highly scenic rail corridor with **Montana Rockies Rail Tours,** tel. (800) 519-7245. Trains follow the old Northern Pacific line between Sandpoint, Idaho, and Billings, using comfortable, reclining seat coaches and glass-domed observation cars. The train travels only by day, rolling as far as Missoula the first day and arriving in Billings the next—you can begin the trip from either terminus, and you can also arrange for side tours at either end of the trip. The trips are offered in late July, August, September, and early October, and tickets starts at $399 a person, which includes lodging, breakfasts, and lunches.

TRANSPORTATION PHONE NUMBERS

TRANSPORT	PHONE NUMBERS	SERVICE TO
Delta Airlines	tel. (800) 221-1212	Billings, Bozeman, Great Falls, Helena, Kalispell, Missoula
United Airlines	tel. (800) 241-6522	Billings
Northwest Airlines	tel. (800) 225-2525	Billings, Bozeman, Butte, Great Falls, Helena, Kalispell, Missoula
Horizon Airlines	tel. (800) 547-9308	Billings, Bozeman, Butte, Great Falls, Helena, Kalispell, Missoula
Big Sky Airlines	tel. (800) 237-7788	Billings, Glasgow, Glendive, Great Falls, Havre, Helena, Lewistown, Miles City, Missoula, Sidney, Wolf Point
Sky West Airlines	tel. (800) 453-9417	Billings, Bozeman, Butte, Helena, Missoula, West Yellowstone
Amtrak	tel. (800) 872-7245	runs parallel to Hwy. 2 along northern Montana
Greyhound Bus	tel. (800) 231-2222	covers the I-90 and I-94 corridor, as well as I-15

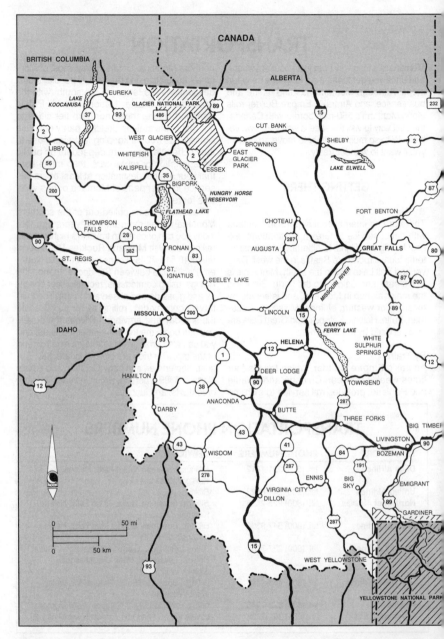

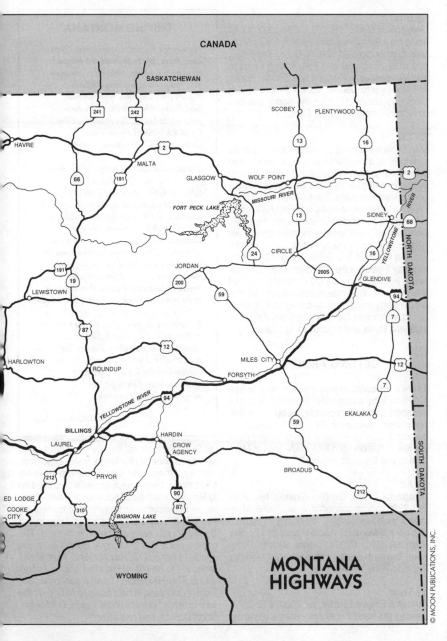

MONTANA
HIGHWAYS

© MOON PUBLICATIONS, INC.

By Bus

Greyhound buses, tel. (800) 231-2222 travel along the national interstate system, linking Montana to other regional centers. Buses travel east and west along I-90 and I-94, linking Chicago and Minneapolis to Portland and Seattle. Buses link Montana to Denver along I-94 and to Salt Lake City along I-15; from the north, one bus daily links Calgary to Great Falls.

By Car

Montana's most traveled roads cross the state east to west. It's no coincidence that these roads parallel early explorer routes; then as now, most travelers come to Montana to get across it as expeditiously as possible. The I-94/I-90 corridor follows the Yellowstone and Clark Fork Rivers and is the most perfunctory route across the state. Dawdlers will prefer to cross the state along more northerly routes. Highway 12 follows the old Milwaukee Railroad line across central Montana; Highway 2 parallels the Canadian border on Montana's Hi-Line, along the old Great Northern rail line. Highway 200 connects the dots between the two. The only major highway cutting north to south is I-15, which links Canada with Great Falls, Helena, and Butte, and extends to Salt Lake City.

GETTING AROUND

There's no question that the best way to see Montana is by automobile. Traveling by public transport is certainly possible, as buses, trains, and planes traverse the state. But the population centers that serve as public transportation hubs are few in number, and who really goes to Montana to see the cities anyway?

By Air

A regional airline, Big Sky Airlines, tel. (800) 237-7788, offers connections to smaller Montana population centers, especially in eastern and central Montana. Another local carrier, Sky West, tel. (800) 453-9417, links Billings, Bozeman, Butte, Helena, with seasonal summer flights to West Yellowstone.

By Train

Amtrak's Empire Builder, tel. (800) 872-7245, crosses Montana's northern extreme along the

---

"DRIVING MONTANA"

The day is a woman who loves you. Open.
Deer drink close to the road and magpies
spray from your car. Miles from any town
your radio comes in strong, unlikely
Mozart from Belgrade, rock and roll
from Butte. Whatever the next number,
you want to hear it. Never has your Buick
found this forward a gear. Even
the tuna salad in Reedpoint is good.

Towns arrive ahead of imagined schedule.
Absorakee at one. Or arrive so late—
Silesia at nine—you recreate the day.
Where did you stop along the road
and have fun? Was there a runaway horse?
Did you park at that house, the one
alone in a void of grain, white with green
trim and red fence, where you know you lived
once? You remembered the ringing creek,
the soft brown forms of far off bison.
You must have stayed hours, then drove on.
In the motel you know you'd never seen it before.

Tomorrow will open again, the sky wide
as the mouth of a wild girl, friable
clouds you lose yourself to. You are lost
in miles of land without people, without
one fear of being found, in the dash
of rabbits, soar of antelope, swirl
merge and clatter of streams.

—Richard Hugo

---

old Great Northern rail line. By doing so, it offers service to none of Montana's major population centers. Unless you simply want to traverse Montana, or have friends or rental cars lined up to ferry you southward (bus links at Havre, Shelby, and Whitefish aren't guaranteed to meet the train), Amtrak isn't a very meaningful way to visit the state: you can't get there from here. The good news is that the Empire Builder skirts the southern edge of Glacier National Park and is reckoned to be one of the most scenic Amtrak routes. The independent traveler bent on kicking loose in Montana is best advised to hop off the train at either Spokane, Washington, or Williston, North Dakota, and rent a car.

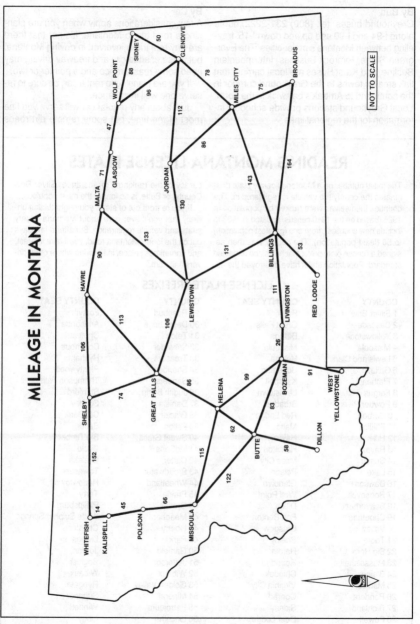

MILEAGE IN MONTANA

NOT TO SCALE

© MOON PUBLICATIONS, INC.

WHITEFISH — 14 — KALISPELL — 45 — POLSON — 66 — MISSOULA

SHELBY — 152 — WHITEFISH

SHELBY — 74 — GREAT FALLS

SHELBY — 106 — HAVRE

HAVRE — 113 — GREAT FALLS

HAVRE — 90 — MALTA

MALTA — 71 — GLASGOW

GLASGOW — 47 — WOLF POINT

WOLF POINT — 88 — SIDNEY

SIDNEY — 50 — GLENDIVE

GLENDIVE — 78 — MILES CITY

GLENDIVE — 112 — JORDAN

MILES CITY — 75 — BROADUS

MILES CITY — 86 — JORDAN

BROADUS — 164 — BILLINGS

MALTA — 133 — LEWISTOWN

JORDAN — 130 — LEWISTOWN

LEWISTOWN — 106 — GREAT FALLS

LEWISTOWN — 131 — BILLINGS

MILES CITY — 143 — BILLINGS

GREAT FALLS — 86 — HELENA

BILLINGS — 111 — LIVINGSTON

BILLINGS — 53 — RED LODGE

LIVINGSTON — 26 — BOZEMAN

BOZEMAN — 91 — WEST YELLOWSTONE

BOZEMAN — 83 — BUTTE

HELENA — 99 — BOZEMAN

HELENA — 62 — BUTTE

HELENA — 115 — MISSOULA

BUTTE — 58 — DILLON

BUTTE — 122 — MISSOULA

By Bus

Greyhound buses, tel. (800) 231-2222, hurtle along I-94 and I-90 and up and down I-15, traveling between Montana's major cities. The Evergreen Stage, Rimrock Buslines, Intermountain Busline, and Karst Buses are local carriers that link smaller towns to the Greyhound corridor in the south and to Amtrak's bailiwick in the north. Local Greyhound stations provide schedule information for the regional lines.

By Car

A few considerations apply when you are planning a road trip to Montana. It's not that there are any real tricks involved in driving Montana, but those used to city and freeway driving may need some reassurance and a pointer or two.

If you are planning to rent a car, be sure to reserve one well in advance.

Just about any regular car will serve you fine most of the time, but some remote dirt roads

READING MONTANA LICENSE PLATES

The initial number on a Montana license plate designates the county the vehicle is registered in. The counties themselves were ranked by population in 1926 (based on the 1910 census, updated in 1933 to include new counties), from one (greatest population) to 56 (least population). The county was then assigned a license plate prefix that has since remained standard. Population shifts have destroyed the accuracy of the rankings; for instance, Silver Bow County, or Butte, is no longer the most populous.

If you're from out of state, you might think it unlikely that you'll ever care about Montana county seats and vehicle registration. But after a few days out on the lonely Montana road, you'll take interest, and sometimes solace, in knowing where other drivers hail from.

LICENSE PLATE PREFIXES

COUNTY	COUNTY SEAT	COUNTY	COUNTY SEAT
1 Silver Bow	Butte	29 Rosebud	Forsyth
2 Cascade	Great Falls	30 Deer Lodge	Anaconda
3 Yellowstone	Billings	31 Teton	Choteau
4 Missoula	Missoula	32 Stillwater	Columbus
5 Lewis and Clark	Helena	33 Treasure	Hysham
6 Gallatin	Bozeman	34 Sheridan	Plentywood
7 Flathead	Kalispell	35 Sanders	Thompson Falls
8 Fergus	Lewistown	36 Judith Basin	Stanford
9 Powder River	Broadus	37 Daniels	Scobey
10 Carbon	Red Lodge	38 Glacier	Cut Bank
11 Phillips	Malta	39 Fallon	Baker
12 Hill	Havre	40 Sweet Grass	Big Timber
13 Ravalli	Hamilton	41 McCone	Circle
14 Custer	Miles City	42 Carter	Ekalaka
15 Lake	Polson	43 Broadwater	Townsend
16 Dawson	Glendive	44 Wheatland	Harlowtown
17 Roosevelt	Wolf Point	45 Prairie	Terry
18 Beaverhead	Dillon	46 Granite	Philipsburg
19 Chouteau	Fort Benton	47 Meagher	White Sulphur Springs
20 Valley	Glasgow	48 Liberty	Chester
21 Toole	Shelby	49 Park	Livingston
22 Big Horn	Hardin	50 Garfield	Jordan
23 Musselshell	Roundup	51 Jefferson	Boulder
24 Blaine	Chinook	52 Wibaux	Wibaux
25 Madison	Virginia City	53 Golden Valley	Ryegate
26 Pondera	Conrad	54 Mineral	Superior
27 Richland	Sidney	55 Petroleum	Winnett
28 Powell	Deer Lodge	56 Lincoln	Libby

ROAD REPORTS AND HIGHWAY INFORMATION

Statewide recording: tel. (800) 226-7623 or (406) 444-6339, or check the Web site at www.mdt.mt.gov.

Local Reports (area code 406):

Billings	tel. 252-2806
Bozeman	tel. 586-1313
Butte	tel. 494-3666
Glendive	tel. 365-2314
Great Falls	tel. 453-1605
Havre	tel. 265-1416
Helena	tel. 444-6354
Kalispell	tel. 755-4949
Lewistown	tel. 538-7445
Miles City	tel. 232-2099
Missoula	tel. 728-8553
Wolf Point	tel. 653-1692

get pretty dodgy without a high-clearance vehicle. Likewise, two-wheel drive will handle most situations, but it's not a bad idea to throw a tow rope on the back seat and, except in the dead of summer, it makes sense to carry tire chains.

Distances are great in Montana: fill your tank frequently, especially in eastern Montana. Along Hwy. 200, hundreds of miles separate gas stations. Plan ahead. Don't assume every little dot on the map will have gas; many are merely pioneer post offices that mapmakers haven't bothered to delete. Ask gas station attendants how far the next gas station is, if you are in doubt. Make sure your vehicle is in reasonable shape. Check tires, oil, and radiator water. Carry extra oil and water.

A less apparent consideration involves foreign cars. By and large, Montana is Ford and Chevy country. If, by Montana standards, you are driving a moderately obscure foreign vehicle, don't anticipate that parts will be readily available should a breakdown occur. If you know that the alternator is failing on your foreign-built car, don't head into rural Montana assuming that repairs will be easy.

If cattle are in the road, just drive slowly toward them and they'll grudgingly move out of the way. Sheep will rarely give way in any logical fashion.

Logging trucks rule the roads in the western forests. Don't be stubborn about keeping your piece of the roadbed when one bears down on you.

When the federal government left it to the states to set their own speed limits in 1995, Montana dropped the daytime speed limit altogether, while cautioning motorists to drive at speeds "reasonable and prudent" for the road conditions. This doesn't mean that you can drive at any speed you like. The traffic cops can and will stop you if you are traveling at speeds they deem unsafe for the conditions. In most cases, it's unwise to travel much over 85, both for personal safety (the roads are frequently winding and in poor condition) and to forestall the possibility of getting a ticket. The nighttime limit is 65 mph on the interstates, 55 mph on secondary roads.

The white crosses along state highways do, indeed, mark the sites of fatal automobile accidents.

The state **highway information number** is (800) 226-7623 or (406) 444-6339, TTD (406) 444-7696, or check the website at www.mdt.mt.gov. During the winter, call this number to find out which passes are closed and what the driving conditions are like. Recordings are updated two to three times daily.

OTHER PRACTICALITIES

CROSSING TO AND FROM CANADA

Of the 15 roads that cross from Montana into Canada, only three are open around the clock. Highways 93 and 15 and Road 16 (in the state's far northeastern corner) have 24-hour ports of entry. U.S. citizens need to be prepared to show a passport to cross the border; however, you may be asked to show only a driver's license or proof of citizenship to cross back and forth (the same goes for Canadians coming this way). Citizens of any other nation should be prepared to show a passport and the appropriate visas. Citizens of any country may be asked to provide proof that they have sufficient funds for their intended length of stay.

U.S. Customs
Customs allows each person over the age of 21 to bring 1 liter of liquor and 200 cigarettes into the USA without paying duty. US citizens are allowed to import, duty-free, $400 worth of gifts from abroad, and non-US citizens are allowed to bring in $100 worth. Should you be carrying more than $10,000—in US or foreign cash, traveler's checks, money orders, or the like—you need to declare the excess amount. There is no legal restriction on the amount that may be imported, but undeclared sums in excess of $10,000 may be subject to confiscation.

Canadian Customs
Adults (age varies by province but is generally 19 years) can take 1.1 litres (40 oz) of liquor or a case of 24 beers as well as 200 cigarettes, 50 cigars and 400 grams of tobacco into Canada (all are cheaper in the USA). You can bring in gifts totaling up to $60 in value. Pistols or handguns cannot be taken into Canada, though hunting rifles can be.

MONEY

Almost all Montana banks have ATMs, making it easy to travel without the hassle of traveler's checks. Credit cards are widely—though not universally—accepted.

Foreign Exchange
In short, don't depend on exchanging foreign currency or traveler's checks in Montana. While banks in the larger cities supposedly offer exchange services, the transaction is so out of the ordinary that you may be told to come back another day after they figure out how to do it. Save yourself time and hassle and change your money before getting to Montana. Or just use ATMs to draw money out of your foreign account.

Sales Tax
There is no sales tax or VAT in Montana. It is one of three American states that do not levy a tax on products at the register (the others are Oregon and New Hampshire). Taxes on property and income, however, are steep.

The frequently dire financial condition of the Montana state government makes the sales tax a tempting revenue enhancer to some politicians, landowners, and advocates of public education. However, voters have repeatedly turned down the sales tax by referendum.

WOMEN TRAVELERS

Though it's not really the expected thing, there's little reason for a woman to feel uneasy about traveling alone around Montana. If you're not up to being outgoing, people will generally leave you alone. But if you get to feeling chatty or flirtatious, you're in real luck. You'll be a curiosity, and men and women alike will sit you down and spin tales, feed you, and make you grin. Of course, you have to look out for weirdos, but they're usually about as much of a threat as grizzly bears, and much easier to deflect. If a place makes you nervous, do the smart thing and leave. On the whole, travel in Montana is, for a woman on her own, exhilarating and ego-boosting.

PRECAUTIONS

Montana is not a particularly menacing place; however, a few considerations may save the traveler unpleasant experiences.

EVELYN CAMERON/MONTANA HISTORICAL SOCIETY, HELENA

Independent women travelers are nothing new in Montana.

Animals

Grizzly bears are found in Glacier and Yellowstone National Parks, and in smaller populations in wilderness areas in much of the Rockies. When provoked—and it doesn't always take much to rile them—grizzlies are vicious. Every year, it seems, someone is mauled by a grizzly, with deaths not infrequent. If you are planning a trip through grizzly country, check with local rangers for bear updates; areas in Glacier are often closed to hikers due to grizzly problems. Make noise as you hike to forewarn nearby bears; small "bear bells" hooked on packs are common noisemakers. Don't sleep near smelly food, such as bacon; hang food from branches away from tents. If at all possible, hike in a large group.

Mountain lions are not as aggressive as grizzlies, but as their territory is progressively whittled away, there is more lion-human contact. Mountain lions live in most of the Rocky Mountain region. While human adults are in little danger from mountain lions, small children—especially if unattended—can attract them. Montana newspapers report regularly on mountain lion attacks and sightings of lions stalking people. Again, safety lies in numbers.

Not all threats come from carnivores. **Moose** are great hulking animals given to spontaneous charges if surprised. **Buffalo,** either at Yellowstone Park or on private land, can be short-tempered if provoked. These animals are not vicious, but are territorial and easily surprised. Be careful.

Rattlesnakes are common over the eastern two-thirds of the state. While a rattlesnake bite is rarely fatal these days, it's no fun either. If you are hiking anywhere in eastern Montana, it is imperative to wear strong boots with high tops. Watch where you step. Be especially careful around rocky promontories: snakes like to sun themselves on exposed rocks.

Rattlesnakes are not aggressive to humans; given their druthers, they will slink away, rattling. If you have never heard a rattlesnake rattle, don't worry that you might mistake it for something else. It is a vestigial human trait to leap backward and shriek when you hear the rattle. When angered, however, rattlesnakes will coil and strike. If you are bitten, immobilize the affected area and seek immediate medical attention.

Be suspicious of overly friendly small mammals. Rabies is, as elsewhere, a real problem. If you are hiking in the vicinity of stock animals, especially cattle, it is wise to remember that bulls can be threatened by the presence of humans. Give them a wide berth.

Health and Wellness

In Montana, you'll find no unexpected health dangers, and excellent medical attention is readily available. However, in rural parts of the state, doctors and hospitals can be quite far apart, so it's a good idea to begin your journey in good health and to take no unreasonable risks while traveling the state. The text gives emergency numbers to call should you need medical attention. *Note that in most rural areas the 911 number is **not** in operation.*

The greatest risks most travelers will face are related to weather and insect bites. Too much summer sun can lead to sunburn, especially at Montana's higher altitudes. Wear sunscreen. Heat exhaustion can also be a problem if you're struggling up a hot hiking trail in full sun. Be sure to drink plenty of water and slow down if you feel yourself overheating.

If you have insect bite allergies, don't mislead yourself into thinking that Montana's dry climate might be bug-free. It's not. An abundance of fierce insects awaits. Mosquito repellent is definitely recommended. Montana mosquitoes do not carry any diseases, but they can be very annoying, and an infected bite can be both unsightly and painful.

Ticks pose some slight risk of diseases such as Rocky Mountain fever and Lyme disease. If practical, wear light-colored clothing so you can spot ticks more easily. When you're hiking through underbrush, wear long-sleeved shirts and long pants tucked into your shoes or boots. Apply an insect repellent containing DEET. Be sure to check your body for ticks after walking in the woods or grassy meadows—and look *everywhere* on your skin—especially in patches of body hair (also be sure to check pets for ticks). If you find a tick with its head imbedded, don't panic. Using tweezers or your fingers, pull gently and steadily on its body until the tick disengages. Do *not* crush the tick, burn it with a match, douse it in alcohol, or any other "home remedy," as these actions can cause the tick to regurgitate bacteria into its bite, increasing your chance of infection.

Under no circumstances should you drink unfiltered or untreated water straight from streams, springs, rivers, or lakes. The microscopic parasite *giardia* lives in mountain streams and will happily take up residence in your lower intestinal tract. Giardia enters streams through the fecal remains of animals—especially beaver (which gives the condition its common nickname, "beaver fever") and is prevalent throughout Montana.

SAY IT RIGHT— A GUIDE TO PRONUNCIATION

When in Montana, you might as well pronounce as the locals do. Don't get caught mispronouncing the following:

Absaroka: ab-SOR-ka
Absarokee: ab-SOR-kee
Charlo: SHAR-lo
Choteau: SHOW-toe
creek: CRIK (almost always)
Ekalala: EEK-a-lak-a
Garnet: gar-NET
Havre: HAV-er
Helena: HEL-en-a
Hysham: HI-sham
Kootenai: KOOT-nee
Laurin: law-RAY
Lima: LI-ma
Makoshika: ma-KOE-shika
Marias: ma-RI-us
Meagher: MAR
Missoula: ma-ZOO-la
Ronan: ro-NAN
Rudyard: RUD-yerd
Spokane: spoe-KAN
Winnett: WIN-et

Symptoms of giardia infection include stomach cramps; nausea; a bloated stomach; watery; foul-smelling diarrhea; and frequent gas. Giardia can appear several weeks after exposure to the parasite; symptoms may disappear for a few days and then return, a pattern which may continue. Tinidazole, known as Fasigyn, or metronidazole (Flagyl) are the recommended drugs for treatment; both are prescription drugs. Either can be used in a single treatment dose. Antibiotics are useless.

Giardia is a fairly common summer affliction in the region. It's even been known to enter the water supply of whole mountain towns.

Weather

Weather extremes are common in Montana. When outdoors in high temperatures, remember to drink plenty of water; native Montanans often take salt pills to prevent dehydration. Listen for weather forecasts—sudden storms can blow in, causing rapid changes in temperature and wind conditions. Certain parts of Montana are known for their windiness: Great Falls ("the Windy City"), Livingston, and Cut Bank each deserve the reputation. If you are driving a high-profile vehicle, listen for wind warnings.

Winter cold is the greatest weather concern. Roads can be treacherous if snow-covered, and incremental melting leaves small, invisible patches of ice on the road. If you travel by automobile in Montana in the winter, make sure you have tire chains, and know how to put them on. Make sure you also have blankets or a sleeping bag, plenty of warm clothing, gloves, shovel, a flashlight (days aren't long in the winter), and maybe even a paraffin heater. Carrying extra food and water is a good idea. Again, pay attention to weather and road reports, and don't take chances.

COMMUNICATIONS

Montana may be remote, but you can use your cellular phone pretty much anywhere in the state. Most towns have a business with a fax machine you can use. Public libraries usually have computers for public use, including Internet and e-mail connections. Larger towns have business centers with computers, e-mail and Internet connections, and fax machines.

Media
The only national newspapers you can count on finding in Montana is *USA Today* and (to a more limited extent) the *Wall Street Journal.* Regional daily papers include the Billings *Gazette,* the Great Falls *Tribune,* the Butte *Standard,* and the *Missoulian.*

Regional newspapers do a poor job of reporting national and international news. If you don't want to lose touch with the outside world, your best bet are the various **National Public Radio affiliates** across the state. These public radio stations are indicated in the text, usually under the "Information" heading. Translator stations carry public radio to pretty remote parts of Montana, so if you are hungry for "Morning Edition" or "All Things Considered," try scrolling around the bottom end of the FM radio dial.

If you want to read up on Montana on a monthly basis, check out *Montana Magazine* a high-quality monthly devoted to history, travel, and

culture in the state. If you can't find it on your newsstand, contact the magazine for a subscription at P.O. Box 5630, Helena, MT 59604-9930, tel. (888) 666-8624.

MAPS

The state highway department puts out a free road map that will suffice if you stick to paved roads. Request a copy from the Montana Promotion Division, Dept. of Commerce, 1424 N. Roberts, Helena, MT 59620, tel. (800) 548-3390.

For a more detailed look, the *Montana Atlas and Gazetteer* is a handy book of topographic maps covering the entire state. It's $14.95 and is available at most bookstores in Montana or from De Lorme Mapping, P.O. Box 298, Freeport, ME 04032, tel. (207) 865-4171. Western GeoGraphics puts out recreation maps of both eastern and western Montana. They include lots of nonpaved roads and some topographic detail. Pick them up for $3.95 at bookstores or order from Western GeoGraphics, P.O. Box 1984, Cañon City, CO 81215, tel. (719) 275-8948.

National forest maps are invaluable for off-the-beaten-path travel in the western part of the state. Day-hikers sticking to established trails will usually be able to navigate nicely with these maps, available at local ranger stations or from the U.S. Forest Service Northern Region Headquarters, Box

REGIONAL MONTANA TOURISM INFORMATION

Contact the following regional tourist offices (area code 406) for information about Montana.

Charlie Russell Country	tel. 761-5036
	or (800) 527-5348
Custer Country	tel. 665-1671
	or (800) 346-1876
Glacier Country	tel. 873-6211
	or (800) 338-5072
Gold West Country	tel. 846-1943
	or (800) 879-1159
Missouri River Country	tel. 653-1319
	or (800) 653-1319
Yellowstone Country	tel. 446-1005
	or (800) 736-5276

7669, Missoula, MT 59807, tel. (406) 329-3511; they're $3.95 from the government, a bit more if you buy them from a bookstore.

Serious backpackers and hunters will want U.S. Geological Survey quadrangle maps. Many sporting-goods stores carry these maps for the more popular areas; they can also be ordered directly from the USGS, Federal Center, Box 25286, Denver, CO 80225, tel. (303) 236-7477. It pays to do a little library research before contacting the USGS; they'll want to know the exact names of the maps you're ordering.

WHAT TO TAKE ALONG

Montana is capable of extreme weather. Winter travel especially demands appropriate cold-weath-er gear. Summer weather can be capricious, but it is usually hot, with afternoon temperatures in the 90s. Evenings can bring thunderstorms and much cooler temperatures. A jacket will make the evenings more comfortable. Few occasions demand formal clothing; besides, what passes for dress-up in Montana won't intimidate casually and comfortably dressed visitors.

Hikers and wilderness campers will need to augment their regular gear with bear bells (to warn bears of their approach). Take along rope to hang food items from trees. Sunscreen and insect repellent are the premier emollients of summer.

While Montana is not backward, small trading towns exist to serve the needs of local farmers and ranchers, not out-of-state tourists. Black-and-white film and even color slide film can be

---

MONTANA FASHION

While fashion may not appear to be much of a preoccupation in Montana, even this low-key style has its system. Here are a few clues to understanding the dictates of Montana chic.

In general, fashion is dictated by function. Ranchers dress the way they do because it's effective. Levi's are eschewed in favor of **Wrangler jeans,** for example. One cowboy claimed that Wranglers fit better over boot tops, but a more understandable reason is the seam: on Wrangler jeans, the seam runs down the outside of the leg; the seam running along the *inside* of a pair of Levi's can get pretty uncomfortable for a cowpoke on horseback.

Boots are still mandatory footwear. They provide necessary protection for the feet and calves while riding on horseback, and their high tops are prophylactic against snakebite. Bootmaking is still a custom trade in most Montana towns.

Neck scarves are not just colorful accessories: they insulate against cold drafts in winter and dust and chaff the rest of the year.

Cowboy hats are still a popular hedge against the sun and wind, straw for summer and felt for winter. The hegemony of the cowboy hat, though, has been somewhat shaken by the rise of the baseball cap, although no one in Montana would consider calling a head covering by that name. Rather, net caps are known by the brand names they feature—call it a "Cat Cap" or a "King Rope Cap"—and they are both identified and justified within Montana fashion.

The prevalence of **pearl snaps** over buttons is as real as it is, sadly, inexplicable.

As in certain ornithological species, the male's attire is often more engaging than the female's. In marked differentiation from the men's, women's clothing tends to be made of synthetic fibers. Wardrobes are put together with something more like abandon than intention or a sense of proportion and coordination. It is probably a judgment on Western culture that women's fashion generally reaches its apex in the menswear department. Women often look their best when they dress in the same clothes as men: jeans, plaid shirts, and boots.

There is some regional variation in dress. West of the Continental Divide, flannel shirts and Birkenstocks are common, particularly among college students.

Warning: *Do not try to duplicate Montana fashion.* Most attempts look as staged as they are. Getting yourself up in full western regalia is probably not going to win you any extra points. While in Montana, just dress comfortably and—especially if you want to win the confidence or friendship of native Montanans—observe a few simple rules:
• Don't wear anything really trendy or goofy. This will put an extra barrier between you and the residents.
• Hot summer weather doesn't necessarily mean shorts for men.
• Shirtlessness is almost taboo.
• Err on the side of comfortable modesty. In Montana, this is considered an element of stylishness.

SURFING MONTANA: TREASURE STATE WEB SITES

Visit cyber-Montana at the following World Wide Web sites.

Start your browsing at **http://travel.mt.gov/** to find Travel Montana, the state tourism bureau.

http://www.ism.net/montana lists information on several Montana cities, including history, educational and economic opportunities.

http://www.mt.gov contains listings on state government bureaus, state job listings, and travel information.

http://www.montana.com provides links to Montana businesses, publishers, organizations, and legislators.

http://kusm.montana.edu links you to Montana Public Broadcasting and lists children looking for e-mail pen pals.

http://aetherserv.com/peaks/ takes you to *Peaks,* an online magazine, which details Montana-based literature and arts, and runs articles on Montana geology and hydrology.

http://nris.msl.mt.gov a service of the Montana Natural Resource Information System, provides data on the state's natural resources; your graphical browser will allow you to download detailed maps.

Reach the University of Montana at **http://www.umt.edu** and Montana State University at **http://www.montana.edu.** In addition to enrollment information and links to various departments, you can also reach each university library through these addresses.

---

hard to find outside the cities. If you have special dietary needs, don't assume that small towns will stock items beyond the most basic of food-stuffs.

GENERAL INFORMATION AND SERVICES

The **area code** throughout Montana is **406.** The entire state is on mountain time.

Liquor stores are operated by the state and are closed on both Sunday and Monday. However, most bars are also licensed to sell liquor, beer, and wine, so you should have no trouble keeping in alcohol while in Montana. Wine is also for sale in grocery stores.

Most businesses are open from 9 a.m. to 6 p.m., Mon-Sat. In smaller towns, don't count on stores being open on Sunday.

Governmental Organizations

The following federal, state, and regional services can provide detailed information on Mon-

tana. They will be happy to fill your mailbox with free informational brochures.

U.S. Forest Service, Northern Region, P.O. Box 7669, Missoula, MT 59807, tel. (406) 329-3511.

Bureau of Land Management, 222 N. 32nd Ave., Billings, MT 59101, tel. (406) 255-2888.

Dept. of Fish, Wildlife, and Parks, 1420 6th Ave., Helena, MT 59620, tel. (406) 444-2535.

Glacier National Park, West Glacier, MT 59936, tel. (406) 888-7800.

Yellowstone National Park, YNP, WY 82190, tel. (307) 344-7381.

Montana Historical Society, 225 N. Roberts, Helena, MT 59620, tel. (406) 444-2694.

Montana Outfitters and Guides Association, P.O. Box 1248, Helena, MT 59624, tel. (406) 449-3578.

For statewide **road conditions,** call (800) 226-7623.

For handicap-access information, contact **DREAM,** NW Montana Human Resources, First and Main Building, P.O. Box 8300, Kalispell, MT 59904, tel. (406) 758-5411.

Travel Montana

The state's tourism bureau can answer most questions about travel in Montana. Some of their brochures are invaluable. Especially vital is the *Montana Travel Planner,* which contains complete listings of all the lodgings, campgrounds, outfitters, resorts, golf courses, and ski areas, and pertinent addresses and phone numbers of institutions in the state. Contact Travel Montana, (800) 847-4868, (406) 444-2654, or TDD (406) 444-2978. Write Travel Montana at 1424 9th Ave., P.O. Box 200533, Helena, MT 59620-0533. The website is really invaluable: http://travel.mt.gov.

In addition, Travel Montana has divided the state into six regions. Each local unit also produces brochures about sites, history, and amenities.

DOVER PUBLICATIONS, INC.

SOUTHEASTERN MONTANA

INTRODUCTION

INDIANS, CAVALRY, AND COWBOYS

Southeastern Montana is the most "Western" of Montana's regions. Historically, it is the West of the early trapper and hunter, and of the clash between Indian and infantry. It was the Montana of the cattle drover and the great cattle barons. Today, it is still home to thousands of American Indians, and it is still unembarrassedly cowboy country.

The Yellowstone River is the locus of the entire region. As the principal avenue of entree and exit in Montana, the Yellowstone took out the region's wealth of furs, brought in soldiers, and transported cattle and sheep to eastern markets. Towns like Miles City, Glendive, and Billings grew up on its banks as railroads extended up the valley. Within memory, ranchers on the "North Side," up to Jordan country, and on the "South Side," down the Powder River, trailed livestock to the "Valley." In these river towns, they partied, visited, and stocked up on groceries before heading out to their far-flung ranches.

The dominant social unit in southeastern Montana today is still the working ranch and family farm, and the same Yellowstone Valley towns are still the center of trade, shopping, and social life. This is about as real as the West gets, but it's not a western theme park. Today, cowboys are stockmen, Indians are Native Americans, and the spirit of the Wild West has grown up into agribusiness.

Southeastern Montana is not a highly developed tourist destination. But for the traveler with patience, a sense of humor, and an interest in wildlife, pristine landscapes, Native America, and the lore of the West, this corner of Montana has few equals.

THE LAND

As the Yellowstone moves eastward through the prairies, it picks up the waters of three major southerly tributaries: the Bighorn, the Tongue, and the Powder. As it debouches into the Mis-

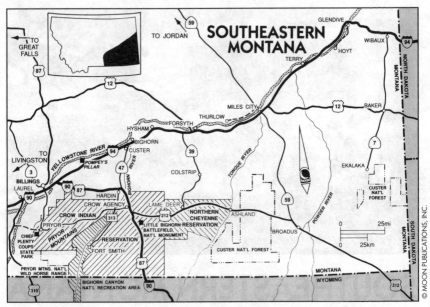

souri, the Yellowstone is the largest free-flowing river in the United States.

It's hard to believe, looking at the dry and dusty buttes and rolling prairies of southeastern Montana, that amphibious dinosaurs and palm trees were once native to this area. For millions of years this was the shoreline of vast inland seas. Southeastern Montana's most distinctive geologic formations—badlands, prairies, and sandstone bluffs, as well as the coal and oil they mask—all date from primeval maritime past.

The seas left deposits of sand, mud, and peat thousands of feet thick. Because exposed sedimentary formations were soft and easily eroded by wind and water, much of the terrain has relaxed into a uniform flatness. More resistant sandstone or clinker (coal-fire-hardened sandstone) provided protection from erosion and now tops buttes and caprocks, protecting softer subsoil from erosion. In other areas, the sedimentary uplands have been carved into deep canyons and sharp bluffs, called badlands. The distinctive barren gray soil is locally called "gumbo."

Vast coal deposits, in veins up to 40 feet thick, underlie most of southeastern Montana. Stripmining the coal has meant displacement of tra-

ditional agricultural interests. One person's overburden is another person's ranch land. In the 1970s and '80s, large strip mines, such as the aptly named Colstrip, brought forth some of the New West's keenest legal sharpshooting, when ranching and environmental interests vied with the onslaught of corporate mining.

Climate

Southeastern Montana has a climate of extremes. The highest and one of the lowest temperatures in the state are recorded here (117° at Glendive, and -65° at Fort Keogh). The shortgrass prairies of the region bake in mid- and late summer; Miles City annually registers some of the highest temperatures in the state. Expect temperatures in the 90s and 100s, and feel lucky if you find cooler weather. You can expect sunshine most of the summer, with frequent and spectacular thunderstorms. Evenings should be cool enough for a light jacket.

Winters are uniformly cold. Winter travel in eastern Montana is not for the faint of heart. Even though the snow and frost often lend the area a unique beauty, frequent use of the road conditions phone line, tel. (800) 226-7623, is recommended. Ideal travel seasons are the late spring and early fall, when warm days and cool evenings can be expected.

Flora

Ubiquitous plants of the high prairies include: blue grama grass; the prickly pear cactus, with beautiful yellow/pink flowers in June; the prairie coneflower, with a few yellow petals around a central column of tiny flowers, which provided the makings for a hot beverage for the Indians; and sunflowers that grow along the broken soil of roadways, alongside several varieties of thistle.

Gullies are the home to shrubs whose fruit would be disdained in more generous climates. However, the chokecherry and buffaloberry possess virtues that made them a food source for both Native Americans and early settlers. Riverbottoms are home to graceful cottonwood trees and willow. Juniper and ponderosa pines grow along the bluffs of sandstone uplands.

prairie coneflower,
Echinacea pallida

Fauna

With the exception of free-ranging buffalo, the wildlife of western lore still thrive in southeastern Montana. Coyotes, foxes, and rattlesnakes live in the hills, and large populations of pronghorns and mule and white-tailed deer make the region one of the state's premier hunting areas. The Pryor Mountains Wild Horse Range boasts Montana's only remaining herds of wild horses.

The region is especially of interest to birdwatchers. Golden eagles and the occasional bald eagle are seen, floating on updrafts, watching for their prey of cottontail rabbits and mice. Many other raptors, such as merlins, prairie falcons, red-tailed hawks, and great horned owls, are also easily spotted.

The Central Flyway crosses southeastern Montana, making it both a great birdwatching and bird-hunting region. Teal, canvasback, wood, and mallard ducks are frequently seen, as are Canada geese. Blue herons are common sights.

During the migration season, sandhill cranes, swans, and pelicans make short appearances.

Somewhere near Billings, the Yellowstone ceases being an oversized trout stream and becomes a prairie river. Although rainbow and brown trout are still found as far south as Miles City, sport species such as northern pike, walleye, and channel catfish are more common as the river slows and warms up.

The lower Yellowstone also yields one of the West's oddest fish. The paddlefish is an ancient species, related to the sturgeon, which has somehow survived in the Yellowstone. Its trademark long flat snout is useful for nosing around the riverbottom in search of plankton.

HISTORY

Southeastern Montana's history is closely tied to the history of the Yellowstone River. The Yellowstone was the avenue that brought in explorers, soldiers, and settlers, and the corridor that took out the furs, cattle, and coal.

Before the white man, however, the Yellowstone Valley was the ancient hunting grounds for Native Americans, especially the Crow Nation. The valleys of the Yellowstone and rivers that feed it were rich with game and furs, and the prairies that adjoined the rivers teemed with buffalo. As the Sioux and Cheyenne were forced into this corner of Montana, fierce intertribal rivalries flared.

The Yellowstone was not explored until 1806, during Lewis and Clark's return voyage. Clark and his party floated most of the way down the river in dugout canoes. Upon reaching the confluence of the Missouri, he noted that, due to the enormous abundance of game along the rivers, the location would be advantageous for a trading fort. By the next year, Fort Ramon was established at the mouth of the Bighorn, and trade with the Crows flourished. White settlers moved in to exploit the

WHEN THE BUFFALO ROAMED

The buffalo, or the American bison *(Bison bison)*, as it is properly known, once ranged over most of the North American continent. Between Pennsylvania and the Continental Divide, and from the lower Mississippi and the Arkansas River north to the northern Alberta border, these shaggy members of the cattle family roamed over 40% of the continent in herds of up to a million animals. They were migratory creatures, following the seasons north to south.

Eastern Montana was ideal buffalo country, no matter the season. Huge herds that summered on the Canadian plains moved south to winter on the Montana prairies, while equally numerous herds from the grasslands of Colorado and Wyoming migrated north to summer on the plains of Montana. Perhaps as many as 60 million of these animals once roamed the continent, and as many as four million lived in Montana alone.

As previously agricultural Indians entered Montana from the east, the vast herds of buffalo soon changed the lifestyle of the Native Americans. Bison had always been an element of the Indian culture, but when the Indians were forced onto the plains, the buffalo's importance altered.

In ways that are difficult to imagine today, the buffalo provided the means of life for the early Plains Indians. The hide provided tepee coverings and leather for moccasins; the flesh was eaten fresh in season and also preserved for later consumption (steaks from the hump were delicacies). The bones were used to create a number of tools, from bone-splinter awls (with buffalo sinew for thread) to shoulder-blade hoes. Dried manure was used in campfires. Even the dried tail was used—as a flyswatter.

buffalo, Bison bison

Before the introduction of horses and firearms, the Indians hunted buffalo with bow and arrow, often using buffalo "jumps," or *pishkuns*. The unsuspecting animals were stampeded off cliffs in large herds, after which the tribe harvested the dead and wounded. When the rifle and the horse met on the plains of Montana, the destruction of the vast herds began in earnest.

The development of new tanning techniques in the East allowed tanners to turn dried buffalo hides into soft, marketable leather, changing forever the lives of the prairie Indians. In the 1840s, most of the fur-bearing mammals of the West had been trapped out; by the 1860s and '70s, the great buffalo hunt was on. Waves of new white settlers (many displaced by the Civil War) moved west and joined the slaughter. Entire herds were completely wiped out in the course of a summer, as sharpshooters picked off the animals as they grazed. The animals were skinned, the hides shipped east by steamboat or rail, and the carcasses left to rot. Areas of the northern plains were white with bleached bones where the large herds had been slaughtered, and as the buffalo became scarce, a trade developed in dried buffalo bones (for fertilizers).

By 1884, the buffalo was effectively extinct in the United States. In 1908, when the government created the National Bison Range near Moiese, in northwestern Montana, it was stocked mostly with animals from Canada.

As the buffalo passed, so did the life of the Plains Indian founded on the buffalo. The basis for a nomadic, warrior society was gone, leaving the Indian no source of food, shelter, or support—except the U.S. government.

rich Yellowstone country, and others, with gold prospecting in western Montana on their minds, followed the Bozeman Trail north to the Yellowstone Valley across Sioux and Cheyenne tribal land. The resulting conflicts with these tribes generated some of the most famous battles of the western Indian Wars, including the Battle of the Little Bighorn.

The eradication of the buffalo and the incarceration of the Indians left the prairies empty, but by 1880 huge herds of Texas cattle filled the "open range." The Northern Pacific Railroad pressed up the Yellowstone Valley at the same time, bringing in settlers and establishing trade centers like Billings and Miles City. Homesteaders replaced cattle barons, but they made only a tentative impact on this vast and arid, almost hostile and ungiving land. The coal and oil development of the last 20 years has done as much to change the landscape and character of southeastern Montana as a century of agriculture.

RECREATION

Hunting and Fishing

Southeastern Montana is a hunter's dream. Trophy-size mule deer haunt brushy coulees, and game birds such as pheasant and wild turkey are abundant. Obtaining hunting access is relatively easy. The Dept. of Fish, Wildlife, and Parks' Region 7, which encompasses most of southeastern Montana, has the state's highest number of landowners signed up in the Block Management Program. The program opens and maintains access to 2.4 million acres of private land for recreation purposes. (A list of participating farmers and ranchers is available from the Dept. of Fish, Wildlife, and Parks office in Miles City.) An increasing number of ranchers run outfitting and guide services.

As the Yellowstone River winds through its wooded valley, it attracts anglers with its wealth of walleye, northern pike, smallmouth bass, ling, channel catfish, the occasional trout, and sauger. The river's lower reaches, especially near Glendive and Sidney, are home to the paddlefish. Public fishing sites on the Yellowstone are plentiful, as the Dept. of Fish, Wildlife, and Parks is in the process of locating access areas every 12 miles along the river.

For trout fishers, the Bighorn River is the real news in southeastern Montana; below Yellowtail Dam, the Bighorn becomes one of the state's best trout-fishing areas, and Yellowtail Dam itself in the Bighorn Canyon has got to be one of the most awe-inspiring brown trout and walleye holes in the West. Because much of the Bighorn flows through the Crow Reservation, access is limited. The upper reaches of the Tongue River also provide good trout fishing.

Agate Hunting

The moss agates of the Yellowstone Valley are known around the world for their quality. Starting at the mouth of the Bighorn and continuing to its confluence with the Missouri, the Yellowstone passes through gravel beds rich with the semiprecious stones. It takes a trained eye to spot the matte, yellowish exterior of an agate in the rough, but often the jostling of the river will have chipped the surface, and its translucent interior will be visible. Stop at a fishing-access area or along a bridge, to search for agates. The **Glendive Chamber of Commerce** also offers guided boat tours on the Yellowstone specifically tailored for agate hunters.

Tours

A couple of companies offer tours of historic and cultural sights and recreational areas in southeastern Montana. Contact **Fun Adventures,** P.O. Box 21905, Billings MT 59104, tel. (406) 254-7180, www.montana.net/funadventures, or **Frontier Adventures,** P.O. Box 85, Colstrip, MT 59323, tel. (406) 748-2630 or (888) 665-1631, www.exploremontana.com. Both offer tours of major sites including the Little Bighorn Battlefield, Bighorn Canyon, and others.

INFORMATION

For general information on southeastern Montana, write for the **Custer Country Regional Tour Guide,** Room 40, Route 1, Box 1206, Hardin, MT 59034, or call (800) 346-1876 or (406) 665-1671. The guide is a helpful free source of addresses, travel information, and activities.

The **Custer National Forest offices** can be reached at P.O. Box 2556, Billings, MT 59103, tel. (406) 657-6361. The regional **Dept. of Fish, Wildlife, and Parks** office is at 2300 Lake Elmo Dr., Billings, MT 59105, tel. (406) 247-2940.

Getting Around

Greyhound runs along I-90 and I-94. Two flights daily on **Big Sky Airlines** link Miles City and Glendive with Billings.

BILLINGS

Billings (elev. 3,117 feet) is Montana's largest city, with a population of over 120,000 in the greater urban area. Billings's physical setting is striking: the Rimrocks—sandstone cliffs several hundred feet high—ring the city; from them, five mountain ranges are visible. The Yellowstone Valley here is wide and green. Billings is primarily a sales and trade center, with some oil refining and energy generation enlivening its economy.

Billings makes much of being the largest city in the vector north of Denver and between Spokane and Minneapolis, and boasts of being the capital of the "Midland Empire," a vague principality consisting of eastern Montana, northern Wyoming, the western Dakotas, and, on an expansive day, maybe even some of Canada's prairie provinces. Certainly, to judge by the license plates at the stockyards or at one of the shopping malls, Billings is the service center for much of the northern plains. It's a city that is proud of its wealth and growth, and as the center of a vast agricultural area it has a strong sense of purpose and vitality.

However, the old center of Billings has largely been abandoned. The commercial focus of the city has shifted to malls and developments along Grand Avenue and 24th Street West, quite a ways west of the old downtown. A few businesses hold on downtown, but gentrification has yet to revitalize the old city center.

Billings is also home to two institutions of higher learning. The state's old Rocky Mountain College was founded in 1878. Rocky Mountain, affiliated with the United Methodist and Presbyterian Churches and the United Church of Christ, has 800 students. Montana State University at Billings, formerly Eastern Montana College, offers two- and four-year degrees to some 4,300 students.

HISTORY

The Yellowstone Valley at Billings has been at the crossroads of inter-Indian trade and warfare for years. Prehistoric Indians lived in this area

beginning about 10,000 years ago, as the valley's abundant game and fertility made this a rich homeland, and caves in the Rimrocks gave shelter. Later, mountain tribes from the west, like the Shoshone, ventured down the Yellowstone on hunting trips to the buffalo-laden prairies. The Crow Indians moved into Montana in the 17th century and settled just south and east of Billings. A century later, when the Blackfeet moved in from the north and west and the Sioux moved in from the east, this part of the Yellowstone Valley became a contested hunting ground.

The first white settlement in this area was Coulson, a trade center and ferry crossing founded in 1877. When Frederick Billings brought the Northern Pacific Railroad to the Yellowstone Valley in 1882, the early settlers of Coulson were ready. These enterprising citizens assumed that the railroad would want (and pay amply for) access to the booming hamlet. Not so. Coulson wanted too much money for the right of way to the town, and the railroad bypassed it and established Billings a few miles north as its railhead. By 1884 Coulson was a ghost town, outpaced by prosperous Billings.

The history of Billings thereafter is the story of its growth as a regional trade and agricultural center. The wide valley above and below the city was developed into irrigated fields, and sugar beet cultivation was so successful that a sugar refinery was built here in 1906. The energy boom of the 1960s and '70s brought more wealth to Billings, as both oil and coal reserves in eastern Montana were increasingly tapped.

Billings propelled itself into the news with the great Montana Centennial Cattle Drive of 1989. As part of the Montana Centennial celebrations, an "old-fashioned" cattle drive wended its way south from Roundup to Billings, a distance of about 60 miles. The 3,000 longhorn cattle brought in for the event were outnumbered by the 3,500 riders from all over the world. The five-day drive and concurrent media fair occasioned such festivities that even Billings, which has seen a party or two, stood up and noticed.

SIGHTS

Tours of Billings

Get an entertaining overview of Billings' sights by taking the two-hour **Billings Trolley Tour,** tel. (406) 254-7180. Stops include historic downtown Billings, Black Otter Trail on the Rimrocks, Boot Hill, and several museums. All entrance fees are included in ticket prices—$12 adults, $10 seniors, and $5 children 10 and under. Unfortunately, the trolley only runs on Tuesdays and Thursdays, and reservations are required.

The people who operate the trolley, Fun Adventures, also offer walking tours of downtown, as well as longer theme tours (to Little Bighorn Battlefield, Lewis and Clark sites, etc.) Call to schedule these outings, or visit the company's website at www.montana.net/funadventures.

Downtown Billings

The **Western Heritage Center,** 2822 Montana Ave., tel. (406) 256-6809, is housed in the old Parmly Library, built in 1901 by Frederick Billings in honor of his brother Parmly. The center is a museum of the history and culture of the Yellowstone Valley. Historical photos, period clothing, art, western crafts, historic artifacts, and interpretive exhibits are featured. The center is open Tues.-Sat. 10 a.m.-5 p.m. and Sunday 1-5 p.m., free admission.

The **Yellowstone Art Museum,** 401 N. 27th Ave., tel. (406) 256-6804, located in the old county jail, mounts up to 20 exhibits a year in its five galleries. The center is devoted to securing and displaying contemporary regional and western art, though it houses international and historic pieces as well. There's also a museum shop with local gifts and books. The center is open Tues.-Sat. 11 a.m.-5 p.m., Sunday noon-5 p.m., and Thursday until 8 p.m. Between Memorial Day and Labor Day it opens at 10 a.m.; $3 adult, $2 seniors and students, and $1 for children.

Just west of the downtown area is a district of beautiful old homes. Only one of these is open to the public, but for anyone interested in turn-of-the-century architecture, a walk along these streets (between Division and 3rd Streets, and Lewis and Yellowstone Streets) is a pleasant diversion.

The **Moss Mansion,** at 914 Division St., tel. (406) 256-5100, was built by an early Billings bank president, who engaged Henry Hardenberg, the architect of the Waldorf-Astoria Hotel in New York, to design his Billings home. Completed in 1903, the three-story sandstone mansion has pronounced European touches. In fact, each room seems to be designed to reflect a different European country, from the Moorish entry hall to the Tudor dining room. Most of the original furniture and fixtures remain. Guided tours are offered on the hour, 10 a.m.-3 p.m. in summer (open year round, but call for hours in the off season), $6 adults, $5 seniors, $4 children.

The **Billings Historic District** stretches along Montana Ave. from 23rd to 26th Streets. Here, paralleling the old Northern Pacific tracks, is the heart of old Billings. Turn-of-the-century hotels and commercial buildings crowd in around themselves, though the entire area has gone pretty seedy. The **Rex Hotel,** once frequented by Buffalo Bill Cody, is a major island of gentrification, though galleries and cafes are also making a stand, and the historic, refurbished Northern Pacific Railroad depot buildings stand ready for upscale new tenants.

The Rimrocks

The Rimrocks are worth a visit, if only for the views from the top. From **Black Otter Trail** off Airport Rd., five mountain ranges are visible. To the southeast are the Bighorns, farther west are the Pryors, to the southwest are the Beartooths, and northwest are the Crazies and Snowies.

On the Rimrocks along Black Otter Trail is **Yellowstone Kelly's Grave,** placed here at his request at a site overlooking the Yellowstone River. Luther Kelly was an adventurer of an old-fashioned sort, better suited to fiction than reality. He came west after the Civil War and found the rough-and-ready life here to his liking, despite his cultivated eastern background. He learned both the Crow and Sioux languages and campaigned with General Miles when the Army

---

THE LEGEND OF SACRIFICE CLIFFS

Dominating the skyline south and east of Billings, across the Yellowstone, are the Sacrifice Cliffs. These 200-foot escarpments figure in a Crow legend. As recounted by Mark Brown (in *The Plainsmen of the Yellowstone*), Crow storyteller Old Coyote told of two brothers, both warriors, who returned to their village to find it ravaged with smallpox.

They saw the dead on scaffolds. These brothers were courting two sisters. They saw many scaffolds on a cliff and climbed up there. One said to the other, "Take a look at these dead. What if they were the girls we were courting?" They recognized the sisters.

Their oldest brother was one of the chiefs. He was dead. There was no one to care for the people. They dug into their parfleches. They took out their best clothes and put them on. One had a grey horse. This was his best horse. They got on this horse, rode double. They rode through the camp and sang songs just like when there was no sickness, some lodge songs, and lastly their brothers' songs. After this ride, they went up to the cliff and rode along the rimrock singing their own songs. Then they blindfolded the horse and turned toward the edge of the cliff singing the Crazy Dog Lodge song. They were still singing when the horse went over the cliff.

forced the Indians onto reservations following the battle at Little Bighorn. Kelly later ventured to Alaska and later still became a provincial governor in the Philippines. Back on this continent, he became an Indian agent in Nevada, where he also mined for gold. He died in California, and his body was returned to this site in 1928.

Follow Black Otter Trail to the eastern base of the Rimrocks to find **Boothill Cemetery,** one of the only reminders of the old town of Coulson. Fifty-two early residents are at rest here, many after meeting violent ends. Coulson's sheriff, "Muggins" Taylor, is buried here, as is Henry Lump, the man who killed him. Taylor was the Army scout who brought news of the Custer massacre to the world, via Fort Ellis, in 1876.

Also on the Rimrocks, near the airport, is the **Peter Yegen Jr. Museum,** commonly known as the Yellowstone County Museum. This community museum features an old steam engine from the Northern Pacific, a sheepherder's wagon, a roundup wagon, and homesteader and Indian artifacts. Diorama fans will be uplifted by its display of life in the early years of Yellowstone settlement, and outdoors near the picnic tables is a telescope for viewing Billings and vicinity. Open Tues.-Sat. 10:30 a.m.-5 p.m., Sunday 2-5 p.m., free admission, tel. (406) 256-6811.

The most unusual of Billings's Rimrock attractions is the **Pictograph Cave State Monument,** tel. (406) 247-2940. Located southeast of Billings on the south side of the Yellowstone, the caves were inhabited for about 10,000 years. A succession of cultures have lived here, beginning with a tribe of prehistoric hunters. Excavations have yielded almost 30,000 cultural artifacts of early Paleo-Indians, making this one of the richest archaeological sites in Montana.

The road into the monument passes by spectacular cliffs and ponderosa pine forests. At the site, three caves have been cut into the sandstone by water erosion. The best-preserved cave paintings are in Pictograph Cave. Here, buffalo, elk, prehistoric animals, and figurative and abstract designs are just visible on the sandstone walls of the cave. That the paintings have survived at all is amazing, especially after repeated assaults by vandals with spray paint. However, nature has eventually washed off the spray paint, and the colors of the painting, made from plant resins, cherry juice, animal fat, charcoal, and soil, once again show through. The other two caves, Ghost Cave and Middle Cave, were also inhabited by prehistoric Indians.

A hard-surface, 1,000-foot trail links all the caves from a central parking lot. A very nice picnic area (no camping sites, though), water, and toilets make this a great place to stop and explore. The abundance of birdlife along the rims and the presence of typical prairie flora make the monument grounds a mini nature hike. To find Pictograph Cave State Monument, take exit 452 from I-90 and follow the signs south along Coburn Road for five miles. The monument is open daily 8 a.m.-8 p.m., April 15 through October 15. Admission is $4 per vehicle.

ZooMontana

Billings' small zoo is devoted to northern hemisphere temperate species. Although the zoo is still under development, it remains the only real zoo in the state, and kids will enjoy seeing native animals including river otters, owls, and ferrets, as well as more exotic species such as a Siberian tiger and Seca deer. The Discovery Center features hands-on exhibits and educational displays.

To reach ZooMontana, take I-90 exit 446, and follow the signs west to 2100 Shiloh Road. Admission is $4 adults, $3 seniors, $2 children ages 3 to 15. The zoo is open daily 10 a.m.-5 p.m. April 15 through October 15, weekends only in winter, weather permitting. Call (406) 652-8100 for details.

RECREATION

The **Billings Mustangs,** a farm team for the Cincinnati Reds, train in Billings and constitute just about the only organized spectator sport besides rodeo. The Mustangs play at Cobb Field, at 9th Ave. N. and N. 27th St.; call (406) 252-1241 for a schedule. City parks cater to the casual athlete. **Pioneer Park,** between 3rd and 5th Streets on Grand Ave., is a beautiful old park near the downtown area, featuring tennis courts, jogging paths, and plenty of picnic space. The swimming pool is at **Athletic Park,** N. 27th at 9th Ave. North. **Riverfront Park,** located along the Yellowstone River just off I-90, has picnic tables, jogging paths, fishing access, boat access for nonmotorized boats, and lots of room to romp. No overnight camping.

Take exit 446 north to King Ave., follow it to S. Billings Ave., and follow S. Billings Ave. to the park. **Lake Elmo State Recreation Area,** 2400 Lake Elmo Rd. in Billings Heights, tel. (406) 254-1310, offers swimming, fishing, nonmotorized boating, and picnic areas. Boat rentals are available. There's a $1 per person entry fee (to a maximum of $4 per vehicle). No overnight camping.

There are several public golf courses in Billings. **Briarwood Country Club,** 3429 Briarwood Blvd., tel. (406) 248-2702, has 18 holes and is south of Billings along Blue Creek. The **Par Three Golf Course** has 18 holes and is on Central Ave. at 19th St. W, tel. (406) 652-2553. The **Lake Hills Golf Course** is near Lake Elmo State Park in Billings Heights. Follow Lake Elmo Rd. past Lake Elmo and turn at Wickes Ln.; tel. (406) 252-9244. A new golf course, the **Peter Yegen Golf Course,** is at 3400 Grand Ave., tel. (406) 656-8099.

ACCOMMODATIONS

Generally speaking, Billings features two major centers for accommodations: downtown and the I-90 freeway exits, where you'll find a great many chain hotels.

Downtown

For inexpensive rooms in downtown Billings, try the **Budget Host Inn,** 2601 4th Ave. N; tel. (406) 245-6646 or (800) 283-4678, with rooms at $39 s, $49 d. The **Esquire Motor Inn,** 3314 1st Ave. N., tel. (406) 259-4551, $30 s, $39 d, has a pool, guest laundry, and kitchenettes.

Across from Deaconess Hospital and an easy walk to downtown, the **Billings Inn,** 880 N. 29th, tel. (406) 252-6800, $45 s, $49 d offers continental breakfast, a guest laundry, and nicely furnished rooms. In the same neighborhood, the **Cherry Tree Inn,** 823 N. Broadway, tel. (406) 252-5603 or (800) 237-5882, has rooms at $34 s, $39 d; small pets permitted. Just down the hill from the airport, the **Rimview Inn,** 1025 N. 27th St., tel. (406) 248-2622 or (800) 551-1418, features large, well-equipped rooms starting at $37 s, $40 d. Included is a complimentary continental breakfast; all rooms have refrigerators, some have full kitchens.

Also comfortable is the **Best Western Ponderosa Inn,** 2511 1st Ave. N, tel. (406) 259-5511, (800) 628-9081, with rooms starting at $50 s, $60 d.

Right downtown, this motel offers a pool, sauna, exercise room, and a guest laundry. A charming alternative to the large and generally more expensive downtown hotels is the **Dude Rancher,** a small and venerable motel with a pronounced and delightful Western atmosphere. Rooms start at $46 s, $48 d. The coffee shop here is a popular place for breakfast. The Dude Rancher is at 415 N. 29th St., tel. (406) 259-5561 or (800) 221-3302. Pets are allowed.

If the privations of the prairies have you hankering for room service, then Billings has a couple of top-flight hotels to pamper you. The **Radisson Northern Hotel** is Billings' lodging doyen. Established in 1904 by banking magnate P.B. Moss, the Northern was conceived as the finest hotel north of Denver and west of Minneapolis. It's still a great hotel (although, unfortunately, its historic character was largely obscured in a 1940s fire and subsequent reconstruction), and it offers some of the best food in Billings at the Golden Belle Restaurant. The Northern is at 19 N 28th St., tel. (406) 245-5121 or (800) 333-3333; rooms start at $79 s, $89 d.

A block up is the **Sheraton Billings Hotel.** The Sheraton offers the service and amenities you'd expect (such as an indoor pool, health club, and hot tub), but with the added privilege of doing so in Montana's tallest building (23 stories). The Sheraton is located at 27 N. 27th St., tel. (406) 252-7400 or (800) 588-7666, with room rates running $96 s, 106 d.

Along I-90

If you're just passing through Billings, you might prefer to spend the night out along the freeway. Just off I-90 exit 446, you'll find at least a dozen large motels; barring a major event, you should have no trouble finding rooms without reservations. If you want to call ahead, try one of the following. **Billings Super 8 Lodge,** 5400 Southgate Dr., tel. (406) 248-8842 or (800) 800-8000, has rooms at $49 s, $65 d. **Kelly Inn;** 5425 Midland Rd., tel. (406) 252-2700 or (800) 635-3559, $40 s, $60 d, has a pool, sauna, hot tub, and pets are okay.

At I-90 exit 450 are more major motels, including the **War Bonnet Inn,** 2612 Belknap Ave., tel. (406) 248-7761 or (888) 242-6023. The War Bonnet is nicer than many freeway motels, with a good restaurant and lounge, a pool and hot tub, and some rooms accessible for guests with disabilities. Rates are $39 s, $44 d. The **Howard Johnson Express Inn,** 1001 S 27th St., tel. (406) 245-4656 or (800) 654-2000, has rooms at $52 s, $56 d.

B&Bs

The Josephine, 514 N. 29th St., tel. (406) 248-5898, (800) 552-5898, is in a historic home close to downtown. Five rooms—including one two-bedroom suite—are available, with prices starting at $58 s, $68 d. Included are guest passes to a local health club.

Campgrounds

The **Billings Metro KOA** has 115 RV sites, 60 tent-camping sites, and a pool, playground, and mini-golf course, all right next to the Yellowstone. The KOA is off exit 450 at 3087 Garden Ave. (follow the signs), tel. (406) 252-3104 or (800) 562-8546. The Billings KOA has the honor of being the first KOA in North America. The **Big Sky Campground** is north of exit 446 at 5516 Laurel Rd., tel. (406) 259-4110, and accommodates 100 RVs and 40 tent campers.

FOOD

For breakfast, those who make the **Dude Rancher** their Billings base of operations have only to wander over to the coffee shop, 415 N. 29th St., tel. (406) 259-5561. If eggs and taters seem too much, try the **Grand Bagel Company,** at the corner of N. 30th St. and 4th Ave. N. Another good place for a light breakfast is **Maxine's,** 221 N 29th St., tel. (406) 254-2200, a combination bakery, coffeehouse, and sandwich shop. For espresso, **Cafe Jones,** at 2712 2nd Ave. N, tel. (406) 259-7676, stays open late, as does **Artspace,** a coffeehouse at 2919 2nd Ave. N, tel. (406) 259-7676.

The Billings restaurant scene is diverse, featuring several ethnic cuisines. But don't fool yourself. This is really red meat country. Not far from downtown is the **Granary,** 1500 Poly Dr., tel. (406) 259-3488, a light and airy restaurant in an old mill with good beef, a selection of chicken dishes, and seafood.

Steaks share top billing with gourmet fare at several downtown restaurants. One of Billings' top restaurants, the **Golden Belle,** at the Radis-

son Northern Hotel, 1st Ave. N and Broadway, tel. (406) 245-2232, offers a varied menu of beef, lamb, and fresh seafood. The delicious salmon with anchovy sauce is a holdover from the restaurant's original 1910s menu. There's a good view of the city from the 20th-floor **Lucky Diamond,** in the Sheraton Billings, 27 N. 27th St., tel. (406) 252-7400. The **Rex Hotel,** 2401 Montana Ave., tel. (406) 245-7477, combines excellent aged beef with Italian dishes, game, and fresh fish in a refurbished and elegant old hotel in the downtown historic district. **Jake's,** 2701 1st Ave. N, tel. (406) 259-9375, combines a lively bar with tasty eclectic cuisine.

Another historic building turned good restaurant is **George Henry's,** 404 N. 30th, tel. (406) 245-4570. The 1882 home, not far from downtown, is now in the business of serving tasty steaks, seafood, salads, and light meals.

If you're looking for a break from steaks, Billings is also the place to be. One of the best restaurants in town, **Walker's Grill,** has good gourmet pizzas and pasta in the Chamber Building at 301 N. 27th St., tel. (406) 245-9291. Excellent Greek food is available at **The Athenian,** 18 N. 29th, tel. (406) 248-5681. In addition to familiar Greek specialties, leg of lamb is featured on the weekends. The local brewpub, **Montana Brewing Company,** 113 N. Broadway, tel. (406) 252-9200, offers a large menu of well-prepared pub food.

Billings is blessed with good Asian food. **Thai Orchid** is right downtown at 2926 2nd Ave. N., tel. (406) 256-2206, and has a number of vegetarian dishes. The **Great Wall of China,** 1309 Grand Ave., tel. (406) 245-8601, features good Chinese food at the right price. Near the hotels off exit 446 is **Jade Palace,** 2021 Overland, tel. (406) 656-8888, which mixes Cantonese and Sichuan cuisine in an attractive setting. If you're itching for sushi, you'll find it at **NaRa Oriental Restaurant,** 3 Custer Ave., near the corner of Division and Montana Aves., tel. (406) 245-8866. NaRa also serves Korean dishes in addition to Japanese specialties.

Less formal dining is of course available. Grand Avenue is the "strip" where all the fast-food places huddle.

Bars and Nightlife

Like any other Montana community, Billings has a nightlife centered on bars and restaurants.

The **Rex Hotel,** 2401 Montana Ave., tel. (406) 245-7477, began as an experiment in urban renewal through drink. By putting a trendy bar in an old hotel in the dilapidated historic district along the tracks, the developers began a process of refining both the building and the menu. It is still one of the most pleasant places in Billings for a drink, but it was more charming when there was still an element of raffishness to it.

Jake's, 2701 1st Ave. N, tel. (406) 259-9375, is one of the liveliest bar scenes downtown. Jake's is the kind of bar where, after a couple drinks, everyone seems single. In a city, this would seem threatening. In Billings, it seems endearing.

Other nightspots of note include: the **Monte Carlo,** 2828 1 Ave. N., tel. (406) 259-3393, a horseshoe bar and casino with piano entertainment; **Casey's Golden Pheasant,** 109 N. Broadway, a handsome old bar that now features live jazz; **The Western,** a rowdy watering hole on the "wrong" side of the tracks at 2712 Minnesota Ave., tel. (406) 252-7383, that starts early and goes late. There's an alternative scene at **ArtSpace,** 2919 2nd Ave. N., tel. (406) 245-1100, where occasional poetry readings occur in the coffeehouse/gallery. The local brew pub, **Montana Brewing Company,** keeps things lively at 113 N. Broadway, tel. (406) 252-9200.

EVENTS

MetraPark is the major venue in Billings for concerts, rodeos, fairs, and just about any other event that requires extensive seating and exhibition space. The **Midland Empire Fair** is a large agricultural affair with a rodeo, a carnival, and horse racing; it's held during the middle of August. The **Northern International Livestock Exposition** (NILE) is a large and prestigious livestock show held in October, featuring five nights of rodeo. For exact dates contact the chamber of commerce or call MetraPark at (406) 256-2422, and check the local newspaper for concert dates or sports engagements.

Live theater is presented in a number of venues. The **Alberta Bair Theatre,** 2801 3rd Ave. N, tel. (406) 256-6052, hosts a number of performance events, including theater by the Fox Committee for the Performing Arts, the Billings Symphony, and events featuring visiting artists. **Billings Stu-**

dio Theatre, 1500 Rimrock Rd., tel. (406) 248-1141, is a local community theater featuring old and new favorites of the popular stage.

SHOPPING

The downtown area of Billings hasn't fared so well, as shoppers have deserted older businesses in favor of new shopping centers on the city's fringes. A few older businesses persist in their original locations.

Billings is a good place to get "outfitted" with western goods. **Lou Taubert Ranch Outfitters,** 114 N. Broadway, tel. (406) 245-2248, is an established western store with a wide selection of boots, hats, and gear. **Al's Bootery,** 1820 1st Ave. N, tel. (406) 245-4827, offers a wide selection of boots as well as silver jewelry.

Indian art and crafts are available at a couple of local galleries, though oddly these shops seem to feature more Southwest Indian art than local Indian products. **Buffalo Chips Indian Trading Post,** located in the Rimrock Mall, tel. (406) 656-8954, seems to specialize in southwestern artifacts; **Center Lodge Native Arts,** 121 N. 29th St., tel. (406) 252-9994, has more local work.

Several art galleries in Billings emphasize western and Montana art. **American West Galleries,** 2814 2nd Ave. N, tel. (406) 248-5014, open Mon.-Fri. 9:30 a.m.-5:30 p.m., Saturday 9:30 a.m.-3:30 p.m., features limited-edition prints and some original western-themed art. **Toucan Gallery,** 2505 Montana Ave., tel. (406) 252-0122, Mon.-Sat. 10 a.m.-5 p.m., is located in the historic district and features contemporary local art and crafts.

You can also find a vast selection of Montana-made products online at www.virtualwest.com. Or call (406) 652-8331 to reach Billings-based **Old Montana Virtual West** by phone.

INFORMATION

The **chamber of commerce** is at 815 S. 27th, P.O. Box 31177, Billings, MT 59107, tel. (406) 245-4111 or (800) 735-2635, http://travel.state .mt.us/billingscvb. The main **post office** is directly behind the chamber of commerce at 26th Ave. S and 9th Ave. South. The downtown branch is at 2602 1st Ave. North.

Speedy Wash is downtown at 2505 6th Ave. N, tel. (406) 248-4177; open daily 6 a.m.-11 p.m. **The Laundry Room** is near exit 446 at 3189 King Ave. W, tel. (406) 652-2993; open daily 7 a.m.-9 p.m.

For a **local forecast** call (406) 652-2000. For **road conditions** information, call (406) 252-2806.

The **Fish, Wildlife, and Parks** office is at 2300 Lake Elmo Dr., Billings, MT 59105, tel. (406) 247-2940. The **Custer National Forest headquarters** is at 2602 1st Ave. N, tel. (406) 248-9885. The **BLM** office can be reached at Box 36800, Billings, MT 59107, tel. (406) 255-2888.

Deaconess Medical Center is at 9th Ave. N and Broadway, tel. (406) 657-4000. **St. Vincent's Hospital** is at 1233 N. 30th, tel. (406) 657-7000.

Listen to Montana Public Radio at 91.7 FM.

TRANSPORTATION

Billings is the largest airlink in Montana. Horizon, Delta, and Northwest each fly into Logan Field several times daily. In addition, Big Sky Airlines and Sky West Airlines connect Billings to smaller centers within the state. Logan Field sits atop the Rimrocks at the junction of Airport Rd. and N. 27th. **Hertz, Avis,** and **National** all operate car rental agencies at the airport.

Greyhound, 2502 1st Ave. N, tel. (406) 245-5116, is the only form of public ground transportation in and out of Billings. **MET** is the city's public transport system; call (406) 657-8218 for information.

EAST TOWARD MILES CITY

Between Billings and Miles City lies an area of rich farm- and pastureland, fed by the waters of the Yellowstone and shaded by cottonwoods. Irrigated farming is the mainstay of local economies, with corn, sugar beets, and soybeans the most prevalent crops. Feedlots, where cattle are wintered or fattened, are also common.

Past the steep sandstone bluffs that rise out of the valley floor, beyond the reach of the center-pivot sprinklers, the badlands and prairies begin. Out here, it's suddenly sagebrush and cactus, dusty roads and cattle country. After a drive across these unrelenting plains the traveler realizes the real value of the Yellowstone Valley to the natives: water, and a green thought in a green shade.

When traveling the Yellowstone Valley, one is always following in someone's footsteps. The wide, fertile valley cut by the river has been used for centuries as a thoroughfare, first by foot and horseback, then later by steamboat, railroad, and, most recently, by automobile along I-94.

History

Initially, it was the wildlife that brought people to the valley. Archaeological remains indicate that prehistoric Indians have lived here for thousands of years. Following Lewis and Clark, trappers exploited the region's abundance of fur-bearing animals and established trading forts at favorable points. By the end of the century, the range

was being settled by big cattle and sheep outfits, then the valley itself began to fall to the plow.

Coal-fired electricity-generating plants built at Colstrip by the Montana Power Company in the 1970s sparked a huge debate in the state, as ranches sitting atop coal reserves were tempted and coerced to sell their mineral rights. Ecologists found allies in Indians and cowboys alike as the effects of the coal-fired plants on the environment became known. In the end, the plants went in. But not before families and neighbors divided over the issues surrounding economic growth, environmental damage, and rapid change in traditional communities.

POMPEY'S PILLAR

Pompey's Pillar has always been a landmark. Indians used it as a lookout and for sending smoke signals. But it was the Corps of Discovery that put Pompey's Pillar on the map. In July 1806, William Clark and his party were paddling down the Yellowstone when they sighted this 200-foot-high sandstone outcropping in the middle of the wide valley. Clark named the formation after Jean Baptiste, the son of Sacajawea and Charbonneau, the French trapper and adventurer who accompanied the Corps. Clark had nicknamed Jean Baptiste Little Pomp, meaning Little Chief. Clark wrote:

July 25th, 1806 at 4 P M arived at a re-
markable rock situated in an extensive bot-
tom. this rock I ascended and from its top had
a most extensive view in every direction. This
rock which I shall call Pompy's Tower is 200
feet high and 400 paces in secumpherance and
only axcessable on one Side. The nativs have
ingraved on the face of this rock the figures of
animals &c near which I marked my name
and the day of the month and year. From the
top of this Tower I could discover two low
Mountains and the Rocky Mts covered with
Snow one of them appeared to be extencive.

Some of the Pillar's petroglyphs still remain and are reckoned to be the work of the
Shoshone Indians who lived in this area before the current Plains tribes moved west.
But the real curiosity here is Clark's signature,
carved in the rock and still legible after almost 200 years. Clark was not the last to
sign Pompey's Pillar. A pair of crossed hatch-
ets, insignia medallions worn by members
of the corps, were probably carved by an enterprising corpsman while Clark finished his
signature. Captain Grant Marsh, pilot of the
steamship *Josephine,* added his graffiti in
1875.

POMPEY—SACAJAWEA'S REMARKABLE SON

The child that William Clark knew as Pompey was
born to a destiny usually reserved for heroes of
fiction. He was born to Toussaint Charbonneau—a
French trader living with the Mandan Indians in
North Dakota—and one of his three wives, a 15-
year-old Shoshone named Sacajawea, who had
been stolen away from her tribe in Montana. His
birth was difficult; after many hours of labor, the delivery was hastened by giving Sacajawea a potion of
rattlesnake rattle and river water. Ten minutes later,
she delivered young Jean Baptiste. Two months
later, the Corps of Discovery, with the papoose
Pompey, set out for the Pacific.

Captain Clark grew very fond of the young child
during the course of the journey. After the successful
completion of the trip, the Corps once again reached
the Mandan villages that were home to the Char-
bonneaus. Clark urged them to allow him to take the
young Baptiste to rear as his own. They declined.

Later the same year, however, Clark wrote Charbonneau to repeat his offer, saying, "if you bring
your son Baptiste to me, I will educate him and treat
him as my own child." And this time it worked. Charbonneau, Sacajawea, and Baptiste moved to St.
Louis, where Clark educated the boy in a Catholic
academy.

When Baptiste was 18 years old, he met Prince
Paul of Württemberg, a German aristocrat-cum-sci-
entist intent on exploring Montana. The prince was intrigued by the well-educated half-breed (Baptiste
already spoke three languages), and after ascending
the Missouri in his company, the prince asked Clark
if Baptiste might accompany him back to Germany.

Baptiste spent the next six years living with the
prince in his castle near Stuttgart and accompany-

ing him on his travels to England, France, and North
Africa. His education continued, and he learned
two more languages. When the prince returned to
America in 1829, Baptiste returned as well. This
time, however, after journeying to the headwaters of
the Missouri and back down the Yellowstone, Baptiste remained in the West.

Thereafter, he renounced the refinements of European court life for the rigors and adventure of the
American frontier. He earned a living as a trapper for
the American Fur Company until the fur trade declined in the early 1830s. By the 1840s, Baptiste was
working as a guide for traders, explorers, and foreign visitors. He consorted with such famous mountain
men as Solomon and Andrew Sublette, Jim Bridger,
and Joe Meek. He led more hunting trips for European
noblemen, including a well-documented expedition
by the Scot Sir William Drummond Stewart in 1843. A
contemporary judged him to be "the best man on foot
on the Plains or in the Rocky Mountains."

In 1847, Baptiste was in California, after guiding a battalion of Mormons across the southwestern
deserts during the Mexican War. He was appointed
alcalde for the mission at San Luis Rey, until he
resigned after being accused of "favoring the Indians more than he should," according to contemporary legal documents. In 1848, the lure of gold
drew Baptiste northward to the prospecting country
near Sacramento, where he lived for 18 years. Stories of gold strikes in Montana excited the old trapper, and he set out to revisit the scenes of his youth.
However, he made it no farther than the Owyhee
Valley in eastern Oregon before he died, in 1866.
Jean Baptiste Charbonneau is buried near Dan-
ner, Oregon.

cattle branding near Custer

The BLM operates a visitor center at Pompey's Pillar, and a $3 fee is charged for each vehicle. The park is open between Memorial Day and Labor Day. Climb the boardwalk staircase to see Clark's signature; continue on to a good vista of the Yellowstone Valley and surrounding rimrock hills. There are picnic tables near the river, but no overnight camping is allowed.

The closest facilities are in Ballantine, where the **Longbranch,** alongside the freeway, has a reputation with the locals for good, inexpensive food. The closest motels are in Billings and Custer.

I-94 BETWEEN POMPEY'S PILLAR AND FORSYTH

Between Pompey's Pillar and Forsyth, I-94 parallels the Yellowstone River through a region of farms, ranches, and, near Hysham, badlands. The valley here is wide and, where not under cultivation, forested with cottonwoods. At the edge of the river valley, steep sandstone cliffs rise, fringed with pine and juniper trees.

Although little remains to indicate it, this stretch of the Yellowstone saw much of the early history of Montana. At the mouth of the Bighorn, near present-day Custer, traders erected the territory's first structures. Beginning with Fort Ramon, established by Manuel Lisa in 1807 and named after his infant son, and soon followed by other forts, this location drew adventurers and frontiersmen who came to trade, trap, and to explore the wilderness.

The list of those who passed through these forts reads like a who's who of the early West: Jim Bridger, Father deSmet, John Bozeman. The mouth of the Bighorn River was traditionally the head of navigation for steamboats on the Yellowstone River. It is also the beginning of the agate-rich Yellowstone gravel that stretches downstream to the Missouri.

Nothing remains of the various trading forts along the Yellowstone, but from the fishing-access site at the mouth of the Bighorn River (exit 49), appropriately called Manuel Lisa, you can see where the forts must have stood, and imagine this deserted riverbank as one of the hotbeds of activity west of St. Louis.

For back-road enthusiasts, or anyone who wants a break from the freeway, there is a nice side-road alternative to I-94 beginning at the little community of Custer and continuing to Forsyth. The road, gravel at first, then paved, passes through the small farming and ranching communities of Myers, Hysham, and Sanders. The road keeps much closer to the Yellowstone than the freeway does and offers more interesting scenery.

There are limited but completely adequate tourist facilities. In Custer, the **D & L Cafe and Motel,** 311 2nd Ave., tel. (406) 856-4128, offers inexpensive rooms and good food. Call ahead in winter months; it closes during the off-season. Six miles east of Hysham off I-90's Sarpy Creek exit, the **Sarpy Creek Guest House,** tel. (406) 342-5668, offers guests a two-bedroom country house complete with kitchen.

For two, the house is $75; each additional person is an extra $10. The house can sleep a maximum of 6 people. The **Hysham Hills Supper Club,** tel. (406) 342-5434, has great food, including a Sunday buffet.

COLSTRIP

South of the bluffs of Yellowstone Valley proper, the underlying sandstone changes from Eagle Formation to Fort Union Formation sandstone. While there are no visual differences between the two, there is a vast difference in mineral wealth. In the 15 million years between the two sandstone-making periods, tropical forests laid down vast deposits of peat alongside the ancient seas and riverbanks. When the climate changed, these deposits in turn were covered by others, and the peat slowly turned to coal.

The coal in this part of Montana is highly prized. It is covered by a modest layer of overburden (rock and soil) and makes for easy strip-mining. Strip-mining removes the overburden by levels, revealing the coal seam, which is then gouged out by enormous power shovels. The coal itself is low-sulfur bituminous, which burns cleaner and at a higher temperature than soft coal from other parts of the country.

These considerations have made Colstrip, astride huge coal deposits, appealing to mining and energy interests. When Montana Power began to build coal-fired generators at Colstrip in the 1970s, Montanans were galvanized around the issues of progress, ecology, and heritage.

History

Colstrip (pop. 3,000, elev. 2,540 feet) began in 1924 as a source of coal for the engines of the Northern Pacific. Having depleted its original source of coal at Red Lodge, the Northern Pacific began to extract cheaper, more efficient coal from the eastern plains.

The Northern Pacific was one of the last major railroads to switch from coal- to diesel-fueled engines. After it did, in the 1950s, it sold its coal leases at Colstrip to a subsidiary of the Montana Power Company, called the Western Energy Company. Equipment was updated and coal development was expanded. In 1969, a coal-fired electric generator was built in Billings, operated by the Montana Power Company and fueled by Colstrip coal.

The success of the plant fueled plans for more electric generators. In tandem with the oil crunch of the 1970s, the Western Energy Company revealed plans to build four more huge generators. The power was to be sold to out-of-state markets in the Pacific Northwest and Midwest. But rather than ship the coal to generators near the markets, the Western Energy Company planned to build all four generators in Colstrip.

The amount of coal to be mined was enormous. Entire ranches would be devoured by the strip mines. The generators would pollute the air, which in almost the entire eastern part of Montana is pristine. However, the plants would bring economic growth to some of the state's most marginally successful agricultural communities.

Instantly, battle lines were drawn. Environmentalists concerned with air quality joined with ranchers worried about wells and the lowering of the water table. (Coal seams function as aquifers, as coal is porous, and the water table in this part of Montana is often the shallow layer of coal underlying almost everything in the eastern third of the state.) Other farmers and ranchers, who had struggled for decades against the weather, insects, and bad markets, were understandably excited by the prospect of finally earning a living from the land, albeit by a troubling method.

Even the Indian tribes divided: the Cheyenne fought to cancel coal leases on the reservation and filed to have the reservation reclassified as an area with Class 1 air standards, usually granted only to wilderness areas. The Crow, on the other hand, sold mineral rights and watched strip mines operate on the reservation.

Grassroots opposition found its focus in the Northern Plains Resource Council and its leaders in articulate farmers and ranchers who feared the changes in environment and community that the growth of large-scale mining would entail. Development at Colstrip was a deeply divisive issue to rural Montanans. As traditional "leave me alone" libertarians who resented environmentalists as cowardly predator-lovers, these farmers and ranchers found the same mistrusted environmentalists to be allies against the juggernauts of big business and big development.

In the end, Colstrip electric generators 1 through 4 went in after many delays and courtroom battles. However, the state instituted tough reclamation laws and levied a severance tax on coal sold out of state. The generators have left as many scars on rural Montana culture as they have on the plains near Colstrip.

In the late 1990s, the future of the generators has come into question. Several of the utilities that funded the original development of Colstrip are threatening to pull out. A scant 20 years after they were built, the enormous coal-fired generators seem destined to be mothballed.

Sights

After crossing Montana, the approach to Colstrip is a bit of a shock. The 29-mile drive south from I-94 crosses a countryside of barren, dry valleys and rocky buttes. It seems a marginal, rough piece of real estate. Then the land, without really changing, becomes a bit too smooth, too manicured, as if it had recently been mowed, revealing the good work of the reclaimers. Suddenly smokestacks fill the air. At 692 feet high, they are the tallest structures in Montana. Pipelines and rail lines converge at mammoth generators spewing out smoke. Piles of overburden rise above gashes in the earth, where man and machine render coal from flat fields of black and place it in railcars.

Tours are available to the curious, showing the workings of a modern strip mine and coal-fired generators. The Rosebud open-pit mine tour takes the visitor to the bottom of a working strip mine. The enormous power shovels have to be seen to be believed. The second part of the tour goes to the generating plants. Tours are free, but call ahead to reserve a time; tel. (406) 748-5406 or 748-2990.

Almost as interesting is the town itself. Built almost totally from scratch since the 1970s (remnants of '20s-era buildings are labeled the "historic district"), Colstrip is what other Montana prairie towns might look like if they had money. The town is confusing to drive around in, as you expect to come upon some sort of business area. But the town planners seemingly allocated one store, one restaurant, and one gas station to Colstrip, and the rest is a suburb without a city. Bike paths, manicured lawns around new homes, artificial lakes, lots of parks and sports facilities, even an ice-skating rink, all in a setting of rocky gumbo, make Colstrip seem almost surreal.

Colstrip's 1924 schoolhouse is now the **Schoolhouse History & Art Center,** 400 Woodrose St., tel. (406) 748-4822. Featured are photos of Colstrip over the years, as well as changing art shows. The gift shop sells local crafts.

Practicalities

Override Park on Water Ave. offers basketball courts, tennis courts, a swimming pool, water slide, and a playground. There are also picnic tables at the visitor center just off Hwy. 39.

The new, nine-hole **Ponderosa Butte Golf Course,** tel. (406) 748-2700, is reportedly quite challenging. It's across the street from the high school.

The comfortable **Fort Union Inn** is at 5 Dogwood, tel. (406) 748-2553, (800) 738-2553. Rooms are $39 s, $49 d. There's also a **Super 8** at 6227 Main St., tel. (406) 748-3400 or (800) 800-8000. Camping is available at **Colstrip Community Services,** tel. (406) 748-5057. **Bob's Place,** 17 Cherry, tel. (406) 748-2566, is the locals' favorite for steak, sandwiches, and pizza.

The **visitor center** is open Mon.-Fri. 9 a.m.-5 p.m., Memorial Day to Labor Day, and from 10 a.m.-3 p.m. the rest of the year at 6200 Main St., tel. (406) 748-2990.

Civilization has its merits. Tune in to **Yellowstone Public Radio** at 88.5 FM.

FORSYTH

Forsyth (pop. 2,141, elev. 2,515 feet), nestled beneath a rim of rough gumbo badlands along the banks of the Yellowstone, is a pretty little town with lots of trees and western character. The presence of Colstrip to the south has elevated Forsyth above the general economic malaise assailing other small Montana towns, without developing it into an affluent parody of its historic self. For the traveler, Forsyth offers recreational opportunities and a friendly place to spend the night.

History

Forsyth is named for Gen. James Forsyth, a U.S. Army officer who first landed here in 1875, before the town existed. Steamers stopped here to refuel their engines from the abundant stands of cottonwood. The town was established in 1880 and earned its own post office when the

Northern Pacific arrived in 1882. The elaborate buildings along Main Street, including the imposing Rosebud County Courthouse, indicate the wealth of the young community during the early years of this century.

Forsyth grew into its own as a trading hub after the Milwaukee Road extended north from Forsyth into the Musselshell and Judith Basin country in 1910, opening up a vast new territory for settlement.

The railroads still fuel the Forsyth economy. Much of the coal that Burlington Northern ships out of state from Colstrip and other mines south of Forsyth pass through the rail yards here.

Sights

The **Rosebud County Pioneer Museum,** 1300 Main, tel. (406) 356-7547, houses artifacts from the area's early years of settlement and photographs of pioneer days. Open Mon.-Sat. 9 a.m.-7 p.m., Sunday 1-7 p.m., May-September.

Recreation

Forsyth is well placed to serve as a center for hunters, as it is the hub of many country roads that quickly take the outdoorsperson into prime big-game territory. Pronghorn, mule deer, and white-tailed deer are the usual quarry. Also, with the fields that line the river and the river itself both serving as a temptation, bird hunters are rewarded with ample prey.

With fishing-access sites practically within city limits, Forsyth also welcomes anglers. The **Rosebud State Recreation Areas,** directly east and west of the city, offer fishing and boating access and camping. If you stop for a picnic, don't forget to look for agates.

The **Forsyth Golf and Country Club,** three miles west of Forsyth, exit 93 (Frontage Rd.), tel. (406) 356-7710, has nine holes, rentals, and a clubhouse. The course winds up a steep gumbo canyon in the badlands just outside of town. There

is also an indoor Olympic-size **swimming pool** in Forsyth.

Accommodations

Best Western Sundowner Inn, 1018 Front St., tel. (406) 356-2115 or (800) 332-0921, has rooms for $52 s, $70 d (senior discounts available). All rooms are equipped with refrigerators and coffeemakers; pets are allowed. You get nicely furnished but less-expensive rooms at the **Restwel,** convenient to freeway travelers at 810 Front St., tel. (406) 356-2771. Rates are $34 s, $40 d, and include continental breakfast; some rooms have kitchenettes. **Westwind Motor Inn,** W. Main at Hwy. 12, tel. (406) 356-2038, (800) 356-2038, $37 s, $42 d, has a pretty location near fishing access along the Yellowstone. The inn provides a continental breakfast; pets are permitted in the rooms. At 3rd and Front St. The **Rails Inn,** tel. (406) 356-2242, (800) 621-3754, has single rooms for $40, doubles for $50 (senior and corporate discounts), a hot tub, and lounge. Rooms come with a complimentary hot breakfast the motel's cafe.

There are campsites at both of the **Rosebud State Recreation Areas** on the east and west ends of town. **Wagon Wheel Campsites,** exit 95, tel. (406) 356-7982, welcomes both tent and RV campers.

Food

For food 24 hours a day, go to the **Speedway Diner** in downtown's vintage Howdy Hotel, 811 Main St., tel. (406) 356-7987. **M&M Pizza &Café,** 1425 Front St., tel. (406) 356-7181, offers a complete menu as well as excellent pizza.

Services

The **Rosebud Health Care Hospital** is at 383 W. 17th St., tel. (406) 356-2161. **Emergency** is 911. The **chamber of commerce** can be contacted at P.O. Box 448, Forsyth, MT 59327, tel. (406) 356-2141.

MILES CITY

Miles City (elev. 2,371 feet) is an attractive town located at the confluence of the Tongue River and the Yellowstone. Gumbo buttes vaguely fringed with juniper ring the town. Miles City is the second-largest city in southeastern Montana, with almost 8,900 inhabitants. It's a major trade center for farmers and ranchers who, in their pickup trucks, converge on the city for livestock sale days, during harvest for parts, or as often as an excuse can be found to "go to Miles."

HISTORY

Miles City was born in the aftermath of the Battle of the Little Bighorn. After the defeat of Custer's Seventh Cavalry, the Army decided to establish a permanent military presence in eastern Montana to protect settlers and to drive the Sioux back onto reservations. In the fall of 1876, six companies of the Fifth Cavalry under the command of General Nelson Miles established a military cantonment at the mouth of the Tongue River and arranged for the building of Fort Keogh. The civilian settlement that grew up downriver was initially known as Milestown. Fort Keogh, the largest military fort built in Montana, was finished in 1878, and Miles City reestablished itself on the Tongue River's opposite shore.

Miles City quickly became important as a trade center. The military payroll made for a relatively

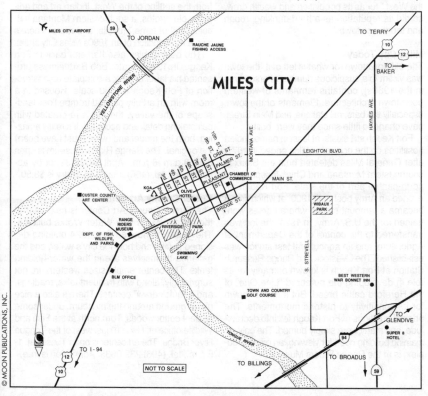

affluent citizenry, encouraging a stable base for the trades and mercantile. Steamboats were the vehicle for almost all transportation in the early days, and Miles City was an important port. The steamboats brought up goods for Fort Keogh and the young community of Miles City and took out a wealth of buffalo bones and hides.

After the Army had subdued the Sioux in 1877, and after the buffalo hunters had completed their own devastation, the vast prairies along the lower Yellowstone drainage were opened up for grazing. The first of the huge trail drives north from Texas was in 1879, and for the next 10 years Miles City was the center of a grazing region that summered tens of thousands of southern cattle. The Northern Pacific Railroad arrived in 1881, providing a railhead to eastern slaughterhouses and markets. These boom years in the 1880s justified Miles City's swaggering boast of being the "Cow Capital of the West," for as its population and wealth grew, so did its reputation as a hard-drinking, rough and tough cowtown.

Miles City Today

The old downtown, or what is left of it (the town was victim to a suspicious number of arson fires in the 1980s), contains remnants of western boomtown architecture. Elements of the town, especially the bars, rail stations, and Main Street, have changed little since they were built.

Fort Keogh still exists, at least in name. Indian hostilities on the northern plains ended in 1877, after General Miles defeated both the Sioux in southeastern Montana and Chief Joseph in the north-central part of the state. Fort Keogh remained an Army post until 1900, at which time it became a remount station where horses were trained for the U.S. Army. In 1924, the fort was transferred to the control of the Department of Agriculture, and an agricultural test station was established. The Livestock and Range Research Station at Fort Keogh is known primarily for its role in developing the purebred "Line One" of the Hereford cattle breed. But it is not known for its sensitivity to historic monuments. The original buildings of Fort Keogh fell into decrepitude, and many were simply burned. The only remaining building open for viewing, an officers' duplex, is at the Range Riders Museum.

SIGHTS

Range Riders Museum

Every community in eastern Montana has a local museum. If you see only one, make it the Range Riders Museum in Miles City. Located at the western edge of the city, near the confluence of the Tongue and Yellowstone Rivers, it contains enough items to impress even the most jaundiced of museum-goers.

A one-room school, a frontier cabin, tepees, and a sheep wagon have been moved onto the grounds and maintained in period condition with authentic furnishings. A building from Fort Keogh, officers' quarters, is open to visitors and is a vivid reminder of just how civilized life was on the Yellowstone in 1878.

Inside the museum is an excellent gun and weapon collection, artifacts and memorabilia from the settling of the West, Indian art and artifacts, old photos, a southeastern Montana settler's "hall of fame," fossils, and more. There's also a reproduction of an 1890s Miles City street.

The best display also harkens back to Fort Keogh. In 1990, curator Bob Barthelmess presented his labor of love: a complete reconstruction of Fort Keogh at 1:80 scale. Housed in a room with an artfully painted trompe l'oeil landscape of the valley, the fort is re-created with painstaking detail and accuracy. It's really amazing, both the model and (what must have been) the original. The Range Riders Museum is open daily 8 a.m.-8 p.m., April 1-Oct. 31, or by appointment, tel. (406) 232-6146. Entry is $3.50.

Custer County Art Center

The Custer County Art Center is next door at the historic Miles City Water Works building. The gallery is housed in a 1924 building designed to filter and hold the city's water, and the galleries themselves are in the water-holding tanks. The center emphasizes western art, not surprisingly, along with frequent talks, readings, and a "quick draw" contest. There's also a nice picnic ground around the museum, under some ancient cottonwoods. Turn north at the Fish and Wildlife office off Hwy. 10 just west of the Tongue River Bridge. The art center is open Tues.-Sat. 1-5 p.m., tel. (406) 232-0635. Admission is free.

Downtown
Downtown Miles City is still intact enough, despite the efforts of arsonists, to look like the cattle-trading capital it once was. There's an undeniably western flavor to the city, with its old bars, saddleries, cafes, and the clientele to appreciate them. Most of the downtown area is now listed on the National Register of Historic Places.

Recreation
Riverside Park, on W. Main at the Tongue River Bridge, has tennis courts and swimming in a natural lake. **Wibaux Park** has a good playground for kids and is easy to find from the freeway by following S. Haynes Ave. from the Broadus exit toward town and turning south two blocks at S. Strevell. The **Town and Country Golf Course** is a private nine-hole club open to the public at Montana Ave. and S. 4th Street. Call (406) 232-1600 for information.

Twelve miles southwest of Miles City, on Hwy. 12, **Woodruff Park** has picnic sites in grassy swales and pine trees. Although there are no formal trails, a nice wander along the ridges is enjoyable. Overnight camping is also allowed, although no water is provided, and garbage has to be carried out. Cross-country skiers make use of the park in winter.

White-tailed and mule deer are abundant in the countryside around Miles City, making it a good headquarters for hunters. Consider an outfitter if you are new to the area. **Ray Perkins Outfitters Service** offers game-bird and big-game outfitting, 1906 Main, Miles City, MT 59301, tel. (406) 232-4283.

PRACTICALITIES

Accommodations
A clutch of chain hotels is located at the Broadus exit (exit 138) off I-94. The **Super 8** is south of the interchange on Hwy. 59, tel. (800) 800-8000 or (406) 232-5261 in the area. Single rooms are $48, doubles $54. **Motel 6** is north toward town, 1314 S. Haynes Ave., tel. (406) 232-7040; rates here are $34 s, $41 d. Along the same strip, the **Days Inn,** 1006 S. Haynes Ave., tel. (406) 232-3550 or (800) 525-6303, has a pool and hot tub; rooms are $35 s, $48 d. **Custer's Inn Budget Host,** at 1209 S.

Haynes, tel. (406) 232-5170 or (800) 456-5026, has an indoor pool, saunas, and rooms for $35 s, $43 d. The **Best Western War Bonnet Inn,** at 1015 S. Haynes Ave., tel. (800) 528-1234 or (406) 232-4560, is one of the city's best. Single rooms start at $64, doubles at $69. The newest hotel on the strip is **Holiday Inn Express,** 1720 S Haynes, tel. (406) 232-1000, with complimentary breakfast, indoor pool, and guest laundry; $69 s and d.

Downtown is the **Olive Hotel and Rodeway Inn,** 502 Main St., tel. (406) 232-2450 or (800) 228-2000, $34 s, $41 d, the only old original Miles City hotel in operation. The Olive is so well established that even fictional characters (such as Gus McCrae of *Lonesome Dove*) stay there. You can choose to lodge in the old hotel or in the more modern motel to the side. Either way, you are staying at a Montana institution and are seconds away from very good steaks in the main hotel. The Olive's 1899 lobby is listed in the National Register of Historic Places.

For camping, the **Miles City KOA** is near the Tongue-Yellowstone juncture at 1 Palmer St., tel. (406) 232-3991. It features a pool, tent sites, laundry, and hot showers from May to November. The **Big Sky Campground,** tel. (406) 232-1511, is just off the Baker interchange (exit 141) and is open to both RVs and tents from May to November. Not much shade, though.

Food
There's a large concentration of fast-food restaurants, a truck stop, and a dependable 24-hour **4-Bs,** tel. (406) 232-5772, at the Broadus exit off I-94. For tasty food at extremely reasonable prices, go to the buffet at the **Boardwalk,** 9065 S. Haynes. At the Baker interchange, there's **Thad's Restaurant,** part of a truck stop whose cafe, tel. (406) 232-5910, has a good local reputation. There are no surprises on the menu, but the food is tasty.

There's more character and probably better food uptown. Here, amongst the easily recognized fast-food and sandwich joints, are more authentic Miles City eating experiences. The **Olive Hotel Dining Room,** 502 Main St., tel. (406) 232-2450, has great steaks. Another landmark is the old diner-like **600 Cafe,** 600 Main St., tel. (406) 232-3860, full of character and characters, both local. It's a great place to catch the pulse of this old cow town.

Right next door is the more upscale **Hole in the Wall,** 602 Main St., tel. (406) 232-9887, featuring fairly authentic western decor and steaks. **Club 519,** 519 Main St., tel. (406) 232-5133, features steaks in the historic First National Bank building (1910).

Entertainment
A night out in Miles City is a great way to experience one of the legacies of the Old West. Miles City started as a watering hole for thirsty soldiers, and it still is a major meeting place for stockmen and ranch hands. Miles City is a city exceptionally blessed with great old bars, and some of them have not changed appreciably (except for the addition of the ubiquitous gambling machines).

The **Montana Bar** is probably one of the greatest bars in the state, remarkably unchanged since it opened in 1902. You can imagine the many tall tales told and livestock trading that went on here at 612 Main Street. Other good bars are the **Range Riders,** 605 Main St., the **Bison,** 618 Main St., the **Log Cabin,** 710 Main St., and the bar at the **Olive Hotel,** 501 Main Street. Also check out the **Golden Spur,** 1014 S Haynes, tel. (406) 232-3544, where you can taste Miles City's own microbrew, Milestown Draught.

Events
The **Jaycee Bucking Horse Sale** is the one event that Miles City is known for throughout the West. On the third weekend of May, rodeo stock contractors and bacchants from just about everywhere gather in Miles City to watch young untamed horses buck. The most promising of these mounts are then sold at auction as rodeo broncs.

The Bucking Horse Sale is one of the biggest parties in the state, though the actual rodeo is now the central event in a weekend's worth of events including horse racing, a street dance, a barbecue, cowboy poetry readings, and the like. Don't let these more civilized pursuits fool you: this is a flat-out celebration of the Dionysian element of the Old West. Admission to the rodeo is $10 a head for reserved seats; general-admission seats are $7; children under 12 get in $2 cheaper in either section.

The third weekend of June is set aside for the **Balloon Roundup,** Montana's largest hot-air balloon rally. Events include balloon races and games, a barbecue, a parade, and parties. The Balloon Roundup is held on S. Haynes Ave., near the Broadus interchange.

Shopping
Where better to buy your western togs than in the Cow Capital of the West? The **Miles City Saddlery** will outfit you (and the horse you rode in on) with quality western gear. From boots, cowboy hats, spurs, and pearl-snap shirts to handmade saddles, it's all here, 808 Main St., tel. (406) 232-2512. In a happier era, Main Street was lined with shops, each peddling its own handmade boots and saddles. Wilson brand boots were once the lo-

The Jaycee Bucking Horse Sale is one of Montana's most popular rodeos.

cal's boot of choice. Although the boots are now made elsewhere, **Coggshell Boot and Wilson Saddlery,** 519 N Montana St., tel. (406) 232-2800, is still in operation.

In the back of every saddlery was once a grandfatherly man crafting saddles for local ranchers and cowhands. Nowadays, if you hanker after a custom-made saddle, be prepared to pay a small fortune. **T-Bone Saddle Shop,** tel. (406) 232-5176, is one of the few saddle makers left in Miles City, at 114 N 7th Street.

Check out the local arts and crafts scene at the **Wool House Gallery,** 419 N 7th St., tel. (406) 232-0769. The gallery is located in a former railroad wool warehouse and now features woodworking, steel sculpture, paintings and drawings, and a small railroad museum of Miles City.

Services

The **Post Office** is at 106 N. 7th Street. The **Holy Rosary Hospital** is at 2102 Clark St., tel. (406) 232-2540.

If the sky is threatening, call the **weather service** for an update, tel. (406) 232-2099, and check the **road conditions** by dialing (406) 232-2099. **Montana Public Radio** is heard locally on KEEC 90.7 FM.

Information

The Miles City **Chamber of Commerce** is located at 901 Main St., Miles City, MT 59301, tel. (406) 232-2890, www.inetco.net/mcchamber.

The **BLM** office is across from the Miles City Sales Yards, about a mile west of the Tongue River Bridge. The mailing address is P.O. Box 940, Miles City, MT 59301, tel. (406) 233-4333. The **Dept. of Fish, Wildlife, and Parks,** tel. (406) 232-0900, is just south of the BLM office.

Getting There

Big Sky Airlines has daily flights from Frank Wiley Field into Miles City. A roundtrip flight from Billings is about $70. The **Greyhound** station, tel. (406) 232-3900, is at 2210 Valley Dr. East.

THE LOWER YELLOWSTONE

Between Miles City and its confluence with the Missouri, the Yellowstone becomes a languid prairie river flowing through increasingly arid badlands. The trees and the small towns thin out, and a kind of sullen barrenness grips the landscape.

This is ranch country, rugged and desolate. Since the days of the big cattle drives in the 1880s, the plains along the lower Yellowstone have been home to large holdings of livestock. Towns such as Terry, Glendive, and Wibaux had their beginnings as trade and rail centers in the early days of the West. Their economies are still largely tied to agriculture, although oil and gas production have bolstered them somewhat in the recent years of poor cattle, sheep, and grain markets.

This area is also home to curious opportunities for the traveler. Makoshika State Park near Glendive offers startlingly rugged badlands filled with fossils, hiking trails, and wildlife. It also offers the chance to pull into old towns like Terry and Wibaux and experience the life of the modern stockmen on their own turf.

HISTORY

Until the end of the Indian Wars of 1876-77, this was Indian country, with the Sioux harassing travelers on the Yellowstone as they passed through. When the Northern Pacific was surveyed, hundreds of soldiers were needed to protect the engineers from the Indians. At this time, the only whites living in this part of Montana were rough-hewn loners who cut cottonwood for steamer fuel by summer and shot buffalo by winter.

By 1877 the Indians were mostly incarcerated on reservations and the land opened to exploitation. One of the last great herds of buffalo on the open range was slaughtered in the Terry area in the early 1880s, just in time to be shipped east on the first trains running east and west on the Northern Pacific.

The prairie was soon overrun with herds of Texas longhorns. Glendive and Wibaux were major railheads for the shipment of the cattle to eastern markets, and were rough-and-ready "cow towns" in their day. After the hard winter of

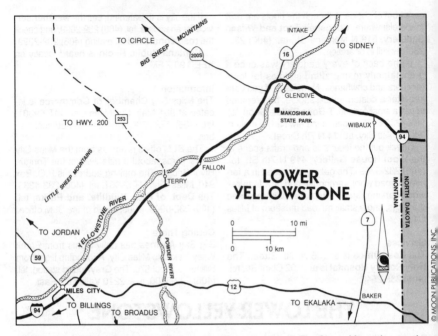

1886, when vast herds of "free range" cattle died, the cattle industry was reborn in areas like Wibaux, where the cattle barons of the open range then founded ranches.

The Cedar Creek Anticline, which lifts the Makoshika Badlands above the plains, also traps natural gas and oil in domes beneath the prairies. Development of these fuels prompted a boom in Glendive in the 1970s.

TERRY

This little ranch town sits along the Yellowstone, with prairies to the south and rugged badlands to the north. If you are traveling east, it's time to realize that you're well and truly on the plains of Montana. At Miles City, the Yellowstone is a wide green valley with irrigated pastures and fields. At Terry, 40 miles downstream, only a fringe of green isolates the river from the encroaching prairies.

Terry (pop. 665, elev. 2,244 feet) is a friendly town where ranchers meet to drink coffee or a

beer and to talk. The Sheep Mountains, gumbo breaks to the north, provide a scenic vista over badlands and river valley, and offer wildlife viewing. As ever, the Yellowstone is good for fishing and boating.

Terry has a tradition of producing rodeo stars. Terry-born rodeo rider and showman Bernie Kempton toured the world in Wild West shows early this century. In Australia he drew local attention by roping not one but two kangaroos per loop. Kempton retired to the Terry area where he ran a popular guest ranch. The Fourth of July Terry Rodeo is considered one of the best rodeos in the state.

History

The mouth of the Powder River, five miles upstream from Terry, is one of those locations that everyone noted when passing through. William Clark camped across the Yellowstone from the Powder on the last night of July 1806. Sir George Gore made camp here on his big-game safari of 1856. General Custer passed through here on his way to destiny in 1876.

Terry began as a refueling station for the steamers bringing soldiers and supplies up the Yellowstone during the Indian Wars of the 1870s. The rough life during these early years is illustrated by a tombstone epitaph at a small pioneer cemetery on the Powder River: "Killed in a quarrel at Top Foley's Roadhouse, 1880."

Sights

The **Sheep Mountains** directly north of Terry are not mountains at all. Rather, they are rugged gumbo badlands that form the watershed between the Yellowstone and the Missouri River drainages. Especially in spring and early summer, when the striations are moist and highly colored and the wildflowers are in bloom, they seem almost forlornly beautiful.

Although the Sheep Mountains are not developed as a destination, Hwy. 253, a gravel road, continues on to Brockway and Hwy. 200.

From a turnout high in the Sheep Mountains, two miles north and six miles west off Hwy. 253, a scenic viewpoint overlooks the Yellowstone. Called the **Terry Badlands,** this is a designated wildlife-viewing area. The usual big-game animals are here, as well as predators, golden eagles, and songbirds. Watch out for snakes.

Several historic sites are commemorated near the mouth of the Powder River. A small **pioneer graveyard** sits on the west bank of the river at the Hwy. 10 bridge (Hwy. 10 is the old highway, now the local access road). A roadside sign describes the graveyard and its three headstones, which lie about 100 feet off the road. Another sign describes the old **Terry Supply Station,** which stood on the Yellowstone and furnished fuel to steamers as they brought soldiers into Montana during the Indian Wars. Two soldiers of Custer's Seventh Cavalry are buried here. A road, suitable for high-clearance vehicles, leads to the site.

The **Prairie County Museum,** 105 Logan, tel. (406) 637-5595, is housed in an elegant turn-of-the-century bank building. Its exhibits include horse-drawn carriages, rebuilt offices and businesses, and historical photographs. The museum staff can direct the traveler to several Indian tepee rings and buffalo jumps in the hills around Terry.

Evelyn Cameron, a pioneer photographer, took spectacular pictures of Terry and the surrounding area around the turn of the century. Some of her photos hang in the **Cameron Gallery,** next door to the county museum. Both the historical museum and gallery are open Memorial Day through Labor Day.

Accommodations

One of Terry's original hotels, the **Kempton Hotel,** 204 Spring St., tel. (406) 635-5543, $22 s, $30 d, is still in operation and makes a stopover in Terry more intriguing. Except for the neon sign, the Kempton has changed little for decades, with

Homesteaders establish themselves near Terry in the city's early years.

EVELYN CAMERON/MONTANA HISTORICAL SOCIETY, HELENA

its white clapboard exterior and second-floor balcony. The **Diamond Motel,** just off I-94, tel. (406) 635-5407, is a more modern alternative, with some RV hookups (and showers) available in summer. Singles start at $26, doubles are $30.

The **Terry RV Oasis,** just off exit 176, tel. (406) 635-5520, has tent camping and is closer to the freeway.

Food
Try the **Overland Restaurant,** 316 E. Spring St., tel. (406) 635-5830, for light meals—the restaurant's owner is also a good source of information on the Terry area.

Services
The **chamber of commerce** can be reached at P.O. Box 667, Terry, MT 59349, tel. (406) 635-2126. The **sheriff** can be reached at (406) 635-5738. The Terry area is famous for big-game and game-bird hunting. For **guide service,** contact **Robert Dolatta Outfitters,** HC 77, Terry, MT 59349, tel. (406) 486-5736.

GLENDIVE

Like other towns on the Yellowstone, Glendive (pop. 4,557, elev. 2,069 feet) seems like an oasis of green and trees after crossing the sere plains that surround it. Although agates are common all along the Yellowstone, Glendive probably has the best agate hunting in the state. One of the best collections of this beautiful stone can be found here, and organized float trips on the river are available to the would-be collector. And although the paddlefish lives in much of the lower Yellowstone, the Glendive area is the paddlefish capital of Montana. Makoshika State Park, a preserve of colorful and austere badlands at the southeastern edge of town, offers camping, hiking, wildlife viewing, and fossil hunting.

History
Glendive began as Fort Canby, a military camp built to protect railroad workers as they laid the track for the Northern Pacific up the Yellowstone

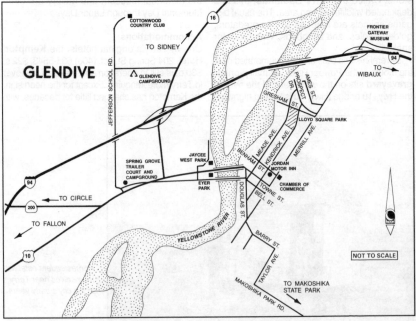

YELLOWSTONE MOSS AGATES

Agates and sapphires are Montana's two official gemstones. Although agates occur worldwide, dendritic agates from the Yellowstone Valley are highly valued for their unusual figurations. Often called moss agates, the interiors of these stones reveal startlingly realistic mini-landscapes when correctly cut and polished.

Agates are made when gases form bubbles within cooling igneous strata. These cavities are slowly filled with water carrying a silica solution tinted with mineral traces (usually iron). As the silica hardens, it forms regular bands of color of varying intensity. Successive layers of colored silica are laid down within the cavity. As the overlying rock is eroded, the nodes of agate are freed from their setting.

Moss agates are different from banded, or riband, agates because of the presence of plume-like formations within the stone. Small fractures allow the penetration of minute amounts of water-borne minerals into the silica node, which, as it hardens, forms tree- or featherlike apparitions in the translucent stone. Combined with bands of color within the agate, these formations make landscape images of trees and sunsets, or trees along a lakeside. The verisimilitude of moss agates can be uncanny.

These agates, often called picture agates, occur almost exclusively in the Yellowstone Valley between the mouth of the Bighorn River and the Missouri. Why this should be so is a matter of speculation. As the Bighorn, Tongue, and Powder Rivers drain a common area of Wyoming, some theories propose that the agates formed in volcanic ash and lava beds near the watersheds of these rivers and later washed downstream to the Yellowstone. This explanation seems rational, but no appropriate igneous formations have been found in Wyoming.

If you know what you are looking for, agates are not hard to find, but it takes a trained eye to spot them in the rough. Only if they are scuffed or broken do they reveal their translucent interior; otherwise they are a dirty yellow-white.

Agate hunting is a favorite pastime for many locals, and many shops carry baskets of cut agates or agate jewelry for those not willing to hunt for their own. The same locals and shopkeepers are usually willing to lend advice to novice agate hunters. The best agate-hunting seasons are early spring and midsummer, when snowpack runoff scours out the gravel beds. Inquire at the local chamber of commerce to find out if there are guided agate-hunting tours. Just be sure not to cross private property without permission.

Valley in the late 1870s. The train actually arrived in the settlement on July 4, 1881. The name Glendive is apparently a corruption of "Glendale," the name given to a nearby creek by Sir George Gore on his hunting trip in 1856. (A more colorful story maintains that the name is a reference to a particularly earthy bar on the site named Glen's.)

Glendive was a division headquarters for the Northern Pacific. The grazing land around Glendive made it a railhead for cattle and, as the land fell to the plow, for grain and sugar beets as well.

Glendive is at the northern end of the Cedar Creek Anticline, whose rich oil and gas fields brought sporadic wealth and development to the area. Most recently, during the 1970s, oil exploration brought a quick boom in growth, followed by the inevitable bust.

Makoshika State Park

Makoshika contains 8,800 acres of heavily eroded badlands, whose rugged beauty and facilities make it the area's premier attraction. The same geologic buckling that formed the Cedar Creek Anticline raised these badlands hundreds of feet above the prairie. As water eroded the exposed land, it cut through the layers of the Fort Union Formation and revealed a lower, earlier stratum, the Hell Creek Formation. Imbedded in the Fort Union Formation is a rich record of fossil life, including the enormous remains of such beasts as triceratops and tyrannosaurus. In 1990, a volunteer paleontologist sat down for a lunch break on what turned out to be a huge triceratops skull. The excavated skull is now on display at the park visitor center.

Today, in Makoshika Park, deep ravines have been cut from ridgetops into box canyons whose walls contain fossils. Although fossil hunting is not encouraged in park lands, the park offers stunning overlooks onto the badlands and many opportunities for recreation. Park admission is $4 per vehicle, plus $11 to camp.

As the road leaves Glendive, it quickly climbs up a series of steep switchbacks onto a plateau. From here, the road continues 12 miles along steep ridges and barren canyons with frequent viewpoints and picnic areas. Two maintained trails allow hikers access to the steep canyon walls and valley floors and to the fantastically sculpted formations carved by erosion.

The **Cap Rock Nature Trail** is an interpreted trail that drops 160 feet onto the canyon walls. It passes a short natural bridge, pedestal rocks, fossil beds, and a gumbo sinkhole. A brochure available at the trailhead relates geological history and explains how the formations occurred. About half a mile farther in, the **Kinney Coulee Hiking Trail** winds down a canyon through juniper trees and eroded formations which take on fanciful shapes. This steep trail is about a mile long and puts you onto the valley floor. The brochure also identifies common plants and animals along the path.

Makoshika Park is also a good wildlife-viewing area. Most noteworthy is a summer population of turkey vultures. Golden eagles are common, as are hawks. Coyotes can be heard howling at night. Mule deer hide out here by day and descend to the valley floor by night.

At most overlooks there are picnic tables, and there is a new visitor center at the park entrance. Overnight camping is allowed at the campsite one mile inside the park. Drinking water is available. Trailers are not allowed past the campground, as the road becomes quite steep. A road guide to the park is available at the chamber of commerce or park entrance for $1.

To reach Makoshika State Park, follow Merrill Ave. south from downtown and turn under the railroad tracks on Barry Street. Follow the signs right on Taylor Ave. to the park access road. For more information, contact the Park Manager at P.O. Box 1242, Glendive, MT 59330, or phone the visitors center, tel. (406) 365-6256. The park is open all year; heavy rain or snow may make the roads impassable.

Other Sights

The **Frontier Gateway Museum,** Belle Prairie Rd., tel. (406) 365-8168, has several interesting exhibits. In addition to artifacts of local history, seven historic buildings have been moved to the site, as well as a collection of old fire engines. The museum basement houses a replica of old downtown Glendive. A unique exhibit here is a display of evidence from the area's past murder trials. Hours are Mon.-Sat. 9 a.m.-noon and 1-5 p.m., June-Aug.; Sunday and holidays 1-5 p.m., May and September.

Agate lovers will want to see the **Klapmeier Agate Collection** in the lobby of the Holiday Lodge, 223 Kendrick Avenue. Moss agates are sometimes called "scenic agates," and this collection shows why. The eye is tempted to see land- and seascapes in the thinly cut slices of stone. Many of the agates are made into handsome western jewelry. Peek into the hotel bar to see the mounted paddlefish.

Glendive's community art center, called **The Gallery,** is in the West Plaza mall, tel. (406) 365-6508. The Gallery features works by local artists, including sculpture.

Downtown Glendive has a number of interesting old buildings. A brochure with a walking tour of Glendive is available from the chamber of commerce.

Glendive also has attractive parks. **Lloyd Square Park,** a block and a half west of Merrill Ave. on Gresham St., has an outdoor pool and tennis courts. On the west end of the Bell Street Bridge is **Eyer Park,** with a playground and picnic grounds. On the other side of the road is **Jaycee West Park** with more tennis courts.

Recreation

Intake, an irrigation diversion 16 miles northeast of Glendive, is the center for **paddlefishing,** although paddlefish are found south to Miles City and in the Missouri as well. The State Dept. of Fish, Wildlife, and Parks closely supervises paddlefishing areas to limit abuses and overfishing. The season begins in May and ends July 15, and a special permit, beyond the usual fishing license, is necessary.

Another reason to take to the river is to hunt for agates. From March to October, **guided agate float trips** can be arranged by the Glendive Chamber of Commerce, P.O. Box 930, Glendive, MT 59330, tel. (406) 365-5601.

The **Cottonwood Country Club,** north after Hwy. 16 exit to Highland Park Rd., tel. (406) 365-8797, is a challenging nine-hole course.

PADDLEFISH & MONTANA CAVIAR

Paddlefish occur in only two places on earth: in the upper Missouri drainage and in the Yangtze River in China. No paddlefish had been seen in the U.S. since 1912, and the species was feared extinct. Then, in 1962, a fisherman near Intake landed a grotesque-looking specimen weighing 28 pounds, with no scales and a very prominent snout. Since then, the sport of paddlefishing has become a popular early summer recreation in eastern Montana.

The paddlefish is a member of a primitive family that includes the sturgeon. Among its peculiarities are a three-chambered heart, a skeleton of cartilage instead of bone, a very long life span (up to 30 years), and, of course, its snout, which can be up to two feet long on an adult. It eats only plankton, which it strains out of river water flowing through its gills. This means that the paddlefish won't rise to bait. Instead, it can only be snagged from the river depths where it lurks.

And thus, the *sport*, not art, of paddlefishing. Anglers use heavy rods and line as well as heavy weights (or even spark plugs) to drop the line to the bottom of the river. The line is jerked along the bottom, with the hopes of snagging a paddlefish from its muddy lair. Once on the hook, a tremendous battle ensues, as paddlefish frequently weigh upward of 80 pounds (the record paddlefish, apprehended in the Missouri, weighed 142.5 pounds).

The popularity of paddlefish snagging has begun to worry wildlife experts. In recent years, a disproportionate number of fish taken were huge and old. While exciting for the angler, the ages of the fish being taken has convinced the Fish and Wildlife Department that there aren't sufficient numbers of young fish surviving in the Yellowstone and Missouri. As a result, fewer paddlefish permits are available.

While not all paddlefish flesh is edible (much of it is ominously dark and strong-tasting), a large paddlefish yields an abundance of delicate white meat, which tastes like and shares texture with monkfish.

Since 1989, the Glendive Chamber of Commerce has been authorized to collect paddlefish roe to make into commercially processed caviar. (Actually, paddlefish anglers donate the roe to the chamber, in return for having their fish cleaned.) Although the caviar is not available in Glendive, or anywhere else in Montana (the Fish and Wildlife Department expressly forbids sale of the caviar in Montana to reduce the risks of a caviar black-market), it fetches high prices on the international caviar market. However, anyone can order Glendive paddlefish caviar as long as it is shipped to an out-of-state address. If you'd like to order some, call the Glendive chamber of commerce at (406) 365-5601. The chamber has so far collected nearly a million dollars from the sale of paddlefish roe. Part of the money has been used for county parks and paddlefish research; a full 60% of the proceeds is returned to the community through grants.

KAREN McKINLEY

Accommodations

The **Best Western Jordan Inn,** 223 N. Merrill Ave., tel. (406) 365-5655 or (800) 824-5067, $50-55 s, $65-70 d, is both the local Best Western motel and Glendive's landmark hotel, $45-55 s, $50-65 d. An indoor pool and sauna and a courtyard with pool and ping-pong enliven a stay here. Guests can also use the facilities at a local health club. The **El Centro,** 112 S. Kendrick Ave., tel. (406) 365-5211, $24 s, $33 d, is downtown on a quiet street, and rooms have refrigerators and microwaves. At exit 215 are the **Super 8,** tel. (406) 365-5671 or (800) 800-8000, $42 s, $58 d, and the **Days Inn,** tel. (406) 365-6011, $42 s, $58 d. Pets are permitted at both of these places. The **King's Rustic Inn,** 1903 N. Merrill Ave., tel. (406) 365-5636, is convenient to the freeway, has a pool, and rents rooms starting at $48 d.

A historic prairie style 1912 home at 113 N. Douglas St. is now **The Hostetler House B&B,** tel. (406) 365-4505, (800) 965-8456. The two guest rooms ($45 s, $50 d) share a bath and use of a hot tub. Many of the furnishings are handmade and others are heirlooms. The B&B is just a block from the Yellowstone and close to swimming pools, tennis courts, and downtown.

You are guaranteed a friendly welcome from hosts that grew up in the Glendive area.

Another historic home turned B&B is **Charley Montana B&B,** 103 N. Douglas, tel. (406) 365-3207, (888) 395-3207. This 8,000-square-foot mansion, built in 1904, features original family furnishings. Of the five guest rooms, four share a bath. Rates range $65 to $95.

The **Glendive RV Park and Campground,** 206 1st St., Highland Park, tel. (406) 365-6721, has both RV and tent facilities, plus a swimming pool and camping cabins with air-conditioning and TV!. The **Green Valley Campground,** a half mile north on Hwy. 16, tel. (406) 365-4156, has its own fishing pond. There's also a campground at **Makoshika State Park.**

Food
For the best beef in Glendive, head to the **Blue Room Steak House,** in the Holiday Lodge, 223 N. Kendrick Avenue. The dining room features murals by noted western artist J.K. Ralston, and great steaks and prime rib are menu highlights. **Bacio's Italian Ristorante,** 302 W Towne St., tel. (406) 365-9664, offers tasty Italian cooking. This is just about the only Italian restaurant for 300 miles, so load up. For more basic fare, try the **Jordan Coffee Shop** at 221 N. Merrill Ave., tel. (406) 365-2122, or **CC's Family Cafe,** 1902 N. Merrill Ave., tel. (406) 365-8926.

Shopping
Good places to shop for cut stones or agate jewelry are the **Jordan Gift Shop,** 223 N. Merrill Ave., tel. (406) 365-2207; **Big Sky Agates,** 817 Jefferson School Rd., tel. (406) 365-3888; and **Kolstad Jewelers,** 107 W. Bell St., tel. (406) 365-2830. The Jordan Gift Shop also has a good selection of regional books and crafts.

Services
The **Glendive Community Hospital** is located at 202 Prospect Dr. at Ames St., tel. (406) 365-3306. **Emergency** is 911. **Econo Wash,** 1212 W. Towne, is open seven days a week, 6 a.m.-10 p.m.

The **chamber of commerce** is at 313 S Merrill Ave., P.O. Box 930, Glendive, MT 59330, tel. (406) 365-5601. You'll receive a free moss agate just for stopping by.

Getting There
Glendive is 35 miles west of the North Dakota

border on I-94. Glendive has **Greyhound** bus service and daily air service on Big Sky Airlines.

WIBAUX

Wibaux (WEE-boh) is a quintessential cattle town (pop. 605, elev. 2,634). This small eastern Montana community has seen some of the West's most colorful characters, and it has been an actor in some of the West's most colorful periods. Today, it is a comfortable corner of Montana whose past feels relatively recent.

History
The Northern Pacific passed through this area in 1881, spawning a tiny community called Mingusville. It became the railhead for the huge cattle ranches that grew up along the North Dakota–Montana border. (It was also the local party town, since neighboring Dakota counties were "dry.") This area was coveted grazing land in the days of the open range, but the disastrous winter of 1886 spelled the end of the trail-drive days.

Among the investors who made a successful change to rancher was a Frenchman, Pierre Wibaux, who arrived in Montana in 1883. He is rumored to have made it through 1886 by feeding his cattle cottonwood branches and, with an influx of French capital, was able to buy up livestock at low prices from desperate fellow cattlemen. By the mid-1890s, 65,000 head of cattle bore his brand, the W Bar.

So it was no mere act of hubris when Wibaux in 1894 presented the Northern Pacific authorities a petition asking that Mingusville, Wibaux's ranch's principal railhead, be changed to Wibaux. The authorities sensibly complied.

In this corner of the U.S., these were the days of colorful characters. Just over the border in North Dakota, the Marquis de Mores established the town of Medora. This French nobleman founded a huge cattle ranch and meat-packing plant in the middle of nowhere, built a manor house for his wife, and waited for fortune to come visit. Instead, he welcomed such visitors as Teddy Roosevelt, who had established a cattle ranch nearby after the deaths of both his mother and wife. Wibaux was another fixture in this stylish set.

Wibaux spent his final years in Miles City. His original ranch, with its elaborate home and outbuildings, burned some years ago. Other original ranches still stand; all are privately held. Ask at the tourist office for information about touring the old ranching country.

Sights

Pierre Wibaux left a legacy in Wibaux that, for such a small town, seems very rich. In 1884, Wibaux's father sent him money to build a church. **Saint Peter's Catholic Church** was built the next summer out of native stone and lava rock. Saint Peter's reveals its French background: its quiet rootedness recalls a Normandy churchyard more than a pioneer parish eight miles from North Dakota. It is an imposing structure on the prairies, in summer covered with green ivy, rising above the town that Wibaux built. Consider that when this handsome church was built, places like Glendive and Billings were little more than rail sidings. Beyond the church is a statue of Pierre Wibaux, looking north toward the location of his old ranch.

Wibaux's W Bar Ranch was 14 miles north of the present town. To conduct business in town he built an office and bunkhouse. This small clapboard "town house" now houses the **Wibaux County Museum,** at Orgain and Wibaux Streets, tel. (406) 795-2381; tours are conducted daily at 1, 2, and 3 p.m., Memorial Day to Labor Day. The town house has been returned to its original 1892 condition, including the grounds, which French gardeners had designed with a pond, flower beds, and a grotto. The museum houses personal belongings and furniture as well as items typical of the days of open range.

In 1964, during the New York City World's Fair, Montana sent a railcar containing promotional exhibits about the state, as it was in the same year celebrating its centennial as a territory. Today, the railcar contains the **Centennial Car Museum,** E. Orgain, tel. (406) 795-2289, open 9:30 a.m.-5:30 p.m. Memorial Day to Labor Day. Inside are Indian and pioneer relics, including the museum's pride, a human vertebrae with an arrowhead imbedded in it, which has been unofficially dated to a period at least 2,000 years ago. Admission is free.

Accommodations and Food

The **W-V Motel,** 106 2nd Ave., tel. (406) 795-2446, is $20 s, $29 d. The **Wibaux Super 8,** 400 W 2nd Ave., tel. (406) 795-2666, has rooms at $41 s, $52 d.

The **Anvil Butte Ranch,** tel. (406) 795-2341, puts up guests in the ranch house or in tepees and leads tours focusing on ranch life, dinosaurs, Indian culture, or Custer.

There is a restaurant in the **Palace Hotel** on Main St., tel. (406) 795-2426, and the **Shamrock Bar,** also on Main St., tel. (406) 795-8250, also serves up light meals and good times. **Genie's Kitchen,** at I-94 exit 241, tel. (406) 795-2228, serves up home-style cooking three meals a day.

Information

The **chamber of commerce** can be reached at P.O. Box 159, Wibaux, MT 59353, tel. (406) 795-2412.

Wibaux's French-influenced St. Peter's Church was built in 1884.

W.C. McRAE

THE SOUTHEASTERN CORNER

While the Hi-Line could boast of being Montana's breadbasket, the "South Side" can stake claim to being its cattle range. Initially, this most southeasterly of Montana regions was Indian country; the line between Crow and Sioux territory fell somewhere around the Tongue and Powder Rivers, and this made for hard feelings. The tribes, competing for access to the rich buffalo-hunting grounds, became rivals.

The buffalo were here because of the rich grasses that grew during good years. Once a market was established for buffalo hides, and later for buffalo bones, days were numbered for these enormous animals. But any country good for buffalo was good country for cattle. When the Indians were safely sequestered on reservations and the buffalo were all slaughtered, the rich prairies were open to cattle.

The first cattle drives arrived in the 1870s. Ten years later, the first of the big ranches were in full swing. Miles City was the railhead for the region's livestock. The entire area was thought of as Miles City's "South Side," meaning the rich agricultural area south of the Yellowstone and east of the reservations where livestock grew fat and cowboys and ranchers grew restless for the temptations of a night in town.

Today, this once-vibrant region of the West has its horns tucked in due to years of drought and economic hardship. However, the underlying wealth of its oil and gas reserves has helped to keep these communities stable.

Southeastern Montana is one of the premier hunting areas of Montana. Pronghorn, mule deer, and white-tailed deer range across the entire area; it's also rich in game birds.

BAKER

Located 81 miles from Miles City and only 12 miles from North Dakota, Baker (pop. 1,755, elev. 2,929 feet) is a bustling commercial center with good recreational facilities. Baker first boomed during the early years of its founding, when the railroad came across Montana in the 1900s. Most of the downtown was built during

this time. In the 1960s and '70s nearby oil and gas exploration brought a new spate of civic building. Even though the oil boom has gone a bit bust, Baker has experienced enough prosperity to distance it from its roots as an agricultural trade center.

History

Originally a camping place on the Custer Trail between Wibaux and Camp Crook, Baker took off with the arrival of the Milwaukee Railroad in 1906, which brought homesteaders in its wake. The locals showed their gratitude by changing the name of the old settlement of Lorraine to Baker, to honor the construction engineer of the Milwaukee line. Due to the enormous railroad ad campaigns, which promised "free land" and great futures to immigrants, these Baker-area farmers and ranchers expected rich returns. But they could not have had any idea just how rich.

A driller exploring for water in 1915 instead struck natural gas; the well ignited and burned for six years. Drilling in earnest commenced, and soon Baker was at the center of extensive oil and gas fields. Baker's stable economy has allowed it to develop civic amenities (good schools, parks, athletic complexes) that most urban dwellers consider a necessity of life, but which are rare in poor, rural Montana.

Nearby Ismay decided to celebrate its centennial as a community in 1993 by renaming itself something that would garner some attention. Like Joe. The town's namesake—former San Francisco 49ers and Kansas City Chiefs quarterback Joe Montana—was flattered but didn't bother to attend the festivities.

Sights

The **O'Fallon Historical Museum,** 2nd St. at Fallon, tel. (406) 778-3265, contains artifacts from the area's Indian past and early settlement. The real highlight here is an enormous stuffed steer, at almost 4,000 pounds one of the world's largest.

Recreation

While Baker does not have the western character of some of its southeastern Montana neighbors, it

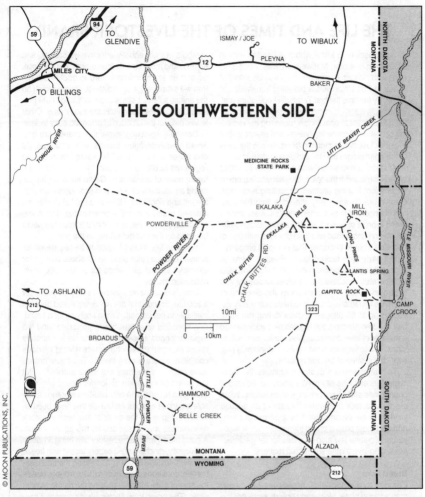

THE SOUTHWESTERN SIDE

does offer the traveler sports and leisure facilities notably absent elsewhere in the region. **Baker Lake** is a reservoir in the center of town that's the focus of summer water sports. At Triangle Park, at the lake's south end, there is a swimming area, a picnic shelter, and a playground. There's fishing access on the lake at the Iron Horse Park. **South Sandstone Lake State Recreation Area,** 13 miles west of Baker on Hwy. 12 and then seven miles south, offers free camping and fishing access.

Baker Recreation Complex, 1015 S. 3rd W, tel. (406) 778-3210, open Mon.-Fri. 6:30-8 a.m., 4-9 p.m., Saturday and Sunday 1-5 p.m., is a modern facility open to the public on the high-school grounds. There are racquetball courts, an indoor Olympic-size pool, and a weight room. The city tennis courts are also located near the high school. The **Lakeview Golf Course,** south on Hwy. 7, tel. (406) 778-3166, has nine holes and a clubhouse.

© MOON PUBLICATIONS, INC.

THE LIFE AND TIMES OF THE LIVESTOCK BRAND

It is impossible to know who first used brands in Montana; however, Meriwether Lewis marked his bags with his own brand, and the 1850 inventory of goods at Fort Union lists a branding iron valued at $2.50. By the time the first Territorial Legislature met, in 1864, livestock numbers were great enough for the government to enact a law regarding the recording of brands. Registering brands was meant to limit livestock loss due to straying (a problem in the days of the open range) and to help prosecute rustlers.

A state commission was formed to regulate brands throughout the state, thus eliminating brand duplication. But the problem of rustling remained. Certain brands are easily altered: a "running iron" can change E-Y to B-K within minutes. Also, since a brand is proof of ownership, any animal stolen while young and unbranded and then branded with someone else's brand becomes that person's property.

But early laws lacked teeth. Rustlers were an especially virulent problem in central Montana, and exasperated ranchers here took enforcement into their own hands. Vigilantes under the direction of Granville Stuart are reported to have summarily executed up to 60 alleged rustlers during the summer of 1884. Alarmed, the legislature quickly passed a number of laws controlling the movement of livestock. Those laws form the basis of Montana's present-day system of brands records.

To halt movement of stolen animals, livestock inspectors examine all animals when moved across county lines and when a change of ownership takes place. Livestock presented for sale at an auction yard must be accompanied by a permit of transport and must pass a brand inspection at the sales yards. Montana law also provides for range detectives, who investigate suspected rustlers.

Brand Lore

Contrary to popular belief, brands are not a cowman's vanity plate. Most early brands were not the owner's initials. One problem is that all characters and symbols are not equally effective as brands, and some brand more cleanly than others. For instance, Bs and 8s are notoriously hard to apply—the hot iron will simply singe an indistinguishable blotch on the animal's flesh. Letters such as Y and N are preferred, since their clean lines are easily read. Other letters present the problem of being too easy to alter.

Generally speaking, two-figure brands are preferred over three-figure brands: to a cattleman, it's one fewer iron to apply. The same brand can be registered to different people if it is applied to different parts of the animal. Cattle have six typical brand areas: the hips, ribs, and shoulders—on both the left and right side. HS—on a right shoulder is a different brand from HS—on a left hip. The same rules apply to horses, except that horses are never branded on the ribs but rather on the jaw.

Montana law allows brands to be registered for animals besides cattle and horses: sheep brands, for example, as well as brands for buffalo, elk, deer, hogs, and mules.

Brands must be reregistered every 10 years, for a $50 fee. Brands that are not reregistered become available to newcomers. When applying for a brand, one specifies what letters are preferred, and the registrar sends a selection of brands not already taken that use those characters. (Most obvious combinations are already taken.) Two-figure brands have cachet, since they are more authentic. But the Brand Commission no longer issues any new two-figure brands. The only two-figure brands available are those established brands that have been allowed to lapse. In the back of Montana livestock newspapers you will see ads for two-figure brands. A good brand with some history can bring $1,500.

Recently, ranchers have experimented with freeze branding. Instead of hot irons searing the flesh, extremely cold irons, dipped in liquid nitrogen, freeze the animal's hair follicles, causing the hair to grow in white. The brand then shows up in contrast. Obviously, this method works best on dark animals.

This entire area is very popular for hunting deer, pronghorn, and game birds, including wild turkey.

Over in Ismay, **Myers Ranch Wagon Trains,** tel. (406) 772-5675 runs three-day wagon train trips through the hills of the Powder River country.

Accommodations

The attractive **Sagebrush Inn,** 518 W. Montana, tel. (406) 778-3341 or (800) 638-3708, $38 s, $50 d, has an older extension with rooms for a few dollars less. **Roy's Motel,** 327 W. Montana, tel. (406) 778-3321 or (800) 552-3321, $28 s, $38 d, has a hot tub and an RV campground. Pets are permitted at both of these motels.

Baker makes tourists welcome with free camping. Tent campers are encouraged to throw up a tent in **McClain Memorial Park,** Hwy. 12 at 3rd St. West. In the same complex is **Walt's RV Memorial Park,** which offers free RV camping with hookups.

Food

Good home-style food is available at **Sakelaris's Kitchen** in the Lakeside Shopping Center, tel. (406) 778-2202, or **Gramma Sharon's Cafe,** 507 W. Montana. **Jane's Home Cookin'** serves homemade soups and pies at 23 S. 1st St. W, tel. (406) 778-3647. If you want a drink with your steak, go to the **Loft,** 19 S. Main, tel. (406) 778-3557, or to the **Corner Bar & Casino,** 1 S Main.

Services

The **Fallon County Hospital** is at 320 Hospital Dr., tel. (406) 778-3331. Call the **sheriff's office,** tel. (406) 778-2879, in case of emergency.

The **chamber of commerce** can be reached at P.O. Box 849, Baker, MT 58313, tel. (406) 778-2266.

EKALAKA

Ekalaka (pop. 433, elev. 3,457 feet) is known affectionately as "the town at the end of the road," for there is only one paved road to it. It is reached by first going to Baker (not exactly the center of the world itself) and turning south for an additional 35 miles. No one just turns up in Ekalaka by mistake, but there are ample reasons to make the trip in.

The Medicine Rocks, an Indian holy site, are 11 miles north of town. Three units of the Sioux Division of the Custer National Forest are within an hour of the town limits. Carter County Museum is nationally known for its collection of local dinosaur skeletons. The town buildings don't bother to hide their age or history.

But the real pleasures of Ekalaka are highly subjective and understated. Ekalaka is for the connoisseur of western towns. Ekalaka is for the traveler who will smile to see a main street on which original stone buildings house bars and museums, and street benches on which natives sit and chat; for a traveler who finds pleasure in a forest of scattered pines atop limestone cliffs; for a traveler content to watch the sun set at the site of ancient Indian rites; for the traveler who enjoys a quiet drink listening to the conversations of ranchers in old bars. Anybody beguiled by the

JIM MASTERSON

Claude Carter,
Ekalaka's founder

languors of the West will find Ekalaka fascinating.

History

While other cities have founding fathers, Ekalaka has a founding bartender. Claude Carter, a Nebraska buffalo hunter who knew the weaknesses of his fellow settlers, was intending to establish a bar along Russell Creek when his wagon of logs bogged down several miles short of his destination. "Hell," Carter was reported as saying, "any place in Montana is a good place to build a saloon." His bar, the Old Stand, was the founding business of Ekalaka, and tradition places the date in the 1860s. In those days, Ekalaka was known as "Pup Town," for a nearby prairie dog town.

David Russell, the first white homesteader in the area, moved to the Old Stand settlement in 1881. His wife was a Sioux woman named Ijkalaka ("Swift One" in Siouan), a niece of Sitting Bull. When the post office came in 1885, it was named for her.

Time, if not prosperity, has been kind to Ekalaka; the town is much as the 1930s left it, for better or worse. Old stone buildings line the street, and an impressive old courthouse stands witness at the end of Main Street. Like Jordan to the northwest, this is still a western town little affected by the trends and happenings of the outside world.

Sights

The **Carter Country Museum,** on Main St., tel. (406) 775-6886, open Tues.-Sun. 1-4 p.m., is worth a detour. For any fan of dinosaur remains this is one of Montana's best museums, as its collection, and curator Marshall Lambert, are nationally known. Ekalaka country is particularly rich in fossil remains, and Lambert, a science

The Medicine Rocks were sacred to the Sioux.

W.C. McRAE

teacher at the local high school, was a keen amateur paleontologist. His discoveries of entire dinosaur skeletons, including the only remains of the *Pachycephalosaurus* found in the world, allow the Carter County Museum to boast a collection of bones to rival the best museums in the country. There's also a good selection of Indian artifacts and minerals.

"One road in" is Ekalaka's motto. However, for the recreationist who has no fear of a gravel road, this corner of Montana offers little gems of beauty and adventure, and other ways out.

The **Medicine Rocks State Park,** 11 miles north of Ekalaka on Hwy. 7, contains a series of sandstone outcroppings carved by the wind into weird and mysterious shapes. Some of the buttes tower 80 feet above the pine-clad prairie, and others wind along the hilltops like trains. The Sioux called the area Inyan-oka-la-ka, or "Rock with Hole In It," for the strange holes and tunnels in the stone. Legend maintains that the Indians used the area for vision quests and other rituals, and considered the rocks to be sacred and full of "medicine," or spirit power. Sitting Bull and his Sioux and Cheyenne warriors reportedly camped here before the Battle of the Little Bighorn, waiting for guidance from their medicine men. The mile-square park welcomes picnickers, campers, and sightseers. At the entrance to the park is a hand pump with good water; tables, fire pits, and latrines are also provided. A word of caution: Beware of snakes.

Three sections of the **Sioux Division of the Custer National Forest** lie within easy striking

range of Ekalaka. South of town, along a well-traveled gravel road, are the **Chalk Buttes.** These stark white cliffs sit atop rocky, forested buttes and can be seen for miles. The Chalk Buttes have long served as landmarks for travelers and stockmen. Fighting Butte, or Starvation Rock, is the most northerly of the Chalk Buttes. Its flat top is inaccessible but for a treacherous, single-track path. According to Indian legend, members of one tribe, seeking to escape pursuers of another tribe, fled up the precipitous path leading to the summit. Once there, the pursuing Indians simply guarded the single-file access to the butte and waited for their foes to die of thirst and starvation.

According to a BLM official, species of grass grow on the top of Fighting Butte that occur nowhere else in the Ekalaka area. One local sheep rancher grazed sheep on these unusual grasses, to his eventual chagrin. A windy storm blew up, and the entire herd of 600 drifted with the wind to fall off the sheer sides to their deaths.

Recreational opportunities are more numerous in the other sections of the Sioux Division of the Custer National Forest. In the **Ekalaka Hills,** southeast of Ekalaka, there are two camping areas. **Macnab Pond** is located in piney hills seven miles southeast of town on Hwy. 323 and one mile east on a gravel road. Watch for signs. Trout have been planted in the pond.

Ekalaka Park is more remote. Follow signs for **Camp Needmore,** three miles southeast on Hwy. 323, and after arriving at Camp Needmore follow Forest Service Rd. 104 (Rimrock Carter

Rd.) five miles. Although there are no official trails, hiking among the ponderosa pines and sandstone outcroppings is easy and interesting. Wildlife is abundant, and during the spring there is a good display of wildflowers.

If you like this kind of lonely, open country sprinkled with buttes and pines, and if you feel adventurous, then a day-trip to **Long Pines,** the third section of the Sioux Division, is well worth it. Follow Prairie Dale Rd. (to Mill Iron) off Hwy. 323 (three miles south of Ekalaka) for about 10 miles, and turn south on Forest Service Rd. 107 (Snow Creek Road). This gravel road follows the main spine of the Long Pines. Wildlife viewing is especially good.

Raptors love the sandstone bluffs (this is the nation's primary breeding range for merlin falcons), as do deer, coyotes, and wild turkeys. Just short of the North Dakota border lies **Capitol Rock,** a huge deposit of volcanic ash eroded into the shape of the nation's capitol. Again, hiking is informal, as there are no maintained trails. Camp at Lantis Spring Campground, about 15 miles into the national forest, where water is available. If you camp informally, make sure you heed fire restrictions and carry garbage out.

If you follow Snow Creek Rd. out, you end up in Camp Crook, South Dakota, on the Little Missouri. Camp Crook was a station on the Deadwood Stage.

Accommodations

The **Midway Motel** is on Hwy. 7 as it enters Ekalaka, tel. (406) 775-6619, $31 s, $42 d. The **Guest House** is an updated hotel on Main St., tel. (406) 775-6337, $30 s, $40 d. Pets are okay here. **Cline Camper Court,** west of town, tel. (406) 775-6231, is open April-Dec. but has no tent sites; **Ekalaka Park** is a Forest Service campground. Go three miles south on Hwy. 323, then follow signs on improved road for another six miles; it's open May-November. **Macnab Pond,** another Forest Service facility, is seven miles south on Hwy. 323, one mile east on improved road; both sites have toilets and water, and Macnab has fishing.

Food

The **Old Stand** is on Main St., tel. (406) 775-6661, and still offers steaks and cocktails. The **Wagon Wheel Cafe,** just up the street, tel. (406) 775-6639, is a friendly place for a lighter meal.

Outfitters

This area offers some of the best deer and antelope hunting in the state. **J & J Guide Service,** HC 51 Box 962, Mill Iron, MT 59324, tel. (406) 775-8891, leads hunts for mule deer, whitetail, and pronghorn; **Mon-Dak Outfitters,** Alvin Cordell, Box 135 Montana Rte., Camp Crook, ND 57724, tel. (605) 797-4539, leads trips into southeastern Montana.

Services

Dahl Memorial Hospital is at 110 Hospital St., tel. (406) 775-8730. The **sheriff** can be reached at (406) 775-8743.

There's a **swimming pool** in Ekalaka Park, just behind Main Street.

The **Custer National Forest Office** can be reached at (406) 775-6342.

BROADUS

There's something about the Powder River that excites the phrasemaker. "A mile wide, an inch deep," "Too thin to plow, too thick to drink," the sayings go. There is some truth: when the Yellowstone discharges into the Missouri, the Powder River has contributed only five percent of the flow but 50% of the silt. The broad grassy valleys of the Powder River and the Little Powder River have been home first to vast herds of wildlife and later to equally vast herds of cattle.

Nestled in the cottonwoods along the river, Broadus (pop. 532, elev. 3,030 feet) is an attractive ranching town. Oil revenue allows the town extras like a good school system and new county offices.

History

The early Indians spent summers hunting here, where buffalo, prairie elk, deer, pronghorn, and game birds were abundant. Later, after westward Indian migration began, these hunting grounds were at the heart of bitter disputes between the Crows, who claimed it as a homeland, and the Sioux alliance.

A sad presaging of the great buffalo annihilation came in 1854 through 1856, when Sir George Gore, an Irish sportsman, came to hunt the Powder River country. Gore was no rugged survivalist: his entourage included several guides, 20 servants, 112 horses, 12 yoke oxen, six wagons, and 21 carts for ammunition. After spending the winter at the mouth of the Tongue River, Gore killed local game in such numbers that finally the Crow protested.

After the Sioux were corralled and the buffalo eliminated from their range, the rich Powder River country became the avenue into Montana for Texas cattle drives. The cattle boom lasted barely 10 years, but survived long enough to form much of the iconography of the Old West.

Market forces, a disastrous winter, and the influx of homesteaders all contributed to the decline of the cattle drover and the establishment of the cattle rancher. By the 1890s, ranches and settlements were springing up along the Powder and its tributaries. Broadus, and euphonious crossroads like Sonette, Olive, Epsie, Liscom, Quietus, Mizpah, and other "South Side" outposts, began as trading centers and post offices.

Located near the confluence of the Powder and the Little Powder Rivers, Broadus became the dominant trading center for the southeastern corner of Montana. Oil was discovered in Belle Creek, south of Broadus, in 1967. Within six years, the field had produced over a billion dollars' worth of oil alone; Belle Creek also produces significant amounts of natural gas.

Sights

The **Powder River Historical Museum,** 102 W Wilson, tel. (406) 436-2862, has a collection of artifacts illustrating local history, along with old cars, an old buggy, and the old Powder River County Jail. The **Mac's Museum** collection of Indian artifacts and seashells is also here now, as is the local visitors center

Cattle Drives

The Powder River country is seeing another surge of cattle droving these day, though this time they're put on for fun. Expect to trail cattle with suitably gentle horses, do chores, eat chuckwagon food, sleep out, and (the one non-genuine amenity) shower. Contact **Powder River Wagon Trains & Cattle Drives,** P.O. Box 676, Broadus, MT 59317, tel. (406) 436-2350, 436-2404, or (800) 982-0710 if a recreational cattle drive sounds like fun. Expect to pay about $1,450 for a six-day drive.

Recreation

Rolling Hills Golf Course, at the junction of Hwy. 212 and Hwy. 59, is a public course with nine holes. The **swimming pool** is at 202 S. Wilbur, tel. (406) 436-2822. In **Broadus City Park,** there are tennis courts, picnic grounds, and a playground.

Accommodations

Both of Broadus' motels are now operated by one office, Broadus Motels, tel. (406) 436-2626. You'll be given a choice of an older or a newer unit, with singles/doubles in the older unit running $44/$52, $4 more for the newer rooms. Both are equally well-furnished and comfortable. Both motels are downtown, at 311 W. Holt and 101 N. Park.

Another lodging alternative is to stay at a guest ranch. In between cattle drives, the folks at **Powder River Wagon Train,** P.O. Box 676, Broadus, MT 59317, tel. (406) 436-2350 or (800) 982-0710, open their ranch to guests, who share ranch chores with the host family. **Doonan Gulch Outfitters,** 25 miles west of Broadus off Hwy. 212, tel. (406) 427-5474, also operates the **Oakwood Lodge B&B** in a spacious new log lodge on their ranch.

Town and Country Trailer Village, one block west of Hwy. 212 E, tel. (406) 436-2595, open April-Nov.; and **Wayside Park,** just south of the junction of Hwys. 212 and 59, tel. (406) 436-2510, both offer tent and RV camping.

Food

The attractive **Judge's Chambers** restaurant, tel. (406) 436-2002, serves three meals a day made from local products, including vegetables and herbs from the chef's garden. This is the most refined food for miles, so do plan to stop. The **Homestead Inn** serves standard Montana fare plus pizza on Hwy. 212 at the east edge of town, tel. (406) 436-2615; the **Montana Bar and Cafe,** 111 E. Wilson, tel. (406) 436-2454, serves three meals a day, with homemade pies a favorite.

Outfitters

The Powder River country is home to an abundance of outfitters. The local twist on hunting is to go after prairie dogs rather than, say, elk. **Powder River Outfitters,** P.O. Box 678, Broadus, MT 59317, offers archery, deer, pronghorn, and game-bird hunting; call (406) 427-5497 ask for Ken. **Doonan Gulch Outfitters,** Russell Greenwood, P.O. Box 501, S. Pumpkin Creek Rd., Broadus, MT 59317, tel. (406) 427-5474, offers hunting for big game and "varmits," rockhounding, hiking, and a B&B.

Services
Powder River Medical Service is at 507 N. Lincoln, tel. (406) 436-2651. Contact the **sheriff** at (406) 436-2333. The **chamber of commerce** is at P.O. Box 484, Broadus, MT 59317, tel. (406) 436-2611.

THE CROW AND NORTHERN CHEYENNE RESERVATIONS

The Crow and Northern Cheyenne Reservations are basically the upper drainages of Montana's Tongue and Bighorn Rivers. The landscape combines the lyricism of rough sandstone bluffs and uplands covered with ponderosa pine forest with the austerity of the high, barren prairies. And underlying everything here are the vast coal deposits of the Fort Union Formation.

Except for the river valleys and small reservation towns, there is scarcely any development. Like the Custer National Forest to the east, the reservation lands seem to be maintained in a kind of ad hoc trust. While this has preserved the beauty and integrity of the area, it has hindered the economic development of the tribes.

This region has always been Indian land, first by tradition, later by decree. The Crow settled here 300 years ago. Later, other tribes vied for room on these rich hunting grounds south of the Yellowstone. When traders first came to barter with the Indians for furs, they came here; when the Army came to subdue the Indians, they came here as well. Some of the most stirring events of western history took place on these plains and in these open forests. And something more than history, as well. The mixed prairies and forests of these reservations have themselves a cultural weight, their openness and limitlessness a statement of animistic potency.

HARDIN

Even though Hardin (pop. 3,225, elev. 2,966 feet) is not on the Crow Reservation, it serves as the primary trading center for residents of the reservation and the ranches to the north and west. It's a pleasant town, with a local museum that's worth a visit, and is a good base for trips to the Little Bighorn Battlefield, Bighorn Canyon, and the Crow and Northern Cheyenne Reservations.

The confluence of the Little Bighorn and Bighorn Rivers was a strategic outpost during the Indian Wars. The steamboat *Far West* maneuvered up the Bighorn to the mouth of the Little Bighorn in June 1876 to pick up wounded soldiers after the Reno-Benteen battle. In 1877, the year after the Custer battle, Bighorn Post was built on the cliffs above the confluence. Renamed Fort Custer, it was apparently rather a grand fort, in the manner of Fort Keogh; it was abandoned in 1898.

By 1906, the Dawes Act opened the area to white settlement. The next year, only nine years after Fort Custer ceased its patrol of the Crows, the Chicago, Burlington, and Quincy Railroad built a spur line down to the present site of Hardin, both to bring in new settlers and to service their needs.

During WW II, many Japanese-American internees were brought into Montana to work sugar beet fields, as farmers were experiencing a labor shortage. A large number worked in the Hardin area; some settled here after the war.

Sights
The **Bighorn County Historical Museum,** just off exit 497, has 20 old restored buildings open for viewing, including a handsome 1917 German Lutheran church, an old post office and store, and old farm buildings, including a 1916 farmhouse that's never been renovated and particularly evokes early-century rural life. The museum contains rotating exhibits and a good selection of books on local history and lore. The museum is open daily 8 a.m.-8 p.m., May-Sept.; Mon.-Sat. 9 a.m.-5 p.m., Oct.-April; tel. (406) 665-1671. The museum also has picnic tables and bathrooms.

Stop by the **Jailhouse Gallery** at 218 N. Center, tel. (406) 665-3239, to see exhibits on Native American culture and art, and works by local artists.

Custer Park has a playground and picnic tables. Take exit 495 south on Crawford St., but resist the urge to veer off to Yellowtail Dam and follow Crawford until 3rd Avenue.

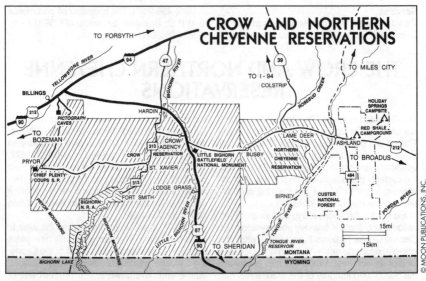

CROW AND NORTHERN CHEYENNE RESERVATIONS

© MOON PUBLICATIONS, INC.

Hardin's community **pool** is Olympic-sized and indoors. Find it at 621 W. 8th St., tel. (406) 665-2346.

Accommodations

The **Lariat,** near downtown at 709 N. Center, tel. (406) 665-2683, $35 s, $47 d, allows pets, as does the **Western Motel,** 830 W. 3rd, tel. (406) 665-2296, with rooms starting at $35 s, $45 d. The **American Inn,** 1324 Crawford, tel. (406) 665-1870 or (800) 582-8094, $45 s, $63 d, has two guest laundries, a hot tub, pool, and 140-foot water slide. Also part of the complex is a lounge, restaurant, and casino, as well as a playground and barbecue area.

A couple of local B&Bs offer interesting lodging options. The **Kendrick House Inn,** 206 N. Custer, tel. (406) 665-3035, is a historic boardinghouse updated to offer five charming guest rooms starting at $50 s, $65 d; an all-you-can-eat breakfast is included. Families and small pets can sometimes be accommodated with advance notice. Just across the street in another historic building, the owners of the Kendrick House have opened a teahouse with light lunch and dessert service.

A historic brick hotel in downtown Hardin has been converted into the **Hotel Becker B&B,** 200 N. Center, tel. (406) 665-2707. There are

seven guest rooms, each with its own bathroom (though some baths are across the hall). The owner/hostess is a good cook and travel adviser. Rooms range from $60 to $70.

The **KOA** is one mile north of Hardin on Hwy. 47, tel. (406) 665-1635. **Grandview Campground** is south of Hardin on Hwy. 313, tel. (406) 665-2489.

Food

Besides the truck stops along the interstate, there are a couple of local favorites. **The Purple Cow,** just north of I-90 on Hwy. 47, tel. (406) 665-3601, is a vintage roadside diner. Downtown, **Golden Cow Chinese Cafe,** 410 N. Center, tel. (406) 665-3145, is a reminder that Hardin was home to several Asian settlers. Locals like the **Merry Mixer,** 317 N. Center, tel. (406) 665-3735, for a steak and a drink (it's also open for breakfast and lunch).

Events

The Hardin Chamber of Commerce yearly sponsors **Little Bighorn Days,** whose main feature is the **Reenactment of Custer's Last Stand.** The event is held on the Friday, Saturday, and Sunday closest to the anniversary of the battle on June 26. In addition to the battle itself, the actors stage the events that led up to the conflict. It's a huge swirl of horses, tepees, and warriors, with over 200 participants, and the drama is matched by the dust. The reenactment is held six miles west of Hardin, not at the battle site. Other events during Little Bighorn Days include a rodeo, an 1876 Grand Ball, Indian dancing, and special tours of the Little Bighorn Battlefield.

Tickets to the reenactment are $10 adults and $6 children. There are two shows on Saturday, and one each on Friday and Sunday. Tickets and information are available through the Hardin Chamber of Commerce, tel. (406) 665-1672 or through Billings' MagicTix, tel. (800) 366-8538. For more information, check out the website, www.mcn.net/custerfight.

Information
The **chamber of commerce** can be reached at 21 E. 4th St., Hardin, MT 59034, tel. (406) 665-1672. The **post office** is at 406 N. Cheyenne. The **Bighorn County Memorial Hospital** is at 17 N. Miles, tel. (406) 665-2310.

THE CROW INDIAN RESERVATION

Before the White Man
The present-day Crow Indians derive from Hidatsa tribes who originally lived along the Mississippi headwaters. Of Siouan linguistic stock, they were an agrarian people who lived in earth lodges and made pottery. Sometime during the 1600s, the Crow left the larger Hidatsa tribe and began to move westward, first settling in the Black Hills area. Increasingly, lands as far west as the Powder, Tongue, and Bighorn river drainages were added to their hunting grounds, and by the 1770s the tribe had settled onto its historic homelands south of the Yellowstone.

When William Clark first traveled through Crow territory in 1806, the Crow were a wandering tribe of hunters living in tepees along the Bighorn. The horse had been introduced to the Crow only about 50 years before, and even though only 3,500 members belonged to the tribe, they already owned about 10,000 horses. The Crow had almost totally given up agriculture (though they continued to raise tobacco) and were nomadic within their hunting grounds. Crow women were famous for their bead and quill work, and Crow men were great horsemen and hunters. They were also

Crow braves

MONTANA HISTORICAL SOCIETY, HELENA

proud of their long hair and may have been "les beaux hommes" ("the handsome men") recorded by the French explorers, the Verendryes. The tribe was organized first by family, then by matrilineal clan. Known as the Absaroka in Hidatsan, or "Children of the Large-beaked Bird," they were considered to be as crafty and enterprising as the raven, hence the English name Crow.

Friendly Relations
From their first contact with white explorers and traders, the Crow have maintained mostly friendly relations with European settlers. Montana's first trading post, Fort Ramon, was built in 1807 at the juncture of the Bighorn and Yellowstone to service beaver-pelt trade with the Crow. Although the Indians initially were not exactly willing partners in the beaver trade (they chafed at trapping and trading pelts for more goods than they had need for), the presence of white traders in Crow territory led to a long-standing and important alliance between the Europeans and the Crow.

In 1833, Fort Cass was built on the same ground as the abandoned Fort Ramon. By this time, the main article of trade was buffalo hide, and this time the Crow were interested. A complex relationship between the Indians and whites emerged: the traders provided tobacco, food, guns, manufactured goods, clothing, and liquor, while the Crow provided pelts and hides and protection from the hostile Blackfeet to the north. The whites and Indians hunted together, sharing knowledge and cultures.

But the Crow became economically dependent upon trade with the whites, a dependency serviced by plundering the riches of their homeland. While Indians like the Crow were instrumental in exterminating the vast herds of buffalo in the West, the buffalo remained their source of food and shelter. By the 1880s, the buffalo had disappeared from its range on the Yellowstone.

The alliance with the agents of the United States was also strategic for the Crow in their ongoing warfare with rival Indian tribes. The warlike Blackfeet to the north endangered their lucrative trade with the whites, while the Sioux and Cheyenne to the east threatened traditional Crow hunting grounds. The treaties of Fort Laramie in 1851 and 1868 guaranteed the Crow homelands against incursions by whites and by other Indian tribes, especially the hostile Sioux confederacy.

It wasn't just geopolitical concerns that provided the bond between the Crow and the white settlers. Their friendship lasted several generations and weathered many altercations. And while the U.S. government was not especially solicitous to the Crow (though they were treated somewhat less abjectly by the U.S. than some other tribes), the Crow remained faithful allies.

The Reservation Today

In 1965, the Bighorn River was dammed near the site of Fort Smith. This beautiful, rugged landscape became the Bighorn National Recreation Area in 1968. By trapping sediment, cooling the water, and maintaining a steady flow, the dam changed the Bighorn from a slow-moving catfish river to a crystal-clear blue-ribbon trout stream, one of the best fisheries for trophy-size trout in the country.

This once-remote corner of the Crow Reservation suddenly became popular with hunters, anglers, and tourists. But the Crow considered the Bighorn Canyon and the adjacent Pryor and Bighorn Mountains to be sacred lands. In 1973, the tribe voted to close all hunting and fishing on the reservation to non-Indians, citing its rights to the Bighorn under the Fort Laramie treaties. The state of Montana took the tribe to court in order to open public access to the river. The case, known as the Battle of the Bighorn, went all the way to the U.S. Supreme Court, which in 1981 found for the state. There are now four fishing-access sites along the river within the boundaries of the reservation.

The present Crow Reservation, much reduced from the 1868 land grant, contains 37,000 square miles of rolling prairie and rugged foothills drained by the Bighorn River, making it Montana's largest reservation. There are about 7,000 tribal members, with a majority living on the reservation. The Crow language, a cousin to Siouan and Assiniboine, is spoken by more than 80% of the tribe. The retention of their native language is a combination of tradition (no Crow addresses another Crow in English) and the fact that the federal government never mandated English-only boarding schools on the Crow Reservation.

Chief Plenty Coups State Park

Chief Plenty Coups, the last of the great Crow war chiefs, is credited with advocating peaceful relations with the whites and for being the first Crow leader to recognize the need to adapt to the new life of the reservation. When the U.S. government opened the Crow Reservation to individual allotments in 1887, the young chief applied for his 320 acres, just west of Pryor off Hwy. 416, along a pretty stretch of Pryor Creek. It had been revealed to Chief Plenty Coups in a vision quest almost 30 years before that he would live out his life there, "where the plums grow."

Chief Plenty Coups attempted to set an example of how the Crow might coexist with the white settlers. He stressed education and mediated conflicts between his tribesmen and the whites. He cultivated his holding and built a two-story log home and a store, symbolically forsaking the tepee and the hunting lifestyle of the prairie nomad. He and his wife lived there until his death in 1932.

A stirring orator, Plenty Coups became a sort of celebrity, traveling to Washington, D.C., frequently to represent his people. While he was staying in Washington he visited Mt. Vernon, home of the first president. He then conceived of dedicating his land on the reservation as a memorial to the Crow Nation. Chief Plenty Coups

Monument was dedicated in 1928 as a "token of my friendship for all people, both red and white." It is now a Montana state park.

The 40-acre park houses a museum of Crow culture, Plenty Coups' home and store, his grave, and a gift shop featuring Crow crafts. The spacious grounds allow plenty of room to stretch your legs, and there is a well-developed picnic area (but no overnight camping). The park is open 8 a.m.-8 p.m. daily, and the museum is open 10 a.m.-5 p.m. May 1-Sept. 30. There is a $4 per vehicle admission charge to the park.

Recreation

The Bighorn River below Yellowtail Dam has become one of the country's most famous trout fisheries. The newfound popularity of the Bighorn has concerned the Crow, who object to the influx of people onto reservation land along the river. The state now maintains four fishing-access sites within the reservation. Do not attempt to fish on private land without getting permission. Anglers should stay within high-water marks, or in or on the river, to avoid trespassing on Indian land. A number of outfitters in the Fort Smith area rent boats and offer guide services.

Events

The **Crow Fair** is the biggest event of the year and is perhaps the largest Native American gathering in North America. During the third weekend of August, the tribal campgrounds near Crow Agency become a sea of tepees, pickup trucks, and RVs as thousands of tribe members and visitors rendezvous to celebrate the Crow heritage. Traditional games are played, including innocent-seeming "hand games," where money is gambled in a variation of the shell game. A number of the Crow dress in traditional garb, which shows off their complex and colorful beadwork. The costumes largely come off during the dance contests. There is also a parade, an all-Indian rodeo, and horse racing. Visitors are welcome, and bead goods and Indian food are for sale. Bring sunscreen and a hat, and be prepared to get dusty. For more information, contact the Crow Tribal Council.

Information

The **Crow Tribal Council** can be contacted at P.O. Box 159, Crow Agency, MT 59022, tel. (406) 638-2601.

Contact the **Bighorn National Recreation Area** at P.O. Box 458, Fort Smith, MT 59035, tel. (406) 666-2412.

LITTLE BIGHORN BATTLEFIELD NATIONAL MONUMENT

The Battle of the Little Bighorn was one of those epochal historical moments when individual strands of fate, personality, and history wove a whole larger and more meaningful than any sum of its parts. Upon hearing the story of Custer and Sitting Bull, an elemental part of the psyche either rejoices at the victory of the American Natives or condemns the triumph of savagery. To stand on the sere slopes of the Wolf Mountains and ponder the events of 1876 is to sense that something much more than a battle between armies and cultures took place. The issues at stake continue to resonate as the historical march of culture confronting culture goes on.

The centerpiece of the monument is the battlefield itself, although the museum and interpretive center are also fascinating. However, change is coming to this remote, historic corner of Montana. The National Park Service, which has supervised the battlefield for decades, has agreed to turn the monument over to a private company, which plans to build a tourist park near the site. The proposed facilities will include hotels, campgrounds, restaurants, more interpretive and theme exhibits, and tours of the battleground. The Crow tribe has recently built a casino, restaurant, and hotel just outside the park boundaries.

George Armstrong Custer

However hackneyed the observation, George Armstrong Custer was, and remains, an enigma. He graduated last in his class at West Point. He served the Union in the Civil War. He became the youngest general in the history of the Army after General Lee surrendered to him; he was later court-martialed for ordering the shooting of Army deserters in Kansas.

Once reinstated, Custer—demoted to a lieutenant colonel—became commander of the Seventh Cavalry. His exploits made him and his wife colorful and frequent guests at New York society functions. He fell afoul of the Grant admin-

George A. Custer

istration for allegations made in congressional hearings about corruption involving the president's brother and Indian trading licenses. Custer was arrested again.

A New York newspaper publisher who championed Custer as a future presidential candidate used his presses to mold opinion in Custer's favor. Rereleased, the 36-year-old Custer led 265 men to death on the Little Bighorn when he went on the offensive against a united war party with upward of 3,000 Sioux and Cheyenne warriors.

The Sioux and Cheyenne

This butterfly of a man confronted representatives of an ancient culture. The Sioux and Cheyenne were settled into one reservation in eastern Wyoming and the western Dakotas by the conditions of the Fort Laramie Treaty of 1868. However, the discovery of gold in 1874 in South Dakota's Black Hills immediately caused the treaty to be broken by gold hunters. Sioux and Cheyenne warriors, responding to these incursions onto their reservation and to the age-old

need to migrate to hunt buffalo, began to leave their reservation. Under the leadership of such warriors as Sitting Bull and Crazy Horse, they camped in the drainages of the Powder, Tongue, and Rosebud Rivers, their numbers growing as more and more Natives became disenchanted with their treatment. Here, for one last reprise, they practiced the centuries-old culture of the Plains Indian.

From here they also raided settlements and harassed travelers. The Commissioner of Indian Affairs ordered the Indians back onto the reservation, threatening military action if they did not comply by January 31, 1875.

The Sioux and Cheyenne did not respond, and the Army was sent to force them.

The Battle of the Little Bighorn

Three separate expeditions were sent out to campaign against the hostiles. These troops were to move from three different directions into the southeastern corner of Montana, where the Indian forces were known to be encamped. Custer's Seventh Cavalry followed the Rosebud River up to its divide with the Little Bighorn, where he was to wait for the two other columns. Instead, he divided his own command into thirds, and on June 25, 1876, took the offensive against one of the largest Indian forces ever gathered.

The details of the engagement at the Little Bighorn are best left for the traveler to discover at the battle site. What actually happened is quite complex and far from certain. It is also very compelling.

Perhaps we learn of Custer and the Sioux too early in life, when complex issues seem too simple. The battlefield is not merely a place for boys of all ages to gloat in the memory of battle. It is as chilling as Civil War battle sites, where you sense the ghosts of the past and somehow recognize the end of a culture and an epoch with a tightened and hollow gut. This is Montana's most haunted ground.

Sights

The battle site is 15 miles east of Hardin, a mile east of Hwy. 90. The visitor center is situated below the crest of the hill where the last stand took place. It contains some very interesting exhibits and should be visited before going on to the battlefields. Exhibits explain the Indian background to the conflict, the military strategies, the contemporary lifestyles of both cultures, and display artifacts of the battle. Probably the most arresting of the exhibits is a raised-relief map of the entire battle area, which uses colored lights (indicating soldiers and Indians) to show the ebb and flow of the battle. There is also a good bookshop where you'll want to pick up further reading or a tape to play in your car as you tour the battlefield. Also interesting is a plaque placed in 1988 by Indian activists on Last Stand Hill Monument demanding recognition of the Indian lives lost in the battle to preserve their homelands. The National Park Service has pledged to erect a memorial to Indian lives and perspectives on the conflict. Downhill from the visitor center is Custer National Cemetery, where some war dead from this and other conflicts are buried.

A quarter mile up the hill is Last Stand Hill Monument, where the last of the Seventh Cavalry died. Grave markers now stand where the bodies of soldiers were found. They were interred in a common grave under the monument, which bears the names of all the dead. Custer is buried at West Point.

To look down the grassy hillside at the markers, some standing alone, others huddled together, many clumped together around the swale

Sitting Bull, Sioux leader

MONTANA HISTORICAL SOCIETY, HELENA

where Custer's own body was found, is to vividly experience the full horror of the battle.

The paved road winds past the monument on a seven-mile loop road to the **Reno-Benteen Battlefield.** Major Marcus Reno and three of the Seventh Cavalry's companies were ordered by Custer to lead the first offensive against the Sioux and Cheyenne village on the Little Bighorn River. They were immediately routed and retreated up to this ridge, where they took up defensible positions. During the melee, the main thrust of the Indian attack was directed north to Custer's command. Reno was joined by Captain Frederick Benteen and the cavalry's pack train, the last third of Custer's original unit. On this hill, behind the bodies of slaughtered pack horses, these soldiers withstood 48 hours of attack by the victorious Sioux and Cheyenne before the Indians, almost inexplicably, retreated. A self-guided walking tour of the battlefield begins at the parking lot.

The visitor center is open Memorial Day to Labor Day 8 a.m.-8 p.m., spring and fall 8 a.m.-6 p.m., and winter 8 a.m.-4:30 p.m. There is a $6 per vehicle fee. In addition, park rangers and Native Americans give free tours and programs on various matters relating to the battle. For information on special programs and on publications sold at the monument write Little Bighorn Battlefield National Monument, P.O. Box 39, Crow Agency, MT 59022, tel. (406) 638-2621.

Personalized tours of the battlefield are available by the half or full day. Contact **Custer Battlefield Tours,** 7 E 5th St., P.O. Box 310, Hardin, MT 59034, tel. (406) 665-1580 or (800) 331-1580.

Down the road in Garryowen is the site of the Reno battle and the new **Custer Battlefield Museum,** tel. (406) 638-2000. The museum has some superb Indian crafts, a collection of historic photos, a recreation of Sitting Bull's campsite, and a tomb to an unknown soldier. There's also a gift shop and gallery. Admission is $3 ages 12 through adult, $2 seniors, free ages 11 and under.

Trail rides near the battlefield are offered by the **7th Ranch** in Garryowen, tel. (406) 638-2438, (800) 371-7963, http://link-usa.com/7thranch.

Accommodations and Food
The Custer Battlefield is about as lonely and forlorn a place as you can imagine. However, some amenities have grown up nearby, and Hardin is only 15 miles away.

The closest motel is **Little Big Horn Camp,** at the Custer Battlefield exit off I-90, tel. (406) 638-2232, $30 s, $35 d. Twenty miles south toward Wyoming is the **Cottage Inn,** 22 Hester, tel. (406) 639-2453, in the community of Lodge Grass.

At the freeway interchange there's a good restaurant/gift shop, the **Custer Battlefield Trading Post and Cafe,** tel. (406) 638-2295. Indian tacos, actually a variety of fried bread, are featured. The gift shop has a nice selection of Indian crafts and books. There's also a restaurant in the **Little Bighorn Casino,** tel. (406) 638-4444, the Crow tribe's casino. The **Sagebrush Inn,** in Crow Agency, tel. (406) 638-2505, offers buffalo burgers and steaks, as well as fry bread. This restaurant is part of the **River Crow Trading Post,** tel. (406) 638-2021, a good place to look for authentic Indian-made items and western gifts.

THE NORTHERN CHEYENNE RESERVATION

Located between the Crow Reservation and the Tongue River, the Northern Cheyenne Reservation was granted to the Cheyenne Indians after a period of wandering and incarceration following the Battle of the Little Bighorn. The Northern Cheyenne Reservation contains 444,500 acres, almost 90% of which is controlled by tribal members. About 3,500 Cheyenne live on the reservation. The land is characterized by patches of dry prairie ringed in by sandstone uplands covered with ponderosa pines. The area is rich in prairie wildlife and game birds, and the Tongue River affords the angler opportunities for walleye, smallmouth bass, and, south near the Tongue River Reservoir, trout.

Highway 212 cuts across the reservation on its way between the Little Bighorn Battlefield and the Black Hills of South Dakota, and it's an absolutely beautiful drive.

Onto the Plains

French traders first encountered the Cheyenne Indians in 1680, when they were living in present-day Minnesota. At that time they were an agricultural people who lived in earth-and-log cabins. The pressure of settlements to the east forced all Indian tribes to migrate west. The Cheyenne, however, were not pushed west by white settlers but by the hostile Sioux, who had themselves been displaced. Driven onto the plains, the Cheyenne lost their agricultural arts and divided into two federations: the Northern Cheyenne in Montana and the Dakotas, and the Southern Cheyenne in Colorado. By the time Lewis and Clark toured the west, the Northern Cheyenne tribe was living near the Black Hills. They lived in tepees and existed almost totally off the largesse of the buffalo. Their agricultural past had faded into tribal myth.

The Northern Cheyenne soon were expeditiously allied with the Sioux due to the presence of two common enemies, the settlers and sol-

a Northern Cheyenne couple beside a sweat lodge

MONTANA HISTORICAL SOCIETY, HELENA

diers, and their traditional rivals the Crow, on whose hunting grounds the two tribes were increasingly interloping.

The Conflicts

When gold was discovered in the Black Hills in the 1870s, treaties barring non-Indians from the area were promptly ignored, and the resulting gold rush and cavalry action forced the Cheyenne (and other Plains tribes) into greater confrontation with the whites. In 1875, when all western tribes were ordered onto reservations, the Northern Cheyenne refused, choosing to live their traditional life on the prairies.

The victory of the Indians over Custer's forces in 1876 earned the Cheyenne only momentary freedom. Within a year of the Battle of the Little Bighorn, all tribe members were forced onto reservations, with the majority incarcerated in Oklahoma with the Southern Cheyenne. During the winter of 1878-79, about 300 of the Northern Cheyenne fled the Indian Territory and attempted to make their way back to rejoin their brethren then sequestered on the Tongue River. After many battles and skirmishes with the cavalry, only 60 of the fleeing Northern Cheyenne lived to be reunited with the tribe remaining in Montana. In 1884, the government granted the tribe its own reservation.

Development

Like other Indian tribes who were settled on what were once considered marginal lands, the Northern Cheyenne have had to fight to resist the development of their lands by outside interests. The reservation sits on the vast coal fields of the Fort Union Formation. In the 1970s, coal companies sought to open up the area for strip-mining. The tribe faced a painful decision: whether to allow the mining and reap the economic benefits, which would bring jobs to the area and allow the building of needed public facilities, or to maintain the integrity of the land in its natural state.

By 1972, energy companies were poised to exploit 70% of the reservation. But the following year, the tribe voted to cancel the leases. After protracted legal maneuvering, the U.S. government upheld the Cheyenne's wishes. During the same period, the Northern Cheyenne sought and finally obtained the first redesignation of air quality (to "pristine") ever granted to a reservation,

thereby inhibiting development of coal-fired generators near the reservation (the enormous generators at Colstrip are 20 miles north). The tribe did decide to allow oil exploration in the 1980s. However, no economically viable reserves were found.

Sights

The tiny town of Busby was the site of an historic and culturally significant **reburial** in 1993, when remains of Northern Cheyenne killed during the Indian Wars were retrieved from the Smithsonian and other east coast museums and reburied in their homeland. The remains got to the museums as a result of an 1880s ballistics study commissioned by the Army—they wanted to see how effectively their new carbines were killing Indians. In 1990, a federal law permitted the remains to be returned to the reservation, where they're now buried in a circle near the Two Moon Monument on Hwy. 212.

The **St. Labre Indian School** was established in Ashland in 1884, after a Catholic soldier stationed at Fort Keogh contacted his bishop to tell him of the woeful state of the Cheyenne, who were wandering, starving and homeless, on the Tongue River. The bishop bought land on the river, and in 1884 four nuns from Toledo, Ohio, established the school and mission.

The mission remains a center of Cheyenne cultural and educational life, currently schooling 700 students. The mission also operates alcohol treatment, employment counseling, and other social services. Its modern chapel, built from local stone in the shape of an enormous tepee, dominates the campus. Tours are available. On the mission grounds the **Cheyenne Indian Museum and Ten Bears Gallery** displays and sells examples of the tribe's fabulous beadwork, open Memorial Day through Labor Day, daily 8:30 a.m.-4:30 p.m., tel. (406) 784-2200.

Accommodations and Food

Although the tribal headquarters for the Northern Cheyenne are located at Lame Deer, Ashland is the reservation's primary trading town and has the reservation's only motel, the **Western 8,** tel. (406) 784-2400, $25 s, $35 d. Camping is available down the road in the Custer National Forest.

Dining opportunities are rather perfunctory. In Ashland, there's the **Justus Inn,** tel. (406) 784-2701, which features a full menu. Snacks and Cheyenne handicrafts are available at the tribe-owned **Cheyenne Depot** in Lame Deer.

Events

There are two powwows, one in Lame Deer on July 4, and another in Ashland over Labor Day. Cheyenne powwows feature dancing contests, Indian singing, and lots of food.

Chief Two Moons was a Cheyenne leader who fought at the Little Bighorn. In his honor, the tribe conducts the **Two Moons Annual World Peace Gathering,** a meeting featuring traditional prayer ceremonies and discussions of issues and events pertinent to contemporary Indians. The gathering is held the last weekend of June. Contact the tribal secretary for details, tel. (406) 477-6248.

Information

Call the Northern Cheyenne Chamber of Commerce at (406) 477-8844 or write to P.O. Box 991, Lame Deer, MT 59043. The Northern Cheyenne Tribal Council can be reached by writing Lame Deer, MT 59043, tel. (406) 477-6248.

CUSTER NATIONAL FOREST, ASHLAND DIVISION

Across the Tongue River from the Cheyenne Reservation is eastern Montana's largest block of national forest. Like other isolated islands of woodland within the vast archipelago of the Custer National Forest, the Ashland Division is largely overlooked by travelers, save the hunters who come to stalk trophy mule deer and wild turkeys.

As in the other forests of southeastern Montana, here ponderosa pine savannahs are interspersed with shortgrass prairie, and isolated sandstone bluffs rise up spookily from the plains. The entire area is rich in wildlife, especially birds.

And like the other Custer forests, this is largely an undeveloped destination for the visitor. But before dismissing these remote areas, the adventurous traveler should consider stopping to enjoy the vast and lonely expanses of these high-prairie grass- and woodlands.

Three areas of the Ashland Division have been designated as riding and hiking areas. They're off-limits to motorized vehicles, making them ideal for nature study and wildlife viewing. While the Forest Service had horses in mind when they called it a riding area, the rough but open landscape is also ideal for mountain-bike exploration. There are no maintained hiking trails, but the nature of the landscape allows for considerable ambling and scrambling.

Red Shale Campground is six miles east of Ashland and has 16 units. Other campsites are more remote. The **Holiday Springs** campsite is of interest not only because it serves as a campground, but because the Forest Service maintains a rental cabin there. Whitetail Cabin sleeps four and has electrical power (though no water): it costs $15 a day. The cabin and campsite are about 18 miles east of Ashland, up the East Fork of Otter Creek.

While cross-country skiing is possible almost everywhere in the area when there's enough snow, the Forest Service has developed two loop trails near Camp's Pass, 20 miles east of Ashland. This area, near the defile where the highway enters the national forest from the east, contains some of the roughest land in this section of the Custer National Forest.

For more information, write Ashland Ranger District, P.O. Box 297, Ashland, MT 59003, or call (406) 784-2344.

BIGHORN CANYON AND THE PRYOR MOUNTAINS

Nothing in the prairies and valleys of the Crow Reservation prepares the traveler for the magnitude and sheer drama of Bighorn Canyon and the Pryor Mountains. The Bighorn River follows a wide, wooded valley from St. Xavier upstream to Fort Smith along Hwy. 313, where suddenly the land ends in upheaval, with bright red clinker stone topping gravel bluffs. The road climbs four miles up a series of steep switchbacks onto a plateau. At the base of the eroded face of the Pryors, an enormous canyon opens up, with the waters of Yellowtail Reservoir a ribbon of blue below thousand-foot cliffs.

Bighorn Canyon isn't particularly on the way to anywhere: you have to really want to be there to get there at all. Much of the land around the canyon is Crow Reservation land and off-limits to most visitors. Despite the information on many road maps, you cannot get from the dam at Fort Smith on the northern end of the canyon to the recreational access areas to the south (a distance of only 25 miles)—unless you have a boat or want to drive a couple hundred miles around and about and down and through Wyoming and back up into Montana, since the Crow do not allow non-tribe members to cross tribal land. This inaccessibility isn't a problem for the locals, who tend to use the reservoir for boating. But a traveler on a schedule will need to make plans to see the entire canyon.

The Land

Bighorn Canyon cuts through walls of limestone between the Pryor Mountains and the rugged Bighorn Mountains in Wyoming, revealing 500

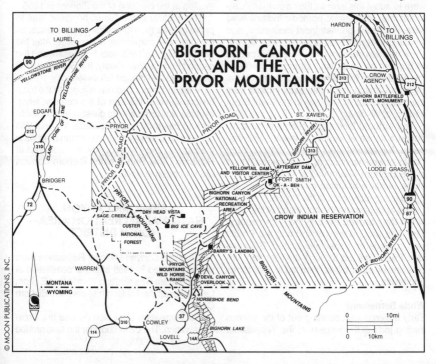

million years of geologic history. Both the Pryors and the Bighorns were formed when Paleozoic-era sedimentary rock was shoved eastward by the rising Rocky Mountains and upward by a bulwark of rising igneous magma. Limestone that had been laid down 300 million years ago was forced to the surface, forming first the Bighorn Mountains in Wyoming and, trailing behind in Montana, the Pryors.

The Bighorn River rises in Wyoming and flows north uneventfully until it comes to the limestone plateau just east of the Pryors. Here the river has cut into the fault line between the two mountain ranges and has carved out one of the deepest and most dramatic canyons in the northern United States.

HISTORY

Early Inhabitants

Bighorn Canyon and the Pryor Mountains were home to many early Indians. Although the Crow were to adopt this land as their own many centuries later, prehistoric nomadic Indians lived here, where the prairies meet mountains, and where limestone caves provided easy shelter. Crow tradition describes the indigenous people of Bighorn as "dwarfish," strong, and without fire. Bad Pass Trail, which skirts the rim of the Bighorn Canyon, led these early Indians from the grassy plains of Montana to the Great Basin country of Wyoming.

The tortured landscape seems to have induced a sense of wonder in these early residents, for several sites appear to have been places of worship (such as the Medicine Wheel in the Bighorn Mountains of Wyoming). The stone remains of vision-quest structures are found along rocky cliffs in the Pryors.

The area became the homeland of the Crow when they arrived here in the 17th century. The land around the canyon and the Pryors was considered especially sacred. Because Bad Pass Trail led through their territory, incursions by other tribes often led to skirmishes and feuds.

White Settlement

Early adventurers operating out of the various trading forts at the juncture of the Yellowstone and Bighorn Rivers trapped in the Bighorn country. John Colter, who "discovered" Yellowstone Park, was the first white to explore the Pryors, and Jim Bridger, tale spinner and backwoodsman, claimed to have been the first to float the Bighorn River. Frontier missionary Father deSmet said the first Catholic mass in the state, under a large cottonwood tree near Fort Smith in 1840.

The first white settlement resulted from the Bozeman Trail. Established by John Bozeman in 1864, it cut off from the Oregon Trail and veered north up to the Yellowstone Valley and thence to the goldfields of western Montana.

The Bozeman Trail crossed into Montana near Decker and crossed the Bighorn River at the northern end of the canyon. In Wyoming the trail crossed Sioux land, which was greatly resented by them. (The Crow tolerated the whites as long as they moved across their land without settling.) A series of forts was built by the military to protect settlers and miners from the Sioux as they passed through the prairies. The most northerly of these, Fort C.F. Smith, was located at the crossing of the Bighorn in 1866.

The hostility of the Sioux, however, was to prove greater than the military's endurance, as the forts were perpetually under siege. After the Hayfield Fight in 1868 near Fort Smith, and the second Fort Laramie Treaty, the Bozeman Trail was closed and the fort left deserted.

A second, more peculiar adjunct to the local history came at the turn of the century, when the area was given over to guest or "dude" ranches and celebrity homesteaders. Writers Will James and Carolyn Lockhart both ran ranches in the Bighorn and Pryor country. The buildings at Hillsboro Dude Ranch along Bighorn Canyon are now open to visitors.

BIGHORN CANYON NATIONAL RECREATION AREA— NORTH DISTRICT

The Bighorn Canyon National Recreation Area was designated in 1968 after the completion of Yellowtail Dam. The resulting 71-mile-long Bighorn Lake extends the full length of dramatic Bighorn Canyon.

The recreation area also divides the Crow Reservation. The Crow consider the land around

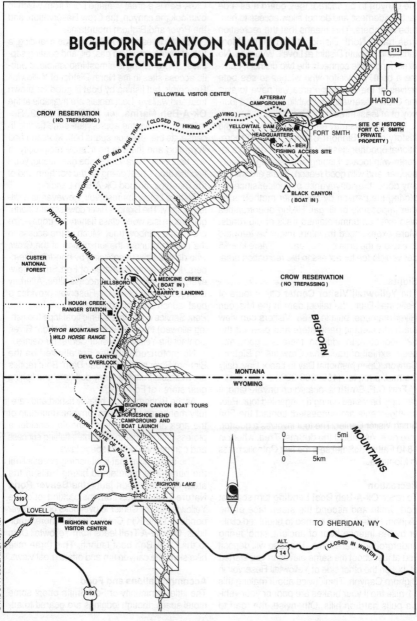

BIGHORN CANYON NATIONAL RECREATION AREA

CROW RESERVATION
(NO TRESPASSING)

YELLOWTAIL VISITOR CENTER

AFTERBAY CAMPGROUND

TO HARDIN

HISTORIC ROUTE OF BAD PASS TRAIL (CLOSED TO HIKING AND DRIVING)

YELLOWTAIL DAM
PARK HEADQUARTERS
OK-A-BEH FISHING ACCESS SITE

FORT SMITH

SITE OF HISTORIC FORT C.F. SMITH (PRIVATE PROPERTY)

BLACK CANYON (BOAT IN)

PRYOR MOUNTAINS

CUSTER NATIONAL FOREST

CROW RESERVATION
(NO TRESPASSING)

HILLSBORO

MEDICINE CREEK (BOAT IN)
BARRY'S LANDING

HOUGH CREEK RANGER STATION

PRYOR MOUNTAINS WILD HORSE RANGE

DEVIL CANYON OVERLOOK

BIGHORN CANYON

BIGHORN

MONTANA
WYOMING

BIGHORN CANYON BOAT TOURS
HORSESHOE BEND CAMPGROUND AND BOAT LAUNCH

HISTORIC ROUTE OF BAD PASS TRAIL

MOUNTAINS

0   5mi
0   5km

37

310

LOVELL

BIGHORN CANYON VISITOR CENTER

BIGHORN LAKE

TO SHERIDAN, WY

ALT. 14 (CLOSED IN WINTER)

310

the canyon to be sacred; they guard it as a de facto wilderness and do not allow access to non-tribe members. This means that the recreation area has a North District at Fort Smith, Montana, and a South District at Lovell, Wyoming. No direct land route connects the two districts. Lacking a boat, the visitor who wishes to see both halves of the recreation area will have to skirt the Crow Reservation by public highway, a journey of at least three hours by car.

While tourists may enjoy the scenery and the history of the Bighorn Canyon, it is the recreational opportunities that make the canyon a favorite with locals. Fishing and boating are very popular, and with good reason. Boats are without any doubt the conveyance of choice, since exploring the canyon by any other method is either impossible or illegal. Hiking opportunities also exist on unmaintained trails or old roads. More experienced travelers might be tempted to explore the area's many caves. There is a $5 per vehicle fee for access to the recreation area.

Sights

The **Yellowtail Visitor Center** offers tours of Yellowtail Dam, the tallest dam in the Missouri River drainage, built in 1968. Visitors can view the hydroelectric generators and peer off the 525-foot dam. In addition, there is a good museum exhibit of traditional Crow life in Bighorn Canyon. Open Memorial Day to Labor Day, daily 9 a.m.-5 p.m., tel. (406) 666-3234.

Fort C.F. Smith is located on private land; it can only be visited during a ranger-led tour. Prior arrangements are suggested; contact the Fort Smith Visitor Center. The tour involves a quarter-mile hike. Ask about the **deSmet Tree,** where in 1840 Father deSmet said the first Catholic mass in Montana.

Recreation

To reach **Ok-A-Beh Boat Landing** turn south at Fort Smith and ascend the steep face of the Bighorn Plateau, here burned to bright red clinker by the intense heat of ancient, smoldering underground coal seams. The road will deposit you at just about the same elevation you started at, but on the other side of Yellowtail Reservoir in Bighorn Canyon. Think twice about making this 11-mile trip if your brakes are poor or your vehicle pulls hard on hills. Otherwise, the road to

Ok-A-Beh is a great vantage point from which to overlook the canyon, the Crow Reservation, and the Pryor and Bighorn mountains.

Boat facilities at Ok-A-Beh include a landing, a fish-cleaning area, and gas, oil, and boating supplies. Shore fishing is almost impossible at public-access sites in the North District of Yellowtail Reservoir, but fishing by boat is good for brown trout and walleye. Boat rentals are available at the **Ok-A-Beh Marina,** tel. (406) 666-2349. Remember to have the appropriate state fishing license, as the reservoir spans both Montana and Wyoming and there is no license reciprocity. If you happen to have your scuba gear along, you'll find the area's best diving off the northern end of the reservoir, around Ok-A-Beh Landing.

Fishing below the reservoir, however, is a different story. The Bighorn River downstream (north) of the dam is a world-class fishery for trophy-size brown and rainbow trout. Much of the access to the river falls under the jurisdiction of the Crow, who do not allow trespassing by non-tribe members. In the immediate area of Fort Smith, however, there are two public-access sites. Afterbay Dam just below Yellowtail Reservoir provides a boat launch and fishing access. From here, the Park Service offers free scenic float trips (no fishing allowed) three miles down the Bighorn River. Contact the Yellowtail Visitor Center for details.

No motorized vehicles are allowed on the Bighorn River below Afterbay Dam. Boat rentals are available from the many outfitters and fishing gear stores at Fort Smith.

As the Bighorn is both heavily fished and carefully monitored for access, anyone uncertain of the area and its conditions should consider a professional outfitter to guarantee fishing success and compliance with trespass laws.

The same laws that limit fishing access limit the number of maintained hiking trails in the area. One very short jaunt, the **Beaver Pond Nature Trail,** leaves from the parking lot of the Yellowtail Visitor Center to overlooks onto beaver ponds in Lime Kiln Creek. For the more ambitious, **Om-Ne-A Trail** leads from Yellowtail Dam to the Ok-A-Beh boat launch. This three-mile hike skirts the canyon rim and offers great views.

Accommodations and Food

The little community of Fort Smith offers some motel space, though lodgings are geared to anglers on package fishing trips. All of the following are found along Hwy. 313, and rooms begin between $40 and $50 a night. The **Bighorn Anglers Motel,** tel. (406) 666-2233, and the **Bighorn Trout Shop Motel,** tel. (406) 666-2375, both offer gear and bait in addition to rooms. **Polly's Place,** tel. (406) 666-2255, promises home cooking to serious anglers. Before you make motel reservations, check with your guide or outfitter—many of the outfitters will offer room and board to their angling guests. For a good burger or steak, head down to the **Ok-A-Beh Marina,** (406) 666-2349.

Camping is a more economical means of spending the night in Fort Smith. The National Park Service maintains a free 30-site campground at **Afterbay. Cottonwood Camp,** tel. (406) 666-2391, offers all the usual niceties, plus boat rentals and shuttle service to fishing-access sites. On Yellowtail Reservoir itself, the Park Service maintains a boat-in-only campsite with minimal facilities at the head of **Black Canyon,** five miles south of Ok-A-Beh by boat.

A larger selection of lodgings is available in Hardin, 42 miles north on Hwy. 313.

Outfitters

The Bighorn River below Yellowtail Dam is blue-ribbon trout fishing. Many outfitters offer fishing, floating, and hunting packages. If it's the trout luring you to the Bighorn, then the following outfitters are serious about fishing and promise results.

Quill Gordon Fly Fishers offers boat rentals, accommodations, and, of course, sage advice with its guide service, P.O. Box 597, Fort Smith, MT 59035, tel. (406) 666-2253. **Bighorn Angler** offers boat rentals, accommodations, a tackle shop, and a full guide service, Fort Smith, MT 59035, tel. (406) 666-2233. **Golden Sedge Drifters,** Greg Childress, P.O. Box 342, Broadus, MT 59317, tel. (406) 554-3464, offers float trips and fishing on the Bighorn River.

BIGHORN CANYON NATIONAL RECREATION AREA— SOUTH DISTRICT

Sights

The South District has its headquarters at the **Bighorn Canyon Visitor Center,** at the junction of Hwy. 14A and Hwy. 310 in Lovell, Wyoming. In this solar-heated building the traveler will find information on the canyon's wildlife, geology, and history. There is also a large raised-relief map of the recreation area that reduces a monumental landscape to a comprehensible scale. Self-guided cassette tours of the history and geology of the area are available. The rangers lead special activities, including campfire programs at Horseshoe Bend Campground. Check the information board at the visitor center for details. Open Memorial Day to Labor Day, 8 a.m.-6 p.m. daily, and the remainder of the year 8 a.m.-5 p.m., tel. (307) 548-2251.

The South District contains the best access to dramatic views onto the canyon. As Hwy. 37 leaves the Lovell area, it climbs onto a plateau with strangely desertlike features such as thorn bushes and barren, rocky slopes. This almost lunar landscape is broken as the road drops onto **Horseshoe Bend,** where a wide expanse of the lake passes into Bighorn Canyon to the north.

Highway 37 (misleadingly known as the Trans-Park Highway; no road connects both halves of the park) then passes into the **Pryor Mountains Wild Horse Range,** where one of America's last herds of wild mustangs runs free.

Within the boundaries of the Wild Horse Range is the most spectacular view onto Bighorn Canyon. Where Devil Canyon meets Bighorn Canyon, sheer, 1,000-foot-high cliffs tower above the waters of the lake. From **Devil Canyon Overlook** atop one of these cliffs, the views are literally breathtaking, as well as vertigo-inducing. Informational signs explain the precipitous landscape.

A short hike off the highway near the campsite at Barry's Landing leads to the remains of **Hillsboro,** a ghost town originally built by an early white settler, G.W. Barry. After several financially unsuccessful attempts at mining and horse ranching in the first decade of this century, Barry converted his settlement into Cedarville Dude Ranch, a guest ranch for tourists. Most of the original buildings are still standing. Highway 37 ends at **Barry's Landing,** a boat launch established by Barry, who offered boat tours of the canyon. Barry's Landing is now maintained as a boat launch and campsite by the Park Service.

After crossing the Montana line, Hwy. 37 parallels the ancient **Bad Pass Trail,** the path used for centuries by Indians as they passed from the plains and valleys of Montana to the Great Basin land of Wyoming. Travois trails and stone cairns are still visible along the trail. You can get a feel for the Bad Pass Trail if you hike or drive up Dryhead Road (an unimproved road that begins where the paved portion of Hwy. 37 dead-ends at the turnoff for Barry's Landing) into the **Lockhart Ranch.**

Carolyn Lockhart was a successful journalist who left the *Boston Post* for the life of a Bighorn Canyon homesteader and western novelist. Lockhart and her companion weathered the Depression years only to fight the government when it claimed that the two women had not improved on the homestead. Lockhart was awarded the title to her land in 1936. The original structures still stand abandoned at her ranch. Dryhead Road continues to parallel Bad Pass Trail for another 12 miles beyond the Lockhart Ranch but is passable only to high-clearance vehicles or hardy hikers.

Recreation

While fishing is certainly a popular pastime on Yellowtail Reservoir, water-skiing, swimming, nautical sightseeing, and even scuba diving are the order of the day. **Horseshoe Bend Campground and Boat Launch** is located on the northern end of Bighorn Lake (a wide abayment of Yellowtail Reservoir), just before it disappears northward into the defiles of the canyon. Besides its role as a boat-in area, Horseshoe Bend serves as a hub of other recreational activities, including supervised swimming. Free canoe trips into the canyon are offered by rangers, as are evening campfire programs. Check the information boards at the visitor center in Lovell for details.

Privately operated **Bighorn Canyon boat tours** are also offered from Horseshoe Bend. For information on the two-hour tours, contact S-S Enterprises, P.O. Box 717, Cowley, WY 82420, tel. (307) 548-6418. Boat rentals are available from the Horseshoe Bend Marina. A second boat launch is located 17 miles farther north, at Barry's Landing.

From Horseshoe Bend Campground, **Crooked Creek Nature Trail** wends a quarter mile through the arid landscape. Self-guiding brochures identify plant and animal life. **Medicine Creek Trail** follows the rim of Bighorn Canyon for almost two miles from Barry's Landing to Medicine Creek Campground. In addition to these maintained trails, options for hiking in the Bighorn Canyon area are

dictated only by the energy and forethought necessary to strike out on your own. The area is full of old mining, logging, and ranching roads. With the help of a ranger and a Forest Service map, much of the area is open for exploration.

Spelunking is another activity offered to the adventurous in the Bighorn region. The entire area is a huge uplift of limestone which has eroded for millions of years. The results are networks of caves, filled not simply with mineral formations but also with the archaeological remains of early Indians. The Park Service and the BLM limit access to many of the caves, but most (such as the Bighorn Caverns) are open to experienced spelunkers upon request. Ask at the visitor center in Lovell, or at the Cody, Wyoming, BLM office for permission, keys, and information on specific dangers. Most will require a four-wheel-drive vehicle for access.

Practicalities

Lovell, Wyoming, is 12 miles south of the recreation area, and is the closest community to the South District. The **Super 8 Motel,** at the east end of Main St., tel. (307) 548-2725, $40 s, $48 d, offers a restaurant and RV park. The **Cattlemen Motel,** 470 Montana Ave., tel. (307) 548-2296, $38 s, $46 d, is comfortable and quiet. The **Horseshoe Bend Motel,** 375 E. Main St., tel. (307) 548-2221, $42 s, $49 d, is on the main road going to Bighorn Canyon.

Campgrounds are available in the recreation area. At **Horseshoe Bend Campground** there are 126 sites, with most modern facilities. Seventeen miles downriver is **Barry's Landing Campground** with 14 sites, but bring your own water. **Medicine Creek Campsite** is a hike-or boat-in-only area two miles north of Barry's Landing, with primitive facilities.

THE PRYOR MOUNTAINS

Rising to the west of Bighorn Canyon are the low, greatly eroded plateaus of the Pryor Mountains. Although these mountains are not very high in the Montana scale of things, they form a very curious destination for the traveler. The Pryors are so extraordinarily rich in Indian tradition and sites that the parts of the range that fall in the Crow Reservation are considered sacred and treated as wilderness. The area is also rich in limestone caves, noted both for their mineral formations and archaeological interest.

The Pryors are surrounded by the Crow Reservation and the Bighorn National Recreational Area. They are therefore not easily accessible. But the difficulty of getting in is more than made up for by the reward of being there. This is really remote country, with tepee rings and ice caves, bighorn sheep and mustangs, views over holy land, all amply served by Forest Service roads. Although a high-clearance vehicle is a good idea, the Pryors cry out for exploration by mountain bike.

Sights

In the mid-1960s, public concern became focused on about 200 wild horses living in the Pryors, remnants of larger herds that roamed the remote areas of the West. In 1968 the BLM established the **Pryor Mountains Wild Horse Range** on 44,000 acres on the Montana-Wyoming border. The ancestry of these animals is mixed. Some horses are merely escapees from ranch herds; others derive from Indian pony stock, which in turn was generated from imported Spanish horse lines. "Tiger stripes" on the legs or back are characteristics derived from Spanish breeds. A dominant stud, his harem of mares, and their foals form common mustang social units.

Wild-horse viewing is easiest along Hwy. 37 coming north from Wyoming into the Bighorn Recreation Area. For the more adventurous, the meadows and box canyons of the Pryors are a more memorable place to see the herds.

Bighorn sheep, for which this entire area was named, have been restocked in the Pryors. Deer and elk are common, and the area is popular in the fall for hunting.

The remoteness of the Pryors makes them tempting destinations for a certain kind of adventurer. Mountain bikers will find this a compelling challenge, because of the flora and fauna (where else can one pedal amongst wild horses?) and also because of the area's archaeological wealth. Most important, there are many deserted roads from the days when these mountains were mined and logged.

The Forest Service map of the Custer National Forest indicates a great number of caves, many open to public access. **Big Ice Cave** was once a popular picnic spot for day-trips in the early years of the century. It was closed for many years except to guided tours by the Forest Service but now is open for informal exploration. There are picnic grounds and wilderness camping opportunities nearby. Big Ice Cave is found at the top of the Pryors, along Forest Service Road 3093. Spelunkers are advised to check with the BLM or Forest Service for details of access to other caves, since some are locked in order to prevent vandalism and to protect the unsuspecting from specific dangers.

Almost the best reason to venture into the Pryors is the last one reached, at least by civilized routes. Past Big Ice Cave, on Forest Service Road 849, is **Dry Head Vista,** a panoramic viewpoint with Bighorn Canyon dropping away 4,000 feet below.

Native American Experience

It can't be called a guest ranch, they're not exactly outfitters, and it's only kind of like going camping—**Sacred Ground** offers something else altogether. Guests spend a week sleeping in tepees and experiencing traditional Native American ways of life, which may mean riding and hiking, observing plants and wildlife, attending ceremonies, meeting tribal elders and teachers, or spending time alone. It's all flexible, with a focus on a personal interaction with nature. The cost for a week is about $600, with some special guest-worker rates available. Contact Sacred Ground at P.O. Box 78, Pryor, MT 59066, tel. (406) 245-6070.

Campgrounds

Within the bounds of the **Custer National Forest** are a couple of camping areas. **Sage Creek Campground** is the most northerly; bringing water is a good idea for the squeamish, even though there are several natural springs with potable water. **Crooked Creek Campground** is farther in (near Big Ice Cave) and more rudimentary, and it requires a more energetic motor vehicle.

Getting There

This isn't as simple as it looks. Maps show a

road south from the little town of Pryor. Called Pryor Gap Road, it is in fact the old roadbed of an abandoned rail spur line. It is not in very good shape, but it is the shortest way into the Pryors from southeastern Montana. It also crosses Crow land, and sometimes access has been denied. It's best to check on road conditions and access before starting up the gap. The standard but somewhat indirect way into the area is from the west, via Hwy. 310, onto Pryor Mountain Rd. two miles south of Bridger, or north and east from Warren, Montana, along Sage Creek. About 20 miles of gravel road later you will arrive in the canyons of the Pryors.

From the Wyoming side, if you have a 4WD vehicle, there are several rough and scenic routes into the Pryors. Cowley Airport Rd. turns into a 4WD road called Crooked Creek Road. In its rough-and-ready fashion it leads past tepee rings and the two highest peaks in the Pryors before reaching Crooked Creek Campground. For the very hardy, a road leads up to (or more prudently, down from) Dry Head Vista, along Sykes Ridge Road. Before attempting either route, ask locals for directions and cautionary tales.

INFORMATION

For details on the Wild Horse Range and other destinations, the **Bighorn Canyon Visitor Center** can be reached at P.O. Box 487, Lovell, WY 82431, tel. (307) 548-2551. It's at the junction of Hwys. 310 and 14A at the east end of Lovell.

Yellowtail Visitor Center is at the end of Hwy. 313, at Fort Smith, MT 59035, tel. (406) 666-2358.

The **Beartooth Division of the Custer National Forest** has jurisdiction over the national forest in the Pryor Mountains, and can be reached at Rte. 2, Box 3420, Red Lodge, MT 59068, tel. (406) 446-2103. The **Custer National Forest Supervisor's Office** is in Billings at 2602 1st Ave. N, Billings, MT 59103, tel. (406) 657-6361.

The **BLM office** in Cody, Wyoming, has the keys to many of the caves in the Bighorn Canyon area. Reach them at (307) 587-2216.

The Lovell, Wyoming, **Chamber of Commerce** can be reached at P.O. Box 322, Lovell, WY 82431, tel. (307) 548-7552.

"CRISIS"

Get the coal out, with a tumult and shout.
Yes, tear it out of the ground.
There's a crisis to smite and cities to light.
There's billions of tons to be found.
And when coal is burned great wheels will be
  turned.
And a shaft from the wheels turns the earth.
It's simple you see (or so they tell me)
As they ravage the land of my birth.

Damn pristine air! There's water to spare!
We'll lower your taxes for you.
We'll pave all your roads. Help shoulder your
  loads.
Their cajoling beats a tattoo.
We'll build swimming pools and public
  schools—
Build an empire upon your Plains.
Just climb in with us, on our omnibus.
Eat our truffles and drink our champagnes.

Don't fret for the grass. If our plans come to
  pass,
You'll have more than you've ever seen.
For we can "reclaim." (At least that's our aim.)
We'll improve what once was pristine.
But if you feel doubt, then we'll buy you out
For more money than you've ever seen!
Enjoy wealth to the hilt. To assuage your guilt,
Wash in dollars if you still feel unclean.

In times such as these, in our energy squeeze,
You must try the "big picture" to see.
If untempted by booty, then think of your duty.
If you're selfless, then you must agree:
Our country must grow or the grey faceless foe
Will surely stalk o'er our grave.
For Growth made us great. It must not abate.
It's no monster, you see, Growth's our slave.

We'll win in a rout, if we get the coal out.
We'll all be the winners, you see.
We'll not freeze in the dark. We'll continue
  our lark.
And coal—good black coal—holds the key.

On their shrill voices go. Drifting, sifting like
  snow.
I resist them with all of my might.
For their cloying sweet song is grievously wrong.
Deep within me, I know that I am right.

—Wallace McRae

DOVER PUBLICATIONS, INC.

NORTHEASTERN MONTANA AND THE BIG OPEN

One of the state's least-visited areas, northeastern Montana is usually dismissed as an unwieldy piece of real estate that has to be crossed to get to more verdant or populated destinations. But this vast region contains enormous reserves of wildlife, the homelands of three Indian tribes, and some of the state's best hunting and fishing. Some of the wildest rodeos in the state are permitted out here; at Fort Union, would-be frontiersmen in buckskins gather to shoot muskets; and local Indians look for new reasons to throw powwows. Memories of the Old West—of the open range, cattle rustlers, and the homestead movement—drift in and out of conversations.

Even though you probably won't plan your vacation around it, what you're likely to remember about this part of the state is the people. In some kind of contrast to the rugged terrain and remorseless weather, the inhabitants of this lonesome corner of Montana are genuinely friendly, if haughtily independent, and are probably some of the most inveterate socializers you'll ever meet.

THE LAND

In few places is the dinosaur fossil record so easily read as in northeastern Montana. Once tropical seacoast, these prairies sprouted exotic vegetation, and dinosaurs of every size and description crowded in hoping to eat and not be eaten. Some still-unknown event eradicated these exuberant life forms about 70 million years ago; sediments continued to accumulate along the marshes, burying the remains of these ancient plants and animals.

After a prolonged altercation with Ice-Age glaciers, the Missouri River cut a new channel across the prairies, revealing hundreds of feet of fossil-rich sediment in the deep, gorgelike Missouri Breaks. The formation, named for Hell Creek near Jordan, where extensive fossil excavations have taken place, continues to yield up its ancient secrets.

The ice sheets of the last ice age did more than divert the Missouri. They ground down the

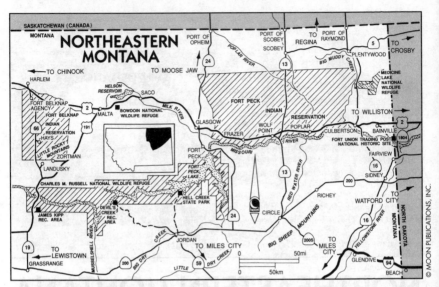

prairies north of the Missouri River's present channel to a uniform flatness.

Climate

In a word, extreme. Winter winds find nothing between the Arctic Circle and here to halt their chilling advance. While winters are not particularly snowy, cold temperatures—Glasgow's average reading in January is 10° F—combine with these winds to produce even more intense chill factors. Summer is very hot, with daytime temperatures usually in the 90s, though Medicine Lake once matched the state record of 117°. Hot parching winds often blow throughout the month of August. Although this is one of the most arid parts of Montana, summer thunderstorms sometimes bring late evening showers. Probably the best time to travel is the fall, when clear, crisp, and dry weather can be expected through mid-November.

ruffed grouse, Bonasa umbellus

Flora

The shortgrass prairie here is rarely interrupted by trees, and only the occasional resilient chokecherries and red-stemmed willows break up the hegemony of the grasslands. Along the Missouri, however, substantial cottonwood groves sway above the river; in the bluffs above Fort Peck Dam, ponderosa pine and juniper cling to a baleful existence.

Fauna

The state's largest wildlife refuge, the Charles M. Russell National Wildlife Refuge sustains populations of elk and bighorn sheep found no where else on the plains. Resourceful fox and coyote proliferate. Smaller but important wetland refuges shelter migrating waterfowl.

Much of the rest of this region might as well be a refuge. Wildlife is common. Mule and white-tailed deer abound, as do pronghorn; even the most casual observer can see dozens of each along the roads. Waterfowl, pheasants, and grouse are equally pervasive. It's no surprise that this is paradise for hunters.

HISTORY

The Sioux, Assiniboine, and Blackfeet Indians shared these buffalo-rich plains in shifting, suspicious alliances. The development of transportation corridors across Montana's northern tier—first with steamboats on the Missouri River in the 1830s, then with the Great Northern Railway up the Milk River valley in the 1880s—set the stage for the Indians' removal to reservations.

The homestead era brought the greatest changes to northeastern Montana. With a farm family on every half-section, these arid plains were forced momentarily to yield up a bounty of grain. Scandinavians and other northern Europeans were especially attracted to this unsettled area, and many small villages, dominated by a Lutheran or Methodist church spire, were settled with vague, utopian aspirations. The profoundly varying climate, leagued with Depression-era drought and insect infestations, brought an end to most homesteads.

Many of the unemployed farmers and tradesmen did find local work, however. The greatest of all Public Works Administration projects was Fort Peck Dam on the Missouri River. Employing tens of thousands of workers and flooding 250,000 acres of riverbottom, Fort Peck is one of the world's largest dams and an important source of hydroelectricity.

INFORMATION

Travel Montana's **Missouri River Country** region covers much of northeastern Montana. Write for their free travel information at P.O. Box 387, Wolf Point, MT 59201, or call (406) 653-1319 or (800) 653-1319.

TRANSPORTATION

Amtrak's Empire Builder traverses northern Montana, with service east from Portland and Seattle and west from Chicago. There are four stops weekly in each direction at Wolf Point, Malta and Glasgow. Call (800) 872-7245 for information and reservations.

Big Sky Airlines flies into Wolf Point, Glasgow, and Sidney from Billings. Call (800) 237-7788 for schedule information.

Automobile travelers need to be aware that parts of northeastern Montana are very remote: not every dot on the map has a gas station, nor in fact does every dot exist in a form helpful to travelers. Along Hwys. 2 and 200, gas up frequently. Don't count on 24-hour service stations to help you cross the area at night.

THE LITTLE ROCKY MOUNTAINS AND THE FORT BELKNAP RESERVATION

The Little Rockies are the easternmost of central Montana's volcanic outlier mountains. The core of the range, blanketed by displaced, tilted layers of limestone, contains significant deposits of gold. The usual mix of prospectors, ne'er-do-wells, and colorful characters rushed in during the 1890s, founding Zortman and Landusky. Outlaws from the Missouri badlands, a kind of resort community for rapscallions, made these mining camps their local watering holes. Such criminals as Kid Curry and Butch Cassidy were habitués of the remote and lawless Little Rockies.

THE FORT BELKNAP INDIAN RESERVATION

From the Little Rockies north to the Milk River lies the 645,000-acre Fort Belknap Reservation, home to the Gros Ventre and Assiniboine Indians. These two tribes were rivals in the complex intertribal politics characteristic of the 1800s. The Assiniboine are a Siouan people that drifted west as settlement to the east displaced them from their traditional home near Lake Winnipeg. After arriving on the plains, the Assiniboine be-

THE LEGEND OF SNAKE BUTTE

Snake Butte, southwest of Harlem, figures in a Gros Ventre legend. In ancient times, the nomadic Gros Ventre had no single place to bury their dead, as they followed game across the prairies. According to legend, when hunting buffalo near Snake Butte, a child died, and the bereaved parents prepared the body and left it high on a lonely cliff on the butte.

When the parents returned to visit the body, as was customary, they found that it had disappeared. The child's father found a wide trail leading from the burial area to a deep ravine in the side of the butte. The eerie trail bore the sign of scales, as if fashioned by a huge snake. The frightened parents returned to camp and related their story to a medicine woman. She vowed to visit the butte and spend the night on its peak.

The next morning she returned. Spirits had told her that deep beneath the butte lived a huge and evil snake; it had taken the child's body to warn the Gros Ventre that anyone who visits the butte will likewise disappear.

The exemplum obviously had little effect on the U.S. Corps of Engineers when they built Fort Peck Dam. They needed a source for riprap on the dam's face, and the igneous rock of Snake Butte (a diatreme radiating from the Little Rockies) was perfect. Workers quarried one million cubic yards of rock from the front of the butte and transported it 130 miles to the dam site.

The bad news is that the face of Snake Butte has been devastated; the good news is that the snake of Gros Ventre legend eluded capture.

came fierce rivals of the Blackfeet Indians. After smallpox decimated their numbers in the 1830s, the tribe settled along the Milk River to hunt the disappearing buffalo.

How the Gros Ventre (French for "Big Belly") came by their name is something of a mystery; not only the French but the Blackfeet and Shoshone referred to the tribe as the "Belly" people. One theory holds that in sign language the tribe was indicated by gesturing to the ribs, where early Gros Ventre tattooed symbols.

The Gros Ventre were allied with the powerful Blackfeet Nation. This Native American cartel roamed freely across northern Montana, terrorizing Indian and white settler alike. But increasing

trade with the whites, especially for whiskey, demoralized the tribes. Old alliances were scrapped, and the Blackfeet and Gros Ventre fell to fighting. The Gros Ventre soon found themselves siding with their old enemies, the Assiniboine and the U.S. Army, against the marauding Blackfeet. The Gros Ventre settled on the northern slopes of the Little Rockies. The U.S. government built Fort Belknap in 1871—in part to protect the tribes from each other—and in 1887 created the reservation.

Sights

At Hays, along the flanks of the Little Rockies, Jesuit F.H. Eberschweiler founded **St. Paul's Mission** in 1886 to instruct the Gros Ventre. The early church was built of logs and contained instructional paintings; it burned during the 1930s and was rebuilt in stone. Some original log outbuildings (1890s) remain.

Behind Hays, leading up People's Creek into the Little Rockies, is **Mission Canyon.** A gravel road passes beneath steep limestone cliffs riddled with caves. After half a mile, the road leads to a **natural bridge,** where water has carved through the limestone, leaving an arch 60 feet above the valley floor.

Events

Milk River Indian Days, held in Fort Belknap usually on the last weekend of July, features contest dancing, a marathon run, and a giveaway; in mid-June, the **Hays Mission Canyon Dance** is held in the canyon behind the town. The public is welcome to attend these celebrations.

Information

Contact the Tribal Offices, Fort Belknap Agency, Rte. 1 Box 66, Harlem, MT 59526, tel. (406) 353-2205, for information on tribal activities.

THE LITTLE ROCKY MOUNTAINS

On the map, the southern border of the Fort Belknap Reservation looks as if someone took a bite out of it. In fact, that's about what happened. Prospectors found gold in the Little Rockies in 1884; by the 1890s, in contravention of treaties, miners overran the narrow gulches of these low mountains. The federal Indian agent for the reservation was unable to stop the influx, and he urged the Assiniboine and Gros Ventre tribes to sell a strip of land four miles wide and seven miles long to the BLM. The tribes received $350,000 for the land in 1895; in the early 1990s, the mines were producing $25 million a year in gold and silver.

History

Although rumors of gold in the Little Rockies were spreading abroad as early as the 1860s, the Blackfeet discouraged exploration. Development awaited Pike Landusky, a grizzled veteran of past gold rushes, Indian fights, and whiskey trading. He and a companion found gold in 1894 near the town that now bears his name; within months hundreds of miners streamed in. The next year the government bought the land from the reservation, and within a decade, placer mining was replaced by more efficient, but environmentally damaging, cyanide stamp mills.

Even for mining camps, the towns of Landusky and Zortman drew more than their quota of rough characters. Pike Landusky himself was no milquetoast: in 1868, he went to the mouth of the Musselshell to trap and trade with the Indians; instead, he was ambushed by a party of Sioux. The irascible Landusky seized his frying pan and started beating one of the warriors with it; startled, the Sioux braves ceased their advance, and Landusky jerked the breechcloth off another and commenced lashing him in the face with it. Sensing a demonic presence, the Indians withdrew, leaving this dervish two ponies as an offering.

In an altercation with the Blackfeet, Landusky was shot in the jaw. The bullet shattered the bone and teeth; Landusky simply fished the fragments out of his mouth, discarded them, and went on fighting.

Landusky was representative of other rough-and-tough characters in this neighborhood: this was not a delicate society. Jew Jake was the local barkeeper; his leg had been shot off by a lawman in Great Falls, and he used a Winchester rifle for a crutch. The Curry Gang, three brothers who skirted civility and the law, owned a ranch just south of town. Pike Landusky fell afoul of the Curry Gang when he objected to the wooing of his daughter by the youngest Curry, Lonnie. Sensing a slight, Kid (the eldest Curry) rode to town and shot Landusky dead at Jew Jake's bar. As a final humiliation, the other Curry brother, Johnny, moved in with Mrs. Landusky.

The Currys gained national prominence after they formed the Wild Bunch with Butch Cassidy and the Sundance Kid, and went on a spree of bank and train robberies.

Mining in Landusky and Zortman peaked in the 1910s; the second-largest cyanide mill in the world was erected in Zortman to leach gold out of quartz ore. By 1940, almost all activity had ceased, but in the 1980s the price of gold was high enough to justify reopening the mines at Zortman. In 1998, the Pegasus Mine closed again.

Sights

Both **Zortman** and **Landusky** have preserved the flavor of old gold camps and are protected as national historic sites. Although nominally considered ghost towns, neither has developed its old buildings as a tourist attraction. In Zortman, the original jail still stands, and the Buckhorn Store and Bar still minister to the hungry and thirsty. The trailers and campers of today's miners contrast oddly with the rough log cabins of yesteryear. Landusky shows even fewer signs of life: a mining town is probably in extremis when its bar has closed.

Ten miles south of the Little Rockies lie the Missouri River Breaks. This province of rough badlands and river frontage has been included in the Charles M. Russell National Wildlife Refuge. Just about the only easily accessible part of the refuge is reached by a **self-guided auto tour** off Hwy. 191 a half mile north of the Robinson Missouri River Bridge. This 20-mile drive along good gravel roads passes great wildlife viewing and scenic landmarks.

Practicalities

In Zortman, the **Buckhorn Store**, tel. (406) 673-3162, offers cabins ($33-37), campsites ($$8 to $12), and groceries. The **Zortman Garage**, tel. (406) 673-3160, also offers RV hookups and cabins. One mile north of Zortman, the BLM maintains **Camp Creek**, a streamside campground.

Another BLM campsite, **Montana Gulch**, is one-half mile west of Landusky.

THE MILK RIVER VALLEY

Between Malta and Glasgow, Hwy. 2 unrolls between cottonwoods and willows and the green thread of the Milk River. The prairies of northern Montana continue their expansive, monotonal rhythm. Occasionally a ridge of uplands infringes, outriders from the wild Missouri Breaks just south, causing the horizon to hike up its skirts.

Ice-age glaciers covered this part of Montana, homogenizing the prairie surface and obstructing the old Missouri River course. When the ice sheets retreated, about 10,000 years ago, the Missouri found a more southerly valley to its liking. The sluggish and inconsiderable Milk River, so named by Lewis and Clark who thought its waters resembled "a cup of tea with the admixture of a tablespoonful of milk," has borrowed the old channel.

Eastern Montana's only hot-springs resort, a wildlife refuge dense with birdlife, and some of the state's best big-game hunting make a virtue out of these implacable prairies.

HISTORY

The Bad Old Days

First the Plains Indians and the buffalo, then open-range cowboys and cattle claimed this rich rangeland. Just as the Indians entered remote areas of Montana after being displaced by homesteaders elsewhere, so settlement in the Judith Basin during the 1890s pushed untamed cowboys, desperadoes, and loners north into the Milk River valley.

The Missouri Breaks and the Little Rockies were a villainous no-man's land. From rugged hideouts, rustlers trailed stolen cattle to Canada and back, across the law-free expanses of Milk

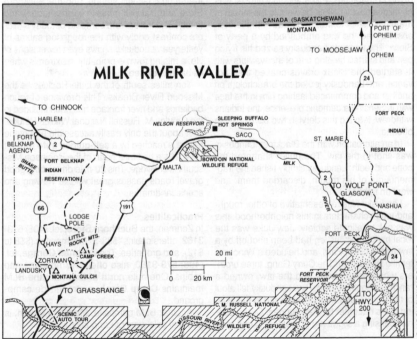

River country. The Hole-in-the-Wall Gang, led by Kid Curry, found cattle and horse theft too facile. In 1901, they held up the westbound Great Northern train five miles west of Malta. After stopping the train and blowing up the safe, the gang fled with worthless unfranked banknotes.

Painter Charlie Russell rode with other cowboys along the Milk River. One of his most famous paintings, *Loops and Swift Horses are Surer Than Lead*, re-created a 1904 episode that occurred just south of Saco. Early-rising cowpunchers found that 40 horses were missing from the remuda. A quick search revealed that a grizzly bear had entered camp, charged the horse covey, and was chasing the frightened horses across the prairie. The cowboys gave chase, and, within seconds, lassoed the furious bear.

Settlement

The Great Northern Railway pushed up the Milk River valley in 1887. Initially, it brought little settlement to this part of the state, except for villages where cowboys loaded cattle onto railcars. The seclusion of northern Montana ended in the 1910s, when the homestead land rush brought in thousands of dryland farmers. Throughout the Milk River valley, homesteads sprang up every 320 acres. The Great Northern actively promoted the cheap land of northern Montana in Central and Eastern Europe; these immigrants founded ethnically homogeneous enclaves. Amongst the most resilient are the Hutterites and Mennonites, who maintain several communities in the area. These Amish-like settlers were originally German/Russian Anabaptists, who emigrated to Montana after experiencing religious intolerance on the steppes.

MALTA AND VICINITY

Yes, Malta (pop. 2,303, elev. 2,254 feet) was named for the Mediterranean island. No, Malta was not named for or by Maltese immigrants. As the Great Northern built across unpopulated northern Montana in 1887, enterprising employees spun the globe and then stopped it with a jab of the finger. Thus were deserted sidings along the Great Northern saddled with exotic names.

The siding at Malta jump-started. Ranchers whose herds of cattle ranged the unfenced prairies needed a railhead, and thirsty cowboys needed a

town to carouse in. Irrigated farms along the Milk River notwithstanding, this is still cattle country: Malta is a rancher's, not a farmer's, town.

Sights

Housed in the old Carnegie library is the **Phillips County Museum**, 133 S. 1st St. W, tel. (406) 654-1037, open Tues.-Sat. 10 a.m.-noon and 1-5 p.m., mid-May to mid-September. With displays of cowboy gear, Indian beadwork, and homesteader-era artifacts, it commemorates the area's history.

Just two miles east of Malta is the **Bowdoin National Wildlife Refuge**, tel. (406) 654-2863. Founded in 1936, this marshy lake is a major stopover for both migrating and nesting waterfowl. White pelicans are commonly seen (there are over 800 nesting pairs), as are rarer white-faced ibises and night herons. In the spring watch male sharp-tailed grouse as they drum their chests to impress the females. Access is by canoe or along a six-mile auto tour.

Fossil Digs

The **Judith River Dinosaur Institute**, tel. (406) 654-2323, Box Y, Malta, MT 59538, is an independent paleontological research organization that, amongst other projects, sponsors fossil excavations involving serious and qualified lay participants. There are five five-day summer sessions, each of which each take on only ten to 12 individuals, and the focus is on providing a field experience to educators; educational credit is available for working on the dig. Non-educators are welcome to apply and join the digs when space is available.

Digs operated by the Judith Basin Dinosaur Institute are noteworthy for their level of participation. Rather than being a grunt for researchers who have all the fun, as is commonly the case when the public pays to be a part of an excavation, here participants get involved in all parts of the process, including learning field and extraction skills, and helping with lab work. Current excavations are on a duck-billed dinosaur bone-bed, which ends up being much more interesting than hauling buckets of dirt for scientists mining for micro-fossils.

Spaces go very quickly, so if you're serious about paleontology, inquire as soon as you start planning your Montana trip. Costs are $575 for five days of work (considerably more if you want college credits). This price does not include lodging or meals in Malta.

Accommodations

The nicest place to stay in Malta is the **Great Northern Motor Hotel,** 2 S. 1st Ave. E, tel. (406) 654-2100, (888) 234-0935, $42 s, $49 d, with a bar, restaurant, casino, and steak house. The hotel also offers inside parking: just the thing if you're visiting in winter. The pleasant **Maltana Motel,** 138 S. 1st Ave. W, tel. (406) 654-2610, $34 s, $43 d, is a well kept-up older motel just a block from downtown on a quiet street. This comfortable motel underwent a complete renovation in 1998.

Out on Hwy. 2, the **Edgewater Motel,** tel. (406) 654-1302, $46 s, $51 d, offers an indoor pool, sauna, and campsites. The **Sportsman Motel,** 231 N. 1st St. E, tel. (406) 654-2300, $30 s, $34 d, has a comfortable older units, some with kitchenettes. The Sportsman also rents RV spaces.

Food

For steaks, try the **Great Northern Motor Hotel,** 2 S. 1st Ave. E, tel. (406) 654-2100. For a lighter meal, go to the **Westside Restaurant** west of Malta on Hwy. 2, tel. (406) 654-1555, or the **Hitchin' Post,** east of Malta, tel. (406) 654-1882. The **Mustang Cafe,** 122 S. 1st St., tel. (406) 654-1895, is a good locals' kind of eatery; if you need a stretch, you can bowl a few strikes in the adjacent bowling alley while you wait for lunch; open 10 a.m.-11 p.m.

Information and Services

Contact the **Malta Chamber of Commerce** at Box GG, Malta, MT 59538, tel. (406) 654-1776 or (800) 704-1776. The **Phillips County Hospital** is at 417 S. 4th St. E, tel. (406) 654-1100. For emergencies, call the **sheriff** at (406) 654-1211.

For a local **road report,** phone (406) 265-1416.

SACO AND VICINITY

Saco (pop. 247, elev. 2,184 feet) is a little agricultural trading center named, like Malta, by the globe-spinners at the Great Northern for Saco, Maine. Chet Huntley, the late TV newscaster, was born and educated near Saco; the country grade school he attended now stands in a city park and serves as the local museum.

Accommodations and Food

There's one motel in town, **O'Brien's,** at 203 Taylor, tel. (406) 527-3373, $24 s, $29 d. **O'Brien's Cafe** is down the street at 507 Taylor, tel. (406) 527-3537, open 6 a.m.-10 p.m.

Camping and Fishing

Two miles off Hwy. 2 and adjacent to Sleeping Buffalo Resort is **Nelson Reservoir State Park,** a 4,500-acre lake with camping along its banks. Locals use the reservoir for water-skiing and fishing (northern pike and walleye).

Sleeping Buffalo Resort

Unique along the northern tier, this rustic—some might say funky—hot-springs spa combines inexpensive accommodations, water-skiing, and aqua-therapy. Named for large glacial rocks half-buried in the prairies, the hot springs were tapped in 1924 when oil drillers struck a pool of hot, highly mineralized water at 3,200 feet. When the water reached the surface, the mineral gases ignited. The spring burned for six years.

Initially developed as an old-fashioned health spa, the hot springs at Sleeping Buffalo have been somewhat modernized and developed into a family recreational facility. Presently, the resort includes both indoor and outdoor hot pools (106°), a water slide, two bars, a restaurant, a golf course, and rooms in venerable cabins or motel units starting at $31 to $36.

Sleeping Buffalo Resort, Star Rte. 3, Box 13, Saco, MT 59621, tel. (406) 527-3370, lies 10 miles west of Saco on Hwy. 2, then one mile north along a good gravel road. The resort is open year-round.

GLASGOW AND FORT PECK

The largest Public Works project of the 1930s' New Deal era, Fort Peck Dam—holding one of the world's largest reservoirs—is an enormous tribute to the spirit that overcame the Great Depression. The old rail town of Glasgow, now the largest city in northeastern Montana, was the stepping-off point for the dam project and is now the livestock trade center of the region. Vivid history, unparalleled recreational opportunities, as well as tours of the enormous hydroelectric facilities make this northeastern Montana's most enticing stopover.

GLASGOW

The Great Northern established a wide spot along the rails called Siding 45 in 1887. The town, originally just a series of tents, became Glasgow in 1889. Glasgow (pop. 3,656, elev. 2,216 feet) grew fitfully as homesteaders and ranchers made use of the rail connections.

During the 1930s, Glasgow boomed as it became the primary trade and transport center for the shifting population of workers at Fort Peck Lake. Little shanty towns sprang up to serve the needs of the 10,000-strong labor force. This period of growth lasted less than a decade, and although few dam workers permanently settled in the area, Glasgow remains the focus for anglers and holidaymakers at the reservoir.

More problematic for the city was the Glasgow Air Force Base. During the mid-1960s, the population of Valley County nearly doubled with Air Force personnel and their families. Glasgow built new schools, redesigned the old downtown for more traffic, and prepared for sustained growth. When the Air Force pulled out in 1969, the city planners were left with a facility that, unlike Fort Peck, had no apparent afterlife. Currently, Boeing rents the base for flight training and equipment testing. The 1,200 living units on the base are being marketed as St. Marie's, a retirement community for military personnel.

Sights
The **Valley County Pioneer Museum,** Hwy. 2 at 8th Ave. N, tel. (406) 228-8692, is one of east-

ern Montana's best museums. Diorama fans should prepare to be giddy, as the museum utilizes a number of these well-done displays to present local history. An authentic teepee is the focus of the Indian exhibit, a sheepwagon and chuckwagon commemorate the life of the early stockman, and there's also a re-creation of a frontier town.

Accommodations
Glasgow's largest and newest motel complex is the **Cottonwood Inn,** east on Hwy. 2, on the edge of town, tel. (406) 228-8213 or (800) 321-8213. There's a good restaurant, pool, sauna, hot tub, guest laundry, meeting and small convention facilities, and nearly 100 rooms. Rates are $50 s, $68 d; pets are okay.

On the west end of the Hwy. 2 strip, just across from the Pioneer Museum, is the **Star Lodge Motel,** tel. (406) 228-2494, with in-room coffee makers, refrigerators, and some microwaves. All this, pets okay, and rooms are a thrifty $26 s, $37 d. The **La Casa Motel,** 238 1st Ave. N, tel. (406) 228-9311, is convenient to a number of chain and local restaurants, allows pets, and has rooms at $31 s, $42 d.

Glasgow's downtown area offers a couple of lodging options. The excellent **Campbell Lodge,** 534 3rd Ave. S, tel. (406) 228-9328, is in easy walking distance of downtown shopping and offers discounts for AAA, AARP, and commercial travelers. The Campbell Lodge is two blocks from the city pool and recreation center; rates are $29 s, $34 d. The **Roosevelt Hotel,** at 412 3rd Ave. S, tel. (406) 228-4341, is Glasgow's old downtown hotel. It's been totally remodeled and refurbished, and all rooms have 35-channel TVs and refrigerators; there's also a hot tub on premises. The Roosevelt stands in a quiet location one block from Main Street, rates are $25 s, $29 d.

For a campsite, consider driving the 17 miles to Fort Peck, or head to **Shady Rest RV Park, in Glasgow,** tel. (406) 228-2769.

Food
If you like a good steak and you like a western bar atmosphere, then you'll treasure **Sam's Supper Club,** 307 1st Klein, tel. (406) 228-4614. The

clientele, a mix of cowboys, anglers, and businessmen, converge here for the outstanding charbroiled beef and good salad bar. Sam's is now open for Mexican lunches. Another Glasgow institution is **Johnnie Cafe,** 433 1st Ave. S, tel. (406) 228-4222, an old 24-hour downtown diner where locals gather. The dining room at the **Cottonwood Inn,** east on Hwy. 2, tel. (406) 228-8213, is open 6 a.m.-10 p.m. and offers chicken and pork dishes in addition to the compulsory steaks. **Eugene's Pizza,** 193 Klein, tel. (406) 228-8552, is open 4 p.m.-midnight, and serves Glasgow's best pizza.

Information
Contact the **Glasgow Chamber of Commerce** at 110 5th St. S, Glasgow, MT 59230, tel. (406) 228-2222. The **Dept. of Fish, Wildlife, and Parks** is at Hwy. 2 W, Glasgow, MT 59230, tel. (406) 228-3700. The **BLM** office is west on Hwy. 2, tel. (406) 228-4316.

Transportation
Amtrak passes through Glasgow four times a week each way. Call (800) 872-7245 for information; the depot, at 424 1st Ave. S, is operated by the Burlington Northern and endures Amtrak traffic without promoting it. Three flights a day link Glasgow to Billings on **Big Sky Airlines,** tel. (800) 237-7788. **Budget Rent-A-Car** is at 626 2nd Ave. S, tel. (406) 228-9325.

FORT PECK

History
Early traders built the original Fort Peck as an Indian trading post in 1867. Located right on the banks of the Missouri River for ease in loading and unloading steamboats, the trading post did a bang-up business with the Sioux and Assiniboine. The Great Northern Railroad in 1887 chose to build through the gentle Milk River valley rather than traverse the intemperate badlands of the Missouri River, thereby bypassing the old fort.

In the fall of 1933, workers began to clear brush in preparation for the building of Fort Peck Dam. The largest and most ambitious of Franklin Roosevelt's Public Works projects, construction of the dam created jobs for tens of thousands of

---

FORT PECK FACTS

• Construction crews at Fort Peck moved 130 million cubic yards of dirt and replaced it with four million cubic yards of gravel and 1.6 million cubic yards of riprap.

• The reservoir has the capacity to store 19 million acre-feet of water (the runoff from one-third of Montana).

• The maximum depth of the lake is 220 feet.

• The dam stretches from bluff to bluff across the Missouri, a distance of 3.5 miles.

• The construction technique that built Fort Peck Dam is called "hydraulic fill." The sediment from the Missouri River bottom was pumped to the dam face as slurry, where it was drained into rock structures that trapped the mud and let the water drain away. More rock was then layered on top of this earth embankment.

---

people during the Great Depression and altered the face of Montana. At the time of its completion, Fort Peck was the world's largest reservoir. Fifty years later, at 150 miles long, with a shoreline longer than California's, it is still the planet's second-largest earth-fill reservoir.

The Army Corps of Engineers justified the expense of Fort Peck ($150 million) by promising better river navigation, flood control, hydroelectric generation, and irrigation possibilities. But Fort Peck's biggest impact on Montana was the amount of jobs it provided. During the seven years of construction, at one time or another 50,000 people worked at the dam.

The Corps of Engineers built a showpiece town to house its personnel and serve as the dam headquarters. Named after the old trading post, Fort Peck also contained an enormous theater and a grand hotel, each built in the arts-and-crafts style characteristic of New Deal architecture.

But handsome, well-planned Fort Peck was not where the workers lived or played. The towns that grew up to service this largely young, energetic, and migratory workforce quickly accrued reputations for wild times that would have made Bannack jealous. Shanty boomtowns like Wheeler, New Deal, and Park Grove shot up, invigorated with government cash and hard-won 1930s *jouissance*. For its first issue (Nov. 23, 1936), *Life* magazine sent Margaret Bourke-White to Fort Peck to chronicle life on this new frontier. Little remains of this short and incandescent moment of Montana's development except derelict buildings and memories of landmarks like the Buckhorn Bar, destroyed by fire in 1983.

Sights

The **Fort Peck Power Plants** near the junction of Hwys. 24 and 117, tel. (406) 526-3411, offer tours of the turbines and electrical-generation facilities. Call ahead for times; the facilities sometimes close for repairs. The main power plant also houses the **Fort Peck Museum,** tel. (406) 526-3421, which contains an excellent collection of fossils and Indian relics discovered while building the dam.

While the town of Fort Peck will not overwhelm the visitor with sheer size, some of the old Public Works buildings are astonishing relics. The **Fort Peck Theater** on Main St., tel. (406) 228-9219,

At a cost of $150 million and taking seven years to complete (1933-1940), Fort Peck Dam was the largest project of Franklin Delano Roosevelt's Public Works Administration.

MONTANA HISTORICAL SOCIETY, HELENA

was built in 1934 as a cinema in an imposing and somewhat squatty chalet style, all the better to accommodate its 1,100-patron capacity. It's hard to imagine a grander example of rustic New Deal architecture. For over 20 years, the theater has been home to one of the state's best summer theater companies. The shows run June through August; call (800) 828-2259 for details. The **Fort Peck Hotel** on Missouri Ave. and the dam's **administration building** on Kansas Ave. were built at the same time, and share the 1930s' grandiose architectural vision.

There's excellent wildlife viewing just downstream from the dam. Starting at the Downstream Campground, the **Beaver Creek Nature Trail** winds along brushy streams and ponds; interpretive signs point out habitat and help identify species. Larger mammals, like deer, pronghorn, and buffalo, can be seen along an auto trail at the **Leo B. Coleman Wildlife Exhibit,** which begins on Big Horn St. just across from the Fort Peck Theater.

If there's any question in your mind about the meaning of the term "badlands," then continue south of Fort Peck on Hwy. 24 toward Hwy. 200. Like a boat cresting waves, the road peaks and troughs through sandstone uplands and spectacular badland ridges and valleys. This land is adjacent to the C.M. Russell National Wildlife Refuge and offers opportunities for viewing pronghorn, mule deer, coyote, and other prairie residents.

Recreation

The Fort Peck area offers the best recreational opportunities in eastern Montana. The 245,000-acre reservoir contains sturgeon, northern pike, walleye, paddlefish, sauger, channel catfish, and lake trout. Locals also use the lake for water-skiing, sailing, parasailing, and windsurfing. There are six recreation areas within four miles of the dam itself and a dozen others farther afield. The best and most accessible fishing areas are south along Hwy. 24, along the Big Dry Arm.

If you're a compulsive walleye fisher, consider entering the Montana Governor's Cup, a very popular walleye fishing tournament held the second weekend of July at Fort Peck Lake. Hundreds of people from all over the West converge on Fort Peck to compete for $40,000 in prizes. Contact the Glasgow chamber of commerce for information.

If you'd like hire a guide for fishing on Fort Peck Lake, contact Billingsley Ranch Outfitters, P.O. Box 768, Glasgow, MT 59230 or call (406) 367-5577. For boat rentals, contact the Fort Peck Marina at (406) 526-3442. Boaters need to pay attention to storm and wind warnings: intense thunderstorms build quickly along the prairies, and high winds can create waves high enough to endanger small boats.

Fossil Hunting

From the mouth of the Musselshell River on, the Missouri River cuts down through the Hell Creek Formation, a geologic layer containing one of the richest records of prehistoric life in the world. Few anglers or boaters go to Fort Peck Lake without keeping an eye open for fossils, and others, taken by the area's Cretaceous-era outcroppings, come to the lake expressly to hunt fossils. Although vertebrate fossil excavation isn't allowed on the C.M. Russell Wildlife Refuge without a permit, nonvertebrate plant or shell fossils can be removed from public land. Often banks of sandstone and shale offer up fossils for viewing, particularly petrified fish, mollusks, and leaf imprints.

For a number of years, Earthwatch has coordinated public participation in the Fort Peck area **dinosaur digs** of Dr. J. Keith Rigby, a professor at Notre Dame University. Three two-week long sessions are held in July and August, during which volunteers help scientists dig and prepare fossils. For more information, contact Earthwatch, 680 Mt. Auburn St., Watertown, MA 02272, or call (617) 926-8200.

A word of warning: if you are exploring Fort Peck environs on back roads, head back to pavement at *the first sign* of rain; the gumbo hills quickly become impassably slick.

Accommodations

The **Fort Peck Hotel,** on Missouri Ave., tel. (406) 526-3266, built to house visitors during Fort Peck dam's heyday, is one of Montana's most unusual lodgings. This venerable three-story hotel contains 47 rooms, a bar, and a dining room. The spirit of the hotel hasn't changed much since the New Deal '30s, but that is all the more draw for anyone who hankers for a taste of bygone days; however, the rooms are more modern after a thorough refurbishing in 1993. Rates are $43 s, $48 d.

Camping

Numerous campgrounds are scattered around Fort Peck Dam, all with access to fishing. Just under the bluff from the Fort Peck townsite on Hwy. 117 is the **Downstream Campground;** it's in a great location, but bring the insect repellent. Likewise, the **Rainbow Campground** is three miles north of Fort Peck on Hwy. 117, where there's good fishing for walleye and northern pike. On the lake itself is **West End Campground,** three miles west of Fort Peck off Hwy. 24.

Food

The **Fort Peck Hotel,** tel. (406) 526-3266, offers tasty and imaginative food in a great dining room reminiscent of summer camp; it's open 6:30 a.m.-9 p.m. For a short-order meal with cocktails, try the **Gateway Inn,** "The best dam bar by a dam site," west of Fort Peck on Hwy. 24, tel. (406) 526-9988.

Information

For more information on Fort Peck Dam, contact the **Corps of Engineers,** E. Kansas St., Fort Peck, MT 59223, tel. (406) 526-3411.

The Fort Peck office for the **C.M. Russell National Wildlife Refuge** is north along Hwy. 117, tel. (406) 526-3464.

Fort Peck Theater

THE FORT PECK INDIAN RESERVATION AND VICINITY

East of Fort Peck Dam, the Missouri River flows down a wide fertile valley lined by cottonwood trees. Extending north and south of the river are the relentless and austere plains. Also north of the river is the Fort Peck Indian Reservation, the state's second largest, home to the Yanktonai Sioux and Assiniboine tribes. Highway 2 follows the Missouri, linking old river-freighting centers and ranch towns like Wolf Point and Poplar.

HISTORY

The Assiniboine Indians moved south out of Canada into Montana in the late 1700s, where they lived along the Missouri River. They became willing partners with the early white traders. In 1837, smallpox raged through the Assiniboine Nation, killing an estimated two-thirds of the tribe.

Greatly weakened as a society, the Assiniboine quickly agreed to the constraints and protections of early reservation treaties and settled along the Missouri. When smallpox again broke out amongst the Indians upriver at Fort Belknap, these Assiniboine quickly moved farther down the Missouri to live with the Yanktonai Sioux near Fort Peck, thereby avoiding the epidemic.

The Sioux Nation was one of the greatest of the Indian tribal confederations. The branch that came to inhabit the northern prairies of Montana is called the Yanktonai Sioux. They originally roamed the prairie provinces of Canada until forced into Montana. Here, rolling waves of displaced Indians came to a congested, chaotic halt.

The Yanktonai were part of the alliance that fought Custer in 1876; this triumph didn't forestall their enclosure in the huge Indian territory north of the Missouri the following year. When the Great Northern sought to put a railway across northern Montana in the late 1880s, the U.S. government renegotiated the reservations to allow the railway right-of-way. The Sioux and Assiniboine were assigned to their present reservation in 1888.

Fort Peck Reservation was one of the worst-affected reservations under the Dawes Act. Seeking to turn these nomadic tribesmen into agrarian landowners, this federal program allocated homestead-sized pieces of land to individual Indians. The surplus land then became available to non-Indians. Because of the size of the Fort Peck Reservation (2.1 million acres) and the paucity of Indians (about 2,000 at the time), only 46% of the reservation is now owned by Native Americans.

WOLF POINT

History

Wolf Point (pop. 2,874, elev. 2,004 feet) began as a trading post on the Missouri. The thick groves of shady cottonwoods were home to early "wood hawks," who made a rugged living felling trees to feed the engines of steamboats that trundled the river between St. Louis and Fort Benton.

Along this stretch of the Missouri, the local Indians quickly learned that there was money to be made in selling wood. Cedar wood fetched a higher price than cottonwood; the canny natives would paint the ends of cottonwood logs red and then demand cedar prices for them. When the river was too low for the boats to approach the bank where the Indians were trying to sell wood, they would squat in the shallow water with only their heads above water to give the impression that the river was shoulder deep.

The name Wolf Point apparently derives from an event in the fur-trading days. During an especially harsh winter, trappers had good luck trapping and poisoning wolves. However, the wolves froze solid before they could be skinned, so the trappers piled the carcasses along the river's edge, to be skinned in the spring. But when the trappers returned, Indians had taken control of the landing, and the trappers were forced to abandon their booty. The putrefying wolves became a landmark for steamboat crews.

Wolf Point is now a trade town for local farmers and ranchers and a center for the Sioux and Assiniboine. Grain-storage facilities here can warehouse 1.5 million bushels of grain, making Wolf

Point one of the state's most important terminals. The Wolf Point Wild Horse Stampede is the state's oldest organized rodeo, and one of the best.

Sights
The **Wolf Point Area Historical Society Museum,** 220 2nd Ave. S, tel. (406) 653-1912, contains artifacts from its early frontier and homesteading days, plus a reliquary devoted to native-son trick roper Montie Montana (and his horse Rex).

If old tractors and farming implements are of interest, one of the nation's most complete collections of John Deere tractors is located north of Wolf Point. With over 500 tractors, the **John Deere Tractor Collection & Museum** contains an example of every John Deere manufactured from 1923 to 1953. Although the collection is private, the owner is happy to show the tractors to interested visitors. Call tel. (406) 392-5224 and ask for Louis Toavs to set up a time to visit.

Accommodations
In downtown Wolf Point, the **Sherman Motor Inn,** 200 E. Main St., tel. (406) 653-1100 or (800) 952-1100, $30 s, $40 d, offers a good restaurant, a lounge and casino, a health club, and convention facilities on-site. Other motels string along Hwy. 2. The **Homestead Inn,** 101 Hwy. 2 E, tel. (406) 653-1300 or (800) 231-0986, $30 s, $39 d, is closest to the old center of town. With clean and comfortable rooms, complimentary coffee and donuts in the morning, queen-size beds, guest laundry, cable TV, and direct dial phones, this is another good lodging deal; pets are okay.

Rancho Campground is one mile west on Hwy. 2, tel. (406) 653-1940. At the junction of Hwys. 2 and 13 (seven miles east of Wolf Point) is **R.B.W. Campground,** tel. (406) 525-3740.

Food
A number of drive-ins and fast-food parlors are strung along Hwy. 2, but it's worth driving downtown to find better atmosphere. The restaurant at the **Sherman Motor Inn,** 200 E. Main St., tel. (406) 653-1100, is the nicest in town, with a menu that offers alternatives to the beef pervasive in most eastern Montana eateries; it's open 6 a.m.- 10 p.m. For Wolf Point's best steak, go to the **Elk's Club,** 302 Main St., tel. (406) 653-1920.

The **Wolf Point Cafe,** 217 Main St., tel. (406) 653-9910, recalls a time when times, and foods, were simpler. Kick start your morning at **Espresso Madness,** near the junction of Hwy. 2 and 4th Ave.

Events
The **Wolf Point Wild Horse Stampede** began in Wolf Point as a Native American celebration of horse racing and horsemanship. Early cowboys found the event to their liking and joined in. The Stampede became a full-blown rodeo in 1915, after it was sanctioned by the Rodeo Cowboy Association. Today, it is the oldest and one of the most prestigious rodeos in Montana, where rodeo events alternate with Indian dancers in a mutual celebration of shared culture. The Wolf Point Stampede is held the second weekend in July, with three separate rodeos and parades. Contact the chamber of commerce for further details.

The Assiniboine celebrate **Red Bottom Day** west of Wolf Point at Frazer the third weekend of June. The powwow involves singing, traditional dancing, a giveaway, and a display of handmade wares.

Information
Contact the **Wolf Point Chamber of Commerce** at 201 4th Ave. S, Wolf Point, MT 59201 tel. (406) 653-2012.

Getting There and Around
Amtrak's Western District ends in Wolf Point, and four trains a week pass through in each direction. The depot is on Front St., tel. (406) 653-2350. **Big Sky Airlines** flies between Billings and Wolf Point two times a day; call (800) 237-7788.

POPLAR

Poplar (pop. 920, elev. 1,963 feet) is the agency town for the Fort Peck Indian Reservation. Like many a Missouri River town, Poplar had its fitful beginnings as an Indian trading post and freighting center for furs and buffalo robes. Its pulse quickened when the Great Northern went through in 1887, and the Fort Peck Reservation was carved out and centered here the following year.

Poplar is also home to **NAES College,** a tribal community college, and **A & S Industries.** A & S, a tribally owned business, employs over 400 people to make camouflage netting and medical chests for the U.S. government. A large and heavy-producing oil field lies just north of town.

Sights

The **Poplar Museum,** open Memorial Day to Labor Day, daily 11 a.m.-5 p.m., tel. (406) 768-5223, is located east of Poplar on Hwy. 2, in the old tribal jail. In addition to Indian artifacts, the museum also relates the history of the Assiniboine and Sioux reservation.

The **Fort Peck Assiniboine and Sioux Cultural Center & Museum,** tel. (406) 768-5155, ext. 2328, focuses on tribal history. It's open May to September on Hwy. 2 east of town.

Accommodations and Food

Lee Ann's Motel, 150 F St., Hwy. 2, tel. (406) 768-5442, $25 s, $33 d, offers clean, snug rooms, some with kitchenettes. **Bud's RV Park,** one mile east on Hwy. 2, tel. (406) 768-3392, is open April through November.

Try the **Buckhorn Cafe,** 217 2nd Ave. W (behind the bar) for light meals—the Indian tacos are a favorite. Steaks, and good ones, are the specialty at the **American Legion Supper Club,** 127 A St. E, tel. (406) 768-3923.

Events

The **Iron Ring Celebration,** held the third weekend of July in Poplar, commemorates the last Sioux chief with dancing and a powwow. The Assiniboine and Sioux collectively host **Oil Discovery Celebration,** a powwow held the last weekend of August to memorialize the 1950s discovery of oil on the reservation.

Information

Contact the Fort Peck Tribal Council at P.O. Box 1027, Poplar, MT 59255, tel. (406) 768-5155.

THE NORTHEAST CORNER

In Montana's northeast corner, the center does not hold. Up here the locals keep one eye on Canada, one on North Dakota, and their back to the rest of Montana.

Saskatchewan is at least as important to Plentywood and Scobey as is, say, western Montana. Canadians pour over the border by the thousands, both to shop and to carouse. Considering that goods are already significantly cheaper in the U.S. than in Canada, and that Montana doesn't even *have* a sales tax, for many Canadians shopping in northern Montana isn't a weekend's amusement but an economic necessity. (Also, many local businesses take Canadian money at par.)

Montana has some of the nation's most relaxed liquor laws, while Saskatchewan has some of Canada's most restrictive. Montana allows gambling in many forms; Saskatchewan doesn't. Add up this equation and you have, in the middle of these arid unpopulated prairies, a couple of the most unlikely holiday towns in the country.

But this corner of Montana isn't just festivities and holidaymaking on the northern plains. Surrounding Plentywood and Scobey is rich farmland, pressed flat as table linen by ancient glaciers, with an occasional divot carved out for small farm ponds. Medicine Lake Wildlife Refuge is one of the state's foremost areas for viewing migratory waterfowl and other prairie species. Both Scobey and Plentywood offer fine museums that commemorate the homesteaders who helped tame the Wild West.

SCOBEY

With sufficient rain, Scobey (pop. 1,101, elev. 2,450 feet) is at the center of some of the state's most productive wheat-growing land. As in Saskatchewan, the growing season is too short to depend on the grain to ripen for combining. When the seed heads are fully grown but not yet dried and golden-colored, farmers cut the grain into windrows. The wind and sun quickly dry the plants into straw and ripened kernels, and the grain is then combined off the ground.

Scobey, like many other towns along the Great Northern Railroad, was settled principally by Scandinavians; it's now a trading town for local farmers and ranchers, as well as for visiting Canadians. Only 17 miles from Saskatchewan, the Canadian influence is strong. Canadian radio is pervasive on the airwaves, the occasional "Eh?" sneaks into conversations, and—most

Scobey's outstanding
outdoor museum,
Pioneer Town

W.C. McRAE

damning—Scobey is home to Montana's only curling rink.

Sights
Pioneer Town, a project of the Daniels County Museum, is one of the state's best walk-through museums. Basically a recreation of an early homesteader town, the 20-acre site contains 40 buildings, some with period furnishings. Included are a restored schoolhouse, barbershop, blacksmith shop, and undertaker's office, and a two-story hotel, two churches, vintage automobiles and farm equipment. The county historical archives are also kept here. Pioneer Town lies just west of town off 2nd Avenue. It's open Memorial Day to Labor Day, daily 1-5 p.m. or by appointment the rest of the year. Call the Daniels County Museum at (406) 487-5965 for details.

Janus Park, with playgrounds, a swimming pool, and picnic tables, is located at Park St., between 2nd and 3rd avenues.

Accommodations and Food
The **Cattle King Motor Inn** at the south edge of town on Hwy. 13, tel. (406) 487-5332 or (800) 562-2775, $44 s, $50 d, offers free continental breakfast, guest laundry, commercial and senior discounts, and there's one handicapped suite; pets are $5 extra. The **Juel Motel,** 514 Main, tel. (406) 487-2765, $28 s, $38 d. is the older and less expensive alternative.

The **Ponderosa,** 102 Main, tel. (406) 487-5001, is a bar and grill that also serves pizza. The

Slipper Lounge, next to the Cattle King Motel at 608 Main, tel. (406) 487-9973, is the local casino, supper club, and salad bar; it's closed Mondays.

Information and Services
The **Daniels Memorial Hospital** is at 105 5th Ave. E, tel. (406) 487-2296. Contact the **sheriff's office** at (406) 487-2691. The **U.S. Border Patrol** can be reached at (406) 487-2621 in the Port of Scobey. The border with Canada is open 8 a.m.-9 p.m.

For area information, contact the **Scobey Chamber of Commerce** at P.O. Box 91, MT 59263, tel. (406) 487-5502.

PLENTYWOOD

Located just about as far as it could get from the centers of Montana trade and power, Plentywood (pop. 1,989, elev. 2,024 feet) is closer to Winnipeg than to Helena; Minneapolis is closer than Dillon. But Plentywood isn't any the less Montana-like for it. In fact, Canadians love to visit Plentywood precisely because it is so much more Wild and Western—that is, Montanan—than their prairie provinces.

By the way, only on a vast and treeless plain would a cowboy be reduced to calling a place Plentywood simply (so the story goes) because he found enough wood to build a fire.

History
For such a far-flung locality, Plentywood is in the mainstream of Montana history. The Sioux

chief Sitting Bull and his followers passed through this area after the Battle of the Little Bighorn in 1876. After living safely for five years in southern Saskatchewan, they moved south and surrendered to U.S. Army officials at the present site of Plentywood.

After the military evacuated the Indians, the plains of northern Montana became rangeland. However, the presence of valuable cattle and horses, combined with the absence of any effective law enforcement, made the area popular with rustlers. The Outlaw Trail, so named by Butch Cassidy, crossed the Canadian line just north of Plentywood. Gangs of rustlers drove stolen Canadian cattle across the border here and followed Cassidy's trail across the most lawless and inaccessible parts of Montana on their way to markets in the Southwest.

During the early 1900s, a number of shady characters lived in the gulches north of Plentywood. Unembarrassed to smuggle whiskey, to alter brands after ferrying livestock back and forth across the border, or to rob a train, these denim-collared criminals earned the area a reputation, according to an early brand inspector, as the "most lawless and crookedest" in the state.

After the Great Northern brought in homesteaders in the 1910s, Plentywood gained quite a different reputation. Not finding either of the two major political parties to their liking, early homesteaders formed the Farmer-Labor Party. Throughout the 1920s, this socialist-leaning party

controlled county politics. In the 1930 general election, 300 Sheridan County residents voted straight-ticket Communist Party.

Today, the county's progressive politics are expressed in the quality of its public institutions, parks, and recreational facilities.

Sights

The **Sheridan County Museum** tel. (406) 765-2219, at the fairgrounds on the east side of Plentywood, contains memorabilia from frontier and homesteading days. On the museum grounds is the **Old Tractor Club,** a huge collection of vintage tractors and farm equipment.

Accommodations

The handsome **Sherwood Inn,** 515 W. 1st Ave., tel. (406) 765-2810, \$40 s, \$50 d, continues the illusion that there are forests here—a theme perpetuated by the presence of local lounge **Robin Hood's** and restaurant **Fryer Tuck's.** These businesses take Canadian dollars at face value. Free campsites are available at the city park at the north end of Box Elder Street.

Food

For light meals, try the **Alta Vista Cafe,** 564 W. 1st Ave., or **The Dairy Lunch,** 121 N. Main, tel. (406) 765-2441. For steaks, drinks, and dancing, try the **Sundance Diner,** 105 S. Main, tel. (406) 765-2350, or the **Blue Moon Supper Club,** an archetypal Montana steak house east of Plentywood on Hwy. 5, tel. (406) 765-2491.

Fort Union

Gravestones at Fort Buford hint at the turbulence of life (and death) on the frontier.

W. C. M⁀RAE

Information and Services
Information is available through **Plentywood Chamber of Commerce** at P.O. Box 4, Plentywood, MT 59254, tel. (406) 765-1607.

The **sheriff's office** can be contacted at (406) 765-1200. **Sheridan Memorial Hospital** is at 440 W. Laurel Ave., tel. (406) 765-1420.

Reach the **U.S. Border Patrol** at the Port of Raymond, tel. (406) 765-1852. The border is open 24 hours daily.

MEDICINE LAKE
NATIONAL WILDLIFE REFUGE

Medicine Lake lies in an old channel of the Missouri River. Before the ice ages, the Missouri flowed north from near Culbertson along this watercourse, eventually to empty into Hudson's Bay. Ice sheets blocked this channel about 15,000 years ago, and the Missouri sought more southerly outlets. Now the broad valley once dominated by the river holds a series of shallow lakes.

Established in 1935, the Medicine Lake National Wildlife Refuge, tel. (406) 789-2305, is a superior example of a prairie lake ecosystem. Containing 31,000 acres of lake, wetlands, and prairie, the refuge is home to enormous numbers of ducks (10 different species) and geese, as well as pelicans, herons, grebes, and cranes. Pronghorn and white-tailed deer are common along brushy coulees. In an area called the Sandhills are stands of chokecherry, buffalo berry, and native prairie grasses; hiking trails cross the rolling hills.

In 1976, 11,360 acres of the refuge were designated a wilderness area; no motorized boats are allowed on the lake. On the 18-mile auto tour around the lake, one of the 10 stops is the **Tepee Hills Site.** Here, rings of stone indicate the sites of ancient Indian lodges perhaps 4,000 years old.

FORT UNION AND VICINITY

"A judicious position for the purpose of trade" is what Capt. William Clark recorded at the confluence of Montana's two mighty east-flowing rivers, the Missouri and the Yellowstone. And traders quickly agreed. The American Fur Company built the region's grandest fur-trading post here in 1828, overlooking the juncture of the two rivers. Fort Union prospered in the 1830s and '40s as it became the undisputed focus of the Montana fur trade.

Today, the site is administered by the National Park Service, which is in the process of reconstructing the fort as it stood in 1851.

FORT UNION

History

Lewis and Clark camped at the confluence of the Missouri and Yellowstone rivers on their way into Montana and again as they exited a year later. Upon arriving in late April 1805, they were glad to have made it to this famous landmark, where the forks of the Missouri divide. The captains allotted each member of the Corps of Discovery a dram of whiskey in celebration; the fiddle came out, and the evening was spent in song and dance. The expedition continued up the Missouri River.

Though overwhelmed with mosquitoes, on his return trip Clark recognized the strategic nature of this site. These two enormous, easily navigable rivers drained a vast region rich in wildlife. Whoever controlled the Missouri and Yellowstone confluence controlled the wealth of the two river basins.

During the early 1800s, although the Americans controlled the trade on the Yellowstone and had made friends with the Crow Indians, the Missouri River all the way to Three Forks was controlled by the Blackfeet, who, through trade for firearms, were allied to the English in Canada. The Americans attempted again and again to establish trade with the Blackfeet, with uniformly bloody results.

In 1828, John Jacob Astor (of the American Fur Company) ordered Kenneth McKenzie to build a trading fort at the confluence of the Yel-

lowstone and Missouri, and to break the British hegemony over trade in the Missouri. McKenzie dispatched a trapper who spoke the Blackfeet language to induce warriors to accompany him back to Fort Union. Showered with gifts, the Blackfeet shortly entered into trade at Fort Union. With the Blackfeet suddenly compliant, and with steamboat service (starting in 1832) to Fort Union, all of Montana was open for exploitation. Until the 1850s, Fort Union reigned undisputed over Montana trade.

McKenzie, powerful, unscrupulous, and vain, built up Fort Union to be the most elegant habitation west of St. Louis. Liveried servants poured French wines into crystal goblets at his table; bagpipers piped as he entered his dining room; Native chiefs were sometimes greeted by McKenzie in full chain mail. The list of guests at Fort Union reads like a who's who of the American West: painters Karl Bodmer, George Catlin, and J.J. Audubon, Germany's Prince Maximilian, Father deSmet, Jim Bridger, and Governor Isaac Stevens.

The enormous success of Fort Union was not based solely on geography. Although it was illegal to sell alcohol to the Indians, McKenzie established a still at Fort Union and used alcohol to cement Native loyalty to his trading post and the United States. This was not a fine single malt that he traded to the Indians for furs: an early recipe for "Indian whiskey" cut McKenzie's homemade liquor with river water, cayenne pepper, tobacco, sagebrush, and a dash of strychnine.

The damage to the Plains Indians begun by alcohol at Fort Union was hastened by the arrival of the steamboat *Saint Peter* in 1837. The Assiniboine camped at Fort Union contracted smallpox from the crew; from here it spread quickly amongst the Indians in northern Montana. An estimated 15,000 of them—two-thirds of the tribe—died from the disease that year.

As fur-bearing animals in Montana approached extinction, Fort Union waned. By 1867, it had fallen into disrepair; some buildings were dismantled to build Fort Buford two miles downstream, and the remainder was sold by wood hawkers as steamboat fuel.

Sights and Events

Behind 20-foot-high palisades situated on the high banks of the Missouri River, the reconstructed **Fort Union Trading Post National Historic Site,** Buford Rte., Williston, ND 58801, tel. (701) 572-9083, is located only yards east of the Montana border in North Dakota and is again the focus of traffic at the Yellowstone and Missouri confluence. The **Bourgeois House** was the home of the fort's factor, or governor. The building was reconstructed as an exact replica of the surprisingly elegant 1851 house seen in paintings of the time; it now houses the visitor center and a good museum detailing the history of trade and early frontier life on the Missouri.

The National Park Service is in the process of rebuilding the rest of Fort Union. With the fortifications erected, the **Indian Trade House,** where Natives swapped beaver, mink, and marten skins for rifles, trinkets, and whiskey, is next scheduled for completion.

From the palisades, the Missouri and Yellowstone confluence can be seen, and it's easy to imagine steamboats pulling up to the embankment to load up with furs.

During the summer the **Fort Union Rendezvous** takes place. At this reenactment of an 1800s trappers' gathering, hundreds of buckskin-clad, musket-bearing, teepee-dwelling people gather to celebrate frontier-era skills and fortitude. There're also hatchet-throwing contests, food cooked à la frontier, and black-powder rifle shooting. Contact the fort for dates.

It's important to note that Fort Union Trading Post National Historic Site is not a commercial reconstruction: this isn't a theme park, and it's not just for kids. The fort is one of the most informative and satisfying stops in this part of Montana, definitely worth a detour. The Fort Union Trading Post National Historic Site is open daily 9 a.m.-5:30 p.m. central time. In summer, guided tours are offered; call ahead for a schedule, (701) 572-9083.

FORT BUFORD AND THE MISSOURI-YELLOWSTONE CONFLUENCE

Two miles farther into North Dakota are the remains of Fort Buford. Built in 1866 in the midst of hostile Sioux territory, the fort was conceived less as a military staging site than as a thorn in the side of the Sioux. About half the buildings at old Fort Union were dismantled and brought here to be rebuilt. Little remains but a few frame buildings and the fort's 1860s graveyard; reading the tombstones gives a fascinating glimpse of what life—and death—was like at this frontier outpost.

Just east of the ruins of Fort Buford along the same road is the confluence of the Yellowstone and Missouri rivers. A nice picnic area on a broad embankment overlooks this historic crossroads. A respectful stillness seems to encroach: these two prodigious rivers, meeting beneath yellow bluffs in a tangle of cottonwoods, willows, and a crisp dialogue of waters, have embraced almost all of Montana.

During the heyday of Fort Union, the confluence was farther upstream, near the fort. But in compliance with some fluvial law, their junction has drifted eastward.

There's a pleasant and free campground near the old cemetery.

CULBERTSON AND VICINITY

As the valleys of the Yellowstone and Missouri prepare to meet, a ridge of high, gray badland buttes rises to the south. To the north, the prairies begin their flat sweep to Canada.

The land here is rich, and grain production has dominated the local economy since the Great Northern Railroad brought homesteaders here to plow. If good soil wasn't enough in itself, nature also found time to bury a wealth of oil here.

Culbertson (pop. 819, elev. 1,921 feet) has come a long way since the day in 1892 when a young woman stepped from the train at Culbertson station and spent some time looking for the town; where she came from, two buildings did not constitute a town. Early ranchers engaged in horse ranching; the many military forts along this length of the Missouri demanded a large number of mounts. Now a pleasant farming town, Culbertson sits at the crossroads between northern Montana and Saskatchewan.

Cattle Drives

Join a Wild West cattle drive in the ranch country near Culbertson. Foss Cattle Drives, HC 69 Box 97, Culbertson, MT 59218, tel. (406) 787-

5559 offers five day drives in June, July, and August. The $1,350 charge includes all costs, including meals, lodging, horses, and activities.

Accommodations and Food
The **King's Inn,** 408 E. 6th, tel. (406) 787-6277 or (800) 823-4407), $30-35 s, $40-45 d, is a modern, attractive motel along Hwy. 2 with all queen beds. There's free camping in the city's **Bicentennial Park,** off 3rd Ave. E, you'll also find a playground and picnic area.

The **Wild West Diner,** 20 E. 6th, tel. (406) 787-5374, is a classic roadside cafe with a pleasingly unassuming menu. **M & M's Place,** 14 E. 6th, tel. (406) 787-5362, is a family restaurant/drive-in near the junction of Hwys. 2 and 16.

Information and Services
Contact the **Culbertson Chamber of Commerce** at P.O. Box 639, Culbertson, MT 59218, tel. (406) 787-5275. **Roosevelt Memorial Hospital** is at 818 2nd Ave. E, tel. (406) 787-6281.

HIGHWAY 200: FAIRVIEW TO CIRCLE

The highway system in Montana almost exclusively follows river valleys or old rail lines, but there's one marked departure from the general rule. Highway 200 enters eastern Montana near the Yellowstone-Missouri confluence and, like a sensible highway, follows the Yellowstone Valley to Sidney. Then, perversely, it lights off west across the prairie, toward nowhere in particular.

Between Sidney and Lewistown—a distance of almost 300 miles—Hwy. 200 passes through only three towns with gas pumps (Circle, Jordan, and Grassrange); their *combined* population approaches 1,500 people. As it connects up these remote enclaves of humanity, Hwy. 200 intersects a part of Montana often called the Big Lonely. Unpopulated, marginally productive, and often starkly beautiful, this is one of the last vast frontiers left in Montana.

Fairview
Squat on the Montana-Dakota state line and 11 miles east of Sidney is Fairview, a small farming town in the heart of sugar beet country. Fairview's principal claim to fame is that half the town is in North Dakota. There's camping in **Fairview City Park,** complete with RV hookups, a playground, a swimming pool, and picnic facilities.

SIDNEY AND VICINITY

Although stockmen had begun to establish ranches along this stretch of the Yellowstone Valley in the 1880s, it took the Lower Yellowstone Project, a federally funded irrigation project begun in 1904, to put Sidney (pop. 4,971, elev.

1,928 feet) on the map. The wide, fertile valley fell to the plow and hip waders. Sugar beets became the principal crop, inducing Holly Sugar to build a refinery here.

In the 1950s, Sidney found itself on the edge of the Williston Basin, a huge oil reserve. Sidney moved from sugar town to oil town seamlessly, accruing the economic benefits.

Sights
One of the largest community museums in this part of the state, the **Mondak Heritage Center,** 120 3rd Ave. SE, tel. (406) 482-3500, open Mon-Fri. noon-5p.m., Sat.-Sun. 1-5 p.m., combines the function of a regional art center and local history museum. In addition to displays of area history, the basement houses a re-creation of an old-time Sidney street.

Accommodations
The oil boom of the 1990s has had an ameliorative effect on the quality of lodging in Sidney. The **Lone Tree Inn,** 900 S. Central Ave., tel. (406) 482-4520, $46 d, and the **Richland Motor Inn,** 1200 S. Central Ave., tel. (406) 482-6400, $49 s, $54 d, are both modern, attractive, hotel-like lodging complexes.

Camping
Six miles east of Sidney on Hwy. 200 is **Richland Park.** This fishing-access area and campground is shaded by cottonwood and elm trees, and it provides latrines, potable water, picnic facilities, and a playground. If you plan to camp overnight, don't leave Sidney until you get permission and buy a $1 ticket from the Richland

SHEEPHERDERS' MONUMENTS

You'll notice them on the tops of gumbo buttes in eastern and central Montana: steep piles of rock rising like parapets against the skyline. Known as sheepherders' monuments, they are the work of Scottish and Irish herders whose sheep-tending jobs gave them lots of free time on hilltops.

In many ways, the open range lasted longer for sheep ranchers than for cattlemen. Before the proliferation of stock reservoirs, sheepherders (Montanans never use the term "shepherd") trailed sheep from pastures near "camp" to water every day. The range may have been fenced, but sheep needed the herder's extra inducement to behave sensibly. While at camp, herders typically kept watch over their flocks from nearby hills, mindful of predators and wayward sheep. Most ranches still employed herders—typically of Basque, Irish, or Scottish origin—through the 1950s.

Sheepherders always claim that they began to build cairns on the tops of high hills as windbreaks, but something more than utility went into it. Herders took pride in building the tallest, or the most tightly fitted, monument. Old-timers can still tell you which herder built every monument on the skyline.

Unfortunately, few ranches employ herders anymore, so remaining monuments have begun to slump a bit in their advanced age. And the monuments' survival is further threatened by the fact that vandals derive pleasure from toppling those convenient to highways. Please respect the age of

these constructions—and the isolation, work, and pride that went into them.

County Sheriff's Department, 110 2nd Ave. NW, tel. (406) 482-7700.

Food

For breakfast and light meals, try the **M & M,** south of Sidney on Hwy. 200, tel. (406) 482-1714, open daily 5 a.m.-7 p.m., or **Gulliver's,** 120 E. Main, tel. (406) 482-5175, open for breakfast and lunch. There's Mexican cuisine at **La Casita,** 102 E. Main, tel. (406) 482-1839, and Chinese at the **New China Restaurant,** 821 S. Central Ave., tel. (406) 482-6188, open 11 a.m.-9:30 p.m.

For steaks or seafood, go to the **South 40,** 209 2nd Ave., tel. (406) 482-4999, open Mon.-Thurs. 11 a.m.-10:30 p.m., Friday and Saturday 11 a.m.-11 p.m., Sunday 9 a.m.-10 p.m.; or the **Triangle,** south of Sidney on Hwy. 23, tel. (406) 482-4709, open nightly from 5 p.m.

Information and Services

Contact the **Sidney Chamber of Commerce** at 909 S. Central Ave., Sidney, MT 59270, tel. (406) 482-1916. **Community Memorial Hospital** is at 216 14th Ave. SW, tel. (406) 482-7700.

Transportation

Big Sky Airlines flies into Sidney twice a day from Billings; call (800) 237-7788 for details.

RICHEY

Between Sidney and Circle, Hwy. 200 climbs up over gravel hills and out of the Yellowstone drainage. The countryside opens up into a wide basin garnished here and there with ranch buildings. In good years, deer and pronghorn are abundant, making this area popular with hunters.

The urban instinct is weak here—the little crossroads of Richey (pop. 245) represents one of this region's few experiments in city living. Richey is a pleasant little hamlet dominated by grain elevators; the **Richey Historical Museum,** tel. (406) 773-5656, commemorates the homesteading boom that followed the Great Northern line into town. The **Farmer's Kitchen Cafe,** tel. (406) 773-5533, serves up tasty food designed to satisfy a ranch hand's appetite; it's open 6 a.m.-7 p.m.

CIRCLE

Circle (pop. 727, elev. 2,450 feet) got its start as a cattle town during the open-range years. The biggest outfit hereabouts had a simple circle for its brand, hence the name for the settlement that grew up beside it. Both the Northern Pacific and the Great Northern schemed about extending into Circle; this alone was sufficient to bring in grain-farming homesteaders who had plans for the flat grazing lands of the Redwater River Valley.

South of Circle are the Big Sheep Mountains, obviously named by people who hadn't seen a mountain recently. Actually little more than a series of high sandstone ridges, they mark the watershed between the Yellowstone and Missouri drainages. At one time, Audubon mountain sheep grazed along these chokecherry-laden bluffs. They live on in the name of the mountains only: like the buffalo, early frontiersmen found them an easy, tasty prey and hunted them to extinction.

Sights
The **McCone County Museum,** west of town on Hwy. 200, tel. (406) 485-2414, contains displays commemorating the Circle's frontier history. On the museum grounds are a restored country schoolhouse, an old church, and a caboose from the Northern Pacific.

Accommodations and Food
The **Traveler's Inn,** at the junction of Hwys. 13 and 200, tel. (406) 485-3323, is Circle's sole lodging option. Rooms are $29 s, $34 d, though you can take $3 off the price if you pay with cash. There's RV parking at **Scheer's Trailer Court** on 1st Ave. N, tel. (406) 485-2285.

It's some kind of judgment when the best place to eat is the **Tastee-Freez,** on the east end of town, tel. (406) 485-3674, but it's a pretty good Tastee-Freez. Otherwise, try the **Wooden Nickel** on Main St., tel. (406) 485-2575, open 10 a.m.-10 p.m.

Information and Services
Write the **Circle Chamber of Commerce** at Circle, MT 59215, tel. (406) 485-2414. For emergencies, contact the **sheriff's office,** tel. (406) 485-3405.

There are two service stations, open till 9 p.m. For **road conditions,** call (406) 365-2314.

THE BIG OPEN

West of Circle, the farms thin out, the landscape coarsens into badlands, and signs of human habitation grow more scarce. From here to the banks of the Musselshell River 150 miles west, Hwy. 200 traverses a vaguely defined region of ranches, gumbo buttes, sagebrush, coyotes, and cowboys. It's known by many names: Big Dry Country, the North Side, Jordan Country, the Big Empty, the Big Lonesome, and the Big Open.

The last of these gained currency a few years ago when environmental activists proposed turning the area into an enormous wildlife park; it's hard to imagine how much more of a wilderness this forlorn and lonesome land could be. Garfield County, nearly the size of Connecticut, encompasses much of this area; it has the lowest population density in the state, with not quite one person for every three square miles of land.

But if you asked one of the locals, you'd be told there's not much room left. Out here, under a trademark big sky, where single farms and ranches engulf a whole township's worth of land, people get used to taking up space.

For better or worse, this is one of the last outposts of the frontier spirit: cowboy hats are mandatory, the bar doubles as the community hall, and the rodeo club is the biggest extracurricular activity at the high school. Here, more than anywhere else in the state, there is still some Wild left in the West.

JORDAN AND VICINITY

No one comes to Jordan (pop. 445, elev. 2,800 feet) because of its interesting history or architecture. Like other late-germinating communities, many of the first settlers were outlaws. Homesteaders drifted through desultorily, recoiling when they discovered what a nasty piece of business the Big Dry Country was. Big ranches and big families have always ruled the rangelands. And now, what makes Jordan exceptional is that it never bothered to change.

Jordan is remote. In 1931, only eight households had running water. Rural homes didn't have electrical service until 1952, and ranches didn't get telephones until 1956. Public transportation? Never had it, probably never will. The most isolated county seat in the lower 48 states, Jordan is 175 miles from the nearest major airport, 85 miles from the nearest bus line, 115 miles from the nearest train line. The local high school serves such a vast area that it maintains one of only two public coed dormitories in the United States.

Once discovered, Jordan has always fascinated journalists. A New York radio station in 1930 identified Jordan as "the lonesomest town in the world." A local ranchwoman for years contributed a column called "Timber Creek Riffles" to the *Wall Street Journal.* Jordan made it to the front page of the nation's papers in the 1970s when, in the aftermath of a break-in at the local drugstore, the sheriff deputized the men in the local bar as his posse. The sheriff got his man, but only after the gun-toting mob gave a visiting Associated Press journalist an eyeful of western color.

A famous TV investigative reporter showed up in town a few years later to film a story about the farm/ranch crisis. Locals in the bar didn't much like his flashy ways; he conducted his on-screen interviews with his nose in plaster.

The Montana Freemen
Unsurprisingly, given the thin veneer of society, the militia-like Freeman's movement has found a number of adherents. Jordan again made the national press in 1993 when the local militia issued "dead-or-alive" bounties for the duly elected county sheriff, attorney, and a Federal Judge. The conflict between the local adherents of Freeman philosophy and local authorities deepened when anti-government zealots from across the West started streaming in to a 920-acre ranch west of Jordan, to hole up and establish a Freeman world headquarters known as "Justus Township." This self-declared free state administered under Freeman authority developed its own court and laws, elected officials, and bizarre banking practices. The Freemen, in general, refused to acknowledge the authority of any governing body except their own.

As the actions of the Freeman swerved from paranoid to nutty, the impact on the community intensified. Many of the people in the Freeman compound had family members who were pro-

Settled by outlaws, hard-scrabble Jordan hasn't changed much since 1900. The most isolated county seat in the contiguous US, it is today 175 miles from the nearest airport.

foundly anti-Freeman. Brother was pitted against brother, father against son, with the Freemen issuing bounties and arrest warrants for old friends and family alike. Many people around Jordan received death threats or were threatened with arrest and trial in a Freeman-style "common-law" court. With the Freemen increasingly wild-eyed and armed to the teeth, it was easy to believe that a bloodbath was imminent.

The FBI had been monitoring the Jordan Freemen for some time (in fact, operatives had infiltrated the compound posing as fellow anti-government kooks). Finally, in early 1996, the federal agents moved against the Freemen, capturing two of the ringleaders. The rest of the Freemen, numbering in the twenties, retreated to their heavily armed ranch compound, and the standoff began.

Within days, almost 600 Federal law enforcement agents were in place in Jordan (the county fairgrounds was Operations Central), and as many as 200 journalists from around the world crushed into the little town, occupying every motel room, spare bedroom, and apartment for miles.

Obviously, life changed pretty quickly for tiny Jordan and its usually sanguine citizens. After enduring interview after interview with visiting film crews and a town suddenly overrun with strangers, many of the locals grew weary of the whole Freeman nonsense—you couldn't get a drink in the bar without a microphone being stuck in your face. After a couple of months without a resolution in sight, an area rancher drew up a petition that urged the FBI to use "reasonable force" to end the standoff. Within a couple of days, more than 200 Jordan-area citizens had signed the document. With the locals obviously growing restless, the FBI finally made a move. They turned off the Freemen's electricity and phone service. Within a matter of days, the Freemen began negotiations to give themselves up.

The standoff lasted 81 days. Remarkably, not a shot was fired during the entire confrontation, robbing the Freemen of guaranteed martyr status, seemingly a goal of hardened anti-government extremists motivated by events at Ruby Ridge, Idaho, and Waco, Texas.

In 1998, the Freemen were tried in Billings. In 1998, a Montana jury found 8 of the Freemen guilty of 23 federal felonies. Notably, only one of the Freemen from Jordan itself was convicted of federal offenses.

The Freeman issue is still a very potent topic of discussion in Jordan, but don't be surprised if the locals don't want to talk about the situation with strangers. Family ties are still strained, and while not many local people agreed with the Freemen's sentiments (don't assume that everyone from Jordan is a sympathizer; in fact, the truth is quite the opposite), the sense of community fragmentation and hostility that the standoff produced will take a long time to dissipate.

Sights
Despite its reputation as the last stronghold of the Old West, Jordan is normally a friendly town with adequate facilities for the traveler. It is central to great hunting and to recreation and wildlife viewing on the C.M. Russell Wildlife Refuge and Fort Peck Lake.

The **Garfield County Museum,** just east of town, tel. (406) 557-2517, offers both historic and prehistoric overviews of the locality. A replica of a triceratops found north of town, an actual triceratops head, and other fossil remains are the highlights here. Also on display are homesteader memorabilia, early photos, and a restored one-room school. Open daily in afternoons, June 1-Sept. 1.

About eight miles west of Jordan is a curious landmark known as **Smokey Butte.** This promontory, which rises a thousand feet above surrounding prairie, is the easternmost of the many igneous intrusions that rose into mountains in central Montana. More curiously, the rock that makes up Smokey Butte, armolcolite, has never been found elsewhere except in rocks collected on the moon.

Accommodations and Food
One of Jordan's old hotels, the **Garfield,** on the corner of Main St. and Hwy. 200, tel. (406) 557-6215, is still in business and offers rooms in the hotel or in newer motel units; $28 s, $32 d. **Fellman's Motel,** on Hwy. 200, tel. (406) 557-2209, $42 s, $47 d, is Jordan's other option. Campers should go to **Kamp Katie,** just west of the bridge, tel. (406) 557-2851, a pleasant-enough campground on the banks of Big Dry Creek.

The **QD's,** tel. (406) 557-2301, west of Jordan on Hwy. 200, is Jordan's only full-service restaurant, open daily 6 a.m.-10 p.m.

Information and Services
Contact the **Jordan Commercial Club** for trav-

DINOSAUR COUNTRY

The dun-colored badlands that rise along the Missouri River, fantastically carved by erosion into sharp canyons and buttes, contain one of the world's richest chronicles of early life on earth. Paleontologists discovered some of the first and most important remains of dinosaurs in these desiccated hills. Today, the annual arrival of the summer "bone diggers" is almost an institution in Jordan.

In 1902, Dr. Barnum Brown, of the American Museum of Natural History, journeyed to the Jordan area to search for dinosaur remains. Brown cut quite a figure: he reported to the digs in a starched white collar and polished knee boots, popping his gold pince-nez on and off. The existence of large dinosaurs was still a matter of conjecture in scientific circles—the giant reptiles certainly didn't form part of the popular imagination.

What attracted Brown to this area was its Cretaceous-era badlands. Laid down by shallow, marshy seas about 70 million years ago, these layers of mudstone, shale, and sandstone were normally covered by thick layers of more recent sediment. When the Missouri River cut its way through the badlands, it opened up a gorge through millions of years of geologic history. Here, in the arid bluffs of Garfield County, the earth had stored its memories of vanished life. In the stratified layers of sediment revealed by erosion, Brown reasoned, one should be able to find the band corresponding to the "Age of the Dinosaurs."

In a gumbo escarpment on Hell Creek, Brown found much more than he was looking for: two skeletons of *Tyrannosaurus rex*. The fossil-rich Cretaceous sediments, now called the Hell Creek Formation in honor of Garfield County's dinosaur haven, has continued to yield specimens. In 1988, a Jordan couple found the most complete tyrannosaurus skeleton to date (the seventh found in the area) along the shore of Fort Peck Lake. Triceratops has almost become Jordan's dinosaur mascot. And

aquatic duck-billed dinosaurs and the mosasaurus—a sea-serpent-like dinosaur—have also been found in the Hell Creek Formation. Smaller finds—dinosaur eggs, petrified mollusks, and fish—are common.

Later scientists have come to Jordan not to dig bones but to research theories. It was commonly known that dinosaurs (and, in fact, most early lifeforms) were found only below a smudgy black band in the gumbo buttes, for instance. This thin layer of lignite coal in fact demarcates the Hell Creek and Fort Union sedimentary formations. Dr. Walter Alvarez, from UC Berkeley, analyzed this layer closely, found that it contained traces of iridium embedded in similar sediments worldwide, and in 1979 proposed his asteroid-impact theory. According to Alvarez, a massive asteroid struck the earth, throwing dust into the atmosphere in such vast quantities that it caused a global winter during which the dinosaurs became extinct.

Other scientists dispute the asteroid theory. Eager to prevail, two research groups are currently accumulating evidence—here in the badlands—for competing dinosaur-extinction theories.

JIM MASTERSON

---

el info at P.O. Box 370, Jordan, MT 59337, tel. (406) 557-2232. For emergencies, call the **sheriff's office** at (406) 557-2882. The **C.M. Russell Wildlife Refuge** maintains a wildlife station in Jordan along Hwy. 200; tel. (406) 557-6145. Contact the **BLM** at (406) 557-2376; the office is on Main Street.

For local **road conditions**, call (406) 365-2314.

THE CHARLES M. RUSSELL NATIONAL WILDLIFE REFUGE, EASTERN UNIT

Known to locals, with widely varying degrees of affection, as the "C.M.R.," the 1.2-million-acre Charles M. Russell National Wildlife Refuge flanks the entire northern edge of Garfield County along the Missouri River. One of the largest refuges in the nation, the C.M.R. is home to an abundance of wildlife, including elk and bighorn sheep, which were once common on the prairies.

Garfield County contains more of the refuge than any other county; feelings run high here about having such a huge wilderness area (and its champion, the Federal Government) for a neighbor. Many local residents are still bitter about being displaced from their land along the Missouri when Fort Peck was built and about their grazing land in the Breaks being turned into de facto wilderness, and are unhappy when what land they have left is overrun by errant herds of deer, pronghorn, elk, and worst of all, coyotes.

Unfortunately, heavy-handed interference on the part of the government and sheer old-fashioned cussedness on the part of the locals combine to make the C.M.R. much less accessible to visitors than it should be. Quite apart from the incredible wealth of wildlife—lacking only grizzly bears and wolves to replicate the Missouri River flora and fauna experienced by Lewis and Clark—the Missouri Breaks are dramatic and austere badlands still full of outlaw lore. And at the center of the refuge is Fort Peck Lake, one of the largest manmade lakes in the world, important as a migratory waterfowl stopover, to say nothing about its stellar fishing and recreational possibilities.

There is public access to the refuge and Fort Peck Lake at two sites in Garfield County. The most popular is **Hell Creek State Park,** 26 miles north of Jordan, tel. (406) 232-0900 for information. Developed as a recreation area for local anglers and boaters, Hell Creek offers a campground, marina, tel. (406) 557-2345, store, and cabins. The road in, best attempted in dry weather, passes through rugged badlands. Elk, deer, waterfowl, eagles, foxes, and coyotes are pervasive. Entrance is $4 per vehicle, camping $11 per night.

Farther afield, along a dodgier road, is **Devil's Creek Recreation Area,** with undeveloped campsites, about 40 miles northwest of Jordan. Here, the gumbo buttes, fringed with ponderosa pines, drop away in canyons to the lake's shore. Both sites offer good scouting for fossils.

Information and Services
A regional office for the Charles M. Russell Wildlife Refuge, tel. (406) 538-8706, is in Lewistown. The mailing address is P.O. Box 110, Lewistown, MT 59597.

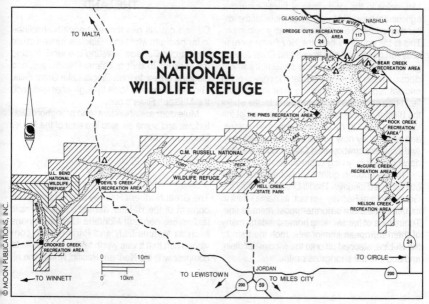

DOVER PUBLICATIONS, INC.

NORTH-CENTRAL MONTANA

From the dramatic eastern front of the Rocky Mountains to the long views of the Hi-Line, this agricultural heart of Montana has more for the visitor than a look at a topographic map would imply. This is the country where the Nez Perce were finally run down by Army troops and Chief Joseph gave his remarkable surrender speech. It's where dinosaur nests have revised scientific opinion of the ancient reptiles, transforming their image from flesh-ripping brutes into loving parents. It's where the Blackfeet have held fast to a small part of the land they used to race across with their horses, and where they now host a big annual powwow. And it's where cowboy artist Charlie Russell settled down to work in his log-cabin studio.

There's enough quiet history here to keep a buff occupied for days. The Hi-Line was built by the Great Northern Railway—in fact, its name refers to its being the state's northernmost railroad line. Thousands of hardworking homesteaders, many of them European immigrants, took the train to the Hi-Line, stepped off onto the windswept plain, and dug into the shortgrass prairie.

THE LAND

Oil and natural gas formed beneath anticlines in far northern Montana. Glaciers moved down from arctic Canada, leveling the land, forcing the Missouri to shift its channel southward, and plugging outlets to form Glacial Lake Great Falls. The Milk River now flows through what was once the Missouri River's bed.

Mule deer are abundant, and pronghorn, waterfowl, and some elk also live east of the Rocky Mountain Front.

HISTORY

The Great Northern Railway defined the development of the Hi-Line. James J. Hill had rails laid across northern Montana after Montanans such as Marcus Daly and Paris Gibson convinced him that it was worth taking the trouble to compete with the Northern Pacific, whose line al-

THE MISSILES ON THE PRAIRIE

Scattered among 23,000 acres of prairie surrounding Great Falls, tucked away in fields or meadows, are some 200 unremarkable enclosures of chain-link fencing and cement, more or less perfectly innocuous in appearance. But each of these facilities is home to a Minuteman intercontinental ballistic missile. Malmstrom Air Force Base, in Great Falls, is the headquarters for the Minuteman missiles.

The missiles were located in Montana for a number of reasons. Their fuel is very sensitive to humidity, making the arid prairies a natural habitat. Also, the average elevation of 3,500 feet gives the missiles a head start, yielding a six-percent fuel savings. And the

fact that not many people live hereabouts probably didn't hurt, either.

Each subterranean silo consists of an 80-foot-deep tube, launch equipment, and missile. The silo door *alone* weighs 108 tons. The launch facilities are controlled from a nearby underground chamber. Launch-control chambers have walls 4.5 feet thick and dangle in a 90-foot-deep pit, suspended by cables that allow the chamber to swing three feet in any direction.

Since the end of the cold war, the Minutemen have been deactivated. Once staffed 24 hours a day in readiness for enemy attack, the sites now slumber, awaiting the arrival of another superpower threat. A flick of a switch would bring the system back to full readiness.

---

ready ran across the southern part of the state. In order to keep the railcars filled, settlers were recruited, both for Gibson's town, Great Falls, and for the northern tier, which would be coaxed into producing grain.

Hill and Professor Thomas Shaw were proponents of dryland farming. Shaw developed a theory that called for deep plowing and unrelenting cultivation of the land, a method that was practiced widely and led to wide-scale erosion. Precious topsoil, catching a windy ride, blew completely out of the state.

Between 1910 and 1918, homesteaders, sometimes derogatorily called "honyockers," swarmed to Montana for free land. Typically a family would get off the train, which had a boxcar full of their possessions, pay a "finder" $20 to lead them to their homestead, and start plowing. During the middle of the decade, the homesteader's life looked good. Wet weather helped crops to flourish, and WW I inflated the price of grain. But when drought set in in 1918 and didn't let up for years, homesteaders scattered almost as fast as the dry topsoil.

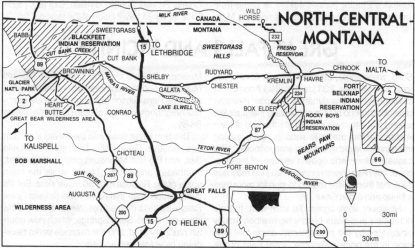

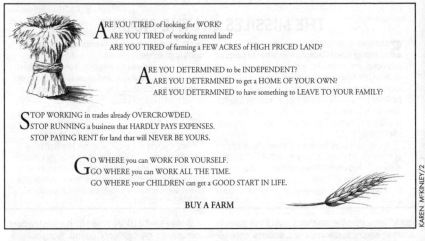

ARE YOU TIRED of looking for WORK?
ARE YOU TIRED of working rented land?
ARE YOU TIRED of farming a FEW ACRES of HIGH PRICED LAND?

ARE YOU DETERMINED to be INDEPENDENT?
ARE YOU DETERMINED to get a HOME OF YOUR OWN?
ARE YOU DETERMINED to have something to LEAVE TO YOUR FAMILY?

STOP WORKING in trades already OVERCROWDED.
STOP RUNNING a business that HARDLY PAYS EXPENSES.
STOP PAYING RENT for land that will NEVER BE YOURS.

GO WHERE you can WORK FOR YOURSELF.
GO WHERE you can WORK ALL THE TIME.
GO WHERE your CHILDREN can get a GOOD START IN LIFE.

BUY A FARM

KAREN MCKINLEY/2

Wheat farming has remained a major part of the local economy, and one way of dealing with the dry, windy climate is the strip agriculture you'll see wherever wheat's been planted, in which one strip of land is cultivated and the adjoining strip lies fallow.

PRACTICALITIES

Transportation
Amtrak's Empire Builder, taking its name from James J. Hill's sobriquet, crosses northern Montana four times a week traveling between Chicago and the west coast with stops in Havre, Shelby, Cut Bank, and Browning. Four major airlines serve Great Falls, and **Rimrock Stage** buses, tel. (406) 453-1541, connect Great Falls with Havre, Shelby, and Cut Bank.

Information
Travel Montana provides excellent free travel information. Most of the Hi-Line falls within their Charlie Russell Country division. Call (800) 527-5348 for a free travel guide of the region.

GREAT FALLS AND VICINITY

Solid, wholesome, and prosperous, Great Falls (pop. 57,758, elev. 3,333 feet) suffers if compared to Montana's more dynamic and cosmopolitan cities. It's the kind of uneventful place that feels like a good place to raise a family. It's the kind of town whose citizens prefer to shop in malls, leaving the handsome old downtown area to molder. The casual explorer who doesn't venture off the long, bleak 10th Ave. South commercial strip may well think that there's little reason to stop for more than a fill-up and a diet Coke.

However, look again. To start with, there's rich Lewis and Clark history here, albeit mostly obliterated by the hydroelectric dams that now rope in the once-awesome Great Falls of the Missouri. There's also the Charles M. Russell Museum, and the unexpected—contemporary art at the Paris Gibson Museum. There are beautiful neighborhoods full of mansions, many now B&Bs.

The Sun River flows into the Missouri at 10th Ave. South in Great Falls. The Highwood, Little Belt, and Big Belt Mountains crop up to the east, southeast, and south of town, while the main spine of the Rockies runs 50 miles west. But it's the Missouri River that has always defined Great Falls—the falls themselves, remembered in the city's name, the Giant Springs, which now nourish hatchery trout, and the riverside parks beckoning bicyclists and anglers.

HISTORY

When sheets of glacial ice covered the northern Montana plains 15,000 years ago, present-day Great Falls was under 600 feet of water. Ice dams backed up Glacial Lake Great Falls between Great Falls and Cut Bank, spilling out into the Shonkin Sag. Blackfeet controlled the area when Lewis and Clark spent June 15-July 15, 1805, negotiating the Great Falls of the Missouri, actually portaging 18 miles in 13 days. A grizzly bear chased Lewis into the Missouri at one point; he was also impressed that there were "not less than 10,000 buffalo in a circle of two miles."

Paris Gibson first visited the river-bend site of present-day Great Falls in 1880 and quickly set to building a city there. He conferred with James J. Hill, of the Great Northern Railway, and in 1887 the Montana Central Railroad was built through Great Falls, connecting the Great Northern line to the mining centers farther south.

The Anaconda Company came into town in 1908 and built a copper-reduction plant, powered by a dam on Black Eagle Falls. The cheap electricity generated by the Black Eagle Dam and the others that followed on other falls spurred Great Falls early on to an industrial economy, with attendant labor union and political imbroglios.

SIGHTS

Be warned that street addresses are a little confusing in Great Falls. Avenues run east and west, streets run north and south, and both are named almost exclusively with numbers. Central Ave. divides north from south; most of the city lies east of the Missouri River; streets west of the river wear a "W" as part of their names.

Lewis & Clark National Historic Trail Interpretive Center

In 1998, the 5,500-square-foot Lewis & Clark National Historic Trail Interpretive Center, tel. (406) 791-7717, opened on a cliff overlooking the Missouri's Great Falls. This $6 million facility instantly transformed Great Falls into a major Montana destination, giving the local tourist trade a badly needed focus.

The center itself doesn't break new ground for anyone familiar with the Lewis and Clark Expedition, and the displays often seem a little cursory, given the complexity of the history involved. But it's

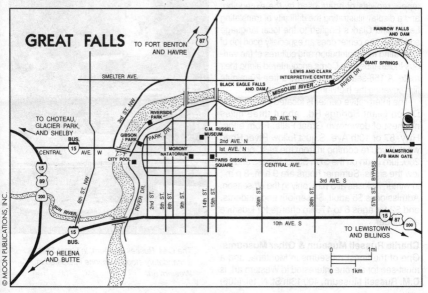

a laudable enterprise just to *present* the complex issues represented by the Corps of Discovery: Enlightenment high ideals, American cultural imperialism (especially over Native Americans), the devastating extractive economic practices that followed, and the sheer catch-your-breath adventure, to name a few.

The exhibits follow the course of the journey, from St. Louis up the Missouri, into Montana and to the Great Falls, which the explorers reached in June of 1895. The Corps spent a hellacious month portaging their boats around the Falls of the Missouri River, which is here lined by cliffs. The two-story diorama of Corps members pulling canoes up the cliff is an especially vivid illustration of the fortitude of these early explorers. Try your hand at pulling a specially weighted rope meant to reproduce the effort required in the portages, and let your thoughts marvel that these men—dressed in just moccasins and buckskins, and living on rations—had the strength to pull these boats for 18 miles, filled with a total of about a ton of gear.

The maze-like exhibits follow the expedition's journey across the Rockies, to the Pacific, and then back down the Missouri through Montana and back to St. Louis. Along the way, the center features a Mandan Indian earth lodge, a Shoshone Indian tepee, replicas of boats used by the expedition, and a display illustrating the difficulty of translating Lewis' and Clark's English to the local language and back. The center does an especially good job of illustrating the contribution and cultures of the various Indian tribes the Corps encountered along their route. A 158-seat theater shows a free 20-minute film covering the highlights of the expedition.

The interpretive center is located just off River Dr, on Giant Springs Rd., about three miles northest of downtown Great Falls. From either Hwy. 87 or 10th Ave. S, just follow River Road west. If you're coming in from the east, on Hwy. 200, turn north on the 57th Street bypass and follow the signs. Summer hours are 9 a.m.-8 p.m.; in winter, it closes at 5 p.m. only in the off season. Admission is $5 adult, $4 seniors and students, and $2 for ages 6 to 17. No charge for kids five and under.

Charlie Russell Museum & Other Museums

One of the finest museums in Montana, and a must-see for anyone interested in Western art, is **C.M. Russell Museum,** 400 13th St. N, tel. (406)

727-8787. Charlie Russell's brilliant colors are astounding and complex, and seeing the original paintings is a real treat. The museum complex includes Russell's log-cabin studio and house; there's also a good bookshop and reproduction gallery. Admission is $4 for adults, $2 for students, and $3 for seniors. Summer hours are Mon.-Sat. 9 a.m.-6 p.m., Sunday 1-5 p.m. Winter hours are Tues.-Sat. 10 a.m.-5 p.m., Sunday 1-5 p.m.

A few blocks from the Russell Museum, at 1400 1st Ave. N, tel. (406) 727-8255, the **Paris Gibson Square Museum of Art** mounts some surprisingly forward-thinking art exhibits. Housed in a handsome old school, the gallery is open during the summer Mon.-Fri. 10 a.m.-5 p.m. and Tuesday 7-9 p.m.; from Labor Day until Memorial Day, hours are Tues.-Fri. 10 a.m.-5 p.m.; free admission. Two gift shops in the art center specialize in local crafts; there's also a great lunch spot.

The C.M. Russell Museum, in Great Falls, is a mandatory stop for anyone interested in Western art.

The **Cascade County Historical Society,** tel. (406) 452-3462, shares the Paris Gibson building and the museum space there includes historical exhibits. Historical Society members also conduct tours of the Ulm Pishkun, Fort Shaw, and other local historic sites.

Other Sights
Malmstrom Air Force Base has a museum and park open to the public Mon.-Sat. noon-3 p.m., tel. (406) 731-4044. Tours of the base leave from the main gate (2nd Ave. S) on Friday noon-2:30 p.m. Call (406) 731-2427 for tour information.

Twelve miles north of town on Hwy. 87, the 12,300-acre **Benton Lake Wildlife Refuge** harbors nearly 200 bird species, including shorebirds, snow geese, tundra swans, burrowing and short-eared owls, and mammals such as rabbits, deer, and long-tailed weasels. Visitors can stop by April 1-Oct. 31 during the daytime.

Turn off I-15 at the Ulm exit, 15 miles south of Great Falls, and follow the state park signs six miles along good gravel roads to the **Ulm Pishkun State Monument.** Tepee rings abound near the 30-foot-high buffalo jump, and there are supposed to be some pictographs there, too. Poke around the base of the cliff for decaying buffalo bones, but wear boots to guard against the prickly pear and rattlesnakes, and don't carry off any souvenirs—the area is protected by the State Antiquities Act. A prairie-dog town and picnic area share the *pishkun* site (steep cliffs that the Indians drove the buffalo over), which is closed Oct.-May.

Springs, Rivers, and Dams
Everywhere you turn in Great Falls, there's a park, and the keynote one—the River's Edge Trail, a greenway along the Missouri and River Drive—is worth a special visit (see below).

The **Giant Springs Heritage Park** is three miles from downtown, and the Fish, Wildlife, and Parks Visitor Center there has good brochures describing Lewis and Clark's portage of the falls, as well as information and exhibits on fishing and hunting.

Giant Springs, a gushing natural springs that captured the attention of Lewis and Clark, is part of the Giant Springs Heritage Park. The genesis of this 134,000-gallon-per-minute fountain is in the Little Belt Mountains southeast of Great Falls. Exposed Madison limestone absorbs mountain

Ulm Pishkun buffalo "jump" is a state monument.

snowmelt and rain, which then drains and flows through fissures to Great Falls, where it surges up and spews into the Missouri River. The mineral-rich water has proven to be a good fish-breeding medium, and there's a trout hatchery a stone's throw away from the springs. This is an enchanting place to picnic or just relax amid leafy lawns and the sounds of rushing water.

Downstream from the springs are overlooks onto the dams that harness Black Eagle and Rainbow falls. Both of these dams have preserved the essential nature of the waterfalls. From the roadside overlook, look across the Missouri to the town of **Black Eagle,** a company town that was built up around the turn of the century to serve the copper-reduction works.

Head north on Hwy. 87 to visit the **Ryan Dam,** which marks the site of the Great Falls of the Missouri, described by Meriwether Lewis as "the grandest sight I ever beheld," with its roily cascades, foamy spray, and spiky rock projections.

RECREATION

Bike or jog along the Missouri River on the **River's Edge Trail,** stretching from the 10th Ave. Bridge to Giant Springs Heritage State Park and on past Crooked Falls. This rails-to-trails path has just been lengthened by an additional 6,000 feet. With over eight miles of paved pathway and an additional 17 miles of single-track trail suitable for hiking or mountain biking, the River's Edge Trail is a great recreational asset to the city, and a good place for travelers to take in the both the urban and natural history of the area.

Swim outdoors (or take one of the water slides) at **Mitchell Pool,** just south of the 1st Ave. Bridge on River Drive. Open swimming hours are 1-8 p.m., adult swim is noon-1 p.m. Admission is $2 for adults, 75 cents for children. Serious lap swimmers may prefer the beautifully named, carefully maintained **Morony Natatorium** at 12th St. N and 1st Ave. North.

The Great Falls **Dodgers** are the Pioneer League farm team of the Los Angeles Dodgers. Minor-league baseball fans can catch them throughout the summer at Legion Park. Call (406) 452-5311 for schedule and ticket information.

The **R.O. Speck Golf Course** is a busy 18-hole public course on River Rd. next door to Legion Park. Across the river in Black Eagle, the **Anaconda Hills Golf Course** has recently expanded to 18 holes.

Some 25 miles south of town in Cascade, the **Lazy D Flyfishing Lodge,** tel. (406) 468-9391 offers both full fishing packages and budget trips (rooms run $65 d on this plan). Most of the fishing is on the upper Missouri and Smith rivers. During the winter, call the Lazy D at (503) 458-6083.

For fishing gear and tips, stop by the **High Plains Outfitter,** at 205 9th Ave. S, tel. (406) 727-2119.

LODGING AND FOOD

B&Bs

Great Falls' B&Bs are in a beautiful residential neighborhood between downtown and the C.M. Russell Museum. The best of them, the **Old Oak Inn,** 709 4th Ave. N, tel. (406) 727-5782 or (800) 888-727-5782, is a 1908 mansion. The four guest rooms and one suite range $55-95.

Hotels and Motels

Great Falls lodgings are found basically in two areas. A number of older well-maintained hotels and motels are downtown, while along the 10th Avenue strip, amid the casinos, car lots, and malls, you'll find a great number of inexpensive motels, as well as several new upscale motel complexes.

Downtown: These hotels and motels are older and offer substantial savings over the establishments out on the strip. The pleasant **Mid-Town Motel,** 526 2nd Ave. N, tel. (406) 453-2411 or (800) 457-2411, $42 s, $47 d, has a local's-favorite restaurant and bakery on-site and accepts pets. **Triple Crown Motor Inn,** 621 Central Ave., tel. (406) 727-8300 or (800) 722-8300, $43 s, $49 d, offers complimentary continental breakfast, tanning beds, and a casino/lounge.

O'Haire Motor Inn, 17 7th St. S; tel. (406) 454-2141 or (800) 332-9819; $49 s, $65 d, features an indoor pool, restaurant, lounge, and indoor parking. Some two-bedroom suites available. **Best Western Ponderosa Inn** is right downtown at 220 Central Ave. tel. (406) 761-3410 or (800) 266-3410. With rooms for $54 s, $62 d, the Ponderosa offers an outdoor pool, sauna, restaurant, lounge, casino, microwaves and refrigerators in all rooms, and small dogs are okay.

10th Ave. S.: All the usual chain hotels have properties along the 10th Ave. S. strip. You'll also find a lot of older motor-court motels. In all but the busiest weekends, you'll have no trouble finding a room without reservations. Just remember that most of 10th Ave. S. is a busy six-lane highway. Here's a cross-section representing some of the better choices. **Budget Inn,** 2 Treasure State Dr (I-15 and 10th Ave. S.), tel. (406) 453-1602 or (800) 362-4842, has rooms at $49 s, $55 d, and offers a continental breakfast. **Wagon Wheel Motel,** 2620 10th Ave. S., tel. (406) 761-1300 or (800) 800-6483, $42 d, has an indoor pool and some theme rooms. The **Super 8 Lodge,** 1214 13th St. S, tel. (406) 727-7600, $61 d, sits back off the strip and offers a continental breakfast. A good mid-price choice.

Two of Great Falls' best lodging options are also along the strip (both allow pets). The **Best Western Heritage Inn,** 1700 Fox Farm Rd., tel. (406) 761-1900 or (800) 548-8256, $66 s, $72 d, is a quarter-mile off the highway and is the city's largest hotel. The recreational facilities are noteworthy, with two indoor pools, hot tubs, saunas, and a game room. Also on site is a restaurant and a lounge/casino. Rooms are nicely furnished; executive suites with kitchenettes and ironing boards are available. The **Town House Inn,** 1411 10th Ave. S, tel. (406) 761-4600 or (800) 442-4667, $80 s or d, has stylish rooms (including some that are in effect efficiency apartments), plus a casino, pool, sauna, hot tub, and restaurant. The Town House is near Holiday Village Mall, the area's largest shopping center.

Food and Drink

For a morning jump start, **Morning Light Coffee Roasters,** 900 2nd Ave. N., tel. (406) 453-8443, has espresso drinks and pastries and is a convivial place to start the day. They have a second location in a small downtown mall at 525 Central Ave., tel. (406) 453-3206. Another good downtown spot for a light breakfast is the **Daily Grind,** at 320 1st Ave. N, tel. (406) 452-4529. Order breakfast 24-hours a day at **Tracy's,** 127 Central Ave., tel. (406) 453-6108, a Great Falls institution.

In some ways, Great Falls is a better place to eat lunch than dinner. The **Museum Cafe** at the Paris Gibson Square Center for Contemporary Arts is a gem of a lunch spot, open Tues.-Fri. for lunch only. The well-thought-out set menu changes weekly; a three-course lunch is $7. Reservations, tel. (406) 727-8255, are mandatory. **Club Gourmet** serves Mexican food and light entrees for lunch only at the venerable and well-preserved old bar, Club Cigar, 208 Central Ave., tel. (406) 727-8011. New and recommended is **Penny's Gourmet To Go,** 815 Central Ave., tel. (406) 453-7070. The storefront end of a catering business, Penny's offers soups, sandwiches, pasta, and salads at lunchtime. You can choose to eat in or take out.

At night downtown, dining choices are limited. The Great Falls branch of **Bert and Ernie's,** is located in an old brick storefront at 300 1st Ave. S, tel. (406) 453-0601. Stick to the burgers and microbrewed beers. **Mama Cassie's** is a casual downtown Italian restaurant and deli with spaghetti dinners starting at $8, deli sandwiches, and good homemade bread. It's at 319 1st Ave. N, tel. (406) 454-3354.

Great Falls' unflappable sense of tradition extends to its favorite restaurants. For generations, two restaurants in Black Eagle, the old union town located on the north bank of the Missouri, have served up old-fashioned ethnic fare with a high-minded zeal. At **Borrie's,** 1800 Smelter Ave., tel. (406) 761-0300, massive servings of Montana steaks and traditional Italian pastas laden with the hearty sauces of our immigrant forebears lead out the menu. At **3-D International,** 1825 Smelter Ave., tel. (406) 453-6561, ethnic ecumenicism is practiced, with half the menu devoted to Chinese food and half to traditional Italian. The menus at Borrie's and 3-D International say a lot about the early labor currents in industrial Great Falls, and besides that, the food is quite good. Considered the best restaurants in the city by the stolid middle classes, you'll need reservations to get in the door. There aren't many restaurants like these left, so do go.

Otherwise, Great Falls has steaks, steaks, and steaks to offer its evening diner. **Jaker's Steak, Ribs, and Fish House** just about says it all, except that the place is also a casino. Find it at 1500 10th Ave., tel. (406) 727-1033. Not as fancy, **Eddie's Supper Club,** 3725 2nd Ave. N, tel. (406) 453-1616, is the steakhouse for meat lovers: more care is taken in the kitchen than on stylish redecoration. Expect cracked red vinyl booths and great food. If you're up to a short drive, head out to the **Bar-S Supper Club,** seven miles east of Great Falls on Hwy. 200, tel. (406) 761-9550. Again, don't let appearances deceive. This venerable roadhouse has been serving up magnificent steaks for years.

EVENTS

The **C.M. Russell Auction of Original Western Art** is an annual March event benefitting the C.M. Russell Museum, and bidders descend from all over the country. Contact the museum at (406) 727-8787 for details.

With tons of Lewis and Clark history in the area, it's natural for Great Falls to host the **Lewis and Clark Festival** in late June or early July. Frontier cooking, flintlock demonstrations, and firemaking are some of the things you'll see at the living history encampment at Giant Springs State Park, where actors and docents in period dress re-create the daily life of the expedition's soldiers. Mini float trips and longer dinner float trips down the Missouri take in some of the river's historic sites, while other guided tours visit more out of the way Lewis and Clark and naturalist destinations. Other festival events include dramatic readings, academic lectures on the Corps of Discovery, children's events, a buffalo barbecue, and a western art show and sale. This is quickly becoming a major event in Great Falls; with the completion of the Lewis and Clark Interpretive Center in 1998, it is sure to become even more popular. Many of the events are free. For more information, contact Lewis and Clark Festival, P.O. Box 2848, Great Falls, MT 59403, or the chamber of commerce.

Beginning the last Saturday of July and lasting eight days, the **Montana State Fair** takes over the town and the fairgrounds, located just west of downtown, across the Missouri. Through the summer the fairgrounds also host **horse races**.

INFORMATION AND SERVICES

The **Great Falls Chamber of Commerce** can be reached at 815 2nd St. S, or P.O. Box 2127, Great Falls, MT 59403, tel. (406) 761-4434. The

new **visitor center** is located just east of the 10th Avenue Bridge, beneath the "big flag" on Upper River Road.

The **public library** is at 301 2nd Ave. N, tel. (406) 453-0349. Listen to **Montana Public Radio** at 89.9 FM.

Transportation

Southwest of town, **Great Falls International Airport** is the region's largest, and serviced by major airlines.

Intermountain Bus and **Rimrock Stage** also use the airport as a headquarters, tel. (406) 453-1541; between the two lines, buses travel from Great Falls to Shelby, Havre, Lewistown, Billings, Bozeman, Helena, Butte, Missoula, and Kalispell.

Great Falls Transit System runs buses in and around town. Call (406) 727-0382 for schedule information. Hail a **Diamond Cab** by calling (406) 453-3241.

FORT BENTON AND BIG SAG COUNTRY

East of Great Falls, the Rockies fade from view, the buttes and peaks of central Montana loom, and the Missouri leaves its wide valley to plunge into a badlands gorge. This transitional landscape between the prairies of eastern Montana and the foothills of the Rockies contains some of the most interesting history, geology, and scenery in the state. Here, too, are seldom-visited back roads leading to pleasant, isolated towns like Highwood, Stockett, and Eden.

The region is also home to the oldest town in Montana—Fort Benton. Steamboats from St. Louis docked here 125 years ago (it was known as the "innermost port"), making it the stepping-off point for thousands of settlers and their chattel.

THE LAND

Geologically speaking, relatively recent events created the distinctive landscapes of the Big Sag area. About 20 million years after the Rockies formed, a vast surge of volcanic activity forced molten rock to the surface in many parts of central Montana.

Not all lava erupted; some molten rock squeezed up through fissures and faults or fed into underground reservoirs, called laccoliths. Erosion has exposed these formations—steep vertical ridges of volcanic stone, called dikes, running in straight lines across the landscape. One of the most prominent laccoliths in Montana, Square Butte, rises spectacularly from the plains near Geraldine.

Ice-age glaciers trapped river flow and glacial meltwater, forming Glacial Lake Great Falls. The present site of Great Falls was flooded by 600 feet of melted ice; water stretched from the Highwood Mountains to the Rocky Mountain foothills. As the lake grew and the glaciers receded, this vast body of water cut a new spillway. About 10,000 years ago, the overflow of Glacial Lake Great Falls roared through this channel—until the melting glaciers revealed a lower watercourse. The glacial lake spillway, called the Shonkin Sag by geologists and the Big Sag by locals, remains a deep U-shaped valley, 500 feet deep and a mile wide, along the base of the Highwood Mountains and Square Butte. All that's left of the huge river that once flowed here are the awesome canyon that it cut and a few shallow lakes.

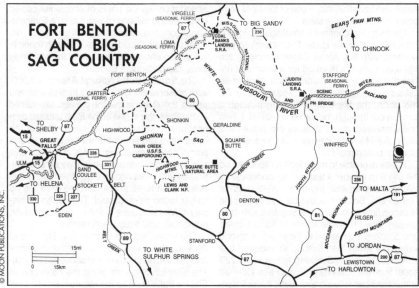

FORT BENTON AND BIG SAG COUNTRY

HISTORY

The mix of rich prairie grassland, mountain pastures, and easy access to supplies at nearby Fort Benton gave this area prominence in the early days of open-range ranching. The Milwaukee Road established rail service to the area in 1908, laying track along the Shonkin Sag's old riverbed and opening the region to the homesteader.

Montana's first commercial coal production began in 1876 at Belt. The high-quality lignite coal extracted was hauled to Fort Benton, whose steamboats demanded a source of fuel. The abundance and quality of the lignite drew the attention of Marcus Daly, whose Anaconda Copper Company smelters also needed coal. Daly gained control of coal production in Belt in 1893 and established the town as a center for coal refining. One hundred coke ovens and a coal washhouse lined Belt Creek; a branch line of the Great Northern daily carried 1,500 tons of coke to smelters at nearby Great Falls and Anaconda.

The fuel needs of the Great Northern itself led to the development of coal mines at Sand Coulee and Stockett, just west of Belt. All these mining centers fell on hard times when the smelters converted to natural gas and the railroads converted to diesel fuel. There is no coal production in the area now.

SIGHTS

The Shonkin Sag

Today, the Shonkin Sag is home to the small community of **Highwood,** numerous shallow lakes, and scattered farms and ranches. To reach the Shonkin Sag, follow Hwy. 228 east from Great Falls or Hwy. 331 north from Belt. Highwood sits at the mouth of the sag. From here, gravel roads continue on to Geraldine or Fort Benton—both are well-signed and in good condition.

The more scenic choice is the Geraldine road. It continues up the Shonkin Sag to the little crossroads of Shonkin, then cuts south into a steep valley in the Highwood Mountains. The road leaves the mountains and again crosses the Shonkin Sag; Square Butte looms to the south across several marshy lakes, and a spiky palisade of igneous rock (a volcanic dike) marches across the valley. The county road ends at Geraldine and Hwy. 80. The landscape is curiously spare and beautiful; this is one of the most compelling side trips in the state.

Shonkin Sag continues southeast, following Hwy. 80 past Square Butte. Then it turns abruptly north, with tiny Arrow Creek borrowing the Missouri's ancient riverbed for a short and uneventful journey northward. Prominent white cliffs cap the ridges east of Square Butte. To the north, the Missouri is flowing through a canyon cut through the same formation. Lewis and Clark were much taken by the White Cliffs along the Missouri, calling them "seens of visionary inchantment."

Travelers unable to make the full circuit around the Big Sag can get a taste of the landscape by taking a shorter side trip to Stockett, south of Great Falls. Before the last ice age began, the Missouri flowed in a channel slightly south of its present flow. The little towns of Sand Coulee and Stockett are nestled in the round-bottomed valley left when the Missouri abandoned this channel. To reach Stockett, follow Hwy. 227 south from the outskirts of Great Falls. Off-road enthusiasts can follow gravel roads through gently rolling landscapes, with great views onto the Rocky Mountain Front and the central Montana mountains, by continuing on to Eden, the Smith River valley, and Ulm.

Highwood Mountains

The Highwood Mountains are the deeply eroded remnants of isolated volcanoes that erupted about 50 million years ago. Although not tall—Highwood Baldy reaches 7,625 feet—these old craters host good trout streams. Like the other ranges of central Montana, the Highwoods don't overwhelm the traveler with size or severity; more meadow than peak, they are islands of green in a sea of grainfields. The Forest Service maintains a popular **campground** on Thain Creek.

Away from the main cluster of peaks, a series of isolated buttes marches to the east. While explosive volcanic events formed the Highwoods, unerupted pools of magma are responsible for these symmetrical but craggy peaks.

The most notable of these lava formations are **Round Butte** and **Square Butte,** east of the Highwoods. The unusual magma that formed these extrusions is a dark, crystal-flecked rock called shonkinite, rare enough to be named after the central Montana area where it occurs in abundance. As the pools of shonkinite cooled underground millions of years ago, a lighter igneous rock floated to the top of the laccolith, like cream on milk. Called syenite, it's much lighter in color than shonkinite and forms the startlingly white cap on Square Butte.

The **Square Butte Natural Area** is a 2,000-acre preserve along the butte's high plateau and peaks, 2,400 feet above the prairies. Maintained by the BLM, this is one of the most unusual destinations in Montana. The steep sides of the butte have protected the native grasses and plants from overgrazing; Lewis and Clark saw such stands of grasses when they crossed the prairies 200 years ago. In a good year the plants reach waist level; some varieties here are no longer found on rangeland. The wildflower display in May and June is astonishing, and deer, pronghorn, and birds are abundant.

The views, too, are spectacular. The core of the laccolith rises in cliffs and ridges of shonkinite and syenite, hundreds of feet above the plateau. The Shonkin Sag runs along the north side of Square Butte (look for the escarpment of an ancient waterfall in the watercourse). Here, as at few other places, one can truly grasp the expanse of the plains. The mountains of central Montana perforate the otherwise limitless flat horizons stretching outward for hundreds of miles.

Although ascending to the Square Butte Plateau is relatively easy (given a high-clearance vehicle and a little chutzpah), getting to the top of the volcanic plug itself requires a rigorous scramble up very rough terrain. Square Butte is much more rugged than it looks from a distance. Don't attempt to climb it alone, and don't feel as if you have to. Heroism isn't required to enjoy the plant and animal life; a good picnic will do as well.

Square Butte is accessible only through private land. The landowners ask that you check in with them before starting up the butte. The road is a 4WD track, and although adequately maintained, it is quite rocky. Cars with narrower axles than pickup trucks will need to straddle the tracks; the trademark shonkinite can easily puncture the oil pan of a low-bellied car. Although a high-clearance vehicle is preferable for this road, at least one Honda Accord has made it up and back.

To reach Square Butte Natural Area, turn at the community of Square Butte and follow the signs.

The road passes through a ranch yard; from here, the top of the plateau is about three miles.

Accommodations and Food

The Big Sag area is within easy driving distance of Great Falls, Lewistown, Stanford, and Fort Benton, each of which offers a full range of lodgings and amenities. To reach **Thain Creek Campground,** follow road signs for Highwood from Hwy. 200, then turn up Highwood Creek for 18 miles on a good gravel road.

In Highwood, the **Willow Tree Cafe,** tel. (406) 733-2383, serves breakfast and lunch. In Geraldine, the local eatery is **Mike's Bar and Grill,** tel. (406) 737-4541.

FORT BENTON

Once the bustling head of Missouri River navigation, Fort Benton (pop. 1,654, elev. 2,600 feet) is now a quiet, even sleepy town. When the fur trade boomed, steamboats struggled up the narrow, sandbarred waters of the Missouri to discharge fortune-seeking trappers and prospectors and load up with furs. The Great Falls of the Missouri, 25 miles upstream, barred further river travel.

Fort Benton was built in 1846 and served primarily as a fur-trading post. By 1859, the Mullan Road linked Fort Benton with Walla Walla, Washington, the easternmost outpost on the Columbia River system. The Whoop-Up Trail led from Fort Benton to Alberta and was used to supply western Canada with illegal "Indian whiskey"; incongruously, the fort was also supply depot for Canadian Mounties charged with bringing order to the wild, whiskey-sodden western provinces.

Of the trading forts built in mid-19th-century Montana, only Fort Benton survives as a town today. History is well displayed in Fort Benton's long, green riverside park. And the Missouri River still flows by, wide and muddy as ever, headed for an area still barely touched by roads.

Sights

Start Fort Benton's walking tour in the city park. The remains of the original fur-trading fort are here, as is the **Museum of the Upper Missouri,** tel. (406) 622-3766, which focuses on the fur trade and steamboat era. Hours are 9 a.m.-7

p.m. daily May 15-Sept. 15. The museum shuts down Oct. 15-May 1 and stays open 1-5 p.m. the remaining days of the year. Excavations are currently underway in the park to uncover the foundations of the fort, and hopeful plans exist to build a replica of old Fort Benton one day.

Continue walking down the levee to find a statue of Lewis, Clark, and Sacajawea, sculpted by Browning, Montana, artist Bob Scriver; a keelboat replica built in the early 1950s for the movie *The Big Sky;* and the 15th St. Bridge, which has spanned the Missouri since 1888. Historical signs along the grassy riverside strip discuss riverboats, the fur trade, and wild times in the streets of 19th-century Fort Benton.

Facing the river at 1718 Front St., the **Wild and Scenic Upper Missouri Visitor Center** has wildlife and archaeological exhibits and a Lewis and Clark slide show.

Among the town's historic buildings, the **Grand Union Hotel,** 1302 Front St., stands out. It was indeed grand when it was built, in 1882—just as the railroad was poised to eclipse the steamboat as a means of transportation. The hotel has finally reopened to overnight guests (see below).

In front of the hotel is a bronze statue of **Shep,** Fort Benton's most famous canine denizen and an object of near obsessive veneration for some (a Web search reveals some surprising websites). Shep was a faithful workmate of a local sheepherder. The herder died, and his body was ferried away by rail. Shep, however, kept vigil. The dog met every train into town for over five years. Shep's story became known across the country, and he became the darling of travelers and locals alike. However, Shep was eventually run over by a train and buried on a hill overlooking the depot. Read his story and weep.

Three blocks from the river, on 20th and Washington Streets, the **Museum of the Northern Great Plains,** tel. (406) 622-5316, has an agricultural focus; open daily May 15-Sept. 15, 9 a.m.-7 p.m.

Recreation

The Missouri River provides the recreational, as well as the historical, focus for Fort Benton. A visit to the BLM's information center at 1718 Front St. will make all but the most hydrophobic start planning a float down the Missouri.

Just down the park from the remains of old Fort Benton is the **swimming pool**. It's a nice, big pool, worth the fee ($2 adult, $1 children). The **Signal Point Golf Course**, out St. Charles St., is reportedly the state's most challenging nine-hole course.

Fish the Missouri from Fort Benton's levee for sauger, freshwater drum, and goldeye.

Accommodations
The **Grand Union Hotel**, at 704 14th Ave., tel. (406) 622-3228, reopened as a lodging in late 1998. This beautiful Historic Register building from 1882 adds a real touch of class to any stay in Fort Benton.

The **Pioneer Lodge**, 1700 Front St., tel. (406) 622-5441, is the best place to stay in town, though you may drive right by it the first and maybe even the second time. The building used to be a general store. The rooms ($35 s, $50 d) are comfortable and full of character; they have TVs but no telephones.

RV campers can pull up and spend the night for free in the city park, but there are no amenities. Tent campers are not encouraged to do the same.

W.C. McRAE

Missouri River Breaks

Food and Drink
While the **3-Way Cafe,** 2300 St. Charles St., tel. (406) 622-5681, may have the more titillating name, you'll want to go to **Loving's Pizza,** tel. (406) 622-5102, 1050 22st St., for homemade pizza, pasta, and Mexican food. The **Banque Club,** tel. (406) 622-5272, 1318 Front, is the local steakhouse.

Events
A **summer celebration** is held the last weekend of June. Labor Day weekend brings the **Chouteau County Fair.**

Information and Services
Dial (406) 622-5451 for **emergency** services.

Write the **Fort Benton Community Improvement Association,** P.O. Box 879, Fort Benton, MT 59442, tel. (406) 622-3864, for information. Or stop in at **Karen's Insta-Print Studio,** 1402 Front St. (by C-J's Diner) for tourist brochures.

"SEENS OF VISIONARY INCHANTMENT": THE WILD AND SCENIC MISSOURI RIVER

East of Great Falls, the Missouri River leaves its valley and begins to burrow below the prairie surface. The sluggish river and the deep canyon it cuts were designated a Wild and Scenic River in 1976; 149 miles of river and 131,840 acres of adjacent land are preserved much as Lewis and Clark encountered them. Today, this makes for one of the great float trips in the nation, with tons of wildlife viewing enhancing the historic and scenic value of this last remnant of free-flowing Missouri River.

The Land
The austere gorge cut by the Missouri between Fort Benton and Fort Peck Dam is a relatively recent accomplishment. Until the most recent ice ages, the Missouri flowed north from this point until it debouched into Hudson's Bay. But when ice sheets blocked that outlet, huge ice-age dams, filled with the Missouri's flow and glacial melt, spilled over the plains. Almost surreptitiously, the Missouri began to flow along the southernmost face of the glaciers, slowly cutting

a channel all the way to the Mississippi. When the ice sheets began their last retreat, 10,000 years ago, the Missouri remained in this new channel.

The precipitous and highly eroded walls of much of the Wild and Scenic Missouri's canyon are known locally as "breaks" or "badlands." These strata, sedimentary remains of ancient seas, began to wash up in eastern Montana 80 million years ago. The 1,000-foot-deep gorge cuts through most of this geologic history. Erosion has isolated monoliths of sandstone, craggy outbursts of rock, and sheer cliffs of startlingly white limestone.

The soils are extremely infertile—rich in alkali and salt, they support little plantlife except for occasional junipers and ponderosa pines. Along the river, however, there are beautiful groves of shade-giving cottonwoods.

In its lower reaches, the Wild and Scenic Missouri merges with the C.M. Russell National Wildlife Refuge. Here, elk, bighorn sheep, deer, beaver, mink, coyotes, and birds in abundance live along the riverbanks.

Exploring the Wild and Scenic Missouri by Boat

Only one road crosses the Missouri between Fort Benton and the Fred Robinson Bridge, north of Grassrange, 150 miles away. Only remote, ranch-access dirt roads even come close to it. Without any doubt, the best way to see the Wild and Scenic Missouri is by boat.

A float trip on the Missouri takes two forms—a guided trip with a guide and outfitter or a well-planned float on your own. Each has its advantages.

While a traveler's independent streak might initially value a go-it-alone attitude, consider the following. Remember that there are no towns along the river, no shops, no restaurants, and no motels. You have to bring your own water—even boiled, the water of the Missouri, while potable, is far too muddy to be appealing for drinking. There are no telephones or ambulances waiting if accidents occur (actually, heat stroke and sunburn are the greatest dangers). The Missouri is not a fast, shoot-the-rapids river; it takes seven days to float all the way from Fort Benton to the Fred Robinson Bridge. And, when it's all over, you still have to get back to your vehicle, several hundred road miles back upstream.

If you do decide to float on your own, remember to sign in at the BLM visitor center in Fort Benton before putting in to the river. The stretch of the Missouri between Fort Benton and Loma is an easy one-day trip and is the most heavily used segment of the Wild and Scenic Missouri. For more information, contact the **BLM River Manager,** Airport Rd., Lewistown, MT 59457, tel. (406) 538-7461. During the summer, the BLM maintains an office at 1718 Front St., Fort Benton, MT 59442, tel. (406) 622-5185.

Outfitters

The following outfitters are among the best for guided trips on the Missouri; each offers different packages involving trips of varying lengths (a minimum number of floaters is also usually demanded), and both rent canoes. The BLM provides a complete list of permit-holding outfitters.

Missouri River Outfitters, P.O. Box 762, Fort Benton, MT 59442, tel. (406) 622-3295, was one of the first to offer trips down the Missouri; these outfitters have been in business for over 30 years. The most popular trips are on special motorized riverboats (these are canopied for bad weather and have toilets on board). There are several choices of put-in spots and destinations, and depending on your schedule and interests, you'll choose either a three- or a five-day trip. On overnight trips, the outfitters provide all food, tents, and camping gear; you'll be expected to bring a sleeping bag and pad. Rates are $200 per day. You can also rent canoes, or just arrange shuttles back to your vehicles, from sthe company. For $100 a day, they will outfit and guide canoe trips. The most popular of these is the three-day paddle from Coal Banks Landing to Judith Landing.

Missouri River Canoe Company, HC 67 Box 50, Loma, MT 59460, tel. (406) 378-3110, is a unique operation based out of the all-but ghost town of Virgelle, once a railhead for Missouri River traffic. The old general store is now an antique store and the headquarters for this canoe outfitting and rental operation. The four boarding rooms above the store, plus five homesteaders' shacks scattered around the old townsite, are offered to canoe clients on a B&B basis. As you might guess, any B&B operated by an antiques dealer is well-done and beautifully authentic; the as-was homesteaders' homes are especially evocative of bygone days.

Canoe trips are available in three forms. Guided and outfitted trips range from four to 12 days, including all transportation, food, and gear except a sleeping bag and personal effects. Outfitted but unguided trips are also available, at $150 per day per person, including canoes, food, camp gear, and shuttle. Simple canoe rentals are also available at $35 a day. Bed and breakfast ranges $40-70.

Exploring the Wild and Scenic Missouri by Car

While there's no substitute for a float trip down the Missouri, travelers on a tight schedule or fearful of water retain interesting options. On this section of the Missouri, only one gravel road bridges the river; other less-traveled roads cross the river on ferries.

The **Missouri River ferries** are among the last river ferries in the country. Licensed by the U.S. Coast Guard, these cable-drawn ferries connect obscure county roads for ranchers and farmers who live in this lonesome stretch of Montana.

The ferries are free during the day; simply pull up to the landing and drive onto the small plank barge. If the ferry is on the other side, the operator will cross to pick you up. If there is no sign of life, honk your horn. Out of consideration, plan to use the ferries within normal waking hours (also, there's sometimes a fee for late-night crossings). The ferries normally operate April to Thanksgiving; the rest of the year the river freezes over.

Ferries operate at Carter, Virgelle, and Stafford. The Carter Ferry links up with a network of country dirt roads in the Fort Benton—Highwood area, making a loop trip easy (if dusty).

Loma is where the Marias River flows into the Missouri. In 1805, when Lewis and Clark were traveling up the Missouri to its headwaters, they spent several puzzling days camped at the confluence. Their Mandan informants had not mentioned this particular river coming in from the north, and most of the men in the party believed that this large river was actually the main stream of the Missouri. (If you wonder how the corps could have been so flummoxed by so small a river as the Marias, remember that it was once much larger and is now impounded for irrigation by Tiber Dam.) Lewis, and eventually Clark, thought otherwise, and led the corps south, along what really *was* the Missouri. The mouth of the Marias became the site of **Fort Piegan**, established in 1831 for trade with the Blackfeet.

SIGHTS ALONG THE MISSOURI

Downriver from Virgelle, the Wild and Scenic Missouri passes beneath the White Cliffs, escarpments of white limestone looming above the river. Passing through the limestone are dikes of volcanic rock radiating from mountain ranges in central Montana.

Erosion has dealt harshly but creatively with these formations, incising them into landmarks for river travelers. The White Cliffs are often compared to the fortifications of ruined cities, with isolated towers and spires emerging in bas-relief from the canyon. Imaginative minds have accorded the formations fanciful names: Eye of the Needle, Citadel Rock, Steamboat Rock, Hole in the Wall.

Once past the PN Bridge, the river enters the Missouri Breaks. Here, in a badlands gorge hemmed by outcrops of sandstone, erosion has segregated colorful but barren gumbo soil into buttes, bluffs, and canyons. Gangs of rustlers menaced early stockmen from these inaccessible ravines. Today, the fringe of pine and juniper shelters elk, deer, mountain sheep, and birds of prey.

In 1805, Lewis and Clark paddled upriver along this same expanse of the Missouri River. The beauty and monumentality of the canyon overwhelmed them. No self-respecting travel writer would dare attempt to match Meriwether Lewis's elegiac prose (or his spelling):

May 31st, 1805: The hills and river Clifts which we passed today exhibit a most romantic appearence. The water in the course of time has trickled down the soft sand clifts and woarn it into a thousand grotesque figures, which with the help of a little immagination and an oblique view are made to represent eligant ranges of lofty freestone buildings, having their parapets well stocked with statuary; collumns of various sculpture both groved and plain, in other places with the help of less immagination we see the remains or ruins of eligant buildings; some collumns standing and almost entire with their pedestals and capitals; As we passed on it seemed as if those seens of visionary inchantment would never have an end; for here it is too that nature present to the view of the traveler vast ranges of walls of tolerable workmanship.

Downstream from Virgelle is the most scenic portion of the Missouri Breaks; **Coal Banks Landing State Recreation Area** is a popular departure point for float trips. For cars, the landscapes are dramatic, but there is no road access to the nearby White Cliffs area along the river.

The **Stafford (or McClelland) Ferry** is the most remote of the Missouri River ferries, linking dirt roads north of Winifred with a gravel road south of Chinook. It's a long road—about 80 miles—but it passes through breathtaking badlands, along the trail of Chief Joseph's last flight and battle, and through the lonesome and lovely Bears Paw Mountains. It's countryside not often seen by travelers. Note, however, that you should *not* attempt this road if rain threatens.

There's a bridge now at the site of the old PN Ferry, at the juncture of the Judith River and the Missouri. The Judith adds its deep valley to the Missouri's gorge, making this a precipitous confluence. It's easily reached north of Winifred, or south of Big Sandy, by good all-weather gravel roads.

Practicalities

There aren't many lodging options in this remote stretch of badlands. You can call and ask for one of the charmingly authentic rooms at the Virgelle Mercantile now operated by **Missouri River Canoe Company,** tel. (406) 378-3110, though their canoe clientele have dibs. Otherwise, the closest lodgings are in Fort Benton and Big Sandy. Great Falls and Havre are close enough to serve as bases for day-trips.

There are undeveloped campgrounds at the ranger stations at **Coal Banks Landing,** near Virgelle and at Judith Landing north of Winifred.

THE HI-LINE

More than any other part of Montana, this is the country the railroad built. James J. Hill, head of the Great Northern Railway, mounted an aggressive campaign to bring European immigrants to the Hi-Line—by train, of course. Towns named Zurich, Malta, Inverness, and Kremlin were supposed to welcome Europeans.

Today, this is the Montana known by Amtrak passengers, wheat farmers, and few others. Almost nobody comes here on vacation, unless it's to help their parents out with the harvest. Glacier Park-bound easterners zip past the grain elevators and filling stations, seldom turning from Hwy. 2 to explore the old downtowns.

However, the area does warrant a second glance. Havre's tours of its "underground" city and its Native American buffalo jump are definitely worth taking in, and the Bear Paw Battleground has been elevated to National Monument status, with a visitor's center and better facilities hopefully on the way.

HAVRE

You wouldn't know it by the pronunciation, but Havre (HAV-er, pop. 10,232, elev. 4,167 feet) does take its name from the French city Le Havre. Originally it was called Bull Hook Siding, but James J. Hill pleaded for a name befitting the dignity of a Great Northern town. The locals complied, as Hill was ensuring the town's prosperity by making it a railway-division point.

Raucous boom times came to town with the railroad and with cowboys in the 1890s. Gambling and prostitution both swelled to legendary proportions, some of which took place "underground," in Havre's basement carousing and shopping district. By 1910 homesteaders were piling into the land office at Havre to claim their 160-acre plots. They were, as a whole, a much more serious bunch than railroad workers and cowboys and the bartenders, card sharks, and whores who'd gathered around Hill's esteemed division point, but Havre did its best to resist the new morality imposed by farmers and prohibitionists.

Traces of this heritage linger in the drive-up bar and the gambling joints still thriving in downtown Havre. And why Havre's high school teams are called the Blue Ponies is anyone's guess.

Sights

A century ago, a number of Havre's pioneer businesses, including brothels, bars, opium dens, as well as bakeries, butchers, laundries, and pharmacies were located beneath the city streets. The tunnels that run through downtown Havre have been partially restored and opened as **Havre Historical Underground Tours,** one of the state's most interesting history lessons. Many of the businesses are re-created with the exact fixtures and objects that originally were used in the underground district at the turn of the 19th century, making this a fascinating snapshot of a bygone era. Access to the underground area is by tour only, and last approximately one hour. Tours are offered throughout the year, Monday through Saturday. Call ahead for scheduled tour times and reservations. Tickets are $6 adult, $5 seniors, and $4 children. You'll need to be able to negotiate steep stairs to get access to the tour, though wheelchairs are available once underground. For more information, contact Havre Beneath the Streets, 100 3rd St., tel. (406) 265-8888.

The **H. Earl Clack Museum,** toward the west end of town at the Hill County Fairgrounds, is free and open from Memorial Day through Labor Day daily 9 a.m.-9 p.m. The **Wahpka Chu'gn Buffalo Jump** provides the fodder for the museum's most interesting exhibits. At this archeological site, which is directly behind the Holiday Village Shopping Center in Havre, Native Americans from three different prehistoric cultures, dating from 2,000 to 600 years ago, drove herds of bison off a cliff and then processed the slain animals for meat, hides, and tools. Excavations of the *pishkun* have uncovered Indian campsites, stone tools, and piles of buffalo bones. The site is open for tours only, which are operated by the nearby Clack Museum. Tours run mid-May through Labor Day Tues.-Sun. and cost $3.50 adult, $3 seniors, and $2 students. Call (406) 265-6417 for details.

The remains of **Fort Assiniboine** are south of the intersection of Hwys. 2 and 87. The Clack Museum leads tours out to the old fort, built in 1879 to protect U.S. citizens from both the Blackfeet and the feared return of Sitting Bull from his exile in Canada. The fort was converted to an agricultural research station in 1913 and was used to house transients during the Depression.

MSU-Northern, formerly Northern Montana College, has a well-tended campus south of downtown and is a good place to sit in the shade. The Math-Science Building houses natural history displays, including a stuffed specimen of the extinct Audubon mountain sheep once displayed above the bar of one of Havre's bygone high-class joints.

Ten miles south of Havre on Hwy. 234 is **Beaver Creek Park,** the nation's largest county park. With 10,000 acres of rolling hills and streams, the park is a popular place for picnics, camping, and for getting a sense of the lovely and remote Bears Paw Mountains. These low mountains are 50-million-year-old volcanic humps that rise just enough above the surrounding prairies to provide welcome relief from the heat, and to sustain plants, wildlife, and streams otherwise absent from the plains. From the park, follow back roads to the Chief Joseph Battleground, or to the Rocky Boys Reservation.

Rocky Boys Reservation

On the western edge of the Bears Paw Mountains south of Havre is the reservation named for Chippewa leader Stone Child, called Rocky Boy by the whites. Almost 2,000 Chippewa and Cree share this 108,015-acre reservation, which is owned entirely by tribal members.

Cree Indians came from the Upper Great Lakes area to the northern plains in the late 1700s and were allies of the Assiniboine and foes of the Sioux and Blackfeet. When bison began to disappear from the plains, the Cree became drifters in search of the last herds. They became known for their wandering on the northern plains and for their alignment with Louis Riel and his band of Metis.

U.S. authorities repeatedly tried to force the Cree to settle in Canada, and for many years the tribe was homeless. The Cree teamed up with another homeless group, Rocky Boy's band of Chippewa, who had been shorted out of reservation land in North Dakota. When Fort Assiniboine was abandoned in 1911, part of its acreage was set aside as a reservation for the Chippewa-Cree. Reservation life was not easy for these tribes, and employment on the reservation is still difficult to come by.

The tribes own and operate the Bears Paw Ski Bowl, a small downhill ski area (see below).

Recreation

When the sun beats down on the Hi-Line, consider a dunk in Havre's **city pool,** 420 6th Ave., tel. (406) 265-8161.

Fish **Fresno Reservoir,** northwest of Havre, for walleye, crappie, and northern pike. In **Beaver Creek Park** there's good fishing in two small lakes for pike and trout. Buy a fishing permit ($5) at the park headquarters, located at the park entrance, 10 miles south of Havre on Hwy. 234.

Tribal fishing and camping permits are issued by the Chippewa-Cree at their business office, tel. (406) 395-4282, in Box Elder. The tribes also run the **Bears Paw Ski Bowl,** a small downhill ski area on the flanks of the Bears Paws, 26 miles south of Havre, on the **Rocky Boys Reservation.** It's usually open mid-Dec. through April 1.

Accommodations

Havre's old downtown hotel, the **Park Hotel,** 335 1st St., tel. (406) 265-7891, has been refurbished and offers rooms starting at $31 d; it's convenient to the train station. Also downtown, the attractive **El Toro Inn,** 521 1st St., tel. (406) 265-5414 or (800) 422-5414, has a Spanish motif and rooms from $36 s, $47 d. Conference rooms are available, convenient for shopping and dining options, and the city pool is just two blocks away; pets okay.

A little farther from downtown, the **Budget Inn Motel,** at 115 9th Ave., tel. (406) 265-8625, is a good deal, with well-maintained rooms starting at $35 s, $40 d. Commercial rates available, pets okay. **The Duck Inn,** 1300 1st St., tel. (406) 265-9615 or (800) 455-9615, is part of a dining and entertainment complex, with three restaurants, a casino, and gift shop. RV spaces are also available; rooms in the motel are $41 s, $46 d. Likewise, **Townhouse Inns of Havre** is a large motel complex at 601 1st St. W, tel. (406) 265-6711 or (800) 442-4667. Single rooms start at $64 s,$74 d, and there's an indoor pool, sauna, and fitness room, with an adjoining casino and lounge. Convention rooms are also available; bring your pet along for $4 extra.

On the west end of town, near the fairgrounds and buffalo jump, is the **Havre Super 8 Motel,** 166 19th Ave. W, tel. (406) 265-1411 or (800) 800-8000; $39 s, $51 d, and pets are allowed with permission.

By the museum, the **Lions Campground,** tel. (406) 265-7121 or (888) 265-7121, is okay for RVs, but tent campers are better off heading toward the Bears Paw Mountains. It's only about 15 miles south on Hwy. 234 to the campgrounds at **Beaver Creek County Park,** tel. (406) 395-4565, a huge park with 250 sites in several discreet campgrounds. Purchase a $5 camping permit at the park office, 10 miles south of Havre on Hwy. 234.

Food and Drink

Pizza Hut, McDonald's, and **Kentucky Fried Chicken** all rear their heads on the west end of town, but there are a few alternatives. Chinese restaurants have a long history in Havre—in the early days there was always Chinese food to go with the hell-raising. Today, the **Canton Chinese Restaurant** at 439 1st St. W, tel. (406) 265-6666, carries on the tradition. **Nalivka's Original Pizza Kitchen,** 1032 1st, Havre, MT 59501, tel. (406) 265-4050, is the local's favorite for pizza and pasta.

Andy's Supper Club, 658 W. 1st St., tel. (406) 265-9963, is Havre's best steakhouse. You won't need to spend much time studying the menu, as it's basically just a list of steaks. Count on a massive meal, served in traditional Old Montana courses, complete with relish trays, salads, and pasta courses, all before the truly enormous steak arrives. Try the **Mediterranean Room** at the Duck Inn, 1300 1st St., tel. (406) 265-6111, for an exercise in amazing kitsch. Classical statues gaze at you as you ponder the pricey but admirably extensive (for northern Montana) menu. And, while a bit predictable, **4-Bs** rarely disappoints; they have a place at 604 1st St. W, tel. (406) 265-9721.

For a less nutritious view of Havre stop by the **Oxford Bar,** 329 1st St., where drinks are swallowed unnoticed when the gambling gets hot. Across the street at the **Palace Bar,** 281 1st Ave., there's a wonderful back bar and generous drinks.

Events

The **Rocky Boy Powwow** is held in early August near Box Elder on the Rocky Boys Reservation.

The **Hill County Fair** is in mid-August, and mid-September brings **Havre Festival Days.** For more information, call the chamber of commerce at (406) 265-4383.

a homesteader's cabin on the Hi-Line

JUDY JEWELL

Information and Services

You'll notice the streets in Havre run parallel to the railroad tracks (Hwy. 2 is 1st St.); avenues are perpendicular to the tracks. Names for both rely principally on numbers, leading to maximum confusion.

The **chamber of commerce** is at 518 1st St., P.O. Box 308, Havre, MT 59501, tel. (406) 265-4383. Find the **post office** at 306 3rd Ave., just across from the lovely courthouse. The public **library** is just a couple of blocks away at the corner of 3rd St. and 4th Avenue. In the same neighborhood, **Big Sky Books,** at 301 3rd Ave., tel. (406) 265-5750, has piles and piles of used books and several tidier shelves of new books, many about Montana.

The **Chippewa-Cree Business Committee** is at Rocky Boy Rte., Box 544, Box Elder, MT 59521, tel. (406) 395-4282.

Transportation

Amtrak's Empire Builder makes a brief layover in Havre, as it is a restocking point. Trains arrive four times a week: contact the station, tel. (406) 265-5381, at 235 Main Street.

Rimrock Stages provides bus service to the Hi-Line and Great Falls, and stops at the Park Hotel in Havre, 335 1st St., tel. (406) 265-6444. The one daily bus to Great Falls leaves at 12:45 p.m., in time to meet the eastbound Amtrak train, on those days when it's on time. Westbound Amtrak passengers will need to stay overnight to catch a bus south to Great Falls.

The **Havre Hill County Airport** is serviced by Big Sky Airlines. **Budget Rent-A-Car** has an office at the airport, tel. (406) 265-1156. **Enterprise Rent-A-Car** is at 1991 W US Hwy. 2, tel. (406) 265-1156. **Rent-A-Wreck,** tel. (406) 265-1481, is at 1219 3rd St. N.

CHINOOK

Chinook (pop. 1,586, elev. 2,310 feet), the Hi-Line's remaining cattle town on the Milk River, is named after the warming wind that's saved many a cow from freezing or starving to death.

Bear Paw Battleground

The site of the Chief Joseph battlefield is 16 miles south of Chinook on paved Hwy. 240, in view of the Bear Paw Mountains.

This is where Gen. Nelson Miles overtook the Nez Perce, who were less than 40 miles from sanctuary in Canada. And it was here that Chief Joseph gave the speech for which he is most remembered:

It is cold and we have no blankets. The little children are freezing to death. My people, some of them, have run away to the hills, and have no blankets, no food; no one knows where they are—perhaps freezing to death. I want to have time to look for my children and see how many I can find.

Maybe I shall find them among the dead.
Hear me my chiefs. I am tired; my heart
is sick and sad.
From where the sun now stands, I will
fight no more forever.

The windswept patch of prairie has a few plaques and a trail through the grass that leads to small markers strewn over the battlefield, marking the sites of deaths and camps. The battlefield has recently been taken over by the National Park Service, as part of the Nez Perce National Historical Park. There's talk of building a visitor center if funding can be found.

In the meantime, there's a good local museum, the **Blaine County Museum,** at 501 Indiana, tel. (406) 357-2590, that's able to provide information about the battlefield. A mural and a slide

---

THE NEZ PERCE AND THE BATTLE AT BEAR PAW

After the Nez Perce crossed the Missouri on their 1877 flight to Canada, they changed command and slowed down. They'd been on the run for four months and were tiring. Poker Joe, who'd proven himself to be a strong strategic leader, let Looking Glass, who pressed for a more relaxed pace, take over.

This pause gave General Nelson Miles and his battalion from eastern Montana the opportunity to attack the Nez Perce while they were still in U.S. territory. The Nez Perce were caught off guard, but they fought hard on the cold, snowy prairie for six days before finally agreeing to lay down their arms.

Chief Joseph negotiated a cease-fire with Miles in which the Nez Perce would surrender their weapons but would see the return of their horses and their homeland in eastern Oregon. That night, White Bird—the only other Nez Perce chief still alive following the Bear Paw battle—led a band of Nez Perce toward Canada. Over 200 escapees made it to Canada, where they joined Sitting Bull and his Lakota followers.

Those who remained with Joseph were sent to Miles City, then to Kansas, and then to Oklahoma. Not until 1885 were they allowed to return to reservations in the Northwest.

---

show on the Nez Perce Battle of the Bear Paw are featured. From May through Sept., hours are Tues.-Sat. 8 a.m.-5 p.m., Sunday 2-4 p.m. Winter hours are Mon.-Fri. 1-5 p.m.

Practicalities
Bear Paw Court, 114 Montana Ave., tel. (406) 357-2221 or (800) 357-2224, is a well-maintained court motel with cool neon and rooms at $35 s, $47 d. At the attractive **Chinook Motor Inn,** 100 Indiana Ave., tel. (406) 357-2248 or (800) 603-2864, rooms are $44 s, $52 d; there's also a restaurant and lounge/casino.

The **Pastime Lounge and Steakhouse,** tel. (406) 357-2424, and the restaurant at the Chinook Motor Inn are the best bets for a meal in this small town.

The **Blaine County Fair and Rodeo** and an accompanying art show and auction are held in mid-July. Contact the **Chinook Chamber of Commerce** at P.O. Box 744, Chinook, MT 59523, tel. (406) 357-2100, for more information.

WEST OF HAVRE

Every six miles or so, Hwy. 2 passes through yet another tiny town dominated by grain elevators and Lutheran church spires; many are fancifully named (by the Great Northern) and most are just hanging on to existence. This is marvelous farmland for high-protein wheat, which fetches premium prices from bread makers.

Small towns like Joplin, Hingham, and Gilford don't have much in the way of facilities for travelers, but there's invariably a bar, a grocery store, and a coffee-klatch cafe in each town that would be glad to see a stranger.

Don't just whiz through **Kremlin.** Stop and look hard for the onion domes rising above the prairie—they're what give the town its name. (Actually, *nobody's* ever seen 'em, except a homesick Russian homesteader back in 1910 or so.)

The unenlightened may pass south of **Rudyard** on Hwy. 2 and dismiss it as a real hayseed town, but Rudyard natives have ended up doing such diverse things as running restaurant chains in France, creating art installations at the Whitney, and selling paintings in the western art world that are valued into the six-digits. Stop by and have a look at their new museum.

Inverness offers the **Inverness Supper Club,** tel. (406) 292-3801, a favorite watering hole and steakhouse for local farmers and ranchers; it's also open for lunch.

Chester

A dam on the Marias River forms **Tiber Reservoir** (aka Lake Elwell) southwest of Chester (pop. 952, elev. 3,283 feet). It's the only recreational area for miles around, and is a haven for those seeking **campsites.** Boating is popular, fishing is mediocre for rainbows and perch, and there seems to be a largely untapped potential for windsurfing. A float trip along the Marias from below the dam to the Missouri River passes badlands and white cliffs not unlike those of the "wild and scenic" stretch of the Missouri.

If you're not a camper, perhaps you'd like to stay in a motel named after a local point of interest. The **MX Motel** on Hwy. 2, tel. (406) 759-5564, reminds passers-through that some missile silos slumber just off the highway around here.

Shelby

A boxcar was thrown from a Great Northern train here in 1891, and the site was named after Montana's general manager of the Great Northern, who swore the place would never amount to much. Shelby (pop. 2,704, elev. 3283 feet) developed into a trade center, supplying cowboys and sheepherders with food and wild times. Oil was discovered north of town in 1921, and though the town's population swelled, it didn't quite live up to its own expectations. In 1923, Shelby hosted a prizefight between Jack Dempsey and Tommy Gibbons. A 45,000-seat arena was erected for this occasion; unfortunately, only 7,000 were filled for the fight.

The **Marias Museum of History and Art,** 206 12th Ave., tel. (406) 434-2551, has memorabilia from the big fight and displays concerning the region's oil wealth.

Sweetgrass border crossing, 24 miles north of Shelby on I-15, is open 24 hours and is the state's busiest port of entry.

Shelby has a quite a number of motels and sees a lot of Canadian travelers. Downtown, **O'Haire Manor Motel,** 204 2nd St. S, tel. (406) 434-5555 or (800) 541-5809, $32 s, $44 d, has a fitness room and hot tub, guest laundry, and some two-bedroom units. The entire facility has been remodeled within the last couple of years; pets are okay. The **Comfort Inn,** tel. (406) 434-2212 or (800) 442-4667, at the junction of I-15 and Hwy. 200, $59 s $69 d, has a lounge and casino, pool, pets are okay. Also nice is the **Crossroads Inn,** Hwy. 2 at I-15, tel. (406) 434-5134, with a pool; $50 s, $64. Campers may want to swing seven miles south of town to **Williamson Park,** on the Marias River.

Hong Kong Chan's, a Chinese restaurant at 200 Front St., tel. (406) 434-2646, is not as improbable as its name. **Dixie's Inn & Dining Room,** west of Shelby, tel. (406) 434-5817, is the spot for a night out on the town.

Like many hot Hi-Line towns, Shelby has a city **swimming pool,** at 105 12th Ave. N, tel. (406) 434-5311.

Conrad

Conrad (pop. 2,873, elev. 3,500 feet), though 24 miles south of the Hi-Line proper on I-15, shares an agricultural heritage and economy with the towns along Hwy. 2. Dryland farming and big irrigation projects took off here and made it a productive wheat-growing area. Conrad is within easy striking distance of Lake Elwell, a minor mecca for recreationists on the prairies.

There's a **Super 8 Motel** 215 N. Main tel. (406) 278-7676 or (800) 442-4667, $51 s, $60 d., handy to the freeway; the motel also features some kitchenettes and executive suites. There's also a casino and convenience store.

BLACKFEET INDIAN RESERVATION

Just east of Glacier National Park and the Rocky Mountains, shortgrass prairie rolls across the Blackfeet Reservation, a high plain cut through by creeks and dotted with lakes. Strong west winds, long cold winters, and short hot summers make it difficult to ignore the weather here.

Among the reservation communities, **Heart Butte** is the most traditional; **East Glacier, St. Mary,** and **Babb** cater to tourists, with many businesses owned by non-Indians. **Cut Bank,** on the reservation's eastern border, has more in common with the Hi-Line towns to the east.

Meriwether Lewis hoped to find the headwaters of the Marias River mingling with those of the Saskatchewan River, up above the 50th parallel. On their return from the Pacific, Lewis and a small party of men traced Cut Bank Creek from its confluence with the Two Medicine River. (These two streams combine to form the Marias.) Unfortunately for Lewis, Cut Bank Creek comes out of the Rockies west of Browning, and, due to cloudy weather, he couldn't see the stars well enough to get an exact reading of how far north he was. All in all, it was enough to cause him to name their terminus "Camp Disappointment." A highway marker and a wind-tossed hilltop picnic area now mark the site.

Lewis's side trip is also notable because it marks the only time anybody was killed during the expedition. Two Blackfeet were killed when, after sharing a campsite with Lewis's group, they tried to steal guns from the white explorers.

HISTORY

The Blackfeet, originally from north of the Great Lakes, moved west in the 1600s and established southern Alberta as their territory. What is now known as the Blackfeet Nation is composed of three distinct tribes: the Northern Piegan (Pikuni), the Southern Piegan or Blackfeet (Siksika), and the Blood (Kainai). By the 1700s, bands of Blackfeet had settled in what is now Montana. The Northern Piegan and the Blood mostly remained in Canada.

The Blackfeet formed tentative alliances with the neighboring Cree and Assiniboine, and considered the more distant Shoshone and Crow their enemies. When they first arrived on the northern plains, the Blackfeet had neither horses nor guns. They drove buffalo over *pishkuns,* steep cliffs, to kill them.

Horses, acquired from either the Shoshone or the Flathead, Nez Perce, and Kootenai tribes, made a tremendous difference in the everyday life of the Blackfeet. Buffalo were much easier to hunt from horseback and, once the tribe began trading for guns, were a snap to shoot down. The Blackfeet became skilled riders, and their fierce reputation was enhanced as they were able to stage wide-ranging raids.

When white explorers and mountain men arrived in the 1800s, the Blackfeet controlled the northern plains. White settlers feared the Blackfeet's raids as much as they vied for their business at trading posts. Early trading posts in Blackfeet country included Fort Piegan on the Missouri River near present-day Loma.

Contact with white traders and soldiers brought more of the valuable guns and ammunition, but also conflict and disease. The Blackfeet were decimated as much by disease as by battle. Thousands were killed by smallpox and scarlet fever.

The U.S. government was eager to confine the Blackfeet and, in order to start the process along, marked the land north of the Yellowstone and south of Canada's Saskatchewan River, east of the Continental Divide and west of the confluence of the Missouri and Yellowstone Rivers, for a Blackfeet reservation. Of course, pressure from whites wanting the land for their own uses resulted in an incredible shrinking reservation. The Blackfeet Reservation now comprises 1.5 million acres, with over a third of that owned by non-Indians.

Oil drilling on tribal land has provided revenue for the Blackfeet since the early 1900s. Oil and gas now supply the tribe with most of their income and much controversy. Ranching, farming, and a pencil factory also contribute to the reservation economy.

WHY "BLACKFEET"?

Two legends tell of how the Blackfeet got their tribal name.

The first, and oldest, is a story about a man and his three sons. Obeying a vision, the man sent his sons west to hunt buffalo. The buffalo were where they were supposed to be, by the thousands, but they were difficult to approach. The Sun appeared in a second vision and provided the father with black medicine with which to paint his oldest son's feet. It worked—the son was able to run down the buffalo. His descendants are called Blackfeet. (The man's other two sons weren't ignored. One became a warrior—his painted red lips earned his descendants the name "Bloods." And the third son returned home with clothes of distant tribes; his descendants became the Pikuni, or "Far-Off Clothing." Whites transformed this into "Piegan.")

The less visionary explanation points to the fact that the tribe's long travels across scorched prairies to reach what is today Montana probably blackened their moccasins.

Lakes dot the Blackfeet Reservation, and many of them are worth fishing. The tribe has a fishing information line at (406) 338-7413; they'll provide advice on the necessary permits and current fishing conditions.

CUT BANK

This foothills oil and gas town of 3,508 souls was named by the Blackfeet for "the river that cuts into the white clay bank," or Cut Bank Creek. There was an initial burst of development when the Great Northern Railway came through in the 1890s, and another big spurt in the 1930s when oil and gas were discovered nearby. Cut Bank is actually on the eastern edge of the Blackfeet Reservation, but, unlike Browning, it's not a thoroughly Indian town.

Practicalities
The **Glacier Gateway Inn,** 1121 E. Railroad St., tel. (406) 873-5544 or (800) 851-5541, is new and comfortable for this part of the world; $44 s, $54 d gets you a clean and well-appointed room.

You can't miss it—it's next to the 27-foot penguin. There are three theme rooms, one with a two-story tepee inside! The **Northern Motor Inn,** 609 W. Main, tel. (406) 873-5662, with rooms at $44 s, $57 d, also has an indoor pool and hot tub.

The venerable **Glacier Motor Inn,** 15 1st Ave. SW, tel. (406) 873-5555 or (800) 546-5554, has rooms in the older hotel building ($28 s, $34 d), and in a newer motel ($37 s, and $42 d). There's also a dining room and casino on premises, and a guest laundry.

Golden Harvest Cafe, 13 W. Main, tel. (406) 873-4010, is the local's breakfast and lunch hangout. Get sandwiches at the **Smokehouse Deli,** 5 N. Central Ave., tel. (406) 873-4747. For dinner, look to the **Village Dining and Lounge,** tel. (406) 873-5005, in the North Village Shopping Center near the Northern Motor Inn.

The city's heated outdoor **swimming pool** is at 320 2nd Ave. W, tel. (406) 873-2452.

The last weekend of July brings Cut Bank's **Lewis and Clark Expedition Festival.** The **chamber of commerce,** P.O. Box 1243, Cut Bank, MT 59427, tel. (406) 873-4041, can supply details.

BROWNING

Browning (pop. 1,220, elev. 4,462 feet) is the headquarters of the Blackfeet tribe. It's 18 miles east of Glacier National Park and many park-goers zip through, in a hurry to get to the mountains. Though Browning is not a fancy place—it can be hard to find a pay phone that works, and the cafe fare is no more compelling than the highway motel rooms—there is a certain spirit to the place, and there are reasons to stop here.

Sights
Browning's main attraction is the **Museum of the Plains Indian,** near the intersection of Hwys. 2 and 89. The exhibits of cultural artifacts are well curated and professionally displayed, the slide show is vivid, and the gift shop is a good place to buy Indian art and jewelry without fear of getting inferior or inauthentic goods, and with the assurance that the artist is being fairly com-

pensated. June-Sept. the museum is open daily 9 a.m.-5 p.m. Winter hours are Mon.-Fri. 10 a.m.-4:30 p.m., tel. (406) 338-2230.

At the same highway intersection, the **Museum of Montana Wildlife** is a jumble of taxidermy, dioramas, and bronze sculptures. It's joined by the **Hall of Bronze** and artist **Bob Scriver's studio and gallery.** Though a bit of a mishmash, it's worth visiting along with the Museum of the Plains Indian. The museum is open daily, May 1 through Labor Day, 8 a.m.-5 p.m. Adult admission is $2, reduced rates for children and families, tel. (406) 338-5425.

The back roads of the reservation pass homes (with an occasional tepee pitched out back), lakes, oil and gas rigs, and a ceremonial sun lodge (a polygonal log-limbed structure). While common manners dictate that one shouldn't trespass, it is especially important not to enter tribal religious sites, such as a sun lodge.

Accommodations and Food
The **War Bonnet Lodge,** at the intersection of Hwys. 2 and 89, tel. (406) 338-7610, has double rooms for $59; there's also a dining room and lounge. The **Western Motel,** 121 Central Ave. E,

tel. (406) 338-7572, offers clean rooms at a relative savings.

Browning's no culinary mecca, but there is the 24-hour **Montana Casino and Restaurant,** tel. (406) 338-5576, as well as the **Glacier Restaurant,** at the junction of Hwys. 89 and 2, tel. (406) 338-7509.

Events
North American Indian Days are held the second week of July at the powwow grounds behind the Museum of the Plains Indian. Dancing and drumming are the highlights of the weekend activities. Teams of drummers come from all over the West to compete at this powwow, and their drumming is frequently rhapsodic. Stick games, jewelry peddlers, and the bustling encampment of tepees, tents, and pickups round out the scene. Spectators will quickly realize that this is *real,* not something trotted out for tourists, and, while non-Indians are welcome, events aren't geared toward them.

Information
Information is available from the **Blackfeet Nation,** P.O. Box 850, Browning, MT 59417, tel. (406) 338-7276.

ROCKY MOUNTAIN FRONT

The Rocky Mountains hoist themselves off the plains just west of Choteau and Augusta. It's as dramatic a transition as you'll find in any landscape: flat rangeland to the east, wilderness mountains rising abruptly to the west. In winter, chinook winds blow down off the mountains to warm the plains; the rest of the year, the wind just plain blows.

In this spectacular setting is found some of the state's best loved and long-standing guest ranches. Many also operate as outfitters for fishing and hunting trips, and lead pack trips back into the Bob Marshall Wilderness.

Natural-gas pumps and missile sites dot the fields stretching out from the Rocky Mountain Front. Controversy has erupted between those who want to develop natural gas (and feel that it can be balanced with wilderness) and those who fear such gas exploration and mining will harm the Front's environment.

CHOTEAU

Choteau, at the feet of the Rocky Mountains, is not in Chouteau County; it's the county seat of Teton County. The town (pop. 1,791, elev. 3,800 feet) is built around the county courthouse, smack where Hwy. 287 crosses Hwy. 89.

The town has become known as a paleontological hot spot. Dinosaurs used this area as a breeding ground, and paleontologists (led by Jack Horner, now based in Bozeman at the Museum of the Rockies), have pieced together revolutionary dino-life theories based on bones and eggshells excavated at nearby Egg Mountain.

The Old North Trail was an important migratory trail for proto-Indians running from the Arctic to Mexico over 8,000 years ago. Traces of it are still visible at the Pine Butte Preserve just west of present-day Choteau.

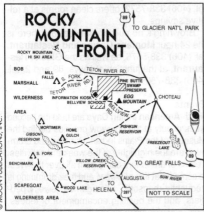

ROCKY MOUNTAIN FRONT

TO GLACIER NAT'L PARK

ROCKY MOUNTAIN HI SKI AREA

BOB

MILL FALLS

MARSHALL

TETON RIVER RD.

S. FORK RIVER RD.

PINE BUTTE SWAMP PRESERVE

WILDERNESS

TETON

INFORMATION KIOSK BELLVIEW SCHOOL

EGG MOUNTAIN

CHOTEAU

AREA

BELLVIEW RD.

MORTIMER

GIBSON RESERVOIR

HOME GULCH

PISHKUN RESERVOIR

S. FORK

WILLOW CREEK RESERVOIR

FREEZEOUT LAKE

BENCHMARK

TO GREAT FALLS

89

SCAPEGOAT WILDERNESS AREA

WOOD LAKE

TO HELENA

AUGUSTA

SUN RIVER

287

NOT TO SCALE

© MOON PUBLICATIONS, INC.

Catholic missionaries preceded the fur traders who started white settlement here; the town was named after Pierre Chouteau, who was associated with the American Fur Company. The first "u" in the name was dropped to distinguish the town from Chouteau County. When fur trading died out, the economic mantle was picked up by cattle ranchers.

Choteau was home to novelist A.B. Guthrie until his death in 1991. Guthrie, best known for *The Big Sky,* was an environmentalist in this land of ranchers and natural-gas speculators.

Teton Trail Village
Standing on Choteau's main street this cluster of old refurbished cabins loaded with period artifacts is hard to miss, and you shouldn't. The biggest draw (besides the ice cream shop) is the **Old Trail Museum,** tel. (406) 466-5332. While the main exhibits at the museum have to do with the area's fossils, including dinosaur bones and eggs, other displays focus on more recent Choteau history, such as the Old North Trail and the story behind a contentious trial and hanging in the 1920s.

The museum has recently received a major grant, allowing it to expand its services and hire a full-time curator/paleontologist. The museum also operates two-day **paleontology workshops,** where, for a fee, interested bone diggers literally get to work in the field with the museum curator. Pre-registration is strongly suggested; costs are $145 per person. The Old Trail Museum also offers 10-day paleontology courses for college

credit in conjunction with the College of Great Falls.

Egg Mountain
Egg Mountain, a nondescript hill west of Choteau, is where paleontological history was made. In the 1970s, a local rancher discovered a cache of dinosaur remains in a shaley outcrop. When the site, a 80-million-year-old formation of mud and ash, was excavated by paleontologist Jack Horner, the soil didn't just yield the bones of adult dinosaurs, but also hundreds of bones from juvenile dinosaurs. The most revolutionary find was nests of fossilized eggs, which strongly suggest that the dinosaurs here—dubbed *maiasauras* "good mother lizards"—were nurturing animals. Rather like modern social bird species, the finds at Egg Mountain indicate that female dinosaurs laid their nests in colonies, protected the nests from predators (pesky albertasaurs), and cared for their juvenile young.

Staff members at the "dinosaur school" run free tours of the dig sites. These tours, held at 2 p.m. every day of July and August, are the *only* times the sites are open to the public. It is imperative that unescorted visitors not trespass on Egg Mountain or the bone beds.

To reach the dinosaur fields, turn off Hwy. 287 south of Choteau at the Triangle Meat Packing plant. Follow the little green Dinosaur School signs; when the road forks, don't take the road to Pishkun Lake—veer right. There are two big digging sites here—Egg Mountain, where evidence of many dino nests has been unearthed, and the "bone beds," final resting place of many maiasaurs.

If you want to take the tour of Egg Mountain, it's a good idea to check in first at the Old Trail Museum in Choteau to make sure the tour is running. It's a rather long detour on dirt roads out to the site, and you can't see much from the road.

Fossil Digs: Serious amateur paleontologists may find that an afternoon tour is not enough. Students at the dinosaur school, supervised by staff from the Museum of the Rockies, are turned loose with jackhammers and screwdrivers, the tools of the paleontological trade here on the eastern front of the Rockies. Daylong workshops are offered at $125 for adults, $95 for kids. Weeklong adult only courses cost $1,450. Students board in the camp tepees, eat the camp food, and, presumably, some drink the camp brew—Jack

Horner's first grant was $10,000 from Rainier Beer. Contact the Museum of the Rockies at (406) 994-6618 for information on these field courses.

Pine Butte Swamp
Nature Conservancy Preserve

Nestled between the Front Range and a missile silo, this preserve stretches from the mountains to the plains across a rare (for this area) wetland. (More precisely, it's a fen, which means that the water actually flows.) Grizzly bears forage here and have historically used the brushy swamp as a corridor to the plains; this is now one of the easternmost outposts of the grizzly, which was native to the plains. Access to the preserve is limited.

Summertime tours are conducted at 3:30 p.m. each weekday, starting from the Bellview Schoolhouse, now the preserve's education center. The schoolhouse is five miles west of Egg Mountain on the same road, and the Pine Butte tours are designed to follow the ones conducted on Egg Mountain.

To visit the swamp at other times, drive past the schoolhouse and turn right on a cut-across road. Drive northwest on this road for about two miles to an information kiosk. Park here, read the posted information, and take the trail starting directly across the road from the kiosk. It's a short easy hike up a flower-strewn ridge to a view of the glacier-carved Pine Butte, wetlands, glacial moraines, faint traces of the Old North Trail, and the Rocky Mountain Front.

The Pine Butte Preserve runs summer workshops for both children and adults. Most of these courses run for several consecutive days and focus on the region's natural history, but nature writing and puppet-making have also been offered. Contact the Pine Butte Swamp Preserve, HC 58 Box 34B, Choteau, MT 59422, tel. (406) 466-5526, for schedules and course descriptions.

Another good wildlife area is **Freezout Lake,** a waterfowl area and wetlands southeast of Choteau, a rest stop for migrating birds. Pelicans, blue-winged teal, and marsh hawks reside here, as do snow geese in the spring and tundra swans each fall. Nearby Priest Butte was the site of a Catholic mission for the Blackfeet.

Recreation

Take your pick of trails on the South Fork of the Teton River—many of them lead into the Bob

Marshall Wilderness. **Our Lake** (called Hidden Lake on the trailhead sign) is three miles up and in. Mountain goats are often visible above the lake. The hike to **Headquarters Pass** starts at the same trailhead (near the Mill Falls Campground) and passes a high waterfall on the Sun River on the way to expansive views. Grizzly bears are sometimes spotted in the area, so take precautions. It's not unusual to run into snowfields on the higher trails even in July.

Rocky Mountain Hi Ski Area has cross-country and downhill trails at Teton Pass. The relatively small downhill area has lift tickets for $17. Cross-country skiers headed for the Bob Marshall Wilderness Area often start from Choteau, as roads are plowed all the way to the mountains.

Fish **Pishkun Reservoir,** southwest of town, for kokanee salmon, northern pike, and rainbow trout.

Accommodations

None of Choteau's motels will bust a traveler's budget—most rooms are less than $35. The attractive **Hensley 287 Motel,** 20 7th Ave. SW, tel. (406) 466-5775, is located on Hwy. 287. Some rooms have kitchenettes. The cheery **Belle Vista Motel,** 614 Main Ave. N, tel. (406) 466-5711, has rooms from $28 and is located just across from the museum. At the **Big Sky Motel,** AAA member, 209 S. Main, tel. (406) 466-5318, rooms start at $45 and have microwaves and cable TV (some also include kitchens). The new **Best Western Stage Stop Inn** tel. (406) 466-5900, 1005 Main Ave. N., has handsomely furnished rooms, with a pool and hot tub. Complimentary continental breakfast included. Rooms are $60 s, $65 d.

The free **Choteau city park campground** is right in town; turn off Hwy. 89 at the blinking light and follow the KOA signs. The city park is closer in than the **KOA,** which is farther east, tel. (406) 446-2615. Choose the city park if flush toilets and running water are amenities enough; for hookups, showers, and campground fees, continue on to the KOA.

Mill Falls Campground is small, free, and well situated for hikers. Follow Hwy. 89 north out of Choteau and turn down the road to Teton Canyon.

B&Bs

The **Country Lane Bed and Breakfast,** on Hwy. 89 1.5 miles north of Choteau, tel. (406) 466-2816, is a very pleasant and spacious contemporary home adjacent to a 58-acre game preserve. There are four guest rooms with king or queen-size beds, a heated indoor pool, and gift shop. The country-style breakfast is especially tasty. Rooms range from $50-70.

If you're looking for historic character, then you'll love the **Inn Dupuyer**, tel. (406) 472-3241, located 34 miles north of Choteau in the little community of Dupuyer (the setting for several Ivan Doig novels). The original inn is a hundred-year-old two-story log home that the owners carefully refurbished by constructing a modern home around the older building, largely encasing the log structure. While the dining room, kitchen, and a parlor area are new and commodious, the bedrooms and the common room are all in the historic log home. All four rooms have private baths and are carefully decorated with local period furnishings; the antique beds all have down comforters. The upstairs common room, with an old wood-burning stove, saddle tack, and rustic furniture, will make you feel as if you've just settled into a very stylish 1890s ranch house. Off the back is a deck with great views onto the Front Range. Rooms are $65-85, open all year. The only drawback is that there's no real restaurant in the town of Dupuyer, although you can drive to Pendroy, 15 miles south, to the **Rose Room,** tel. (406) 469-2205, a Montana original with steaks, chicken, and seafood. Or ask your hosts for advice on local dining.

Guest Ranches
Two of Montana's best guest ranches are tucked in behind the Rockies Front Range, west of Choteau.

For an old-fashioned horse-based guest ranch, it's hard to beat the **Seven Lazy P,** P.O. Box 178, Choteau, MT 59422, tel. (406) 466-2044. In operation for 40 years, this beautifully located ranch offers lodging in comfortable log cabins large enough to sleep an entire family; each has private bath and toilets. Meals are served in the gracious lodge headquarters, reached by a short bridge across a stream. The lodge common room, dominated by a stone fireplace and filled with comfortable rustic furniture, is an atmospheric place to hole up with a book or talk about the day's adventures. Activities include daily organized horseback riding, hiking, and fishing trips—or plain old relaxing. If you're considering a long-distance pack trip into the Bob Marshall Wilderness, the

Seven Lazy P offers seven to 10 day backcountry excursions (owner Chuck Blixrud was elected Montana outfitter of the year in 1995). Rates run $140 a day (three-day minimum), which includes all meals and horseback riding; the weekly rate is $900. Pack trips run $190 a day, or $1,750 for 10 days. Closed in winter.

Visitors are in for a slightly different experience at the **Pine Butte Guest Ranch,** HC 58, Box 34C, Choteau, MT 59422, tel. (406) 466-2158. Stunningly located on the South Fork of the Teton River, with steep escarpments rising on all sides, Pine Butte has been a dude ranch since 1930. The original owners sold it to the Nature Conservancy, which is dedicated to preserving plants, animals, and natural communities by protecting the land and waters they need to survive. Consequently, in addition to traditional dude-ranch activities like trail rides, the ranch also sponsors daily naturalist hikes and programs along the Front Range, focusing on the area's unique natural history. During the spring and fall, the ranch sponsors a series of longer, hands-on workshops on topics like grizzly bears, the local dinosaur digs, or nature photography. You'll leave the Pine Butte Ranch not only saddle sore, but wiser about the natural world of Montana.

Lodging is in very comfortable single and duplex cabins, each with private bathrooms and fireplaces; there's even a swimming pool. Meals are served in the lodge, which is filled with handmade furniture made by the ranch's original owner. Summer rates are $1,075 a week for adults, $825 for children (one week minimum, Sunday to Sunday stays only). During May and September, weekly rates are substantially less, and guests may come for shorter stays (two-night minimum) at $116 a night. Room, board, naturalist tours, and during the summer season horseback riding, are included in the fee, as is Sunday transportation to and from Great Falls Airport. The workshops cost $1,250.

Food and Drink
Summers heat up east of the Rockies, and Choteau is a good place to cool off with an ice-cream cone. There's an ice-cream parlor in the **Teton Trail Village** and another one right across the street at the **OutPost Deli,** 819 7th Ave. N, which is also a good spot for a sandwich, tel. (406) 466-5330. The **Circle N,** 925 N. Main Ave.,

tel. (406) 466-5531, is open for breakfast, lunch, and dinner, and serves steaks, burgers, and a Sunday buffet.

Events
The **Choteau rodeo** takes place on the Fourth of July.

Information
The Forest Service **ranger station** is on Hwy. 89 at the northern edge of town, tel. (406) 466-5341. An information kiosk is set up in Choteau during the summer, and the **Old Trail Museum** is another good source of information, especially for dinosaur details.

The **post office** is at 103 1st Ave. NW.

AUGUSTA

Even more so than Choteau, Augusta is spectacularly located and is a good way in to the Bob Marshall Wilderness Area. As you head south on Hwy. 287 from Choteau, past mounded glacial moraines, the east face of the Rockies becomes closer and more dramatic. The road crosses the Sun River seven miles north of Augusta as it flows from the Rockies to the Missouri. Blackfeet referred to the Sun as the Medicine River: mineral deposits from a side gulch were used medicinally. Gibson Reservoir, named after Paris Gibson, the founder of Great Falls and initiator of hydroelectric power on the Missouri, is on the Sun River right where the Rockies jut up from the plains. The dam was built in 1913 primarily to store and divert water for irrigation.

Augusta is home to the American Legion Rodeo, the state's oldest. It's also one of the best regarded, and people drive hundreds of miles to attend. The rodeo is held on the last Sunday of June.

Sights
Gibson Reservoir is 26 miles northwest of Augusta. Reach it via the road toward the south end of town with the sign to Willow Creek Fishing Access Site (Rd. 1081). On the way to the Rocky Mountain Front, the road crosses a moraine strewn with glacial erratics—boulders carried in glacial ice and then dropped where the ice melted. Once the road meets up with the Sun River, you come right up against the rocks, and the whole geologic idea of "overthrust" becomes startlingly clear.

The road ends just past the dam, and trails continue the length of the reservoir, past medicine springs and Native American pictographs, into the Bob Marshall Wilderness. Bighorn sheep, elk, and deer winter north of the reservoir.

The state bought land for **Sun River Wildlife Management Area** in the 1940s to provide wintering ground for the Sun River elk herd. Previous to that, the elk had competed with cattle on the plains and with bighorn sheep in the mountains. Thousands of elk now winter on the moraine between the Gibson Reservoir and Augusta. Hunting is permitted here, though it's prohibited in the Sun River Game Preserve, part of the Bob Marshall Wilderness Area. The range is closed in the winter (though elk are often visible from nearby roads) and open in the summer to birdwatchers, hikers, and mountain bikers.

Recreation
The trail from Mortimer Campground on Gibson Reservoir goes into the Bob Marshall Wilderness Area.

Other trails into the Bob Marshall and Scapegoat wilderness areas start from Benchmark and South Fork Campgrounds. A trail starts at the South Fork Campground and passes through the Sun River Game Preserve on its way to the spectacular Chinese Wall, a 13-mile-long, 1,000-foot-tall escarpment on the Continental Divide.

Accommodations and Food
The place to stay in Augusta is the **Bunkhouse Inn,** 122 Main St., tel. (406) 562-3387 or (800) 553-4016, a 1912 hotel that started out in Gilman, which is now a ghost town. The old hotel was moved to Augusta, then renovated into a one-of-a-kind rustic inn. It has nine rooms, all with shared baths (the owners point out that this is an improvement over the outhouses of the original hotel). Singles are $25, doubles $35. Restaurant choices are pretty much limited to the cafe at the Wagons West Motel, tel. (406) 562-3295.

Settle in and contemplate geology at **Home Gulch Campground** below Gibson Reservoir on the Sun River, 21 miles from Augusta. Five miles down the road, **Mortimer Campground** perches above the reservoir. A trail leads from Mortimer into the Bob Marshall Wilderness Area.

Three campgrounds south of Gibson Reservoir are on Road 234 (Benchmark Rd.) west of Augusta. **Wood Lake** is 25 miles from Augusta, **Benchmark** is another five miles down the road, and **South Fork** is yet another mile on, at the end of the road. For information, call the ranger station at (406) 562-3247.

Guest Ranches

The mountains behind Augusta harbor a clutch of excellent guest ranches. One of the state's most famous and beloved is **Klick's K Bar L**, in the Sun River Game Preserve. Founded in 1927, this Montana original likes to boast that it's "beyond all roads": no roads lead to the ranch, so to reach the ranch in summer, you'll need to ride a jet boat up Gibson Lake. Lodging is in attractive cabins with one to three rooms; bathrooms are nearby. The main log lodge, with a dining room and large sitting area, is a rustic beauty. There's a natural warm-water swimming pool, along with fishing, trail riding, cook-outs, and wildlife viewing. The Klicks also operate pack trips into the Bob Marshall Wilderness. Contact the ranch at (406) 562-3551 (summer) or 562-3589 (winter), or write care of P.O. Box 287, Augusta, MT 59410. Rates begin at $148 a day, all inclusive, with a six-day minimum.

For a real outback Montana ranch experience, try the **Benchmark Wilderness Ranch**, tel. (406) 562-3336, P.O. Box 190, Augusta, MT 59410. The Benchmark Ranch is located deep in the Lewis and Clark National Forest, so far back that there are still no phones and no electricity (the otherwise modern, comfortable cabins and lodge are powered with propane appliances and lights). The advantage of this remote site is that you don't have to go far from your cabin to arrive in real wilderness. Benchmark specializes in horseback fishing trips ($95 per day adult), either day trips from the ranch or overnight camping trips to even more isolated backcountry lakes and streams. Benchmark also offers long-distance packtrips into the Bob Marshall. These last a minimum of five days; $150 adult per day, $75 children under 11. In the fall, there are guided hunting trips. You'll get a friendly welcome at the Benchmark—the ranch has been in operation since 1928, and you can rest assured that the stock and the hands here are some of the best in the state.

The **JJJ Wilderness Ranch**, P.O. Box 310, Augusta, MT 59410, tel. (406) 562-3653, located on Gibson Reservoir, operates a full-fledged dude ranch, with horseback riding, nature photography, swimming in the heated pool, and fishing. Exploring the Front Range on horseback is the specialty of the Triple J, and you'll get plenty of hands-on instruction from the wranglers. Kids get a special welcome—there's even a special Kids Wrangler to supervise rides and games. Lodging is in cabins, all with modern bathrooms and ample sitting room. Rates are $1,073 per person or $2,044 per couple, per week, Sunday to Sunday only, and include all meals (including steak barbecues) and activities. The Triple J also runs five- to eight-day pack trips into the Bob Marshall for $205 per person per day.

Information

The Forest Service operates a **ranger station** just down Willow Creek Rd., tel. (406) 562-3247.

BOB MARSHALL WILDERNESS AREA

The Bob Marshall Wilderness Area was created in 1940, when three national forest primitive areas were combined and named for a New Yorker who was a strong advocate for wilderness and an inveterate hiker.

The Land

The eastern face of the Bob Marshall is characterized by overthrust—old rocks on young. The Sawtooth Range, which forms the Rocky Mountain Front, shows off faults, folds, and overthrusts in the layers of limestone jutting into the prairie. The rocks here are generally younger than those to their west. Oil and gas speculators have been petitioning the Forest Service since the 1940s for the right to drill in the Bob Marshall and Great Bear wilderness areas.

The eastern Sawtooth side of the Bob Marshall is, as expected, drier, windier, and more sparsely vegetated than the western Swan Range side. Bears, mountain goats (native, not transplants), elk, and bighorn sheep all thrive in this wilderness area.

Getting In

Despite its imposing appearance, the Rocky Moun-

The Sun River flows from the Bob Marshall Wilderness Area.

JUDY JEWELL

tain Front has a number of entrances to the Bob Marshall Wilderness Area. Roads west from Choteau and Augusta end at trailheads, some right near the wilderness boundary. There's a real visual punch gained by entering over the Front Range, where escarpments are pronounced, rather than from the west, across the trailing ends of the propped-up rocks.

The Benchmark trailhead west of Augusta is a particularly popular one, especially with horse

packers. Just to the north, trails from Gibson Reservoir lead right into the wilderness.

From the Headquarters Pass Trail, west of Choteau, continue on to Rocky Mountain Peak, the Bob's highest peak at 9,392 feet. This trail can also be followed to the Chinese Wall (see below).

Backpackers should plan to spend a minimum of five days to a week—distances are great. The Forest Service puts out a topographical map of the Bob Marshall, Great Bear, and Scapegoat Wilderness Complex. Use this map or USGS topos to select a route.

Destinations

Hikers and packers can start at virtually any trailhead and reach the Chinese Wall. This 1,000-foot-high escarpment near the Continental Divide is the hallmark of the Bob and can see a surprising amount of traffic during the summer. For solitude, it's worth studying the maps and consulting with rangers to pick a less traveled area.

West of the Divide, the South Fork of the Flathead River cuts through the Bob and is a favorite with floaters and anglers, who usually come in from Holland Lake on the western border.

East of the Bob Marshall's divide, anglers go after rainbow, brown, lake, golden, and cutthroat trout. Grayling are here too, but they must be released when caught.

The **Sun River Game Preserve** was established in 1912 to protect and develop big-game herds. It now covers much of the eastern half of the Bob Marshall Wilderness Area—the only part of the Bob where hunting is prohibited.

Information

Contact the Forest Service at the Choteau Ranger Station, Rocky Mountain National Forest, Choteau, MT 59422, tel. (406) 466-5341.

DOVER PUBLICATIONS, INC.

THE JUDITH BASIN AND CENTRAL MONTANA

Central Montana is the state's hybrid province: here, hundreds of miles from the Rocky Mountains' front range, isolated mountain peaks rise up like islands from the surrounding prairie. Called outliers, these ranges are literally habitat "islands" to plants and wildlife otherwise found only in the fastness of the Rockies.

Between the mountains are prairielike plateaus—the Judith Basin is the largest and most central of these—that were an ample home first to buffalo, and then, in the same pattern as the rest of eastern Montana, to livestock and farmers. But the mountains inevitably intrude, and nowhere on the central Montana prairies are they out of sight.

Central Montana managed to experience, almost headlong and after the fact, every phase of the state's history. Prospectors followed cattle barons, who were hurried out by the railroads and homesteaders. Fossil-fuel exploration followed giddily, and the region's hub city, Lewistown, is now quickly becoming a retirement community.

It seems odd that such a rich, central, and practical region should be one of the last settled in Montana. But the area's potent amalgam presents the traveler with a telescoped menu of the state's best offerings in hiking, hunting, fishing, wildlife viewing, scenery, and flat-out western culture.

THE LAND

Central Montana is a half-mountain, half-prairie region of high plateaus and mountain valleys, roped in by the rivers that circle, feed, and drain the region. The Missouri River, rising from the south before turning sharply east, borders the area to the west and north; the Musselshell River, flowing east and then abruptly north, delimits central Montana to the south and east. Within this oblong of land has occurred some of Montana's most curious geologic history.

About 50 million years ago vast amounts of magma began to rise randomly along faults and fractures in overlying rock. In some cases, as in the Highwood Mountains, volcanic eruptions occurred. Sometimes the magma pooled under existing sedimentary levels, bulging these strata up to mountain height (the Big Snowy Range). In other cases, magma flowed along fractures until lakes of lava formed at their ends. Erosion has eaten away the softer sedimentary casts, leaving spiny lava outcrops (like Square Butte). Surrounding these mounds and spurs of rock are the rolling prairies.

The molten rock that hardened into mountains in central Montana is quite unusual. Not only has it proved to be rich in gold, silver, and lead, it contains minerals quite rare elsewhere. Shonkinite, a peculiar basalt that makes up the Highwood, Adel, and Bears Paw Mountains, is named for Shonkin, Montana. Some of the world's bluest and most valued sapphires are mined on Yogo Creek in the Little Belt Mountains.

During the last ice age, central Montana's mountains stood above and helped block further advance of the continental ice sheet. Huge lakes formed when rivers like the Missouri and Musselshell, which drained northward, could find no escape for their waters. When these lakes burst and formed new river channels, they cut deep valleys.

Around Great Falls particularly, minor streams today flow through enormous spillways meant to contain the Missouri.

Climate

The mountains of central Montana are not high by world, or even Montana, standards. However, they are very effective in trapping weather. Winters are harsh, and snowfalls are very heavy. In fact, the state record snowfall—33 feet in one year—was recorded in the Little Belt Mountains. Winter can come early and stay late, especially in mountainous areas.

Central Montana does not suffer the same extremes of summer heat as does eastern Montana. Frequent summer thunderstorms keep the region green long after the prairie grasses have withered elsewhere.

INFORMATION

Travel Montana's central Montana district is called Charlie Russell Country. For free travel information contact them at P.O. Box 3166, Great Falls, MT 59403, tel. (800) 527-5348.

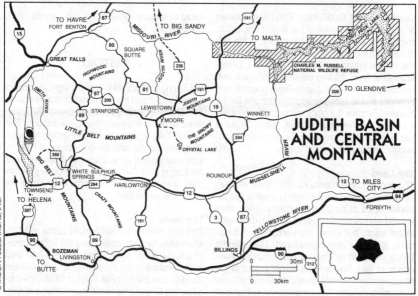

The **BLM office** is on Airport Rd., Lewistown, tel. (406) 538-7461. Most of the mountains in the area are part of the **Lewis and Clark National Forest,** Jefferson Division. The Forest Supervisor's Office can be reached at P.O. Box 871, Great Falls, MT 59403.

GETTING THERE AND AROUND

Great Falls and Billings are the closest airports served by major air carriers, although **Big Sky Airlines** has two flights a day into Lewistown from Billings. Call (800) 237-7788 for schedules; one-way fares between Billings and Lewistown can be as low as $38.

Intermountain Buses offers service between Great Falls and Billings, via Stanford, Lewistown, and Roundup. For schedules, contact the Lewistown depot, 102 W. Main St., tel. (406) 538-3380.

Auto Tours
If you're a fan of Charlie Russell paintings or

Montana history, or are just looking for a theme for your central Montana explorations, consider taking the **CM Russell Memorial Trail.** Charlie Russell spent most of his life between Great Falls and the Judith Basin, and images of the unique landscape, as well as noted events from the area's early history, made their way onto his canvases. A number of private and public sponsors worked together to produce an interpretive guide to central Montana that brings the paintings and landscapes back together. The free guide, available from most tourism offices, or directly from the Russell Country office listed above, keys 25 of Russell's most famous paintings to the landscapes and stories that were part of their genesis. The interpretive points, marked by signs, stand mostly along Hwy. 200 between Great Falls and Lewistown, with a profusion around Russell's old stomping grounds at Utica. It's a great day-trip through beautiful country, one that makes Russell's achievement even more meaningful.

LEWISTOWN

Lewistown (pop. 6,380, elev. 3,960 feet), nestled along Big Spring Creek at the foot of the Judith, Big Snowy, and Moccasin Mountains, is the hub of central Montana (actually, the exact center of the state is located at 1105 W. Main St.). Lewistown is a lively trading center for farmers and ranchers in the fertile Judith Basin country, and provides ample facilities and temptations for the traveler. Besides the city's many buildings of historic and architectural interest, within 30 miles are hiking trails, mountain lakes, trout streams, wildlife viewing, and ghost towns.

The Land
The Big Snowy Mountains (and their eastern extension, the Little Snowies) form a broad, domed arch rising from the plains. They were formed when magma pushed up from deep within the earth; but rather than erupting as a volcano, it pooled and crystallized. This magma blister elevated its limestone overburden thousands of feet. Today the sharper peaks of the Moccasins and Judiths reveal clusters of magma intrusions; erosion has stripped the softer rock

away to expose igneous granite, syenite, and, occasionally, gold.

HISTORY

Big Spring Creek Valley was strategically located as settlement and trade entered central Montana. Fort Sherman trading post, founded in 1873, serviced hunters, trappers, and Crow Indians. The Carroll Trail, a stage route connecting Missouri River steamboats with the gold camps at Helena, was established a year later and passed near the trading post. Camp Lewis, a temporary military post, was built to protect commerce along the trail in the same year.

The Metis
The first permanent settlement came in 1879, when Metis families settled along Big Spring Creek. The half-French, half-Chippewa Metis had lived in the prairies of the northern U.S. and southern Canada until the Riel Rebellion of 1870. Dislocated by the English, the Metis fragmented and drift-

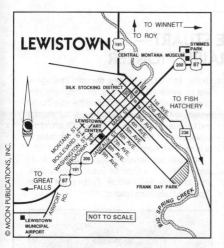

© MOON PUBLICATIONS, INC.

LEWISTOWN

TO WINNETT
TO ROY

CENTRAL MONTANA MUSEUM

SYMMES PARK

SILK STOCKING DISTRICT

TO FISH HATCHERY

LEWISTOWN ART CENTER

TO GREAT FALLS

FRANK DAY PARK

BIG SPRING CREEK

LEWISTOWN MUNICIPAL AIRPORT

NOT TO SCALE

ed westward in search of a homeland. Louis Riel joined the Big Spring Creek Metis in the early 1880s, but in 1884 he returned to Canada with most of his people to organize and resist English Canadian incursions against the Canadian Metis.

After the second Riel Rebellion failed in 1885, the Metis drifted back into Montana as "landless Indians," most of whom were eventually settled on the Rocky Boys Reservation. Some Metis remained on Big Spring Creek and established homesteads. Francis Janeaux opened a store and platted part of his land for the town that eventually became Lewistown.

Taming the Territory

Meanwhile, the Judith Basin was opening up. Granville Stuart established the DHS, a huge open-range cattle ranch, east of Lewistown in 1880. Other ranchers moved in to graze the rich prairies. Prospectors discovered gold at Maiden in the Judith Mountains the same year. The central Montana gold rush was on, and mining camps like Gilt Edge, Maiden, and Kendall boomed.

Even though the Indian Wars of 1876-77 had effectively crushed the fighting force of the Native Americans of Montana, in 1880 the Army established Fort Maginnis to protect fledgling settlements from Indian attack. None occurred, and the indolent soldiers became more of a problem to local residents than the hostiles they purported to deter. The fort was closed in 1890.

Lewistown remained a rough-and-ready frontier town longer than comparable Montana communities. Rustlers preyed on local ranches, finding ample shelter in the rugged Missouri Breaks north of town. A shoot-out on Main Street ended the careers of two suspected ringleaders (known to contemporaries as Rattlesnake Jake and Longhair Owen) in 1884.

Lewistown was incorporated in 1899, and in 1903 the Central Montana Railroad (bought in 1908 by the Milwaukee Railroad) reached this center of mining and ranch trade. What was taken out in cattle or gold was dwarfed by the numbers of homesteaders who came in. The Judith Gap and Lewistown area was quickly and heavily settled by hopeful farmers: nearly 6.5 million acres of land were opened for settlement. The hegemony of the open-range ranches was broken, and by 1920 mining had declined in importance. The fertile countryside of central Montana sheltered homesteaders from some of the vicissitudes encountered by settlers elsewhere, and the gracious homes and buildings of Lewistown bear testimony to the community's long-standing stability.

SIGHTS

Historic Lewistown

Lewistown has one of the prettiest physical settings in the state, and almost matches its natural attributes with its graceful turn-of-the-century architecture. There are three neighborhoods listed as historic districts in the National Register of Historic Places. The chamber of commerce, 408 N.E. Main St., provides brochures with walking tours of Lewistown. Not to miss: The **Fergus County Courthouse,** at 8th Ave. and Main, built in 1907 in mission style; behind it, on Broadway and 7th, is a wooden frame building that originally served as officers' quarters at Fort Maginnis; immediately next door is a wonderful example of a sandstone "four square" home. The **Silk Stocking District,** an area bounded by Boulevard and Washington Streets at 2nd and 3rd Avenues, contains a mix of arts-and-crafts style and neo-Georgian homes built by early haberdashers (hence the name). Dominant throughout, and especially downtown along Main St., are buildings made of sandstone bricks carved by immigrant Croatian stonecarvers.

GRANVILLE STUART— AMBITIOUS PRAIRIE PIONEER

Granville Stuart, statesman, rancher, vigilante, writer, ambassador, and librarian, was among those early Montana settlers who thrived on challenge. Born to Scottish parents in West Virginia in 1834, Stuart accompanied his family to California during that state's gold rush. While returning east, he and his brother James detoured north through Montana. On Gold Creek, near Drummond, they discovered gold in 1858 and essentially started the Montana gold rush. But Granville was canny enough to realize that the *real* way to make money in a gold camp was to supply goods to miners, and he opened a store in Bannack in 1862. He also operated a small farm and soon ran a lumber company as well. He saved his money and began to dabble in ranching in the Deer Lodge Valley.

Stuart was elected to the Territorial Council in 1871 and to the lower house twice, in 1876 and 1879. By 1879, he moved cattle out of western Montana and onto the plains of the east. He helped found the DHS Ranch east of Lewistown, the first large ranch in this part of the state.

Entire towns of rustlers sprang up in the inaccessible Missouri Breaks to prey on these early ranches. At a meeting in Helena in 1884, the Montana Stockgrowers Association named Stuart—a founding member of the association—president. Stuart presented the cattlemen's concerns about rustling to the legislature and to the administrators of Fort Maginnis, which the Army had built in the hay yard of the DHS Ranch. When the branches of the government failed to adopt appropriate measures, Stuart and other fed-up ranchers founded "Stuart's Stranglers," a vigilante gang that broke the back of organized rustling. Estimates of the number of suspected rustlers killed in 1884 vary, but at least 25 died, and perhaps as many as 100.

The winter of 1886-87 dealt with Stuart as sternly as others on the Montana prairies. He swore that he would never again winter an animal he couldn't

shelter. In 1891, he became the state land agent, and he selected 600,000 acres of government land—whose proceeds still support the state school system. In 1894, he was named envoy to Paraguay and Uruguay by President Cleveland. Stuart retired to Montana in 1899 and became the Butte public librarian until his death in 1918.

Although not formally educated, Stuart was an avid reader with a taste for Byron, Shakespeare, and the Bible. His memoir, *Forty Years on the Prairie,* is fascinating reading.

MONTANA HISTORICAL SOCIETY, HELENA

Granville Stuart ca 1883

Central Montana Museum
Located in the same complex as the chamber of commerce, 403 N.E. Main St., tel. (406) 538-5436, this local museum features Indian relics, homesteader memorabilia, and reminders of life on the open range.

Lewistown Art Center
Specializing in Montana art, this small gem of a gallery, 801 W. Broadway, tel. (406) 538-8278, mixes traveling shows of regional art with a good selection of art and crafts in its gallery shop.

Ghost Towns

Note that most of the following ghost towns are located on private land. Landowners have reportedly been restricting access for a number of reasons, including liability and to keep people from packing everything off. If you're keen on actually investigating one of the following gold camps first-hand, call the chamber of commerce to find out what the current state of access is. Otherwise, just driving the public roads to the ghost towns makes for a nice afternoon drive.

Gold was discovered in 1880 in the Judith Mountains; by 1881 **Maiden** claimed a population of 6,000, making it larger than Lewistown, with which it vied for county seat when Fergus County was formed in 1882. To reach Maiden, take Hwy. 191 north from Lewistown for 10 miles, then turn east on a good secondary road, the Maiden Road, for nine miles. This gold camp burned in 1905, making the inevitable ghost town a bit more spectral.

The road up Warm Springs Creek in the Judith Mountains to Maiden is very scenic, and it continues five miles over a very steep pass to **Gilt Edge**, another gold camp gone bust (this is not a road for trailers). Gilt Edge boomed when gold was discovered in the early 1890s. Calamity Jane Cannary claimed that Gilt Edge was her favorite town; she also claimed that she was the local law enforcement. A few intact brick buildings and more disintegrating plank buildings remain. Gilt Edge can also be reached by traveling Hwy. 200 east from Lewistown for 14 miles; turn north another mile.

Farther west in the Moccasin Mountains is **Kendall**, a gold camp that reached its zenith in the first years of this century. The foundations of the union hall and a bandstand are amongst the remains. Take Hwy. 191 north to Hilger, then turn west for about six miles.

Charlie Russell Chew-Choo

It's a real groaner of a pun, but this dinner train through farm and ranch land north of Lewistown has proved to be a popular summer weekend activity. The train, made up of historic dining cars, leaves from Spring Creek Junction and travels to Denton, a three and a half hour ride through some lovely country filled with wildlife, and over the vertigo-inducing Hanover Trestle.

A prime-rib dinner is included in the $69 ticket, along with western entertainment. During Lewistown's Cowboy Poetry Gathering, the trip is accompanied by cowboy rhymes. At present, the train runs only on Saturday evenings. Call (406) 538-2527 or (800) 735-7886 ahead for reservations.

RECREATION

Fishing

The Lewistown area offers great trout fishing. Big Spring Creek issues forth from a spring five miles south of town, and locals consider it one of the best fishing streams in the state. Turn south on 1st Ave. and follow signs to Heath or the State Fish Hatchery. Warm Springs Creek is also good trout fishing, in a more rural setting. Take Hwy. 191 north 10 miles to the intersection of Warm Springs Creek Road.

Lake anglers are also in luck. **Crystal Lake**, high in the Big Snowy Mountains, affords excellent recreational opportunities, including good fishing for rainbows. No motorized boats are allowed. Good hiking trails, overnight camping, and picnicking make Crystal Lake a popular destination for locals. Crystal Lake is 35 miles south of Lewistown; follow Hwy. 200 west seven miles, then follow well-signed gravel roads 28 miles south (or turn off at Moore; it's 21 miles to the lake from here).

Hiking

The gentle, domed peaks of the Big Snowy Mountains provide surprisingly challenging and rewarding hikes. From the south end of Crystal Lake, **Uhlhorn Trail** leads up an initially steep grade to the Big Snowy Crest. High, moderately flat alpine meadows open out across the saddle of the mountains, with great views across the plains of eastern Montana. At the crest, the trail divides. To the west, a two-mile-long trail leads to Ice Cave, cool and exciting to explore with a flashlight. A longer hike involves following the crest trail to the east. The trail continues through meadows until, about six miles in, the ridge narrows to Knife Blade Ridge. The trail skirts abrupt drops on both sides before reaching Greathouse Peak, about 10 miles from the crest trailhead.

CHOKECHERRIES

The chokecherry is one of the few fruits native to the northern prairies. This large deciduous shrub produces sour, aptly named fruit that played a large part both in traditional Plains Indian culture and in the lives of early settlers.

Chokecherries are a large component of pemmican, a staple of the Plains Indian diet. Ground chokecherries were added to powdered dried buffalo meat to form a compound that was both nutritious and portable. For long journeys, nomadic Indians stored pemmican in buffalo-skin vessels, or in their parfleches. Pemmican could be eaten out of hand by people on the move, and it could also be fed into boiling water to make a flavorful soup. Indians also made cakes of dried chokecherries, which were saved and eaten in winter. Chokecherries provided one of the only sources of vitamin C in the plains diet.

As notable as the chokecherry's gastronomic virtues were its emetic properties. Sufferers of stomach complaints or diarrhea made and drank a tea of chokecherry twigs and bark; relief was quick—and lasting. Captain Lewis drank chokecherry tea when he developed intestinal distress along the Missouri and recovered within hours.

Indians also used chokecherry wood for arrow shafts and bows. War and hunting parties used chokecherry wood to build fires because the burning wood produced little smoke.

Homesteaders carefully gathered and processed the fruit into jellies and syrups. To an old-timer, the thought of pancakes and chokecherry syrup brings back happy associations of simpler times.

Mountain ravines and streamsides around Lewistown are still home to stands of chokecherry; recognize them by their pale green-white tufts of flowers and hanging clusters of dark fruit.

Lewistown is host to the Chokecherry Festival the second weekend of September. There's a street dance and a marathon run, and judges award a prize for the best chokecherry recipe. Try one of those recipes, or consider making a batch of chokecherry jelly—just pick the fruit and prepare it according to any recipe for sour cherry jelly. Be careful of the leaves, however—they contain cyanic acid and can be poisonous.

chokecherry,
Prunus virginiana

KAREN McKINLEY

Parks

A scenic place for a picnic is the **State Fish Hatchery** on Upper Big Spring Creek. The eponymous Big Spring is the world's third-largest freshwater spring, discharging 62,700 gallons of water a minute, over three million gallons per hour. Near the hatchery, along the stream and amongst trees, there's a picnic area; tours of the hatchery are available. Follow 1st Ave. south to Country Club Rd. and follow signs for the hatchery.

Closer to town, **Symmes Park** has a picnic area, tennis courts, and a playground, and is located right behind the chamber of commerce and museum at Hwy. 200 and Prospect Avenue. The city swimming pool and water slide is in **Frank Day Park,** 6th Ave. and Cook St. (12 blocks south of Main Street). Also at Day Park is Open Market, a farmers and crafters market held on summer Saturday mornings.

Along Denton Rd., 10 miles north on Hwy. 191, then west on Hwy. 81, lies **Warm Springs,** a natural spring of warm water diverted into a swimming pool. Adjacent is a picnic area. There is a $3 fee for use of the pool and grounds.

Golf

The **Lewistown Elks Country Club,** south of Lewistown on Spring Creek Rd., tel. (406) 538-7075, is a nine-hole course situated above a pastoral mountain stream. The **Judith Shadows Golf Course,** off Marcella Rd., tel. (406) 538-6062, is the town's new 18-hole course.

ACCOMMODATIONS AND FOOD

Hotels and Motels
The **Yogo Inn,** 211 E. Main St., tel. (406) 538-8721 or (800) 860-9646, is Lewistown's most comfortable lodging. The Yogo was developed out of the old train station by a consortium of local citizens, and it caters to the small conven-

tion trade. The Yogo has the kinds of amenities (indoor and outdoor pools, a spa, good restaurant, lounge, meeting rooms) that dignify this class of motel ($59-69 s, $69-79 d).

On the east edge of town is the well-maintained **B & B Motel,** 520 E. Main St., tel. (406) 538-5496 or (800) 341-8000, with rooms at $37 s, $45 d. Pets are okay with a $3 charge. The **Super 8,** 102 Wendell, tel. (406) 538-2581, $42 s, $47 d, stands on the hill west of town, as does the **Mountain View Motel,** 1422 W. Main St., tel. (406) 538-3457 or (800) 862-5786, $31 s, $41 d. The Mountain View is located near a number of restaurants and convenience stores, and also has two two-bed-room houses and one two-bedroom suite, all fully furnished, for daily or weekly rent; pets are okay.

The **Historic Calvert Hotel,** 216 7th Ave. S, tel. (406) 538-5411, $17 s, $29 d, is Lewistown's remaining older hotel, and it's listed on the National Registry of Historic Places.

Campgrounds

Mountain Acres is principally an RV park, located just north of Lewistown on Hwy. 191, tel. (406) 538-7591. Tent campers will prefer **Crystal Lake,** 35 miles south of town.

Food

The **Garden Restaurant,** at the Yogo Inn, 211 E. Main St., tel. (406) 538-8721, has Lewistown's most varied menu, featuring local trout along with beef, pasta, and seafood. Combining Southwestern cooking and a used bookstore, **Poor Man's Book and Southwest Cafe,** tel. (406) 538-4277, 413 W Main St., is an unusual mix for Lewistown. The food is very good as well as inexpensive, and you can browse the bookshelves while you wait. Open for lunch only. The **Main Street Bistro,** 122 W. Main St., tel. (406) 538-3666, adds continental flavors to the Lewistown dining scene, with pasta dishes, salads, and fresh vegetables.

Elsewhere, steaks are the order of the day. The **Hackamore Casino,** two miles west of Lewistown on Hwy. 200, tel. (406) 538-5685, and the **4 Aces,** 508 1st Ave. N, tel. (406) 538-9744, are both good supper clubs (with menus heavily weighted to beef) that can't quite decide if they are restaurants, casinos, or nightclubs.

Go to the **Whole Famdamily,** 206 W. Main St., tel. (406) 538-5161, for home-style cooking; this is the kind of place that has great pies and huge sandwiches. Visit your food roots at a classic Lewistown diner, such as the homey **Empire Cafe,** 214 W. Main St., tel. (406) 538-9912.

EVENTS

Lewistown's biggest summer festival is the **Montana Cowboy Poetry Gathering.** Every year the number and quality of the poets increase, with home-spun artists coming in from all over the western U.S. and Canada. Headquartered at the Yogo Inn, but with events held at a variety of locations around Lewistown, the gathering happens in mid-August. It's a great time to be visit Lewistown, as the festival is really taking off in popularity and reputation, with new functions and activities added every year. Be sure to make reservations well in advance. For more information, contact the chamber of commerce.

SERVICES

The **Lewistown Area Chamber of Commerce** stands at 408 N.E. Main St., Lewistown, MT 59457, tel. (406) 538-5436 or (800) 216-5436.

The **Central Montana Medical Center** is at 408 Wendall Ave., tel. (406) 538-7711. **Emergency** is 911.

Winter storms can be intense in the local mountains. To check **local road conditions,** call (406) 538-7445.

If dirty clothes are getting you down, go to the **Sun Shine Laundry,** 511 E. Main St., tel. (406) 538-9919.

The **Carnegie Public Library** is at 701 W. Main St., tel. (406) 538-5212. The **post office** is at 204 3rd Ave. N, tel. (406) 538-3439.

GETTING THERE AND AROUND

Two flights daily on **Big Sky Airlines** link Lewistown with Billings. One-way fare can be as cheap as $30. Contact Big Sky Airlines at (800) 237-7788 for schedules; their number at the airport is (406) 538-2311.

Rimrock Stage Buses run between Billings, Lewistown, and Great Falls. The Lewistown depot is at 513 1st Ave. N, tel. (406) 538-9227.

Cars are available from **Budget Car Rental,** 519 W. Broadway St., tel. (406) 538-7701.

EAST OF LEWISTOWN

Once the traveler descends from the pass of the Judith Mountains 10 miles east of Lewistown, unadulterated eastern Montana lies ahead. The ponderosa pines quickly thin and give way to shortgrass prairie; mountain valleys flatten into wide coulees surmounted by sandstone bluffs. Ranches displace farms, and gray rain clouds from the west veer upwards, cauterized by heat rising off the prairies. Somewhere hereabouts, the Great Plains begin in earnest.

This part of Montana is more often traversed than visited: even by Montana standards, this is pretty forlorn country. Nonetheless, it bears the memories of a violent history, sporadic development, and early settlement. Today, in the tradition of the glory days of the West, this outpost of central Montana supports large ranches, a vast wildlife refuge, and tiny communities known mostly for their watering holes.

THE LAND

Within the arm formed by the Musselshell River flowing north to meet the Missouri, flat but eroded prairies stretch between Grassrange and Winnett. The plains belie their beginnings as sedimentary seabeds, and, especially north along the present-day Missouri you can see the effect of Glacial Lake Musselshell.

Geologists discovered one of the first and richest oil fields in this part of Montana in 1920. The Cat Creek Anticline, a buckling of sedimentary layers caused at the same time the mountains rose in central Montana (about 50 million years ago), contains domes of oil-rich sandstone at a depth of about 1,200 feet.

An earlier but less productive oil discovery was made in the impressive Devil's Basin, 27

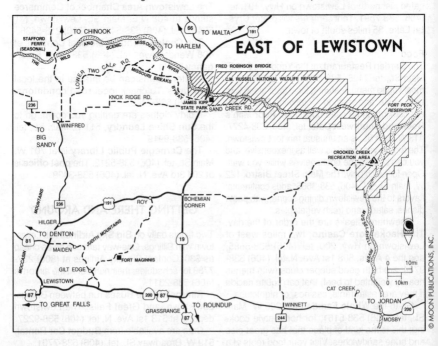

miles south of Grassrange on Hwy. 87. Here, sandstone layers are so tightly folded by underlying faults that they rise in steep ridges and stalk across a wide, barren valley.

HISTORY

As with the Big Open region just to the east, here the requisite historical phases of boom and development came late and peremptorily. There was little settlement—of a law-abiding sort—until this century, making this one of the last areas of Montana to be settled.

As early as the 1860s, Fort Musselshell, established at the Musselshell and Missouri river juncture, was a busy trade center with the Gros Ventre Indians. By the 1870s, the more hostile Sioux forced abandonment of the trading post. Another trading outpost, Carroll, was established just up the Missouri in 1874. From here, freighters established a stage route west to the gold camps at Helena, in hopes that Carroll's downstream location would displace Fort Benton as the hub of steamboat trade, at least in low-water years. The stages stopped rolling after only one year.

Trappers, wolf hunters, and woodchoppers (for the steamboats) were the only permanent residents of this remote country, and they lived together in rough camps that passed for towns. As steamboat trade dwindled, the settlements increasingly became hideouts for rustlers and outlaws; Kid Curry and his gang had a pied-à-terre in a knocked-together river town called Rocky Point. The Breaks, as this rough country was known, became synonymous with rustlers and ne'er-do-wells. An 1870 census found 170 people living along the Missouri from Fort Benton to North Dakota; the count included only one white woman.

The Open Range

On the prairies that spread out eastward from the Judith Mountains, cattlemen like Granville Stuart soon established huge open-range ranches. By the 1880s, lawlessness was so rife that Fort Maginnis, raised on the flats next to Stuart's DHS Ranch, spent more time pursuing rustlers than intimidating Indians.

The mouth of the Musselshell hosted numerous rustler gangs: in this wild country of brushy badlands, box canyons, and primitive settlements, wayward cowboys could trail stolen cattle and horses into secret ravines, alter their brands, and sell them to traders or trail them to Canada. Once in Canada, they would steal other livestock and trail them south into the States.

As the situation worsened, Stuart and a posse of like-minded vigilantes met at a bar in Gilt Edge and decided to take matters into their own hands. During the summer of 1884, "Stuart's Stranglers," as the vigilantes called themselves, took the offensive against the rustling rings along the Missouri. In a series of shoot-outs and hangings, at least 17 men were killed by the vigilantes in Rocky Point, at the mouth of the Musselshell, and other hideouts along the Missouri. Spurred on by their success, Stuart's Stranglers took their show on the road, and in secret raids in other parts of eastern Montana killed an estimated 100 more suspected thieves.

So the ranchers rid themselves of the threat of rustlers; but as these stockmen did not own the land they grazed, soon homesteaders carved the open range into half-section parcels.

CHARLES M. RUSSELL NATIONAL WILDLIFE REFUGE, WESTERN UNIT

The Western Unit of the Charles M. Russell National Wildlife Refuge forms the northern border of much of this area. Created in 1936, the 1.2-million-acre C.M.R., as it is known locally, is the second-largest wildlife refuge outside of Alaska. Highway 191 is one of two paved roads into the refuge; the other is 125 miles east. Anyone who wishes to visit the refuge must be willing to drive, sometimes for great distances, on gravel and dirt roads. The rustlers and outlaws who holed up here did so for a reason: it's hard country to navigate. However, isolation conducive to thieving is also conducive to wildlife.

Travelers without high-clearance vehicles are advised to cross the Fred Robinson Bridge on Hwy. 191 and take the **Self-Guided Nature Trail,** a 20-mile loop north of the Missouri. Those with more versatile vehicles can explore the back roads of these rugged, isolated, and uninhabited badlands on the south side.

Sand Creek Road leaves the pavement four miles south of the Fred Robinson Bridge, at the refuge headquarters, and winds through badlands, with several side roads giving onto the riverbottoms. A much longer road (and in bad weather one of more dubious passability) leaves Hwy. 191 near the crossroads at Bohemian Corners (and runs north from Hwy. 200 at Winnett) and leads into some of the roughest and most historic wildlands in the refuge. **Crooked Creek Recreation Area** is located at the mouth of the Musselshell River, where the waters of Fort Peck Lake meet steep gumbo canyons.

Many travelers will find this rugged but eerily beautiful country reason enough to visit the refuge, but don't forget the wildlife. Deer, pronghorn, and elk range through the refuge in profusion. Bighorn sheep, coyotes, and prairie dogs can be seen by the sharp-eyed, and over 200 bird species have been sighted.

Back Country Byways
The BLM has designated some scenic off-road routes under its protection as "Backcountry Byways." The **Missouri Breaks Back Country Byway** makes a loop west of Hwy. 191 and travels through rough badlands, with views onto the Missouri River and its canyon. The byway begins within the Charles M. Russell National Refuge and continues along the boundary of the Upper Missouri Wild and Scenic River area. Turn west on Knox Ridge Rd. one mile south of the Fred Robinson Bridge. The most questionable part of the entire route immediately looms as the dirt road climbs up a very steep grade to the top of the breaks. After this point, the road becomes much less stressful; however, do not attempt this route if it's at all wet.

The BLM's designated route splits off Knox Ridge Rd. and turns north toward the river along Lower Two Calf Road. From it, several side roads drop onto the riverbottom. Sweeping views of the Missouri and wildlife sightings make this byway both instructional and awe-inspiring. The route rejoins Knox Ridge Rd. and returns to Hwy. 191 across high prairies.

The entire loop road is 73 miles long; at the western junction of Knox Ridge and Lower Two Calf roads, the traveler can also continue 12 miles to Winifred and paved Hwy. 236.

Campgrounds
Informal camping is allowed in most areas of the

C.M.R., with established campgrounds at **James Kipp State Park,** at the Fred Robinson Bridge on Hwy. 191. The campgrounds at **Crooked Creek** have a boat launch, but not fresh water.

Information
Contact the Charles M. Russell National Wildlife Refuge at P.O. Box 110, Lewistown, MT 59547, tel. (406) 538-8706.

WINNETT AND VICINITY

History
Walter Winnett's ranch along McDonald Creek evolved in 1909 from an open-range camp to a small town as homesteaders who settled the valley needed a center for commerce. The Milwaukee Road extended to Winnett (present pop. 190, elev. 2,960 feet) in 1917, just as drought hit. The community began to fray, then in 1919 oil was discovered at Devils Basin, the first oil strike in central Montana. Despite the bad years for farmers, Winnett's population boomed with the hope of more oil strikes. At Cat Creek, on the Musselshell, drillers discovered significant reserves of oil in 1920. A pipeline was laid to Winnett, a refinery was established, and the railroad shipped out the first tanker of oil in 1921. By 1923, Winnett had a population of 2,000 people.

But the boom was short-lived; within 10 years, Winnett had lost three-quarters of its population, even though Cat Creek continued to produce oil. Ranching and farming, much of it on arid and marginal land, again took over as the area's primary economy.

Accommodations and Food
In this vast unpopulated area, there are few lodging options. In reality, only bad luck, car trouble, or the spirit of adventure should catch you spending the night out here. The **Northern Hotel,** tel. (406) 429-7781, is one of Winnett's originals; $15 d. In the tiny community of Grassrange, the motels vie for the trucking trade. The grimly efficient **Grassrange Motel,** tel. (406) 428-2242, is part of a bar/cafe complex. Also in Grassrange, the **Little Montana Truckstop,** tel. (406) 428-2270, has an RV park and showers.

Winnett has seen good times and bad.

In Winnett, the **Kozy Korner,** tel. (406) 429-2621, is open 6 a.m.-9 p.m. At the crossroads of Hwys. 87 and 191, there's the **Bohemian Corner Cafe,** tel. (406) 464-2321, open 7 a.m.-9 p.m. The **Grassrange Bar,** tel. (406) 428-2242, also serves food, as do the truck stops.

WHITE SULPHUR SPRINGS AND THE BELT MOUNTAINS

The wide basin of the Shields and Smith Rivers stretches between the Missouri and Yellowstone drainages. Although hemmed in by five mountain ranges, the valleys are vast and flat: prairie wanna-bes.

White Sulphur Springs lies at the center of this valley network. The hot springs for which the town is named were first enjoyed by Indians; by the turn of the century, developers advertised them as America's answer to Europe's famous spas in Baden-Baden.

As elsewhere in central Montana, the mountains drew early settlers to mining camps; one of the richest gold strikes in the state was in the Big Belts. The valleys provided ranching, which proved to be a less transitory occupation.

The basin offers unparalleled recreational opportunities. The Shields and Smith Rivers, and also Belt Creek, hold pedigrees as great trout streams. The Smith River passes through a deep limestone canyon, making it inaccessible to land vehicles for 61 miles; this section has become a favorite for river floaters.

THE LAND

The basin drained by the Smith and Shields Rivers is flanked by mountains that rose in conjunction with volcanic activity in central Montana. The exception are the Big Belt Mountains, which formed as recently as 25 million years ago when bedrock buckled, forcing very old sedimentary layers to the surface. Across the valley, the Little Belt Mountains were formed earlier. The Castle Mountains just to the south erupted about the same time. The molten core of the Crazy Mountains pushed up through still-wet layers of sediment to form serrated peaks. The Bridger Range is a buckle of sedimentary rock that rose as the central Montana volcanoes erupted.

Also forced upward as the Big and Little Belts buckled were plateaus of Madison limestone. The Smith River cuts a long canyon through this formation; Belt Creek leaves the Little Belt Mountains through an escarpment of limestone.

HISTORY

Diamond City in Confederate Gulch in the Big Belt Mountains was the site of one of the state's earliest and richest gold strikes. Three veterans of the Civil War found the placers in 1864; by 1867 the town's population had swollen to 5,000, with a reputation for wildness and wealth.

The gravels were extraordinarily rich. Legends tell of single pans containing a thousand dollars' worth of gold; in one day miners claimed 700 pounds of gold from one strike. But the diggings were shallow; by 1870 the boom was over and the gold camp deserted. But not before prospectors extracted an estimated $16 million from the gulch.

Miners decamped to the Little Belts and Castle Mountains, and moved onto silver, lead, and copper. Prospectors discovered copper east of White Sulphur Springs in 1866; the mining camp, called Copperopolis, had to send its ore to Wales to be smelted. Production of silver began at Neihart in 1881 and wavered until the Great Northern Railway built a line up Belt Creek in 1891. Monarch grew up as a commercial and smelting center for local miners. There has been little significant mining activity in the Little Belts since 1900, however.

The Army built Fort Baker on the Smith River in 1869 to protect the thriving mining camps of Confederate Gulch from Indian reprisal. It was relocated upstream in 1870 and renamed Fort Logan. The fort was never called on militarily, and it was abandoned in 1880. Several original log buildings remain.

Real settlement of the Smith and Shields valleys awaited the railroads and the Homestead Acts. Richard Harlow's much-ballyhooed Montana Railroad bypassed White Sulphur Springs, which angered residents who fancied their town to be a major spa waiting to happen. Harlow instead linked the Missouri River to the silver camp of Castle in 1895. The Milwaukee Railroad bought Harlow's "Jawbone" Line in 1908.

White Sulphur Springs finally got its railroad in 1910, when local entrepreneurs built the ambitiously named White Sulphur Springs and Yellowstone Park line. Despite the moniker, the line merely linked White Sulphur Springs to Ringling, 18 miles away.

WHITE SULPHUR SPRINGS AND VICINITY

White Sulphur Springs (pop. 964, elev. 5,200 feet) was named for the white deposits left by the hot water that burbles up in the city's public park just off Hwy. 12. The 115° waters only faintly smell of sulphur, but weary travelers have soaked in them for centuries. Today, the flow is tapped for use in the Spa Hot Springs Motel; it also heats the town bank.

History

White Sulphur Springs had been a popular hot springs for local Indians for many years; Crow chief Plenty Coups recalled pilgrimages by warriors to the medicinal mud baths. James Brew-

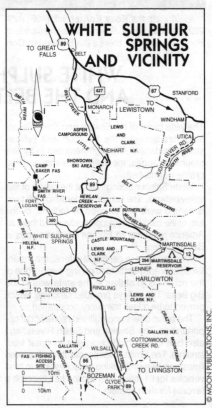

er chanced onto the area in 1866, as stagecoaches rumbled through along the Carroll Trail. Brewer developed the hot springs as a stage stop for travelers; references to Baden-Baden, whose famous German springs the waters here are said to resemble, dot his early promotional literature. However, the grand hotel and spa envisioned by early boosters never materialized.

Notoriety of another sort has clung to White Sulphur Springs. Two noted Montana writers, Walt Coburn and Ivan Doig, hail from local ranches. The latter's *This House of Sky* is autobiographical and is set hereabouts.

White Sulphur Springs' 1892 granite mansion the Castle now serves as the Meagher County Historical Museum.

Sights

The gracious homes built in White Sulphur Springs during the 1890s are testimony to the wealth of open-range ranchers who found the wide valleys hospitable for cattle and sheep raising.

The Castle, a mansion built in 1892 out of locally carved granite, now functions as the **Meagher County Historical Museum,** 310 2nd Ave. NE. It contains a selection of artifacts from the region's early history and some beautiful period furniture. The mansion itself is well restored; the carved wood and moldings are to die for. Open Memorial Day to Labor Day 10 a.m.-6 p.m., $3 admission, tel. (406) 547-2324.

Eighteen miles northwest of White Sulphur Springs along Hwy. 360 are the remains of **Fort Logan,** the military post built in 1870 to defend local mining camps. The log blockhouse still stands on the banks of the Smith River, surveying the valley.

Floating and Fishing the Smith River

The Smith River gets off to an easygoing start in the wide basin around White Sulphur Springs but soon passes into a narrow canyon cut through extensive limestone formations. Between old Camp Baker and Eden Bridge, a 61-mile stretch, the river can only be reached by boat. The extreme remoteness of this portion of the Smith,

along with excellent wildlife viewing and old-fashioned excitement, make this float very popular.

The Smith also offers excellent fishing for brown and rainbow trout. The state maintains two fishing-access sites and campgrounds in otherwise inaccessible portions of the river north of White Sulphur Springs. Take Hwy. 360 west and follow signs to Smith River (18 miles) or Fort Baker (26 miles).

Due to increased traffic on the river, the Dept. of Fish, Wildlife, and Parks, tel. (406) 454-3441, has begun to limit the number of **float trips** down the Smith. Only 73 commercial launches are allowed during the summer, and permits for public, non-outfitted float trips are now distributed in a lottery. Even the campsites are available by reservation only. Most outfitters will offer four-, five-, and six-day trips down the Smith; the difference in the length of trips is the pace of the trip. Four days is break-neck and exhausting, six days is leisurely and suited to anglers. A full Smith River trip costs around $2,500.

The following outfitters are amongst the best and most environmentally sensitive; some of the other major float trip companies on the Smith have made a habit of trashing the campsites and the river in their haste to make a buck. Some of the better Smith River outfitters include **Paul Roos Outfitters,** tel. (406) 442-5489 or (800) 858-3497, Box 621, Helena, MT 59601, and the **T Lazy B**

Ranch, tel. (406) 682-7288, 532 Jack Creek Rd., Ennis, MT 59729.

One of the best local fishing and hunting outfitters is **Avalanche Basin Outfitters**, tel. (406) 547-3962, P.O. Box 17, White Sulphur Springs, MT 59645, which offers guided fishing trips on the Smith and other local rivers. **Castle Mountain Fly Fishers**, P.O. Box 404, White Sulphur Springs, MT 59645, tel. (406) 547-3918, is another good fishing outfitter that specializes in remote fly-fishing camp trips.

Accommodations

The **Spa Hot Springs Motel**, 202 W. Main St. or P.O. Box 370, tel. (406) 547-3366, $42 s, $52 d, has White Sulphur Springs' trademark hot water piped into indoor and outdoor pools. Nonguests can drop by for a swim and soak for $4.50. Under new ownership (a retired chiropractor), the motel and springs are going through a renaissance. All beds have been fitted with Sealy Posturepedic mattresses, and the entire facility, including the guest rooms, have been extensively remodeled. The mineral pools are drained and cleaned nightly, making this a very clean spa. The **Tenderfoot Motel**, W. Main St., tel. (406) 547-3303 or (800) 898-3303, $25 s, $33 d, offers small cabins with kitchenettes as well as motel rooms. All the units have recently been remodeled; some rooms are accessible to guests with disabilities.

Very nice bed-and-breakfast accommodations are also available. The imposing **Foxwood Inn** is a 105-year-old, 28-room mansion about a mile southwest of town off Hwy. 360; tel. (406) 547-2224 or (800) 508-5225. There are 15 guest rooms, $45 s, $62 d. All rooms have phones and mountain views and have been newly redecorated.

At the **Montana Mountain Lodge,** 22 miles north of White Sulphur Springs at 1780 Hwy. 89 N, tel. (406) 547-3773, the focus is on recreation. Equal parts a outdoorsperson's lodge and a B&B, this modern five-bedroom guesthouse (all with private baths) is located in a lovely and secluded spot in the Belt Mountains. It's an easy walk to a fishing stream, and the proprietor, once a field organizer for the Aubudon Society, doesn't need much encouragement to strike out on a birdwatching expedition. In winter, there's no end to the action, as the lodge is close to Showdown Ski Area, and cross-country plus snowmobile trails. Not only is the owner is a fountain of knowledge

about the region, and indeed about all things Montanan, she's able to put together impromptu expeditions and horseback rides—even great meals—with short notice. Rooms begin at $70.

Campgrounds

The **Springs Campground,** on Hwy. 89, tel. (406) 547-3921, is convenient for RV campers. Consider camping lakeside at **Newlan Creek Reservoir,** 10 miles north of White Sulphur Springs, or along **Sutherlin Reservoir,** 12 miles east on Hwy. 12.

Food

The locals' favorite place for coffee and pie is the **Truck Stop Cafe** on the east end of Main St., tel. (406) 547-3825; it's open 5:30 a.m.-10 p.m. For a good steak, go to the **Connexion,** tel. (406) 547-9994, just south of town.

Information

The **Meagher County Chamber of Commerce** can be reached at P.O. Box 365, White Sulphur Springs, MT 59645, tel. (406) 547-3366. The **Lewis and Clark National Forest** office's address is P.O. Box A, White Sulphur Springs, MT 59645, tel. (406) 547-3361.

For information about floating the Smith River, contact the **Dept. of Fish, Wildlife, and Parks,** 4600 Giant Springs Rd., Great Falls, MT 59404, tel. (406) 454-3441, or contact the outfitters listed above.

NORTH OF WHITE SULPHUR SPRINGS ON HIGHWAY 89

Actually anything but little, the Little Belt Mountains ramble across 1,500 square miles of central Montana. Formed by underlying folds in the bedrock, these broad arches expose rocks from a hodgepodge of sources, including Precambrian sedimentary rock, limestone, and igneous intrusions. Silver has been mined in the Little Belts since the 1880s, but now more famous are the sapphire mines on Yogo Creek. Originally considered to be detritus from gold placer mining, the blue stones were analyzed and discovered to be sapphires of unusually high quality and a startlingly dark blue color. They occur, like diamonds in South Africa, in a "pipe" only eight feet across and three miles long. Sapphires have been mined commercially since 1896; the mines are not open to the public, but Yogo sapphires are available from local jewelers.

Recreation, however, and not mining, seems to be the future of the Little Belts. Skiing, hiking trails, snowmobile tracks, and great fishing now characterize these pretty but undramatic mountains. **Showdown Ski Area,** high in the Little Belts, holds the state's record snowfall—33 feet of snow in one winter. For your $25 lift ticket, you get access to 34 runs with a vertical drop of 1,400 feet. Facilities include a cafeteria, a bar, ski rentals, and a pro shop. Showdown is eight miles south of Neihart, tel. (406) 236-5522 or (800) 433-0022; call (406) 771-1300 for the 24-hour snowline.

Neihart

There's not much life left in the old mining town of Neihart. It began in 1881 when silver was discovered; the rail line to Great Falls would have ensured growth if the silver market had remained stable. Neihart was marginalized after the silver crash of 1893. Victorian-era homes and a log school testify to its more affluent days.

One oasis in Neihart is **Bob's Bar and Grill,** tel. (406) 236-5955, which also sells hunting and fishing licenses. Forest Service campgrounds abound along Hwy. 89 in the Little Belts: **King's Hill,** nine miles south of Neihart, and **Aspen,** six miles north of Neihart, are convenient to the highway.

The Lewis and Clark National Forest's **Belt Creek Information Station** is on Hwy. 89 in Neihart, tel. (406) 236-5511.

Monarch

Born a mining camp, Monarch has developed into a tourist center. Its sylvan character, access to fishing in Belt Creek, and bars and restaurants make this a favorite stop for hikers and skiers from Great Falls.

As Hwy. 89 drops out of the Little Belts and onto Belt Creek, 10 miles north of Monarch, a roadside stop overlooks Belt Creek as it issues out of a canyon of white limestone cliffs. At the **Sluice Box State Monument,** trails lead up the creek beneath these cliffs. It's a good spot for a picnic, or to try for a trout.

Accommodations are offered for $50 single, $60 double at the **Cub's Den,** tel. (406) 236-5922, an all purpose enterprise with a grocery store, gas station, and restaurant. The restaurant boasts a full lunch and dinner menu, from peanut butter sandwiches to steak and lobster. Next door is a casino and bar. The motel has a pool and hot tub, and a poolside continental breakfast is served; pets are okay. The **Lazy Doe,** tel. (406) 236-9949, serves lunch and dinner, and overlooks Belt Creek.

Recreation

The Little Belts along Hwy. 89 have been mined and logged. To explore the range on foot, travelers should hike into the headwaters of the Judith River—the South Fork, Lost Fork, and Middle Fork of the Judith are each served by good trails. The drainages cut through limestone canyons and are de facto wilderness areas.

For access to the hiking trails, follow the Judith River southwest from Utica along a good gravel road toward **Fred Ellis Memorial Recreation Area.** Follow signs to the trailhead.

SOUTH OF WHITE SULPHUR SPRINGS ON HIGHWAY 89

The Shields River

From the western slopes of the Crazy Mountains flows the Shields River. Highway 89 follows the river as it drains southward through lush farm and ranch land. In the 1860s frontiersman Jim Bridger led settlers up the Shields River and over Battle Ridge Pass into the Gallatin Valley to western Montana gold camps. Settlement spread up the valley after the Northern Pacific reached Livingston in 1882; a stage line soon linked Clyde Park to the Yellowstone Valley, and a spur line of the NP extended to Wilsall in the first decade of this century.

In the saddle between the Shields and Smith Rivers is Ringling, named for John Ringling, of circus fame, who settled and ranched near here. A division point on the Milwaukee Road, it now contains a grain-alcohol plant that converts local wheat and barley to gasohol. St. John's Catholic Church sits on a bluff above the town, dominating the skyline.

There's good fishing in the Shields River and its Crazy Mountain tributaries. Hiking trails to high mountain lakes in the Crazies depart from trailheads on Cottonwood Creek.

HIGHWAY 12 AND THE MUSSELSHELL VALLEY

The Musselshell River rises in the peaks of the Crazy, Castle, and Little Belt Mountains and flows east through a wide wooded valley, lined with farms and ranches. Here is some of the gentlest beauty in Montana; shaded by majestic cottonwoods, cattle graze along a rushing river flanked by steep sandstone cliffs. And, as everywhere in central Montana, mountains loom in the distance like ramparts.

Rarely in Montana does the integrity of the natural landscape seem so little in conflict with the pursuits of agriculture. The compromise that nature has made with the rancher seems only to have made the landscape more gracious.

Almost nowhere else in Montana have a region and a railroad been so closely linked as the Musselshell River Valley and the Milwaukee Railroad; the solid towns built alongside the railroad reflect the confident dreams of settlers that it brought west. Roundup and Harlowton have endured as trade centers; however, the scope and solid stylishness of their old town centers contrast oddly with their present, chastened realities. They wear their pasts awkwardly, like ill-fitting clothes—modest communities occupying towns built for larger purposes.

Other settlements—Shawmut, Twodot, Ryegate—didn't fare as well. Today all but ghost towns, these old communities are stone and brick monuments to the poignant, and mostly unrealized, dreams of an entire generation of Montanans.

Highway 12 parallels the old Milwaukee Road and serves the farming, ranching, and mining communities that sprawl across this piece of Montana. This is one of the most beautiful drives in the state; east to west, it's more direct than the freeway.

Fishing

The Musselshell River affords good fishing for trout in its upper reaches west of Harlowton. From Roundup to Fort Peck Lake, catfish, northern pike, and smallmouth bass predominate. Lake fishing at Sutherlin, Martinsdale, and Deadman's Basin reservoirs is excellent for rainbow trout.

THE LAND

The Castle and Little Belt Mountains formed when magma shot up from deep in the earth, pushing up the earth's surface in broad domes. Eventually, erosion exposed the mountains' granite cores.

The Crazies tell a more unusual creation story. They too were formed by the intrusion of magma, but here the molten rock projected into still-moist sediment. The enormous heat of the magma baked the wet sand and mud into hard metamorphic deposits. Erosion has washed away the softer deposits, leaving the jutting igneous intrusions and their husks of baked sandstone. Glaciers later carved steep valleys into the sharp peaks.

After leaving the mountain valleys, the Musselshell passes into a wide prairie valley with sandstone bluffs flanking the river. Near Roundup, the river cuts into the Fort Union Formation. Its rich veins of coal were mined during the early years of this century.

As Hwy. 12 climbs up out of the Musselshell Valley and into the lower Yellowstone drainage, it crosses a broad saddle of land punctured here and there with oil wells. The bleak prairie surface disguises an anticlinal arch in the bedrock, that trapped significant reserves of oil.

HISTORY

The Musselshell Valley was a rich hunting ground for early Indians, but it didn't historically belong to any single tribe; it was either shared or battled for. In the 1830s, part of the Crow tribe moved north from the Bighorn River Valley, settled along the Musselshell, and became known as the River Crow. Subsequent treaties established the Crow Reservation south of the Yellowstone, and the River Crow were removed from the Musselshell.

By the 1870s, open-range cattle companies grazed the valleys of central Montana. The Army established a trail linking Fort Custer on the Bighorn and Fort Maginnis near Lewistown; it crossed the river near the present town of Musselshell. Texas drovers considered this ford to be the last stop in the long trail from the south; thereafter, cattle fanned out to graze the rich prairies to the north. The Musselshell Valley and Judith Basin remained the province of open-range ranchers for almost 30 years. Two of these ranches—the Twodot and the Seventynine—have passed into western lore. Uncharacteristically, the big cattle outfits here shared the range with enormous sheep ranches, especially near Martinsdale and Sumatra.

Mining began in the 1880s at Castle, where a rich vein of silver was intermittently exploited. However, central Montana was far from any railroad—ox teams hauled the ore to Helena for smelting—which made further development of minerals unprofitable. Local residents began to call for a central Montana railroad. During the 1890s, Richard Harlow built the Montana Railroad, in fits and starts and as financing allowed, eventually linking Lombard, on the Missouri River, to Harlowton and Lewistown in 1903.

The Chicago, Milwaukee, St. Paul and Pacific Railroad, on its way to Seattle, laid tracks up the Musselshell in 1908. The firm bought the Montana Railroad from Harlow, thereby extending into the Judith Basin. Coal deposits at Roundup were developed to fuel the Milwaukee's engines.

In 1915 the Milwaukee announced that it would electrify its engines between Harlowton and Avery, Idaho, which made it at the time the longest stretch of electric railroad in North America. The engines that pushed the trains uphill ran backwards downhill, working both as brakes and as generators to recharge up to 60% of the electricity expended on inclines.

Ad campaigns from the railroad convinced prospective settlers of the richness of central Montana. Towns sprang up along sidings, and farmers claimed the bottomland, half section by half section, signaling the end of the open range. The media trumpeted the bumper crops raised by these first-time farmers, and many immigrants responded, choosing new, seemingly secure lives and opportunities on the Montana prairies.

The decline of central Montana began with the droughts of the late 1910s and continued as later droughts combined with the Great Depression of the 1930s. Nature in Montana proved to be cruel: of the tens of thousands who moved to central Montana during the homestead era, only the frugal, driven, and lucky endured until the 1940s. The rural population decamped; coal mining at Roundup ended in the 1950s, and the Milwaukee Railroad itself, struggling since the 1940s, ended its central Montana service in 1980.

Today, agriculture nevertheless remains the backbone of local economies. Although large farms and ranches have replaced homesteads, for many in central Montana rural life is as unsure nowadays as it was for earlier, perhaps more naive, settlers.

FORSYTH TO ROUNDUP

Highway 12 crawls out of the Yellowstone Valley and across an arid plain before it drops into the

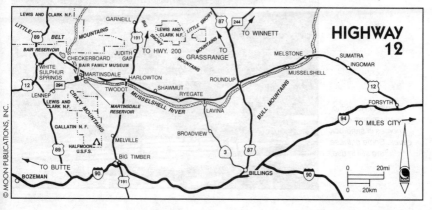

Musselshell River Valley. Forsaken little towns like Vananda follow the old Milwaukee Road. They indicate both the hope and the disillusion of early homesteaders. This is historically sheep and cattle country. The early prosperity of now-flagging communities like Ingomar and Sumatra was linked to vast, nearby stretches of open prairie. which needed a railhead for shipping livestock to outside markets.

Within the Musselshell Valley, irrigated farm-land replaces the arid plains. Little towns like Melstone (pop. 166, elev. 2,897 feet) and Mus-selshell, once centers for homesteaders, are today crossroads and gas stations for travel-ers and local farmers. West of Melstone, the sandstone cliffs and bluffs of the Fort Union Formation shelter the valley; their rich coal veins enriched the local economy when the steam engines of the Milwaukee Railroad crossed the West.

Practicalities

One of the most famous bars in Montana is the **Jersey Lily** in the little community of Ingomar. The bean soup here is the pièce de résistance and enjoys statewide fame. The Jersey Lily is the only business left in town, and only local ranch-ers and the occasional traveler keep the bar from going the way of the rest of the town. Plank sidewalks, hitching posts, and tumbleweeds in the street aren't added for effect: they're real.

Enthusiasts of western lore can test their mettle at the authentic outdoor privies.

ROUNDUP

History

Roundup (pop. 2,049, elev. 3,184 feet) was, by dint of etymology, the beginning of the Great Montana Roundup, the centennial cattle drive in 1989. In this it mimicked its frontier role as a center of livestock roundups in the 1880s.

The Milwaukee Railroad put Roundup on the map. In 1908 its steam engines arrived to create a demand for cheap coal in central Montana. The Bull Mountains, an uplift of sedimentary sandstone containing significant amounts of coal, are south of Roundup. Mines here became the Milwaukee's fuel source.

At Roundup, Hwy. 87 intersects north to south. Klein, a largely defunct community just across the Musselshell from Roundup, was once a vibrant mining community. Early immigrants solved the housing problem by building lodgings into the cliffside. Some of these cave-homes are now used for livestock; some still house people. Watch for electric lines and TV antennas.

Sights

The **Musselshell Valley Historical Museum,** 524 1st St. W, tel. (406) 323-1403, contains re-

South of Roundup, early miners made homes in sandrock caves. Some of these are still in use.

W.C. McRAE

minders of Roundup's dual heritage as pioneer cowtown and mining camp. Open Memorial Day to Labor Day daily 9 a.m.-6 p.m.

Recreation
Pine Ridge Country Club, one mile west on 13th Ave. W, tel. (406) 323-2880, is a nine-hole course with a log clubhouse dating from 1908. The municipal **swimming pool** is at 700 3rd Ave. W, tel. (406) 323-1384.

Practicalities
The **Big Sky Motel,** 740 Main, tel. (406) 323-2303, $31 s, $39 d, has air-conditioned rooms with cable TV (and Showtime). Nonsmoking rooms are available, and dogs are okay. On the north end of town is the **Ideal Motel,** 926 Main, tel. (406) 323-3371 or (888) 323-3371, $29 s, $35 d; some rooms have kitchenettes. The Ideal also offers RV hookups. At **Cowbell Park,** off Hwy. 12 south of town, there is free overnight camping along the Musselshell River.

The best choice for a quick bite in Roundup is the **Busy Bee** on Hwy. 87, tel. (406) 323-2204. It's principally a diner open 24 hours a day; the large parking lot explains its popularity with truckers. The **Vault,** 201 Main, tel. (406) 323-1229, is the town's pizzeria. For the best steaks in the area, try **Stella's Steak House & Supper Club,** 123 Hwy. 87 N, tel. (406) 323-1166. Roundup likes good coffee; try a cup at the **Morning Grind,** 119 Main, tel. (406) 323-1579.

Information
Contact the **Roundup Chamber of Commerce,** P.O. Box 751, Roundup, MT 59072, tel. (406) 323-1966.

ROUNDUP TO HARLOWTON

History
The traveler is rarely out of sight of ponderosa pines on sandstone buttes or of the cottonwood-lined Musselshell on this length of Hwy. 12. As elsewhere on the Milwaukee Road, community hopes ran high; the huge, now defunct hotel at bypassed Lavina testifies to the ambitions of homestead-era settlers. At Barber, among the deserted storefronts is Grace Lutheran Church. Built in

1917 by German homesteaders, it could be the prototype for the Little White Church in the Vale; it is also the smallest active Lutheran congregation in the nation.

Just east of Ryegate, Chief Joseph and the Nez Perce crossed the Musselshell in 1877 as they fled northward to Canada.

Practicalities
Near Lavina, the **Lavina Crossing Cafe,** south on Hwy. 3, tel. (406) 636-2112, is open 6 a.m.- 8 p.m. If you want a break in Ryegate, try the **Ryegate Cafe,** 107 1st St., tel. (406) 568-2279.

At **Deadman's Reservoir,** north of Hwy. 12 between Barber and Shawmut, there are free undeveloped campsites, along with good fishing and views of the Big Snowy Mountains.

HARLOWTON

The original settlement at this valley crossroads was called Merino, indicating the importance of sheep and wool production in the area. When Richard Harlow's Montana Railroad reached the village in 1900, the jubilant citizens renamed their town in his honor.

Harlowton (pop. 1,127, elev. 4,167 feet) was a division station for the old Milwaukee Line; this and a flour mill provided a suitable basis for substantial early growth. Harlo (as it is known to locals) has one of the best-preserved town centers in Montana, a perhaps unwelcome benefit of limited recent growth. Immigrant stonesmiths cut sandstone from nearby quarries to build storefronts. Three blocks of the downtown area, now a historic district, are built of this handsome native stone.

At Harlowton, Hwy. 191 cuts through north to south. Access to the Judith Basin and the Yellowstone Valley make Harlowton a hub of local travel.

Sights
The **Upper Musselshell Historical Society Museum,** 11 S. Central Ave., tel. (406) 632-5519, contains local memorabilia, the requisite pioneer schoolroom re-creation, old conveyances, and an interesting display of serving vessels carved from 200 different kinds of wood. It's open May 1-Nov. 1, Tues.-Sat. 10 a.m.-5 p.m., Sunday 1-5 p.m.

downtown
Harlowtown's historic
district

W.C. McRAE

On the corner of Central Ave. and Hwy. 12 is a circa 1915 Milwaukee Road Electric Locomotive. Trains pushed by engines like this were the first to climb the Rockies under electric, not steam, power.

Recreation
The **Jawbone Creek Golf Course,** one-half mile north on Central Ave., tel. (406) 632-9960, is a nine-hole course that incorporates an old cemetery as a hazard.

Accommodations
The **Country Side Inn,** 309 3rd Ave. NE, tel. (406) 632-4119 or (800) 632-4120, $38 s, $47 d, is a handsome log motel with a new hot tub, sauna, and exercise room. In addition to non-smoking rooms and king-bed rooms, there's also one room that's handicapped accessible; pets are okay. The **Corral Motel,** tel. (406) 632-4331 or (800) 392-4723, $35 s, $45 d, is located a quarter-mile east of town at the junction of Hwys. 12 and 191. There are three kitchenette rooms, plus three units with suite-style separate bedrooms.

There's camping at **Chief Joseph Park** near the eastern junction of Hwys. 191 and 12. This three-acre city park also offers a playground, picnic sites, and a fishing pond.

Food
The **Cornerstone,** 11 N. Central Ave., tel. (406) 632-4600, a bakery and cafe featuring pizza; it's open for breakfast and lunch. At the cross-roads of Hwys. 191 and 12 is **Wade's Cafe,** tel. (406) 632-4533, a truck stop open for three meals a day; during the summer, there's a drive-in. For a steak, head to the **Sportsman's Bar & Steakhouse,** tel. (406) 632-4848, just east of Harlowton.

Information
Contact the **Harlowton Chamber of Commerce,** P.O. Box 694, Harlowton, MT 59036, tel. (406) 632-4694. The **Musselshell Ranger District Office** is just west of town off Hwy. 12, and can be contacted at P.O. Box F, Harlowton, MT 59306, tel. (406) 632-4391.

HARLOWTON TO THE CRAZY MOUNTAINS

West of Harlowton the horizon is punctuated by the rugged peaks of the Crazy Mountains, the most dramatic of central Montana's ranges. Highway 191 cuts south along the eastern face of the Crazies to Big Timber and the Yellowstone Valley.

The Musselshell River skirts the northern edge of the Crazies; its headwaters are in the more modest peaks of the Castle and Little Belt Mountains. Highway 12 follows the Musselshell until it divides; it then follows the North Fork through a canyon and past Checkerboard, a pretty community sadly turned trailer court. Highway 294 follows the South Fork of the Musselshell and the old Milwaukee tracks, between the Castle and Crazy Mountains.

This is rich agricultural land: the wide green valleys provide open winter pasture, while nearby mountain slopes afford rich summer grazing.

History

The upper Musselshell has traditionally been livestock range, especially for sheep; in 1910 Charles Bair, the local sheep baron, shipped 44 train-car-loads of wool out of Martinsdale, the largest single shipment of wool in the state's history. A famous local ranch was the Twodot, named for its cattle brand. Today, the little settlement of Twodot, little more than a school and a bar, serves Montana townfolk as a short-hand epithet for any rural eastern Montana community.

At the tiny community of **Lennep,** one of the Milwaukee's electric powerhouses sits idly beside the road, a remnant of that railroad's early electrified service. Along a gravel road seven miles north of Lennep is the ghost of Castle, a silver-mining town that ran its boom-to-bust cycle in the last decades of the 1800s. Lennep was the site of the first Lutheran church service held in Montana, in 1891; the present church, built in 1910, commands a broad view over the valley.

MONTANA'S LATE, GREAT BAIR FAMILY

Charles Bair came to Montana in 1883 as a conductor on the Northern Pacific Railroad and went into ranching in 1891. At the time, the land in central and southern Montana was just opening up to agriculture. Bair was able to acquire a sizable holding in the Musselshell River Valley—and grazing rights to acreage on the Crow Reservation. On these properties he amassed one of the largest herds of sheep in the world. At one point in the 1910s, he owned 300,000 head.

A large part of the Bair fortune was made in the Yukon. In 1898, Bair sold 25,000 head of sheep and invested in a company that developed a machine to heat and pressurize water. This hot water was then pumped into the gold-bearing permafrost along the Klondike River, freeing the gold from the frozen earth. Bair came back from the Yukon a much richer man. As befitted a man of power and influence, Bair was friends with many of the celebrities and politicians of his era, including most of the U.S. presidents. He also cultivated the friendships of artists, including Charlie Russell and J.K. Ralston (whose works he began to collect), and Will James and a number of early film stars. While operating on the Crow Reservation, Bair became acquainted with Chief Plenty Coups, the great chieftain who lead the Crow toward a more agrarian life. Bair began to collect Crow artifacts, many of which were gifts from the chief himself.

Bair had two daughters, Marguerite and Alberta, who were educated at Bryn Mawr. On their grand tours of Europe, the women began collecting the fine furniture and art that distinguish the Bair collection today. In time, the art and furniture collection outgrew the family's original ranchhouse, at which time the daughters simply added more rooms. Eighteenth-century French furniture was a particular passion of the Bairs, as was Paul Storr silver.

Charles Bair died in 1943. Marguerite married the ranch foreman, Scotsman Dave Lamb, in 1938, and they continued to live at the ranch until their deaths,

C.M. RUSSELL MUSEUM

Alberta Bair, 1980

(continues on next page)

MONTANA'S LATE, GREAT BAIR FAMILY
(continued)

in the 1970s. Alberta, who never married, also continued to live in the family mansion. She was a well-known and very colorful character, equally at home sealing a lamb sale in a Miles City bar as dining with royalty in an English county manor. Alberta was known for her proclivity for red hats, fine automobiles, vodka, and outspoken views on nearly everything. She lived until 1993, when she died, at 98.

By the end of her life, Alberta had become a fixture on the Montana cultural scene. The Bairs were one of the most philanthropic families in the state, funding museums, hospitals, libraries, colleges, and charitable organizations. The Alberta Bair Theater in Billings, the city's performing arts center, was one of their gifts. Each year, four students from each of four rural Montana counties are given full-ride four-year academic scholarships, also courtesy of the Bair family.

Alberta's will stipulated that the Bair family home be left as a museum for the people of Montana.

C.M. RUSSELL MUSEUM

Bair Family
Museum

Charles M. Bair Family Museum

The Bairs were one of Montana's most wealthy and unusual ranch families, and their home opened in 1996 as a museum. This is easily one of Montana's most intriguing sites, and you should make whatever detours necessary to see this unique piece of history.

To say that the museum is in the family ranchhouse is to become involved in the kind of understatement that makes describing this collection so difficult. Certainly this house started out as a ranchhouse, but by the time the Bairs were through with it, the house had been added to sporadically until it was several hundred feet long and contained 26 rooms, many built just to house the family's art and furniture collections. Charles Bair's clout with the rich and powerful at the turn of the century in Montana made it easy for him to amass his astonishingly wide collection of Native American artifacts, including headdresses, beaded clothing, and parfleches from the last of the Montana tribes' great chiefs. He also accumulated an impressive collection of Western paintings by Charlie Russell, J.K. Ralston, and J.H. Sharp, as well as a gallery of inscribed photos of presidents and celebrities.

Charles Bair's penchant for collecting paled beside his daughters' enthusiasm for it. In their 20 trips to Europe, Marguerite and Alberta indulged in a passion for Louis XV furniture, Scottish china, Sevre pottery, antique textiles, English silver, and that's just for starters. The Bair daughters were also smart enough to buy up a collection of late French Impressionist paintings by

Edouard Cortes. When they couldn't find upholstery fabric opulent enough (or one could opine, sufficiently gaudy), they hired French mills to custom weave designs to their specifications.

This is not your average Montana ranchhouse, and no matter what your preconceptions, you will be bowled over by the collection. It's not just the sheer abundance of priceless antiques and fine art from all over the world, it's also that, in the Bair's democratizing artistic vision, a Charlie Russell oil painting of cowboys should hang over a 18th century marble commode that once graced Versailles, or that a Crow porcupine quill-, feather-, and bead-embroidered vest belongs next to an Impressionist masterpiece. And when you think you've seen it all, there's always the White Bathroom.

The Bair Family Museum is open May 1-Sept. 30, Wed.-Sun. 10 a.m.-5 p.m., for tours only. Admission is $3 adult, $1.50 under 16, or $10 for a family. The museum is located one mile south of Hwy. 12 at Martinsdale. For more information, call the **C.M. Russell Museum** in Great Falls, which operates the Bair Family Museum; tel. (406) 727-8787.

Recreation

The Crazy Mountains' heavily glaciated peaks loom miragelike above the surrounding plains; isolated and spectacular, they are amongst Montana's undiscovered gems for hiking and high mountain lake fishing. Legends abound as to how they got their name, but they all have to do with women gone crazy with grief.

Hiking trails into the east side of the Crazies depart from the **Halfmoon U.S. Forest Service Campground,** 15 miles west of Hwy. 191 on a good gravel road. There are a number of steep ascents, and the snow lasts well into June at higher elevations, so plan your hikes carefully. A short day-hike of five miles roundtrip from the campground takes the hiker to views of jagged peaks rising impertinently from deep-blue lakes; there's even good trout fishing in the lakes, though not all are easily accessible. Mountain goats were transplanted here in the 1940s and have flourished.

To reach Halfmoon Campground, travel eight miles south of Melville on Hwy. 191; the road passes through bucolic ranch lands before entering the Big Timber Canyon on its way to the trailhead.

Accommodations and Food

In Martinsdale, **The Crazy Mountain Inn,** 100 Main, tel. (406) 572-3307, offers rooms ($21 s, $31 d) in a carefully renovated turn-of-the-century hotel. The inn serves the best food—steaks, chicken, and homemade soups—in this part of Montana.

Free lakeside camping is available at **Martinsdale Reservoir,** two miles east of town on a local access road, and at **Bair Reservoir,** 11 miles west on Hwy. 12.

Guest Ranches

With the Crazy Mountains as a backdrop, it's no wonder that some of Montana's best guest ranches have developed such devoted audiences.

The **Sweet Grass Ranch,** Box 161, Melville Rte., Big Timber, MT 59011, tel. (406) 537-4477 summer, tel. (406) 537-4497 winter, welcomes guests to live the good life at the base of the Crazy Mountains; it's been in the same family for five generations and still operates as a cattle ranch. Horseback riding is the principal activity, with daily trail rides on the ranch's mountain trails, or out onto the high plains. This is a working ranch, so when the angus need to be moved or checked on, guests are invited to go along to help; the ranch provides a variety of other real-life activities as well, including milking the cows and riding the fence line. Guests are welcome to fish local streams and lakes or hike in the Crazies; cookouts and rodeos are featured, and outfitted trips into the Crazy Mountain backcountry can also be arranged. The original lodge, where meals are served, is listed on the National Register; lodging is either in the lodge (bathrooms down the hall), in secluded cabins with woodstoves and private baths, or in small cabins à la frontier. There is a seven-day minimum stay, with rates beginning at $800 a week.

Bonanza Creek Guest Ranch, tel. (800) 476-6045 or fax (406) 572-3366, Lennep Rte., Martinsdale, MT 59053, is a large, long-time cattle ranch with a new focus on guest ranching. If your idea of a guest ranch stay is horseback riding by day and lounging in a private log cabin by night, then Bonanza Creek is a good bet. Unlimited horseback riding is the main activity here, and as the ranch maintains a herd of 1,500 cattle, you'll probably have the chance to use a horse as God intended—to push cows around.

Of course, guests are free to explore on mountain bikes, to head out fishing, or simply relax. Lodging is in four new family-sized log cabins, each with full bath, or you can opt for the tepee and the kids can camp out in the sheep wagon. Meals are served in the cathedral-ceilinged main lodge. Six night stays are preferred ($1,100 adult, $800 12 and under), though shorter three-day stays are considered if the schedule allows ($600 adult, $450 12 and under).

The **Lazy K Bar Ranch,** Box 550, Melville Rte., Big Timber, MT 59011, tel. (406) 537-4404,

is the state's oldest dude ranch, and one of its most exclusive. Writer Spike Van Cleve wrote about his humorous misadventures here with errant guests and horses in *A Day Late and a Dollar Short,* and in fact the Van Cleve family still owns the ranch.

Information

For information on the Crazy Mountain area, contact the **Gallatin National Forest, Big Timber Ranger District,** P.O. Box A, Big Timber, MT 59011, tel. (406) 932-5155.

THE JUDITH BASIN

Bounded by the mountain ranges of central Montana, the broad basin of the Judith River contains some of the state's richest agricultural land. Streams course through fields and meadows; abundant crops and well-nourished livestock share this fecund domain.

For centuries, this open prairie supported hundreds of thousands of buffalo. After their decimation, the first open-range ranches of Montana prospered here. The Milwaukee Road and the Great Northern vied for supremacy in the Judith Basin, each luring settlers (and hence passengers and freight) by extensive advertising campaigns. The dryland farms were so successful that the Judith Basin became the poster child of the Montana homestead movement. Unfortunately, even here farmers could not survive on homestead allotments during cycles of bad years.

History

Though not "ghost towns" to the popular mind, many stillborn little rail-side towns are almost completely deserted. Some have become incorporated into nearby farms or still support a roadhouse. Stop and examine these old towns to understand the lives of the thousands of people who tried to extract a living from the prairies.

Often made of brick, buildings were built to last. Banks were especially solid, much more so than the institutions they housed. Quality schools were also a source of pride to homesteaders, and early automobile garages were sometimes stylish additions to young towns. Unlike in comparably sized mining ghost towns, saloons and hotels are much rarer in these agri-

cultural and ranching towns. In comparison to civic architecture, private homes were usually small and unprepossessing; in many cases, farmers stabled livestock in more attractive lodgings than they themselves lived in.

Two hundred Minuteman missiles are buried in silos across this area of Montana. Currently, their presence is menaced more by superpower friendliness than by enemy attack.

Information

For information about the Judith Basin area, contact the **Judith Ranger District, Lewis & Clark National Forest,** P.O. Box 434, Stanford, MT, tel. (406) 566-2292.

STANFORD AND VICINITY

Stanford (pop. 533, elev. 4,200 feet) was the Judith Basin's most important trade center for grain and livestock in the early 1900s. It has managed to survive the vicissitudes of drought and bad markets better than its neighbors, and the town's wide streets and well-kept homes make it a handsome anomaly in central Montana.

Sights

Stanford's **Judith Basin Museum,** 203 1st Ave. S, tel. (406) 566-2281, is open Memorial Day-Labor Day and features a collection of over 2,000 salt and pepper shakers and frontier-era household items. Stop at the **Basin Trading Post** along Hwy. 200 to see an exhibit on a dastardly white wolf from homesteader days.

Accommodations and Food
The **Sundown Motel,** west along Hwy. 200, tel. (406) 566-2316, stands next to Stanford's best steak house, the **Sundown Inn** tel. (406) 566-9911. A single room goes for $25 s, 34 d.

The **By Way Cafe,** south of Stanford on Hwy. 200, tel. (406) 566-2631, is that uniquely Montanan institution, the combination truck stop, restaurant, and liquor store. In the center of town is the **Wolves Den,** 81 Central Ave., tel. (406) 566-2451, open for breakfast and lunch.

Hobson and Utica
The **Judith Basin Cattle Pool** was one of the earliest open-range outfits in the state. During the boom years of the 1880s, investors bought cattle and then pooled them together to be run by hired cowboys. Calves were branded with the same brand as their mothers; in the fall, they were sold, trailed to railheads, and shipped to feedlots for fattening.

Utica was the hub for open-range cowboys in the Judith Basin during the 1880s; here, they gathered the immense herds of cattle to divide them according to brand. It was a raucous time: after a summer of sometimes lonely cattle herding, the cowboys had a chance to kick up their heels and celebrate. Painter Charley Russell worked the ranges here, and many of his paintings feature the unique skyline of the Judith Basin.

Not much is left in Utica except a bar and a museum, both appropriate memorials to the ghosts of cowboys past. When the Great Northern line went through, Utica was bypassed for Hobson (pop. 227, elev. 3940 feet), 10 miles down the Judith River.

Art of another sort has its heyday around here in late summer. Hobson-area businesses have recently sponsored hay-bale decorating as a fun and humorous diversion (there's also a sizable pot of prize money awarded). Watch for large round hay bales wearing clothing, paint, old tires, hats, and whatever makes a good visual joke.

Sights: The **Utica Museum,** tel. (406) 423-5208, preserves Utica's cowboy heritage with tools, saddles, and wagons from last century.

Food: Light meals are served at Utica's old bar, the **Oxen Yoke Inn,** tel. (406) 423-5560. In Hobson, there's breakfast and lunch at **Cathy's Cafe,** Main St., tel. (406) 423-5312. The **Hobson Supper Club,** tel. (406) 423-5639,

is the local steak house. At the junction of Hwys. 200 and 191 is **Eddie's Corner,** tel. (406) 374-2471, a popular truck stop, open 24 hours a day.

The Judith Gap
Named for the wide and desolate divide between the Big Snowy and the Little Belt Mountains, the Judith Gap has been a transportation corridor for centuries. Crow Indians crossed the gap to hunt buffalo in the Judith Basin; Blackfeet warriors later pushed south across the area to menace the Crow along the Musselshell. Traders used this notoriously windy pass to reach erstwhile settlements and gold camps in central Montana. Both the Great Northern and the Milwaukee lines laid track over the Judith Gap to reach homestead towns.

The first settlement in the area was the old crossroads of U-bet, which thrived as a stop on the old Carroll Trail stage line during the 1870s. U-bet was a well-loved watering hole for early cowboys. When Richard Harlow's Montana Railroad pushed through the Judith Gap in 1903, it too named its station U-bet.

During the homestead rush, a telling division of sentiment regarding alcohol led to the establishment of two communities. North Garneill was "dry"; nearby South Garneill (incorporating U-bet) had a guesthouse, saloon, and the accoutrements of an Old West town. In some kind of victory, today only North Garneill survives, if only diffidently and under the abridged name of Garneill.

The **U-bet and Central Montana Pioneers Monument** at Garneill is a huge block of granite on a concrete base. Embedded in the base is an array of local rocks. There are two large, nearly identical pear-shaped stones here, found by early settlers near Winnett. Apparently carved by Indians, unfortunately their meaning has been lost.

Food: The **Carroll Trail Inn,** in the town of Judith Gap, tel. (406) 473-2325, is open 7 a.m.-7 p.m.

Winifred
The mouth of the Judith River was an important stop for Missouri River steamboats. Camp Cooke was built here in 1866 both to protect travelers from the hostile Blackfeet Indians and to defend the thriving community of Judith Landing, which grew up from selling wood to the steamers en route to Fort Benton.

Although not much is left at the old site of Judith Landing, the drive to the confluence of the Judith and Missouri rivers is a spectacular side trip into the Missouri Breaks. Proceed to Winifred along Hwy. 236 north of Lewistown and follow a good gravel road toward the PN Bridge. Soon the farmland falls away in 1,000-foot drops to the rivers below; directly west, an abandoned channel of the Missouri River slumps into the Judith Valley and across the present Missouri. After crossing the PN Bridge, the only span on the

"wild and scenic" stretch of the Missouri, Hwy. 236 continues through farmland to Big Sandy, 40 miles distant.

From Winifred a right turn on Knox Ridge Rd. leads to other views of the Missouri Breaks and to the C.M. Russell National Wildlife Refuge.

Food: The **Winifred Tavern and Cafe,** tel. (406) 462-5426, provides for the needs of local farmers, ranchers, and the occasional traveler, serving three meals a day Wed.-Sun. 8 a.m.-8 p.m., also Mon.-Tues. 7 a.m.-2 p.m.

DOVER PUBLICATIONS, INC.

SOUTH-CENTRAL AND THE MISSOURI HEADWATERS

More than any other part of the state, this country of broad valleys, rugged mountains, lush ranches, and trout-laden rivers is what people expect to find in Montana. And it doesn't disappoint. From the Yellowstone River, the longest undammed river in the lower 48 states, to the Beartooth Highway, declared by the late Charles Kuralt one of America's most spectacular drives, to the serene, history-laden Missouri Headwaters, this is country that cuts deep to the soul.

THE LAND

The Missouri headwaters, where the Jefferson, Madison, and Gallatin Rivers merge and create the Missouri, anchor the northwestern corner of this region. In the northeastern corner, the Crazy Mountains rise wildly from the plains. The Beartooth and Yellowstone Plateaus are at the southern edge. Rivers roll off south-central Montana's mountain ranges—the Beartooths, the Absarokas, the Gallatins, Madisons, Gravellys, and the Tobacco Roots—and course north to the Missouri.

Montana's highest spot is in the Beartooths, and, not surprisingly, a *lot* of snow falls in the high country near Yellowstone.

Over the course of the last 600,000 years, Yellowstone's volcanoes covered the Absarokas with lava and ash, and glaciers pushed and carved their way across the region's higher peaks. Faults cut across the mountain ranges, and mountains still tumble.

Flora and Fauna
Lodgepole pine is the predominant tree species in most of the forests in the headwaters region. These trees are particularly prone to fatal infestation by pine beetles. Dead, dry, and brittle, the stands become easy fodder for fire, which is the necessary ingredient to break open the pine cones and allow the seeds to germinate.

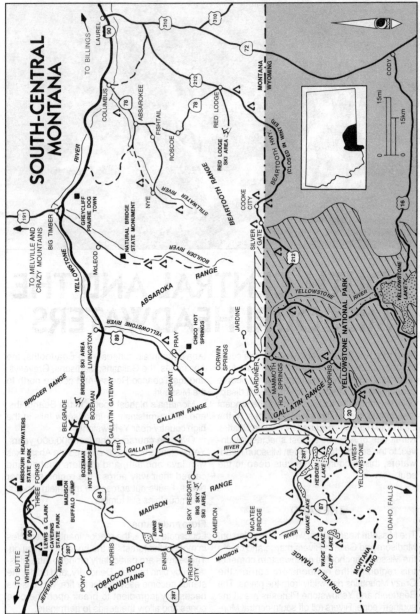

SOUTH-CENTRAL
MONTANA

TO MELVILLE AND
CRAZY MOUNTAINS

TO BILLINGS

LAUREL

COLUMBUS

ABSAROKEE

FISHTAIL

ROSCOE

RED LODGE

RED LODGE
SKI AREA

MONTANA
WYOMING

CODY

BEARTOOTH HWY.
(CLOSED IN WINTER)

15mi

15km

YELLOWSTONE RIVER

COOKE
CITY

SILVER
GATE

YELLOWSTONE NATIONAL PARK

YELLOWSTONE
LAKE

BIG TIMBER

GREYCLIFF
PRAIRIE DOG TOWN

McLEOD

NATURAL BRIDGE
STATE MONUMENT

NYE

STILLWATER RIVER

BEARTOOTH RANGE

BOULDER RIVER

ABSAROKA
RANGE

JARDINE

YELLOWSTONE RIVER

PRAY

CHICO HOT
SPRINGS

EMIGRANT

CORWIN
SPRINGS

GARDINER

MAMMOTH
HOT SPRINGS

NORRIS

GALLATIN RANGE

LIVINGSTON

BRIDGER RANGE

BRIDGER SKI AREA

BOZEMAN

BELGRADE

GALLATIN GATEWAY

GALLATIN RANGE

GALLATIN RIVER

MISSOURI HEADWATERS
STATE PARK

THREE FORKS

LEWIS & CLARK
CAVERNS STATE PARK

BOZEMAN
HOT SPRINGS

MADISON
BUFFALO JUMP

GALLATIN

MADISON
RANGE

BIG SKY RESORT

BIG SKY
SKI AREA

CAMERON

ENNIS
LAKE

McATEE
BRIDGE

MADISON RIVER

HEBGEN
LAKE

QUAKE LAKE

WADE LAKE

CLIFF LAKE

WEST
YELLOWSTONE

MONTANA
IDAHO

TO IDAHO FALLS

TO BUTTE

WHITEHALL

JEFFERSON RIVER

PONY

NORRIS

TOBACCO ROOT
MOUNTAINS

ENNIS

VIRGINIA
CITY

GRAVELLY RANGE

MADISON RIVER

© MOON PUBLICATIONS, INC.

Plains habitats crop up between the mountain ranges, and there's some tundra on the high peaks. Cottonwood and aspen line the streams; serviceberries provide the locals with the makings of purple serviceberry pie.

Trout are south-central Montana's most famous fauna, but plenty of deer dot the hillsides, and, at the eastern edge of the region, there's a freeway-side prairie-dog village.

HISTORY

The hunting ranges surrounding the Missouri headwaters were coveted and often fought over by Native Americans. Bannock, Blackfeet, Crow, Flathead, and Shoshone all considered it sacred hunting ground. As the Blackfeet gained control of the northern plains, they drove other tribes out of the Missouri headwaters area. The Shoshone moved south and west, the Crow tended to stay off to the east, and the Flathead crossed over from the Bitterroot Valley less often.

Lewis and Clark arrived at present-day Three Forks in July 1805 and declared it the headwaters of the Missouri. Clark and his party returned to the forks on their way back east; from the headwaters they traveled up the Gallatin, crossed Bozeman Pass at Sacajawea's suggestion, and reached the Yellowstone River near the site of present-day Livingston. They floated the Yellowstone to its confluence with the Missouri, where they were joined by Lewis and his men.

Fur-bearing animals quickly caught the eyes of white trappers and mountain men. Miners made some forays into the mountains, but homesteaders and ranchers were ultimately more successful. Tourism, spurred on by the dude ranches and fly-fishers, is now evident in most towns, and television and movie celebrities have joined the artists and writers who have set down roots in south-central Montana. Ted Turner and Jane Fonda, Dennis Quaid, Meg Ryan, Michael Keaton, Jeff Bridges, Tom Brokaw, Brooke Shields, and Whoopi Goldberg all own land in this most celebrity-studded area of Montana.

RECREATION

The Madison, Gallatin, and Yellowstone Rivers lure anglers with trout. People do run rivers, hunt, and mountain bike here, but it's the fishing that draws pilgrims from around the world. The hatches of salmon flies and caddis flies are as closely watched as the seasons, and most everyone knows brown from rainbow from cutthroat. See specific sections below for more information.

Bitterroot to Beartooth, though a bit dated, is still an excellent resource for hikers in the mountains of the headwaters region. Author Ruth Rudner focuses on wilderness areas and land nominated for wilderness designation in the 1980s. Discussions of the ecology of the specific areas are an important part of this Sierra Club totebook (see **Booklist**).

THREE FORKS AND THE MADISON RIVER VALLEY

Even if the notion of the Missouri headwaters doesn't automatically stir your blood, a visit there probably will. There's something *big* about the place where three lively trout streams join up to make their way across the plains that gives the spirit an almost geological uplift.

The Madison, the middle fork of the Missouri, starts in Yellowstone Park and joins with the Jefferson and the Gallatin at Three Forks. Mention of the Madison quickens the pulse of anglers across the U.S.; people come from all over to

fish here, and the valley sports a number of guest ranches to accommodate them.

THE LAND

All three of the Missouri's forks come straight from the mountains. The Madison Range flanks the Madison Valley to the east; to the west are the northerly, batholithic, and glacier-cut Tobacco Root Mountains and the low, southerly Gravelly Range.

WHIRLING DISEASE

Madison River anglers are catching fewer rainbow trout today than they were just a few years ago. Lots fewer. Rainbow populations are running only 10% of their 1991 levels, and it's likely that whirling disease is to blame.

Whirling disease, a fish disease characterized by tail-chasing, was somehow introduced into the Madison in late 1994 and has been spreading downriver ever since.

The disease is thought to have originated in Europe, where brown trout have largely developed an immunity to it. It was introduced to the United States in the 1950s, via frozen trout, and now has been detected in 20 states. In other western states, the infestation tends to move downstream at the rate of 15 to 20 miles a year, and there's little indication that the infection will go away.

Montana Fish, Wildlife, and Parks has been studying the disease and its effects on wild trout populations (in other places where it's found, whirling disease has affected mostly hatchery fish), resulting in clo-

sure of some stretches of the river. They have also instituted preventive measures, aimed at halting the spread of *Myxobolus cerebralis,* the protozoan spore that causes the illness, to other rivers. Since there is no known cure for the disease, it is important that anglers follow these precautions:

• Remove all mud and aquatic plants from your vehicle, boat, anchor, trailer and axles, waders, boots, and fishing gear *before* departing the fishing access site or boat dock.
• Drain all water from your boat and equipment— including coolers, buckets, and live wells—*before* departing the fishing access site or boat dock.
• Dry your boat and equipment between river trips.
• Don't transport fish from one body of water to another.
• Don't dispose of fish entrails, skeletal parts, or other by-products in any body of water.
• Don't collect sculpins (also known as bullheads) or use sculpins as bait.

The northern valley is wide; indeed, between Three Forks and Ennis, Hwy. 287 skirts well west of the Madison, following the Jefferson for a while, through wide open and rolling plains.

The Gravelly Range is well named. These mountains aren't particularly high, but they do have a fair amount of geology packed into their rubbly composition. For one, the marble that underlies parts of this range has further metamorphosed into talc in some places, making this a major talc-mining area.

The Madison Range has obvious recent geologic activity. The eastern front is moving along a fault. A lurching move in August 1959 jacked the mountains up and dropped the valley floor. The southern end of Hebgen Lake rose, the northern end dropped, and a rock slide buried campers and blocked the Madison River, forming Quake Lake.

FISHING

Fish the lower Madison (below Ennis Lake) for brown trout or the upper river for the now-scarce rainbow trout, and be prepared to catch a gen-

erous number of whitefish as well. The state once stocked the Madison with hatchery trout, but this practice was discontinued and wild populations were doing well on their own until whirling disease came along.

Along with the beautiful riffled water and trout come crowds. To avoid them, look for spots far from Hwy. 287 and fish early or late in the season. Although the high waters make most stretches of the Madison too turbulent for fly-fishing until late June, some stretches (especially inside Yellowstone Park) are okay for flies by early June, and turbulent waters don't seem to deter anglers when the salmon flies hatch around the end of June.

July and August are when the caddis hatch, and anglers flock to the upper Madison. North of Ennis Lake, the river warms up too much for good summer fishing; try this area in the spring or fall. Fly-fishing is usually good through mid-October on most of the Madison.

Some areas of the Madison River are closed to fishing from a boat; bait fishing is prohibited along some stretches, and for a 30-mile stretch of the upper river, catch-and-release fishing is mandated. Special regulations will usually be posted at fishing-access areas, but check ahead with the Dept. of Fish, Wildlife, and Parks or your fishing guide.

THREE FORKS AND VICINITY

Three Forks (pop. 1,481) gets its name from the confluence of the Gallatin, Madison, and Jefferson Rivers, which occurs on a wetland plain surrounded by mountains just north of town.

Just west of Three Forks, Hwy. 287 follows the Jefferson River through fossil-ridden limestone that's been jostled into a tilted position. For a few miles the land is open and dry; past Lewis and Clark Caverns, the Madison River flows through a gorge of high, buff-colored hills. This road, which eventually leads to Cardwell, is a pleasant alternative to the interstate.

History

Before Lewis and Clark camped at the Missouri headwaters, the Three Forks area was already well traveled. It was a disputed hunting area and the site of frequent battles between the Crow and the Blackfeet. The mountain and river bands of the Crow had regular rendezvous at the headwaters, where they'd hunt, fish, and, later, trade with whites.

When the Corps of Discovery reached the Missouri headwaters on July 27, 1805, Lewis and Clark concluded that none of the three rivers was sufficiently larger than any other to warrant calling it the Missouri and the other two feeder streams. They solved this dilemma by declaring them "three noble streams," and took the opportunity to name them after the President (Jefferson), the Secretary of State (Madison), and the Secretary of the Treasury (Gallatin). Actually, river-naming was not

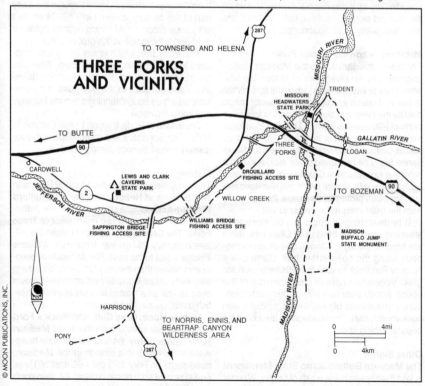

foremost in Lewis and Clark's minds—they were far more preoccupied with meeting the Shoshone, from whom they hoped to obtain horses.

The Blackfeet thwarted the business of a small trading post established in 1810 on the spit of land between the Jefferson and Madison Rivers. Gallatin City was built near the mouth of the Gallatin headwaters in 1864 and prospered for a few years. The settlement was established here under the premise that steamboats could navigate the Missouri to this point. Of course, the Great Falls of the Missouri were not properly taken into account, and when Fort Benton became the head of navigation on the Missouri, Gallatin City foundered. Some of the buildings were moved from the original site across the Madison-Jefferson, and this second Gallatin City, with its ferry service to the mining towns to the west, became an important food supplier. Bozeman ultimately outstripped Gallatin City as a commercial center, and when the railroad skirted the three forks in 1883, the town was pretty much abandoned.

Missouri Headwaters State Park

Try to visit this site, where the Madison, Jefferson, and Gallatin Rivers join up to form the Missouri, early or late in the day, when the light comes in low and opens you up to some special magic held by the rivers and bluffs. The park is four miles north of I-90 near the town of Trident. Good information stations discuss local flora and fauna as well as Corps of Discovery history. There's a $4 entrance fee. The headwaters site includes an old hotel and log cabin from Gallatin City. There's also a small cave with several faded and damaged Native American **pictographs;** follow the trail south from the main interpretive center to see it.

If birdwatching appeals to you more than steeping yourself in Lewis and Clark lore, there are herons, ospreys, Canada geese, and songbirds along the headwaters trail. Climb Lewis Rock or Fort Rock to scan the cliffs for golden eagles. Vegetation here is characteristic of the plains: prickly pear and pincushion cacti, bluebunch wheatgrass, big sagebrush, saltbush, and buckwheat brush. The headwaters area is also a popular fishing spot.

Other Sights

The **Madison Buffalo Jump State Monument** is less than seven miles south of Logan. Wander around the steep cliff, contemplate the bone

shards, and wait for the landscape to turn rich with buffalo, deer, and pronghorn. The same $4 fee admits you to both the Headwaters State Park and the Madison Buffalo Jump.

Headwaters Heritage Museum, 202 S Main St. in Three Forks, is open Mon.-Sat. 9-11 a.m. and 1-5 p.m., Sunday 1-5 p.m. mid-May through mid-Sept., tel. (406) 285-4778. A good collection of historical photographs and an archaeological display are among the exhibits.

Pony, just below the Tobacco Root Mountains about 30 miles southwest of Three Forks and six miles up a paved road from Harrison, comes off as something of a ghost town, but it actually has 115 residents. There are a few fancy new houses on the hills above the abandoned Victorians and brick bank building. Pony took its name from Tecumseh "Pony" Smith, who mined gold here in 1868. Gold, silver, and some tungsten were mined in Pony through the early part of this century, and an early 1990s attempt at cyanide-process gold mining netted virtually no gold and left cyanide in the groundwater.

The Pony Bar, which is still doing business, used to be a boardinghouse for men. When the second-floor residents got tired of running downstairs and out back to the outhouse, they constructed a "pee trough" running down the hallways and into a drainpipe.

Southwest of Pony, through Potosi Canyon, is Potosi Hot Springs, a site undeveloped save for a small Forest Service campground.

Fishing

There's fishing access to the Missouri River and its tributaries at **Headwaters Park. Drouillard Fishing-Access Site** offers entry to the Jefferson River on Hwy. 10 two miles west of Three Forks. The **Sappington Bridge** crosses the Jefferson on Hwy. 287 at Hwy. 10, and the **Williams Bridge** is just to the east. The Jefferson is deeper and slower than the riffly Madison, but fishing very early or late in the day will often yield brown trout as well as a host of less prestigious whitefish, carp, chubs, and suckers.

Cobblestone, Grey Cliff, and **Black's Ford** fishing-access sites are on the lower Madison River between Hwy. 84 and the Missouri headwaters. To reach this stretch of the Madison, head south on Hwy. 286 (off I-90 east of Three Forks) or east from Norris on Hwy. 84, then north on Hwy. 286. Camping is permitted at these undeveloped riverside spots, but care should be taken not to stray onto the surrounding private land without permission. The relatively warm lower Madison, while popular, does not share the incredible reputation of the river's cooler upper reaches.

There are several pulloffs on Hwy. 84 near the bridge nine miles east of Norris, and the more ambitious angler can head up the trail into Beartrap Canyon (see below).

Other Recreation

Beartrap Canyon, a BLM wilderness area east of Norris, is a steep gorge cut by the Madison River. A hiking trail starts three miles down a dirt road from the Red Mountain Campground (about nine miles east of Norris on Hwy. 84) and runs seven miles up the canyon. A dam at the southern end holds back Ennis Lake; hiking is prohibited around the dam, forcing hikers to retrace their steps to leave the canyon. The trail is popular with both hikers and anglers and can get crowded on summer weekends.

Bear Trap Hot Springs is just east of Norris on Hwy. 84; it's $4 for a soak ($3 children). At this funky spot, the pool is small and lined with wooden boards. Hot water shoots into the air and showers down onto a corner of the pool.

Accommodations

The **Sacajawea Inn,** 5 N. Main St., tel. (406) 285-6515 or (800) 821-7326, is the best place to stay for miles around. The huge old hotel was built in 1910 by John Q. Adams (no known relationship to the former president) to serve passengers and crew of the Milwaukee Railroad and has been completely and beautifully refurbished. Rooms, all with phones, private baths, and use of the inn's outdoor hot tub, run $69 s, $99 d, with significant off-season savings. Pets are welcome with a $5 additional charge.

Alternatives are the **Broken Spur Motel,** a perfectly comfortable place with free continental breakfast at 124 W. Elm, tel. (406) 285-3237 or (888) 354-3048, $44 s, $52 d, or **Fort Three Forks Motel,** on Hwy. 287 near I-90, tel. (406) 285-3233 or (800) 477-5690, with rates in line with the Broken Spur (they're owned by the same folks). Pets are accepted at both places for a small fee. Just past "downtown," find the **Lewis and Clark Motel** at 510 Main St., tel. (406) 285-3454.

the Sacajawea Inn, in Three Forks

JUDY JEWELL

Camping

The **Missouri Headwaters State Park campground** has brushy riverside sites perfect for those on a Lewis and Clark pilgrimage. Read their journals first if you doubt the importance of bringing mosquito repellent. The $11 fee includes day use.

There's also a large state park campground west of Three Forks at **Lewis and Clark Caverns,** open May through September.

The campground at **Bear Trap Hot Springs** is convenient, if occasionally boisterous. If you find it tough to leave the hot springs, or if the combination of a hot bath and a cold beer proves a little too seductive, plunk down $15 for a tent or trailer site. Head east on Hwy. 84 for nine miles to find **Red Mountain,** a free BLM campground near the bridge over the Madison River. For a secluded spot, try **Potosi,** a free primitive Forest Service campground about eight miles south of Pony.

Food and Drink

Of the three good dining bets around Three Forks, the particularly surprising one is the **Willow Creek Café & Saloon,** six miles southwest of Three Forks in Willow Creek, tel. (406) 285-3698. Breakfast, lunch, and dinner are all a cut above what you'd expect to find out here, and both the restaurant and the bar are easy spots in which to while away a couple of hours. The menu is a combo of "international" dishes, such as seafood fettucine, and "country cookin'," like chicken-fried steak; a large breakfast runs $4-5; dinners are about $12.

The **Sacajawea Inn's** restaurant goes a step farther in the gourmet direction—appetizers of Provençal-style pizza and $12-18 dinners of rosemary-garlic lamb chops or chicken with sauterne sauce can make one inquire about long-term rentals at the inn. The dining room is open for dinner year-round and, in the summer, for breakfast and lunch as well.

It's only six miles from Three Forks to Logan, where the **Land of Magic Dinner Club**, tel. (406) 284-3794, serves renowned steak dinners.

The **Prairie Schooner**, not far from Main St. at 10770 Hwy. 287 in Three Forks, tel. (406) 285-6948, has inexpensive cafe breakfast, lunch, and dinner food, including buffalo burgers and huckleberry shakes.

Events

The Three Forks **rodeo** is held the third weekend of July. A **Lewis and Clark Pageant** is staged also in July, right around the time of year the Corps of Discovery first passed through.

Each September, Headwaters Park is the site of the **John Colter Run,** a seven-mile dash through the prickly pears commemorating Corps member Colter's 1808 feat of survival when he was stripped and hunted by Blackfeet Indians and still managed to escape (clothing and shoes are permitted on the run).

Information

Reach the **Three Forks Chamber of Commerce** at P.O. Box 1103, Three Forks, MT 59752, tel. (406) 285-4556. The local **visitor center** is housed in a railroad caboose just around the corner from the Sacajawea Inn. Visit the **library** at 121 2nd Ave. E, tel. (406) 285-3747.

ENNIS AND VICINITY

Ennis (pop. 1,000, elev. 4,927 feet) is known for its superb fishing, for Ted Turner's nearby buffalo

ranch, and for its lively Fourth of July rodeo and popular October Wild Game Cookoff.

Originally founded as a supply station for the gold towns of Virginia City and Nevada City shortly after gold was discovered in Alder Gulch, ranching has become Ennis's economic mainstay. Many of the area's ranches are now owned by wealthy (and sometimes famous) investors who hire real ranchers to manage and run the cattle (or buffalo). Anglers flock to Ennis in the summer, when they outnumber the cowboys on Main Street.

Indeed, Ennis's Main St., not long ago a small strip with a couple of rancher bars, a cafe, and a fly-fishing shop, is now lined with gift and antique shops and real estate offices.

Sights

The **Ennis National Fish Hatchery** breeds rainbow trout 12 miles south of Ennis. It's open to visitors, tel. (406) 682-4847.

It takes all day to drive from Ennis to Sheridan if you dip south of Hwy. 287 and follow the scenic Forest Service roads through the Gravelly Range, but you'll likely see elk, moose, pronghorn, many deer, grouse, and a sheep or two. Stop at the Ennis Ranger Station and pick up their brochure on the Gravelly drive. Don't figure on taking your two-wheel-drive Dodge Dart on this 60-mile rangeland tour if the road is wet or snowy; it gets pretty steep.

Fishing and Floating

The 50-mile stretch of the Madison River from Quake Lake (near Yellowstone Park) north to Ennis is an almost continuous riffle, and trout are eager to grab passing morsels. This makes for good fishing for beginning fly anglers.

The state maintains several fishing-access sites on the Madison River near Ennis. **Ennis FAS** is on Hwy. 287 just south of Ennis; **Burnt Tree Hole** is a mile west of Ennis on Hwy. 287, then two miles south on the county road; **Eight Mile Fork** is four miles down the same county road; **Varney Bridge** is another six miles down the road. All these spots except Ennis have informal, no fee, camping sites; there's a small fee to camp at Ennis. To reach **Valley Garden FAS,** turn north onto the county road from Hwy. 287 a quarter mile south of town and travel two miles. **McAtee Bridge,** 18 miles south of Ennis, also provides access to the Madison.

Ennis Lake (a.k.a. Ennis Reservoir or Meadow Lake) is a silty, shallow reservoir backed up by a rather small Montana Power dam on the Madison just below the lake. Because it's so shallow, Ennis Lake gets very warm during the summer. The warm water makes for pleasant swimming but causes rampant algae growth and is generally rough on fish downstream. Resorts and ranches surround Ennis Lake.

Float the Madison, but take care where you go. Beartrap Canyon is for whitewater experts, and the segment between Cameron and Ennis is tough for a novice to navigate. A popular and easy trip runs 30 miles from Quake Lake (put in at the Hwy. 87 bridge four miles from the lake) to the Varney Bridge in Cameron. This stretch of the river passes several campgrounds. Fishing from a boat is restricted on certain stretches of the Madison. Check the current regulations before casting a line.

Yellowstone Raft Company runs day-long trips on the Madison through Beartrap Canyon ($85). Call them at (406) 848-7777 (Gardiner), 995-4613 (Big Sky), or (800) 348-4376. They also offer fishing float trips on the Madison.

Other Recreation

Madison Meadows is a public, nine-hole golf course just west of town, tel. (406) 682-7468. Public tennis courts are adjacent to the golf course.

Many old logging roads in the hills south of Ennis are closed to motorized traffic and make good mountain-bike routes. Get the current road-closure information at the Ennis Ranger Station. The Gravellys are popular with elk hunters, but the recent road building and logging have threatened elk habitat, partly because all the logging roads have brought more hunters to previously remote areas.

September brings upland game-bird hunters to the area for Hungarian partridge and sharptail, blue, and ruffled grouse.

Accommodations

Dude ranches surround Ennis, and there are some more conventional motels here too. Riverside Motel and Outfitters, 346 E. Main St., tel. (406) 682-4240 or (800) 535-4139, is a good budget choice—it's right by a little riverside park and has a large grassy area for fly casting as well as a kids' fishing pond. Rooms run $35 s, $50 d (somewhat lower in the fall, winter, and spring); in-room

pets are permitted for a $3 fee, and motel guests can arrange free horse boarding. One of the Riverside's owners is a fishing guide; let him know if you're interested in fishing the Madison, Big Hole, Jefferson, or Yellowstone Rivers.

At the Sportsman's Lodge, north of town on Hwy. 287, tel. (406) 682-4242 or (800) 220-1690, you have a choice of regular motel units or rustic cabins, all set in a nicely landscaped property. Rates are $42-48 s, $56-60 d.

A couple of Ennis's nicest motels are just south of town. The El Western Resort, tel. (406) 682-4217 or (800) 831-2773, on Hwy. 287 S, sits on 17 wooded acres near the river. Accommodations are in duplex log cabins, either "sleeping cabins" or more luxurious cabins complete with kitchens and fireplaces. Some of the cabins are practically lodges, with up to four bedrooms. Rates begin at $65. The El Western is open April 15-Oct. 31. Right next door on Hwy. 287, the Rainbow Valley Motel, tel. (406) 682-4264 or (800) 452-8254, has a pool and rooms for $60 s, $80 d and up, with lower winter rates. The rooms are large and nicely furnished in a Western style. You have a choice of two-bedroom units, kitchen units, and rooms with patios overlooking the river.

The Fan Mountain Inn is on the north edge of town at 204 N. Main, tel. (406) 682-5200, and charges $38 s, $54 d. All of Ennis's motels except the Rainbow Valley accept pets.

Lake Shore Lodge, P.O. Box 160, McAllister, MT 59740, tel. (406) 682-4424, rents fully equipped housekeeping cabins on Ennis Lake for $40 s, $50 d and up. Camping space for RVs and tents, outfitter services, and boat rentals are all available here.

Ranch Stays

The Old Kirby Place, south of Cameron, is noted for its log lodge and bunkhouse dating from the 1880s, its great location, and its celebrity guests. Fishing is the focus here, though there are opportunities to ride horses and hike. Rates run $175 per day per person, with a three-day minimum (includes all meals). Contact Walter Kannon, West Fork Bridge, Madison River, Cameron, MT 59720, tel. (406) 682-4194. During the winter, Mr. Kannon is at P.O. Box 104, Sugar Loaf, NY 10981, tel. (914) 469-4380.

Also near Cameron is the CB Ranch, P.O. Box 604, Cameron, MT 59720, tel. (406) 682-

4954. Rates are $850 a week for a single person or $750 per person for a double room. It's not a big outfit; only about a dozen guests are here at a time. The CB is a working family-owned cattle ranch and, though most guests come to fish (women's fly-fishing lessons are a specialty), horses are available.

Diamond J Ranch, P.O. Box 577, Ennis, MT 59729, tel. (406) 682-4867, 14 miles east of Ennis, has 10 cabins available June-Sept. for three-day or weeklong stays. In addition to fishing, horseback riding, and early autumn bird hunting, the Diamond J has indoor tennis courts and a swimming pool.

Ennis's **T Lazy B Ranch,** tel. (406) 682-7288, has log cabins and a lodge on a private stream.

Camping

Ennis Fishing-Access Site, just out of town on the south side of the bridge, is a more developed campground than most of the state's fishing-access sites. The camping fee includes such amenities as pit toilets and running water.

Once you get south of Cameron there are plenty of public campgrounds. **West Madison** BLM campground is three miles west of the McAtee Bridge (the bridge spans the Madison a few miles south of Cameron); **South Madison** is another BLM campground, about six miles south of the McAtee Bridge and a mile off Hwy. 287.

About 34 miles south of Ennis, near the West Fork rest area, find both **West Fork** and **Madison River** Forest Service campgrounds ($9 fee). In the same area, find **West Fork Cabin Camp,** a private outfit with housekeeping cabins and an RV campground. Since it's on the Madison River, fishing is taken seriously. Call (406) 682-4802 for reservations.

Food and Drink

Ennis's restaurant of note is the **Continental Divide,** where creative, sophisticated meals are served in a setting that's not too intimidating to be a real treat. Dinners run $15-20, with a logical emphasis on steak and seafood, but with influences from Asian and European cuisine. Call (406) 682-7600 for reservations, but don't expect to find it open during winter months.

For a quick bite, **Bettie's Cafe** is off the main drag by a couple of blocks, tel. (406) 682-7744. Local ranchers hang out at the **Silver Dollar**

Saloon, tel. (406) 682-7320. Pizza and sandwiches are on the bar menu, and in the adjoining steak restaurant (tel. 406-682-7770), a prime-rib dinner goes for $8.95. The **Long Branch Saloon and Supper Club,** tel. (406) 682-9908, has a hand-carved bar and good dinners.

Down the road in Cameron, find the **Cameron Cafe,** tel. (406) 682-4950, and, for a spirited Saturday night, the **Blue Moon Saloon.**

Events

Mid-June brings **Pioneer Days** to Ennis. The Fourth of July weekend **rodeo** is taken seriously here. Mid-October, shortly after the start of hunting season, Ennis holds its **Wild Game Cookoff.** Visitors can taste the dishes and vote for their favorites. Both the rodeo and the cookoff are known statewide as happenin' events. Call the chamber of commerce at (406) 682-4388 for details.

Shopping

Like much else in Ennis, shopping revolves around fishing. There are several fly-fishing shops in town, including **Madison River Fishing Co.,** 109 Main St., tel. (406) 682-4293, and **The Tackle Shop,** tel. (406) 682-4263. These shops can also recommend guides.

If the fishing is off, would-be anglers can head west on MT 287 to Twin Bridges for a shopping spree at the **R.L. Winston Rod Company,** where the extremely well-regarded rods are handcrafted.

Information

The **Madison Valley Public Library** is at 210 E. Main St., tel. (406) 682-7244. Ennis's **Chamber of Commerce** can be reached at P.O. Box 291, Ennis, MT 59729, tel. (406) 682-4388. The **ranger station** is just west of town at 5 Forest Service Rd., tel. (406) 682-4253.

Contact the **sheriff** at (406) 843-5351, the **fire department** at (406) 682-4800, and the **ambulance** service at (406) 682-4222. Call the **Madison Valley Hospital** at (406) 682-4274.

CLIFF AND WADE LAKES

If you aren't able to make the drive in to Red Rock Lakes Wildlife Refuge but would like to see some wildlife, try Cliff Lake and Wade Lake. These turquoise lakes are about six miles west of

JUDY JEWELL

view from route to Cliff Lake

Hwy. 287 via Forest Service Rd. 8381 (find this road just north of where Hwy. 87 joins Hwy. 287).

The road into the lakes passes the ghost town of Cliff Lake, crosses the "Missouri Flats," a high sagebrush prairie with abundant birdlife, and climbs to the forested lakeshores. Trumpeter swans sometimes appear here in the winter, and raptors live and nest around the lakes. Moose are also common. Wade Lake has good trout fishing.

The southern road to Cliff and Wade Lakes snakes in through humpy sagebrush and pine-covered hills from Hwy. 87, north of where Raynolds Pass crosses the Continental Divide at a remarkably level 6,834-foot pass into Idaho. It takes its name from Captain Raynolds, who headed a scientific expedition in 1860. Jim Bridger was the scientists' guide. There's now a fishing-access site just south of Hwy. 287 near Raynold's Pass.

Accommodations and Food

The utterly charming **Wade Lake Resort,** tel. (406) 682-7560, has simple housekeeping cabins (each with its own outdoor gas grill in addition to the more traditional kitchen set-up) for rent year-round. Bathrooms are in a separate, shared bathhouse. At Wade Lake, the focus is on low-impact recreation. During the summer, anglers come to fish the lakes, known for their huge rainbow and brown trout. A wood-fired hot tub is especially welcome in the winter, when the resort caters to cross-country skiers, grooming 35 miles (55 kilometers) of trails. Winter visitors are especially likely to see wildlife; lots of animals winter in the area. Cabins run $60-80 a night, with a two-night minimum stay. Canoes and motorboats are available for rent at the lodge.

Over on the far side of Cliff Lake, **Cliff Lake Resort,** tel. (406) 682-4982, also has several rustic cabins with kitchens and a shared bath, which rent for $30-40 a night. There are also two larger, more modern houses, which sleep up to 12 and rent for $180 and up a night, and an in-between three-bedroom house going for $90 and up. Dogs are permitted in the rustic cabins but must stay out of the larger houses. The resort can arrange fishing trips and horseback rides.

Just up the hill from the Cliff Lake Resort, the **Saddlehorn Restaurant and Bar** serves the area's only food. Lunchtime burgers and salads run $5-10; beef makes up most of the dinner menu, which runs $15-18.

There are three very pleasant Forest Service campgrounds in the area: **Wade Lake, Hilltop,** and **Cliff Point,** all near Wade Lake Resort.

QUAKE LAKE AND HEBGEN LAKE

South on Hwy. 287 toward Hebgen Lake, the mountains rise off the plain of the Madison Valley. Hebgen Lake is the reservoir formed by the damming of the Madison River in 1915. The lake's north side has a smattering of resorts and private campgrounds; several public campgrounds are on the lake's less-trafficked south side.

Late on the night of Aug. 17, 1959, the Madison River Canyon shuddered as an earthquake measuring 7.5 on the Richter scale started a giant landslide. A 7,600-foot-high mountain collapsed into the river, burying campsites at the Rock Creek Campground and damming the Madison to form Quake Lake. Twenty-eight people were killed. A couple of large fault blocks dropped and tilted north. A huge tidal wave swept across Hebgen

Lake, over Hebgen Dam (six miles away), and into the Madison River Canyon. Amazingly, Hebgen Dam held.

Dead trees now stand in Quake Lake, the Madison River is still choked with rubble, and a "ghost village" near the east end of Quake Lake is a jumble of buildings swept up and dropped by floodwaters. Reach the ghost village via the road across from Cabin Creek campground.

A visitor center now overlooks the site of the landslide. It's open Memorial Day to Labor Day, tel. (406) 646-7369.

Recreation

The **Lee Metcalf Wilderness Area,** just north of Hebgen Lake, and the adjacent **Cabin Creek Wildlife Management Area** are crisscrossed with trails. Several trails start at the end of Beaver Creek Rd., and a trail heads out from Cabin Creek Campground to the wilderness area and other trails. Consult a Gallatin National Forest map, available from the ranger station in West Yellowstone or Ennis before setting out.

Even when the lake is iced over, fishing continues on Hebgen Lake. Brown and rainbow trout predominate, and can be quite large. Smaller populations of cutthroat, whitefish, and arctic grayling also live here. Fishing is not quite as good on Quake Lake, which, before the 1959 earthquake, was one of the Madison River's prime fishing areas.

Hebgen Lake is a popular boating and water-skiing spot and, though people do windsurf on the lake, it's probably not worth planning an entire vacation around it.

There's backcountry cross-country skiing on Hebgen Mountain and less challenging trail skiing at Refuge Point on Hebgen Lake. Stop by the ranger station in West Yellowstone for more information.

Accommodations

Parade Rest Guest Ranch, near Hebgen Lake at 7979 Grayling Creek Rd., West Yellowstone, MT 59758, tel. (406) 646-7217, caters to anglers and their families. All meals and horseback riding are included in the $125 per person per day tariff (lower rates for children). Parade Rest has close ties to many local fishing guides, and while the ranch can set you up with a guide, it's best to arrange this well in advance. **Firehole Ranch,** 11500 Hebgen Lake Rd., tel. (406) 646-7294, is a luxurious fishing-oriented vacation ranch, with in-house fishing guides and a full complement of other recreational activities. Rates are all-inclusive and begin at $250 per person per day.

Moderately priced lodgings dot the north shore of Hebgen Lake. (Hebgen Lake Rd. here is the same as Hwy. 287.) None of these are fancy, but they're good resting places, just enough removed from the hubbub of Yellowstone National Park to afford real relaxation. **Lakeview Cabins,** 15570 Hebgen Lake Rd., tel. (406) 646-7257, is next to the lake and the U.S.S. Happy Hour Bar. **Kirkwood Ranch Motel,** 11505 Hebgen Lake Rd., tel. (406) 646-7200, is on Hebgen Lake and rents boats. **Campfire Lodge Resort,** 8500 Hebgen Lake Rd., between Hebgen and Quake Lakes by Cabin Creek, tel. (406) 646-7258, has cabins, sites for tents and RVs, a cafe, and boat rentals. On Hwy. 191, just south of where Hwy. 287 comes in, the **Madison Arm Resort,** tel. (406) 646-9328, has an RV campground and a marina.

Cabin Creek and **Beaver Creek** Forest Service campgrounds are on the Hwy. 287 side of Hebgen Lake. To the east, **Rainbow Point** (on the Grayling Arm of Hebgen Lake) and **Bakers Hole** (on the Madison River above Hebgen Lake) are public campgrounds close to West Yellowstone, and often full of RVs. **Spring Creek, Rumbaugh Ridge,** and **Lonesomehurst** are Forest Service campgrounds on the less-traveled south shore of Hebgen Lake.

A lot of snow falls here in the winter, and virtually all of these places shut down between late September and early May. Winter travelers can reserve a Forest Service cabin on Hebgen Lake Road by calling (406) 646-7369. It's available from Nov. 20 to April 1.

Food and Drink

The resorts along the north shore of Hebgen Lake offer what there is to be found in the way of food and drink. The **U.S.S. Happy Hour Bar,** 15400 Hebgen Lake Rd., tel. (406) 646-7281, is a particularly appealing bar with a view of Hebgen Lake. If it's choice you want, head down the road to West Yellowstone, where restaurants proliferate.

Information

A deluxe **visitor information center** sits above Quake Lake. The **Hebgen Lake Ranger Station** is actually on the northern edge of West Yellowstone, tel. (406) 646-7369.

BIG SKY AND THE GALLATIN VALLEY

Highway 191 follows the swift west Gallatin River (generally referred to simply as the Gallatin) north from Yellowstone Park through a narrow valley speckled with dude ranches and resorts. The Madison Range, including Spanish Peaks, is west of the Gallatin Valley; the Gallatin Range rises to the east.

In the rugged northern part of the Madison Range, Precambrian basement rock juts up as high as 11,000 feet. Legend has it that these "Spanish Peaks" were named for Spanish trappers from Mexico who showed up in the area in 1836 and, in 1863, had a run-in with some Crow Indians.

Just below the Madison and Gallatin Ranges, the West Yellowstone Basin is a high plain layered with obsidian sand from volcanic eruptions and silt deposits from melting glaciers. It was the site of the Bannock Trail, which led Indians to eastern buffalo-hunting grounds. Highway 191 follows the route of a road cut in 1911 from Bozeman to West Yellowstone.

Tourism is not new to the Gallatin Valley. The Milwaukee Pacific Railroad built the Gallatin Gateway Inn in 1927 at the terminus of its tourist spur line down from Three Forks. Tourists generally dined at the hotel but slept in their train cars before boarding buses to Yellowstone Park. Once tourists began traveling more by car than by train, the railroad was forced to sell off the elegant hotel, which passed through a series of owners and foundered for many years; fortunately, it was never the victim of remodeling and is now an elegant Historic Landmark.

SIGHTS

Big Sky, Montana's largest ski resort, is on Lone Mountain about an hour north of West Yellowstone. The slopes of Lone Mountain have been grazed since the 1890s, and dude ranches began to spring up a few years later. When native son Chet Huntley retired from the newscasting business, he started up Big Sky Resort in what he figured was the ideal spot to blend development with the natural environment, though at the base of the lifts, the Huntley Lodge and its

swarming parking lot now teeter on the edge of overwhelming nature.

Development here has not led to wide use of street addresses—businesses are located by the "village" they occupy: the Huntley Lodge and ski lifts are in the development known as Mountain Village; Meadow Village is toward the base of the mountain.

To experience Huntley's ideal, stay in one of the many well-appointed hotel rooms, but try to escape the network of shops and pizza parlors for at least a little while.

Soldier's Chapel commemorates Montana's native sons who died in the infantry in WW II. The log chapel is on Hwy. 191 near Big Sky. Sunday services are held here.

RECREATION AND EVENTS

Skiing

Big Sky has excellent downhill skiing. Eighty trails lace two mountains, an average of 400 inches of snow falls each year, and there are enough lifts, including a new tram to the top of Lone Peak, to keep lines fairly short. The tram, with its two 15-passenger cars, stops just 16 feet short of the summit and opens up lots of steep terrain. The vertical drop is an amazing 4,180 feet, and the longest runs go on for three miles. Lift tickets are $47 a day for adults; children 10 and under ski free. Half-day and multiday rates are also offered, as is night skiing Dec. 26 to March 31. Big Sky's season runs from mid-Nov. through mid-April. Call Big Sky at (406) 995-4211 or (800) 548-4486.

Cross-country skiers can buy daily passes for the trail network at **Lone Mountain Ranch,** tel. (406) 995-4644. The 45 miles of groomed trails cross a variety of terrains with some good views of the Gallatin Valley. Lessons and naturalist-guided tours into Yellowstone National Park are also offered. Cross-country skiing is usually possible from early Dec. through mid-April.

Cross-country skiers can also head to the Spanish Creek Cabin on the edge of the Lee Metcalf Wilderness Area, about 10 miles north of Big Sky. It's rented out Dec. 1-April 30 for $20 a night. Call the Bozeman Ranger Station at (406) 587-6920 for reservations.

Floating

The Gallatin is popular with whitewater enthusiasts; it's a challenging river to float. Don't put into the Gallatin without plenty of whitewater experience under your belt. The 20-mile stretch between Big Sky and the mouth of Gallatin Canyon is particularly wild. Two rafting outfitters have their headquarters on Hwy. 191 near the Big Sky turnoff. **Yellowstone Raft Co.,** tel. (406) 995-4613 or (800) 348-4376, and **Geyser Whitewater Expeditions,** tel. (406) 995-4989 or (800) 922-7238, both run daily whitewater trips. Expect to pay about $75 for a day-long trip (includes lunch), and $35 for a half day. Geyser Whitewater also runs half-day trips in inflatable kayaks for $45.

Fishing

Fishing access to the Gallatin River is easy; the road runs alongside it much of the way from Yellowstone to Bozeman, and there are many pulloffs—de facto fishing-access sites. There's an official site at the Axtell Bridge, between Gallatin Gateway and Bozeman Hot Springs. Fish don't grow large in the cold waters of the upper Gallatin, but most anglers pull something from the riffly waters of this stretch. The West Fork comes in near Big Sky, and the combined waters flow through a canyon with exceptionally good fishing. Fishing from a boat is prohibited on the Gallatin.

The salmon flies hatch from late June through early July on the Gallatin, but there's good fishing for brown and rainbow trout April through October. **Gallatin Riverguides,** P.O. Box 160212, Big Sky, MT 59716, tel. (406) 995-2290, leads fishing trips year-round. **Lone Mountain Ranch** and **320 Ranch** (see below) also provide fishing guides, as does **Wild Trout Outfitters,** tel. (406) 995-4895.

Other Recreation

Hikers flock to the **Lee Metcalf Spanish Peaks Wilderness Area** during the summer. Trails, most more suitable to overnight backpacking than to day-hiking, cross the peaks. Trailheads sprout on Hwy. 191 between Big Sky and Bozeman; the Cascade Creek hike is especially popular, and the trail can be crowded on the weekends. The Squaw Creek trail heads out of the Squaw Creek campground and follows the creek 11 miles to the Gallatin Divide.

In Big Sky proper, hike along the North Fork trail, a mile off the main road, just above Lone Mountain Ranch. This ridgeline path heads deep into the Spanish Peaks, where it connects with other Forest Service trails.

Backpackers can hike up almost any creekside trail and catch the **Gallatin Divide Trail,** which runs north-south along the divide between the Gallatin and Yellowstone Rivers from the Yellowstone National Park boundary to Hyalite Peak, just outside Bozeman. The trail passes lakes, petrified forest, and badlands; lucky hikers will see moose and possibly bears.

Stop at the Squaw Creek Ranger Station for trail tips, or pore over the Gallatin National Forest map to construct a long backpacking trip in this spectacularly scenic area.

The **Arnold Palmer Golf Course,** a challenging riverside course at the Meadow Village, was indeed designed by Palmer. It's open to the public; call (406) 995-4706 for a tee time.

Jake's Horses, tel. (406) 995-4630, offers guided rides on the trails around Big Sky on gentle horses. Find the stables three miles south of Big Sky on Hwy. 191.

Rent bikes at **Grizzly Flats,** between Meadow Village and Hwy. 191.

Long, multipitched climbs right near the highway make the Gallatin Canyon popular with climbers, even though the rock is crumbly and rather unstable.

Events

During the second weekend of January, Big Sky holds a winter carnival. In July, the **Big Sky Arts Festival** sponsors a concert series, bringing classical, jazz, and country music to the slopes every weekend. Call (406) 995-5000 for exact dates and details.

ACCOMMODATIONS

There are several lodging options at Big Sky. Motel rooms, cabins, and condominiums are all available at different elevations on Lone Mountain. A shuttle bus runs between all the lodging spots and the ski lifts. Room prices are somewhat fluid and can vary greatly by season and by the day of the week. Additionally, each place will have a number of different room types available. It's best to call and see what's available to fit your needs.

At the bottom of the hill, **Best Western Buck's T-4 Lodge,** on Hwy. 191, tel. (800) 822-4484 or (406) 995-4111, is a very nice lodging with two large outdoor hot tubs and rooms starting at $89-99 single, $99-109 d. The restaurant here is also notable. Pets are permitted with a $5 fee.

The **Golden Eagle Lodge and Condominium Rentals,** at the Meadow level of the the mountain, tel. (406) 995-4800 or (800) 548-4488, There's a staggering array of lodging choices, ranging from reasonably priced suites that can accommodate up to eight people, plus many condos and homes for nightly rental studios begin at $75 in winter, $130 in winter. Add extra bedrooms, Jacuzzis, and saunas, and the prices increase accordingly. A pool is available for lodge guests, and many of the condos are equipped with hot tubs and/or have access to a swimming pool.

Somewhat apart from the Big Sky bustle is the **Rainbow Ranch Lodge,** tel. (406) 995-4132 or (800) 937-4132 on the Gallatin River at the base of the mountain. The lodge's 13 newly renovated rooms all have balconies overlooking the river, and there's a shared deck with a fireplace and large hot tub. Rates run $115-195 for rooms and suites.

Between Meadow and Mountain, the **River Rock Lodge,** tel. (406) 995-2295 or (800) 995-9966, has Big Sky's most comfortably elegant lodgings. The tasteful western-craftsman decor has a practical note, like the handsome wool blankets and down comforters on each bed. Rooms come with sink, coffeemaker, and mini-bar, and start at $90 s, $115 d during the summer and fall, going up to $140 s and $155 d during the height of ski season.

Rooms at the **Huntley Lodge and Shoshone Condominium Hotel** in the Mountain Village, tel. (800) 548-4486 or (406) 995-5000, begin at $132 during the winter and $115 in the summer; condos begin around $200. There are two swimming pools, a steam room, hot tubs, and great access to the slopes.

Many families prefer to rent condominiums for their ski vacations, and several agencies will arrange rentals from about $150 a night and up. Try **Big Sky Condominium Management,** tel. (406) 995-4560 or (800) 831-3509; **Triple Creek**

Realty, tel. (800) 548-4632; or **Big Sky Chalets,** tel. (406) 995-2665 or (800) 845-4428.

North of Big Sky, in the town of Gallatin Gateway, the historic **Gallatin Gateway Inn** has been beautifully restored to landmark status. Rooms in the old hotel start at $95 during the summer, $60 in the winter; spacious suites run $115 summer, $85 winter. There's a very nice outdoor pool and hot tub, as well as a casting pond and tennis courts. Reserve by calling (406) 763-4672 or (800) 676-3522.

Ranch Stays

Lone Mountain Ranch, halfway between the highway and the ski lifts, tel. (406) 995-4644, is a little different from the other Big Sky lodgings. Originally a working cattle ranch, it has become a great cross-country ski resort (some say the nation's best) and, during the summer, a dude ranch with special programs for anglers and for children learning to ride. Any number of different packages are offered, but a standard summertime seven-day stay in a small cabin costs $1,900 s, plus $1,150 for each additional person. Winter rates are $1,535 s, plus $860 for each roommate.

Another noteworthy guest ranch, the **Nine Quarter-Circle Ranch,** specializes in families and has plenty of children's activities, tel. (406) 995-4276 or 995-4876. The Nine Quarter-Circle has been in operation since 1912. Guest accommodations are in log cabins, all with private baths and wood stoves. Meals are served in the handsome central lodge. Activities include horseback riding, fishing, overnight pack trips, and square dancing. Weekly rates are $1,092 per person double occupancy.

320 Ranch, a guest ranch since the turn of the century, is 12 miles south of Big Sky and six miles north of Yellowstone Park, tel. (406) 995-4283 or (800) 243-0320. Cabin rentals begin at $83-108 a night, depending on season (summer is the most expensive). Cabins with kitchenettes and larger log houses are also available, and weekly or monthly rentals and activities such as horseback riding and fishing can be easily arranged. Even if you're not sleeping at the 320, it's a good place to stop for a meal.

Campgrounds

At the southern end of the valley, **Bakers Hole** is the closest public campground to West Yellowstone. It's just three miles north of town on Hwy. 191 and is one of the few public campgrounds that accepts advance registration, tel. (800) 283-CAMP. Blue herons nest on the Madison River just across from the campground.

Spire Rock is a small, free Forest Service campground about 15 miles southeast of Gallatin Gateway. Another good bet is **Moose Flat,** five miles north of Big Sky on Hwy. 191 and **Squaw Creek,** just north of Moose Flat.

FOOD AND DRINK

There's no dearth of good food around Big Sky. Down in Meadow Village, **First Place,** tel. (406) 995-4244, is reckoned to serve some of the mountain's best dinners, including chicken with black bean salsa for about $15 and charbroiled pork tenderloin with huckleberry sauce for about $16. Another good dinner spot is halfway up the hill, where the **Lone Mountain Ranch** serves dinner each night at 6:30 p.m.; reserve by calling (406) 995-2782. The views from the comfortable Lone Mountain bar are especially seductive after a few times around the cross-country ski trails. Big Sky's third place for a good, if somewhat spendy, dinner is down on Hwy. 191, at **Buck's T-4 Best Western,** just south of the Big Sky turnoff. Buck's specializes in wild game dinners, like ringneck pheasant stuffed with pistachio and pheasant pâté, or Texas antelope. Call (406) 995-4111 for reservations.

For lunch or a take-out dinner, try the **Gallatin Gourmet Deli,** tel. (406) 995-2314, in the country store in the Meadow Village. They make delicious soups, sandwiches, and salads. Moderately priced Italian and Mexican dinners share the bill at **Rocco's,** yet another Meadow Village eatery, tel. (406) 995-4200.

Between Meadow and Mountain, the Westfork area has a couple of good places to stop for a quick bite. The **Blue Moon Bakery,** tel. (406) 995-2305, serves soup and sandwiches in addition to bread, bagels, and breakfast pastries. At **By Word of Mouth,** tel. (406) 995-2992, the soup, sandwiches, and salads are geared toward a gourmet's palate, though it's still possible to get a good veggie sandwich for less than $4.

At the top of the hill, **Huntley Lodge** has a fancy dining room. Sandwich shops, pizza joints, Chinese food, and cafeterias are all well represented and easy to find in Mountain Village.

Reasonably priced meals and western atmosphere abound at the **Corral Steakhouse Cafe,** five miles south of Big Sky on Hwy. 191, tel. (406) 995-4249. The **Half Moon Saloon,** three miles south of Big Sky on Hwy. 191, is a comfortable place to stop for a beer, and the **Rainbow Ranch Lodge** serves elegant dinners just south of the Big Sky turn-off. Almost to Yellowstone, the **320 Ranch** is worth a stop for good Montana-style steak, trout, and fish dinners, tel. (406) 995-4283.

In the northern part of the valley, almost to Bozeman, the **Gallatin Gateway Inn,** tel. (406) 763-4672, serves elegant yet robust dinners for $15-20.

PRACTICALITIES

Shopping
Stop by **Moose Rack Books,** just north of the Big Sky turnoff on Hwy. 191, tel. (406) 995-4521. It's one of the region's best bookstores, with a good selection of used books on Montana and the West. They also have a small shop up by the ski area in the Mountain Mall, tel. (406) 995-2551.

Information and Services
Big Sky Resort Association is at P.O. Box 1, Big Sky, MT 59716, tel. (800) 548-4486 or, in Montana, (800) 824-7767.

Contact the **sheriff** at (406) 585-1475, the **fire department** at (406) 585-1390, and the **ambulance service** at (406) 585-1480.

Transportation
Northwest, Horizon, Sky West, and Delta airlines all fly into the Bozeman airport. **4X4 Stage** tel. (406) 388-6404, (800) 517-8243 runs a shuttle from the airport to Big Sky. Reservations are required; fare is $36.50 one way. Shuttle buses run frequently between Big Sky's Meadow and Mountain villages. See below for car rentals in Bozeman.

BOZEMAN AND VICINITY

Bozeman (pop. 28,522), home of Montana State University, lies at the foot of the Gallatin Valley, with the Gallatin Range (and its Spanish Peaks) and Madison Range to the south, the Bridger Range to the northeast, the Tobacco Roots farther west, and the Big Belts way off north and west.

It's a lovely setting, and Bozeman makes the most of its physical attributes, with hiking and skiing practically out the back door. However, what makes Bozeman such a great destination for a traveler is the town itself. More than any other Montana city, Bozeman has maintained its handsome old downtown as a business center, which makes the city seem centralized and community-focused. Add some excellent restaurants, art galleries, an outgoing, youthful population, and inexpensive lodging options and you've got a recipe for Montana's most beguiling urban experience.

It's safe to wear sandals in Bozeman—its elevation of 4,754 feet puts it just high enough to be inhospitable to rattlesnakes.

HISTORY

Native Crow, Blackfeet, Bannock, Shoshone, and Flathead referred to this area as the "Valley of the Flowers." It was a sacred hunting ground and neutral territory.

White settlers named the city for John Bozeman, mountain man and immigrant guide of the 1860s. Bozeman's trail, essentially a spur of the Oregon Trail leading to Montana's gold country, ran along what is now a section of I-90. Frequent attacks by Sioux and Cheyenne bands plagued sojourners on the Bozeman Trail. Bozeman himself was killed, perhaps by Blackfeet (or perhaps by a business colleague, perhaps by a jealous husband), near Livingston in 1867. Largely as a reaction to Bozeman's murder, Fort Ellis was established in 1867 at the site where William Clark and his party camped in 1806. It was the supply post for the Cavalry during the Battle of the Little Bighorn in 1876 and provided military escort for railroad surveyors in the 1880s.

Even before the Northern Pacific Railroad came through in 1883, Bozeman had the bearing of a civilized town set down in the wilds. One fortune seeker who passed through Bozeman in 1882 claimed it was the nicest place he'd been since St. Paul. In a letter to his sister, he told of "2 Churches, Court house, fine large brick school and the nicest lot of small dwelling houses all painted white with green lawns and level as a floor. There are lots of brick store buildings here. That is something you don't see the whole length of the Yellowstone River."

DOVER PUBLICATIONS, INC.

three Crow—a secondary chief, a warrior, and a wife of the warrior

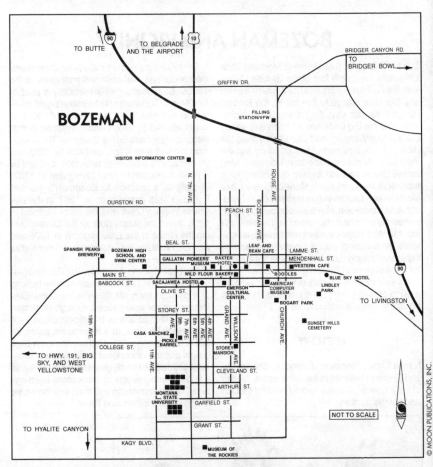

BOZEMAN

Bozeman is still more upscale than the rest of the state and has become the nexus of, or at least the market town for, Montana celebrities. It's a fun, lively place to visit and is well situated for recreationists, but it's not to be confused for the Real Montana.

SIGHTS

Historic Bozeman

To embark on a historical downtown walking tour, with a foray into residential areas, start at the large brick building at Main and Rouse; it once housed city hall, but was first the opera house, with the original sign remaining over the front door for years afterward. Historic business buildings along Main St. include the **Baxter Hotel** (eat in one of the restaurants it now houses, or simply step in and admire the lobby), the **Hotel Bozeman,** the **Ellen Theatre,** and **Holy Rosary Church.** Historic homes cluster in the neighborhood between Main St. and the university, especially along Willson Avenue. The Sigma Alpha Epsilon fraternity house at Willson and College is known locally as the **Storey**

Mansion. It was the home of the son of Nelson Storey, the first cattleman to drive cattle up from Texas to the Gallatin Valley.

Sunset Hills Cemetery, immediately south of Lindley Park, is now home to John Bozeman, Chet Huntley, and most of the people that Bozeman's buildings and streets are named for. The old part of the cemetery is off to the west; if you're really interested in exploring the graves, stop in a bookstore and pick up a copy of the cemetery guide produced by MSU art students.

Montana State University

Montana State University, founded in 1893, is the state's oldest university. Originally the "Ag School" in the state system, it is now a haven for some 10,000 outdoorsy students with a technical bent. The university, located south and west of city center (take 7th Ave. south from Main Street to find the campus) is dominated by unremarkable modern buildings and isn't really much of a destination unless you're visiting someone living in the dorms.

The good-natured rivalry between Bozeman's MSU Bobcats and Missoula's University of Montana Grizzlies can be widened in scope to encompass a rivalry between the two university towns.

Museums

At the southeast corner of the MSU campus, S. 6th Ave. and W. Kagy Blvd., find the **Museum of the Rockies.** The collection is eclectic, but most people know the museum for its significant collection of dinosaur bones, including the **Tyrannosaurus rex** skull excavated in eastern Montana in 1990. There's also a sampling of modern art, pioneer history, and astronomy. It's a good place to take the kids, and adults may want to prepare by reading Jack Horner's book, *Digging Dinosaurs,* before their visit. Horner is a renowned paleontologist in charge of the museum's impressive paleontology department.

Admission is $6 for adults, $4 for children 5-18 (kids under five get in free); the popular planetarium is another $2.50 apiece. The museum is open daily 8 a.m.-8 p.m. from Memorial Day through Labor Day; during the winter, hours are Mon.-Sat. 9 a.m.-5 p.m., Sunday 12:30-5 p.m.; tel. (406) 994-2251.

The **Gallatin Pioneers' Museum,** in the old county jail at 317 W. Main St., tel. (406) 582-3195, is open weekdays June-Sept. 10 a.m.-4:30 p.m.

and Saturday 1-4 p.m. Winter hours are weekdays 11 a.m.-4 p.m. and Saturday 1-4 p.m. The museum only took over from the jail in 1982, and there are still jail cells and a gallows amongst the Indian artifacts, old household items, and barbed wire collections. Look for the display of tiny carved Montana agates, the products of a Gallatin County couple's lifelong hobby. A dollhouse-size bar, complete with back bar and bottles, is particularly charming.

Fort Ellis, the site north of town where Clark and his party camped July 14, 1806, and which later became an Army fort, is no longer standing, but local guys with metal detectors have turned up a number of relics, which are on display at the Gallatin Pioneers' Museum.

Lest you think that all historical museums in Montana focus on early settlers, take note of the **American Computer Museum,** 234 E. Babcock St., tel. (406) 587-7545. You'll not see one old kitchen utensil in this surprisingly absorbing museum. Instead, ponder computers that seem immense and confusing and realize that they are little more than a dozen years old. It is worth being guided around; the curator's talk is understandable and interesting, even to one for whom computers are little more than smart typewriters. Summer hours are daily 10 a.m.-4 p.m.; winter hours are Tuesday, Wednesday, Friday, and Saturday noon-4 p.m. Admission is $3 ages 13 and over, $2 for children 6 to 12.

A few blocks west of the computer museum, at 111 S Grand, the **Emerson Cultural Center** houses artists, craftspeople, performers, and a cafe. Visitors can browse the studios and galleries, stop for lunch at the Cafe Internationale, and attend evening performances. Call (406) 587-9797 for a schedule of events.

RECREATION

Pools and Parks

The **city pool** is adjacent to the high school at 1211 W. Main St., tel. (406) 587-4727. Regular morning, noon, and evening lap swims are scheduled. For a relaxed paddle around a somewhat dilapidated hotsprings pool, **Bozeman Hot Springs KOA,** 133 Lower Rainbow Rd., tel. (406) 587-3030, charges $3 adults, $2.50 children. During the summer, the outdoor pool in **Bogart Park** is open afternoons and evenings.

Lake swimmers may prefer Glen Lake at **East Gallatin State Recreation Area** on Manley Rd. in the northeast corner of town.

Of the many parks in Bozeman, the visitor is most likely to spend time in **Lindley Park** on the south side of E. Main St., just out of downtown. The Sweet Pea Festival overruns the park early each August, and it's a good spot for a picnic at other times. **Bogart Park,** on S. Church Ave., has an outdoor swimming pool, an ice rink, and a summertime Saturday-morning farmers' market. Just south of Bogart Park, pick up the **Gallagator Linear,** a walking, running, skiing, and biking trail that runs from S. Church Ave. and Storey St. to 3rd Ave. and Kagy Boulevard.

Hiking
Hyalite Canyon is about half an hour south of town via S. 19th Ave. and Hyalite Canyon Road. Drive to the end of the road to launch a five-mile hike past nearly a dozen waterfalls to Hyalite Lake, then go another two miles to reach Hyalite Peak. One drainage over from the Hyalite Lake hike, Emerald Lake is another five-mile hike to a pretty lake in a high cirque. Turn left off the road shortly after the youth camp at Hyalite Reservoir to reach this trailhead.

The trails in this area are well maintained and well signed. Indeed, many of the trails, campgrounds, and fishing-access points in Hyalite Canyon are designed to allow people of differing physical abilities to use them. The trails are rated from easiest to most difficult; one of the easy trails is a half-mile paved loop from Langhor Campground with nature trail signs in both type and braille.

North of town, the **Bridger Foothills National Recreation Trail** starts at the **M Picnic Area** on Bridger Dr. (head north on Rouse; it becomes Bridger Dr.) and continues for 21 miles to the Fairy Lake Campground. From there, it's a two-mile hike to **Sacajawea Peak.** To drive to the **Fairy Lake Campground,** take Bridger Dr. for 24 miles to Forest Rd. and go another seven miles to the campground. If you're just up for a short hike, start at the same place and hike up to the "M" for a great panorama of Bozeman and the Bridger Canyon.

Another good view of the city and surrounding mountains comes from Peet's Hill, right in town

at the corner of S. Church and Storey, across the road from the entrance to the Gallagator Linear trail. It's a short and rewarding climb up the hill.

Skiing
Big Sky, one hour to the south, is the state's largest downhill ski resort and is the site of good cross-country skiing at **Lone Mountain Ranch,** tel. (406) 995-4644.

Bridger Bowl, 16 miles northeast of town up Bridger Canyon Rd., tel. (800) 223-9609 or (406) 586-1518, is Bozeman's local nonprofit ski mountain. It's just as snowy as Big Sky and less glitzy and less expensive (lift tickets are $29 for adults, $12 for children, and $20 for seniors). Call (406) 586-2389 for a ski report.

Cross-country skiers can head up Bridger Canyon to **Bohart Ranch Cross Country Ski Center,** 16621 Bridger Canyon Rd., tel. (406) 586-9070. During the summer the trails are used for mountain biking, hiking, and horseback riding. There are also cross-country ski trails at Hyalite Reservoir, 18 miles south of town, Bozeman Creek, five miles south of town, and Stone Creek, 10 miles northeast of Bozeman. Call the Forest Service at (406) 587-6920 for details on these trails.

Chalet Sports, at Main St. and Willson Ave., tel. (406) 587-4595, rents both skis and bikes. Cross-country skis are also rented out at Bohart Ranch and Lone Mountain Ranch.

Fishing
Though there aren't any major trout streams flowing through Bozeman, the town is close enough to the Gallatin, the Yellowstone, and the Madison Rivers to support several good fly shops and outfitters. **River's Edge,** 2012 N. 7th Ave., tel. (406) 586-5373, is a fly-fishing shop with a guide service. **Montana Troutfitters,** 1716 W. Main St., tel. (406) 587-4707, is an Orvis shop, and guides are available from **Montana Flycast Guide Service,** 1431 S. 3rd Ave., (406) 587-5923.

Other Activities
Rent rafts, kayaks, and other recreational equipment from **Northern Lights,** 1716 W. Babcock St., tel. (406) 586-2225. The staff here can also supply recreational information, especially concerning climbing routes in Hyalite Canyon, Gallatin Canyon, and at Bozeman Pass.

Pick up a map of the Gallatin National Forest's **mountain bike trails** at any bike or outdoor store.

Golf **Bridger Creek,** 2710 McIlhattan Rd., tel. (406) 586-2333 or **Cottonwood Hills** on River Rd., tel. (406) 587-1118.

For those who aren't fans of the fairways, perhaps the **Skate Palace** at 2015 Wheat Dr., tel. (406) 586-7770, holds more appeal.

ACCOMMODATIONS

Hostel

Travelers who prefer not to stay in standard motel accommodations have a choice in Bozeman. The **International Backpackers Hostel,** at 405 W. Olive St., tel. (406) 586-4659, has $12 rooms in what could pass for a big MSU group house, with no curfew. Shuttle transportation to trailheads is available through the hostel, which also has some mountain bikes for rent. Staff can also give you information about hosteling and special transportation through Yellowstone Park.

Bed and Breakfasts

The **Voss Inn,** in a 120-year-old mansion at 319 S. Willson Ave., tel. (406) 587-0982, www.wtp.net/go/vossinn, is Bozeman's premier bed and breakfast. The six guestrooms range in price $75-85 s, $85-95 d, are furnished with antiques, and all have their own private bathrooms. Breakfast is served to guests in their rooms, and afternoon tea is served in the parlor.

Each of the three rooms at **Torch and Toes,** 309 S. 3rd Ave., tel. (406) 586-7285 or (800) 446-2138, www.avicom.net/torchntoes, evidences a personal touch from the proprietors' family. If you're traveling with a group or a family, consider the carriage house, which can accommodate up to six people. Rooms run $70 s, $80-90 d and up; the inn, like the Voss, is in a historic neighborhood between the university and downtown Bozeman. The **Lindley House,** near downtown at 202 Lindley Place, tel. (406) 587-8112, www.avicom.net/lindley, is a Victorian manor home with a lovely garden and rooms for $75-250.

Cross-country skiers and sledders can head right out the door at **Bergfeld B&B,** 8515 Sypes Canyon Rd., tel. (406) 586-7778, www.avicom.net/bergfeld. Downhill skiers will have a 20-minute drive to the slopes, and there's a hot tub to come home to. The B&B, decorated with a fly-fishing motif, doubles as a llama ranch and is a few miles north of town with great mountain views. Rooms run $75-100.

Hotels and Motels

Many motels are strung along both Main St. and 7th Ave., but they do have a tendency to fill up on summer weekends or when the MSU Bobcats have a big home game.

Most convenient to shopping and dining downtown are the following motels. Inexpensive and friendly, the **Imperial Inn,** 122 W. Main St., has a prime downtown location, tel. (406) 587-5261 or (800) 541-7423. Rates are $52 s, $62 d, with considerably cheaper off-season rates.

A step up in facilities and price, the **Best Western City Center,** 507 W. Main St., tel. (406) 587-3158, is on the edge of downtown, not far from the university. Rooms are $74 s, $89 d. There's a pool, plus a restaurant and lounge.

On the east side of Bozeman are several pleasant lodging choices, all of which as an easy stroll or drive to downtown; from the freeway, take exit 309. **Blue Sky Motel,** 1010 E. Main St., tel. (406) 587-2311 or (800) 845-9032, has nicely maintained units and a hot tub, and is next door to a city park. Rooms are $49 s, $59 d. **Bozeman's Western Heritage Inn,** 1200 E. Main St., tel. (406) 586-8534 or (800) 877-1094, is a good deal, with spacious rooms at $53-63 s, 58-68 d, plus a fitness room, hot tub, steam room, suites with jacuzzis, free light breakfast, and pets okay. There are also kitchen suites. All rooms have king or queen beds, and singles have recliners. The **Ranch House Motel,** 1201 E. Main St., tel. (406) 587-4278, has clean rooms for $27 s, $37 d.

On the other end of Main Street is a clutch of motels close to the MSU campus. Most convenient is **Lewis & Clark Motel,** 824 W. Main St., tel. (406) 586-3341 or (800) 332-7666, a large complex that includes an indoor pool, fitness center, sauna, hot tub, plus a restaurant and lounge. Rooms are $62 s, $72 d. Farther out but newer, the **Bobcat Lodge,** 2307 W. Main St., tel. (406) 587-5241, features all kitchenette suites at $33 s, $49 d. There's an indoor pool, sauna, and laundry room, making this another good lodging deal.

The rest of Bozeman's lodging choices are along N 7th Ave., the commercial strip that leads to I-90 exit no 306. Right at the exit is a bundle of chain motels.

The **Bozeman Inn,** 1235 N. 7th Ave., tel. (406) 587-3176 or (800) 648-7515, has rooms at $45-55 s, $65-75 d, pets are okay. The **Econo Lodge,** 805 Wheat Dr., tel. (406) 587-2100 or (800) 800-7089, has rooms at $54 s, $62 d, and a sauna, hot tub, and continental breakfast. The **Super 8,** 800 Wheat Dr., tel. (406) 586-1521 or (800) 843-1991, prices rooms at $56 s, $70 d. **Best Western GranTree Inn,** 1325 N. 7th Ave., tel. (406) 587-5261 or (800) 624-5865, with rooms at $89 s and d, offers an indoor pool, hot tub, laundry room, restaurant and lounge, and an airport shuttle.

The **Holiday Inn,** 5 Baxter Ln., tel. (406) 587-4561 or (800) 366-5101, has spacious rooms starting at $89 s or d. Services and amenities are outstanding and include an indoor pool, hot tub, exercise and game rooms, restaurant and lounge, room service, laundry room, and massage therapist; kids stay—and eat—free, and pets are welcome, too. Another first-rate lodging is the **Days Inn** 1321 N. 7th Ave., tel. (406) 587-5251 or (800) 987-3297, with a fitness room, hot tub, sauna, cooked-to-order hot breakfast, one- and two-bedroom suites, and business work areas. Rooms are $74 s, $83 d.

Closer to MSU and downtown, but on the Strip is the **Rainbow Motel;** 510 N. 7th Ave., tel. (406) 587-4201. One of the few real deals in Bozeman, rooms are $38 s, $50 d, and there's an outdoor pool and free continental breakfast.

Gallatin Gateway Inn

Even though it's 15 miles from town in the Hwy. 191 hamlet of Gallatin Gateway, travelers to Bozeman shouldn't overlook the historic Gallatin Gateway Inn. The old railroad hotel has been extensively renovated, though not substantially altered from the original. Huge arched windows and ocher walls give the lobby an airy Mediterranean feel, and the quarters, which range from smallish standard rooms in the hotel proper ($90 and up in the summer, $60 and up during the winter) to spacious suites in buildings behind the main lodge ($115 summer, $85 winter) are graceful and comfortable. There's an outdoor pool and hot tub, a

casting pond, tennis courts, and places to hike or mountain bike just out the back door. Call (406) 763-4672 or (800) 676-3522 for reservations.

Forest Service Cabins

The Bozeman Ranger District rents out a number of rustic cabins in the Gallatin National Forest. They're generally equipped with wood stoves but have no running water, and they cost $20 a night. For a list of cabins, call the ranger station at (406) 587-6920.

Camping

Tent campers will almost certainly want to head for one of the three campgrounds in Hyalite Canyon: **Langhor** is 11 miles south of town on Hyalite Canyon Road. **Blackmore** and **Hood Creek** are another five and six miles down the same road. Reach Hyalite Canyon Rd. by heading south on 19th Avenue.

Another reasonable camping bet is the **Bozeman Hot Springs KOA,** eight miles south of town on Hwy. 191, tel. (406) 587-3030. The springs fill one large and several small indoor pools; outside the bathhouse, it's a KOA campground. Camping fees start at $15, with an extra dollar fee to swim (it's $2.50 for noncampers to use the hot springs).

FOOD AND DRINK

Bozeman's prosperous trendiness is reflected in its restaurants—not a bad thing for the hungry traveler. In fact, Bozeman has a higher concentration of great restaurants than any other city in the state. That doesn't mean that all the best meals are served in posh new cafes, however. But the emphasis on fresh ingredients and vivid flavors resonates even in more modest venues.

Casual Meals

At the **Western Cafe,** 443 E. Main St., tel. (406) 587-0436, cinnamon rolls come out of the oven at 8 a.m., tabs must be paid before the first of the month, the grill cook's quick, and there's a jackalope head mounted above the milk dispenser. They open at 5 a.m.

For those who would rather drink coffee than eat, the **Leaf and Bean** is a good place to hunker down with the morning paper. It serves some pastries and a full range of espresso drinks at 35 W. Main St., tel. (406) 587-1580. **Wild Flour Bakery,** 19 S. Willson Ave., tel. (406) 587-8110, and **Bozeman Bagelworks,** 708 W. Main St., tel. (406) 585-1727, are both great places to stop for some early morning carbohydrate loading.

In the heart of downtown, in the old Baxter Hotel building at 105 W. Main St., tel. (406) 586-1314, the **Bacchus Pub** is a casual spot for a pint of beer and a burger or salad. For downtown's best pizza and good local ales, go to **MacKenzie River Pizza,** 232 E Main, tel. (406) 587-0055.

A couple of good, homey, and inexpensive spots are tucked behind W. Main St., on Babcock. **Carito's Authentic Mexican Restaurat** is at 1511 W. Babcock, tel. (406) 586-3547. **La Parrilla** is a multi-ethnic grill serving "wraps" at 1533 W. Babcock, tel. (406) 582-9511.

For a real brewpub atmosphere, go to **Spanish Peaks Brewery and Italian Caffe,** 120 N. 19th Ave., tel. (406) 585-2296. Their gourmet wood-fired pizzas are a good foil for a tall glass of Black Dog Ale. Pasta, fresh fish, and rotisseried meats are other specialties.

Near the university, there are some casual places catering to students and locals. The **Pickle Barrel** is not much bigger than the genuine item. All they've got are sandwiches, but they're giant, satisfying things, with any of the steak-and-cheese sandwiches getting a special recommendation. There are picnic benches out front so you can hang around and eat, then finish the gorge with an ice-cream cone from the equally tiny place next door. (It's actually part of the Pickle Barrel, but the buildings are too small to fit main course and dessert in the same place.) They're across from the university at 809 W. College St. (and also downtown at 209 E. Main, and, during the winter, at Bridger Bowl). Open for lunch and dinner, with free delivery, tel. (406) 587-2411.

For a full sit-down-inside meal, **Casa Sanchez** is right around the corner at 719 S. 9th Ave., tel. (406) 586-4516. It's a pleasant place in an often-crowded small house serving moderately priced Mexican lunches and dinners.

Columbo's Pizza and Pasta, 1003 W. College St., tel. (406) 587-5544, features cheap, filling, and generally quite tasty dinners (some less than $5).

The deli at the **Community Food Co-op,** 508 W. Main, tel. (406) 587-4039, serves very tasty vegetarian soups, salads, and casseroles.

Fine Dining

The old Baxter Hotel is home to several eating and drinking options. For pasta, seafood, grilled meats, and continental-style dishes, try the **Pasta Company,** 105 W. Main, tel. (406) 586-1314. In summer, the same menu is available in a garden setting behind the hotel, in the dining area called **The Outback.** Another good downtown dinner house is **O'Brien's,** 312 E. Main St., tel. (406) 587-3973, where northern Italian and French dinners are prepared with an eye toward health. Breakfasts are also popular here.

John Bozeman's Bistro, downtown at 242 E. Main St., tel. (406) 587-4100, serves lunch and dinner daily, and weekend breakfast. The food is good American-bistro-ex-hippie style, there's plenty of it, it's easy to eat for less than $10, and the atmosphere is comfortable if not stimulating.

Bozeman's most ambitious menu is found at Boodles, 215 E Main, tel. (406) 587-2901. The very cosmopolitan atmosphere is just right for contemplating a selection of New American dishes featuring duck breast, lamb, porterhouse steak, game, and other up-to-the-moment choices. Live jazz on weekends. Open for dinner only. Entrees range $15-25.

Jadra's, 101 E Main, tel. (406) 582-0393, brings modern Asian cooking to Main Street Bozeman. Featuring a sushi bar and serving Thai, Indian, and Japanese cuisines, Jadra's will please most palates. At the same address, just below Jadra's but half a world away in cooking style, **Looie's Down Under,** tel. (406) 522-8814, is a branch of the popular Livingston restaurant, featuring high-quality Italian and Continental cuisine.

If you're staying on the 7th Ave. motel strip and lack the energy to leave your street, there are alternatives to McDonald's and Taco Bell. **Ferraro's,** 726 N 7th Ave., tel. (406) 582-1651, features classy Italian dining and a great wine list. At the Bozeman Inn, 1235 N. 7th Ave., **Santa Fe Red's** serves good southwestern-style food, tel. (406) 587-5838.

If you're hankering for roasted rack of lamb with lavender and thyme honey mustard glaze, pick up and drive out to the **Gallatin Gateway Inn,** on Hwy. 191 at Gallatin Gateway. The food is very good, and the atmosphere sublime. Call (406) 763-4672 for reservations.

NIGHTLIFE

The 1939 WPA *Montana, A State Guide Book* characterized Bozeman as "an old and decorous town. Local ordinances prohibit dancing anywhere after midnight and in beer halls at any time. It is illegal to drink beer while standing, so all Bozeman bars are equipped with stools."

Well, things have loosened up a little bit since the '30s. College students have a nasty habit of standing up to drink, and the electronic gaming machines now endemic in bars threaten to make barstools obsolete.

The **Robin Lounge** in the old Baxter Hotel, 105 W. Main St., tel. (406) 586-1314, is not too far from what you'd expect in an old and decorous town. The architecture is great here, and the bar scene is not too scary.

Hop over a couple of blocks to the **Crystal Bar** at 123 E. Main St., tel. (406) 587-2888, and both the decor and decorum become a bit more tenuous. The Crystal's rooftop terrace is surrounded by chickenwire to keep patrons from tossing beer bottles onto the sidewalk below. At the **Rockin' R**, 211 E. Main St., tel. (406) 587-9355, the mixed crowd is usually sprinkled with poets and lefties. Head down to the corner of Main and Rouse, to the old Bozeman Hotel building, to find both the **Zebra Club**, with cocktails and indie bands, and **The Point After**, a sports bar focusing on the MSU Bobcats.

Go north to 2005 N. Rouse Ave. to the **Filling Station VFW**, tel. (406) 587-5009, for music from local bands, many playing alternative western music. It's also at least a quasi-official stop for scores of Harley riders on their way to the annual Harley-Davidson Festival in Sturgis, South Dakota. The **Cat's Paw**, 721 N. 7th Ave., tel. (406) 586-3542, is a band bar with a space large enough to sponsor big shows.

For three more hanging-out bars, head back to Main St., where the **Hofbrau, Molly Brown's,** and the **Scoop** all cluster near the intersection of 8th and Main.

If what you're after is good, gutsy microbrewed beer and a spiffy clean black-and-white-tiled setting, visit the **Spanish Peaks Brewery** at 120 N. 19th Ave., tel. (406) 585-2296, and quaff some Black Dog Ale.

Nightlife doesn't necessarily include alcohol at the **Leaf and Bean** or the **Emerson Cultural Center,** both of which often have music in the evenings.

EVENTS

The Gallatin County Fairgrounds is the site of the **Montana Winter Fair** late each January. Unlikely as it may seem, it's a wintertime version of a state fair.

One of Bozeman's pleasant surprises is the **Intermountain Opera,** tel. (406) 587-2889, which stages one production a year (with two performances). Pablo Elvira, a Gallatin Valley resident who sings with New York's Metropolitan Opera, is frequently featured in these mid-May productions.

The **College National Finals Rodeo** is traditionally held in mid-June at the MSU field house, but the event now changes location annually. Wherever it is hosted, it's a popular show and tickets can be hard to come at the last minute, so reserve tickets in advance whenever possible. For more information contact the College National Finals Rodeo, 502 S. 19th Ave. #303, Bozeman, MT 59715, tel. (406) 994-4813.

The **Sweet Pea Festival** dominates Bozeman's social scene during the first weekend of August. Booths from local restaurants line up along Main St. for the **Taste of Bozeman,** a big picnic-cum-dinner party that kicks off the festival weekend. As the arts festival bustles in Lindley Park, people gear up for the Sweet Pea Ball, held at the Gallatin Gateway Inn. A parade and plenty of musical and arts events are scheduled for the festival weekend. For specifics on any events, call the chamber of commerce at (406) 586-5421 or (800) 228-4224.

September marks the start of the season for the **Bozeman Symphony Orchestra and Symphonic Choir.** Performances occur approximately once a month through April. Call (406) 585-9774 for the season's schedule.

SHOPPING

There's plenty of shopping to be done on and around Main Street.

T. Charbonneau Trading Company, with its allusion to Sacajawea's husband, is an upscale "western lifestyle" shop with bent-willow furniture and designer cowboy clothes. It's at the corner of Main and Rouse, tel. (406) 587-9198. For stylish leather jackets with a western twist, try **Rising Sun Leather** at 307 E. Main St., tel. (406) 586-0222. Even budget travelers can get outfitted at **Take 2,** a used-clothing shop in the basement at the corner of Main and S. Tracy Streets, downtown. For real western duds—the kind that actual ranchers and barrel racers wear—go to McCracken's, 131 E Main, tel. (406) 586-9570.

Northern Lights, 1716 W. Babcock St., tel. (406) 586-2225, has equipment and clothing for hikers, climbers, campers, and cross-country skiers. It's located near the Patagonia mail-order headquarters and often has good deals on Patagonia clothing.

Montanaphiles, baseball lovers, and jazz buffs alike will thrill to the collection at **Vargo's Books,** 6 W. Main St., tel. (406) 587-5383. The shelves are packed with new and used books on topics both mainstream and obscure. **Country Bookshelf** is an exceptionally good general bookstore with many books autographed by their Montana authors at 28 W. Main St., tel. (406) 587-0166.

If you need special camera supplies, stop by **f-11,** 16 E. Main, tel. (406) 586-7218. It's one of the best photo supply shops in the state, and camera repairs are done in-house.

Main St. is also home to a great many art galleries, many featuring local artists.

SERVICES AND INFORMATION

The **Bozeman Area Chamber of Commerce** is at 1205 E. Main St., tel. (406) 586-5421 or (800) 228-4224.

Dial 911 for the **police** or **fire** departments; (406) 587-0911 reaches the **ambulance** service. **Bozeman Deaconess Hospital** is at 915 Highland Blvd., tel. (406) 585-5000.

Find the **public library** at 220 E. Lamme St., tel. (406) 586-4787; it's open Tues.-Saturday. Pick up **Yellowstone Public Radio** at 102.1 FM in and around Bozeman. Good alternative tunes come out of KGLT, 91.9 FM.

The **Montana Dept. of Fish, Wildlife, and Parks** has an office at 1400 S. 19th Ave., tel. (406) 994-4042.

The **post office** is in the Federal Building at 32 E. Babcock Street.

TRANSPORTATION

Gallatin Field is eight miles west of town, near Belgrade. Serviced by Delta, Horizon, Sky West, and Northwest airlines, flights come in daily from Salt Lake City and Denver.

Automobile rentals are available at the airport through **Budget Rent-A-Car,** tel. (406) 388-4091 or (800) 527-0700; **Avis,** tel. (406) 388-6414 or (800) 311-1212; **Hertz,** tel. (406) 388-6939 or (800) 654-3131; and **National,** tel. (406) 388-6694 or (800) 227-7368. There's also bus service between Gallatin Field and downtown Bozeman.

Greyhound stops in Bozeman on its way across I-90/94; catch it at 625 N. 7th Ave., tel. (406) 587-3110 or (800) 231-2222. **Rimrock Trailways,** provides bus service to Helena and Missoula from the same bus terminal.

Classic Limo, tel. (406) 585-5466, offers another way of shuttling around town or to Big Sky or Yellowstone.

LIVINGSTON AND THE PARADISE VALLEY

Back when passenger trains still crossed southern Montana, Livingston was the gateway to Yellowstone National Park. Parkgoers would change trains at the Livingston depot and take the rail spur to Yellowstone.

Nowadays, travelers with a little time to pass can stock up on some of the world's most coveted flies in Livingston, cast them into the Yellowstone River, soak in the hot springs at Chico, or wander out of the broad, sun-filled Paradise Valley into the Absaroka-Beartooth Wilderness Area. There's really no sense in a pell-mell dash to often-hectic Yellowstone Park when there are so many places to linger around just to the north.

LIVINGSTON

Livingston's a weird place. Stand by the jukebox at a downtown bar and a lovely woman in evening dress may invite you to party with Tom McGuane and Peter Fonda. Or maybe you'll be the lucky person to meet the guy dressed in full buckskins, up visiting from Los Angeles. At the very least you'll hear a good fishing story.

While Bozeman quickly gained a reputation as a straitlaced town, Livingston, 26 miles east, never had any such opprobrium to live down. It's a town with a history of such Wild West legends as Calamity Jane and Kitty O'Leary, a.k.a. Madame Bulldog. (Calamity Jane's reputation must have softened over the past century, for there's now a beauty salon named for her in Kalispell, offering brow arching and facial waxing as well as haircuts.)

Few towns have seen the gentrification boom as much as Livingston. What was, a few years back, a sleepy and rough-edged town with a local artist and a writer or two, is now a mandatory waystation on the glam tour of Montana. For lively Livingston-based fiction, read Jamie Harrison's *The Edge of the Crazies* or any of Thomas McGuane's books set in Montana.

Livingston, the Park County seat (pop. 7,509, elev. 4,490 feet), is situated at the wind-tossed northern end of the Paradise Valley on the banks of the Yellowstone River. The Absaroka Range, rising up in the south, dominates the town, and the Crazy Mountains show up to the northeast. After its northerly run up from Yellowstone Park, the Yel-

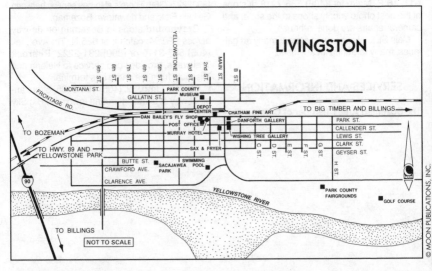

lowstone River turns east at Livingston, where I-90/94 meets the river and ushers it from the state.

History
Mt. Baldy (a.k.a. Mt. Livingston), southeast of Livingston in the Absaroka Range, was the site of winter vision quests by Crow braves. William Clark camped on the Yellowstone River south of Livingston on July 15, 1806. Several days later, Crows stole his party's horses, forcing the explorers to build dugouts and bullboats.

Livingston's comparatively mild climate led Nelson Storey to select it for the terminus of his cattle drive from Texas in 1866 á la Larry McMurtry's *Lonesome Dove*—a trip prescient of Montana's development as cattle country.

Tourist development began in the 1860s when a physician established a hotsprings resort east of Livingston near Springdale. In 1867, trail guide John Bozeman was killed in a narrow part of the Yellowstone Valley 13 miles east of Livingston. A highway marker on I-90 commemorates him.

The Railroad
The Northern Pacific laid rail tracks across the Yellowstone in the early 1880s. Two merchants bent on supplying the railroad promptly founded Clark City, on the southeast side of present-day Livingston. They didn't realize that the NP had already planned to build the town of Livingston in the same area. Within months, Livingston (named for a railroad official) sprouted right next to the railroad tracks, and the Clark City entrepreneurs moved to the new townsite.

Livingston became a major railroad division point and locomotive-repair site, and a boom set in. Ever since then, Livingston's history has been a cycle of booms and busts. When tourists flocked to Yellowstone Park via train, rail passengers debarked the main Northern Pacific line to catch the Park Branch Line to Gardiner and Livingston flourished.

With the good times came legendary rambunctiousness:

The old Bucket of Blood, *113 Park St., one of the many old-time Montana saloons so named, was probably a little rougher than most. It . . . was the center of a group of resorts of the same kind including a gam-* *bling dive run by Tex Rickard, Kid Brown, and Soapy Smith until the Klondike rush took them off to the Yukon. Madame Bulldog, once Kitty O'Leary, ran what was euphemistically known as a dance hall. Her joint, she said, was a decent one. Announcing that she would stand for no damfoolishness, she saved the wages of a bouncer by polishing off roughnecks herself. Her dimensions, like her sensibilities, were pachydermal; she tipped the scales at 190, stripped. And stripped she was most of the time. Calamity Jane was one of her associates for a time, but legend has it that they fell out, whereupon Madame Bulldog tossed Calamity into the street, "as easy as licking three men." When asked whether Calamity Jane really tried to fight back, one who knew both women replied succinctly, "Calamity was tougher'n hell, but she wasn't crazy!"*

—From the WPA's
Montana, A State Guide Book

When the Burlington Northern closed down its southern Montana lines in 1986, things looked grim. Since Montana Rail Link bought the southern Montana line and its shops in 1988, there's been a bit of an upturn, helped along by a boom in tourism.

Sights
The Northern Pacific Railroad Depot, built in 1901-02, resembles an Italian villa. It's now called the **Depot Center** and houses the Livingston Chamber of Commerce and a well-curated historical, cultural, and art museum. The Depot Center, 200 W. Park St., tel. (406) 222-2300, is open from June through mid-Oct. Mon.-Sat. 9 a.m.-5 p.m., Sunday 1-5 p.m.; winter hours are Thurs.-Sun. 1-5 p.m. Admission is $3 for adults and $1 for children and seniors.

The other historical museum in town, the **Park County Museum,** is tucked into an old schoolhouse and a hundred-year-old Northern Pacific car across the tracks from downtown at 118 W. Chinook St., tel. (406) 222-4184. Among the displays are a room devoted to railroading and a bicycle collection. The Park County Museum is open June 1 to Labor Day, noon-5 p.m. daily.

CALAMITY JANE

It's a little hard to pin down many facts on Martha Jane Cannary (better known as Calamity Jane), largely because she was one of the West's most notorious liars.

Martha's father moved his wife and children west from Missouri in the early 1860s. He was ostensibly a Mormon lay preacher bound for Salt Lake City, but the Cannarys seem to have landed in Virginia City, Montana, during the 1865 gold rush. As a teenager, Martha Jane set to wandering around the west, picking up what work she could.

Like many other women of the West, she became a prostitute. But she demonstrated both an aptitude for and interest in such male-dominated pursuits as Army scouting and prospecting. And she often showed her more tomboyish side. Says the WPA's *Montana, A State Guide Book,* "She was given to shooting up saloons, and to raising hell with tongue and quirt."

She may have been a lover of Wild Bill Hickok's, but it's unlikely. Stories of her secret marriage to Wild Bill, and of a daughter, Janey, resulting from it are unsubstantiated. But her theatrical bent did lead to a stint with Buffalo Bill's Wild West Show. Her theatrical career, however, as well as many other projects, was cut short by her alcoholism.

Castle, Harlowton, Big Timber, and Livingston were all her haunts. She lived in Livingston off and on—she had a cabin at 213 Main Street for several impoverished and unhappy years. She was 51 when she died outside Deadwood, South Dakota, in 1903. According to her wishes, she was buried next to Wild Bill in the Deadwood cemetery.

MONTANA HISTORICAL SOCIETY, HELENA

Martha "Calamity" Jane Cannary

For a fact-based, eloquent novel, try Larry Mc-Murtry's *Buffalo Girls,* which chronicles the lives of Calamity Jane and her comrades.

Livingstonians ran amok in the late 1970s, listing every eligible site on the National Register of Historic Places. There's great pride taken in the restoration of downtown buildings to their original western look, and it does look splendid. Much of the restoration has been accomplished by public grants with matching funds from local businesses. Look for elaborate brickwork and faded signs painted on the sides of the downtown buildings. Wander down some of the residential streets. Yellowstone St., three blocks west of Main, was a very tony address around the turn of the century. The east side of town, near G and Callender, was the figurative "other side of the tracks," where the blue-collar rail-road workers lived. To round out the tour, visit the 300 block of South B Street. The four matching houses on the east side of the street were once Livingston's brothels.

Recreation

Fishing is, of course, Livingston's recreation of choice. The Yellow Pages list nearly 40 outfitters and fishing guides. **Dan Bailey's Fly Shop,** 209 W. Park St., tel. (406) 222-1673 or (800) 356-4052 is a good first stop for any angler; the staff can also set you up with a guide. Two local guide services are **Anderson's Yellowstone Angler,** which also has a shop just south of town on Hwy. 89, tel. (406) 222-7130.

Because the Yellowstone is such a popular and accessible floating river, shuttle services have sprung up to transport floaters' cars from the put-in point to the take-out point. Check with fishing and tackle shops for the details and phone numbers.

The city **swimming pool** is near the foot of Main St. just east of Sacajawea Park.

Timber Trails, 309 W Park, tel. (406) 222-9550, builds specialized mountain bikes and rents and repairs cycles.

The nine-hole **Livingston Golf and Country Club** is a public course on River Dr. at the foot of Main St., tel. (406) 222-1031.

B&Bs
Remember When, near downtown at 320 S. Yellowstone St., tel. (406) 222-8367, is a Victorian house on the National Register of Historic Places, with rooms for $50-60. Just out of the bustle of town, on an island in the Yellowstone, **The Island,** 77 Island Dr., tel. (406) 222-3788, has two rooms renting for $85-90 in the summer, $50 during the rest of the year. Three miles south of town, the **Blue-Winged Olive,** 5157 Hwy. 89, tel. (406) 222-8646 or (800) 995-1366, caters mostly to anglers, who appreciate its proximity to the Yellowstone and to several spring creeks. It's open April-Oct., with rooms running $70 single, $85 double.

Hotels and Motels
The **Murray Hotel,** across from the Depot Center at 201 W. Park St., tel. (406) 222-1350, has enough character to hold its own in a lively, quirky town like Livingston. Like much of the rest of downtown, the Murray is listed in the National Register of Historic Places, and its interior architecture recalls the grander side of the Old West. After years of neglect, the Murray has recovered its panache, retaining the eccentricities that have traditionally made it a haven for "writers, artists, and film people." (Film director Sam Peckinpah lived in a Murray Hotel suite in the 1970s and reputedly shot up the ceiling—rent it now for $170 a night.) Standard rooms run $54 s, $72 d, suites start at $75, and dogs are permitted. (Be sure to visit the rooftop hot tub.)

A block down from the Murray, the **Guest House Motor Inn,** 105 W. Park St., tel. (406) 222-1460 (888) 222-1460, has doubles from

$36 s, $48 d. On the east end of town on Hwy. 85, the **Rainbow Motel,** tel. (406) 222-3780 or (800) 788-2301, allows most pets and charges $39 s, $49 d and up. There's a nice grassy area with some picnic tables outside this friendly motel, which is a block from the Yellowstone River. An adjacent campground and RV park is run by the same folks.

Most of Livingston's motels are west of downtown, near the intersection of I-90 and Hwy. 89, the road to Yellowstone. **Budget Host Parkway Motel,** 1124 W. Park St., tel. (406) 222-3840 or (800) 727-7217, has a heated outdoor pool and rooms from $48 s, $59 d, with much lower winter rates (kitchenettes are available for an extra charge, and there's in-room coffee in the standard rooms). Pets are permitted for an extra $3.

There's a pool, a playground, and in-room coffee at the **Del-Mar Motel, Inc.,** I-90 Business Loop W, tel. (406) 222-3120 or (800) 450-3120, $53 s, $59 d. Pets are permitted with some restrictions.

Doubles are $83 at the **Best Western Yellowstone Inn,** 1515 W. Park St., tel. (406) 222-6110 or (800) 826-1214. Facilities include a restaurant, lounge, heated indoor pool, and convention meeting rooms. Rooms run $55 s, 65 d at the **Paradise Inn,** near the freeway exit on the west end of town, tel. (406) 222-6320 or (800) 437-6291; there's an indoor pool.

The **Forest Service** rents several cabins in the Livingston district for about $25 a night. Call the ranger station at (406) 222-1892 for details and reservations.

Camping
Unless you're looking for RV camping, it's better to drive a ways up the Paradise Valley to find a site. But, in a pinch, there are private campgrounds in Livingston: try the one associated with the **Rainbow Motel,** tel. (406) 222-3720; the **Livingston Inn Motel and RV Park,** near the freeway at 3053 A Rogers Ln., tel. (406) 222-3600; or the **Rock Canyon Campground,** which has tepees for rent three miles south of town on Hwy. 89, tel. (406) 222-1096. A little farther south, **Yellowstone's Edge,** 3501 Hwy. 89 S., tel. (406) 333-4036, is a particularly well equipped and well situated RV park with tent sites.

Food and Drink

Livingston's best food is at the Murray Hotel's **Winchester Cafe,** 201 W. Park St., tel. (406) 222-1350. Local trout and leg of lamb are some of the elegant but hearty entrees (there are even some vegetarian offerings). Dinners run around $15; breakfast and lunch are also served.

Martin's Restaurant, next to the depot, at 108 W Park, tel. (406) 222-2311, remains a traditional 24-hour railroad cafe. If it's breakfast you need, stop by the **Beartooth Bakery & Diner,** 104 N. Main, tel. (406) 222-2920.

Two Bozeman eateries have Livingston outposts at 113 W. Park Street. Get caffeinated at the **Leaf and Bean,** tel. (406) 222-8472, and eat a huge sandwich at the **Pickle Barrel,** tel. (406) 222-5469. Next door is **The Wok,** 117 W. Park, tel. (406) 222-9009, with fresh and tasty Asian fast food. Also in this cluster of eateries is **Stromboli's Pizzeria,** tel. (406) 222-4747, 106 E. Park, with a terrace dining area open in good weather.

Step downstairs at 119 W. Park St. to **Uncle Looie's,** tel. (406) 222-7177, for tasty, traditional Italian dinners from $9.

The back bar at the Livingston Bar is now **Chatham's Livingston Bar and Grill,** 130 N Main St., tel. (406) 222-7909. The bar dates to the early 1900s and was supposedly Calamity Jane's favorite spot in Livingston. Calamity probably wouldn't recognize much on the menu today, which—reflecting the tastes of its owner, renowned painter and epicure Russel Chatham—specializes in upscale preparations of gourmet ingredients such as boned poussin, loin of rabbit, lamb, fresh fish, and veal, in addition to steaks. And she probably wouldn't know her way around the extensive wine list, either. This is one of the finest restaurants in these parts; open for dinner only.

Don't be surprised to find yourself propped up against a bar in Livingston. The town's wild reputation is supported by a wealth of bars. The **Mint Bar** on Main and Callender has a card room and the ubiquitous electronic gambling machines. The bar at the **Murray Hotel** may host tea-drinking hotel guests early in the evening, but it eases into rowdiness later at night. Spot Livingston's literati at the Murray or the **Owl,** 110 N. 2nd, tel. (406) 222-1322.

The **Sport,** a bar with good burgers, was reputedly Robert Redford's hangout when he was in town filming *A River Runs Through It.* And, if you come in with a creel full of fish, the Sport will cook them up for you. Next door is **The Sport Next Door,** tel. (406) 222-8221, 116 S. Main St., with live music and a sports-bar atmosphere.

Wilcoxson's, Livingston's home-town ice cream, is available in most grocery stores throughout the state.

Events

The **Livingston Roundup Rodeo** is on the Fourth of July weekend. It kicks off with a parade and segues into a lively Professional Rodeo Cowboys Association (PRCA) rodeo. Reserved seats at the rodeo cost $8, general admission is $5, children $3.

The **Yellowstone Boat Float,** a three-day mid-July event, runs 110 miles from Livingston to Columbus, following the route of Captain Clark and his party on their return from the Pacific. The float is open to all, any sort of boat is permitted, and, like the river, it's "wet, wild, and dam free." Contact Yellowstone Boat Float, Inc., P.O. Box 1000, Laurel, MT 59044, for more information and exact dates.

During the second week of August, Livingston hosts the **Park County Fair.**

Arts

It may be a little surprising that a scrappy railroad town like Livingston has become something of an artists' colony. But the beautiful light and stunning scenery (not to mention the trout fishing) of the Paradise Valley work in counterpoint to Livingston's raucous edge to make this one of the state's most prestigious addresses.

Russell Chatham is Livingston's most renowned artist. His oils and lithographs evoke the places where the plains come up against the mountains. Chatham's work is represented in town by **Chatham Fine Art,** 120 N. Main St., tel. (406) 222-1566. Other galleries along the same stretch of Main St. are the **Danforth Gallery,** 106 N. Main St., which focuses on contemporary Montana artists, and the **Wishing Tree,** 113 W. Callender St., tel. (406) 222-7528, with a good selection of high-quality crafts and art.

Shopping

Sax and Fryer, 109 W. Callender Street is Livingston's landmark book and stationery store. **Gil's** carries every variety of western souvenir at 207 W. Park Street. Next door, fly-tiers start early at **Dan Bailey's Fly Shop,** an angler's supply mecca. Bailey's flies are so renowned they're practically pedigreed; they're also available by mail order from 209 W. Park St., Livingston, MT 59047, tel. (406) 222-1673. Just south of Livingston on Hwy. 89, **Anderson's Yellowstone Angler,** tel. (406) 222-7130, is another source of tackle and guidance.

Information and Services
The Livingston **Chamber of Commerce** is housed in the old baggage room of the Livingston Depot Center, 208 W. Park St., tel. (406) 222-0850.

For information on hiking, camping, Forest Service cabin rentals, and fishing, stop by the ranger station on Hwy. 89 about a mile south of Livingston, tel. (406) 222-1892.

Livingston Memorial Hospital is at 504 S. 13th St., tel. (406) 222-3541. The **post office** is at the corner of Main and Callender. **Olson's Laundry,** at D and Park, tel. (406) 222-7428, is open daily 8 a.m.-10 p.m.

Transportation
The **Greyhound** depot is at 105 W Park. Three eastbound and three westbound buses pass through daily. For schedule information call (406) 222-2231. **TW Services** buses use the same depot and run to Yellowstone Park during the summer months. A TW bus leaves Livingston each morning at 8:15 a.m. It arrives in Mammoth at 9:35 a.m. and continues on a tour through the park. Bozeman and Billings have more car rental agencies, but **Rent-A-Wreck** has an office at Park and 6th, tel. (406) 222-0071 or (800) 255-0071. Reach **VIP Taxi** at (406) 222-0200.

PARADISE VALLEY

The Land
The never-dammed Yellowstone River flows through the Paradise Valley and separates the eastern Absaroka Range and the western Gallatin Range. The valley starts narrow, squeezing through Yankee Jim Canyon near Yellowstone Park, then broadens enough for ranches to spread out on the valley floor.

Yellowstone's volcanoes spat out the Absaroka Range—a high lava field with relief etched by erosion from water and glacial ice.

The Absarokas are lush, wet mountains, more characteristic of western Montana than the dry peaks east of the Divide. The same Yellowstone lava flows covered folded sedimentary rocks of the Gallatin Range.

History
The Crow lived along the upper Yellowstone for 200 years before white explorers and mountain men, including Jim Bridger, began cutting up and down the valley in the 1800s.

Gold, but not much of it, was mined in the 1860s. Emigrant Gulch was the site of the first strike in 1864, and a short-lived mining town called Yellowstone City sprouted on the hillside of the gulch. Old Chico was another mining

CELEBRITY RESIDENTS

In Hollywood, everyone is a star. In Montana, everyone from Hollywood is a rancher. Among those who have or are rumored to have holdings in Montana are:

Mel Gibson, who has owned a cattle ranch near Red Lodge

Peter Fonda, who owns land near Livingston

Tom Brokaw, who fishes the West Fork of the Boulder River

Brooke Shields, another Boulder River resident

Ted Turner and Jane Fonda, who rile up the neighbors on the Madison River

Michael Keaton, Paradise Valley rancher

George C. Scott, who lives in the Bitterroot Valley

Goldie Hawn and Kurt Russell, who maintain a residence near Hamilton

Huey Lewis, also in the Bitterroot

Jeff Bridges, who has land near Livingston

Keifer Sutherland, who has a home near the slopes at Whitefish

Liz Claiborne, who has a vacation home in the Swan Valley

Tom Selleck, who owns land near Bigfork

Tom Cruise, who has a pied-á-terre in Whitefish

Sydney Pollack, who keeps a home in Hamilton

Andie McDowell, who tried to get along with her neighbors in Missoula

camp, where one of the world's largest gold dredges scraped a trickling stream.

By the 1880s, coal had replaced gold as the valley's main lode. Coke ovens were built west of Livingston to produce fuel for the smelters in Anaconda.

Both cattle and sheep ranching have long been important in the Paradise Valley, but subdivisions have carved big outfits into a panoply of ranchettes near Livingston.

The **Church Universal and Triumphant** (known locally as CUT) has bought over 25,000 acres of land north and west of Gardiner. This spiritual community believes in furthuring harmony between the land and its inhabitants, but has drawn criticism for its land use and environmental track record. When the church began geothermal drilling, environmentalists feared that Yellowstone Park geysers would be affected. A USGS study has since concluded that this tapping won't harm the park's geysers, but a National Park Service study wasn't able to conclude what the effects would be. The church has taken steps to work with the local community (and they've capped the geothermal well, which is the subject of pending congressional legislation), but suspicion of CUT still goes beyond the usual wariness of outsiders.

Sights

Come to the Paradise Valley for the Yellowstone River, its valley, and the surrounding mountains. A few miles south of Livingston, the paved but potholed East River Rd. leaves Hwy. 89. Both roads along the Yellowstone are lovely, but East River Rd. gives a better view of the way people live in the valley.

The upper Yellowstone River cuts through the gneiss of narrow **Yankee Jim Canyon** 15 miles north of Gardiner. Jim George, a.k.a. Yankee Jim, built the first road into Yellowstone National Park. He charged a toll to travel the road, and when the Northern Pacific claimed its right to the roadbed, the railroad was forced to build Yankee Jim another road farther up the hill.

Jardine, an old mining ghost town five miles up Bear Gulch from Gardiner, has seen several spurts of mining activity. Both gold and arsenic were mined here, with arsenic production continuing until the end of WW II. The late 1980s saw another attempt to mine gold from Jardine, but the town is notable chiefly as home to some

JUDY JEWELL

Even with increased development and a sizeable celebrity presence, in the Paradise Valley, some of the old ways live on.

well-preserved mining relics. Hiking trails starting in Jardine lead into the Absaroka-Beartooth Wilderness.

Fishing

The Yellowstone River is a blue-ribbon trout stream. Most everybody who fishes here uses flies, and the local fishing shops are quick to advise you on what'll work best. Summer and fall are the most popular seasons to fish the Yellowstone. Early in the summer, the salmon flies and caddis flies hatch. Later on, around August, trout feed on grasshoppers near the river's edge. Numerous fishing-access sites dot both Hwy. 89 and East River Road.

Besides the Yellowstone, there are a couple of "spring creeks" that challenge the skillful angler. The two most notable of these, Nelson's and Armstrong's, are on private land and a fee is charged for fishing them. For details, ask at Dan Bailey's Fly Shop in Livingston or at any other local angler's shop. Another good source for advice, gear, or access to private fishing spots is **Big Sky Flies,** on Hwy. 89 at Emigrant, tel. (406) 333-4401.

Hiking

Mill Creek reaches into the Absaroka-Beartooth Wilderness Area. The lower stretches of Mill Creek Rd., from the town of Pray to the wilderness boundary, are good for mountain biking, and the foot trail continues into the wilderness area. Thompson Lake, Elbow Lake, Mt. Cowan, and Passage Creek Falls are some of the destinations for hikers. Snow Bank campground is a handy jumping-off point.

In the Gallatin Range, hike or cross-country ski just about any drainage: **Trail Creek** (there's cross-country skiing in the vicinity of the Forest Service cabin there), **Big Creek** (28 miles south of Livingston, then west up Big Creek Road), **Rock Creek** (with access to a trail network), or **Tom Miner Basin** (and the nearby Gallatin Petrified Forest).

Other Recreation

Swimming: Even if you're not staying at the lodge, stop by Chico Hot Springs for a swim ($4.75 adult, $3.25 child, for a day pass). The pool is huge, and it's always a great place to people-watch.

Bicycling: The East River Road is for cyclists who don't mind a few potholes. Mountain bikers will want to turn off the main road and head up into the hills. Rent bikes from Big Sky Flies in Emigrant—after a day on the bicycle saddle, the pool at Chico is hard to pass up.

Floating the Yellowstone: The upper stretches of the Yellowstone River, particularly through Yankee Jim Canyon, have some challenging whitewater. After the river leaves the canyon and enters the Paradise Valley, it calms down enough for novice floaters to navigate it without much difficulty. Gardiner's **Yellowstone Raft Company,** tel. (406) 848-7777, runs raft trips on the Yellowstone. Half-day trips are $27 for adults, $15 for children; full-day trips are $53 adults, $35 children.

Accommodations

Chico Hot Springs, halfway between Livingston and Gardiner in Pray, is the sort of spot you want all your friends to know about and everybody else

to ignore. The lodge here is built around a large hot springs-fed swimming pool. The rooms in the circa-1900 lodge are cramped and spartan, but the rooms aren't where most guests spend their time (and rooms in the new lodge-like condos and motels are spacious and very nicely furnished). Yellowstone Park is right down the road, and there's plenty of hiking and fishing in the Paradise Valley, soaking and swimming in the pool, elegant dinners in the hotel dining room, and rowdy good times in the lively bar. There's an outfitter on the premises with horses, fishing gear, and bicycles for rent. Rooms in the lodge start at $60 d; there are motel rooms and cabins ranging from $85 to $105; the condos ($125-275) are very comfortable. Dogs are permitted in the rooms at Chico. (All the prices go down a few dollars in the winter.) Call (406) 333-4933 or (800) 468-9232 to reserve rooms or meals (see below).

Though Chico is the most renowned place to stay in the Paradise Valley, there are several other perfectly fine places to stay between Livingston and Gardiner. **Pine Creek Store & Lodge,** 12 miles south of Livingston on East River Rd., tel. (406) 222-3628 or (800) 746-3990, rents quintessential Montana resort cabins in a friendly community with easy fishing access to the Yellowstone. Cabins, all with electric heat, sleep two to six people, run $52-65 a night, and pets are allowed. The excellent **Pine Creek Café,** tel. (406) 222-5499, is also part of the complex.

The Forest Service has a cabin for rent up Trail Creek, 20 miles southwest of Livingston. The cabin is rented year-round for $25 a night; winter visitors may need skis or a snowmobile to navigate the final three miles of the road.

At the **Yellowstone Valley Ranch,** 14 miles south of Livingston on Hwy. 89, tel. (406) 333-4787, (800) 626-3526, www.destinations-ltd.com, anglers stay in tastefully decorated cabins perched just above the Yellowstone, affording wonderful river views and good fishing. This is emphatically a fly-fishing lodge, where anglers spend their days with some of the Paradise Valley's best guides. Beginning fly-fishers are welcome, and benefit from the two-to-one guest/guide ratio. The ranch offers weeklong packages, focusing on fishing but also including horseback riding, mountain biking, canoeing, and excursions to Yellowstone. Prices are all-inclusive and range $1,995-2,150 per person for double occupancy.

Mountain Sky Guest Ranch is a family-oriented guest ranch set up Big Creek with great views of Emigrant Peak, across the Paradise Valley in the Absaroka Range. Riding is one of the core activities here, but fishing, tennis courts, a pool, hot tub, and sauna are also available, and there's a well-developed program for kids, from infants to teens. Each guest is matched with a horse to ride for the week's stay, and either breakfast rides or 9 a.m. rides are scheduled daily. Ranch staff run van trips into Yellowstone Park for hikes and wildlife viewing, and can assist anglers on ranch streams and ponds. The food at Mountain Sky is first rate, and the "rustic" cabins are a far cry from the typical Montana rustic cabin (there are also modern cabins available). Rates run $2,205-2,345 a week per person, with reduced rates for children. The ranch offers shorter stays and corporate retreats at the season's shoulders and shuts down between early Oct. and mid-May. It's best to book far in advance; write or call P.O. Box 1128, Bozeman, MT 59715, tel. (406) 587-1244 or (800) 548-3392.

Camping

There's a Forest Service campground two miles up **Pine Creek** from the hamlet of Pine Creek. Pine Creek Falls is a short hike from the campground, and Jewell and Pine Creek lakes are three miles up the trail.

Snow Bank Forest Service campground is 20 miles south of Livingston on Hwy. 89, then another 15 miles east on Mill Creek Road. Closer to Gardiner and Yellowstone Park, **Tom Miner/Petrified Forest** Forest Service campground is eight miles west of Hwy. 89 on Tom Miner Rd. (36 miles south of Livingston). The Gallatin Petrified Forest is a two-mile hike from the campground. The many fishing-access sites on the Yellowstone are de facto campgrounds.

Food and Drink

The restaurant at **Chico Hot Springs** is known statewide for its gourmet fare ($15-22 dinners; reservations highly recommended). Open daily for dinner only and Sunday for brunch also. Penny-pinchers can eat at the snack bar out by the swimming pool (summer only) or at the Poolside Grille. Or run down the road to the **Emigrant General Store,** with good morning muffins and an even better selection of wines.

The other good choice for a more informal meal is the **Pine Creek Café,** tel. (406) 222-5499, down the road at Pine Creek. You'll enjoy old-fashioned favorites such as chicken and dumplings, burgers, and steaks; desserts are good, and in good weather there's deck seating.

Breakfast, lunch, and dinner come with local color at the **Old Saloon** on the west side of the highway in Emigrant.

Down the road at Corwin Springs, the **Ranch Kitchen** offers both a peek into the lives of Church Universal and Triumphant members and good home cooking, including vegetarian meals, tel. (406) 848-7891. Summertime brings a weekend dinner theater and country music revue to the restaurant.

GARDINER

Gardiner is a year-round route into Yellowstone National Park, but it's become known for its Church Universal and Triumphant neighbors (who are not your run-of-the-mill western neighbors, even in the "New West") and gained additional notoriety in the early 1990s as the place to go to shoot Yellowstone Park buffalo. Buffalo frequently carry brucellosis, a bacterial infection that causes abortions in newly infected cattle. For several years, bison straying from Yellowstone Park were hunted by wildlife officials and private hunters. After an uproar, state and federal agencies began working on an Environmental Impact Statement focusing on the management of buffalo both inside and outside the park. Until a conclusion is reached, rangers continue to shoot bison caught damaging property or creating a nuisance outside the park. Designated Crow tribal members butcher the animals and keep the meat.

But, for the average traveler, Gardiner (pop. 600, elev. 5,314 feet) isn't far removed from what is expected at the gateway to America's oldest national park. The motels and souvenir shops are somewhat less daunting than those in West Yellowstone, and elk and deer wander from the park to graze on ornamental shrubbery and linger on lawns. Gardiner's small enough not to need real street addresses—just squint hard and you'll find what you're looking for.

The Gardiner entrance to Yellowstone is marked by the Roosevelt Arch, dedicated in

1903 by Theodore Roosevelt. It's the only park entrance open to cars year-round. The road between Gardiner and Cooke City is plowed during the winter.

Events and Recreation
The rodeo comes to Gardiner in mid-June. Call the **chamber of commerce,** tel. (406) 848-7971, for the exact date.

Boats aren't allowed on Yellowstone Park's rivers, but **Yellowstone Raft Company,** headquartered in Gardiner, runs trips on the Yellowstone, Gallatin, and Madison Rivers, tel. (406) 848-7777.

Local outfitters guide visitors on a wide variety of trail rides and fishing trips. **Hell's A Roarin' Outfitters** is based in Jardine, tel. (406) 848-7578; **Parks' Fly Shop,** tel. (406) 848-7314, operates out of Gardiner.

The Gallatin National Forest has a **ranger station** in Gardiner near the park entrance, tel. (406) 848-7375.

Accommodations
During the summer, many of the accommodations in Gardiner are expensive—even the **Super 8,** Hwy. 89, tel. (406) 848-7401, charges $85 a night. Parkgoers may prefer to reserve in advance and stay in the lodge or cabins at Mammoth Hot Springs, which has more moderate prices.

From mid-September through May, lodging prices drop significantly.

For those who don't mind spending $85 and up during the summer, the **Absaroka Lodge,** tel. (406) 848-7414 or (800) 755-7414, is well situated on the banks of the Yellowstone River. Kitchenettes are only $5-10 extra. The **Best Western by Mammoth Hot Springs** is set back off the highway just north of Gardiner on Hwy. 89, tel. (406) 848-7311 or (800) 828-9080. The comfortable rooms run $84 s, $94, and there's an indoor pool.

At the **Yellowstone Village Inn,** tel. (406) 484-7417 or (800) 228-8158, there's an indoor

pool and sauna and rooms starting at $65 s, $79 d. The inn can also arrange tours and activities for guests.

On Hwy. 89, the **Flamingo Motor Lodge,** tel. (406) 848-7536, and **Hillcrest Cottages,** tel. (406) 848-7353, have lodgings for around $50-60. In the same price range is the **Yellowstone River Motel,** just east of Hwy. 89 near the park entrance, tel. (406) 848-7303 or (800) 797-4837, and the **Jim Bridger Court,** tel. (406) 848-7371 or (888) 858-7508, with cabins at $50-60.

Paradise, tel. (406) 848-7684, and **Rocky Mountain,** tel. (406) 848-7251, are RV-style campgrounds right in Gardiner. **Eagle Creek** is a Forest Service campground four miles northeast of town.

Food and Drink
The gamut of tourist restaurants is represented in Gardiner. **Cecil's Restaurant,** tel. (406) 848-7561, is open for breakfast, lunch, and dinner a stone's throw from the Roosevelt Arch. For sandwiches, try the **Sawtooth Deli,** tel. (406) 848-7600, or the **Town Cafe,** tel. (406) 848-7322, or grab a burger at the **Corral Drive Inn,** tel. (406) 848-7627. Gardiner's fancy restaurant is the **Yellowstone Mine** in the Best Western, tel. (406) 848-7336. It's open daily for breakfast and dinner. For something a little bit Western, head to **Red's Blue Goose Saloon, Barbeque & Steakhouse,** at Park St. and Hwy. 89, tel. (406) 848-7037. If you're hungry, but don't feel compelled to stop in Gardiner, try the **Ranch Kitchen,** seven miles north of town in Corwin Springs, tel. (406) 848-7891.

Transportation
One of Yellowstone Park's concessionaires, TW Services, runs bus tours of the park. From late May through mid-September, buses leave Gardiner every morning at 8:30, tour the Grand Loop of Yellowstone's roads, and return to Gardiner at 6:15 p.m. The fee is $32 adults, $16.50 children. Call (307) 344-7311 for reservations.

BIG TIMBER TO LAUREL

The Boulder River falls between the Absarokas and the Beartooths to Big Timber, passing ghost towns, church camps, and dude ranches on the way. Around Big Timber, the Boulder pours into the Yellowstone River, which around here changes from a cold-water trout stream to the broad, warm home of paddlefish.

History

This whole area was Crow territory before white settlers moved in. It's reckoned that the French Verendrye party passed by the Boulder River and Big Timber Creek in 1741 as they traveled down the Yellowstone from the Musselshell River. The next white explorers were Captain Clark and his brigade, who camped near Hunter's Hot Springs in July of 1806.

It wasn't until 1873 that a rancher settled in the area. When the railroad came through, a small settlement sprang up near the mouth of the Boulder River. This town, called Dornix (meaning "Rock Pile"), never made it as a railway station. In 1883, the town of Big Timber was founded just to the west. Ranching, especially sheep ranching, tourism and recreation, now support the local economy.

BIG TIMBER AND VICINITY

Big Timber (pop. 1,698, elev. 4,072 feet), a mostly quiet ranch town, is not a forested spot. William Clark named Big Timber Creek for the stand of cottonwoods shading its confluence with the Yellowstone. Today, it might be called "Big Wind" or "Crazyview," for the frequent gusts and the nearby mountain range are far more noticeable than the trees.

Sights

Like nearby Livingston, Big Timber has an abundance of art galleries. For a look at Sweet Grass County art, stop by **Sweetgrass and Sage Gallery** a mile west of town, tel. (406) 932-5307. The late Spike Van Cleve, a rancher from Melville, was a raconteur of ranch life, and his granddaughter Barbara, a photographer now based in

New Mexico, has stunning black-and-white photos hanging in the Grand Hotel. **Cabin Creek Studio,** on Hwy. 10 E, tel. (406) 932-5115, houses sculptures of Lyle Johnson, who is known for his western bronzes.

There are also several good antique stores in Big Timber, not to mention **Victorian Village,** a large and well-tended historical museum and antique store begun as a Washington man's private collection; it is now continued by his family. Summer hours are daily 9 a.m.-5 p.m.; the museum is closed Oct.-Feb. and open Saturday and Sunday 10 a.m.-4 p.m. during the spring and early fall.

The **Sweet Grass County Museum,** 120 McLeod St., is open Tues.-Sat. 10 a.m.-4 p.m. It features displays of the area's geology and natural history.

Yellowstone cutthroat trout of all ages live in the pools of the **Fish Hatchery** north of town on McLeod St., tel. (406) 932-4434. Trout are taken from the hatchery to stock lakes across the state.

Pull off the freeway at Greycliff to visit the communal burrows of **Greycliff Prairie Dog Town.** It may not sound like much, but prairie dog behavior is kind of a kick to watch, and even the most jaded wildlife observer is likely to leave with half a roll of film exposed with shots of chortling prairie dogs. From May 1 to Sept. 30 there is a $4 per vehicle entrance fee.

The **Crazy Mountains,** north of Big Timber, are a spectacular, isolated range. To reach them from Big Timber, drive north on Hwy. 191 (the road to Harlowton) and follow signs for Big Timber Canyon. **Halfmoon campground** and a trailhead into the mountains are about 15 miles from the pavement.

Events and Recreation

Sunbaked I-90 travelers may enjoy a stop at the **Big Timber Waterslide,** nine miles east of Big Timber at exit 377, tel. (406) 932-6570. The water park is open June 1 through Labor Day, 10 a.m.-7 p.m.; admission is $10.95 for ages seven and above, $8.50 for ages two to six.

The nine-hole public **Overland Golf Course** is a mile east of Big Timber on Hwy. 10, tel. (406) 932-4297.

Boulder River **fishing-access sites** include **Big Rock,** four miles south of Big Timber, and **Boulder Forks,** at the confluence of the Main Boulder and West Boulder Rivers in McLeod. Fish the Yellowstone from **Grey Bear,** six miles west of Big Timber on the frontage road, or **Pelican,** just east of the Greycliff exit on the frontage road.

In the Crazy Mountains, hiking trails start from the **Halfmoon campground.**

The **rodeo** is held the last weekend in June. Equally popular is the **cutting horse show,** held at the fairgrounds during the last weekend in July. Cutting horses are trained to separate specific cattle from a herd without causing a fracas. For more information call the chamber of commerce at (406) 932-5131.

Accommodations

The **Grand Hotel,** tel. (406) 932-4459, a 100-year-old hotel at 139 McLeod St. in Big Timber, has been restored as a bed and breakfast. This is a great place to stay—the rooms are cozy, the full breakfasts are staggeringly good, there's a sauna in the upstairs hallway, and the adjoining restaurant and bar are good places to while away an evening. Rates (including breakfast) range from $59 (room with shared bath) to $145 (suite with a private bath), dropping about $20 in the off season.

The **C.M. Russell Lodge and Motel,** tel. (406) 932-5245, and the **Lazy J Motel,** tel. (406) 932-5533, are both on Hwy. 10 (the old highway through town) in Big Timber and have rooms starting around $45 d. Out by the freeway exit, the **Super 8** has double rooms for $50 and up.

Spring Creek Camp and Trout Ranch, tel. (406) 932-4387, has cabins and some tent sites but is essentially an RV park two miles south of Big Timber on Boulder River Road. They also run an outfitting service, with an emphasis on big-game hunting (including bow hunting).

The **Big Timber KOA** is near the Greycliff exit, nine miles east of Big Timber, tel. (406) 932-6569. Besides tent and RV sites, there are cabins for rent, a swimming pool, and hot tubs.

Nineteen miles north of Big Timber, up Big Timber Canyon, **Halfmoon campground** features hiking trails into the Crazy Mountains.

Food and Drink

You can breakfast at the **Grand Hotel** only if you're a guest there, but lunches and dinners are served up to the public, and there's a friendly bar off to the side of the lobby. Northern Italian entrees are interspersed among the steaks on the dinner menu (dinners run about $15). The Grand's bar is an easygoing place for a drink and a chat. Next door, **Prospector Pizza,** tel. (406) 932-4846, is a popular and inexpensive place to eat, as is the **Madhatter Grill and Saloon,** also on McLeod.

Frye's, the cafe at the C.M. Russell Lodge, is a traditional place to stop for a meal in Big Timber.

Information

Write to the **chamber of commerce** at P.O. Box 1012, Big Timber, MT 59011, or call (406) 932-5131. Reach the **Forest Service** at (406) 932-5155.

BOULDER VALLEY

It's hard to pick Montana's most beautiful river valley, but this one's a strong contender. Small wonder, then, that celebrities and novelists have become the modern-day homesteaders here.

Sights

Drive up the Boulder River Valley 25 miles south of Big Timber to the **Natural Bridge State Monument.** The limestone cliffs have been warped, lifted, dropped, and eaten away by weak river-water acids, leaving a spectacular gorge with a 100-foot waterfall. The eponymous natural bridge across the falls collapsed in 1988. Trails course the park, but there are no campsites.

Just down the road from the natural bridge, the **Main Boulder Ranger Station** dates from 1905. There are pictographs in the caves west of the ranger station.

Forty miles up the Boulder River from Big Timber, the ghost town of **Independence** recalls a past of gold mining and stock-promotion schemes. The final four miles to Independence are best driven in 4WD.

Accommodations

The Boulder Valley didn't support miners or farmers for long, but dude ranchers have done well by it. The **Hawley Mountain Guest Ranch,** 45 miles south of Big Timber, www.hawleymountain.com, has reasonably priced weeklong Sunday to Sunday packages including cabin, meals, horseback

Big Timber's Grand Hotel, now a grand bed and breakfast

JUDY JEWELL

riding, fly fishing, and river floating. Accommodations are either in the lodge or in one of two cabins. Weekly all-inclusive rates are $1,420 s, $2,015 d; cabins are about $300 more per week. Information is available by writing to P.O. Box 4, McLeod, MT 59052 or by calling (406) 932-5791.

For less expensive lodgings, the tidy **McLeod Resort,** P.O. Box 27, McLeod, MT 59052, tel. (406) 932-6167, has a campground ($15), cabins ($17.50 and up), and apartments ($50 and up). The cabins and the apartments have cooking facilities, but in the cabins cooking utensils are not provided.

The Gallatin National Forest is studded with campsites south of Big Timber, but you've got to drive a ways to get to them. **Falls Creek Campground** is 30 miles south of town on Boulder River Rd., with **Aspen Grove, Chippy Park,** and **Hell's Canyon** campgrounds all within the next 10 miles. **Hicks Park Campground** is 50 miles south of Big Timber on the same road. Turn right at McLeod to reach the **West Boulder Campground,** 30 miles southwest of Big Timber, with a trail into the Absaroka-Beartooth Wilderness.

Food and Drink
If the name of the **Road Kill Bar and Cafe** makes you grin, and if their motto, "From your grille to ours," doesn't put you off, you'll find heaven in McLeod. This Boulder Valley landmark is a convivial place to stop for a drink or a meal. During the summer, there's often a band—drop by on a Thursday night for two-step and polka lessons, and don't forget to look up and admire the arched

plank ceiling in the bar. The Road Kill is 15 miles south of Big Timber, tel. (406) 932-6174.

Events and Recreation
McLeod is the base for the late-August **World's Champion Pack Horse Race** on a six-mile-long trail. Call (406) 222-3168 for information.

When the Yellowstone River is brimful of muddy water, the rocky Boulder River usually runs clear. Upriver from the Natural Bridge, the Boulder is populated with rainbow and cutthroat trout; below the tall falls at the bridge, browns and rainbows predominate.

Follow Boulder River Road to its end to pick up a trail into the **Absaroka-Beartooth Wilderness Area.** This remote, high country is studded with alpine lakes and covered with wildflowers late in the summer. It's a good spot for a week of backpacking.

In the winter, the Boulder River Road is maintained for snowmobiling starting about 30 miles south of Big Timber and continuing to the wilderness boundary. Snowmobilers often spot the many elk and moose that winter in the Boulder Valley. For more information on snowmobiling, call the Forest Service in Big Timber at (406) 932-5155.

COLUMBUS AND BEYOND

Columbus, (pop. 1897) 37 miles east of Big Timber at the mouth of the Stillwater River, is renowned for the **New Atlas Bar,** which has a great back bar and more animal heads than most non-Montanans have seen in a lifetime. Before the New Atlas,

Columbus was known for its frequent name changes. Before landing on the present name, it was called Eagle's Nest, Sheep Dip, and Stillwater.

The jagged peaks of the Beartooth Range form the jawline of the horizon to the south. On the road down from Columbus, through Absarokee to Red Lodge, the fine views of former Crow country recall buffalo hunts and lost freedom.

If merely hanging around this lovely country sounds too unstructured, sign on with **Beartooth Whitewater,** tel. (406) 446-3142, and run a few Stillwater River rapids. For those who are a little more confident of their paddling abilities, they also offer guided trips in one-person rafts.

Eat, drink, and listen to live music at the **Five Spot,** tel. (406) 328-6566.

Fishtail

A lovely little town with one of the state's great names, Fishtail is worth a stop, if only for a Coke at the mercantile. Of course, a brief stop will only make you wish you'd stayed longer, so plan on hanging out for a while. There's some western eating and drinking that go on here at the **Cowboy Bar and Supper Club,** tel. (406) 328-4288. Just down the road in Dean, the **Trout Hole Restaurant,** tel. (406) 328-6780, and **Stillwater Saloon** are part of a spread known as **Montana Hanna's.**

Camp at Pine Grove or Emerald Lake campgrounds out of Fishtail, or at Jimmy Joe or East Rosebud Lake out of Roscoe.

LAUREL

Located at a transportation crossroads, Laurel (pop. 6,125) is a town often passed through by history. What with railroading and refining, it maintains an industrial ambience at odds with the fruitful valley it sprawls in. Boosters of Billings repeat a mantra about the day when Billings stretches clear to Laurel. It's not clear that there's

---

LEWIS AND CLARK MEET THE PRAIRIE DOG

The Corps of Discovery first encountered prairie dogs in what is now Nebraska. Foreshadowing their future relationship with dogs in general, the captains had one of the animals cooked for dinner. Lewis gave roasted prairie dog a favorable review, declaring it "well flavored and tender." The corps soon decided, however, that the burrowing rodents were too difficult to shoot, and the enlisted men spent the better part of September 7, 1804, pouring barrels of water into prairie dog burrows in an effort to flush out a specimen to send to President Jefferson. Finally, one popped out alive, and the study commenced.

Lewis recorded:

ther mouth resemble the rabit, head longer, legs short, & toe nails long ther tail like a ground Squirel which they shake and make chattering noise ther eyes like a dog, their colour is Gray and Skin contains Soft fur . . . the Village of those animals Covs. about 4 acrs of Ground on a Gradual decent of a hill and Contains great numbers of holes on the top of which those little animals Set erect make a Whistleing noise and whin allarmed Slip into their hole—we por'd into one of the holes 5 barrels of water without filling it . . . .

Lewis called the critter a dog because of its bark; Clark pressed for "ground rat" or "burrowing squirrel." It was soon commonly known as a "barking squirrel," except by the French, who stuck with *petit chien,* little dog.

prairie dog,
Cynomys ludovicianus

A live prairie dog was shipped from Fort Mandan to the White House, and, though it arrived on the East Coast in sickly condition, it soon regained its health. One can only imagine Thomas Jefferson's delight at finding a barking squirrel at his door.

THE LEGEND OF THE STILLWATER RIVER

Looking at this lively tributary of the Yellowstone River, you may think that it's been poorly named. But Crow legend explains that the name applies to *part* of the river, not the whole thing.

Legend has it that a beautiful young Indian woman died while searching for food for her hungry party. Her body was placed in a tree above the river, but during a violent storm it fell into the water. The man she had chosen to become her husband jumped into the torrent to rescue her body and he, too, died. When the storm abated, a small, quiet bayou had formed on that stretch of the otherwise rapid river.

much to gain or lose for either city; it's hard times for the farms in between, however.

History

As the Nez Perce Indians fled from the Battle of the Big Hole in 1877, they struck eastward toward Yellowstone National Park. Here they hoped to encounter their allies the Crow and seek asylum in southeastern Montana. By this time, however, the Crow were working closely with the Army. They repudiated the Nez Perce, whose leadership realized they had but one choice remaining: escape to Canada.

They pressed up the valley of the Clark Fork of the Yellowstone and crossed the Yellowstone at Laurel. Colonel S.D. Sturgis and the new Seventh Cavalry caught up with the Nez Perce on September 13, about nine miles north of Laurel, in Canyon Creek. Indian sharpshooters took positions in the sandstone bluffs above the valley and held off the infantry until the Indian car-

avan was safe in the Musselshell Valley. At the Battle of Canyon Creek, the Army lost three men, the Nez Perce claimed three wounded.

Laurel grew up as the railhead for the Red Lodge-area coal mines that fueled the Northern Pacific's Montana steam engines. Laurel became the railroad hub of the entire Yellowstone Valley after the Great Northern and the Chicago, Burlington, and Quincy railroads made Laurel a division point. Access to rail lines made Laurel a candidate for other industry. Currently, a Cenex oil refinery dominates the skyline.

Sights

Follow Hwy. 532 north of Laurel nine miles to visit the scene of the Canyon Creek battle. The **Chief Joseph–Sturgis Battlefield Monument** commemorates the event.

Closer to town, in **Fireman's Park,** a newly unveiled statue of Chief Joseph serves as a memorial to the combatants at the battle.

Accommodations and Food

The classiest place in town is **Best Western Locomotive Inn,** 310 S. 1st Ave., tel. (800) 210-5626 or (406) 628-8281, with a pool, nice restaurant, and sauna; rooms are $55, $70 d. A health club is adjacent. The **Welcome Travelers Motel,** 620 W. Main St., tel. (406) 628-6821, has rooms at $35 s, $42.50 d; kitchenettes are available.

The **Locomotive Inn Restaurant,** 216 1st Ave. S., tel. (406) 628-4030, is Laurel's nicest place to eat, with the fairly requisite menu of steaks, chicken, and seafood.

Information

Contact the **Laurel Chamber of Commerce** at P.O. Box 395, Laurel, MT 59044, tel. (406) 628-8105.

ABSAROKA-BEARTOOTH WILDERNESS

THE LAND

This is Montana's high country: Granite Peak, towering 12,799 feet in the Beartooth Range, is the state's highest point and a formidable climb. Geologically and ecologically different, the Absaroka and the Beartooth ranges share a plateau and a

wilderness area. The accommodating Beartooth Plateau tilts from a low northwestern Absaroka corner to the soaring Beartooths in the southeast.

The Beartooths were uplifted, eroded, partially blanketed with lava from Yellowstone's volcanoes, and covered with glaciers. The limestone cliffs of the Beartooth Range rise from high tundra cut through by steep canyons.

TOM VANDEL

Beartooth Mountains

The weather in the Beartooths can change quickly and with arctic severity. Come prepared for a snowstorm, even in midsummer.

The Beartooths are largely above the timberline, and alpine meadows are the characteristic vegetation. The growing season here is about 45 days, and the plants and the soil are sensitive to trampling. During the late summer, snowbanks sometimes turn pink as microorganisms on the snow's surface die and turn red.

RED LODGE

Red Lodge (pop. 2,204, elev. 5,555 feet) is perhaps best known as the start of the Beartooth Highway.

Purportedly, a band of Crow Indians settled in the Beartooths and decorated their lodges with red clay. Once part of the Crow Reservation, this area was taken from the Indians in 1882 and coal mining commenced a few years later. The mines became the basis for the town, and many immigrants came to work in Red Lodge; Finns were particularly well represented. Mining dropped off in the 1930s, and an explosion at the nearby Smith Creek Mine in 1943 halted large-scale coal mining in the area. Red Lodge is now a resort for travelers on the Beartooth Highway and is also visited by many Montanans for its good spring skiing.

Sights

Red Lodge's turn-of-the-century downtown remains vital and is a showcase of historic preser-

vation. Pick up a walking-tour map from the chamber of commerce and ramble through the sandstone and brick edifices of the late 1800s. Red Lodge's Old Town, near the high school, was the town's business center from 1886 to 1893.

The **Carbon County Historical Museum,** tel. (406) 446-3914, 1011 S. Broadway, open during the summer, has all the expected pioneer paraphernalia, and an additional tidbit—Liver Eatin' Johnson's cabin. It's probably apocryphal, but Mr. Johnson was said to have avenged his Flathead wife's death by eating the livers he'd ripped from Crow Indians.

Coal Miner's Park, at the north edge of town, is home to the **Beartooth Nature Center** (a.k.a. the Red Lodge Zoo), 900 N. Bonner Ave., tel. (406) 446-1133, and hiking, biking, and cross-country skiing trails. Admission to the petting zoo is $4 adults, $2 children (free under age two). Hours are daily 10 a.m.-6 p.m. during the summer. The precursor of the present-day zoo was the See 'Em Alive Zoo, operated by a fox farmer in the 1930s.

Recreation

Red Lodge Mountain is a ski resort six miles west of town, with a vertical drop of 2,016 feet and five chairlifts to ferry skiers up the 30 slopes. Snowmakers are used early in the season, which runs from early December through mid-April. Spring skiing is especially popular at Red Lodge. Lift tickets are $32 for adults, $12 for children. Call (406) 446-2610 or (800) 444-8977 for more information, including information about special packages. Nearby **Red Lodge Nordic Ski Area,** tel. (406) 446-1070, has nine miles of groomed trails, with lessons and rentals available.

Head up the West Fork of Rock Creek for hiking and fishing. The often-crowded **Wild Bill Lake,** six miles from Red Lodge on West Fork Rd., is wheelchair-accessible for fishing. Toward the end of the road, trailheads sprout up. Just out of Basin Campground, the **Basin Lakes National Recreation Trail** is an easy day-hike leading to two lakes (with some brook trout) and a few tumble-down prospectors' cabins. At the road's end, the **West Fork Trail** puts you at the Absaroka-Beartooth Wilderness boundary, a one-mile hike from a waterfall, five miles from a mountain lake, and 10 miles from Sundance Pass.

Many of the area's Forest Service campgrounds are near hiking trails. The **Corral Creek Trail** starts near Sheridan Campground, and Parkside Campground is on the high, winding road to the trailhead for the **Hellroaring Lakes Trail,** which leads to a lovely chain of mountain lakes.

Golf at beautiful and challenging **Red Lodge Resort and Golf Club,** southwest of town on Red Lodge Mountain Rd., tel. (406) 446-1812.

Accommodations

The old downtown hotel choice in Red Lodge is, without question, the **Pollard Hotel,** at 2 N. Broadway, tel. (406) 446-0001 or (800) 765-5273. Back when it was known as the Spofford, it hosted Calamity Jane and Buffalo Bill. Now, after extensive renovation, there are even racquetball courts, a health club, and a sauna. Rooms are very comfortable—many include in-room steam baths and Jacuzzis. Rates begin at $95 s, $150 d.

Best Western LuPine Inn, 702 S. Hauser, tel. (406) 446-1321 or (800) 528-1234, $68 s, $75 d, is off main drag on a stream and has an indoor pool, fitness center, hot tub, sauna, indoor playground and game room, and guest laundry; pets are okay. The chalet-like **Chateau Rouge,** 1501 S. Broadway, tel. (406) 446-1601 or (800) 926-1601, offers rooms in studios ($68 d) or condos ($75 d). These rooms can be made out to sleep a crowd, if necessary. There's an indoor pool.

On a nice location on Rock Creek, **Eagle's Nest Motel,** 702 S. Broadway, tel. (406) 446-2312, has rooms from $36 s and d. There are some kitchenettes and a hot tub, and pets are okay. **Super 8 of Red Lodge,** 1223 S. Broadway, tel. (406) 446-2288 or (800) 813-8335, $55-

65 s, $66-98 d, has an indoor pool, indoor and outdoor hot tub, guest laundry, some kitchenettes, and pets are okay.

There are a few less-expensive places to stay in Red Lodge. With an indoor pool, the **Red Lodge Inn,** 811 S. Broadway, tel. (406) 446-2030, charges $50 d. The alpine-looking **Yodeler Motel,** 601 S. Broadway, tel. (406) 446-1435, has rooms for $45 s, $58 d.

Home Rentals

Four distinctive houses constitute **Pitcher Guest Houses,** tel. (406) 446-2859. They range from a turn-of-the-century four-bedroom house to one-bedroom log cabins.

Resorts

For a full-scale, full-service resort, the **Rock Creek Resort** is four miles south of town on Hwy. 212, tel. (406) 446-1111 or (800) 667-1119, www.rcresort.com. Single rooms start at $88, and accommodations include two-bedroom townhouses for $285 a night, with lots of other rooms available for prices in between. During ski season, Rock Creek offers packages including bed, breakfast, and skiing. A pool, tennis courts, health club, volleyball and croquet, horseback riding, and mountain-bike rentals keep Rock Creek's guests occupied. The resort also features two restaurants.

Willows Inn bed and breakfast at 224 S. Platt, tel. (406) 446-3913, is an old Victorian home with a supplemental two-bedroom cottage.

Camping

The Red Lodge **KOA,** four miles north of town on Hwy. 212, tel. (406) 446-2364, has a swimming pool and sites for both RVs and tents at $15 a night. **Perry's RV Park and Campground** is 1.5 miles south of town, tel. (406) 446-2722. To find Forest Service campgrounds, head south on Hwy. 212. Reach **Cascade** and **Basin** campgrounds via Red Lodge Mountain Rd., which starts right near the ranger station. These are good spots for hikers heading into the Absaroka-Beartooth Wilderness.

Farther south on Hwy. 212, find turnoffs for **Sheridan** and **Ratine. Parkside, Limber Pine, Greenough Lake,** and **M-K** are all part of the Rock Creek Recreation Area 11 miles south of Red Lodge and virtually at the foot of the Beartooth Highway. All these spots but Cascade, Ratine, Sheridan, and M-K have running water and charge a few dollars to camp.

Food and Drink

It's not hard to find a meal in Red Lodge—the town boasts of having more restaurants per capita than any other place in Montana. **Natali's Italian Pasta & Steakhouse,** has reasonably priced breakfasts, lunches, and dinners with good burgers and some European touches at 119 S. Broadway, tel. (406) 446-4025. The **Red Lodge Pizza Company,** 115 S Broadway, tel. (406) 446-3333, also brews its own beers, making this a great eating and quaffing destination.

Serrano's (a.k.a. The Restaurant), 17 Broadway, tel. (406) 446-2900, offers good Mexican and Southwestern-style dishes.

For a casual lunch or dinner, **Bogart's** has good pizza and Mexican food in a comfortable, relaxed setting at 11 S. Broadway, tel. (406) 446-1784. Breakfasts, particularly the sourdough pancakes, are the highlight at **P.D. McKinney's,** open for breakfast and lunch at 407 S. Broadway, tel. (406) 446-1250. **Genesis Natural Foods and Deli,** 123 S Broadway, tel. (406) 446-3202, is a good place to stock up on health foods and picnic items.

A bright spot for coffee snobs afoot in Montana, the **Coffee Factory Roasters,** 6 S. Broadway, tel. (406) 446-3200, roasts beans and serves up espresso and desserts.

Red Lodge's finest dining is at **Greenlee's,** at the Pollard Hotel. Steaks, chops, fresh seafood, pasta, and game dishes highlight the menu (entrees are about $18). There's also a prix fixe menu with four courses for $32. The wine list has been awarded *Wine Spectator*'s Award of Excellence for four years running.

Western bands stop by the **Bull 'n Bear,** 19 N. Broadway Ave., tel. (406) 446-3753.

Events

The **Red Lodge Music Festival** brings top high-school musicians to train with professionals. Both students and faculty perform over a nine-day span in mid-June.

The **Red Lodge Rodeo** is on Fourth of July weekend.

Mountain men descend on Red Lodge in late July and early August. Spend a week at the rendezvous for $15 ($25 family rate) or come in on a day pass for $3 (children $1). The en-

campment on the south end of town features music, dance, black-powder shoots, and trade goods, including buckskin garments, black-powder rifles, Indian beadwork, and pewter ware. More information is available from the chamber of commerce, tel. (406) 446-1718.

Ethnic diversity is celebrated each August during the nine-day **Festival of Nations.** Since the focus is on cultures that make up Red Lodge, expect to celebrate Scandinavian Day, Scottish Day, German Day, Finnish Day, Yugoslavian Day, English-Irish Day, Italian Day, Montana Day, and All Nations Day. An international cooking pavilion is set up at the Labor Temple at the north end of town, and games, dancing, and parades are choreographed throughout downtown. The town fills up for this celebration, so be sure to book rooms in advance if you want to stay in Red Lodge during the second week in August.

It may take an early March trip to Red Lodge to really believe that there is such a sport as skijoring. Visit the rodeo grounds for the **National Ski-Joring Finals,** and watch horses pull skiers around a circular course loaded with jumps and gates. The town's **Winter Carnival** happens around the same time of year.

A personalized event can be yours at the **Canyon Wedding Chapel,** four miles south of Red Lodge, P.O. Box 605, Red Lodge, MT 59068, tel. (406) 446-2681. Both religious and civil wedding ceremonies are held here.

Shopping

Red Lodge supports a surprising number of gift shops with a Native American bent—there are more bear claws and porcupine quills for sale along Broadway than, probably, any place else in the United States. **Broadway Bookstore,** 13 S. Broadway, tel. (406) 446-2742, continues this theme with a good selection of books on Native American topics.

Magpie Toymakers is a particularly charming shop at 115 N. Broadway.

Stop in at the old Northern Pacific depot to visit the **Carbon County Arts Guild,** 11 W. 8th St., with both studio and gallery space, tel. (406) 446-1370.

Information and Services

The **Chamber of Commerce Visitor's Center** is on the north edge of town, tel. (406) 446-1718. Write them at P.O. Box 988, Red Lodge, MT

59068. The **ranger station** is on Hwy. 212, tel. (406) 446-2103.

Carbon County Memorial Hospital is at 600 W. 21st St., tel. (406) 446-2345. Call the **police** a. (406) 646-7544; the **ambulance** and **fire department** are at (406) 446-1212.

The **Carnegie Library** is at 3 W. 8th St., tel. (406) 446-1905.

If you're setting out to drive the Beartooth Highway, be sure to gas up in Red Lodge.

Transportation

Fly into Billings on Northwest, Horizon, Delta, Sky West, or Big Sky. Car rentals are available at the Billings airport or at **Anderson Chevrolet,** tel. (406) 446-2720 or (800) 608-2720, in Red Lodge.

Cody Bus Lines has service between Billings and Cody, Wyoming, via Red Lodge. Call them at (406) 446-2304 or (800) 733-2304 for schedule information.

BEARTOOTH HIGHWAY

Make sure there's gas in the tank, film in the camera, an extra sweater in the back seat, and at least three hours to spare before setting out on the 68-mile-long Beartooth Highway. Built in 1936 and recently designated a National Scenic Byway, the road climbs to 10,942 feet and crosses alpine meadows and snowfields. The road's summit is called the "Top of the World," and, once each July, on an unannounced date, the Red Lodge Chamber of Commerce serves free drinks by the side of the road. The alcoholic beverages of yore have been replaced by soda pop.

The road climbs Rock Creek Canyon out of Red Lodge and switches back four times, crossing as many vegetation zones. Douglas fir and lodgepole pine grow in the valley; the first switchback brings Engelmann spruce into view; up toward the timberline subalpine fir grows in bunches on dry, scrabbly cliffs; where they let off, alpine meadows sprout boulders and wildflowers. Near Beartooth Pass, pink snow betrays the presence of high-elevation algae.

This drive is a veritable geology lesson; watch for the Bear's Tooth, a tall spire left after a glacier devoured the rest of the peak. The Beartooth Range itself takes its name from the eerily ursine appearance of its grinning limestone cliffs. North

of the summit of Beartooth Plateau, Granite Peak juts above the landscape.

The high country around the Beartooth Highway is crossed by hiking trails and speckled with lakes. Hiking trails across fragile alpine terrain are rarely forged paths; rather, they're less precise routes marked by rock cairns. For a short hike through an alpine meadow, drive up to the fire lookout on **Clay Butte** and hike a little over a mile along the ridge.

For a longer trek, take **Trail #614** at the switchback in the road up to the lookout and hike about four miles (generally downhill) around Beartooth Butte to Beartooth Lake. There's a lovely campground at Beartooth Lake, and a loop hike around the butte passes several other lakes in its seven-mile course.

Remember that the road dips down into Wyoming here—buy a Wyoming fishing license in Cooke City or at the Top of the World store before going after the rainbow, cutthroat, and brook trout in Beartooth Lake.

Many of the alpine lakes on the Beartooth Plateau have been stocked with trout. The hikes in are lovely, the fishing's generally good, and Pat Marcuson details every fish-bearing Beartooth lake and stream in *The Beartooth Fishing Guide,* published by Falcon Press.

Campgrounds

The only motel along the road from Red Lodge to Cooke City is a tiny and basic place connected to the **Top of the World Store,** but there are plenty of places to pitch a tent along the Wyoming stretch of the Beartooth Highway. High on the Beartooth Plateau, **Island Lake,** about 40 miles west of Red Lodge, and **Beartooth Lake,** three miles farther west, have trails leading to the many alpine lakes to the north. **Fox Creek,** seven miles east of Cooke City, and **Crazy Creek,** about three miles farther east, don't have the alpine quality of the higher campgrounds, but they are convenient and attractive wooded riverside spots.

COOKE CITY AND SILVER GATE

John Colter was the first white in the area, leading the 19th-century parade of mountain men, traders, prospectors, and speculators. Until 1882 this was still recognized as Crow land, and relatively few

MOTHER LODE OF CONTROVERSY: THE NEW WORLD MINE

For several years, controversy was brewing above Cooke City, the proposed site of a huge gold mine operated by Crown Butte Mine, Inc. The company, a subsidiary of the Canadian conglomerate Noranda, encountered a groundswell of concern from environmental groups, Yellowstone Park officials, and others, including the *New York Times* and President Bill Clinton, who argued that the area is too sensitive for such a project.

The proposed New World Mine would have straddled three major watersheds, bordered on three sides by the Absaroka-Beartooth Wilderness Area, and lain directly in the path of grizzly bears. The miners planned to store acidic waste rock slurry from the mine in a massive impoundment, which critics feared would have been vulnerable to natural forces such as earthquakes, floods, erosion, and landslides—and which would have displaced 56 acres of rare high-elevation wetlands in any event. The mine's advocates maintained that the project would have cleaned up messes left by unregulated miners in the past—and ultimately benefited the Yellowstone ecosystem.

The controversy subsided in August of 1996, however, when President Clinton announced that the federal government would itself purchase the mineral rights to the site. In a deal finalized in August of 1998, the government paid the company $65 million and the project was officially withdrawn.

But the years-long debate may have been instrumental in raising awareness of the environmental hazards of leach mining in general. In the November 3 election of 1998, Montana voters passed the so-called "Cyanide Initiative," establishing a statewide ban on the use of cyanide in open-pit mining of low-grade ores.

whites intruded. By 1883, however, Cooke City, named after the son of a Northern Pacific financier, was a booming mine town. Gold, silver, and lead were extracted from the mountains but, because of the remoteness, the boom didn't last. Unmined lodes remain around Cooke City, but it's still hard to get to them, and, until recently, the mining costs were reckoned to be too high to maintain much of an operation.

Mining speculation started anew in 1991 when Noranda, a Canadian-owned company, came to town. Plans are now well afoot to mine gold, copper, and silver from a site just north of Cooke City. Some local businesses renamed themselves to attract the prospective miners and construction workers, and local environmentalists have formed the Beartooth Alliance, a branch of the Northern Plains Resource Council, to address concerns about wildlife habitats, water quality, and conflicts with recreation and community values. The Greater Yellowstone Coalition, based in Bozeman, is convinced that it is reckless to conduct large-scale mining here near the headwaters of many rivers.

Otherwise, Cooke City (elev. 7,651 feet) is a tourist town. There's just one street to reckon with here, and it's easy to walk from one end of it to the other. Even in the summer, when drivers spill off the Beartooth Highway, there's an easygoing, rustic flavor. During the winter, when the Beartooth Highway shuts down, Cooke City is open via the road through Yellowstone Park to Gardiner. Silver Gate, three miles west of Cooke City, was established as a resort town shortly after construction of the Beartooth Highway. Together, the two towns have about 75 year-round residents, though this, and much else, may change with the advent of large-scale mining.

Recreation

There is some gold in the hills around Cooke City, and fortune seekers may enjoy panning in the local streams.

Beartooth Plateau Outfitters, P.O. Box 1127, Cooke City, MT 59020, tel. (406) 838-2328 or (800) 253-8545, runs hunting, fishing, and horsepacking trips. **Skyline Guide Service,** tel. (406) 838-2380 in summer, (406) 664-3187 in winter, also leads trips into Yellowstone Park and the Absaroka-Beartooth Wilderness Area. Down the road in Silver Gate, **Castle Creek Outfitters,** tel. (406) 838-2301, has similar services.

Rent mountain bikes at the **Cooke City Bike Shack.**

For a short forest hike to a waterfall, start at the Range Riders Lodge in Silver Gate.

Northeast of Cooke City, on the edge of the Absaroka-Beartooth Wilderness, there's a **"grasshopper glacier,"** a glacier with dark bands of grasshoppers frozen into it. Apparently, the grasshoppers were migrating to the plains when overcome by fierce mountain weather. The frozen grasshoppers are cloaked by snowfall during most of the year, but in August the previous year's snow has usually melted away, exposing the would-be migrants. To reach the glacier, drive a high-clearance 4WD up the LuLu Pass–Goose Lake Rd. (near Colter Campground). The road stops at the Absaroka-Beartooth Wilderness border. Continue on foot (or horseback) along the old road to Goose Lake, then take the trail northeast to the saddle between Sawtooth Mountain and Iceberg Peak. Turn right at the saddle and climb the first rock ridge, from which the glacier is visible on the north side of Iceberg Peak. The hike from the road's end to this point is four miles. Topographical maps of the area are available at the Cooke City Store. Hikers should prepare for harsh weather any time of year.

Accommodations

Most accommodations in Cooke City are serviceable, but neither fancy nor expensive, with cabins and motel rooms running $45-60. **Bearclaw Cabins,** tel. (406) 838-2336; **Alpine Motel,** tel. (406) 838-2262, offers rooms at $50 s, $60 d; open all year; HBO available. **High Country Motel,** tel. (406) 838-2272, has rooms at $40 s, $47 d. Kitchen rooms are $50 to $60; one room has a fireplace. **Antlers Lodge,** tel. (406) 838-2432; and **Elkhorn Lodge,** tel. (406) 838-2332, are all basic lodgings (most with kitchenettes) right along the main drag of Hwy. 212. **Hoosier's Motel,** tel. (406) 838-2241, has the added attraction of the **Hoosier Bar,** a 7,651-foot-high paean to Indiana. At **Big Bear Lodge,** tel. (406) 838-2267, the focus is on fly-fishing.

With double rooms going for $70, the **Soda Butte Lodge,** tel. (406) 838-2251 or (800) 527-6462, is a bit more expensive and a bit less spartan than the other lodgings in town. Family rooms and jacuzzi suites are available.

Down the road in Silver Gate, the historic **Range Riders Lodge,** tel. (406) 838-2359, is joined by the **Grizzly Lodge,** tel. (406) 838-2219. Rooms begin at $35 s, $45 d. **Silver Gate Cabins,** tel. (406) 838-2371, has both cabins (each with a queen- and a full-sized bed, plus kitchenette and bathroom) for $40-65, and motel rooms at $39 to $65 d. There are cabin accommodations in the same price range at **Pine Edge Cabins,** tel. (406) 838-2222; and, just off the highway, **Whispering Pines Cabins,** tel. (406) 838-2228. All these places are simple, set in a pleasant woodsy town.

Camping

Chief Joseph, Soda Butte, and **Colter** are Forest Service campgrounds just east of Cooke City on the Beartooth Highway.

Food and Drink

Sit, dizzy from the elevation, on the front porch of the **Beartooth Cafe,** tel. (406) 838-2475, gobble carrot cake, and stroke the town dogs. Wander down the street to the **Hoosier Bar,** or stop in for pie at **Joan and Bill's,** tel. (406) 838-2280. As evening falls, Cooke City takes on the aroma of fried chicken—either **Ma Perkins** or Joan and Bill must be offering it as a $6 dinner special. Dinners at the Beartooth Cafe are trendier and more expensive, with a good selection of imported beers.

Pick up basic groceries and a truckload of ambience at the **Cooke City Store,** tel. (406) 838-2234, a historic general store and de facto community center.

YELLOWSTONE NATIONAL PARK

Most of Yellowstone National Park is in Wyoming, but three of its entrances—West Yellowstone, Gardiner, and Cooke City—are in Montana. For an excellent, in-depth guide to the entire park, see the *Wyoming Handbook* by Don Pitcher (Moon Publications).

Entrance to Yellowstone costs $20 per car, or $10 per person on bicycle or foot. Motorcy-

clists and snowmobilers pay $15 per person. Passes are good for seven consecutive days in both Yellowstone and Grand Teton National Parks. A Golden Age Passport ($10) gives U.S. citizens over age 62 free admission to national parks.

The park is set up for motorists—spin through a couple of loops, watch Old Faithful spew, cruise by

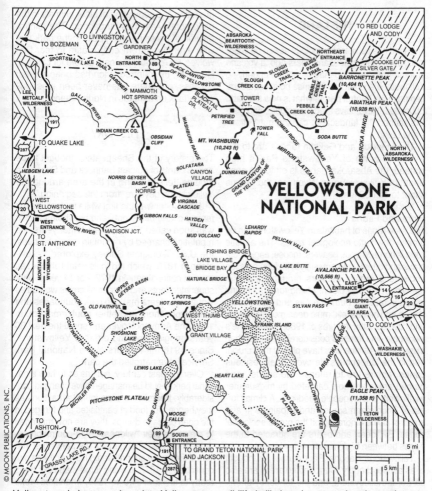

Yellowstone Lake, peer down into Yellowstone Canyon. If you're lucky, maybe you'll see some wildlife. This is all reasonably satisfying, but perhaps not worth the veritable pilgrimages people make to Yellowstone.

There are plenty of ways to make a park visit more enriching. Classes at the **Yellowstone Institute** can provide focus (see below). Read up on natural history and geology. If you're anything of an angler, bring fishing gear and pick up a free fishing permit at a visitor center or ranger station. Find out from a ranger where

wildlife is likely to be spotted and spend some time there with binoculars and perhaps a camera or sketchpad. Follow the trail of the Nez Perce through the park, or become obsessed with the exploits of mountain men such as John Colter.

Yellowstone Park closes for a couple of weeks early in Dec. and from mid-March until May, but for those willing to make the effort to get in there during the winter months, there's a wilder park to explore than most summertime visitors glimpse. Winter snows drive the animals down to lower elevations where they find easier winter grazing.

THE LAND

This land has as violent a geology as can be imagined. Six hundred thousand years ago, a volcano erupted from the deep magma pocket underlying Yellowstone and left an immense hole, or caldera, gaping in the central part of what is now the park. Subsequent lava flows filled the caldera, and glaciers refined the landscape, carving out Yellowstone Lake.

The Madison and Gallatin ranges are to the west and north of Yellowstone Park's high plateau; the Absaroka Range is off to the east. South of Yellowstone, in Wyoming, the Tetons shoot to 12,000 feet.

Flora and Fauna

The wide range of habitats in Yellowstone can be broken down into ecological zones: The aquatic zone is home to trout, beavers, moose, eagles, ospreys and otters. Low grasslands include grasses and shrubs, rabbits, badgers, pronghorn, and, in the winter, elk and bison. Mixed forest contains aspen in recently burned areas and Douglas fir, shrubs and berries, elk, mule deer, mountain lions, and coyotes. After the fires of 1988, Yellowstone's lodgepole pine forest is considerably sparser than it used to be, but the fires have played their crucial part in the lodgepole's life cycle (their resinous cones require fire to release the seeds), and burned areas are now carpeted by midsummer wildflowers and lodgepole seedlings. A climax forest of Engelmann spruce and subalpine fir and areas of alpine tundra top off the park's ecological zones. Elk, deer, and bears are attracted to the edges between high meadows and forests.

Yellowstone National Park cannot be thought of as a distinct entity. Surrounding areas are also part of the ecosystem, and the tendency of animals to naturally walk across unnatural park boundaries can be a source of conflict. Witness the buffalo, host to brucella, a microorganism benign to infected buffalo but which causes abortions in cattle. Neighboring ranchers are in favor of shooting buffalo found straying from the park, and whether this should be permitted, and by whom, has caused no end of brouhaha in the area around Gardiner.

The reintroduction of wolves into Yellowstone has also made area ranchers uneasy. Because of fear of their predatory instincts, wolves were exterminated in the early 1900s. Without their predation, the population of other animals in the park, notably elk, has burgeoned. The reintroduction of breeding wolf packs in the park met with everything from enthusiasm to fear that wolves would make the park unsafe for children. However, the reintroduction has been a great success, and there has never been a serious wolf attack on humans in North America.

HISTORY

The history of the Sheepeaters, thought to be descendants of outcast Bannock and Shoshone Indians, tells of being in the area around the Yellowstone geysers "from the beginning."

John Colter was the first white to describe the fantastic land of fire pots and blowholes, which was soon called "Colter's Hell." After years of a reputation charged by mountain men's tall tales, the U.S. Geological Survey explored Yellowstone in 1870, which led to its establishment as the first national park in 1872. For 14 years, park superintendents and their small crews worked as virtual volunteers marking park boundaries and routing poachers and other troublemakers. In 1886, the Army took over and spent the next 30 years bringing law and order to Yellowstone. Since 1916 the rangers of the National Park Service have patrolled the park.

Over the past century, notions as to how a national park should be managed have changed considerably. Bears were once tourist attractions as they begged for food at campsites and foraged in the open garbage dumps; they are now managed to maximize their "wildness." Fire-control procedures have also changed; for the park's first 100 years, fires were suppressed. This policy was discontinued in 1972, leaving large stands of trees ready to fuel a wildfire. In 1988, when fires broke out, they were initially allowed to burn uncontrolled, but when hot, dry weather looked unlikely to break, fire crews were sent in to the park. Ironically, it was the first snowfall that finally quelled the fires, which burned 36% of the park.

INFORMATION

The **Yellowstone Association** sells books in park visitor centers, and it runs educational programs and the **Yellowstone Institute,** with classes ranging from Yellowstone history to wildlife photography to astronomy. The institute is based in the old "Buffalo Ranch" in the Lamar Valley. For information on the association or the institute, write to P.O. Box 117, Yellowstone National Park, WY 82190, or call (307) 344-2294.

For good information concerning issues affecting the entire Yellowstone ecosystem, contact the **Greater Yellowstone Coalition,** 13 S. Willson Ave., Bozeman, MT 59771, tel. (406) 586-1593.

WEST YELLOWSTONE AND VICINITY

West Yellowstone (elev. 6,666 feet) is the west entrance to the park and the site of a stiff competition between nature and motel space. The 1939 WPA *Montana, A State Guide Book* characterized West Yellowstone as a town "full of eager competition and alert service . . . [where] every variation of western costume appears." There's all the tourist schlock you'd expect, and the out-of-doors is purveyed as recreation, a commodity that'll bring people here and make them spend money. But never mind. It's great country, and if tourism gets you down, come in the off-season (spring) and share the place with buffalo grazing on south-facing hills, huge crows, relaxed locals, and false-fronted buildings shut down until the crowds return.

History

Though the town of West Yellowstone was not incorporated until 1966, white homesteaders started to dribble into the West Yellowstone basin in the mid-1870s when a road was built into the newly formed national park. When the Nez Perce crossed the park in 1877, they nabbed several of the early park tourists, killing a couple but treating the survivors well.

In 1907 West Yellowstone became an official park entrance, and a town was platted. A tourist train from the main Union Pacific line in Ashton, Idaho, began operating in 1909 and the train depot became a hub of West Yellowstone. By 1915, park visitors were arriving by car, and the railroad was eventually supplanted by the highway down the Gallatin Valley from Bozeman.

Sights

Yellowstone National Park itself is the main reason to come to "West," and the **Museum of the Yellowstone** offers a good preview of the park.

Wildlife, historical, and art exhibits are housed in the old Union Pacific Railroad Depot at 124 Yellowstone Ave., tel. (406) 646-7814. The bookstore here is worth a browse; it has a strong regional section and a good selection of field guides.

The **Federation of Fly Fishers' International Fly Fishing Center,** 200 Yellowstone Ave., tel. (406) 646-9541, has fly-fishing displays, a library, and a casting pond. It's open June 15 - Sept. 30, and admission is free.

Just outside the national park entrance, a huge statue of a bear heralds the entrance to the privately owned **Grizzly Park.** The proprietor of this enterprise is attempting to gather "problem bears" from all over the world and confine them with fences and moats to provide a walk-through wildlife-viewing experience. It's generated controversy around the Yellowstone region. Though some bear experts feel that it's better than killing problem bears, other environmentalists worry that the imported bears will draw local grizzlies down toward town, spelling trouble for them. The center also houses a small gray wolf pack (all the wolves were born in captivity) in a one-acre compound. The park comprises an IMAX theater, a museum and interpretive center, a shopping mall, restaurants, lodgings, and nine resident bears. For current info, call the **Grizzly Discovery Center** at tel. (406) 646-7001, open 8:30 a.m.-8:30 p.m. in summer, till dusk the rest of the year, $7.50 admission for adults to the exhibits, $6.50 seniors, $3.00 children.

The IMAX theater, which shares a building with a Taco Bell just inside the Grizzly Park entrance at 105 S. Canyon St., tel. (406) 646-4100, features an eye-popping presentation on Yellowstone's natural history on a six-story screen. The cost here is $7.50 adults, $4.50 children, and the show starts on the hour.

Recreation

Wagons and Trails West, on Yellowstone Ave. next to the information center, offers summertime trail rides and stagecoach tours.

Rent bikes from **Yellowstone Bicycles and Video,** 132 Madison Ave., tel. (406) 646-7815. The Rendezvous Cross-Country Ski Trails (see below) are well suited to summer mountain biking. A bicycling and walking route runs along the old Union Pacific rail bed from West Yellowstone to Island Park, Idaho.

To find a horse for hire, head west on Hwy. 20 (Targhee Pass Hwy.) toward the Idaho border. There you'll find guided rides at **Diamond P Ranch,** 2865 Targhee Pass Hwy., tel. (406) 646-7246 and unguided rides at **Lone Rider Stables,** 1111 Targhee Pass Hwy., tel. (406) 646-7900.

Winter Recreation

During the winter, the only ways into the park from this direction are via cross-country skis, snowmobile, or snowcoach. Heated, 10-passenger coaches equipped with ski racks ferry passengers to Old Faithful and other thermal basins. **Yellowstone Alpen Guides,** 555 Yellowstone Ave., tel. (406) 646-9591, runs several tours, including one with a bit of cross-country skiing worked in; prices run $70-80. Snowcoaches also leave regularly from the **Stagecoach Inn,** 209 Madison Ave., tel. (406) 646-9575. For those who don't want to just ride around in the coach, drivers are accustomed to serving as skiing advisors and shuttlers.

Rendezvous Cross Country Ski Trails comprise 15 miles of trails groomed for both traditional cross-country and freestyle (skating) skiing. The trailhead is just off Yellowstone Ave., about three blocks west of Canyon Street. Loops can be selected according to skill and stamina, and, for that special Montana touch, there's a biathlon loop for gun-slinging skiers. During the summer, the mountain bikers use the Rendezvous' trails.

The **Riverside trails** start where Madison Ave. ends (at Boundary). These trails aren't as meticulously groomed as those at Rendezvous, but they offer a little more scenic punch. The trail network goes right into the park, where it runs along the Madison River. It's easy skiing, with a basic trip of about 2.5 miles. There's a good chance of seeing wildlife from these trails.

West Yellowstone has promoted itself as the "Snowmobile Capital of the World." There are hundreds of miles of snowmobile trails, and it's a good way to explore large areas of Yellowstone Park in the winter. Snowmobiles can be rented at **Rendezvous Snowmobile Rental,** 429 Yellowstone Ave., tel. (406) 646-9564, or from **Yellowstone Adventures,** 131 Dunraven St., tel. (406) 646-7735 or (800) 231-5991. Also, many hotels and motels rent snowmobiles; ask when you make reservations. Expect rentals to start at about $85 a day.

Fishing

West Yellowstone is a good hub for fishing the area's trout streams. The Madison, both in and out of the park, is the most celebrated river, but there are smaller streams worth fishing: Grayling, Duck, and Cougar Creeks, and the South Fork of the Madison. Venture into nearby Idaho and try Henry's Fork of the Snake River. Fishing season gets going on Memorial Day weekend (except on Yellowstone Lake and its tributary streams, where the season opens June 15) and runs through the first Sunday of November. State fishing licenses aren't needed inside the park, but a Yellowstone fishing permit, available free from any park visitor center or ranger station, is required.

If you need someone to initiate you into the mysteries of fly-fishing, find a guru in a guide. Even experienced anglers can benefit from a guide's knowledge of local conditions. They don't come cheap, however; expect to pay $250 a day for a guided float or wading trip. **Bud Lilly's Trout Shop,** 39 Madison Ave., tel. (406) 646-7801, employs some of West Yellowstone's best guides. **Madison River Outfitters,** 117 Canyon St. (P.O. Box 1106), tel. (406) 646-9644, is another good source of fishing expertise in West Yellowstone, as are **Jacklin's,** 105 Yellowstone Ave., tel. (406) 646-7336 and **Arrick's Fishing Flies,** 121 Madison Ave., tel. (406) 646-7290.

Hostel and Cabins

The budget hotel choice is the **West Yellowstone Hostel@Madison Hotel,** a log-hewn cross between an old downtown hotel and a youth hostel at 139 Yellowstone, tel. (406) 646-7745 or (800) 838-7745. It was built in 1912 and remains open Memorial Day-Oct. 5. Hostel rooms provide bunks at $17, while private rooms are $26 s, $45 d. The rooms at the adjacent Madison Motel are less charming but equipped with TVs and bathrooms, beginning at $45 s, $63 d. (Register for both spots in the gift shop.)

The **Gallatin National Forest** rents rustic (no electricity or bathrooms) cabins for $25 a night at Beaver Creek, Cabin Creek, and Basin Station. Contact the Hebgen Lake Ranger District, P.O. Box 520, West Yellowstone, MT 59759, tel. (406) 646-7369, for directions and reservations.

Hotels and Motels

The motels belonging to the West Yellowstone Chamber of Commerce offer one number to call from out of state to book a room in any of the member motels: (800) 521-5241; the local number is (406) 646-7832. Since West Yellowstone fills up so fast, even during the "off" season, it's a good idea to call this number in advance and let them set you up with accommodations. Rates are much lower in spring, fall, and winter; note that not all hotels remain open in mid-winter.

The **Alpine Motel,** 120 Madison Ave., tel. (406) 646-7544, $45 s, $59 d, is a small, centrally located motel with nice rooms, closed Nov. 1-April 30; no phones in rooms. **Al's Westward Ho,** 16 Boundary St., tel. (406) 646-7331, has rooms (some with kitchenettes) at $40-48s, $48-56 d; closed Nov. 1-April 30. **Big Western Pine Motel,** 234 Firehole Ave., tel. (406) 646-7622 or (800) 646-7622, $53-65 s, $57-85 d, has a pool and hot tub, pets are okay, and there are snowmobile rentals in winter. At the **Lazy G Motel,** 123 Hayden St., tel. (406) 646-7586, standard rooms are $43 s. $53 d; for an extra $10, you can rent a room with a kitchenette. The motel also has a picnic area with gas grill.

Roundup Motel/Dude Motor Inn, 3 Madison Ave., tel. (406) 646-7301 or (800) 833-7669, offers rooms at $66 s, $76 d; there are also some two-bedroom units and kitchenettes; closed mid-March through April and late October to mid-December. **Stage Coach Inn,** 209 Madison Ave., tel. (406) 646-7381 or (800) 842-2882, has rooms at $69 to $120; there's also a hot tub and sauna. Enjoy the historic lodge atmosphere with great lobby; also headquarters for snowcoach tours.

The newly renovated **Best Western Desert Inn,** 133 Canyon Ave., tel. (406) 646-7376, has rooms at $79-102 s, $79-121 d; there's a pool. **Best Western Executive Inn,** 236 Dunraven, tel. (406) 646-7681, with rooms from $81 s, $90 d, has a pool, and pets are okay. **Best Western Cross Winds Inn,** 201 Firehole Ave., tel. (406) 646-9557, $79 s and d, and up, has large, nicely furnished rooms, plus an indoor pool and hot tub. **Best Western Weston Inn,** 103 Gibbon Ave., tel. (406) 646-7373 or (800) 528-1234, $80 s, $90 d, has a seasonal outdoor pool, year-round outdoor hot tub, and small pets are okay. The **Brandin' Iron Inn,** tel. (406) 646-9411 or (800) 217-4613, 201 Canyon Ave., offers new rooms at $75 s, $85 d. All rooms come with refrigerators and HBO; there are hot tubs.

Three Bears Lodge, 217 Yellowstone Ave., tel. (406) 646-7353 or (800) 646-7353, $68 s, $83

d, is a nice place with a pool and hot tub. Pets can stay for a $5 surcharge. **Travelers Lodge,** 225 Yellowstone Ave., tel. (406) 646-9561 or (800) 831-5741, $68 s, $84 d, has a pool, sauna, hot tub, guest laundry, and small pets are okay. One of West Yellowstone's most upscale lodgings is **West Yellowstone Conference Hotel & Holiday Inn Sunspree Resort,** 315 Yellowstone Ave., tel. (406) 646-7365 or (800) 646-7365, with rooms at $139 and up. Facilities include indoor pool, sauna, hot tub, and exercise room; there are several two-bedroom units, plus a restaurant and lounge. All rooms have coffee makers, microwaves, and refrigerators.

Camping

The eight campgrounds in the town of West Yellowstone are mostly for RVs, though **Rustic RV Park,** tel. (406) 646-7387, **Wagon Wheel RV Park,** tel. (406) 646-7872, and **Hideaway RV Park,** tel. (406) 646-9049, reserve some space for tent campers. The Wagon Wheel also has cabins for rent for $40-60. Forest Service campgrounds down the Madison Valley offer more options for tenters (though Baker's Hole, three miles north of town, is limited to RVs).

Food and Drink

Bears are the first thing that come to mind when contemplating West Yellowstone's dining venues. For a hearty breakfast or cheap dinner, try the **Running Bear Pancake House,** 538 Madison, tel. (406) 646-7703. The **Three Bears Restaurant** cooks more steaks than pancakes at 205 Yellowstone Ave., tel. (406) 646-7811; open for breakfast and dinner, but not lunch.

Departing from the bear theme, the **Silver Spur Cafe,** 20 Firehole Ave., tel. (406) 646-7013, is a good place to breakfast with the locals—it's open for breakfast, lunch, and dinner. **Nancy P's Bakery,** 29 Canyon St., tel. (406) 646-9737, is *the* place for cinnamon rolls.

Across from the bakery, **Mike's Cafe,** 38 Canyon St., tel. (406) 646-9462, is a good cubbyhole to duck into for a soup and sandwich lunch. Head toward the back of the **Book Peddler,** 106 Canyon St., tel. (406) 646-9358, where soup and sandwiches, pastries, and espresso are served.

Many of West's restaurants are associated with motels; of these, the **Rustler's Roost** in the Big Western Pine Motel, 234 Firehole Ave., tel. (406) 646-7622, stands out. Their menu includes elk and buffalo dinners for about $15.

Head about eight miles west to **Alice's Restaurant,** 1545 Targhee Pass Hwy. (Hwy. 20), tel. (406) 646-7296, for schnitzel or trout dinners for about $10.

Events

The **Rendezvous Cross Country Ski Race** is held early in March. A winter festival has sprung up around this event. The spring months are relatively quiet in West Yellowstone. Plowing the roads into the park provides jobs for weeks, and they're usually clear by May. There's a steady pitch of activity all summer long, punctuated by such events as the August **Federation of Fly Fishers Conclave.** Call the chamber of commerce at (406) 646-7701 for more information.

Shopping

Shops line Canyon Street (a.k.a. Hwy. 191, the road to Bozeman). Pick up western or outdoor clothing, fly-fishing paraphernalia, or that souvenir T-shirt. A visit to **Eagle's Store,** at the corner of Canyon and Yellowstone, tel. (406) 646-9300, will give you a chance to buy everything you need to prove you've been in The West. (It's a little overwhelming, but fun.) Two good bookstores are the **Bookworm,** 14 Canyon St., tel. (406) 646-9736, and the **Book Peddler,** 106 Canyon, tel. (406) 646-9358. Add to these the bookshop in the **Museum of the Yellowstone,** and the traveler who's content to curl up and just *read* about Vacationland is headed for pure bliss.

Fishing shops include **Madison River Outfitters,** 117 Canyon St., tel. (406) 646-9644; **Bud Lilly's Trout Shop,** 39 Madison Ave., tel. (406) 646-7801; **Jacklin's Fly Shop,** 105 Yellowstone Ave., tel. (406) 646-7336; and **Eagle's Tackle Shop,** 3 Canyon St., tel. (406) 646-7521. Most of these places also sell outdoor clothing, and most can arrange guided trips.

Entertainment

Playmill Theater, 29 Madison Ave., tel. (406) 646-7757, and **Musical Moose Playhouse,** 124 Madison Ave., tel. (406) 646-9710, both run family-oriented shows on summer evenings.

Information and Services

The **chamber of commerce** at 100 Yellow-

stone Ave., tel. (406) 646-7701, has the expected array of brochures and a friendly staff. Write them at P.O. Box 458, West Yellowstone, MT 59758. **Yellowstone National Park** has an information line at (307) 344-7381, and the **Hegben Lake Ranger Station,** just north of West Yellowstone on Hwy. 191, tel. (406) 646-7369, can provide information on the nearby Gallatin National Forest. **Southwest Montana Avalanche Advisory,** tel. (406) 587-9784, posts daily avalanche reports outside the post office during the winter. The **library** is at 100 Yellowstone Ave., tel. (406) 646-9017.

The emergency phone number is **911.** The **police** and **ambulance** are housed at 124 Yellowstone Avenue. A **medical clinic,** tel. (406) 646-7668, and a **social service center** share the address of 236 Yellowstone Avenue.

The **post office** is on Madison Avenue. Both a laundromat and showers are open every day at the **Canyon St. Laundry,** 312 Canyon St., tel. (406) 646-9733.

Transportation

West Yellowstone Airport is open during the summer, but it's often easier to fly in to Bozeman and catch a bus to West Yellowstone. Greyhound buses run from Bozeman and also up from Salt Lake City.

To rent a car in West, call **Big Sky Car Rental,** tel. (406) 646-9564 or (800) 426-7669. They're located at Randy's Auto Repair, 429 Yellowstone Avenue. **Avis,** tel. (406) 646-7635 or (800) 331-1212, has an office at the airport.

Buffalo Bus Lines runs tours through the park for $30 per person. Call them at (406) 646-7337, or stop by 214 Madison.

Gray Line offers bus tours of Yellowstone Park originating from 633 Madison Ave. in West Yellowstone, tel. (406) 646-9374. Buses run around either the "lower loop" (includes Old Faithful, Yellowstone Lake, and the Grand Canyon of the Yellowstone), or the "upper loop" (Norris Geyser Basin and Mammoth Hot Springs), $36 adults, $20.50 children for either loop. There's also a tour of Quake Lake and the mining towns of Virginia City and Nevada City. Buses swing by the Lionshead Super 8 at 7:15 a.m., then pick up passengers in town at 7:30 a.m. For advance reservations, call (800) 523-3102.

MADISON JUNCTION

From West Yellowstone, follow the Madison River into the park. This is one of Yellowstone's premier fishing areas—the warm water of the Firehole River joins the cooler Gibbon River at Madison Junction, providing an ideal trout habitat.

Nonfishing partners of anglers may want to spend some time at the **Madison Caldera Arts Center,** where summer brings a variety of arts workshops and performances to Madison Junction.

Between Madison Junction and Norris Geyser Basin, the road follows the Gibbon River. Stop at 84-foot **Gibbon Falls.** Like Madison Junction, the falls perch on the edge of the main Yellowstone caldera.

NORRIS GEYSER BASIN

Yellowstone's most spectacular and changeable thermal area, Norris Geyser Basin, may not be as well known as Old Faithful, but it's far more atmospheric and a better place to actually hike past numerous geysers and boiling pools.

Norris is situated over the junction of two major faults (one that runs down from Mammoth Hot Springs and another coming over from Hebgen Lake). These crustal cracks provide conduits for heat to rise to the earth's surface. Steam vents, hot springs, and geysers are all manifestations of this surface heat.

Sights

Between 1886 and 1916, when the Army ran Yellowstone, some troops were based at the remote Norris outpost. The old Soldier Station has been renovated and now houses the **Museum of the National Park Ranger.** History buffs and fans of rustic architecture will enjoy this stop, but for most people, time is better spent hiking around the geyser basin.

Pick up a map of Norris's trail system and strike out through steam clouds, whiffs of sulfur, spurts of water, and brilliantly colored mineral deposits. Since the landscape here is relatively malleable, the map and signposts may not include all the current thermal activity, and it's this unpredictability that is part of Norris's charm. Be

careful, stay on the trail, but do explore at least one of the two loops.

The path around **Porcelain Basin** is less than a mile long but has expansive pale (indeed, porcelain-hued) views of terraced hot springs and geysers. The more forested **Back Basin** loop is about 1.5 miles long and passes a near-boiling pure green spring that takes its color from the combination of the blue spring water and the yellow sulfur of the basin wall. **Steamboat Geyser,** which has rare 300-foot-high eruptions (and more frequent minor spurts), is also on the Back Basin loop.

Camping

There is a park campground across the road from Norris Geyser Basin and another one between Norris and West Yellowstone at **Madison Junction.** Between Norris and Mammoth, there's camping at **Indian Creek.**

MAMMOTH HOT SPRINGS AND VICINITY

The grand arch leading into Yellowstone from Gardiner, dedicated by Theodore Roosevelt in 1903, was the original entrance to the park and is still the only entrance open to cars year-round.

Elk winter around Mammoth, spending much of their time, it seems, in the hotel parking lot.

Sights

Stop by the **visitor center** for an overview, a movie, and, if necessary, fishing or backcountry permits. Schedules for ranger-led hikes and discussions are also available.

A boardwalk climbs the terraced hot pools. The pools are not static; as the flow of hot groundwater through limestone changes, so do the formations. Groundwater combines with burps of carbon dioxide from underground magma to form carbonic acid, which dissolves limestone. Limey carbonated water emerges from the ground at Mammoth Hot Springs and the lime is deposited as travertine. Thermophilic bacteria and algae live in the hot water, tinting the white travertine with their brilliant colors. Pick up a brochure at the foot of the trail to take the self-guided tour of the springs. Take care to stay on the boardwalk; the hot pools are frequently boiling hot, and they may have very thin crusts

elk resting on terraced
hot springs near
Mammoth

JUDY JEWELL

around them. People and animals have died in thermal pools.

The Army was the park's original overseer, and its headquarters, Fort Yellowstone, is behind the visitor center. It has been used as the **National Park Service Headquarters** since 1918.

During the summer, the Mammoth campground amphitheater is the site of nightly talks by park rangers.

For a roadside glimpse of the park, try the TW Services **bus tour of the Grand Loop.** Reserve a $26 seat (half price for kids) by calling (307) 344-7311, or sign up at the activities desk in the Mammoth Hotel. **Gray Line Tours,** tel. (307) 646-9374, also runs tour buses into the park.

Midway between Mammoth and Tower Junction, the **Blacktail Plateau** offers both a scenic drive and hiking trails. Follow the dirt road through grasslands and along a stretch of the old Bannock Trail, used by the Bannock Indians to cross from present-day Idaho to the eastern plains.

Mammoth's steaming pools and ghostly white terraces are particularly appealing in the winter, when it's not unusual to see elk lying in the hot pools. **Snowcoach tours** leave Mammoth daily from mid-December through early March and head to Old Faithful ($75 roundtrip) and Canyon ($68 roundtrip).

Recreation

Hot springs empty into the Gardiner River at the 45th parallel, and this is one place where hot springs bathing is sanctioned. The parking lot is just over the state line into Montana. It's about a five-minute walk down the path to the springs, which are officially open 8 a.m.-6 p.m. Remember to bring a bathing suit.

Register for **trail rides** at the Mammoth Hotel activities desk. A one-hour ride costs $13.

During the winter, the Mammoth Hotel rents **ice skates** and **cross-country skis.** Guided ski tours are available, as is a snowcoach shuttle service to other areas of the park. A shuttle to the Tower area provides access to some good ski trails around Blacktail Plateau, Lost Lake, and Tower Falls ($12 roundtrip).

Snowmobile rentals are also available at Mammoth.

Accommodations

Mammoth Hot Springs Hotel, open for the summer from the third week of May through the third week of September, has both hotel rooms (starting at $60 with bath, $42 without) and cabins (sans bath, $30; with a bath, $60). The winter season at Mammoth runs mid-December through early March, when rooms are $65 with bath, $45 without. Like the other Yellowstone hotels, it's operated by TW Services; call (307) 344-7311 for reservations.

The campground at Mammoth is small by local standards—only 85 sites. It's open year-round and costs $12 a night.

Food and Drink

Mammoth Hot Springs Hotel Dining Room is a *relatively* fancy, relatively pricey restaurant open during the hotel's season. The **Terrace Grill** (a.k.a. Mammoth Fast Foods) is in the same complex, has a slightly longer season from mid-May through late September, and the atmosphere is decidedly casual. The **Mammoth General Store** offers basic foodstuffs year-round. And remember, you didn't come to Yellowstone for a culinary experience.

Information and Services
General park information is dispensed at the **visitor center** in Mammoth, and by telephone, tel. (307) 344-7381.

Dial **911** for emegencies. The **Mammoth Hot Springs Clinic** is near the visitor center and is open on weekdays all year, tel. (307) 344-7965.

The main Yellowstone **post office** is to the side of the Park Service administration building in Mammoth. Foreign currency can be exchanged at the front desk of any Yellowstone hotel, and there is a bank machine in the lobby of the Old Faithful Inn in Mammoth.

TOWER JUNCTION AND VICINITY

Tower Junction is where the Mammoth–Cooke City road is joined by the road to Yellowstone Canyon. There's a small settlement here—a ranger station, a lodge with cabins, and a campground three miles south at **Tower Falls.** The falls, nestled into a rocky gorge, are a popular sight. A more meditative viewing is often afforded by taking the short but steep hike to the bottom. Bannock Indians found a safe place to cross the Yellowstone River just above the falls; it's now referred to as Bannock Ford.

Elk and bison winter in the **Lamar Valley,** east of Tower Junction. Coyotes are also commonly spotted jogging across the valley floor.

Recreation
The **Buffalo Plateau Trail** swings north of the park into Montana on its 21-mile run from the trailhead three miles west of Tower Junction to Slough Creek Campground. It's best to wait until late July for this hike—the varied terrain includes Slough Creek, which can be difficult to cross when it's carrying lots of water. **Slough Creek Campground** is also the trailhead for an 11-mile hike (or wintertime cross-country ski trip) up Slough Creek to the northern edge of the park. Full descriptions of these and other hikes are included in the Sierra Club totebook, *Hiking the Yellowstone Backcountry,* by Orville Bach. Hikers should also check with park rangers to learn about current trail conditions.

In the winter, the road to Tower Falls becomes a **cross-country ski trail.** A private viewing of the falls is worth the three-mile, generally uphill slog.

Specimen Ridge, southeast of Tower Junction, sports a petrified forest; indeed, petrified forests are stacked deep in this area. The mud and ash coughed up by volcanoes provided soil on which new trees could grow, only to be covered when the next volcano erupted. Erosion has uncovered some of the top layers; it's conjectured that 44 layers of forest exist. Naturalists lead daylong hikes on Specimen Ridge during July and August; details are available at any park visitor center.

Accommodations
Prices at **Roosevelt Lodge** start at $23 for a rustic cabin without a bath; a cabin with a bath is $60. Roosevelt's season is short—early June through the end of August. There's an emphasis on things western here—stagecoach rides leave several times a day for a half-hour tour ($8 adults, $5.50 children), and cookouts at nearby Yancey's Hole involve a horseback or church-wagon journey (see below).

Nearby campgrounds include **Tower Falls,** open late May to mid-Sept.; **Slough Creek,** open late May through Oct.; and **Pebble Creek,** open mid-June to early September.

Food and Drink
If you want a meal that's longer on the experience than on the cuisine, try the TW-sponsored **Old West Dinner Cookout.** Jump on a horse or climb into a church wagon at Roosevelt Lodge and ride to Yancey's Hole for a slab of steak and other picnic fare. Dinner and an hour-long horseback ride cost $35 ($23 children). Wagon riders pay $28 ($18 for children). Reserve a space by calling TW at (307) 344-7311.

The **Roosevelt Lodge** prides itself on the ribs served at its family-style restaurant.

DOVER PUBLICATIONS, INC.

SOUTHWESTERN MONTANA

Southwestern Montana is rich in almost every meaning of the word. Early prospectors found some of the richest gold deposits ever discovered here along the flanks of the Rocky Mountains. Hardrock mining earned Butte the sobriquet, "the richest hill on earth." At one time Helena boasted more millionaires per capita than anywhere else in the nation.

The boom that fed this early growth has largely turned bust. Nowadays, residents measure their wealth in the majestic beauty of the mountains, the free-flowing rivers filled with trout, and the potent culture of old cities and towns whose rich culinary heritage is still keenly observed.

Native Montanans know that some of the best recreation in the state is here. The Jefferson and its tributaries provide blue-ribbon trout fishing, whitewater rafting, and streamside campsites. Enormous national forests provide unparalleled camping, hiking, and wildlife-viewing opportunities: the Beaverhead National Forest alone is larger than many Atlantic states.

THE LAND

The area's rich mines extract mineral riches from intrusions of molten granite that punched up through existing mountain formations about 70 million years ago. Although some of the magma erupted as volcanoes, much simply hardened at shallow underground depths. Called batholiths, these bodies of rock are sometimes vast and richly infused with valuable minerals. The mines at Helena, Boulder, Butte, and Silver Star all tapped into the same enormous formation, the Boulder Batholith.

FLORA AND FAUNA

The southwestern corner of Montana contains a unique mix of plant and animal life. In an hour, a hiker can easily pass from an arid prairie environment of sagebrush and pronghorn, through verdant forests of lodgepole pine, spruce, and fir, and explore alpine tundra life along the many crenellations of the Continental Divide.

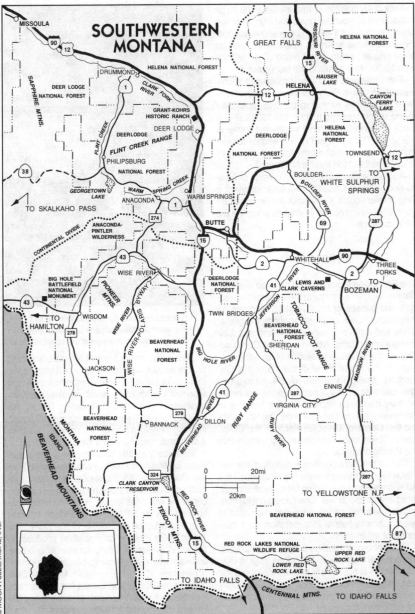

SOUTHWESTERN MONTANA

© MOON PUBLICATIONS, INC.

Especially notable in this area are the large populations of mountain goats and bighorn sheep along the peaks of the Flint Creek and Anaconda-Pintler Wilderness Areas. Prairie fowl, such as sage grouse, seem out of place when sighted with 10,000-foot peaks in the background.

Two otherwise rare species occur in southwestern Montana. Biologists feared that the trumpeter swan was extinct in the U.S. until they found several nesting pairs in the 1930s at Red Rock Lakes in the extreme southwest corner of the state. The lakes are now a wildlife refuge; trumpeters have since reestablished their territory in other parts of the Pacific Northwest.

Another species rarely found outside of Alaska and northern Canada is the arctic grayling, a long-finned cousin to the trout. While not abundant, the grayling occurs in streams along the Big Hole drainage.

HISTORY

The Shoshone Indians, often referred to as the Bannocks, passed through the mountain meadows and passes of southwestern Montana as they passed back and forth between the grasslands and buffalo of central Montana and their homelands in Idaho. When Lewis and Clark paddled up the Missouri in search of an easy passage to the Great River of the West (the Columbia), their Shoshone guide Sacajawea chanced onto a party of natives led by her brother; they had been separated from the time of Sacajawea's abduction as a child. The Shoshone led the Corps of Discovery across the Continental Divide in the Americans' first venture into the Pacific drainage.

One of the most significant battles of the Nez Perce War was fought in the Big Hole, when the Army ambushed the fleeing Nez Perce and suffered a strategic defeat. Chief Joseph then continued to lead his people eastward in an effort to reach Canada before incarceration on a government reservation.

Gold first brought settlers to this part of the state. Beginning at Bannack in 1862, then Virginia City, and then in almost every ravine throughout the area, prospectors found mineral wealth. Gold camps sprang up, the easily panned gold played out, and the settlement moved on.

JUDY JEWELL

Graceful old communities attest to the fact that southwestern Montana has been settled longer than any other part of the state.

This early, colorful era of Montana's mining history ended when silver replaced gold as the mineral of choice. Silver demanded mills and smelters for extraction, which required costly investment. Soon the ripsnorting life of the prospector was replaced by a corporate payroll; panning for gold in a lonely stream was traded for a shift underground with a crew of workers.

Whereas the early transitory life of the placer miner left few monuments, corporate mining from the 1880s to the 1930s built cities of worldwide influence. Butte was perhaps the richest mining center the world has known. Had Butte been a nation, the city would have ranked fourth in world copper production up until the 1930s. During the 1880s Butte was the largest silver producer in the world; William A. Clark, the man who led the development of silver mining, became the eighth-richest man of his day. Helena's Montana Club became the Pacific Northwest's first private club: membership was only open to millionaires (50 Helena citizens in the 1880s qualified).

This wealth built imposing cities; the swaggering, cosmopolitan savoir faire of foreign workers, who came streaming in to work the mines, contributed to their cultural richness.

Three men dominated events in Butte's heyday. William Clark established the city's first fortune in silver mining and smelting. Marcus Daly bought up spent silver mines for the abundance of copper ore that they contained; the advent of electricity and the need for copper wire brought Daly great wealth. Finally, Fritz Augustus Heinze manipulated land ownership laws to take over mining claims of his predecessors.

Life in Butte and other mining communities in southwestern Montana changed dramatically in the early 1900s when, after Marcus Daly's death, his Anaconda Mining Company acquired Clark's Butte holdings and then bought out Heinze's holdings. Suddenly, fractious and rambunctious Butte, and the many mining, logging, and industrial businesses it controlled in the region, were owned by a single, corporate entity. Fierce labor-management battles ensued, with lethal disputes and martial law being more the rule than the exception in 1910s Butte.

Mining went into decline during the Great Depression. Butte, Anaconda, and many other old mining centers are still searching for a stable economic base to replace the copper, silver, zinc, and lead of yesterday.

PRACTICALITIES

Information
Travel Montana, the state tourism bureau, provides good free information on events, sights, and lodgings. Southwestern Montana is contained in their **Gold West Country** region. Call (406) 846-1943 or (800) 879-1159 for details.

Getting There
Helena and Butte are both served by major airlines. **Greyhound** travels along I-90, linking Butte, Deer Lodge, and Anaconda to Seattle and Chicago. **Rimrock Trailways** runs the I-15 route, linking Helena and Dillon to Greyhound at Butte.

Driving can be hazardous in winter; call (406) 494-3666 for local **road conditions.**

BUTTE

Butte (pop. 34,051, elev. 5,755 feet) is at once unique and also Montana's most representative city. Touted as "the richest hill on earth," Butte was the nation's largest single source of silver in the late 19th century and the largest source of copper until the 1930s.

This early and extreme wealth gave Butte a singular history and destiny. The town's politicians utterly dominated Montana government for the first 50 years of statehood. It became the state's first industrialized city, and it was also the largest until the 1960s.

Montanans from other parts of the state have always been deeply ambivalent about Butte: its political infighting, religious rivalries, hot temper, and its wealth and self-importance created a statewide atmosphere of distrust. However, many of the things that now seem typically Montanan—the can-do swagger, spirited politics, the jocular and embracing sociality, its unspoken sense of neighborliness, even its food and drink (and the gusto and quantity in which they're con-

sumed)—reached a zenith in the early days of Butte.

The city's greatest resource was always its people, the swirling mix of Irish, Poles, Italians, Slavs, Chinese, and others who forged the cosmopolitan set of neighborhoods known as Butte. Billings now makes much of being Montana's largest city and enjoys likening itself to a youthful Denver. Early in the 1900s, though, Butte had nearly as large a population tucked into a steep swale on Silverbow Creek; with its bluster and ethnic diversity, Butte was more like Chicago than any other city in the West.

Butte is now the exoskeleton of a much larger city. Some of the charm and much of the history of the old city still remain: people still self-assuredly bustle, good food and drink are unquestionably an elemental part of daily life, and the old mansions and civic buildings that great wealth built still stand beside the ugly smokestacks, head frames, and piles of tailings.

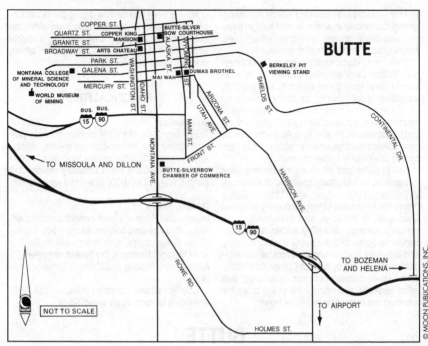

HISTORY

The Copper Kings

When the first placer miners arrived near Butte in 1864, they discovered pits dug with elk antlers: apparently Indians also knew of the area's gold deposits. But prospecting for gold requires water, and here, in this basin just under the crest of the Continental Divide, scarcely a stream runs. The gold camp drifted along until 1874, when the first silver claims were made. Abundant quartz in the Butte area contained an unparalleled richness in silver. The rush was on.

News of the silver strikes spread quickly, attracting miners and entrepreneurs from throughout the West. Two stand out. William Clark, a canny businessman, banker, and former miner from the Bannack gold-rush days, gained control of one of the richest mines. In 1876, Marcus Daly arrived in Butte from Colorado, sent by mining investors to scout out the mines of Butte. Both men controlled enough capital to develop the rich mineral deposits of Butte.

Silver isn't free-occurring, like gold. It must be milled out of the rock, usually quartz, in which it is suspended. This shift in method produced far-reaching changes in the Montana mining West. The gold camps inhabited by free-spirited prospectors quickly evolved into industrial towns dominated by the political and corporate interests of mine and smelter owners—and by organized labor.

Clark became the first of the mining kings of Butte by owning not only mines, but also the supply stores, transportation systems, real estate, banks, and processing plants necessary for the development of Butte.

Daly was the first industrialist to recognize the potential of the Butte copper deposits. He bought up the now-legendary Anaconda Mine and discovered veins of nearly pure copper 100 feet across; this mine alone produced more than 50 million pounds in 1887. Before anyone else realized the value of copper—copper for electric wire was only just becoming a worthwhile commodity—Daly had bought up the mines adjacent to the Anaconda. He built the city of the same name 26 miles west of Butte where he sent copper ore to be smelted.

Besides investment capital, the third component needed to make Butte boom was the railroad. The Utah and Northern reached Butte in 1881, suddenly linking Butte minerals with a world in the midst of industrialization and modernization.

A City of Immigrants

Mining on this scale demanded thousands of miners. Beginning in the 1880s, a vast influx of foreign miners flooded into Butte from eastern and northern Europe, from Italy and Ireland, and from Wales and Cornwall. By 1885, 22,000 people lived in Butte. These men and their families brought to Butte the dreams and enthusiasm of immigrants. Butte was opportunity, financial stability, and excitement.

The social and civic life of Butte was a wild tapestry fashioned from bits and pieces of each incorporated culture. Bars and restaurants were open 24 hours a day, as mines were worked day and night. Each ethnic group had its own neighborhood and customs. Greyhound coursing, Irish football, cockfights, opium dens and secret Chinese societies, fancy-dress balls, a noted opera house, gambling and prostitution, St. Patrick's Day and Balkan feasts combined with a dozen other celebrations and cultural traditions—all these mutated into a uniquely energetic way of life called Butte.

But there was also a dark side. Mining is dangerous work. Quite apart from the obvious risk of cave-ins, the dust and fumes in the mines con-

tributed to everything from respiratory diseases to cancer. Aboveground, air pollution was absolutely treacherous. In the 1890s, smoke and fumes so darkened the air that streetlights burned night and day. Vegetation ceased to grow; dogs and cats were found dead in the streets from ambient poisons.

The Birth of the Anaconda Company

The most noteworthy battles among the Copper Kings, especially Clark and Daly, were not fought over mining claims or wealth, but rather for prestige and politics. Daly connived to deny Clark a seat on the U.S. Senate; Clark won his battle to keep the state capital out of Daly's "company town" of Anaconda. Both men wielded enormous power in the state; each shamelessly manipulated the newborn state government to benefit mining in general, and, when possible, used the government to spite his arch rival's ambitions.

Augustus Heinze, the last of the Copper Kings, arrived in the late days of Butte's zenith. Basically a spoiler, in 1900 he manipulated mining laws and bought judges to press his claim to holdings already developed by Daly. The ploy ultimately made Heinze a wealthy man, but his antagonism forced investors in Daly's Amalgamated Copper Company to rethink and streamline their operations. Amalgamated Copper turned mean. It had already purchased Clark's mining empire; after buying Heinze's holdings, it had total control over Butte. With more benevolent figures like Daly dead and Clark removed from the scene, corpo-

Early mining in Butte wrought environmental havoc.

MONTANA HISTORICAL SOCIETY, HELENA

rate mining triumphed, and the swashbuckling days of Butte were over. Amalgamated Copper, also known as the Anaconda Company or simply "the Company," by 1903 practically ran the state from boardrooms in New York City.

Labor vs. Management

Butte labor was highly organized; the Butte Miners' Union was formed in 1878 and was Local No. 1 of the Western Federation of Miners. Daly and Clark were both tolerant of the unions, and Butte had never seen significant labor-management action.

But when the ownership of the mines moved out of state and became depersonalized, the stage was set for confrontation. Increased rancor characterized the relations of management and labor, but the real battles were fought within the rank and file. Divided between conservative, accommodationist members and more radical workers, some of whom organized for the "Wobblies," or the Industrial Workers of the World (IWW), the labor movement in Butte shattered completely. As conditions in the mines worsened and management demanded lower pay, the two union factions adamantly disagreed about what action to take. Violence broke out: in June 1914, the old Union Hall was bombed in Butte, two men were shot, and miner set upon miner.

Finally, in September, the governor was forced to declare martial law. Left-wing union leaders were tried and imprisoned, and the elected mayor and sheriff of Butte, both Socialists, were removed from office.

Of course, this was music to the corporate ears of the Anaconda Company, which chose this moment to break the back of the union: Anaconda disavowed both union elements and declared the Butte mines an open shop. Events flared up once more in 1917, when 164 miners died in an underground fire. Workers again organized, again with the help of the IWW. Anaconda refused to bargain with the miners, and Butte went out on strike. The Company sent in 200 detectives to infiltrate the movement. One night, masked men forced an IWW leader from his bed, dragged him behind a car to the outskirts of Butte, and hanged him.

The lynching threw Butte into pandemonium. Fearing a renewed shutdown of the mines, the U.S. government declared martial law and sent federal troops into the city. By branding the strikers as antiwar and seditious, the Company and its governmental allies again prevailed. Butte labor remained strongly, but not effectively, organized thereafter.

The Decline of Butte

During the Great Depression, the price of copper fell from 18 cents a pound in 1928 to five cents a pound in 1933. The decline of Butte had begun. The old veins were playing out and the ore was getting more costly to extract. Besides, the Anaconda Company had more cost-effective mining operations in South America.

In 1955 Anaconda opened the Berkeley Pit, an open-pit mine meant to revitalize Butte mineral production. However, surface-mining copper veins several thousand feet deep meant digging a vast hole underneath much of Butte, and some neighborhoods, notably the old Italian district of Meaderville and the vast Columbia Park, toppled into the pit. The Berkeley Pit in its turn reached obsolescence, and in 1983 the Anaconda Company closed its mines in the city of its birth.

Butte struggles on. Denny Washington, a Montana-born industrialist, bought the Anaconda Company properties in 1985 and has developed low-overhead, low-labor methods of extracting profits from the rich ore and rich heritage of Butte.

SIGHTS

For a quick introduction to the sights and history of Butte, take the **Old No. 1 Trolley Tour.** The hour-and-a-half tour leaves the chamber of commerce office, 1000 George St., tel. (406) 723-3177 or (800) 735-6814, daily at 10:30 a.m. and 1:30, 3:30, and 7 p.m., May through mid-Sept.; $5 per adult, $2.50 for children.

World Museum of Mining

Located west of Montana Tech at the end of W. Park St., tel. (406) 723-7211, the museum complex sits on an old mining claim called the Orphan Girl. Included on the grounds is a head frame, ore carts, a locomotive, and other hardware. The indoor museum contains mining tools, steam engines, ore samples, and a large number of old photos and memorabilia from Butte's boom years.

In the same complex is **Hell Roarin' Gulch,** a replica of a mining camp from 1900. A millinery shop, Chinese herb store, bank, church, school, post office, and other period buildings have been faithfully reconstructed. Open daily April 1 to October 31, 9 a.m.-6 p.m.; April to June and Labor Day to Thanksgiving, 10 a.m.-5 p.m.; closed during the winter; free admission.

Montana Tech

Montana College of Mineral Science and Technology, better known as Montana Tech, sits on a bench of Big Butte, the promontory just west of downtown. Established in 1900, the college teaches mineral science and other professional and technical curricula. The four-year institution currently has an enrollment of 1,800 students.

From the ramparts of the campus there are great views over the city to the Continental Divide; a statue of Marcus Daly shares the view from the university's entrance on Park Avenue. Visit the **Mineral Museum,** tel. (406) 496-4414, in Tech's Main Hall, where 1,300 mineral specimens, including a 27.4-ounce gold nugget found near Butte in 1989, are displayed. In a separate, darkened room is an interesting exhibit of fluorescent minerals.

Downtown

Butte's magnificent homes and commercial and civic buildings attest to its early wealth and importance. Increasingly, vacant buildings and boarded up windows are more the norm than the exception, as the downtown sadly slumps into a pre-ghost town torpor.

Much of downtown Butte is protected as a national landmark and many individual buildings are on the National Register of Historic Places; the chamber of commerce provides a brochure with a walking tour of historic buildings. The following are open to the public.

The **Copper King Mansion,** 219 W. Granite St., tel. (406) 782-7580, was built in 1888 by William Clark at a time when he was one of the world's richest men. This three-story brick High Victorian mansion contains 30 rooms, many with frescoed ceilings, carved staircases, inlaid floors, and Tiffany windows. Clark spent $300,000 on the building and imported many craftsmen from Europe. The third floor boasts a 60-foot-long ballroom and a chapel. The mansion is open for tours

daily 9 a.m.-4 p.m., from May 1 through September 30. $5 adults, $3.50 children, under six free.

Clark's son Charles was so taken by a chateau he visited in France that he procured the plans and had it reconstructed in Butte. Now known as the **Arts Chateau,** at 321 Broadway St., tel. (406) 723-7600, it serves as Butte's community arts center. Open Tues.-Sat. 10 a.m.-5 p.m. and Sunday noon-5 p.m., Memorial Day to Labor Day, and Tues.-Sat. 11 a.m.-4 p.m. the rest of the year. Admission is $3.75 adults, $1.25 children.

The showpiece of Butte civic architecture is the **Butte—Silver Bow Courthouse,** 155 W. Granite St., built in 1910. A lovely stained-glass dome tops the four-story rotunda, murals decorate the ceilings, and oak fixtures predominate throughout. Butte leaders spent almost twice as much on this courthouse as the state spent on the Montana Capitol.

Down on Mercury St., the **Dumas** building, 45 E. Mercury, tel. (406) 782-3808, was Butte's longest-lived brothel, in operation from 1890 until 1982. The two-story brick building still has quite a few architectural features that must be peculiar to a house of prostitution, such as windows onto the corridors, and "bedrooms" that the miners more appropriately called cribs. This structure is the only surviving remnant of Butte's once-thriving red-light district. The building has recently been bought by a New York foundation, the International Sex Worker Foundation for Art, Culture, and Education, a nonprofit that works for the rights of prostitutes. Plans are afoot to turn the place into a museum displaying the art of sex workers throughout the world. The Dumas is pretty uniquely Butte—be sure to check it out. Open for a free browse daily from 9:30 a.m.-5 p.m.; $2 tours are available as well.

Also unusual is **The Mai Wah,** tel. (406) 723-3177, a fledgling museum dedicated to telling the story of Chinese miners and workers who pioneered in Butte. The Mai Wah building contained a number of Chinese-owned business—Butte's China Alley, the heart of the old Chinatown, is adjacent. The museum is open Tues.-Thurs. 11 a.m.-3 p.m., but call ahead to confirm times.

Another gem of old Butte architecture is the **Mother Lode Theater,** 316 W Park Street. This magnificent theater has just been refurbished and will serve as Butte's performing arts center. While the theater is not open for regular tours, art events and organizations use the facility, so try to have a look. For scheduled events, call (406) 723-3602.

Our Lady of the Rockies

Overlooking Butte from the fastness of the Continental Divide is *Our Lady of the Rockies,* a 90-foot statue of the Virgin Mary. Completed in 1985, the monument was the result of six years of volunteer community work, including building the access road to the site, 8,510 feet above sea level. There is a viewing point at Continental Drive and Pine. Private vehicles are not allowed on the road up to the statue; you'll need to join a tour bus group (the buses leave from the Butte Plaza Mall, 3100 Harrison Ave.). Tours to the statue are arranged as interest allows; $10 adult, $9 seniors, $5 children. To schedule, call the Our Lady of the Rockies Foundation office, 434 N. Main St., tel. (406) 782-1221.

Berkeley Pit

Veering from the high to the low, there's the Berkeley Pit, the enormous open-pit copper mine just next to downtown Butte. Due to the high costs of hardrock underground mining, in 1955 Anaconda began stripping low-grade copper ore from the surface. Eventually, the Berkeley Pit reached a depth of 1,800 feet; the gulf from side to side is more than a mile across. Mining has ceased here and today the pit is filling with water—Montana's deepest body of water. It is also probably its most toxic water, percolating up as it does through abandoned mineshafts. The poisonous water is a threat to passing waterfowl. A flock of endangered trumpeter swans died in the lake one spring. If left undrained, it's only a matter of time before the rising water will enter the Butte water table, causing further havoc. A viewing stand allows you to look down into the Berkeley Pit and its eerily green water (from dissolved copper and mineral salts). Stand is open March-Nov., at 200 Shields St., tel. (406) 723-3177

Recreation

Stodden Park, at Sampson and Utah Streets, tel. (406) 494-3686, has a swimming pool, picnic grounds, tennis courts, and a nine-hole golf course.

Fourteen miles north of Butte on I-15 (at the Elk Park exit) is **Sheepshead Mountain Recreation Area.** This fishing and wildlife-viewing facility is completely accessible to wheelchairs. It's a stopover for migrating waterfowl, and moose and elk are frequently sighted.

Rock climbers need only look down I-90 to **Homestake Pass,** where the Boulder batholith's granite juts up from the freeway. Head 25 miles south on I-15, turn east at exit 99, and head to **Humbug Spires Wilderness Study Area** to climb the 600-foot granite outcroppings or to merely hike and gawk. **Pipestone Mountaineering,** 829 S. Montana St., tel. (406) 782-4994, has an indoor climbing wall, sells gear, and is a good place to get the inside scoop on local climbs.

ACCOMMODATIONS

B&Bs

Those interested in staying in a grand historic home should check out the **Copper King Mansion B&B,** 219 W. Granite St., tel. (406) 782-7580. In addition to a B&B, the Copper King Mansion—William A. Clark's private Xanadu, built in 1884—also serves as a museum, in fact, travelers stay in the rooms viewed by the public during museum hours. Access to the rooms is structured, so travelers should weigh potential disruptions against their need for seclusion before arranging a stay. Rooms are $55-95.

Butte's other B&B, the **Scott B&B,** 15 W. Copper, tel. (406) 723-7030, is from the other end of the Butte social spectrum. The building is an extensively renovated miners' boardinghouse from 1897. Each of the seven guest rooms has a private bath and phone. Rooms are $75-85.

Hotels and Motels

A number of Butte's inexpensive motels cluster around I-90 exit 127. The **Mile Hi Motel,** 3499 Harrison Ave., tel. (406) 494-2250, is a good deal with pleasant rooms at $31 s, $44 d. There's an outdoor pool, and pets are okay. The **Super 8,** 2929 Harrison Ave., tel. (406) 494-6000 or (800) 800-8000, has rooms at $51 s, $60 d. Pets okay with permission; free continental breakfast; guest laundry. **Butte Comfort Inn,** 2777 Harrison Ave., tel. (406) 494-8850 or (800) 442-4667, $63 s, $68 d, is one of Butte's largest hotels. There's a hot tub, fitness room, generous continental breakfast, and pets are okay.

The **War Bonnet Inn,** 2100 Cornell Ave., tel. (406) 494-7800 or (800) 443-1806, with rooms at $79 s, $89 d, has an indoor pool and hot tub, exercise room, and restaurant and lounge. **Best Western Butte Plaza Inn** 2900 Harrison Ave., tel. (406) 494-3500 or (800) 543-5814, $69 s, $79 d, offers an indoor pool, exercise room, sauna, steam room, and hot tub. The hotel is near shopping, and there's a complimentary breakfast buffet daily.

At the **Ramada Copper King Inn,** 4655 Harrison Ave., tel. (406) 494-6666 or (800) 332-8600. For $77 s, $87 d, you'll get an indoor pool, sauna, hot tub, indoor tennis courts, exercise room, guest laundry, and restaurant and lounge. The Copper King serves as a conference center; pets are okay.

If you'd rather stay in the historic center of Butte, there are a couple pleasant older motels to serve you. **Capri Motel,** 220 N. Wyoming, tel. (406) 723-4391 or (800) 342-2774, has rooms at $40 s, $50 d. The **Finlen Hotel & Motor Inn,** 100 E. Broadway, tel. (406) 723-5461 or (800) 729-5461, $36 s, $40 d, was once Butte's landmark downtown hotel; now only the motor court is open for lodging. Very central for exploring Butte's nooks and crannies.

If you don't mind staying a few miles out of town, consider making **Fairmont Hot Springs** (see below) your base.

Camping

The **Butte KOA** is off I-90's exit 126, two blocks north, tel. (406) 782-0063.

FOOD

Only in Butte could one even begin to make the argument that there is a historic Montana cuisine. Its large ethnic population and its intense urban character gave restaurants a prominence and an enthusiastic clientele that was unusual in

---

THE BUTTE PASTY

O ne of Butte's enduring gastronomic standbys is the pasty (PAST-ee), a meat pie native to Wales and Cornwall. Early miners brought the pasty with them from their Celtic homelands. Here, as there, the savory and resilient pasty made a convenient lunch down in the mine. Pasties are still common in Butte, where they remain a popular alternative to their cousin the hamburger. And, believe it or not, natives really do argue about who makes the best pasty in Butte.

Joe's Pasty Shop, 1641 Grand Ave., tel. (406) 723-9071, bakes highly touted examples of pasty art. On Saturday, the **Butte Hill Bakery,** 7 S. Montana Ave., tel. (406) 723-4828, makes pasties from additive-free ingredients.

However, you needn't call Montana for takeout to enjoy pasties at home. The following recipe is as old as the proverbial richest hill on earth, compliments of Butte.

Dough
1¹/₂ c. white flour
¹/₂ t. baking powder
¹/₄ t. salt
¹/₄ c. butter or shortening
¹/₄ c. cold water

Mix dry ingredients, and cut in butter or shortening with a pastry knife. Add water gradually and stir until a ball of dough is formed. Knead lightly for 10-20 seconds.

Filling
¹/₂ lb. steak, diced into small cubes
1 medium onion, chopped finely
1 small turnip, chopped finely
1 medium potato, diced
2 T. butter

Mix the steak and vegetables. Divide the dough in two, and roll into a circle about the size of a pie pan. Place one-half of the meat mixture on half of the dough circle to within one inch of the edge. Sprinkle the meat with salt and pepper, and put 1 tablespoon of butter on the meat. Enclose the meat by folding over the other half of the dough circle. Seal edges with fork tines. Repeat with remaining ingredients.

Place the pasties on a baking sheet and slit a small hole in the top. Bake at 400° for 45 minutes, occasionally pouring a teaspoon of water in the slit to keep the meat moist. Reduce heat to 350° and bake for another 15 minutes. Serve warm with lots of gravy.

Makes two pasties.

frontier Montana. Butte specialties include the pasty (pronounced "PAST-ee"), brought over from Cornwall, and the pork-chop sandwich. Meals in Butte were traditionally served in courses; the price of dinner included a relish tray, breadsticks, soup and salads, a pasta course, the entree, and dessert. This evening's worth of food and service is called eating "Old Meaderville" style, for the Meaderville Italian neighborhood that collapsed into the Berkeley Pit, fine restaurants and all.

One of the best restaurants in Montana is the **Uptown Cafe,** 47 E. Broadway St., tel. (406) 723-4735, where the best of Butte tradition meets lively up-to-the-minute sauces and ingredients. The wine list is intriguing, the ambience light and friendly, and the fare—with lots of fresh seafood, veal, and pasta on the menu, and a nice selection of homemade desserts as well—superb. Open for lunch buffet weekdays 11 a.m.-2 p.m., Tues.-Sat. 5-10 p.m. for dinner. Most meals range between $17 and $20.

Montana's most famous restaurant is **Lydia's,** 5 Mile, Harrison Ave., tel. (406) 494-2000. Italian food, old-fashioned but highly creditable, is served in an atmosphere of slightly dated chic. Open nightly 5:30-11:30 p.m.

Butte also has good Mexican food. **Cafe La Cosina,** 625 E. Front St., tel. (406) 723-9008, isn't anybody's idea of fancy, but the food is spicy and well prepared; open 11 a.m.-8:30 p.m., Sunday 4-8:30 p.m. **Metal's Bank Grill & Bayern Brewery,** downtown at Park and Main, tel. (406) 723-6160, serves its own beers and ales, as well as a full menu featuring steaks, pasta, and southwestern dishes.

Don't count Butte out for steaks. At the **Lamplighter,** 1800 Meadowlark Ave., tel. (406) 494-9910, open nightly 5-10 p.m., you can have Yorkshire pudding with your prime rib.

For something uniquely Butte, try **Pork Chop John's,** at 8 Mercury St., tel. (406) 782-0812 (downtown), or 2400 Harrison Ave., tel. (406) 782-1783 (on the strip), open 10:30 a.m.-10:45 p.m. The boneless pork-chop sandwich is a Butte original; as you savor it, think of all the hungry miners who also gained satisfaction here. **Nancy's Pasty Shop,** 2810 Pine, tel. (406) 782-7410, can give you a taste of Butte's other culinary gem. **Joe's Pasty Shop,** 1641 Grand, tel. (406) 723-9071, is another favorite for

pasties. For a more traditional bakery, try **European Breads & Pastries,** 127 N Main, tel. (406) 782-5536; closed weekends. And, to start the morning in Butte, hop over to **Java John's,** at 113 Hamilton, tel. (406) 783-7555 for espresso, then swing uptown to the **Butte Hill Bakery,** 7 S. Montana, tel. (406) 723-4828 for bagels or bread.

ENTERTAINMENT

Nightlife

Within a state that already has a rowdy reputation, Butte bears the sybaritic crown; in the Butte equation, bars are elemental. Remember that, in Montana, you don't have to drink alcohol to go out to bars; bars are What You Do. The **M & M** is probably the most famous bar in the state; the mix of gambling, a 24-hour cafe, and a clientele of hardened bar-goers makes this institution one of Butte's most authentic assets. A night out on the town in Butte should also include the **New Deal Bar,** 333 S. Arizona, the **Silver Dollar,** 133 S. Main St., **Irish Times Pub,** Galena and Main, and **Maloney's,** 112 N. Main Street.

Spectator Sports

Butte's minor league baseball team, the **Copper Kings,** a farm team for the Texas Rangers, plays on the Montana Tech campus. Call (406) 723-8206 for schedule and ticket information.

Watch a speed skating race at Butte's **High Altitude Sports Center,** tel. (406) 723-8005, a training center for Olympic athletes.

EVENTS

Butte's biggest annual event is St. Patrick's Day, when uptown is decked out with shamrocks, and a big parade turns the streets into a sea of green. Of course, the parade route heads pretty much straight through the bar doors, or into any of the many restaurants serving special corned beef and cabbage.

The Fourth of July is celebrated in a similarly heady fashion, and there's always a good fireworks display.

Less steeped in tradition, but becoming very popular, is the Winternational Sports Festival, a multisport event that happens every weekend of February, March, and April. Athletes come from across the Northwest to compete in downhill and cross-country skiing, swimming, raquetball, and speed skating. Call (406) 494-5595 or (800) 735-6814 for information on becoming a participant or a spectator.

INFORMATION AND SERVICES

The **Butte–Silver Bow Chamber of Commerce** is at 1000 George St., Butte, MT 59701, tel. (406) 494-5595 or (800) 735-6814.

St. James Hospital is at 400 S. Clark St., tel. (406) 782-8361. **Emergency** is 911.

The main **post office** is at 701 Dewey, tel. (406) 494-2107. The **library** is at 106 W. Broadway St., tel. (406) 723-8262. The **Butte Standard**

is the local daily paper. Montana Public Radio is at 99.3 FM.

The **Suds and Fun Laundromat** is open 24 hours a day at Dewey and Harrison, tel. (406) 494-7004.

TRANSPORTATION

Butte is served by **Horizon, Northwest,** and **Sky West** airlines.

Also at the airport, south off Harrison Ave., are **Avis,** tel. (406) 494-3131, and **Budget,** tel. (406) 494-7573, car rental agencies.

Greyhound and **Rimrock Trailways** bus lines link Butte to other Montana cities. The bus station is at 105 W. Broadway St., tel. (406) 723-3287. For a cab, call **City Taxi,** tel. (406) 723-6511.

THE UPPER CLARK FORK RIVER VALLEY

Silver Bow Creek drains the Butte Basin before charging almost 1,000 feet down a narrow channel to the wide valley below. Here the creek is renamed the Clark Fork River, and it begins to pick up the many tributaries that will eventually make it one of the most important arms of the mighty Columbia.

Early settlers knew this as the Deer Lodge Valley. The state's first ranches grew up when some miners recognized that a quicker and more dependable profit could be made selling agricultural products to the booming mining towns.

Today, this open stretch of the Clark Fork River Valley is the stepping-off point for hikes in the rugged Flint Creek Range. Fishing in the newly vivified Clark Fork River is both popular and possible; in the recent past it was neither. Deer Lodge boasts of being the second-oldest town in the state. Certainly its old prison and ranch museum deserve a visit.

FAIRMONT HOT SPRINGS

This old hot springs spa, just off I-90 halfway between Butte and Anaconda, went through a major facelift to become one of the best-appointed family resorts and conference hotels in Montana. The hot springs here fill four pools. Two of them (one

indoors, one out) are Olympic-sized and heated to 90-100° F; the others run 100-105° F and are meant for soaking weary muscles. The public can swim and soak the day away for $6.50, $3.75 for children 11 and under. There's a separate charge to use the 350-foot-long warm-water waterslide; even for resort guests it costs $8 for a full day pass, $5.50 for a half day, and $1 for a single slide. (A combined pool and slide pass costs $12 adults, $9 kids.)

There are enough other activities to keep a guest plenty busy between dips in the pool. A challenging and well-designed 18-hole golf course is a very big draw (the fifth hole is the state's longest); tennis courts, mountain bike rentals, a fitness room, horseback riding, a petting zoo, and hay- or sleighrides (depending on the season) round out the activities.

Fairmont makes the most of its proximity to hiking and riding in the Deerlodge National Forest and Anaconda-Pintler Wilderness Area, fishing and water sports at Georgetown Lake and skiing at Discovery Basin. Cross-country skiers love Fairmont; after a day skiing the trails around nearby Mount Haggin a good hot soak takes the ache out of tired muscles.

If soaking doesn't do the trick, two massage therapists work at the resort. Call (406) 797-3241, ext. 144, to schedule a Swedish, salt-glow, or shiatsu massage, or inquire at the resort's front desk.

At Fairmont, a full range of rooming options includes suites and kitchenettes; double rooms start at $99-109, dropping to $89 from October to mid-May. The food's good, considering the variety of clientele they have to please. There's dancing and drinks in the lounge.

Some resorts with Fairmont's amenities and potential would discourage kids. Not here. This is a great place to take active children. There are enough supervised activities here that harried parents might even be able to have some time to themselves.

Contact Fairmont Hot Springs at 1500 Fairmont Rd., Anaconda, MT 59711, tel. (406) 797-3241 or (800) 332-3272.

DEER LODGE

Named for a salt lick popular with deer during frontier days, Deer Lodge is the center of a vast valley full of history and recreation.

History
The Mullan Road, a northern version of the Oregon Trail that ran between Fort Benton and Walla Walla from the 1860s to the 1880s, dropped into the Clark Fork Valley near Deer Lodge. The valley, with its abundant water and forage, was popular with pioneers who had just traversed the prairies and Continental Divide.

With as much prescience as savvy, Canadian trader Richard Grant and his sons Johnny and James began trading cattle in the 1850s along the Oregon Trail in Idaho. With cattle fattened on western Montana grasses, the Grants would trade westbound pioneers one fat, healthy cow for two emaciated specimens that had just crossed the plains. It didn't take long for the Grants to amass a huge holding of cattle. In 1862 Johnny Grant established a base ranch in the Deer Lodge Valley, Montana's first. When the gold rush began in the 1860s, cattlemen like the Grants were already in place to sell beef to hungry miners.

When the first influx of prospectors swooped into Bannack in 1862, some disenchanted souls decided to explore the new territory for other options. Among them was a German named Conrad Kohrs. After a stint as Bannack's butcher, he put together his own cattle herd and went

off to Deer Lodge Valley. He bought Johnny Grant's ranch and never looked back. Building on Grant's base, Kohrs was the foremost rancher in Montana for almost 40 years.

The valley was as kind to other farmers and ranchers. Deer Lodge's ornate Victorian homes are witness to the prosperity and aspirations of these early settlers. The fact that early legislatures established the State Home for the Insane in Warm Springs, the State Tuberculosis Sanitarium in Galen, and the State Penitentiary in Deer Lodge is indicative of the valley's political clout.

While the valley prospered due to the proximity to Butte and Anaconda markets, the pollution of these two industrial centers was at odds with the farms and ranches. The WPA's 1939 *Montana, A State Guide Book* described the waters of Silver Bow Creek just above present-day Fairmont Hot Springs as "muddied with the refuse of Butte mines, though in places it is intensely blue from dissolved copper salts." The Clark Fork was unable to support aquatic life until the 1960s, after 10 years of cleanup. In 1903, after cattle began dying in fields from poisoned air, the smelter at Anaconda raised its smokestack 300 feet in order to disseminate its smoke higher in the atmosphere.

Between stricter mining regulations and the decline of mining in general, the valley has returned to a degree of its former integrity. A portion of the Clark Fork by Warm Springs offers such great fishing that it is now regulated by the Dept. of Fish, Wildlife, and Parks.

Old Montana Prison Complex
The Old Montana Prison, 1106 Main St., is the core of a series of contiguous historical exhibits. Montana Territory first established a penitentiary in Deer Lodge in 1871, but the disturbingly attractive buildings now open to the public were begun in the 1890s. The castellated, three-story cell block of red brick was built in 1912. It contains 200 cells, each six feet by seven feet. W.A. Clark financed the construction of the prison theater in 1919. The oldest structure is the quarried sandstone guard wall, 24 feet high and buried four feet below ground, built in 1893.

All these structures, and others, were built by forced convict labor, a practice later outlawed. After a violent prison riot and investigation into the deteriorating conditions at the old prison, a new facility was built in 1979.

Most of the facility is open for self-guided tours. Check out the gun ports in the shower room, the "galloping gallows" for off-premises executions, and maximum-security's Black Box.

The **Montana Law Enforcement Museum** is located in the prison. Here is a memorial to officers slain in the line of duty, as well as curiosities such as Lee Harvey Oswald's handcuffs.

Resist the reaction to find all this really creepy, and do visit the old prison. On the one hand, the perfectly preserved quarters and facilities tell a grim story of prison life in the recent past. But, almost eerily, the handsome architecture and pleasing symmetry of the row upon row of empty cells give the prison a forlorn but intense beauty.

Also in the prison complex is the **Towe Ford Collection,** the world's second-largest antique Ford automobile collection. Edward Towe began his hobby in 1953 with the acquisition of a 1923 Ford Model-T Runabout; the collection now comprises over 100 automobiles. Some of the standout cars: the 1931 A-400 convertible sedan, a 1955 Thunderbird, and Henry Ford's personal "camper," a modified 1922 Lincoln that served as a picnic basket on wheels when Henry Ford went for weekend getaways.

From Labor Day to Memorial Day the prison complex is open daily 8 a.m.-9 p.m. During April, May, September, and October, it's open daily 8:30 a.m.-5:30 p.m.; during the winter it's open Mon.-Fri. 9 a.m.-4 p.m., Saturday and Sunday 10 a.m.-5 p.m. Tickets are $7.95 adults, $4 children; call (406) 846-3111 for details.

Other Museums

Across the street is the **Powell County Museum,** 1193 Main St., tel. (406) 846-3294. It contains dinosaur bones, Indian tools, mining equipment, cowboy gear, and other relics of Powell County's rich history. Nearby is **Yesterday's Playthings,** 1017 Main St., tel. (406) 846-1480, a doll and toy museum. The collection features 1,000 antique dolls from the private collection of Genevieve Hostetter. Deer Lodge's newest museum, the **Frontier Montana Museum,** 1153 Main St., tel. (406) 846-0026, displays Western memorabilia, with a particular focus on saloon memorabilia. Your ticket to the Old Montana Prison includes admission to all the above museums as well.

THE GRANT-KOHRS RANCH NATIONAL HISTORIC SITE

The Grant-Kohrs Ranch, the home and outbuildings of Montana's first ranch, provides a fascinating glimpse into the real life of cowboys and ranchers in the early days of Montana.

Johnny Grant's 1862 log home was considered the finest house in the territory. Conrad Kohrs bought Grant's operation in 1866 and began a series of improvements. To the back of the old house, Kohrs attached a brick addition for a formal dining room, a large kitchen, and second-story bedrooms. The barns and stables were extensive; by the 1880s, Kohrs was grazing cattle on over a million acres of open-range prairie and meadow across four states and southern Canada. Even after the disastrous winter of 1886, Kohrs was able to ship 8,000-10,000 cattle a year to eastern markets.

Kohrs reduced the size of the ranch in the 1910s, but the Deer Lodge holdings stayed in the family until 1972, when the National Park Service bought the ranch to preserve it as a historic monument. The old 23-room ranch house is wonderfully intact, a delightful mix of Victoriana and frontier living. Kohrs's wife Augusta acquired an impressive array of valuable furniture (especially impressive in light of the fact that much of it came to Montana by steamboat and then overland to the Deer Lodge Valley).

The outbuildings contain old tools, horse-drawn conveyances, and period equipment. The old bunkhouse was in many ways the center of the ranch; here, the hired men ate, played cards, and slept while in camp. Their spare rooms and modest environs contrast vividly with life in the Big House.

Find the ranch just north of Deer Lodge on Main St. It's open 9 a.m.-5:30 p.m. daily June 1 to Labor Day, 9 a.m.-4:30 p.m. the rest of the year. Admission is $4 in summer; free from mid-September to May 1. Contact the Grant-Kohrs Ranch Office for more information, 316 Main St., Deer Lodge, MT 59722, tel. (406) 846-3388. The house is open for guided tours only, and no more than 12 people may tour at once, and admission is on a first-come, first-served basis. Apply at the ticket office.

Historic Downtown

Deer Lodge was home to a number of early ranchers and settlers whose fine period houses attest to their wealth and ambition; the city's commercial and civic buildings reflect a shared economic self-assuredness. The state's first college buildings, built in 1878, are now used by the local school district.

At the Courthouse Square stand the Powell County Courthouse, a statue and fountain commemorating John Mullan and pioneers who came west along the Mullan Road, and a Milwaukee Road engine originally built to sell to the Soviet Union. There is an abundance of lovely old homes, including the girlhood home of Jeanette Kelly, the original "Betty Crocker."

Recreation

The Flint Creek Mountains rise directly west of Deer Lodge. These jagged peaks harbor many high mountain lakes linked with good hiking trails; these are also good trails to explore on mountain bikes. From the **Racetrack** Forest Service Campground, a rough road continues eight miles to Indian Meadows trailhead. Here, a series of alpine lakes reposes beneath the 9,000-foot Twin Peaks. The lakes are high enough to be undependable as fisheries. To reach Racetrack, turn west at Warm Springs and continue 10 miles on a good road.

Hikes to other high mountain lakes begin at Tin Cup Lake, eight miles west of Deer Lodge, off Montana State Prison Rd.; and west of Rock Creek Lake, about 15 miles northwest of Deer Lodge on Forest Service Rd. 168. Consult the Deerlodge National Forest Map and the ranger station, 91 N. Frontage Rd., tel. (406) 846-1170.

The city **swimming pool** is at 703 5th Street. **Deer Lodge Golf Club,** tel. (406) 846-1625, welcomes visitors to its nine-hole course just west of town.

Accommodations

Scharf's Motor Inn, near the old prison at 819 Main St., tel. (406) 846-2810 or (800) 341-8000, $35 s, $45 d, has a restaurant, a guest laundry, and allows pets. The **Western Big Sky Inn,** 210 Main St., tel. (406) 846-2590, $45 s, $59 d, has a pool and is convenient to the Grant-Kohrs Ranch. The **Downtowner Motel,** 506 4th St., tel. (406) 846-1021, $32 d, is a quiet block off Main Street. The **Super 8,** 1150 Main St., tel.

(406) 846-2370 or (800) 800-8000, $49 s, $58 d, offers a pool and lies right off I-90. The Deer Lodge **KOA Campground,** tel. (406) 846-1629, is at 413 Park.

Food

For the best steaks in this old ranching town, go to the **Broken Arrow Steak House,** 317 Main St., tel. (406) 846-3400. For family dining try **Scharf's,** 819 Main St., tel. (406) 846-3300; open for three meals a day, it's next door to their motel. The **Old West Bakery,** 321 Main St., tel. (406) 846-2142, offers its version of Butte's pasty in beef or chicken. The **Nickelodeon Cafe,** 502 Main St., tel. (406) 846-3026, combines light meals with ice-cream fountain favorites. As ever, the redoubtable **4-Bs,** 130 Sam Beck Rd., tel. (406) 846-2620, serves good family meals 24 hours.

Information and Services

The Deer Lodge **Chamber of Commerce** is at 1171 Main St., Deer Lodge, MT 59722, tel. (406) 846-2094. The **post office** is at 510 Main St., tel. (406) 846-1882.

The **Powell County Memorial Hospital** is at 1101 Texas St., tel. (406) 846-2212. **Emergency** is 911.

Contact the Deer Lodge **Ranger Station** at 91 N. Frontage Rd., tel. (406) 846-1170.

DRUMMOND

Between Deer Lodge and Drummond, the Clark Fork River is squeezed by the Flint Creek Mountains and the Garnet Range into an increasingly narrow valley. Mining makes a reprise here; at Garrison, phosphate is mined for fertilizer, and near Gold Creek, Granville Stuart made the first gold strike in the state.

History

Settlers during the 1860s rode steamboats to Fort Benton and then continued west to the Columbia on the Mullan Road, a rough trail scouted out by the Army. When gold was discovered in this part of Montana, some travelers were beguiled by the specter of quick wealth and stayed to stake a claim. The Mullan Road wound down the Clark Fork along this valley.

Montana's gold rush began here. In 1860, James and Granville Stuart were panning in

Gold Creek when their pans showed color. Word of the gold strike brought in a flood of prospectors from the spent gold rushes in other parts of the West. Gold Creek was never a rich producer compared with some of the astonishingly fecund diggings elsewhere in Montana, and only a few temporary shacks ever occupied this gold camp. Years later, however, better technology allowed developers to extract the remaining gold with dredges—as the mounds of tailings attest.

Gold Creek had its second day of fame when the Northern Pacific Railroad, built west from Chicago and east from Portland, met here in 1883. Northern Pacific president Henry Villard was present to drive the last spike linking the nation's second transcontinental railroad.

Another note of railroad marginalia: west of Drummond, between mileposts 133 and 132 on the west side of I-5, is the disintegrating shell of a Milwaukee Road electric generating sta-

tion. These stations were built when the Milwaukee introduced electric trains between Harlowton, Montana, and Avery, Idaho. In the 1910s, this was the longest stretch of electric railway in the nation.

Accommodations and Food

The **Drummond Motel,** 170 W. Front, tel. (406) 288-3272, $32 s, $38 d, has large, clean rooms, some with kitchenettes. The **Sky Motel,** east on Main St., tel. (406) 288-3206 or (800) 559-3206, $32 s, $40 d, offers rooms in recently remodeled cabins and has a swimming pool. The **Wagon Wheel Motel and Cafe,** at Front and C Streets, tel. (406) 288-3201 features comfortable rooms ($30 s, $38 d) and good home cooking. All take pets.

The **D-M Cafe,** 112 W. Front, tel. (406) 288-9909, serves three meals a day of hearty food designed to satisfy hardworking ranch hands.

PINTLER SCENIC ROUTE

Montana Hwy. 1 leaves the Clark Fork Valley at Anaconda to wind through high mountain valleys, past ghost towns and old mining centers. The highway plunges down to join the Clark Fork and I-90 at Drummond. This alternative to the freeway doesn't involve any extra mileage, but it does lead to plentiful scenic and historic sites.

Anaconda is the town that Marcus Daly built. As the smelter for Butte's enormous reserves of copper and zinc, Anaconda became a powerful city, very nearly edging out Helena as capital of Montana.

Philipsburg is a convivial old silver town with a wealth of century-old storefronts, private homes, and civic structures. Located in a steep draw beneath craggy peaks, "P-Burg," as Montanans call it, is one of the most picturesque towns in the state.

Recreation ranges from skiing at one of Montana's best ski areas to lake fishing at 5,500 feet, to sapphire hunting and exploring the ghosts of the mining towns that didn't quite make it.

phire Mountains to the west once were sedimentary deposits in present-day Idaho. Great domes of magma bulged up beneath them, forcing these old layers up to great, but unstable, heights. As the underground swellings of magma grew even higher, huge blocks of the rock detached and skidded eastward on seams of molten rock.

The Sapphires came to rest in Montana, leaving the deep Bitterroot Valley in their wake. The land lying in front of the bulldozing Sapphire block became intensely folded and warped, eventually rising up to become the rugged Flint Creek Range.

The magma that lubricated the east-thrusting Sapphire Range apparently oozed out onto the newly formed Flint Creek Range, coating the crumpled landscape with lakes of mineral-rich granite. The silver deposits that sponsored such mining camps as Philipsburg and Granite were mined out of this formation, called the Philipsburg Batholith.

THE LAND

For most of its distance, Hwy. 1 travels along Flint Creek. Its high north-issuing valley is flanked by two very different but related types of mountain ranges. The low, undramatic ridges of the Sap-

ANACONDA AND VICINITY

To the industrialists who built Butte, its incredible mineral wealth was only half the equation. A *lot* of water was needed to refine the ore. Butte, in an arid basin near the Continental Divide, had

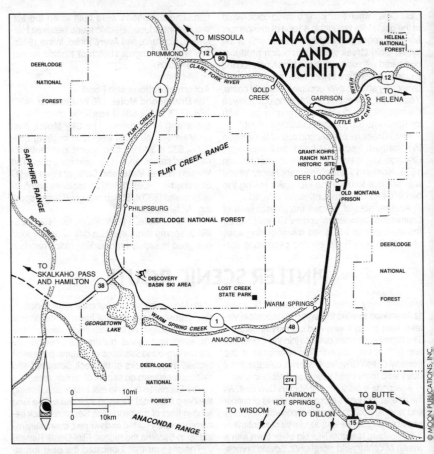

ANACONDA
AND
VICINITY

© MOON PUBLICATIONS, INC.

scarcely enough water for prospectors to successfully pan for gold.

Copper King Marcus Daly decided that, rather than bring the water to the ore, he'd take the ore to a better water source. He went to the Warm Springs Creek Valley, 26 miles west of Butte, to establish a smelter. Daly platted the town in 1883 and named it "Copperopolis." As unlikely as it now seems, Montana already had a settlement with that consonant-rich appellation, and the new town was renamed Anaconda (pop. 10,093, elev. 5,331 feet) for Daly's mine in Butte.

The **Washoe Smelter,** towering on a hill above Anaconda, became the largest copper

smelter in the world. Daly established the Butte, Anaconda, and Pacific Railroad solely to transport the ore from his Butte mines to the Washoe. The smelter could process 1,000 tons of ore an hour; it employed about 3,500 workers. The immense smokestack that rose above Anaconda became a landmark; 585 feet high, nearly seven million bricks were used in its construction.

Anaconda was a classic "company town." Daly was inordinately proud of the town that he founded, and he graced it with fine civic buildings. When Montana became a state in 1889, Daly mounted a huge campaign to name Anaconda the new capital. He immediately clashed with W.A. Clark, who favored retaining Helena, the territorial capital. A classic Copper King feud ensued. Daly spent $2.5 million promoting Anaconda and disdaining Helena and Clark. Clark painted a picture of Anaconda as a grimly obedient company town, and minted copper dollars as exemplars. In 1894, Helena won out, but by fewer than 2,000 votes.

Anaconda was inexorably tied to the fate of Butte. When Butte stumbled, Anaconda also faltered. After years of failing business, the ARCO, which had purchased Anaconda in the late '70s, closed the Washoe Smelter in 1983.

Sights

Anaconda has preserved its historic town center. Stop by the chamber of commerce, 306 E. Park, for a map of historic buildings. One of the most imposing buildings is the old **City Hall,** 401 E. Commercial, tel. (406) 563-2242. Built in 1895, it is made of local materials: pressed brick, Anaconda granite, and copper trim. City and county offices are now housed in the courthouse, along with the historical society and **Copper Village Museum and Art Center.** The **Deer Lodge County Courthouse,** at the south end of Main St., tel. (406) 563-8421, dominates the town. Built in 1898, it features a rotunda, a copper-clad cupola, curving staircases, and a dumbwaiter to convey books from floor to floor.

An art-deco extravaganza, the **Washoe Theatre** at 305 Main St. is one of Anaconda's most stellar showcases. The hammered metal-leaf decorations are almost overwhelming. The imposing **Hearst Free Library,** 401 Main St., was an 1898 gift to Anaconda from William Randolph Hearst's mother, Phoebe.

Catch the 1936 **White bus** at the chamber of commerce, 306 E. Park, tel. (406) 563-2400, for an hourlong tour of Anaconda, $3 adults, $1.50 children. Tours run twice daily Memorial Day to Labor Day, Mon.-Saturday.

Recreation

The biggest thing to hit Anaconda since the smelter is the new Jack Nicklaus-designed **Old Works Golf Course.** The course, built by ARCO on a huge Superfund site, incorporates many historic features of the erstwhile Old Works Smelting Site, including black slag left over from mining, resulting in a strikingly attractive black and green course. This is a long, tough course—seven

miles from start to finish, with some exceptional holes. For tee times, call (406) 563-5989.

Georgetown Lake, 15 miles west of Anaconda on Hwy. 1, provides fabled fishing and water sports access, with plenty of campgrounds (see below). Closer to Anaconda and less crowded with locals are a couple of wildlife-viewing areas. **Lost Creek State Park,** six miles off Hwy. 48, two miles east of Anaconda, is a campground in a narrow limestone canyon. A waterfall, interesting geology, and mountain goat and bighorn sheep make this a nice alternative to urban RV sites.

Mount Haggin Wildlife Management Area offers stunning views onto local mountains and also the chance to see bashful moose and elk. Mount Haggin is popular with cross-country skiers in winter and mountain bikers in summer. To reach Mount Haggin, follow Hwy. 274 14 miles south from Anaconda; watch for the sign for **Mule Ranch Vista.** With 54,137 acres under protection, Mount Haggin is the state's largest wildlife-management area.

Pintler Sled Adventures offers dogsled trips around the Anaconda area. Both hourly and daily rates are available—it's $15 for an hourlong ride, $60 for a full day. For reservations and information call (406) 563-2675 or the Fairmont Hot Springs Resort, tel. (406) 797-3241.

Accommodations

Right downtown is the **Marcus Daly Motel,** 119 W. Park, tel. (406) 563-3411 or (800) 535-6528 in Montana, $38 s, $48 d; it's both comfortable and convenient. Special rates, including a ski package at Discovery Basin Ski Area, are available. The **Vagabond Lodge Motel,** 1421 E. Park, tel. (406) 563-5251 or (800) 231-2660, $48 s, $58 d, is an attractive brick inn across from the city park and within walking distance of the new golf course. The **Trade Wind Motel,** 1600 E. Commercial, tel. (406) 563-3428, $25 s, $32 d, offers kitchenettes, continental breakfast, and a pool and hot tub.

Big Sky RV Park, 200 N. Locust, tel. (406) 563-2967, has fishing access on Warm Springs Creek and is near public parks.

Food

Like a lesser Butte, Anaconda has a reputation for good food and entertainment. **Barclay II Supper Club,** 1300 E. Commercial, tel. (406) 563-5541, is Anaconda's most stylish restaurant, serving large

Italian-influenced meals in many courses; open 5-10 p.m. Another place that's popular with the locals is **Jim & Clara's Supper Club,** 509 E. Park, tel. (406) 563-9963. The **Haufbrau,** 111 Hwy. 1 W, tel. (406) 563-9982, is a good family restaurant with pizza as a specialty.

Information and Services
The **Anaconda Chamber of Commerce** is at 306 E. Park, Anaconda, MT 59711, tel. (406) 563-2400.

The **Community Hospital of Anaconda** is at 401 W. Pennsylvania, tel. (406) 563-5261. **Emergency** is 911.

The **post office** is at 218 Main St., tel. (406) 563-2241.

GEORGETOWN LAKE

Georgetown Lake, at the upper reaches of Flint Creek, is one of the state's oldest hydroelectric projects. The lake is incredibly popular with the locals, and good restaurants and recreation areas ring the shoreline. In winter, the lake is renowned for ice fishing.

Flint Creek was first dammed in 1885 and was further developed in 1891 when the silver mines in Philipsburg demanded a source for electric power. In the 1890s, Marcus Daly's Butte, Anaconda, and Pacific Railroad ran weekend trains to the lake for the workers in Butte and Anaconda. A steamboat plied the lake, offering excursion trips.

Today, boating, windsurfing, and fishing are the preferred pastimes at Georgetown Lake, although many people simply go there to "weekend" at their cabins.

Discovery Basin Ski Area
Located 20 miles west of Anaconda in the Flint Creek Range, Discovery Basin offers a vertical drop of 2,700 feet along 40 runs. Full rental facilities are available, as well as food and beverage services at the ski lodge. A lift ticket costs $22 for adults ($17 for a half-day pass), $11 for children 12 and under and seniors. Discovery is known both for its ski school and for its lack of crowds. There's no lodging at the ski area, but Fairmont Hot Springs Resort offers package deals with Discovery. For more information contact Discovery Basin, P.O. Box 221, Anaconda, MT 59711, tel. (406) 563-2184 or (800) 332-3272.

Accommodations and Food
The following hotel/restaurant combinations offer good food, plus access to the lake and nearby Discovery Basin skiing. **Georgetown Lake Lodge,** Denton's Point Rd., tel. (406) 563-7020, $44 d, is the area's most evolved accommodation; there's also an RV park. The **Pintler Inn,** 13902 Hwy. 1, tel. (406) 563-5072, $27 d, is convenient for passers-through; the restaurant is dependable. To reach The **Seven Gables Resort,** 18 S. Hauser, tel. (406) 563-5052 or (800) 472-6940, $37 d, is just off the road to Discovery Basin, and offers rooms (pets are okay), a restaurant, and a bar.

Camping is easy at Georgetown Lake, with an abundant mix of private and public campgrounds in the area. At **Denton's Point KOA,** west two miles on S. Shore Rd., tel. (406) 563-6030, there's a marina with a bar and restaurant. Just up the road is **Georgetown Lake KOA,** tel. (406) 563-3402, open all year.

PHILIPSBURG

Between Georgetown Lake and Philipsburg, Hwy. 1 follows Flint Creek down precipitous Flint Creek Canyon to the Philipsburg Valley. The terrain eventually becomes more hospitable to ranching, and between Philipsburg and Drummond the landscape becomes increasingly agrarian.

Whether it is the community's isolation or the integrity of its Victorian-era architecture, Philipsburg has recently gained the reputation as a refuge for artists.

History
A lone miner discovered silver ore at Philipsburg (pop. 940, elev. 5,195 feet) in 1864, but he didn't pursue his claim. His boom oratory about the rich deposits, however, attracted more ambitious miners. In 1866, the rich Hope Mine, Montana's first silver mine, was established, and by the next year the camp boasted 700 inhabitants. The silver deposits were rich enough to attract the Northern Pacific's spur line to Philipsburg in 1887.

The Bimetallic Mining Company entered the town in 1885. At the time it was the state's largest silver mill and its smokestacks still tower over Philipsburg. Its demand for power led to the creation of Georgetown Lake.

"DEGREES OF GREY
IN PHILIPSBURG"

You might come here Sunday on a whim.
Say your life broke down. The last good kiss
you had was years ago. You walk these streets
laid out by the insane, past hotels
that didn't last, bars that did, the tortured try
of local drivers to accelerate their lives.
Only churches are kept up. The jail
turned 70 this year. The only prisoner
is always in, not knowing what he's done.

The principal supporting business now
is rage. Hatred of the various grays
the mountain sends, hatred of the mill,
The Silver Bell repeal, the best liked girls
who leave each year for Butte. One good
restaurant and bars can't wipe the boredom out.
The 1907 boom, eight going silver mines,
a dance floor built on springs—
all memory resolves itself in gaze,
in panoramic green you know the cattle eat
or two stacks high above the town,
two dead kilns, the huge mill in collapse
for fifty years that won't finally fall down.

Isn't this your life? That ancient kiss
still burning out your eyes? Isn't this defeat
so accurate, the church bell simply seems
a pure announcement: ring and no one comes?
Don't empty houses ring? Are magnesium
and scorn sufficient to support a town,
not just Philipsburg, but towns
of towering blondes, good jazz and booze
the world will never let you have
until the town you came from dies inside?

Say no to yourself. The old man, twenty
when the jail was built, still laughs
although his lips collapse. Someday soon,
he says, I'll go to sleep and not wake up.
You tell him no. You're talking to yourself.
The car that brought you here still runs.
The money you buy lunch with,
no matter where it's mined, is silver
and the girl who serves your food
is slender and her red hair lights the wall.

—Richard Hugo

Sights

Philipsburg never really changed much after the century turned, and the old town has remained intact. The chamber of commerce passes out a brochure for a walking tour to 32 historic buildings. Note especially the well-preserved Victorian storefronts downtown, many with original signage. The grade school, built in 1894, is the oldest school building in Montana still in use.

The **Granite County Museum and Cultural Center,** tel. (406) 859-3020, houses the **Ghost Town Hall of Fame** at 155 Sansome Street. There are also plenty of ghost towns in the neighborhood; ask for directions to Bearmouth, Black Pine, or Red Lion. The museum also features a thorough exhibit on the hardrock silver mining that enlivened the Philipsburg economy a century ago.

Four miles southeast of Philipsburg on a gravel road is **Granite,** whose rich mines earned it the nickname "Silver Queen." Granite boomed along with Philipsburg; $30 million of silver was mined there during the 1880s. Granite suffered more grievously when the bottom fell out of the gold market in 1893. Within hours of the mines' closing, 3,000 miners and their families reportedly descended on Philipsburg to withdraw their bank accounts and purchase one-way tickets out. The handsome Miner's Union Hall, a three-story brick structure, is one of the few buildings still standing.

Mining hasn't totally gone bust in Philipsburg. Visitors can stop by the **Sapphire Gallery** at 115 E. Broadway, tel. (800) 525-0169, and dig through concentrate from nearby mines for sapphires and garnets.

Accommodations and Food

The **Inn at Philipsburg,** 1005 Broadway, tel. (406) 859-3959, $35 s, $45 d, is open year-round and also has an RV park and meeting rooms; pets are okay. The **Blue Heron B&B,** 138 W Broadway, tel. (406) 859-3856, offers four guest rooms and a suite in a refurbished miners' boardinghouse. Behind the dour storefront at the **Gallery Cafe,** 127 E. Broadway, tel. (406) 859-3534, is good food and the atmosphere of a Richard Hugo poem; open 6 a.m.-8 p.m. The **Rendezvous,** 204 E Broadway, tel. (406) 859-3529, is a coffeeshop and gallery that also offers light Southwest-style lunches. For a more traditional Montana evening meal of steak or prime rib, stop by **Antler's Restaurant and Lounge,** tel. (406) 859-3430,

the Philipsburg jail, where, writes poet Richard Hugo, "the only prisoner/ is always in, not knowing what he's done"

JUDY JEWELL

Information

Contact the Philipsburg **Chamber of Commerce** at P.O. Box 661, Philipsburg, MT 59858, tel. (406) 859-3388. The **Philipsburg Ranger Station** can be reached by calling (406) 859-3211.

THE SKALKAHO PASS ROAD

Six miles south of Philipsburg, Hwy. 38 leaves Hwy. 1 and winds west through the Sapphire Mountains, eventually dropping into the Bitterroot Valley at Hamilton. Travelers should consider this 50-mile drive, partly on gravel roads, for several reasons. The Skalkaho Pass Rd. connects two otherwise distant valleys along a route with great scenic value. On the west side of the divide, the road is forested and steep, often cliff-hanging. The east half is gentler, and runs along the lovely upper reaches of Rock Creek, one of Montana's premier fishing streams.

Anglers will want to leave Hwy. 38 for Rock Creek Rd. and follow it to its confluence with the Clark Fork River. The upper reaches of Rock Creek receive a lot less attention than the more developed areas closer to Missoula, but the fishing is as good.

Amateur prospectors can try their hand at sapphire mining along the banks of Rock Creek. The **Gem Mountain Sapphire Mine,** 13 miles west of the junction with Hwy. 1, tel. (406) 859-

3530, offers buckets of sapphire-rich gravel to process. The sapphires come in a number of shades (classic blue being one of the rarest) and are relatively easy to find. You can choose to wash the gravel yourself, for the real prospector experience, or buy prewashed concentrated gravel by the bucket. The gravel is placed on sorting tables, and then it's up to you to spot the gems. The staff are happy to help—they even offer a faceting and mounting service—and the experience makes a good family outing. There's informal picnicking and camping near the mine along Rock Creek.

West of Skalkaho Pass, 32 miles from Hwy. 1, Skalkaho Falls roars down under the highway and makes a great place to picnic. Although hiking isn't necessary to enjoy the falls, plenty of hiking trails, both formal and informal, sprout from the road. Trail 313, at the divide, is a good one to follow for a short or long hike. Head north along this trail to Dome-Shaped Mountain, home of mountain goats. The trail also passes by the **Skalkaho Game Preserve,** accessible by rough dirt road at Skalkaho Pass. Marshes here are favorite summer habitat for elk; patient visitors may also see mule deer, coyotes, and black bears.

Skalkaho Pass Rd. is closed from mid-October to June. Early or late in the season, call the Highway Department, tel. (406) 859-3932, to be certain the road is open.

THE BIG HOLE RIVER COUNTRY

The Big Hole is known as the "Valley of 10,000 Haystacks" for the stacks of loose, unbaled hay that the local ranchers persist in using for hay storage; ranches don't have much truck with labor-saving technology. Time has not forgotten this isolated valley, but neither has it been thinking of the Big Hole very recently.

The Big Hole River flows north, draining a huge, very high valley lying between the Bitterroot Mountains on the west and the Pioneer Mountains on the east. After bumping into the Anaconda Range, the river does a U-turn and flows south, picking up the east-slope drainage of the Pioneers.

For anglers and floaters, the river's the thing. Fishing in the Big Hole is superlative, and the rafting challenging. And for hunters, this is the best hunting ground for pronghorn in the state, outside of the prairies of eastern Montana. History buffs can hike the trails and war fields of the Battle of the Big Hole, where in 1877 the Nez Perce fought the U.S. Army as the Indians tried to flee incarceration on reservations.

To comprehend the Big Hole's allure, understand that this is still the West. Resorts haven't yet replaced ranches. You can catch trout elsewhere in Montana, but here you can share a drink and tell your fish stories to a hired hand or cowboy—not a conventioneer.

THE LAND

The Big Hole Valley, and the Pioneer and Bitterroot Mountains that ring it, are the result of ancient mountain-moving on an enormous scale. As the North American continent split away from Europe, the collision of the continent and the Pacific Ocean floor produced huge amounts of molten rock. As the landmass continued to flow over the ocean floor, the magma forced up the sedimentary layers that had formed the edge of the old continent.

The enormous pool of magma that formed is known as the Idaho Batholith. It grew so large and forced the older layers of rock so high that eventually, about 70 million years ago, these sedimentary levels skidded off to the east on molten subterranean lubricant, and deep valleys formed in their wake. The Pioneer Range is one of the most easterly of the fragments set adrift by the rising of the new Rocky Mountains; it made its 50-mile journey east in about a million years. The Big Hole Valley is the void left as the old mountains bulldozed eastward.

The Big Hole Valley is some of the highest, flattest land in Montana. Almost all of the farm and ranch land hovers well above 6,000 feet, in wide valley swatches 15 miles across. However, the original gorge left when the rock mass careened eastward was much deeper. Bedrock in parts of the Big Hole is buried beneath 14,000 feet of sediment.

HISTORY

Feeling conceptual, Lewis and Clark in 1805 named the three forks of the Jefferson River Wisdom, Philanthropy, and Philosophy. In time, Wisdom River became the less abstract Big Hole River, so named by later ranchers impressed with the vast real estate hemmed in by towering peaks.

Ranches spread into the valley in the 1880s and the area quickly became synonymous with big cattle outfits. No one has come forward with an explanation for the Big Hole's penchant for unbaled hay. Perhaps it is local pride. The contraption used to stack loose hay, a "Beaver Slide Stacker," which conveys hay up a sloping wooden structure and dumps it onto the stack, was invented by a local rancher in 1910.

BIG HOLE NATIONAL BATTLEFIELD

The Nez Perce

One of the most famous Indian battles in Montana history involved an Indian tribe not indigenous to the state. The Nez Perce homeland was the region where Oregon, Washington, and Idaho meet. There the Nez Perce made their way as seminomadic fishers, hunters, and gath-

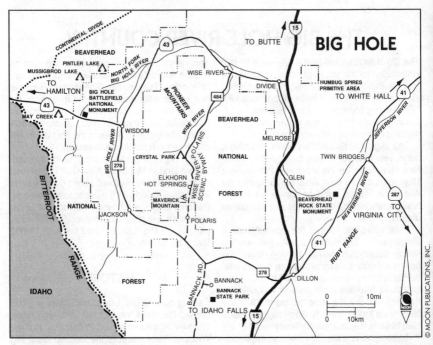

© MOON PUBLICATIONS, INC.

erers. The Nez Perce Nation was a largely peaceable confederation of loosely knit tribal units, each under a powerful chief.

By the 1850s, white settlement began to displace the Nez Perce. An 1855 treaty confined them to a reservation; as the boundaries included their traditional homeland, and since the treaty also restricted white settlement on their land, they complied.

By 1863, however, more stockmen, miners, and settlers were encroaching on Nez Perce land. A new treaty was drawn up, reducing the reservation to one-quarter of its former size. The Nez Perce chiefs whose land was still within the reservation signed the new treaty; those chiefs whose land was being taken away refused. On the pretext that the signature of any Nez Perce chief represented the commitment of the whole tribe, the U.S. government ordered the "nontreaty" Nez Perce onto the new reservation.

While both the Indians and the U.S. Indian Bureau dallied for several years without strict enforcement of the order, increasing pressure

from settlers—especially after Custer's rout in 1876—made compliance a priority. In 1877, the U.S. Army was sent in to compel the delinquent Nez Perce to the reservation.

At this time, a band of young warriors attacked and killed four white settlers in Oregon, whom the Indians believed guilty of earlier murders of Nez Perce elders. Fearing harsh retaliation and foreseeing a dismal future for the tribe, five bands of the nontreaty Nez Perce—about 800 people—fled eastward from the Wallowa Lake area of northeastern Oregon. After two skirmishes in Idaho, where the Indians eluded the Army, the Nez Perce realized they had to leave the area completely. They crossed over to Montana, intent on journeying to Crow country on the Yellowstone, where they hoped to reestablish the tribe.

The Battle of the Big Hole

Once in Montana, the pace of the exodus slowed, and after pushing up the Bitterroot Valley, the Nez Perce camped on the western side of the Big Hole Valley. Here, they considered themselves out of reach of the Army for a few days. They stopped to cut new travois poles and to ready themselves for more traveling.

The Nez Perce knew that the Washington-based Army detachment was two weeks behind them. However, they didn't realize that the Seventh Infantry, under Col. John Gibbon of Fort Shaw, had moved south to ambush them. In the early morning of August 9, 1877, a Nez Perce sentry rode into the advance guard of Colonel Gibbon's forces. He was shot and killed, and the gunfire awoke the rest of the Indian warriors. Mounting a full attack on the Nez Perce as they emerged from their tepees, the infantry killed women, children, braves, and elders indiscriminately.

Indian warriors quickly took up defensive positions, and with sniper fire forced the Army back onto the side hill. Both sides sustained heavy losses.

The Nez Perce successfully besieged the Army troops the rest of that day and night, giving the Nez Perce time to strike their bivouac and flee eastward in search of Crow allies. (The Crow proved to be no allies, and the Nez Perce confronted the Army yet again, in the Battle of Canyon Creek.)

The Battlefield
Hike the trails here not just for their history, but for the quiet beauty of this lush meadow flanked by mountains and a hastening stream.

The **visitor center,** tel. (406) 689-3155, open daily 8 a.m.-8 p.m. Memorial Day to Labor day, 8 a.m.-5 p.m. the rest of the year, provides audio-visual displays that explain the background of the Nez Perce flight and the Big Hole battle. Exhibits include artifacts of the battle and items from the daily life of the early settlers and the Indian tribes who contested here in 1877. Admission is $4 per vehicle.

An extensive network of self-guided hiking trails links the sites of the battle. From the parking lot, a 1.5-mile trail leads to the site of the Nez Perce camp; a shorter trail leads to the siege area. Here, for devotees of military strategy, interpretive signs chart the development of the battle in great detail. A somewhat steeper hike leads to the site of the howitzer captured by the Nez Perce, where there are great views over the battlefield and the Big Hole Valley.

For hiking of a different magnitude, the **Nee-Me-Poo Historic Trail** passes through the Big Hole Battlefield. This 1,500-mile hiking and backpacking trail follows the route of the Nez Perce from Oregon to the Bears Paw Mountains, where the Army finally apprehended the fleeing tribe.

Accommodations
There are picnic facilities at the lower parking lot, along the river, but camping is not allowed. The closest services are in Wisdom, 10 miles east. **May Creek** Forest Service campground is eight miles west on Hwy. 43.

THE BIG HOLE

Although the Big Hole River itself is over 100 miles long, the term "Big Hole," frontier-ese for a deep wide valley, refers to the river's upper basin. Here, between Jackson and Fishtrap, is fabled ranch country, rivaling only eastern Montana for its eternal flatness and traditional western ways. Here too is great fishing for the discriminating angler, with rushing streams full of scrappy brook trout and rare arctic grayling. Almost all river access is through private land; be sure to ask permission from the landowner.

Jackson
Captain Clark and his return party passed through here in 1806 and stopped at the local hot springs. Not content with just a soak, the Corps of Discovery also cooked their dinner in the 138° F water. Now, as then, this little community is known mostly for the springs.

The **Jackson Hot Springs Lodge,** off Hwy. 278, tel. (406) 834-3151, operates a western-style resort at the spot where Lewis and Clark dined. The lodge, which is right on Jackson's main drag, and which dominates the town, is a bit on the fancy side by Montana standards, but as unstuffy as anyplace. Even if you don't stay the night, stop for a swim ($4.50) or a drink at the bar. Open year-round, the lodge caters to summer anglers and tourists but really gears up for winter guests. Nearby are excellent cross-country trails, some groomed and others informal; snowmobilers also use the lodge as a center. Standard accommodations at the resort are in cabin-like motel rooms; rates for these begin at

$68 a night. However, there are some tiny cabins with a shared bath that run $30 a night, and some trailer-like units for $40. If you want to stay in one of the budget options, you'll have to speak up. Very good food, drink, and entertainment are provided at the lodge.

Rose's Cantina, tel. (406) 834-3100, is open for three meals a day and offers an unlikely special: Rose will cook your fresh-caught trout and, for a few dollars, provide hash browns and a salad.

A couple Forest Service campgrounds are west of Jackson. **Miner Lake** is about 10 miles west of town via Forest Rd. 182, which heads off toward the Bitterroots right at the south end of town. The campground itself is not very well marked—look off to your left when you're 10 miles out of town and you'll find at least one of the many de facto campsites in the area. To reach the **Twin Lakes** campground, take Rd. 1290 west from Hwy. 278 about halfway between Jackson and Wisdom and travel for about 13 miles. Both campgrounds are pretty places perched on the east slopes of the Bitterroots. Motorboats aren't allowed on these lakes, but they're great canoe spots.

Wisdom

This little crossroads—more an outpost than a town—is a trading center for the cattle ranches and hay farms that stretch across the wide valley. Higher civilization is making inroads, however. As a sign of changing times, Wisdom supports both watering holes for local ranch hands and a tony fine-art gallery.

Practicalities: The nicest place to stay in Wisdom is the attractive **Nez Perce Motel,** tel. (406) 689-3254, $30 s, $35 d, with some kitchenettes.

Head 10 miles east of town on Rd. 31 to a small campground at the trailhead leading to Sand Lake and Lily Lake. Actually, keep going on the trail system here and you can cross the Pioneers, coming out north of Elkhorn Hot Springs.

The centers of life in Wisdom are its bars and restaurants. **Fetty's Bar and Cafe,** tel. (406) 689-3260, is a local institution serving three meals a day. The **Antler Saloon** is a popular place for a drink; it's not unlike having a beer in a taxidermy shop. Lurid green **Conover's Trading Post** is the community's all-round store and community center.

The really incongruous business in town is the **Wisdom River Gallery,** tel. (406) 689-3400, open daily 9 a.m.-5 p.m. Here, the art of the West rubs cheeks with the life of the West. This fine selection of blue-chip western art, from the likes of Gary Carter and Beverly Doolittle—and some local talents—somehow finds a market in Wisdom. The **Big Hole Crossing Restaurant** serves grilled entrees in the back of the gallery.

Head west from Wisdom on Hwy. 43 to pick up the **Continental Divide Trail** at Chief Joseph Pass. The Bitterroot Ski Club maintains 10 km of cross-country ski trails on the north side of Hwy. 43 at the pass.

Far from anywhere, Wisdom is the place to replenish and refuel in the Big Hole.

W.C. MCRAE

The **Wisdom U.S. Forest Service Ranger Station** can be contacted at (406) 689-3243. **Emergency** is 911.

Wise River

Between Wisdom and Wise River, the Big Hole Valley narrows. The river enters a canyon and picks up speed. Rainbow and brown trout begin to dominate the waters, in numbers and sizes that excite a national audience of fly-fishers. There are a number of fishing-access sites as the river enters its canyon, good for anglers, handy for floaters, and perfect for picnickers. At the town of Wise River, the river of the same name enters the Big Hole. A designated scenic byway along Hwy. 484 begins here.

A couple of lakes in the Anaconda Mountains to the west are of interest to the traveling angler. **Mussigbrod Lake,** 23 miles northwest of Wisdom, has some of the best arctic grayling fishing in the Lower 48. There's also a Forest Service campground. There's a campground too at **Pintler Lake,** 10 miles off Hwy. 43 up Pintler Creek Road. The lake offers good fishing for rainbow and cutthroat, and a very scenic base camp for explorations of the surrounding pine forests.

Practicalities: What passes on the map for a town at Wise River is in fact a couple of bars at the junction of the Big Hole and Wise Rivers. Not to sound dismissive—a couple of bars in fact *do* a town make, at least out here in fly-fisher's heaven.

The **Wise River Club,** tel. (406) 832-3258, is a taciturn old bar full of antiques and stuffed animals. It's still enough of a local's bar to be at once suspicious and friendly. The restaurant is open for three meals a day. The club's motel has rooms at $32 d; there is also limited camping for RVs.

If you get tired of the Wise River Club, then take your patronage to the **H-J Bar and Cafe,** just up the road, tel. (406) 832-3226.

Outfitters and guest ranch resorts provide accommodation options for hunters and anglers. The **Sundance Lodge,** P.O. Box F, Wise River, MT 59762, tel. (406) 689-3611, is a year-round resort that offers hiking, horseback riding, hunting, a hot tub and, of course, fishing, float trips, and a bar. Lodging is in cabins or in the lodge; meals are available in the lodge. Rates begin at $69 a day.

At the **Toussaint Ranch,** guests may stay in a log homestead cabin, tepees, a hayloft, or tents. During the day, there are guided hiking, horseback, and car trips in the Mt. Haggin Wildlife Management Area with the ranch hostess, who has spent 30 years in the area. It's a flexible, low-key, small scale operation, with a variety of options. Cabin-dwelling, full board guests pay about $125 per person per night (including guide service); campers who cook their own meals pay significantly less. Call Chadeayne Roush-Toussaint at (406) 832-3154 for more details.

The **Complete Fly Fisher,** P.O. Box 127, Wise River, MT 59762, tel. (406) 832-3211, promises great fishing, great cooking, and a number of new guest cabins. **Stockton Outfitters,** P.O. Box 9, Wise River, MT 59762, tel. (406) 689-3609, offers fishing and float trips in addition to guest ranch activities.

Big Hole River Outfitters, P.O. Box 156, Wise River, MT 59762, tel. (406) 832-3252, offers accommodations to their angler guests. **Pioneer Outfitter,** 400 Alder Creek Rd., Wise River, MT 59762, tel. (406) 832-3128 or (800) 290-5393, offers big-game hunting as well as fishing expeditions.

The **Wise River Ranger Station** can be reached at (406) 832-3178.

THE LOWER BIG HOLE RIVER

Downstream south from the community of Divide, the Big Hole, heretofore great fishing, becomes a blue-ribbon trout fishery. Brown trout are both huge and abundant. Mid-June, when the salmon flies hatch, marks a frantic season for fish and fishers alike. To the misfortune of trout, there are several good fishing-access sites between Divide and Glen.

Divide

Floaters need beware of a diversion dam just upstream from Divide. Here, water from the Big Hole River is pumped over the Continental Divide to Butte at a rate of five million gallons a day. In its day, the pump station was quite an engineering feat; it's on the National Register of Historic Places.

For hikers, often overlooked is the **Humbug Spires Primitive Area,** a day-hike into an area of geologic interest. Intense faulting has fractured granite extrusions into steep, sharp needles that resemble menhirs. About three miles in, the trail reaches a watershed, and there's a good view over the spiny valley. Exit I-15 at Moose Creek Rd., three miles south of Divide, and turn east.

Melrose

Somewhere near Melrose, the Big Hole leaves its steep-sided canyon and resolutely flows to its appointment with the Beaverhead River. This is a good place to leave the freeway and follow old Hwy. 10. From Glen, off-road enthusiasts can follow a gravel road along the Big Hole River as it trends east to the Beaverhead. It's a pretty drive, becoming dramatic as it approaches historic Beaverhead Rock from its back side.

Melrose lolligags along the old rail sidings that spawned its early growth, a town caught in the midst of a stretching exercise. This pleasant hamlet is known for its fishing; with several fishing-access sites, an attractive motel, a cabin resort, a cafe and bars, it's no wonder that anglers flock here.

Recreation: Head west out of Melrose up Trapper Creek (Rd. 40), then Canyon Creek (Rd. 41) to the Lion Creek trail, a nine-mile loop from the campground at road's end to Lion Lake and back again. From the lake, a hike up nearby Sharp Mountain will give you a pretty good chance of spotting mountain goats.

As elsewhere on the Big Hole, it's easy to find an outfitter to guide you to the fish. **Sundown Outfitters,** P.O. Box 95, Melrose, MT 59743, tel. (406) 835-2751, offers big-game hunting in addition to fishing trips. **Great Waters Outfitting** is based in Melrose, tel. (406) 835-3401, and runs anglers between the Big Hole River and southeastern Montana's Bighorn River.

Practicalities: The **Sportsman Motel,** N. Main St., tel. (406) 835-2141, $38 s, $48 d, is a handsome log motel complex with gas barbecue grills, horse boarding (other pets okay, too), laundry facilities, and an RV park. Two private cabins rent for $80 a night. Head 4.5 miles south of town on the frontage road to **Great Waters,** tel. (406) 835-3401, a cabin resort with a good restaurant in the lodge. Lodging here runs $50-55 a night.

THE PIONEER MOUNTAINS

Surrounded on three sides by the meanderings of the Big Hole River, the Pioneer Mountains are in fact two different ranges divided down a north-south axis, linked yet separated, sort of like the underside of a coffee bean. These out-of-the-way mountains come to life in the winter, as a hot springs resort and a good downhill-ski area combine to bring in the locals. The Wise River drainage is popular with anglers; there are several large Forest Service campgrounds with fishing access along the river.

Highway 484 transects the Pioneer Mountains, from Wise River in the north through Polaris to Hwy. 278 in the south. The Forest Service has designated this part-gravel, part-paved route running down the furrow of the coffee bean as the **Pioneer Mountains Scenic Byway.**

Maverick Mountain Ski Area

The legendary heavy snows of southwestern Montana are put to good use at Maverick, which boasts 215 inches of base snow at the summit of the runs. The vertical drop is 2,120 feet. Maverick Lodge offers a full pro shop, rental, and food facilities; cross-country skiers are welcome. A lift ticket is $19 a day, $11 for children, half price Thursday and Friday. Call (406) 834-3454 for details.

The closest lodging is at the **Grasshopper Inn,** tel. (406) 834-3456, $35 s, $45 d, at the base of the slopes beside the near-ghost town of Polaris. Open 9 a.m.-9 p.m., the restaurant is good, the bar lively, and the motel-style rooms are comfortable. Also very close by is the **Maverick Mountain RV Park,** tel. (406) 834-3452, which has cabins as well as RV hookups. **Elkhorn Hot Springs** (see below) also makes a good base camp for skiers.

Elkhorn Hot Springs

This venerable resort is the other popular lodging for skiers. Cross-country skiers converge here; with 40 kilometers (25 miles) of cross-country trails managed by the resort, an entire mountain range of informal trails to explore, and a good hot soak to come home to, this is near-heaven (at 7,385 feet, literally so). In summer, the hot springs are popular for hikers. There are two outdoor mineral pools, plus a sauna, and it costs $4 for a swim.

Rooms are either in the lodge (bathroom down the hall) or in rustic cabins scattered amongst the trees. The restaurant in the lodge is open for three meals a day. Cabins, with electricity and wood-stoves, but no plumbing (shared outhouse with neighboring cabins) start at $48 d (swimming included). Lodge rooms cost the same. Don't come to Elkhorn expecting a trendy new age getaway—it's funky and remote and, with that in mind, very charming and relaxing. Elkhorn Hot Springs is 13 miles north of Hwy. 278 on Hwy. 484. Contact Elkhorn Hot Springs at P.O. Box 514, Polaris, MT 59746, tel. (406) 834-3434 or (800) 722-8978.

If you want to stop at Elkhorn for a swim and a soak, but would prefer to camp out, there's a Forest Service campground on Grasshopper Creek less than a mile down the road. Pick up the Blue Creek trail just south of the campground and head into the West Pioneers. North of Elkhorn Hot Springs, there are several more campgrounds and trailheads.

Crystal Park

At this Forest Service maintained site four miles north of Elkhorn Hot Springs, rockhounds can dig for quartz crystals. It's a very popular spot, attracting dedicated amateur crystal miners, who come with shovels and screens to sift through the dirt for quartz and amethyst. But even ill-equipped novices can scrape through the topsoil for a few minutes and come up with a small crystal or two.

THE SOUTHWESTERN CORNER

Montana schoolchildren are taught to recognize the state's western boundary as Abraham Lincoln's long-faced profile. The scruff of Lincoln's beard is Beaverhead County, the state's largest and one of its most varied. The Continental Divide careens along towering snowcapped peaks, which ring in valleys so broad, flat, and covered with sagebrush that ranchers from eastern Montana could feel at home: this is western Montana's prairie province. Some of the oldest and largest ranches in Montana stretched across these high flatlands.

History was quick to find this corner of Montana. High on a forgotten pass between Montana and Idaho is Sacajawea Historic Area, where the Corps of Discovery crossed the Continental Divide. Bannack State Park, Montana's best-preserved ghost town, commemorates the state's first city and first territorial capital. Red Rock Lakes National Wildlife Refuge is one of the nation's most important bird sanctuaries. It is a primary breeding ground for trumpeter swans, once feared extinct.

With two million acres of national forest in Beaverhead County alone, and a vast network of streams forming the Missouri's most distant headwaters, southwestern Montana has plenty of room for outdoor recreation. Yet the great fishing, hunting, and hiking opportunities in this lovely corner of Montana are blessedly free of crowds.

HISTORY

The Shoshone Indians were the first Montana-area Natives to acquire horses. They stormed north through the upper Jefferson River drainages to threaten and finally dominate the high plains east of the Rocky Mountain Front in the 1750s. The Blackfeet Federation, moving south from Canada with guns obtained from the British, halted the Shoshone's expansion. The Shoshone were forced back into Idaho by the 1800s, where Lewis and Clark first encountered them.

Monida Pass, now part of I-15, is one of the lowest and gentlest of passes over the Continental Divide. It provided access for some of the earliest migrations of non-Indian settlers. Prospectors found rich gold pannings along Grasshopper Creek in 1862. Bannack sprang up in response, becoming the first real town in Montana. By the time it became the territorial capital in 1864, Bannack boasted hotels, a governor's mansion, churches, and a Masonic temple.

Montana's vigilante movement was born in Bannack. The first elected sheriff, Henry Plummer, was a smooth operator who ran a gang of road agents—deceptively called the Innocents—on the side. They preyed on miners and travelers

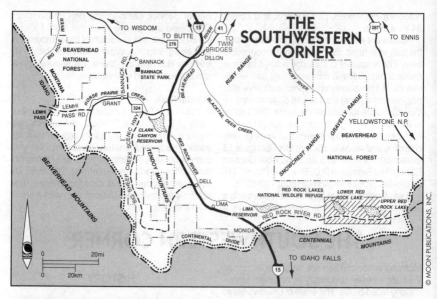

THE SOUTHWESTERN CORNER

© MOON PUBLICATIONS, INC.

until vigilantes prevailed and hanged over 20 suspected outlaws.

The stage line that extended from the Union Pacific in Utah to the Montana goldfields was replaced in 1880 by the first railroad to reach the state, the Utah and Northern. Access to transport made silver camp Butte into a boomtown, and although gold had already played out in southwestern Montana, the railroad boosted the fortunes of nascent stock ranches, expecially sheep outfits. The enormous basins from the Centennial Range in the south to the Big Hole Valley to the west provided rich grazing.

THE RED ROCK VALLEY

The Red Rock River, the Missouri's most distant headwater, drains a broad valley overlooked by the Continental Divide, but not by much. This is high country: the valley stretches out prairielike at elevations above 6,000 feet.

Red Rock Lakes

This remote and beautiful valley, ringed with high but rounded peaks, would probably be ignored by the traveler if it weren't for Red Rock Lakes. At these marshy lakes, biologists discovered trumpeter swans in 1933, once feared extinct in the United States.

Trumpeter swans formerly ranged over much of the continent. However, during the 19th century, hunters found a vigorous market for quill pens, powder puffs, and swan meat. As the homestead movement changed the environment of eastern Montana, with land falling to the plow and marshes being drained, swan populations plummeted. Biologists found only 66 trumpeters in 1933 at Red Rock Lakes, the last individuals of the species in the country.

The U.S. Department of the Interior established the 40,300-acre **Red Rock Lakes National Wildlife Refuge** in 1935. Currently, 600 trumpeters summer here, and, as geothermal activity maintains ice-free water temperatures year-round, the winter population swells to 2,000.

The Defenders of Wildlife, a group concerned with wildlife preservation, has called the refuge one of the most beautiful in America. Upper and Lower Red Rock Lakes are nestled beneath the 9,800-foot Centennial Mountains. This isolated corner of Montana is home to a variety of wildlife, including moose, deer, elk, pronghorn, and fox; 258 bird species have been sighted at the lakes.

To reach the refuge, turn at Monida, just below the Continental Divide on I-15. The reserve begins a rattly 28 miles up a gravel road. Wildlife viewing is best between May and November, which is about the only season the road is dependably passable. The reserve can also be reached in good weather from Idaho, on the Red Rock Pass Rd., from Hwy. 87, 17 miles from West Yellowstone. For more information, contact the Refuge Manager, Red Rock Lakes NWR, Monida Star Rte., Box 15, Lima, MT 59739, tel. (406) 276-3536.

Recreation

Fishing is allowed in most areas of the refuge and provides good sport for trout anglers. Non-motorized boats are allowed on some areas of the lakes; check with refuge managers. Arctic grayling are caught in streams that feed the lakes. Hunting is permitted in designated areas of the refuge for specific species.

Practicalities

The closest motels are in Lima: **Lee's Holiday Motel,** 111 Bailey St., tel. (406) 276-3535, $28 d, and the **Club Bar & Motel,** tel. (406) 276-9996. Up the road in Dell, the **Red Rock Inn,** tel. (406) 276-3501, is a renovated 1895 inn with seven hotel rooms, a bar, and a restaurant. Otherwise, this is camping country. There are two campgrounds at the wildlife refuge, one at each lake,

and each at lakeside, meaning great views but also potential mosquito assault.

Guest ranches and outfitters provide alternatives to camping. **Lakeview Guest Ranch,** Monida Star Rte., Lima, MT 59739, tel. (406) 276-3300, offers a full range of recreation and wildlife-viewing opportunities year-round, plus lodging in luxury cabins. Lakeview is the headquarters of the refuge but offers no amenities. Make sure your gas tank is full before heading up.

Yesterday's Cafe, tel. (406) 276-3308, in Dell, serves superior home-style cooking in a refurbished country schoolhouse; open Sun.-Fri. 7 a.m.-9 p.m. There's also a cafe in Lima.

HORSE PRAIRIE VALLEY

The Red Rock River meets Horse Prairie Creek at Clark Canyon Reservoir, and the Beaverhead River issues forth. While the reservoir is popular with local boaters and anglers, and old ranches fill the wide valley traditionally known as the Horse Prairie, travelers will want to explore the area to relive some of the most stirring moments of the Lewis and Clark Expedition.

History

As the Corps of Discovery pushed up the Jefferson River, searching for the headwaters of

TRUMPETER SWANS

Trumpeter swans are North America's largest waterfowl. A mature male weighs in at 26 pounds, and his wings stretch eight feet. They are pure white, with black beaks. Sometimes, their heads are stained yellowish—a result of diving in iron-rich muds.

Trumpeters mate for life, and their lives are long. Individuals can live for almost 30 years in the wild. The same mated pair often returns to the same nest year after year. Females are called pens, males are called cobs. Swan young, hatched from eggs weighing 12 ounces, are called cygnets.

The continent's largest population of trumpeters occurs in Alaska, although significant numbers of swans can now be found from the mouth of the Columbia River north along the Pacific coast. However, Montana's Red Rock Lakes remains one of the most

trumpeter swans, Cygnus buccinator

beautiful places to observe these rare fowl. Take binoculars, as trumpeters are wary of people. Parts of the refuge may be closed to protect nests.

the Missouri, Sacajawea began to recognize landmarks of her childhood.

Recognizing the need for horses to proceed over the difficult Continental Divide that faced them, Lewis and three men went ahead to scout for the Shoshone, into whose homeland Sacajawea insisted they had entered. Lewis sighted the expedition's first Indian in Montana in the Horse Prairie Valley and continued over Lemhi Pass to encounter a Shoshone lodge near Tendoy, Idaho. After tenuous negotiations for horses, the Shoshone agreed to backtrack with Lewis and his party to meet the rest of the corps.

As the party approached, Sacajawea began to suck her fingers, a sign that she recognized her kin. A Shoshone woman broke rank and ran forward to embrace Sacajawea, recognizing her from her childhood. When Sacajawea was summoned to interpret the dialogue between the Europeans and the natives, she entered the tent where the men were conversing and immediately recognized her brother Cameahwait, who was now chief of the Shoshone.

Consider for a moment what the negotiations for horses and supplies entailed. Sacajawea translated her brother's Shoshone terms into Minataree, which her husband Charbonneau understood. He in turn spoke French to a French-speaking member of the corps, who then translated the terms into English for Lewis and Clark. However circumlocutious, the translations worked. The corps traded for 24 horses, and on August 29, 1805, the entire party climbed over Lemhi Pass and the Continental Divide into Spanish territory.

Lemhi Pass

A drive up the steep, graveled road to Lemhi Pass (elev. 7,373 feet) is a must for any Lewis and Clark buff with a high-clearance vehicle. Turn off Hwy. 324 onto Lemhi Pass Rd., and follow the road, sometimes more rock than gravel, for about 20 miles. From the top, the Montana-Idaho border, mountains stretch to the west as far as the eye can see. A sign commemorates the Corps of Discovery's historic ascent and subsequent descent into Idaho.

Just below the crest of the pass, on the Montana side, the state has established **Sacajawea Historical Area,** with picnic facilities and a small campground. Here, where a tiny spring gushes

out of the rock only yards from the Continental Divide, Lewis thought he had found the "most distant fountain of the waters of the Mighty Missouri." (It's not; that distinction goes to Hellroaring Creek south of the Red Rock Lakes.) The party of four drank from the spring and stood astride it "exultingly," thankful to have lived to put a foot on each side of the "heretofore deemed endless Missouri."

Today's visitor will be unable to resist doing the same. Bring a picnic; this is an enchanting spot and you'll want to stretch your legs before bumping back down to the valley. A steep Forest Service road continues into Idaho; however, it's not advised for cars. Check with the Salmon Ranger Station, tel. (208) 756-2215; sometimes the road is closed due to logging.

Recreation

There's often good fishing for trout in Clark Canyon Reservoir, although the barren, treeless setting and the seemingly always underfilled lake are charm-free. The 5,000-acre lake is popular with boaters from Dillon. The Red Rock River just above the lake is good fishing for cutthroat and rainbows.

Practicalities

Dillon is the closest center for amenities, although at the little crossroads of Grant the Horse Prairie Hilton advertises both beer and welding. There are six free campgrounds on the shores of the Clark Canyon Reservoir.

BANNACK

Bannack is a well-preserved ghost town whose remains commemorate the rich 1862 gold strike on Grasshopper Creek, the scene of some of Montana's most violent early history. Bannack State Park is self-guided and undeveloped; visitors are free to explore this fascinating old territorial capital at will and without threat of gift shops.

History

Prospectors gone bust in the Colorado gold boom came north to southwestern Montana and in 1862 discovered gold at Grasshopper Diggings, about 20 miles west of Dillon. The first of the great Montana booms was on. A sign, written

W.C. McRAE

Bannack, Montana's first capital, is today one of the state's best-preserved ghost towns.

in axle grease, stood at the confluence of the Beaverhead River and Grasshopper Creek:

> *Tu grass Hop Per digins*
> *30 myle*
> *Keep the trale nex the bluffe.*

By winter, a thousand ragtag adventurers, many of them refugees from the Civil War, assembled on the banks of Grasshopper Creek. They named their camp Bannack (symptomatically misspelled) for the native Bannock Indians.

When it came to law and order, which the advent of sudden great wealth demanded, early Montanans just faked it. Henry Plummer was a veteran of California and Nevada gold rushes, and his urbane good looks and considerable charm won the trust of Bannack (and later Virginia City) voters who elected him sheriff.

At the same time, Plummer also secretly led a band of road agents of considerable ruthlessness. These ruffians and killers preyed on travelers, authorities, Indians, and anyone else who got in their way. Bannack in 1863 was the West of Hollywood: gunfights in the street, men gunning each other down over cards, strangers killing strangers for the way they looked. Especially at risk were travelers between Bannack and Virginia City; stage robberies were customary, cold-blooded murder frequent.

Even for the Wild West, violence in Bannack was excessive: during the first year of Plum-

mer's stint as sheriff, the Innocents, as he called his gang, killed over 100 men. As many deaths probably went unreported; in a gold camp of several thousand miners, the summer's orgy of lawless killings claimed a significant percentage of the population.

Once Grasshopper Creek froze up, and panning ceased for the winter, outraged citizens decided to take the law into their own hands. A secret alliance of men formed a Vigilance Committee and codified their own set of laws and punishment (invariably death), a secret oath, and their cabalistic secret number 3-7-77, with which they marked their victims.

The vigilantes moved quickly. In a period of two weeks, 24 of Plummer's gang were summarily hanged. Plummer's last words were "Give me a good drop."

The experience of lawlessness reinforced the need for a stronger civil authority. In 1864, the miners in Bannack and Alder Gulch sent Judge Sidney Edgerton to petition the U.S. government for territorial status, which the Senate granted and President Lincoln signed on May 26. Bannack became the first territorial capital when Edgerton convened the first legislature here; his house became the first Governor's Mansion.

Bannack's prominence had already begun to fade as the far richer colors of Alder Gulch attracted upwards of 10,000 miners by 1864. The territorial capital followed the miners to Virginia City. Little remained of Bannack by 1890.

Bannack State Park

Over 60 structures remain standing at Bannack. The streets, homes, hotels, and civic buildings extend along Grasshopper Creek in various states of disrepair. The entire park is self-guided: explore at will, being careful of dubious stairways and decrepit second stories. The old hotel is rumored to be the most photographed site in Montana. Other buildings of note are the Governor's Mansion, the Masonic Hall, jail, and Methodist church. The third weekend of July is Bannack Days at the state park. Events include a black-powder shoot, horse and wagon rides, and a buffalo-steak barbecue.

Entry is $4 per vehicle, and the park is open all year in good weather, daylight to dark. The park campground costs $11 a site. Call (406) 834-3413 for more information. To reach Bannack, turn off Hwy. 278 and follow a good gravel road for three miles. From the south, Bannack can be reached from Hwy. 324 at Grant, 11 miles along a gravel road.

DILLON

Even if Dillon (pop. 4,382, elev. 5,057 feet) weren't the center of a vast region of broad fertile valleys filled with old ranches and rushing streams brimming with trout; even if Dillon weren't surrounded by national forests and wildlife refuges; and even if Dillon wasn't close to the crossroads of Lewis and Clark, Chief Joseph, Henry Plummer, and a territory's worth of early miners and ranchers, Dillon would deserve the traveler's attention.

Dillon is an authentic old trade town that has managed to endure the recent economic malaise of the agricultural West without facing extinction or resorting to survival as a self-parody for tourists. Filled with historic architecture but kept young by the presence of students at Western Montana College, blessed with fine restaurants, and faithful to the old bars that—then, as now—have consoled cowboys, sheepherders, and miners, Dillon is one of Montana's most bewitching small cities. There may be more urbane entertainment in Helena or Missoula, but in its unassuming way, Dillon keeps itself—and the complicit traveler—happily bemused.

HISTORY

Dillon began in 1880 as the northern terminus for the narrow-gauge Utah and Northern Railroad as it pushed into Montana to service the mines of Butte. Within a year, prosperous Dillon petitioned to take the seat of enormous Beaverhead County from Bannack. The railroad brought a boom to the nascent cattle and sheep industries in the broad valleys that ringed the new city. Rich ranchers soon built mansions in Dillon and invested in commercial ventures. Gold, lead, and silver miners, in their on-again, off-again fashion, found a better market for the metals along the new rail corridor, and they frequented businesses in the new town.

By 1893, Dillon was prominent enough to attract the State Normal School, provided for by the third legislative assembly. The first building, a magnificent Queen Anne extravaganza, was completed in 1897.

Dillon was for many years the railhead for the state's largest wool-producing area, as sheep were especially well suited to the high mountain valleys of southwestern Montana. Irrigated

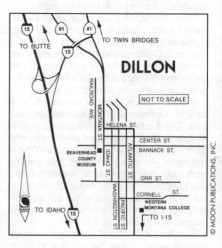

farming, and cattle and sheep ranching, remain the economic backbone of Dillon.

SIGHTS

Historic Dillon
For a city of its size, Dillon has an unexpected array of architectural styles. The Beaverhead County Museum provides a free brochure, *Historical Tour of Dillon,* covering many of the local curiosities.

Some highlights: The **Beaverhead County Courthouse,** Pacific and Bannack Streets, was built in 1889 and contains a four-faced Seth Thomas clock in its tower. The **Dillon Tribune Building,** Bannack and Idaho Streets, housed Dillon's first newspaper; the 1888 facade is made entirely of pressed metal. One of the grandest of all the old hotels in Montana is **Metlen Hotel,** built in 1897 as "one of the best, if not the best, constructed edifices in the state." A little down on its luck today, the Metlen is still an imposing monument to the era of grandiose railroad hotels.

Orr Mansion, at the south end of Idaho St., is flanked by estates of other early entrepreneurs. William Orr was a California cattleman who brought his herd north to the Beaverhead country in 1862. Success was more or less immediate, and by 1864, Orr began to build his Italianate villa.

At the **Beaverhead County Museum,** 15 S. Montana St., tel. (406) 683-5027, a towering Alaskan brown bear (mounted, of course) oversees the exhibits of Indian artifacts, early ranching curios, and mining memorabilia.

Western Montana College of the University of Montana
The 34-acre State Normal School, established to train teachers for Montana's classrooms, was established in Dillon in 1893. The original structure, added to in 1907, forms Old Main, an imposing and distinctive brick edifice incorporating eclectic design elements ranging from Gothic windows to Queen Anne towers.

Recent economic circumscriptions by the state Board of Regents have forced the college to affiliate with the University of Montana in Missoula. Western Montana College specializes in training prospective teachers for Montana's rural schools, and it also organizes the state's Elderhostel program. The campus switchboard can be reached at (406) 683-7011; the mailing address is 710 S. Atlantic St., Dillon, MT 59725.

RECREATION

You can't turn around in Dillon without bumping up against great recreation opportunities. Dillon is the natural hub for the entire south-

downtown Dillon

W.C. McRAE

western corner of Montana, where fishing, hiking, hunting, camping, and exploring the outdoors in general are incarnated in rich abundance.

Fishing

The races and runnels that form the fabric of the Jefferson River are all legendary, highly productive fisheries. The Beaverhead River forms below Clark Canyon Dam; between here and Dillon is some of the most challenging and satisfying trout fly-fishing in Montana. Much of this fast-flowing river is fished best by floating; during high flows, travelers should consider enlisting the aid of outfitters. Of course, one river does not an anglers' paradise make: the Ruby, Big Hole, and Red Rock Rivers, not to mention the mountain streams that feed them, are all within easy casting distance from Dillon. Don't miss Blacktail Deer Creek, just southeast of Dillon, for more leisurely, streamside fishing for brookies and cutthroat.

Hiking

With the Continental Divide arrayed around the perimeter of southwestern Montana, it's no wonder there's great hiking and camping just about everywhere that's uphill. A Beaverhead National Forest map reveals hikes in every direction, but there are a few isolated ranges that avid hikers should try to visit.

The Snowcrest Range contains rugged and seldom-visited 10,000-foot peaks, with large populations of elk and mountain goats. The mountains divide the Ruby, Red Rock, and Blacktail Deer drainages, in a remote area. The Snowcrests are about 20 miles southeast of Dillon along Blacktail Deer Creek Road. Even more remote and rugged are the mountains at the head of Big Sheep Creek (turn west at the Dell exit, 45 miles south of Dillon, and follow signs for Big Sheep Canyon).

Between the Beaverhead Mountains (guardians of the Continental Divide) and the Tendoy Mountains fan out the tributaries of Big Sheep Creek. Trails lead up to glaciated valleys and knife-edge ridges along the Montana-Idaho border. Check with the Forest Service office in Dillon for details.

Outfitters

Bike southwestern Montana with **Bad Beaver Bike Tours,** who run single-day and multiday trips, including a six to 10 day Glacier-Yellow-

stone ride and many off-road rides, out of Bad Beaver Bike Shop at 25 E. Helena St., tel. (406) 683-9292. A daylong mountain bike trip costs about $80 ($85 with bike rental); multiday trips are based out of a backcountry lodge and cost about $150 per person per day, including meals and lodging. Bad Beaver's guides know the area really well, and they stress that even for off-road tours it's not necessary to be a hardcore mountain biker.

In the winter (which can start as early as October in these parts), Bad Beaver changes its focus to **backcountry ski and snowshoe touring.** Multiday tours are again based out of a backcountry lodge, which is equipped with a stock tank turned hot tub.

If you just want to rent a bike and go it alone, Bad Beaver charges $20 a day. Another place in town to rent bikes is **Backcountry Bike & Boards,** 35 E. Bannack St., tel. (406) 683-9696; bike rental runs $20-25 a day.

For horseback rides in the Dillon area, call **Diamond Hitch Outfitters,** (406) 683-5494 or (800) 368-5494. They offer two-hour rides from $25, day-trips for $115, and pack trips for $340-695.

All of the following provide guided fishing excursions on local rivers, and most offer lodging and hunting trips. **Beavertail Outfitters,** Dennis and Jerry Jo Rehse, 2590 Carrigan Ln., Dillon, MT 59725, tel. (406) 683-6232. **Dave Wellborn, Outfitter,** 775 Medicine Lodge Rd., Dillon 59725, tel. (406) 681-3117; he also offers excursions on mountain bikes. **Diamond Hitch Outfitters,** Robert McNeill, 3405 Ten Mile Rd., Dillon, MT 59725, tel. (406) 683-5494; the McNeills offer backcountry pack trips. **Frontier Anglers,** Tim Tollett, P.O. Box 11, Dillon, MT 59725, tel. (406) 683-5276.

PRACTICALITIES

Accommodations

At the **Centennial Inn,** 122 S. Washington St., tel. (406) 683-4454, B&B rooms ($70) are upstairs from the restaurant (see below). **The Creston Motel,** 335 N. Atlantic St., tel. (406) 683-2341, $32 s, $38 d, is clean, quiet, comfortable, and within walking distance to downtown. Pets are permitted for an extra $3.

The **Best Western Paradise Inn,** 650 N. Montana St., tel. (406) 683-4214 or (800) 528-1234, $44-52 s, $50-58 d, is Dillon's plushest motel, with an indoor pool, exercise room, hot tub and restaurant/casino on the premises. The **Dillon Comfort Inn,** 450 N. Interchange, tel. (406) 683-6831 or (800) 442-4667, $51 s, $60 d, has a pool, sun deck, and outdoor recreation area; a full continental breakfast is included in the room rate. The **Super 8,** 550 N. Montana St., tel. (406) 683-4288, charges $47 s, $58 d. The **Sundowner Motel,** 500 N. Montana St., tel. (406) 683-2375 or (800) 524-9746, $35 s, $41 d, across from the Super 8 and four blocks from downtown, has a playground, permits pets in smoking rooms, and serves free morning coffee and donuts.

Guest Ranches

If you want to go native, stay at a guest ranch. The **Pioneer Mountain Farm Inn,** tel. (406) 683-5445, is a huge old log house on a cashmere goat ranch a few miles from town. The owner moved the log house, originally built in Jackson in 1949, to the Dillon area and has updated it with an eye to quirky historical accents, such as the slate floor made from old Beaverhead County school blackboards. The inn caters primarily, though not exclusively, to anglers and is prepared to accommodate people who can't leave their computers at home. The inn's owners also maintain several well-appointed guest lodges at the base of Beaverhead Rock; they cost $750-1,000 per week and sleep four to eight people.

The **Beaverhead Rock Ranch Guest Houses,** run by Gary and Sonja Williams, is at 4325 Old Stage Rd., Dillon, MT 59725, tel. (406) 683-2126. The old log farmhouse and log cabin are at the base of Beaverhead Rock and are part of a working hay farm. Rooms in either the farmhouse or cabin include kitchen and laundry facilities, and run $75 d, with a two-night minimum stay.

At the **Five Rivers Lodge,** perched above the Beaverhead River near spring-fed ponds on Hwy. 41, tel. (406) 683-5000, the emphasis is on fishing, though there are amenities for non-anglers, including a darkroom. Guests stay in comfortable rooms, are fed three meals a day, and

are accompanied by a guide on fishing expeditions. Rates run from $995 for two days of guided fishing and three nights lodging to $2,395 for six days of fishing and seven nights lodging. Non-fishing discounts are available.

Hildreth Livestock Ranch, P.O. Box 149, Dillon, MT 59725, tel. (406) 681-3111, is a working Chiangus ranch that welcomes guests B&B-style. Accommodations are in cabins, which run $90-125 in high season.

Camping

The **Dillon KOA,** 735 W. Park, tel. (406) 683-2749, has a pool, showers, and restrooms. The **Southside RV Park,** exit 62, right on Poindexter, tel. (406) 683-2244, has a lovely location on Blacktail Deer Creek. The **Bureau of Reclamation campground** at Barretts, five miles south of town on the frontage road, sits right on the Beaverhead River as it leaves its canyon. Head 20 miles south of Dillon to **Clark Canyon Reservoir,** where free campgrounds line the shore and are conveniently, but not annoyingly, close to I-15. North of Dillon, on old Hwy. 91, **Skyline RV Park and Campground,** tel. (406) 683-4692, offers fishing and miniature golf.

Food

Start off a day in Dillon with pastries from **Anna's Oven,** 120 S. Montana St., tel. (406) 683-5766. Get a jolt of espresso, pasta lunch or early dinner at **Sweetwater Coffee,** 23 N. Idaho, tel. (406) 683-4141. (Don't go looking for supper here; they close at 6 p.m.) Great Harvest Bakeries are a fixture in the Northwest. The headquarters is here in Dillon. Stop by the home bakery for cookies or a loaf of superior whole-wheat bread (they give away free slices) at 32 S Idaho St., tel. (406) 683-5254.

For a memorable breakfast or lunch, crowd into the **Metlen Cafe,** tel. (406) 683-2335, in the back of the Metlen Hotel on S. Railroad Avenue. The food is good and abundant, and you get to watch expert fry cooks at work.

Some of the best dinners in town come from the **Centennial Inn,** occupying a Victorian mansion at 122 S. Washington, tel. (406) 683-4454. If you're in the mood for high tea, this is only place in Dillon you're going to find it. **The Lion's Den,** 725 N. Montana St., tel. (406) 683-2051, is a supper club serving steaks and seafood; there's dancing later in the evening. The best pizza in town is at **Papa T's,** 10 N. Montana St., tel. (406) 683-6432. The **Paradise Inn Restaurant,** 660 N. Montana St., tel. (406) 683-6422, has an eclectic menu well based in beef. **Blacktail Station,** 26 S. Montana, tel. (406) 683-6611, offers steaks plus daily pasta specials.

INFORMATION AND SERVICES

The well-equipped **chamber of commerce** is in the old railroad depot at 125 S. Montana St., Dillon, MT 59725, tel. (406) 683-5511. The **Dillon City Library** is at 121 S. Idaho St., tel. (406) 683-4544. The **Clean Critter Laundromat** is at 230 N. Montana St., tel. (406) 683-4010.

In case of **emergency** call 911. **Barrett Memorial Hospital,** tel. (406) 683-2323, is at 1260 S. Atlantic Street.

The **Dillon Ranger District,** Beaverhead National Forest, is at 610 N. Montana St., Dillon, MT 59725, tel. (406) 683-3900. The **BLM** office is at 1005 Selway Dr., Dillon, MT 59725, tel. (406) 683-2337.

Shopping

People come to Dillon from all over western Montana to shop at the **Patagonia Outlet,** 34 N. Idaho St., tel. (406) 683-2580, for bargain-priced outdoor clothing.

Transportation

If you're flying to this neck of the woods, check fares on flights into Idaho Falls; it's less than two hours down the freeway and often far cheaper than flying into Montana airports. **Rimrock Trailways** buses connect Dillon with Butte and Idaho Falls. The depot is at 17 E. Bannack St., tel. (406) 683-2344.

ALDER GULCH AND THE RUBY RIVER VALLEY

At Virginia City in Alder Gulch, prospectors stumbled onto one of the richest gold strikes in history. The settlement that sprang up, once called "Fourteen-mile City" for its attenuated slouch down the steep gulch, became the second capital of Montana Territory. Virginia City has survived as other gold camps have not; it's still the governmental seat of Madison County, and amongst the deserted buildings are shops, hotels, and restaurants that belie its guise of a ghost town.

HISTORY

In 1863, one year after the first big gold strike in Montana, a group of prospectors led by Bill Fairweather left Bannack for the Yellowstone Valley. En route, they were harried by Crow Indians and turned back. After pitching camp in the Gravelly Range, the prospectors decided to pan for tobacco money. Their panning turned up rich color, and the miners realized they had discovered a major gold deposit at Alder Gulch.

They vowed to keep silent about their claims, but after they returned to Bannack, their free-

spending ways drew the attention of other prospectors. When they started back to Alder Gulch, hundreds of miners followed them, each hoping to cash in on the presumed new strike. Within a year, 10,000 hopefuls lived in settlements along Alder Gulch.

Gold Camp

The tremendously rich gold-bearing gravels of Alder Gulch lay beneath a considerable weight of overburden. Shafts and tunnels had to be dug and the gravel hoisted out to the surface. The gravel was then shoveled into a "rocker," where water sloshed away lighter materials while the gold nuggets tumbled into baffles on the bottom of the device. If the claim was near streams, water could be diverted into sluice boxes. Dozens of miners could work along a sluice, sometimes hundreds of feet long. During the first five years of mining operations in Alder Gulch, an estimated $40 million was extracted, and by 1928 the total exceeded $100 million, with gold at $16 an ounce.

Although Bannack came first as a gold camp, Virginia City is Montana's first incorporated town; while the gold at Bannack played out quickly,

JIM MASTERSON

mining continued at Virginia City. When the second territorial congress convened in 1865, it met at the state's population center, Virginia City, thereby elevating it to territorial capital. It remained so until 1875.

When Montana became a territory in 1864, an official court system was put in place, though vigilantes retaliated against presumed wrongdoers for several more years. Other institutions soon followed: the state's first school district was established in Virginia City in 1866.

After miners removed the richest deposits of gold in Alder Gulch, more advanced technology allowed the processing of low-grade ore and tailings from early mining to extract trace deposits. The large berms of gravel at the little town of Alder reveal the debris of gold-dredging operations from the early 1900s. Although gold-seekers still pan for gold, and mines south of Virginia City produce gold and silver, the talc mines in the Ruby Range are now the area's largest operations.

INFORMATION

The **Virginia City Chamber of Commerce** can be contacted at P.O. Box 218, Virginia City, MT 59759, tel. (406) 843-5345 or (800) 829-2969. The **Sheridan Ranger District Office** of the Beaverhead National Forest is at P.O. Box 428, Sheridan, MT 59749, tel. (406) 842-5432.

The **Madison County Sheriff** can be reached at (406) 843-5301. The **Ruby Valley Hospital** is at 220 E. Crofoot, Sheridan, tel. (406) 842-5453. Dial (406) 494-3666 for **road conditions.**

VIRGINIA CITY

Montana's second territorial capital, Virginia City (pop. 158, elev. 5,760 feet), is that oxymoronic anomaly, a working ghost town. Five streets of original and restored buildings from the 1860s and '70s define the town, which led to Virginia City's designation as a national historic landmark in 1962. But the town never died. Virginia City is still the county seat, and behind its false fronts and log-frame structures, cafes and shops serve locals year-round.

Sights

Virginia City is best thought of as an open-air museum of the early mining West. While strolling along the board sidewalks, poke into the old buildings. Those that aren't currently in business have been restored and contain artifacts of Alder Gulch's boom years. Most of the following structures lie along Wallace St., now Hwy. 287.

The **Madison County Courthouse,** built in 1876, still serves as the seat of local government. The territorial offices were housed on the second floor of the **Content Corner** building. The **Montana Post Building,** with its display of printing equipment, was home to Montana's first newspaper. Within **Vigilante Barn** the Montana vigilante movement was supposedly born.

The **Pioneer Bar** is an authentic restoration of a mining-era watering hole. The **Bale of Hay Saloon** contains period mechanical peep shows. The **Masonic Temple,** built of cut stone, still houses lodge meetings. The **Madison County Museum** contains artifacts from the Alder Gulch mining days, including furniture, clothing, and photos, and a collection of barbed wire. The **Thompson-Hickman Memorial Museum and Library,** tel. (406) 843-5346, contains the preserved clubfoot of a desperado and other vigilante mementos, as well as ore samples and mining equipment.

Other buildings have been restored to serve their original purposes, as barber shops, grocery stores, and other small businesses of an early mining camp-cum-state capital.

A short walk south on Jackson St. leads to **Alder Gulch Discovery Monument,** which commemorates the original gold strike of 1863. North on Fairweather St. about half a mile to a bluff above town is the **Boothill Cemetery.** Here are

*Virginia City
and Alder Gulch*

buried three road agents who were hanged by vigilantes during their brief tour of duty. Bill Fairweather was buried here until re-interred in a new cemetery with more law-abiding neighbors. Fairweather maintained the respect of the citizens of Alder Gulch by riding along Wallace Street scattering gold dust for children and the less fortunate. From Boothill there is also a good view of Alder Gulch.

Montana's oldest summer-stock theater group, the **Virginia City Players,** performs at two of Alder Gulch's historic buildings. At the **Opera House,** they perform period melodramas and comedies. Tickets are $10 adults, $5 children; the theater is open June 8-Sept. 7; shows start at 8 p.m. At the **Gilbert Brewery** the Players host a vaudeville variety show. Now restored as a bar, Montana's first brewery provides musical cabaret June 21-Sept. 14. Admission to the show is $8 adult, $5 children. For more information on the Virginia City Players, call (406) 843-5377.

Credit for the restoration of Virginia City belongs to Charles and Sue Bovey, who worked hard in the 1940s to preserve the old frontier town. They bought many of the dilapidated buildings and restored them to their original condition. Heirs of the Boveys were forced to sell the properties due to the high cost of insurance and upkeep. After protracted negotiations with buyers as different as Knott's Berry Farm and the National Park Service, the state of Montana "bought" Virginia City and will maintain it essentially as an open-air museum and park.

Accommodations and Food

The **Fairweather Inn,** 315 W. Wallace St., tel. (406) 843-5377 or (800) 648-7588, $45-50 d, is a lovingly restored Victorian hotel. Rooms go fast, so call ahead for reservations. It's open from June to mid-Sept. only. Virginia City's two B&B inns are open year-round in restored and period-furnished National Historic Register homes. The **Virginia City Country Inn,** is a tall, trim Victorian house at 115 E. Idaho, tel. (406) 843-5515, with rooms $45-65. Rooms at the **Stonehouse Inn,** 306 E. Idaho, tel. (406) 843-5504, are $55; the large stone house was built in 1884 by the local blacksmith.

The **Virginia City Campground,** tel. (406) 843-5493, just east of Virginia City, offers miniputt golf and gold panning for the kids.

The **Virginia City Cafe,** 210 W. Wallace St., tel. (406) 843-9997, is open for lunch only. Other establishments close during the winter.

NEVADA CITY

Virginia City's sister city one mile downstream grew up in the boom days of placer mining in Alder Gulch. Abandoned by the 1880s, the ghost town was restored in the 1950s by Charles and Sue Bovey, the driving force behind Virginia City's renovation. The Boveys brought in period buildings from other areas of Montana, creating an outdoor museum of early mining in Montana.

In addition to restored shops and businesses, the **Alder Gulch Short Line Steam Railroad**

Museum contains a collection of rolling stock and engines from the early days of railroading. The $5 admission includes fare on the narrow-gauge rail line running between Nevada and Virginia Cities. Also of interest is the **Nevada City Music Hall,** which houses an astonishing collection of old mechanical music machines. Check behind the Nevada City Hotel to glimpse the renowned two-story outhouse.

Practicalities

The **Nevada City Hotel and Cabins,** tel. (406) 843-5377 or (800) 648-7588, $55 d, is an authentic hostelry restored with an eye to modern comforts. The front part of the log hotel was a stage stop during the gold boom. The cabins are original miners' lodgings. Also in Nevada City, **Just An Experience,** tel. (406) 843-5445, offers B&B rooms and a cabin with a kitchen.

The **Star Bakery Restaurant** is a charming little cafe for light meals. Amenities in Nevada City are open from June to mid-Sept. only.

RUBY RIVER VALLEY

During the 1860s and '70s, the stage route called the Vigilante Trail ran from Alder Gulch down the Ruby River to Twin Bridges, and thence to Bannack or Helena. Thievery along this route led to the establishment of the Vigilantes. Here, too, traders and farmers began communities that would outlast the mining boom.

The Ruby River rises in the gentle peaks north of the Red Rock Lakes. Native Americans called the Ruby Passamari, or "Stinking Water," for the sulfur springs along its banks. The Ruby River, later named for the deceptive red garnets that early settlers mistook for rubies, is interred at Ruby Reservoir, where much of its flow is diverted into irrigation canals.

Alder

After low-tech placer mining extracted the richest gold deposits along Alder Gulch, gold dredges were brought in to rework the displaced, lower-grade gravel. The banks of pebbles at Alder are the remains of this process.

Dredging in the Ruby Valley reached its height during WW I, when Harvard University sponsored the operations and pocketed the proceeds.

Sixty years later, the banks of dredged gravel remain unreclaimed and unproductive.

The Northern Pacific built a branch line from Whitehall to Alder in the early 1900s to take out the dredged gold and other precious metals from the nearby hills. Today, talc mines in the Ruby Range are the area's most important mining operations. Watch for the white mounds near railroad sidings.

At Alder, a gravel road leads south seven miles to **Ruby Reservoir.** There is a free campground and, when the lake's not drawn down by irrigation, boating and fishing. Keep an eye out for garnets. A fair gravel road (eventually becoming Forest Service Rd. 100) continues up the Ruby River, where better fishing and great vistas reward the off-road enthusiast. About 20 miles from Ruby Reservoir is a Forest Service campground, called **Cottonwood Camp.** Forest Service Rd. 100 enters the Red Rock Valley just above the Red Rock Lake game refuge.

Accommodations and Food: Upper Canyon Outfitters, P.O. Box 109, Alder, MT 59710, tel. (800) 735-3973, operates a lodge for anglers, hikers, and horseback riders, and offers fly-fishing lessons on the Ruby River. The **Virginia City KOA,** tel. (406) 842-5677, is in fact just east of Alder, and is open to campers all year.

The **Alder Steakhouse and Bar,** tel. (406) 842-5159, open daily for dinner, and Mon.-Fri. for lunch, is the local supper club.

Laurin

Laurin preserves a hint of this tiny community's Gallic genesis in its pronunciation: with little apparent respect for the original French, you say law-RAY. Jean Baptiste Laurin established a trading post and stage stop along the banks of the Ruby River in the late 1860s and eventually amassed large agricultural holdings in the area. Laurin built St. Mary's Church, a handsome and substantial Catholic church constructed of local stone, as a gift to the town he founded.

The **Vigilante Inn,** tel. (406) 842-5982, is Laurin's sole restaurant, serving breakfast and lunch.

Robber's Roost

Three miles downriver from Laurin, along the old stage route between Alder Gulch and Bannack, is the roadhouse and bar once known as Pete Daly's Place. This log two-story bar and dance hall was built in 1863 and became associated with Henry Plummer and his band of ne'er-do-wells. After two outlaws were lynched by vigilantes nearby, Pete's Place became known as Robber's Roost. Bullet holes in the walls attest to the character of the Alder Gulch bar scene.

A full-length porch with hitching rail gives onto the first-floor bar and gambling hall; upstairs was the dance floor. On the veranda, dancers could catch a breath of air or desperados could plot mayhem as the situation demanded.

Robber's Roost now sits in the yard of a private farm. It's open to the public as an antique store-cum-museum. Call (406) 842-5304 for details.

Sheridan

Sheridan (pop. 723, elev. 5,079 feet) was established in 1866 as mining spread from Alder Gulch northeast to the Tobacco Root Mountains. Sheridan grew into a prosperous trade center for miners and ranchers, reflected in the handsome period storefronts.

Accommodations and Food: The **Mariah Motel,** in the heart of Sheridan at 220 S. Main, tel. (406) 842-5491, has rooms for $30 s, $40 d. **Zak Inn Guest Ranch,** 2905 Hwy. 287, Sheridan, MT 59749, tel. (406) 842-5540, offers access to fishing and other outdoor activities in the lower Ruby Valley.

The **Sheridan Bakery and Cafe,** 201 S. Main, tel. (406) 842-5716, open 7 a.m.-4 p.m., closed Sunday, is a friendly diner with home-baked goods. The **Log Cabin Cafe,** tel. (406) 684-5252, open for three meals a day, lies between Twin Bridges and Sheridan.

THE JEFFERSON RIVER VALLEY

At Twin Bridges, the Jefferson River collects its mighty tributaries—the Big Hole, Beaverhead, and Ruby Rivers—and flows north to its appointment with the Missouri at Three Forks. For much of this 80-mile journey, the Jefferson and its valley are open, wide, and relaxed, as if they too enjoy the spectacular mountain scenery rising above them. The ragged peaks of the Tobacco Root and Highland Mountains contain granite intrusions that are cousins to the mineral-rich formations near Butte.

The Jefferson's deep holes and brushy banks, which hampered Lewis and Clark's journey upriver, now excite sportspeople. Brown trout of storied size lurk in the shade of the overgrowth; river floaters, more captivated by the rugged mountain scenery than challenged by the current, enjoy the river's leisurely pace.

East of LaHood, the river drops into the Jefferson Canyon. Stop and watch for bighorn sheep along the high sheer cliffs. In a limestone formation high on the side of the canyon are the Lewis and Clark Caverns, one of the nation's largest developed cavern systems.

HISTORY

After Lewis and Clark ascended to Three Forks in 1805, their journey then became a series of conjectures about which river fork, and which fork of forks, to follow to the Continental Divide. At Three Forks, the Corps of Discovery chose the Jefferson. They could have saved themselves hundreds of miles of rambling in the upper Jefferson drainages if they had heeded Charbonneau's advice and traveled up Pipestone Creek, near Whitehall. They would have surmounted the Continental Divide in 20 miles and found themselves in the Columbia River drainage.

Near Twin Bridges, the captains chose to follow the Beaverhead River. A few miles upstream, Sacajawea recognized Beaverhead Rock, an immense limestone outcropping rising above the river, as a landmark for her people, the Shoshone.

One of the most stirring stories of the Montana frontier involves corps member John Colter, who could have little imagined the conditions under which he would next see the Jefferson. Colter didn't return to St. Louis with the rest of the corps in 1806, preferring to stay in Montana and lead the life of a mountain man.

In 1808, Colter and a companion were trapping on the lower Jefferson River. Blackfeet Indians ambushed the two men and immediately killed the other trapper. Colter was stripped of his clothing and given a 200-yard head start in a footrace for his life. After killing his closest pursuer with a stolen spear, Colter dived into the Jefferson and hid beneath a shelter of driftwood

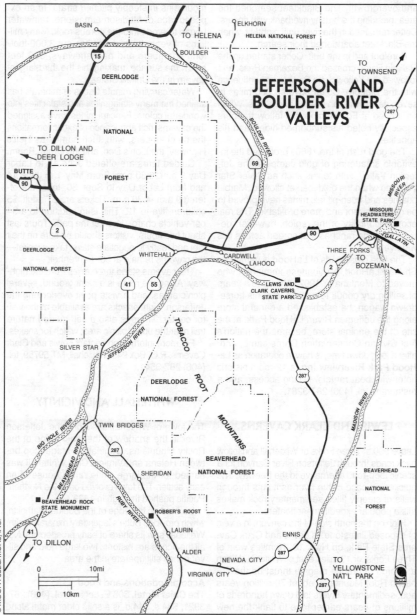

JEFFERSON AND BOULDER RIVER VALLEYS

TO HELENA

HELENA NATIONAL FOREST

ELKHORN

BASIN

BOULDER

DEERLODGE

15

TO TOWNSEND

287

NATIONAL

BOULDER RIVER

69

TO DILLON AND DEER LODGE

BUTTE

90

FOREST

2

MISSOURI RIVER

MISSOURI HEADWATERS STATE PARK

GALLATIN

DEERLODGE

NATIONAL FOREST

WHITEHALL

CARDWELL

LAHOOD

90

THREE FORKS TO BOZEMAN

2

41

55

LEWIS AND CLARK CAVERNS STATE PARK

JEFFERSON RIVER

SILVER STAR

TOBACCO ROOT MOUNTAINS

DEERLODGE

NATIONAL FOREST

287

MADISON RIVER

BEAVERHEAD

NATIONAL FOREST

BIG HOLE RIVER

TWIN BRIDGES

287

SHERIDAN

BEAVERHEAD

NATIONAL

FOREST

BEAVERHEAD ROCK STATE MONUMENT

RUBY RIVER

ROBBER'S ROOST

41

TO DILLON

LAURIN

ALDER

NEVADA CITY

VIRGINIA CITY

ENNIS

287

TO YELLOWSTONE NAT'L PARK

0   10mi

0   10km

© MOON PUBLICATIONS, INC.

and overgrowth. The Blackfeet searched the area, prodding the brushy riverbank with spears. Colter remained in the river until nightfall, when the Blackfeet abandoned their search.

Barefoot and in the buff, Colter started up the Gallatin River, crossed the Bozeman Pass, and followed the Yellowstone River to its confluence with the Bighorn. Colter covered 300 miles in seven days, living on berries and seeds. When he arrived at Fort Remon, his fellow trappers especially noted his sunburned hide—and his appetite.

The gold rush of the 1860s produced the inevitable smattering of gold camps in the Jefferson Valley, with towns such as Silver Star booming when the gold market allowed. Marble quarries and open-pit talc mines have proved to be more resilient and more profitable. The real economic vitality of the region, however, derives from the ranches that spread across this wide valley.

The little crossroads of **LaHood** is named for Shadan LaHood, a Lebanese immigrant who moved to Montana in 1902. After a few years of selling dry goods to settlers from his horse-drawn wagon, he established a general store along the Jefferson River. LaHood Park, at the site of the original store, became the nation's first Civilian Conservation Corps camp, and, after a long down time, is now in operation as **La-Hood Park Riverview Inn,** a 12-room historic hotel with boat rentals, fishing access, and a restaurant, tel. (406) 287-3281.

LEWIS AND CLARK CAVERNS

Leave I-90 at Three Forks or Whitehall and follow back roads through Jefferson River Canyon for a scenic loop-road alternative to the freeway. The quickening pace of the river as it cuts through walls of steeply tilted sedimentary rock makes this a popular expedition for floaters.

High on the north side of the canyon, in a vein of exposed limestone, is Lewis and Clark Caverns State Park, on Hwy. 10, 19 miles west of Three Forks, or 13 miles east of Whitehall. When a ramrod of granite magma thrust up the Tobacco Root Mountains about 70 million years ago, sedimentary layers laid down hundreds of millions of years earlier rose to flank the new

mountains in steeply pitched strata. In an exposed face of Madison Limestone, rainwater began to erode into the porous rock. Many millions of years later, water has cut 3,000-foot-long chambers and passageways, 300 feet below the surface, making this the third-largest cavern in the United States.

Water carrying minute traces of minerals has stained the many stalagmites and stalactites into wonderful colors. Fanciful minds have assigned the caverns' rich abundance of exotic formations theme chambers, with such names as Hell's Highway, the Lion's Den, and the Organ Room.

Guided tours are offered June 15 to Labor Day 9 a.m.-6:30 p.m. From May 1 to June 14 and from Labor Day to Sept. 30, tours are offered 9 a.m.-4:30 p.m. Tickets are $7 adult, $5 children five to 12. This is in addition to a $4 per-vehicle charge to enter the park. Tours last about two hours; visitors should be sure on their feet and ready to negotiate stairs; take a jacket—the caverns remain at 50° Fahrenheit.

The caverns stand three miles from the highway. Along the route is a campground, several picnic areas, and a vista point overlooking the Jefferson. Light snacks are available at the visitor center. There is also a self-guided nature trail near the upper picnic area; watch for snakes.

For more information contact Lewis and Clark Caverns, P.O. Box 949, Whitehall, MT 59759, tel. (406) 287-3541.

WHITEHALL AND VICINITY

The town of Whitehall sits along the Jefferson River in the shadow of the main spine of the Rocky Mountains. Originally a stage stop between Helena and Virginia City, Whitehall was named for the large white ranch house of an early settler. The town evolved once the Northern Pacific pushed through in 1889.

Located on the edge of the Boulder Batholith, which provided Butte's legendary mineral wealth, Whitehall saw its share of early prospectors. Not all the riches are historic: two large gold and silver mines still operate in the area.

Accommodations and Food
The **Chief Motel,** 303 E. Legion, tel. (406) 287-3921, $34 s, $44 d, is a solid older motel along

Hwy. 10. The **Rice Motel,** at 7 N. A St., tel. (406) 287-3895, charges $24 s, $36 d. There's also a **Super 8** at 515 N. Whitehall St., tel. (406) 287-5588 or (800) 800-8000.

Over in LaHood, the **LaHood Park Riverview Inn,** tel. (406) 287-3281, is a historic hotel-cum-fishing lodge.

For good food, the best choice is **Land of Magic Too Supper Club,** 27 W. Legion, tel. (406) 287-5252. Open for three meals a day, it specializes in steaks and seafood.

Silver Star
Silver Star has settled into a gentle doze after an eventful early history. One of the oldest settlements in the state, the town's founder, Green Campbell, was issued Montana land patent No. 1 in 1866. The town sits on the southernmost extreme of the rich Boulder Batholith, and miners extracted hefty amounts of gold, silver, and lead from the Highland Mountains. Silver Star was the only town between Virginia City and Helena during the high-flying 1870s, booming as it serviced the needs of local miners and settlers.

Legend contends that Edward, Prince of Wales, spent three days in Silver Star in 1878. It's been pretty much downhill ever since.

Accommodations: Jefferson River Park, one mile south of Silver Star, tel. (406) 684-5262, is a lovely campground right on the Jefferson River.

TWIN BRIDGES AND VICINITY

Twin Bridges slumbers near the confluence of the Ruby, Beaverhead, and Big Hole Rivers. Lewis and Clark rested here before continuing up the Beaverhead. At Three Forks, the captains named the mightiest of the Missouri forks for President Jefferson. At the forks of the Jefferson, they decided to name each for the cardinal virtues of the president: Philanthropy, Philosophy, and Wisdom. Later settlers waxed less poetic, renaming the rivers the Ruby, the Beaverhead, and the Big Hole. History is silent as to whether the later generation considered these attributes of President Jefferson.

With all these rivers about, the mystery is not which two bridges spawned the town's name, but why there were only two. Twin Bridges found

At Twin Bridges, the tributaries of the Jefferson River join, providing anglers with great sport.

JUDY JEWELL

itself at the center of commerce and transportation for southwestern Montana. By 1884, three daily stagecoaches passed through the town. Reflecting its then centrality, Montana Territory in 1889 built the first normal school in Twin Bridges. After political maneuvering, the state moved the normal college to upstart Dillon in 1893. The school buildings became the State Orphans' Home shortly thereafter. The facility had been home to over 5,000 children before it was closed in 1975. The buildings can be seen just west of town along the road to Dillon.

For many, Twin Bridges is the object of a pilgrimage just to go to the R.L. Winston Rod Company shop. This company makes very well-regarded fly-fishing rods.

Accommodations and Food: King's Motel, 307 S. Main, tel. (406) 684-5639, offers kitchenettes and allows pets. Single rooms begin at $30, doubles at $42—some rooms can sleep up to seven people. Inexpensive accommodations are also available at the **Stardust Country Inn,** 409 N. Main, tel. (406) 684-5648. The **Blue Anchor Bar and Cafe,** 102 N. Main, tel. (406) 684-5655, is open for three meals a day. Just outside of Twin Bridges, on the way to Sheridan, is the **Log Cabin Bakery and Cafe,** 25 Middle Rd., tel. (406) 684-5252.

Beaverhead Rock
Between Dillon and Twin Bridges is Beaverhead Rock, a landmark to settler and Indian alike. The excited Sacajawea recognized the huge outcropping and told the rest of the Corps of Discovery that they were in her homeland. Three hundred feet high, it is apparently the leading edge of land thrust eastward by mountain building to the west.

I-15 CORRIDOR, BUTTE TO HELENA

Between Helena and Butte, I-15 crosses over the Boulder Batholith, an intrusion of magma that shot up from the bowels of the earth like a piston about 70 million years ago. The formation is made largely of granite, but in places it also contains an almost incomprehensible wealth of valuable minerals. Near towns such as Clancy and Jefferson City, gold was panned, mined, and dredged. The orderly dikes of processed gravel tailings from streambeds lie like welts across the landscape.

The old town of Boulder lies at the center of this rich mining area. Its spent mines have recently been put to new use. Radon gas, in low concentrations, occurs naturally in the mineshafts. People who suffer from a variety of ailments—from cancer to asthma to lupus—have found relief descending the mines and breathing the radon-rich air. Called "health mines," these strictly non-AMA-approved facilities have become so popular that peak seasons are reserved for weeks in advance.

HISTORY

About 120 years ago, this forlorn piece of nondescript mountain landscape was one of the busiest and most populated in Montana. Rich but diffident deposits of gold first attracted placer miners in the 1860s. Gold camps sprang up in every gulch. After the surface deposits were exhausted, many camps developed into industrial mining towns, as capitalists brought in more highly mechanized techniques to mine and smelt underground silver, lead, and gold. A final reprise of Montana's mining boom years came in the early decades of this century, when gold dredges reworked the tailings from old mines for the trace

amounts of gold missed by earlier mining methods. By redigesting mining refuse and stream bottoms in a rich muddy soup, dredges were able to isolate what mineral wealth remained, leaving acres of mine tailings.

Between Helena and Boulder, place-names recall important early settlements and boomtowns: Jefferson City, Prickly Pear Gulch, Montana City, Wickes, Corbin—towns that once vied with Helena and Butte in importance during territorial days. Now, little remains, save a citation in a history book and mounds of worked gravel, these towns long ago having slumped from catalepsy into dilapidation.

Boulder and Basin survived the decline of Montana's mining industry by establishing a somewhat more diversified economy. As early as the 1880s Boulder Hot Springs attracted tourists and weekenders to its spa resort. Boulder was also the trade center for ranchers in the Boulder River Valley. Basin struggled on as a rail center for local gold and silver mines until the 1940s, when the presence of uranium met the demands of a changing world. After a brief flurry of activity, these radium-rich mines became the radon health mines that currently energize the local economy.

BOULDER AND VICINITY

Named for the large stones littered around its valley, Boulder (pop. 1,589, elev. 5,158 feet) began as a stage stop between Fort Benton and Virginia City in the 1860s. Its prominence as a trading center was enhanced when the state built the **Montana Home for the Feeble-minded** here in 1892. Now known as the Montana Development Center, the facility houses and trains developmentally impaired citizens.

MIRACLE CURES
IN MONTANA RADON GAS MINES

In 1950, a California woman who suffered from arthritis accompanied her husband into a uranium mine near Boulder. She noted a marked relief from the constant pain to which she had grown accustomed. She related her experiences to a fellow arthritis sufferer. The friend also visited the Boulder mine, and her stay produced the same rapid recovery.

Word of the "miracle cure" soon spread, reaching an early peak when *Life* magazine sent a news team to cover the "stampede" of people arriving to seek this underground cure.

Just why the cure seems to work hasn't been adequately explained. Radon gas is a naturally occurring gas formed when radium, in the process of aging, oxidizes. This radioactive gas occurs in Basin-Boulder mines in levels deemed safe for miners but in concentrations considered therapeutic by the mines' many promoters. Sympathetic researchers contend that radon gas stimulates the pituitary gland to produce health-giving hormones and natural steroids, which can ease or eradicate the pain of conditions caused by hormonal dysfunction.

The recommended "cure" involves a careful regimen of contact with radon gas. Patrons are asked to spend no more than one hour at a time in the mines no more than three times per day. About 30 hours of contact with radon gas is considered to

be the optimum treatment. Within the mines, there are sofas, tables, and chairs for the visitors' comfort; card games and reading are the usual pastimes.

Radon gas therapy is *not* medically accepted in the United States (the European medical establishment is less hostile to radon gas therapy), and the owners stress that the mines are open for people seeking *nonmedical* treatment. There is no guarantee of cure.

There are, however, many moving testimonials from people who have found relief from aggravated and longstanding afflictions. The list of physical conditions for which radon gas may be efficacious grows as the number of afflicted visitors grows. Sufferers of arthritis, migraines, eczema, asthma, diabetes, and allergies have testified to the mines' healing virtues.

If you have questions about the "health mines," contact the **Boulder-Basin Chamber of Commerce,** P.O. Box 68, Boulder, MT 59632, or contact the following mines directly at **Free Enterprise Health Mine,** P.O. Box 67, Boulder, MT 59632, tel. (406) 255-3383; **Merry Widow Health Mine,** P.O. Box 129, Basin, MT 59631, tel. (406) 255-3220.

Radon therapy is very popular; if you are considering a visit, call ahead for reservations, and don't be surprised if the facilities are all booked up.

Old Boulder

The town center of Boulder, with its sprawl of red-brick storefronts, retains much of the flavor of a frontier commercial center. Its most prominent landmark is the **Jefferson County Courthouse,** built in 1889. Its grand scale and gargoyles betray the German education of John Paulsen, who also designed the administration building for the Home for the Feeble-minded. Both are listed on the National Register of Historic Places.

Boulder Hot Springs

One of the earliest tourist facilities in the state, this resort began in 1883 as a spa for the rich and influential in Helena and Butte. Over the years, the lodge has been redesigned and reinterpreted in fashionable, ever more grandiose, architectural vernaculars. The earliest wooden-frame hotel was replaced by a Queen Anne clapboard lodge,

only to be renovated in Spanish mission style. The imposing lodge at Boulder Hot Springs is undergoing another rejuvenation, this time as a New Age-y health and spiritual retreat. A corner of the huge lodge has been renovated and is open as a B&B; rooms run $45-65 single, $70-90 double, including swimming and soaking.

Nonguests can stop by for a swim in the 90-95° outdoor pool, then plunge into indoor hot and cold pools or sit in the steam room for $4, $3 seniors, $2 children. A $11 Sunday buffet lunch includes use of the pools. Boulder Hot Springs is three miles south of Boulder on Hwy. 69. Direct inquiries to P.O. Box 930, Boulder, MT 59632, tel. (406) 225-4339.

Elkhorn

The silver-mining town of Elkhorn began in the 1870s and flourished until the early 1890s, when

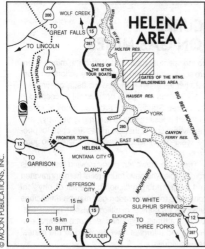

HELENA AREA

the international silver market bottomed out. Although only the ghosts of the town remain, Elkhorn is reckoned to be one of the best-preserved mining camps in the state. Buildings of note: **Gillian Hall,** a two-story bar and dance hall; and **Fraternity Hall,** a meetinghouse in neoclassical style. Elkhorn is six miles south of Boulder on Hwy. 69, then 12 miles north on graveled Elkhorn Road. During winter months, the trip is best made on cross-country skis.

Accommodations and Food

Castoria Inn, 211 S. Monroe, tel. (406) 225-3549, dates from 1889 and is listed on the National Register of Historic Places. It currently offers bed and breakfast starting at $40; rooms in the motel are $34 d. The **O-Z Motel,** 114 N. Main, tel. (406) 225-3364, $30 s, $35 d, is an older motel in the center of historic Boulder.

For campers, the area offers pleasant RV parks with easy access to fishing in the Boulder River. Try the **Sunset Trailer Court,** 4th and Adams, tel. (406) 225-3387, or **Phil and Tim's RV Park,** one-quarter mile south of I-15 on Hwy. 69, tel. (406) 225-3370. Just south of Boulder is the Forest Service's **Elder Creek Campground.**

You'll find **Phil and Tim's Cafe,** open 6 a.m.-2 p.m., in **Phil and Tim's Bowling Alley,** tel. (406) 225-3201. Otherwise, try **Mountain Good Restaurant,** tel. (406) 225-3382, open daily 6:30 a.m.-2 p.m.

BASIN

Located in narrow Boulder River Canyon, Basin is an old mining town that has avoided the narcoleptic destiny of many other mining camps. By luck or connivance, Basin always successfully managed to market what it has.

Gold prospectors such as Granville Stuart helped found the community, but it was silver mines that put Basin on the map during the 1880s.

Basin fell into a long doze after a spurt of gold mining during the 1920s, then reactivated when the uranium market developed during WW II. The radon gas present in many of the old mines is now marketed for its reputed health-giving benefits.

Basin's main street exhibits structures from more prosperous times. The **Masonic Hall** dates from the turn of the century, as does the old boardinghouse in the Sockerson Block. Watch the hillsides near Basin for old flumes and mine adits.

Over the past few years, Basin has attracted artists and musicians, giving the tiny town a lively, alternative feel. Locals have formed the **Montana Artists Refuge,** a residential program for all types of artists. Refuge residents live and work in an old downtown brick building, and they have plenty of chances to collaborate with each other and with the Basin community. The Refuge's big fundraiser, a jazz brunch usually held the first weekend of June, is a lively time to visit. For information on the residency program or the annual brunch, call (406) 225-3525.

Support the local artists with a visit to **Basin Creek Pottery and Gallery,** on Main St., tel. (406) 225-3218.

If you've been hurtling down I-15 and need to stretch your legs, turn off the freeway south of Basin at the Bernice exit (exit 151) and drive a couple of miles east to the Bear Gulch trail. While it's not exactly wilderness, the trail through open forest and meadows is a good break from the road.

Accommodations and Food

Most of the health mines provide accommodations and campgrounds for their guests. Be sure to reserve ahead. The campground at the **Merry Widow Health Mine,** two blocks off Basin Creek

Rd., tel. (406) 225-3220, is open to the public, but spaces go quickly. The Merry Widow also offers motel accommodations at $22 s, $35 d (five-night minimum).

The Silver Saddle Bar and Cafe, tel. (406) 225-9995, open daily 7:30 a.m.-8 p.m., serves good basic food in an authentic western atmosphere.

HELENA

Montana's capital city straddles one of history's richest gold strikes—Last Chance Gulch. Unlike its contemporary boomtowns, Helena (pop. 27,982, elev. 4,124 feet) managed not only to survive but to prevail through good times and bad. Like a snake swallowing its tail, Helena transformed itself from seething gold camp to trade center, then to capital city, and finally into a cultural and tourist center.

In Montana, only Butte can approach Helena in sheer historicity, but history has left Helena a richer legacy of monuments and architecture. From the elegance of the State Capitol and the Cathedral of St. Helena to the stone shacks on Reeder's Alley, the highs, lows, and middlings of the state's history each have here their testimony. Excellent museums and galleries present and preserve the best of Montana's past and present.

People in Helena are both insiders and outsiders. The state is by far the city's largest employer, and Helena's bright, friendly character derives in part from internalizing the lessons of political life. Citizens greet you as if they want to be popularly elected. The real politicians are pretty obvious: spot the ill-fitting western dress jackets, the clumsy handbags and unsensible shoes, and the telltale chummy complicity.

But come the weekend, the insiders go outside. Helena is unbelievably well situated for recreation. With fishing and boating on nearby lakes on the Missouri, hiking and skiing in Helena National Forest, and exploring old ghost towns and other reminders of the past always just nearby, the Helena area tempts the traveler with a rich brew of history and outdoor activity.

HISTORY

Helena began, as did so many other gold camps, as the cry went up, "Just one last chance before we leave." In this case, four Confederate ex-soldiers were panning in 1864 for gold in a narrow gulch called Prickly Pear, just below the crest of the Continental Divide. The "Four Geor-

JEANNETTE RANKIN—
A LIFE OF PRINCIPLE AND PEACE

It's almost a cliche that Montana breeds strong women, but Jeannette Rankin stands out as one of the most forthright of the bunch.

Born in 1880 into a Missoula ranch and timber family, Jeanette was a serious child who considered Chief Joseph a personal hero. After stints teaching at a country school outside Missoula and working in a San Francisco settlement house, she attended social-work school in New York. There she became involved in the women's suffrage movement, and she went on to work in Washington state and Montana to get women the vote. She was a good public speaker, and after a taste of politics she became convinced that politics, not social work, was the most effective way to change the world.

Missoula's own Jeannette Rankin was, among many other things, the first woman representative elected to the U.S. Congress.

In 1916, Rankin ran for Congress, as a Republican, and was elected to the House of Representatives. She was the first woman elected to national office in the United States. The first day she took her seat in the House, President Woodrow Wilson asked Congress to authorize official U.S. entry into WW I. Rankin voted against war, which upset many of her constituents and led to her defeat when she ran for the Senate in 1918.

Fresh out of Congress, and increasingly engaged in the nascent peace movement, she went to Europe and helped found the Women's International League for Peace and Freedom. Upon her return to the States, Rankin worked as a peace activist in Washington, D.C. Sensing that the South was a good place for a peace movement to take root, she also bought a farm in Georgia. Montana remained her voting place, however, and in 1940, the state again elected her to Congress.

After Pearl Harbor, Rankin was the only member of Congress to vote against entry into WW II. She cast her vote saying, "As a woman I cannot go to war, and I refuse to send anybody else."

Rankin was not returned to Congress in 1942, but she remained active in women's, children's, and peace issues, all of which she had supported in Congress. In 1968, she led a group of women in a march protesting the Vietnam War. Rankin died in 1973.

(sidebar credit, vertical:) MONTANA HISTORICAL SOCIETY, HELENA

---

gians," as they were later known, found color in their pans in the draw they called Last Chance Gulch. Word spread and the rush was on. By 1876, the town had grown to 4,000 inhabitants.

At the time, Montana was a territory lacking a cohesive center. Due to the boom-and-bust nature of its initial settlements, the focal point of Montana moved from strike to strike. The earliest territorial capital of Bannack was almost deserted by the time the center of government moved to Virginia City. In turn, Helena attracted the capital in 1875.

Helena had advantages that the other mining centers lacked. The gold, then the silver and lead, were richer in Helena than in other early settlements. Helena was midway on the stage routes between Fort Benton—the uppermost steamboat reach on the Missouri—and Virginia City and other mining areas in southwestern Montana. Newcomers quickly realized that wealth was in trade, not mining, and gravitated to Helena, the largest center of population in the territory. Trade quickly underpinned mining to support Helena's economy. Sometime miners, now important captains of industry, built huge mansions on the city's west side.

Battle for the Capital

Helena first overtook Virginia City in 1875, when

voters chose it to be the territorial capital. The real battle began when Montana was recognized as a state in 1889. The feud between Copper Kings Marcus Daly and William Clark ricocheted across the state. What had been a grudge match of political influence became war as each backed a different city to be capital of the new state of Montana in a statewide election in 1894.

While each of the industrialists had solid power bases in Butte, the wrangle involved Anaconda, the city that Daly built, and the established capital of Helena, where Clark had major mining investments. The attack politics of our time could take lessons from the acrimonious battles of the Copper Kings. Each man controlled newspapers; each shamelessly bought and influenced votes. ("It came through the transom" is an expression still used in Montana to explain a windfall gift from a patron.) In the end, Helena only just won the statewide vote, retaining its hold as the capital.

Helena continued to hold sway over the rich and powerful during the late 1890s and early years of the 1900s, as is witnessed by its elaborate architecture of the period. Be they ranchers, miners, or tradesmen, the rich from across the state hadn't "arrived" until they had engaged in the mansion-building competition that thrived on the west side of Last Chance Gulch. The concentration of wealth in Helena is legendary. In the late 1880s there were more millionaires in Helena per capita than anywhere else in the nation.

SIGHTS

The Montana State Capitol

The State Capitol, 1301 6th Ave., was begun in 1899. This imposing structure, domed with a cupola of Butte copper, was enlarged in 1912 by the extensions containing the present legislative wings. The statue on the dome commemorates an odd episode in Montana history. After the bruising fight for state capital between Helena and Anaconda, the Capitol Commission ran off with the books. When this statue arrived at the railroad station from a foundry in Ohio, no one knew who ordered it, who paid for it, or what it was meant for. The foundry's records were shortly destroyed in a fire, leaving the mysterious statue no history, and no future. The builders of the Capitol needed statuary for the top of its dome, and the *Goddess of Liberty* found its way to the top.

Significant paintings and murals decorate the Capitol. In the House Chambers hangs *Lewis and Clark Meeting the Flathead Indians at Ross' Hole* by Charles M. Russell, one of his largest and most acclaimed works. In the lobby of the House of Representatives are six paintings detailing the state's history, by E.S. Paxson. Tours of the Capitol are given daily on the hour, 9 a.m.-5 p.m. For information call (406) 444-4789.

The Capitol Area

Known in local parlance as the East Side, the

Montana State Capitol

area around the Capitol is directly south of the downtown area and contains many buildings of historic interest.

Probably the first thing a summer visitor should do while in Helena is take the quick city tour offered by **Last Chance Tours,** tel. (406) 442-6880. This open-air tour train does a quick drive-by of most of Helena's historic and scenic properties; the traveler can decide what to explore in further depth. On the route are buildings in the Capitol area, Last Chance Gulch, Reeder's Alley, the mansion district, and Carroll College. Catch the "Last Chancer," as the tour train is nicknamed, just outside the Montana Historical Society at 6th Ave. and N. Roberts St., across the street from the Capitol. Tours begin at 9 a.m. and continue on the hour until 4 p.m.; fare is $4.50.

The **Montana Historical Society,** 225 N. Roberts St., tel. (406) 444-2694, is Montana's premier museum, mixing fine art, an exhibit charting the state's history, and changing exhibits. Of special interest is the **MacKay Gallery of Charles M. Russell Art,** one of the nation's largest public collections of Russell's art. If "western" art seems like an oxymoron to you, come marvel at the brilliant use of color and composition by this unschooled cowboy artist. The **Montana Homeland Exhibit** tells the story of Montana, beginning with Indian prehistory and moving on through the era of settlement. Three rooms contain over 2,000 artifacts. Other galleries change exhibits but often contain fascinating displays of frontier photographs. Of interest to historians and researchers are the **Library and Photo Archives.** Open Mon.-Fri. 8 a.m.-6 p.m., weekends 9 a.m.-5 p.m., Memorial Day to Labor Day; Mon.-Fri. 8 a.m.-5 p.m. and Saturday 9 a.m.-5 p.m. the rest of the year; admission is free.

From 1913 to 1959, Montana's governor lived at the **Old Governor's Mansion,** 304 N. Ewing St., tel. (406) 444-2694. Built in 1883 by a local entrepreneur, the 20-room residence is now owned by the Montana Historical Society, which has restored the ornate building to its historic splendor. Free tours operate on the hour, noon-5 p.m.

The **Cathedral of St. Helena,** 509 N. Warren, tel. (406) 442-5825, was begun in 1908 but wasn't finished until 1924. Modeled after Cologne Cathedral, Helena's largest church dominates the skyline with its 230-foot twin spires. Its stained glass was fashioned in Germany, although the images of the Seven Sacraments seem out of a Burne-Jones Pre-Raphaelite painting. The cathedral is open to visitors 9 a.m.- 5 p.m., unless services are taking place. Free tours are available; call (406) 442-5825.

Last Chance Gulch

In the 1860s, Prickly Pear Creek snaked down from the mountains through a thicket of mining claims called Last Chance Gulch. As mining gave way to commerce, the gulch remained the main street; its winding path, and especially the one-claim-sized business buildings, still reflect its mining past. The old business district of Helena is still impressive, even after a 1933 earthquake destroyed some of its buildings.

Much of Last Chance Gulch is now a pedestrian mall, designed in the 1970s to make this historic main street more attractive to tourists and business. Have a look at the handsome, empty storefronts and decide if it has worked.

The extensive infrastructure of historic business buildings in Helena proves that the capital's most significant occupation was commerce, not mining. Several walking-tour maps to the Last Chance Gulch area are available from the chamber of commerce and from **Downtown Helena,** 121 N. Last Chance Gulch, tel. (406) 442-9869. Notable buildings not to miss:

The Power Block, 58-62 N. Last Chance Gulch, was built in 1889; note that on the southeast corner, each of the five floors has windows grouped in corresponding numbers of panes. The **Securities Building,** 101 N. Last Chance Gulch, built in 1886, is a Romanesque former bank with curious carved thumbprints between the first-floor arches. The **Montana Club,** 24 W. 6th Ave., was Montana's most prestigious private club: membership was open only to millionaires. The club's present building was designed by Cass Gilbert, who designed the U.S. Supreme Court Building.

The **Atlas Building,** 7-9 N. Last Chance Gulch, is one of Helena's most fanciful; on a cornice upheld by Atlas, a salamander and lizards do symbolic battle. **Reeder's Alley,** 308 S. Park Ave., is a winding series of one-room brick shanties built in the 1870s to house the mining camp's many bachelors. Today, it's a theme alley dedicated to shops and places to eat.

Visit the Norwest Bank, 350 N. Last Chance Gulch, tel. (406) 447-2025, to see the **Gold Col-**

lection, displaying gold in many forms, from nuggets to leaves.

West Side Mansions
Montana's grandest historic homes grace the hillside above Helena. In an area roughly bounded by Stuart, Monroe, Dearborn, and Power Streets stand dozens of imposing monuments to the economic clout of their merchant, mining, or ranching owners. The mansions display a bewildering assortment of styles; Mark Twain described these Helena homes as "Queen Anne in front and Mary Ann behind." In all their opulence, these are what money could buy in Helena during the boom years of 1880-1900.

None of the old homes are regularly open for viewing, but a walk through these beautiful old neighborhoods is a must for anyone with an interest in historic homes.

Downtown Environs
Given all the beautiful architecture in Helena, it is ironic that the city's most distinctive building is the **Civic Center,** on the corner of Neill and Fuller, built in 1921 as the Masonic Algeria Shrine Temple. This exercise in high camp is a Moorish revival edifice with a 175-foot minaret, onion dome, and intricately modeled exterior brickwork. It now houses Helena's municipal offices.

Overlooking Helena from the northeast is **Carroll College,** a private Catholic college with a student body of 1,400. Carroll stands on 63 acres atop a bluff still known as Capitol Hill. The site was offered for the state capitol in 1895, but the landowner wanted $7,000 for the real estate, and the frugal Capitol Commission went elsewhere.

Fort Harrison
Established in 1895, Fort Harrison, just north of Helena on Hwy. 12, was one of the Army's last defensive garrisons against ructions in the West. Although the troops were never called out, the fort remained active through WW I. By 1922, the fort was given over to the Veterans Administration and turned into a large veterans' health facility. Fort Harrison still operates as a veterans' hospital, but its most interesting buildings are its 1905 officers' quarters. Built of brick, these imposing three-story duplexes boast wide verandas and gabled roofs. Turn-of-the-century Army life in Montana was extremely genteel,

judging by these lodgings. Buildings at Fort Harrison are closed to the public.

Marysville
Seven miles north of Helena off Hwy. 279, this near ghost town has just enough life left to feed passers by. The **Marysville House,** in the midst of abandoned general stores, churches, and hotels, is housed in the old train depot and is known for its ample meals.

THE ARTS

Theater
Helena is proud of its newest addition to its arts, the **Myrna Loy Center for the Performing Arts,** 15 N. Ewing St., tel. (406) 442-0287. Named for the late film actress who hailed from the Helena area, the center is housed in the revamped 1880s jail. A performance space, gallery, and art-film theater (the Second Story Cinema) combine to make this a jewel in Helena's cultural crown.

The **Grandstreet Theatre,** 325 N. Park Ave., tel. (406) 442-4270, is Helena's community theater. Grandstreet works closely with drama students from Carroll College and conducts a theater school for young people.

Galleries
The **Holter Museum of the Arts,** 12 E. Lawrence St., tel. (406) 442-6400, displays changing exhibits of contemporary art and offers workshops and readings. Summer visitors should check out the Western Rendezvous of Art, a large hanging of noted western artists' works; in the middle of August, the works go on sale. Open Tues.-Sat. noon-5 p.m., Sunday noon-4 p.m.; free admission.

Several private western-art galleries range along Last Chance Gulch, including **Ghost Art Gallery,** 21 S. Last Chance Gulch, tel. (406) 443-4536, and **Cason Gallery,** 7 N. Last Chance Gulch, tel. (406) 443-5919.

The **Archie Bray Foundation,** 2915 Country Club Ave., tel. (406) 443-3502, is a studio workshop, classroom, and gallery for ceramic artists. The brickyard and kilns of **Western Clay Manufacturing Company** have stood just outside Helena for over 100 years. Archie Bray, whose father began the business, was approached by local artists to use the brickyard's huge beehive kilns to fire ceramics. Bray, already active in the Helena arts scene, decided to dedicate a portion of the factory to the ceramic arts. In 1951, he founded the Archie Bray Foundation, now a world-famous facility for training talented young potters and a space in which resident artists can experiment and exhibit.

Visitors can watch potters in workshops and view works for sale in the gallery. The old kilns and outbuildings still stand, while avant-garde ceramics, colorful and abstract, are strewn about with guileless abandon.

RECREATION

Hiking is as close as **Mount Helena,** the city's 620-acre park on the west side of Last Chance Gulch. Seven trails wind up and across the mountainside; some ascend to Mount Helena's 5,468-foot peak, and others dawdle in meadows. To reach the park, follow the ravine behind Reeder's Alley on foot or drive to the top of Adams Street behind the mansion district.

A good diversion for hot kids is **Spring Meadow State Park,** a small lake just west of Helena off Euclid Avenue. A trail rings the lake, but the real attractions are the beaches, lined with swimmers and anglers in summer. Admission is $1 per person.

Great Divide Ski Area, 22 miles northwest of Helena, is a small slope, with 1,330 feet of vertical drop and bargain rates. Adults ski for $20, children and seniors $10. The season runs from mid-Dec. to early April, closed on Tuesdays. Call (406) 449-3746 for more information.

The municipal **swimming pool** is at Memorial Park, 1200 Last Chance Gulch, tel. (406) 449-3483. There are **tennis courts** at the park behind the Civic Center, Neill St. at Park Ave., and at Barney Park, Cleveland and Hudson Streets. Both parks also have picnic facilities and playgrounds.

Holter, Hauser, and Canyon Ferry Lakes in the vicinity of Helena provide excellent fishing, boating, and even windsurfing.

ACCOMMODATIONS

B&Bs

Those who simply can't get enough of Helena's historic homes might consider spending a few

nights at **The Sanders Bed and Breakfast,** 328 N. Ewing St., tel. (406) 442-3309, an impressive mansion built by in 1875 by Montana's first U.S. Senator. This National Registry-listed property is amazingly well-preserved and filled with lovely furnishings, many original to the home. Even though a great deal of care is taken to preserve period authenticity, all of the seven bedrooms have private baths, telephones, and hair dryers, and the entire mansion is air-conditioned. All the rooms have a TV tucked away for inveterate small screen fanatics, though more in keeping with the spirit of the place are the radio alarms, each tuned to the local public radio station. Breakfasts are served in the formal dining room, itself a showpiece of carved oak moldings. Room charges range $80-105.

Just down the street is Helena's other historic inn, **The Barrister B&B,** 416 N. Ewing St., tel. (406) 443-7330 or (800) 823-1148, an 1874 mansion located near St. Helena Cathedral. Its features include ornate fireplaces, antique stained-glass windows, and carved staircases. Modern niceties are also in evidence, including air-conditioning, TVs in rooms, all private baths, and a guest business center with fax machine, copier, and computer. Rooms here are $75-105.

Mountain Meadow Inn, 2245 Head Ln., tel. (406) 442-1909 or (888) 776-6466, with rooms ranging $50-90, is a B&B and a restaurant out by Spring Meadow Lake.

Hotels and Motels

Most of Helena's hotels and motels are located at the fringes of the city at busy intersections. The exceptions downtown are the **Park Plaza Hotel,** tel. (406) 443-2200 or (800) 332-2290, 22 N. Last Chance Gulch, $70 s, $86 d, a well-appointed, nicely renovated downtown hotel, and the more modest but well-situated **Budget Inn Express,** 524 Last Chance Gulch, tel. (406) 442-0600 or (800) 862-1334, $35 s, $45 d.

The **Aladdin Motor Inn,** 2101 11th Ave., tel. (406) 443-2300 or (800) 541-2743, has rooms at $47 s, $61 d, and an indoor pool, hot tub, steam room, and sauna, and an on-site restaurant. Pets are welcome for a $6 fee. **Jorgenson's Holiday Motel,** 1714 11th Ave., tel. (406) 442-1770 or (800) 272-1770, $62 s, $67 d, is near the Capitol and offers an indoor pool, exercise equipment, guest laundry, and restaurant. The newly renovated **Helena Super 8,** 2201 11th Ave., tel. (406) 443-2450 or (800) 848-8888, $55 s, $65 d, has an exercise room, guest laundry, and king rooms with computer hookups. **Knight's Rest Motel,** 1831 Euclid Ave., tel. (406) 442-6384 or (800) 303-6384, is a good value with rooms at $35 s, $43 d; pets are okay.

The **Lamplighter Motel,** 1006 Madison Ave., tel. (406) 442-9200, $36 s, $39 d, offers accommodations in homey cottage units. Some are family units with full kitchens, several are two- or three-bedroom units. Pets are $5 extra.

Best Western Colonial Park Inn, 2301 Colonial Dr., tel. (406) 443-2100 or (800) 422-1002, $69-86 s, $79-97 d, is Helena's most lavish motel complex, with indoor and outdoor pools, sauna, hot tub, free airport shuttle, restaurant, and lounge. The **Shilo Inn,** 2020 Prospect Ave., tel. (406) 442-0320 or (800) 222-2244, $59-89 s or d, has an indoor pool, sauna and steam room. All rooms come with microwave ovens, refrigerators, irons and boards, and video players. Complimentary continental breakfast. The **Days Inn,** 2001 Prospect Dr., tel. (406) 442-3280 or (800) 325-2525, has rooms for $42 s, $68 d.

Camping

The **Helena KOA Campground,** three miles north on Montana Ave., tel. (406) 458-5110, has a pool and playground.

FOOD

Breakfast and Lunch

It makes a certain sense, in a town fueled by the business of politics, that there are as many or more good choices for lunch in Helena as for dinner. Clustered in the Last Chance Gulch area are several good restaurants that serve a busy and boisterous lunch clientele. **Bert and Ernie's,** 361 N. Last Chance Gulch, tel. (406) 443-5680, open 11 a.m.-10 p.m., serves a sandwich-dominated menu with a wide selection of beers.

For lunch in a Helena institution, go to the **Rialto,** 52 N. Last Chance Gulch, tel. (406) 442-1890. Try the burger in this venerable old bar with a cafe up front; the grill is open 11 a.m.-9 p.m. The **Brewhouse Brew Pub and Grill,** 939 1/2 Getchell St., tel. (406) 457-9390, serves up Sleeping Giant beers and ales along with good pub food.

The **Windbag Saloon,** 19 S. Last Chance Gulch, tel. (406) 443-9669, open 11 a.m.-10 p.m., was a brothel named Big Dorothy's until 1973. With this colorful history, and filled with namesake politicians, the Windbag is one of Helena's unique restaurants. The burgers are the thing for lunch, with steaks on the dinner menu; open 11 a.m.-2:30 p.m. and 5-9:30 p.m. The Windbag is about the only decent restaurant open on Sunday night in Helena.

For a snack or pick-me-up, Helena has good coffee and sweet treats. If a sojourn in Montana has you longing for decent coffee, address your needs at **Morning Light Coffee Roasters,** 503 Fuller, tel. (406) 442-5180, open 7:30 a.m.-10 p.m. **Flicker's Coffeehouse,** 101 N. Last Chance Gulch, tel. (406) 443-5567, offers coffee and pastries, and frequent evening entertainment. Helena's most famous sweets sanctuary is **Parrot Confectionery,** 42 N. Main St., tel. (406) 442-1470, a soda fountain and candy factory that isn't just old-fashioned, but actually *old.* Try the handmade chocolates or a malted milk; the Parrot's sole feint to solid food is its renowned chili. Open 9 a.m.-6 p.m. For ice cream, go to the **Ice Cream Parlor,** 718 Logan, tel. (406) 442-0117, open 8 a.m.-11 p.m. It's also a good place to take the kids for a light supper.

Helena has a couple of excellent bakeries. The **Park Avenue Bakery,** 44 S. Park Ave., tel. (406) 449-8424, offers European-style pastries, real French bread, and specialty desserts. A great cheese Danish and a cup of their fine coffee induces a near out-of-Montana experience. Try the **Sweetgrass Bakery,** 322 Fuller Ave., tel. (406) 443-1103, for healthful breads, muffins, sweet rolls, and other baked goods.

Fine Dining

There's also good dining in the downtown area. Northern Italian appears **On Broadway,** 106 Broadway, tel. (406) 443-1929, open 5:30-10 p.m., in a light, airy, red-brick atmosphere; closed Sunday. The menu at the **Stonehouse,** 120 Reeder's Alley, tel. (406) 449-2552, remains firmly grounded in good beef, but it's more cosmopolitan than many of Helena's restaurants. The Stonehouse is located in an 1890s structure listed on the National Register of Historic Places; it's open Mon.-Sat. 11:30 a.m.-2 p.m., Sun.-Thurs. 5-9 p.m. and Fri.-Sat. 5-10 p.m. **Victor's,** in the Park Plaza Hotel, 22 N. Last Chance

Gulch, tel. (406) 443-2200, is open 6 a.m.-10 p.m. and serves an eclectic menu; seating is available on the patio.

The **River Grille,** 1225 Custer, tel. (406) 442-1075, serves an up-to-date menu of specials and seafood, plus good steaks and prime rib.

For dinner in an informal yet comfortable atmosphere, try the **Carriage House Bistro,** tel. (406) 449-6949, 234-1/2 Lyndale. The small but well-thought-out menu has main dishes featuring almost all the major meat groups—chicken breast, lamb fillet, pork loin, shrimp—each served with salad and vegetables. Entrees range between $11-14.

The **Overland Express** was once one of Helena's best restaurants. Since those days it has packed up and left its historic downtown and taken up residence out near the freeways at 2250 11th Ave., tel. (406) 449-2635. Somewhere along the line it became a casino. The steaks are still good, but the atmosphere ain't what it used to be. Still, if you don't want to brave downtown Helena's labyrinthine streets, the Overland beats the fast-food options along the offramps.

One of the Helena area's most unusual dining experiences is in the old near-ghost-town of Marysville. **Marysville House** doesn't even have a phone, and the menu isn't huge, but the steaks, grilled chicken, and seafood gumbo at this rustic frontier-era restaurant keep locals coming back for more. Dinner at Marysville House is a Helena tradition. Summer hours are Tues.-Sat. 5 p.m. till closing, the rest of the year the same hours but closed Tuesday. Marysville is seven miles north of Helena off Hwy. 279.

INFORMATION AND SERVICES

The **Helena Chamber of Commerce** is at 225 Cruse Ave., Suite A, Helena, MT 59601, tel. (406) 442-4120 or (800) 743-5362.

The central **post office** is located at 2300 N. Hastings, tel. (406) 443-3304. The **Lewis and Clark County Library** is at 120 S. Last Chance Gulch, tel. (406) 442-2380.

St. Peter's Hospital is at 2475 Broadway, tel. (406) 442-2480. **Emergency** is 911.

The **Helena National Forest Ranger Station** is at 2001 Poplar St., tel. (406) 449-5490. The **State Fish, Wildlife, and Parks office** is at 1420 E. 6th Ave., tel. (406) 444-2535.

The *Independent Record* is Helena's daily paper. Find **Montana Public Radio** at 91.7 FM and 107.1 FM.

The **Eleventh Ave. Clean and Coin Laundromat** is at 1411 11th Ave., tel. (406) 442-9395.

TRANSPORTATION

Helena is served by Delta, Northwest, Sky West, Big Sky, and Horizon airlines. The **airport** is east on Washington St., or you can take the Airport exit from I-15. **Rimrock buses** link Helena with Missoula, Butte, and Great Falls. You'll find the **bus station** at 5 W. 15th St., tel. (406) 442-5860.

Hertz rents cars at the airport, tel. (406) 449-4162. **Rent-A-Wreck** operates out of 3710 N. Montana Ave., tel. (406) 443-3635. **Budget Car Rental** is at 1930 N. Main St., tel. (406) 442-7011. Call a **cab** at (406) 449-5525.

TOWNSEND AND THE UPPER MISSOURI VALLEY

At Three Forks, the Jefferson, Madison, and Gallatin unite into the Missouri River. Throwing off any trace of its mountain-bred fussiness, the Missouri flows north with stridency.

The country between Three Forks and Holter Dam (the last of the three back-to-back dams that corral the newly minted river) prepares the Missouri for its long journey across the plains. To accustom the river to flatland agriculture, it flows through a wide, prairielike valley divided

into ranches, and three reservoirs within 60 miles impound it, slowing it down. Having learned prudence, the river is released to warm up, bear silt, and shoulder its responsibilities as a prairie river.

It's no wonder, with such an abundance of water around, that Townsend and aptly named Broadwater County boast of their recreational facilities. Perhaps not surprising in an area so close to the state capital, there is an embarrassment of riches in state parks along the Missouri, providing fishing, hunting, boating, and windsurfing opportunities. Visitors can even engage in a more traditional pastime—panning for gold; several old mines provide pay dirt and teach prospecting skills.

TOWNSEND

Townsend (pop. 2,004, elev. 3,833 feet) has always made the most of its location. Platted in advance of the arrival of the first Northern Pacific train in 1883, Townsend was laid out with a deliberate sensibility, as if it were intended for bigger things. Prosperous farmers and ranchers along the Missouri nourished the strapping town; with the completion of Hwy. 12, linking central Montana to the west, Townsend became a transportation crossroads. When the Canyon Ferry Dam was built in the 1940s, Townsend planted its flag over the lakes' recreational opportunities.

Today, Townsend is a pleasant town, filled with trees and parks, seemingly dedicated to recreation on the nearby lakes and along the Missouri River.

Sights

At the **Broadwater County Museum,** 133 N. Walnut, tel. (406) 266-5252, there are relics of the region's history, including early mining tools from Confederate Gulch.

Where the Missouri River enters the Canyon Ferry Lake, just north of Townsend is **Canyon Ferry Wildlife Management Area.** Here, in a 5,000-acre delta wetland, is an exceptional viewing point for migrating waterfowl and nesting birds, including ospreys and loons. Beavers and white-tailed deer are also present. From Townsend, follow Hwy. 12 east to Harrison Rd. and turn north one mile.

Recreation

The upper Missouri Valley is lined by the Elkhorn Mountains to the west and the Big Belt Mountains to the east, each a part of the immense Helena National Forest. While these ranges are not particularly developed for the hiker and camper, the combination of mountain shelter and verdant river meadows makes the area famous for its hunting.

The following outfitters offer both guided fishing trips and big-game hunting expeditions: **Monte's Guiding and Mountain Outfitting,** 16 N. Fork Rd., Townsend, MT 59644, tel. (406) 266-3515 or **Elkhorn Outfitters,** P.O. Box 1339, Townsend, MT 59644, tel. (406) 266-5625.

As elsewhere in Montana, cattle drives have become high recreation around Townsend. **Montana High Country Cattle Drive,** 699 Flynn Ln., Townsend, MT 59644, tel. (406) 266-3322 or (800) 345-9423, organizes a couple of five-day drives each summer; prices run $1,500 per person, including tent lodging, chuckwagon meals, horses, and help from real ranchers and outfitters. During the drive, information programs focus on natural history and issues facing contemporary ranchers.

Accommodations and Food

Lodgings in Townsend are comfortable and convenient for both travelers and water sports enthusiasts. The **Lake Townsend Motel,** 413 N. Pine, tel. (406) 266-3461 or (800) 856-3461, $36 s, $42 d, is in a quiet spot a block off the highway. Each room in this tidy, personable place has its own theme, and there's an outdoor hot tub. Pets are permitted with a $10 deposit. The **Mustang Motel,** 412 N. Front, tel. (406) 266-3491 or (800) 349-3499, $32 s, $40 d, is right along Hwy. 12 and accepts pets for an extra $5. Some rooms have refrigerators and microwaves; one room is accessible to guests with disabilities.

To find campgrounds, follow Hwys. 12 or 284 north along Canyon Ferry Lake; the state maintains 25 of them, mostly toward the north end of the lake.

Good, no-nonsense beef-and-seafood menus characterize the food choices in Townsend. The **Fireside Supper Club,** one mile east on Hwy. 12, tel. (406) 266-3516, is a dependable choice for an evening meal. As much landmark as restaurant/bar is the **Mint,** 305 Broadway, open 6 a.m.-midnight; it also has lighter meals and sandwiches. **Maria's Kitchen** serves Mexican food at 316 N. Front. The **Horseshoe,** 500 N. Front, tel. (406) 266-3800, is open for three meals a day for good, quick food. The **Creamery,** 108 N. Front, tel. (406) 266-5254, is another Townsend institution, serving meals just this side of fast food. Stop by 303 N. Front for coffee at **Two Dagos Espresso.**

If you're up for a drive, then try the **Deep Creek Restaurant,** 11 miles east of Townsend on Hwy. 12, tel. (406) 266-3718; open daily 5-9 p.m. Steaks and fresh fish are served in a remote and beautiful canyon.

Information

Contact the **Townsend Area Chamber of Commerce** at P.O. Box 947, Townsend, MT 59644, tel. (406) 266-4104. Visit the office at 412 N Front St.

The **Helena National Forest Office** is at 415 S. Front, tel. (406) 226-3425.

THE UPPER MISSOURI LAKES

North of Townsend, three dams in rapid succession impound the Missouri. As they are near major population centers and are served by good roads, these lakes are among the most popular and developed in Montana. Canyon Ferry, Hauser, and Holter Lakes are well trod by local anglers, boaters, and campers, but they bear up pretty well, considering their heavy use.

The range of recreational options is boggling—there are 25 state parks on Canyon Ferry Lake alone—which makes a brief overview difficult. Contact the Dept. of Fish, Wildlife, and Parks, 1420 6th Ave., Helena, tel. (406) 444-2535, for more complete information.

Canyon Ferry Lake

Canyon Ferry Dam was built in the 1950s by the Bureau of Reclamation, creating the largest of the three lakes on the upper Missouri. Canyon Ferry backs up 25 miles of reservoir, with almost 80 miles of shoreline. At the south end, nearest Townsend, the lake is widest and the surrounding countryside rolling, gentle, and treeless. To the north, the reservoir narrows and begins to flow into a steep canyon.

On the east side of the lake, about 18 miles north of Townsend, is a sharp ravine in the Big Belt Mountains called **Confederate Gulch.** In 1864, a couple of Confederate soldiers discovered incredibly rich gravel beds here. While it lasted, individual pannings yielded up to $1,000 in gold. A boomtown surged up immediately; called Diamond City, it grew to 10,000 people and was as rowdy and tough as the situation and era allowed. By the 1870s the gold played out, but one last blast with a huge water-cannon-like hydraulic sluice dislodged another million dollars. Today, almost nothing remains of the fabulously rich workings of Confederate Gulch.

There is today, however, popular fishing and boating at Canyon Ferry. The lake is heavily and regularly stocked with rainbow trout, and they are usually hungry and scrappy enough to make a lucky angler feel skilled. Most of the facilities, both public and private, cluster at the northern end of the lake.

Follow Canyon Ferry Rd. (or Montana Ave.) east nine miles out of Helena to reach the lake. If coming north on Hwy. 12, turn on Hwy. 284 eight miles north of Winston. Windsurfers can rent equipment at **Big Sky Windsurfing** at Yacht Basin Marina, 3555 West Shore Rd., tel. (406) 475-3440. The marina also rents all manner of boats, and has a bar and restaurant to boot; tel. (406) 475-3125.

On the southern end of the lake the state parks thin out. The most convenient **campsites** are at Silo, seven miles north of Townsend on Hwy. 12, where there are both public and private campgrounds. At the privately owned **Silo's RV Park** there's **Silo's Inn** bar and restaurant, open 5-9 p.m., tel. (406) 266-5622.

Hauser Lake

Built in 1908 by Montana Power, Hauser Dam is named for Samuel Hauser, an early Montanan who advocated damming the Missouri to harness electricity for regional mining enterprises. At this 3,720-acre lake, heavily used for boating and water-skiing, the fishing is okay for small-mouth bass and kokanee salmon.

There are two scenic, practically adjacent public campgrounds on Hauser Lake. If the beach at **White Sandy,** seven miles northeast off I-15 on Hwy. 453, is full, then continue a few yards farther to **Black Sandy.**

While at Hauser Lake, try your hand at sapphire mining. The **Spokane Bar Sapphire Mine,** 4397 Hart Dr., tel. (406) 227-8989, 10.5 miles east of Helena on York Rd., and the **Eldorado Sapphire Mine,** 6240 Nelson Rd., tel. (406) 442-7960, both offer buckets of sapphire-laden gravel. Here the novice can wash gravel to discover highly colored sapphires as well as garnets, rubies, and gold.

Holter Lake

Holter lake is the most awe-inspiring of the three upper Missouri Lakes. Behind the dam lies the Gates of the Mountains, so named by Meriwether Lewis:

This evening we entered the most remarkable clifts that we have yet seen. These clifts rise from the waters edge on either side perpendicularly to the hight of 1,200 feet. solid rock for the distance of 5³/₄ miles. I entered this place and was obliged to continue my rout until sometime after dark before I found a place sufficiently large to encamp my small party; from the singular appearance of this place I called it the gates of the mountains.
July 19th, 1805

The Missouri cut a deep gorge through thick deposits of limestone; although the flooding of Holter Dam (built in 1913) has lessened the rush of the river through these gates, this is still a startlingly dramatic landscape of geologic and human history.

Do not resist the temptation to take a boat trip through the Gates of the Mountains. Wildlife viewing, historical vignettes, geologic curiosities, and drop-dead beautiful riverscapes make this one of Montana's most compelling side trips.

Gates of the Mountains, Inc., two miles east from the Gates of the Mountain exit off I-15, tel. (406) 458-5241, offers guided open-air **riverboat tours** of the entire canyon. During the two-hour trip travelers usually see bighorn sheep, mountain goats, eagles, ospreys, and deer. Guides point out Indian pictographs along the limestone cliffs. The river cruises begin on Memorial Day and end in September. Call for times. Tickets are $8.50 adult, $7.50 senior, and $5 children.

Plan your day carefully, and disembark the boat at Meriwether Picnic Area. The boat captains allow passengers to break the trip at this point. Here, at the site of Lewis and Clark's 1805 camp, are trails that lead up into the **Gates of the Mountains Wilderness Area,** a 28,560-acre

wildlife reserve within the deep limestone canyons along the east side of the Missouri River. It was back in this remote and precipitous area that 16 young firefighters died in 1959, a tragedy that led to the writing of Norman Maclean's best-selling essay, *Young Men and Fire.*

If you lay over at the wilderness area, be certain to know when to expect a returning riverboat, and save your ticket stub.

B&Bs: Known simply as **The Bungalow,** tel. (406) 235-4276 or (800) 286-4250, Charles Power's 1911 country lodge is now one of Montana's most historically significant bed and breakfasts, located near Wolf Creek, in the Gates of the Mountain canyon country. Charles Power was one of the engines of early Montana capitalism. Beginning rather humbly as a trader at Fort Benton in the 1870s, by the time of his death Powers owned 95 different corporations, controlled four square blocks of downtown Helena (including Helena's most architecturally significant, the Power Block), and was one of the state's richest men. When it came time to build a country home, Power turned to Robert Reamer, the architect who designed the Old Faithful Lodge in Yellowstone Park. For furnishings, Power turned to young interior designer Marshall Fields. Many of the original furnishings remain in the stately log lodge, which offers four guest rooms (one with private bath). Rooms range $85-90.

Campgrounds: There are three public campgrounds along Holter Lake, all on the east side. Turn south from the freeway at the Wolf Creek exit, cross Wolf Creek, then turn north (left) on Recreation Rd. and proceed a few miles to the bridge. Turn south on Bear Tooth Rd. after crossing the Missouri. Continue three miles to **Holter Lake State Park.** Four miles up the same road are **Log Gulch** and **Departure Point State Parks.**

DOVER PUBLICATIONS, INC.

NORTHWESTERN MONTANA

INTRODUCTION

By common perception, the northwestern part of the state is wet, forested, and populous. But, in fact, the main city, Missoula, has only 51,000 inhabitants, gets no more than 13 inches of rain in an average year, and is only particularly well-treed in the Rattlesnake corridor. Indeed, much of this corner of the state has been voraciously logged, and the climate is too harsh for seedling trees to easily reforest the clearcuts.

The other common perception about northwestern Montana is that it's a recreationalist's dream come true. This it is. Not only is it the gateway to Glacier National Park, but there are fishing areas, hiking trails, and public campgrounds galore, particularly in the national forests.

For many visitors, this is archetypal Montana: all these beautiful lakes and soaring mountain peaks are what you came here for. However, you're not alone. The last decade has seen a burgeoning of growth in this area, particularly in

the Flathead Valley, so be prepared to share this corner of Montana with quite a few others.

THE LAND

Northwestern Montana's topography is characterized by a series of forested mountain ranges (the Cabinets, Missions, Bitterroots, Flatheads, Salish, Whitefish, Purcell, Swans), running generally northwest to southeast, and the valleys that separate them. Although this is a mountainous area, it's not particularly high by Montana standards; in fact, Montana's lowest spot (1,892 feet) is where the Clark Fork River enters Idaho near Troy in the state's northwest corner.

Rivers

The Clark Fork of the Columbia is one of the several big rivers in these parts, flowing from its headwaters in the Rockies near Butte, through

NORTHWESTERN
MONTANA

© MOON PUBLICATIONS, INC.

Missoula, and into Idaho's Lake Pend Oreille. The Kootenai River and its reservoir, Lake Koocanusa, drain the state's northwestern corner and spill into the Columbia River in British Columbia. Flathead Lake and the branches of the Flathead River that feed and drain it are other important features of northwestern Montana.

Formation of the Landscape

Most of the exposed limestones, mudstones, and sandstones in northwestern Montana date from the Precambrian era. Many contain fossils of blue-green algae, which were the only lifeform capable of existing in the steamy, carbon dioxide-saturated air.

The Rocky Mountains began to form some 175 million years ago. The westward-drifting North American continent collided with the plate of the Pacific Ocean floor. The resulting crushing pressures, combined with faults, buckled large chunks of the earth's crust into mountain ranges. In other areas, tension across the crust stretched and broke it into a jumble of rocks. Old rocks sometimes landed on top of younger ones, reversing the intuitive order of geology. Once the Rockies had been formed, Montana was left with a topography that we'd recognize, though it's been modified by erosion and glacial action.

During alternating wet and dry geologic periods, layers of soil were laid down, then eroded off the hillsides when the climate dried. This eroded soil filled the valleys and was cut through by rivers that flowed during wetter times.

The glaciers that intermittently crept over northwestern Montana roughly 10,000 to 100,000 years ago refined and honed the landscape into something like its present form. When glaciers plowed through, they scoured out U-shaped valleys; they came from either side of mountain peaks and carved razor-sharp pinnacles; they pushed rocks and soil into gargantuan piles known as glacial moraines.

Glacial Lake Missoula

Glacial ice dammed the Clark Fork River in northern Idaho approximately 15,000 years ago, forming Glacial Lake Missoula, which filled the valleys of western Montana. River water ultimately floated the ice dam like an ice cube in a glass of water, and the lake drained with spectacular force, coursing over the scablands of western Washington and

leaving its mark as far away as the Columbia River Gorge. The ice dam on the Clark Fork settled back down into the riverbed and once again plugged the outlet. The lake filled again, drained again, and was reformed at least 41 times in a little over 1,000 years. Each cycle was shorter, and the lake didn't fill as deep. The record of these successive fillings and drainings can still be seen as a series of faint, perfectly horizontal lines on the sides of Mt. Jumbo and Mt. Sentinel above Missoula.

Climate

This is a moderate area, with considerable Pacific influence. The Rockies shelter the land west of them from frigid continental winds, but snow does pile up in northwestern Montana. The stretch of I-90 just east of Lookout Pass gets particularly snowy. January tends to be the coldest month. Daily minimum temperatures then average around 10-12° F, shooting up to average daily highs of around 28°.

July is ordinarily the hottest month throughout the region, with temperatures normally getting above 80°. Thunderstorms are not uncommon on summer afternoons. May and June are typically the rainiest months. Missoula usually receives about 13 inches of rain a year, Kalispell about 16, and Libby about 18.

Flora

Thanks to the warm wet weather blowing over the mountains of Washington and Oregon from the Pacific Ocean, northwestern Montana's forests resemble those of the Pacific coast with their abundance of conifers, including Douglas fir, western red cedar, and western hemlock. Ponderosa pine, lodgepole pine, and western white pine are other Pacific trees that are important to the landscape and economy of western Montana. There's also a good sprinkling of trees more characteristic of the Rockies, such as Engelmann spruce, western larch, and subalpine fir.

The **bitterroot**, the state flower, was an important food for the Flathead Indians. It is most abundant in the valley that bears its name, where it flowers early in the summer. Subalpine wildflowers bloom wildly on the mountainsides once the snow has melted. Look for glacier lilies, bear grass, Indian paintbrush, and lupine.

Shrubs tend to grow at lower elevations than the wildflower meadows. **Huckleberry** bushes run amok in the open areas of northwestern Montana. Look to meadows, old burns, and clearcuts for the most intense growth. Berries begin to ripen at lower elevations toward the end of July, moving upward as the summer progresses. When in huckleberry country keep an eye out for bears, which love to feast on the tasty fruit.

Oregon grape and kinnikinnick (whose bark was smoked like tobacco by the Indians) are other common shrubby plants in northwestern Montana forests.

Fauna

Grizzly **bears** live in some of the more isolated areas of northwestern Montana, including the Cabinet and Mission Mountains Wilderness Areas. Black bears are more widespread. Don't mess with either.

Bighorn sheep can be spotted on steep hillsides throughout the state's northwestern corner. There's a special bighorn-viewing area on Hwy. 200 just east of Thompson Falls, and a de facto one along Hwy. 2 west of Libby. They also live on the National Bison Range in Moiese, which is also

just about the only place in western Montana you'll see **buffalo,** except those kept in private herds as ranch stock or a tourist attraction. Elk, white-tailed and mule deer, moose, and mountain goats are among the other ungulates, or hoofed animals, that inhabit northwestern Montana.

Mountain lions once had a reputation for being rather elusive, but over the past few years they've been reported to roam the streets of Columbia Falls and send joggers up trees in Missoula's Greenough Park.

There's an astounding variety of **birdlife** in northwestern Montana—bald eagles, ospreys, woodpeckers, dippers, Clark's nutcrackers, western tanagers, great blue herons, hawks, owls, vultures, blue grouse, ruffed grouse, magpies, and hummingbirds. There is a host of waterfowl and shorebirds around Ninepipe and Pablo Wildlife Refuges in the Mission Valley. Loons nest in several lakes near Eureka and in the Swan Valley.

There are three major **trout** species in northwestern Montana: cutthroat, bull, and rainbow. The westslope cutthroat is Montana's state fish and, while not officially endangered, is the object

CAMELS IN THE ROCKIES

Camels in the Rockies? Well, why not? They're strong, they don't drink too much . . . So, anyway, thought the U.S. Army in the 1860s, when some innovative military man began importing camels to use as pack animals. While perhaps more efficient than the customary mules, camels weren't so easy to boss around. Apparently they were harder to recognize, too—several of the camels on the Mullan Road were shot after being mistaken for moose.

of some concern. Catch-and-release fishing is generally recommended, and in some places mandatory, for cutthroat. Bull trout live primarily in the Flathead River system, but their populations have also declined dramatically. In order to protect them from further decline, they are off-limits to anglers on all streams west of the Continental Divide. Rainbow trout are widespread, and are especially prolific in the Kootenai River, where they're native.

Kokanee **salmon** were introduced to the Flathead system in the 1930s and flourished there for about 50 years. In recent years, Flathead populations of this landlocked salmon have declined precipitously, most likely because of competition with mysis shrimp. Kokanee are still plentiful in other lakes, including Lake Mary Ronan (west of Flathead Lake) and Lake Koocanusa.

Dams and development have altered the riparian ecology in northwestern Montana. Native fish, including bull trout, westslope cutthroat, and whitefish, having faced the dams and competition from nonnative species such as lake trout and kokanee salmon, are now seriously threatened by habitat degradation due to logging. In clearcut areas, soil and debris erode into streams, muddying the water and disturbing the delicate chemistry fish need.

HISTORY

Because of the mountainous terrain and dense forests, northwestern Montana wasn't settled or developed by whites as early as other areas of the state. There wasn't a whole lot of activity in this country until the railroad came through in the early 1880s. Other development, particularly the timber industry, was then spurred on, and northwestern Montana became a stronghold of the state's economy.

Native Americans

The original inhabitants of western Montana are known largely through the mythology they've engendered. The Flathead people have stories of those who preceded them in Montana—dwarves, giants, and "the foolish folk," a crass and bumbling bunch who, as the legend goes, died out when the last few fools went over Spokane Falls in a canoe. Anthropologists posit that these early inhabitants were from the Pacific coast. A few traces of jewelry made from saltwater shells have been found, and the people seemed to have a physical stature similar to that of modern coastal tribes. Beyond that, these people and their lives remain a mystery. The Kootenai, Pend d'Oreille, and Flathead tribes took up residence in Montana around the 1500s, a couple of hundred years before Plains Indian culture was established in eastern Montana.

Northwestern Montana is now home to Salish and Kootenai tribes. The term "Salish" refers to a language family common to several Pacific Northwest tribes. Salish speakers in northwestern Montana include the Flathead and Pend d'Oreille. The Kootenai have their own distinct language, which seems to be unrelated to any other (though some anthropologists link it to the Algonquian language group common to many tribes in the northeastern U.S. and Canada).

The **Flathead Indians** came to the Bitterroot Valley from the west. Although they made regular trips to the plains to hunt buffalo, the Flathead also ate many wild roots and berries. During the spring and early summer months, women dug the roots of camas, bitterroot, and wild carrots. The roots were eaten raw, boiled and roasted in stone-lined pits, or sun-dried for later use. Later in the summer they picked serviceberries, chokecherries, and huckleberries. Some of the berries were dried, pulverized, and mixed with dried meats. Flathead men fished for trout, char, whitefish, and suckers with basket traps, weirs, spears, or poles with animal-hair lines and hooks carved from bone or hawthorn.

Confusion abounds as to why the Flathead are called that. Several barely plausible theories exist, but one confusing fact is that they did *not* flatten their heads.

The **Pend d'Oreille** lived in the Mission Valley and westward into eastern Washington. They were on friendly terms with the Flathead tribe; indeed, when the Flathead arrived in the Bitterroot Valley, the Pend d'Oreille who were living there moved north to the Jocko and Mission Valleys so that the Flathead could settle in the Bitterroot.

The **Kootenai** came from the north and settled in and around the Tobacco Plains region (near present-day Eureka), with nomadic bands ranging from southeastern British Columbia, through northern Idaho, and into northern Montana.

There were two main branches: The Upper Kootenai, who lived closer to the Rockies, were frequent buffalo hunters on the plains. The Lower Kootenai were river people who fished more than they hunted, but traded with the Upper Kootenai for horses and buffalo meat. Today, the Kootenai live on the Flathead Reservation, mostly around Elmo on the west side of Flathead Lake, and are part of the Confederated Salish and Kootenai Tribes.

Early White Explorers

Lewis and Clark just skirted the lower corner of northwestern Montana on both legs of their expedition. They met a band of Flathead Indians in the Bitterroot Valley and traded with them for horses. Although they found the Salishan language spoken by these people as bizarre as Welsh, Clark proclaimed the Flathead "the likelyest and honnestst Savages we have ever yet Seen." Lewis and Clark don't seem to be the ones who coined the term "Flathead." In fact, Clark referred to them as the Tushepau, and comments more on their "gurgling" language than on the shape of anyone's head.

On their return trip, the entire Corps of Discovery camped at Traveler's Rest (on Lolo Creek near the Bitterroot River), and Meriwether Lewis cut through the Hell Gate Canyon (in present-day Missoula) with several other men on the way north to explore the Marias River.

Other areas of the state saw quick American fur-trading action soon after Lewis and Clark reported their finds to the nation. But northwestern Montana was dominated by the Canadian fur companies. Many of the trappers and traders were French Canadian; a substantial number of them married Native American women, and today there are still a number of northwest Montanans with French surnames, especially on the Flathead Reservation.

David Thompson, an English-born explorer, astronomer, and geographer for both the Hudson's Bay and North West companies, was the first white person to travel into the northwest corner of Montana. In 1807, he traveled down the Kootenai River from Canada and into Montana. Over the next few years, he set up trading posts along the Kootenai and Clark Fork Rivers and became the first white man to travel the entire length of the Columbia River, which he mapped from mouth to source. Thompson spoke several Indian languages and won the trust and respect of local Indians.

In 1841 St. Mary's Mission was founded in the Bitterroot Valley after repeated requests for Catholicism from the Flathead and Nez Perce of the area. Father Pierre Jean deSmet, the missionary dispatched to found St. Mary's, was also Montana's first agriculturalist. He planted oats, wheat, and potatoes at the mission. This was probably also an initial attempt to make Indians into farmers. Troubles arose between the missionaries and the Flathead, and in 1850, St. Mary's was sold to John Owen, who made it into a trading post.

The St. Ignatius Mission was originally established near the present-day Washington-Idaho border. It foundered there, and when Montana Indians requested another mission, Father deSmet and Father Adrian Hoecken moved St. Ignatius to what is now known as the Mission Valley.

White Settlement

Much of western Montana was opened to white settlement following a reservation treaty enacted in 1855 between Isaac I. Stevens, governor of the Washington Territory (which at the time included Montana), and the Flathead, Pend d'Oreille, and Kootenai tribes. The Hell Gate Treaty established the Jocko Reservation (now known as the Flathead Reservation) in the Jocko and Mission Valleys. The Pend d'Oreille and the Kootenai agreed to live on the reservation but the Flathead chose to remain in the Bitterroot Valley south of Missoula. In 1872, the Bitterroot Valley was opened for homesteading, but some Flathead Indians remained in the area until 1891, when they were forced to move to the reservation.

It took John Mullan and his crew from 1858 until 1862 to build a military wagon road from Fort Benton to Walla Walla, Washington. This was a particularly vital stretch of road, as Fort Benton marked the farthest point that steamboats could travel up the Missouri River, and Walla Walla provided access to the Columbia River. His route has held up well; I-90 follows its course from Deer Lodge to the Idaho line.

John Mullan also has the distinction of having written the first travel guide to Montana. In 1865 he authored the *Miners' and Travelers' Guide to Oregon, Washington, Idaho, Montana, Wyoming and Colorado*. As may be expected, the Montana portion follows the Mullan Road.

Development

The late 1800s brought railroads through northwestern Montana. The Northern Pacific followed the Clark Fork and the Great Northern cut across the northern edge of the state. Timber was needed to construct the railroad lines, and, once the trains were running, they were able to transport the abundant local timber to other areas of the state and nation. The smelter in Anaconda burned endless cords of wood, and large timbers were required to prop up mine shafts.

As the number of homesteaders increased, so did the pressure on the Indians. In 1877, Chief Joseph's retreat led nervous homesteaders in the Bitterroot Valley to petition the government for military forts. Fort Missoula and Fort Fizzle were built to protect the white settlers.

The 1887 Dawes Act allotted parcels of reservation land to individual Indians in an effort to make them understand the concept of owning the land. Unalloted land was often dealt to the U.S. government and then thrown open to white homesteaders. The Dawes Act was repealed in 1934, when tribal, rather than individual, identity was emphasized in the Tribal Reorganization Act. Under these provisions, the Confederated Salish and Kootenai Tribes were incorporated. By that time, much of the land within the confines of the Flathead Reservation was owned by non-Indians, as it remains today.

Northwestern Montana is still one of the wilder areas of the country, with large chunks of public land. Logging roads may crisscross the forests, but it's still easy to find an isolated spot to set up camp or to fish. The economy is still dependent on the vagaries of the timber industry.

PRACTICALITIES

Hunting

Hunters benefit from the vast tracts of public land in northwestern Montana. Most appreciate that it's laced with logging roads, making it easier to get into fairly wild areas. In order to curb the number of hunters in some areas, roads may be closed to motor vehicles during the hunting season. Local ranger stations or state Dept. of Fish, Wildlife, and Parks offices will have information on road closures.

While the thick growth of trees and brush can make hunting difficult throughout much of northwestern Montana, this habitat harbors many animals. Elk, deer (mostly white-tailed, but also some mule deer), and black bear are commonly hunted. It's easy for Montana residents to pick up the necessary licenses for these animals. Nonresidents should apply for a combination sportsman's license well in advance of hunting season. A limited number of tags to hunt mountain goats, bighorn sheep, and moose are awarded by a computer lottery during the summer.

Driving

There's a lot of logging activity in northwestern Montana, and the savvy driver will keep a sharp eye and ear out for log trucks, especially on Forest Service roads. Always give way to the log truck, because the driver cannot make fast stops.

Information

Much of northwestern Montana falls in Travel Montana's Glacier Country region. Contact their office at 836 Holt Dr., Bigfork, MT 59911, tel. (406) 837-6211 or (800) 338-5072.

THE LOWER CLARK FORK

ALONG I-90

Forest-rimmed, hilly, and wild as a freeway ever gets, I-90 follows the Clark Fork and St. Regis Rivers most of the way between the Idaho border and Missoula. From the state line east to Frenchtown (just west of Missoula), I-90 follows the Mullan Road, built by John Mullan and his crew

in the 1860s as a military road from Fort Benton to Walla Walla, Washington.

Pull off the freeway at Haugan (exit 16) to visit the **Savenac Historic Site,** a tree nursery started along the Mullan Road in 1909. A year later, a three-million-acre fire destroyed the new nursery and much else. After the fire, forest rangers stole pine cones from squirrel caches (replacing them with nuts) and replanted the pine seeds. The nursery eventually flourished, providing seedlings to reforest national forests all over the west.

Like De Borgia to the west, St. Regis was named for the Jesuit missionary, St. Regis De Borgia. **St. Regis** is where the St. Regis River flows into the Clark Fork. The St. Regis parallels the freeway to the west of town, the Clark Fork to the east. At the town of St. Regis, the Clark Fork makes a sharp turn to the north. Highway 135 follows it along the lovely stretch to Hwy. 200.

Superior was a mining boomtown. Gold was discovered on a stream called Cayuse Creek in 1869 and, over the next year, 10,000 people swarmed to the mining camp. Other strikes in the area shifted the activity from place to place. In some areas, such as Louisville, Chinese miners moved in to the abandoned shacks and gleaned the remaining gold. Mining booms came intermittently over the next few decades, but pretty much ended in 1910, when a huge forest fire destroyed the Keystone Mine and most everything else for miles around.

Alberton (pop. 396) was originally a railroad town. It was a division point for the Milwaukee Road, whose depot has been restored and is visible from the freeway. Alberton has a packed-to-the-gills used-book store, **Montana Valley Books,** and it has a notorious gorge (see below).

Frenchtown was settled by French Canadians as the Mullan Road was being built. It's now a mill town and a bedroom community of Missoula.

Taft Tunnel Bike Trail

The Taft Tunnel Bike Trail is a rails-to-trails project that has converted 15 miles of Chicago, Milwaukee, and St. Paul Railroad track, tunnel, and tressle into one of the most exhilarating recreation trails in the U.S. The centerpiece of the trail is the 8,771-foot Taft Tunnel, built in 1909 and cut through solid rock from the Montana side of Lookout Pass through to Idaho. As the rail track descends in Idaho, it winds through another nine tunnels and over seven wooden tressles before reaching the valley floor.

For years, the old rail line and abandoned tunnel were popular with in-the-know hikers and bikers, but an upsurge in activity in recent years forced the Forest Service, which controls the access to the rail line, to close the Taft Tunnel and attempt to dissuade activity along the trestles. As there had not been any maintenance for decades, the Forest Service felt it couldn't accept the liability that increased usage brought to recreationalists using the aging facilities. However, lots of grassroots support and backroom political arm-twisting resulted in the Forest Service allocating the necessary funds to clear the tunnel and make the trestles safe for casual recreational use.

Bikers need headlights to traverse the trail, and hikers will want to bring along strong flashlights. Be prepared to get a little wet and chilly in the tunnel. Even though the grade never exceeds 1.7%, vertigo-inducing trestles stand along sheer cliffs and over steep rocky canyons. Whether you're on foot or on a bike, you'll have your heart in your mouth on several occasions.

To reach the beginning of the trail and Taft Tunnel, drive over Lookout Pass on I-90 and take exit 5 for the Taft Area. Turn south and follow Rainy Creek Rd. for two miles, and take the road toward East Portal at the Y-junction. The parking area is immediately ahead, and just beyond is the gate to the tunnel. The trail follows the contours of Loop Creek until it meets the Moon Pass Rd., which leads in 20 miles to Wallace (via Placer Creek Rd.).

A shuttle service ferries cyclists back to Lookout Pass. Plan a full day for this trip, and reserve a spot on the shuttle by calling the Lookout Pass Ski Area at tel. (208) 744-1301. The entire guided ride and shuttle costs $25; the shuttle alone is about $9. Mountain bike rentals are available at the ski area for $15 half day, $20 full day.

For more information about the Taft Tunnel Trail, contact Taft Tunnel Preservation Society at P.O. Box 1222, Wallace, ID 83873; for a $1 donation, they will send a helpful map and informational letter. Rental mountain bikes and information are available from the Lookout Pass Ski Area, tel. (208) 744-1392 on the Montana/Idaho border at I-90 exit 0, and from Excelsior Bikes, tel. (208) 786-3751, 10 W. Portland Ave. in Kellogg.

Other Recreation

Lookout Pass, on the Idaho-Montana border, offers guided horseback rides ($20 for an hour, $50 for a half day, $90 for a full day) and mountain-bike rentals ($15 for a half day, $20 full day). The pass is a hub for hiking, mountain biking, and 4WD/snowmobile trails. During the winter, an average of 350 inches of generally powdery snow falls at Lookout Pass, which offers a small downhill ski area (with free lessons!) and good cross-country trails. Call Lookout Pass at (208) 744-1392.

The attractive, new nine-hole **Trestle Creek Golf Course,** tel. (406) 649-2680, is at the St. Regis exit. There's another nine-hole course in Frenchtown, **King Ranch Golf Course,** tel. (406) 626-4000.

Alberton Gorge (a.k.a. Cyr Canyon) is a 20-mile stretch of whitewater on the Clark Fork River. There are plenty of fishing-access sites along the Clark Fork that can be used to put in and take out boats. It's an especially challenging run when the river is high—only experienced paddlers should attempt it before August. Even when the water level drops, it's not a trip for beginners, though **Lewis and Clark Trail Adventures,** tel. (406) 728-7609, runs regular raft trips through Alberton Gorge. Those who aren't tempted by the whitewater may choose to fish this section of the Clark Fork for brown, cutthroat, rainbow, and bull trout.

Accommodations and Food

Most eastbound I-90 travelers press on to Missoula once they cross into the state, but there are several quite passable lodgings along the freeway. Just west of the state line, in the Idaho town of Mullan, the **Lookout Pass Motel,** tel. (208) 744-1601, has clean, basic rooms (no phones) for $28 single, $34 double.

Down the road from Lookout, there is a string of small towns with (mostly) small motels. In Saltese, the **Elk Glen Store and Motel** provides modest accommodations, tel. (406) 678-4390. You'll know the town of Haugen is coming well in advance from the many billboards heralding **Lincoln's World Famous 10,000 Silver Dollars.** The sprawling Silver Dollar complex has a bar/casino/gift shop/restaurant at its heart and, unlikely as it may sound, it's a good place to stop for roadside refueling. Motel rooms start at $48 s, $59 d, and there's also a large RV park; tel. (406) 678-4271 or 678-4242.

De Borgia's **Hotel Albert,** an old hotel turned bed and breakfast inn, has more charm than any of the other lodgings along this stretch of I-90. A room for two is $64 ($54 s) at the Albert, which has been around since 1911, though it was barely used from the 1920s through the early '90s, when a restoration kept the original character but updated what we've come to consider the essentials. Call (406) 678-4303 for

reservations. Also in DeBorgia, the **Pinecrest Lodge,** tel. (406) 678-4360, rents rustic cabins for $30 s or d, and is the best bet in the area for dinner, especially if you like fish and chips.

In St. Regis, the **Super 8,** tel. (406) 649-2422, is a reliable spot with rooms for $49 s, $59 d. The newly remodeled **Little River Motel,** has rooms from $40 s, $48 d, and also cabin accommodations, tel. (406) 649-2713; pets are okay.

Down the road in Superior, the **Budget Host Big Sky Motel,** with spacious rooms for $44 s, $50 d, tel. (406) 822-4831 or (800) 759-0023, is a good bet for a pleasant stay. Even less expensive are the **Hill Top Motel,** tel. (406) 822-4781, and the **Bellvue,** tel. (406) 822-4692, which offers both motel and hotel rooms (bath down the hall). Neither of these establishments pretends to be anything other than a place to get some sleep.

In downtown Alberton, the **Montana Hotel** was, until recently, a funky old wood-frame hotel. It's been renovated and is now a tidy B&B inn. The charming side garden has a hot tub among the flowers. Rooms go for $65 d (lower winter rates); call (406) 722-4965 or (800) 564-4129 for reservations. When Missoula's motels are booked full, this is a very attractive alternative.

Alberton's **River Edge Resort,** tel. (406) 722-4418, consists of a motel, casino, and campground on the banks of the Clark Fork River, not far from I-90 exit 75. During the summer, rooms are $40 s, $45-50 d. Pets are permitted here. In Alberton, the **Sidetrack Cafe,** tel. (406) 722-3347 serves good breakfasts, burgers, and shakes across from the school.

Camping

For a first chance/last chance Montana campground, there's nothing more convenient than **Cabin City** Forest Service campground. It's a little over two miles off I-90 at exit 22, just east of De Borgia and 22 miles from the state line. Unless you hit a busy weekend, it's relatively peaceful. The campsites are set in a lodgepole pine forest, and there's a three-quarter-mile nature hike down to Twelvemile Creek. The campground is open from late May through early September, $8 per night.

The **Sloway** campground is between exits 37 (Sloway) and 43 (Dry Creek). **Quartz Flat,** another conveniently located Forest Service campground, is at the rest stop east of Superior, near mile marker 58. Rates are $12 a night. It's convenient, but you have to deal with lights and noise from the freeway.

THE ROAD TO PARADISE

Highway 135 follows the Clark Fork River from I-90 at St. Regis to Hwy. 200 just east of Paradise. **Cascade Campground** is a small, basic, roadside Forest Service campground ($8, with smelly pit toilets and hand-pumped water). It's on Hwy. 135 six miles south of Hwy. 200. There's a surprising amount of roadside noise generated by Hwy. 135, but the setting is nice; there is a hike up to a waterfall, the Clark Fork River is just across the road, and if it's chilly, there's a hot springs resort less than four miles up the highway.

Quinn's Hot Spring Resort, three miles south of Hwy. 200 on Hwy. 135, tel. (406) 826-3150, charges from $10 for tent camping up to $17 for a full hookup. For a dip in the 96° outdoor swimming pool, adults pay $2.50 (included in camping fee), $2 for children. There's a small grocery store with washing machines, a bar, and a supper club (with Sunday brunch at 10). Non-campers can get a motel room or a small cabin for $25-50.

PARADISE AND PLAINS

Paradise may have originally been "Pair-o-Dice," after a roadhouse on the road along the Clark Fork. But Paradise isn't such a bad name in itself. There's the river, the mountains, and the banana belt. Not much else, but hey, who needs it?

Plains was originally called "Horse Plains." Its moderate climate made it a favorite spot for Indians and their horses to spend the winters.

Sights
In Plains, the old Horse Plains Jail is at the corner of Blake and McGowan a block north of Hwy. 200. The Wild Horse Plains School House is a log building dating from 1878. It's on the west end of town next to the highway.

Accommodations
While there's no obvious reason to spend the night here, Plains is a pleasant riverside town with several inexpensive motels, including the **Owl Motel,** 304 W. Meany, tel. (406) 826-3691, and the **Tops Motel,** 340 E. Railroad, tel. (406) 826-3412. There are several cafes, restaurants, and bars in Plains.

Recreation
Rocky Point Outfitters is run by Orvall Kuester, tel. (406) 826-3766, who has the reputation of leading good trips for photographers.

THOMPSON FALLS

Thompson Falls (pop. 1,540, elev. 2,463 feet) was named for David Thompson, the geographer and trader who established his Saleesh House here in 1809. The trading post was used, though perhaps not continuously, by Thompson and other North West Company employees until the early 1820s. There's no trace of the Saleesh House left at its original site about two miles east of Thompson Falls on the north shore of the Clark Fork River, but there is a memorial to David Thompson across the highway from the timber-staging area just east of town.

Like many others in Montana's history, Thompson Falls residents of the 1880s decided that a little direct action would enhance their town. They felt that Thompson Falls had been unfairly overlooked by the Northern Pacific Railway, so they piled logs onto the railroad tracks. When the train was forced to stop, the locals boarded it and persuaded the passengers, emigrants from the east, to settle in Thompson Falls.

The falls were dammed in 1916, backing up a two-mile-long reservoir behind the dam. There are two more dams downstream from this one, making the Clark Fork more like a lake than a river for much of its course from Thompson Falls to the Idaho state line.

Sights
Thompson Falls Island, at the foot of Gallatin St., is a day-use park that's closed to automobiles. It's full of bluffs and rocky rises, a good place to hike around and watch the birds, including the osprey nesting on the bridge. Keep an eye peeled for Canada geese. Like the Canadian employees of the North West Company in the early 1800s, they seem to like this area.

bighorn sheep, Ovis canadensis

The local **historical museum** is housed in the old jail, behind the police station on Madison Street. It's open during the summer Mon.-Fri. 9 a.m.-5 p.m.

East of Thompson Falls, the **KooKooSint Mountain Sheep Viewing Area** is a roadside pullout with several informative signs. (KooKooSint is the name given David Thompson by the local Indians. It means "Man Who Looks at Stars.") Bighorn sheep were eaten by the Flathead Indians and by Thompson, who found them a welcome addition to his sparse winter diet. You're most likely to see sheep here in the spring, when they're at lower elevations eating the new grass, or during late November or December, when they descend to feed in the valleys and mate. Open, south-facing slopes provide a winter habitat. The lambs are born in early May on the high ridges, and the sheep summer in the mountains. Mountain sheep have spongy hooves with hard edges to lend traction and support, allowing them to traverse steep slopes easily and quickly.

Accommodations

The vintage **Black Bear Bar & Hotel,** 919 Main, tel. (406) 827-3971, is undergoing renovation and updating, and offers inexpensive rooms (from $18 for a room with bath down the hall, $30 for a private bath). **Falls Motel,** 112 Gallatin, tel. (406) 827-3559 or (800) 521 2184, has a hot tub in a pleasant little solarium and an exercise room; rooms are from $40 s, $48 d. Just west of town, **Rimrock Lodge,** tel. (406) 827-3536, has a good restaurant and rooms for $37 s, $41 d.

Camping

Thompson Falls State Recreation Area is a mile west of Thompson Falls, just off Hwy. 200 on the Clark Fork. The riverside spots have running water but no other amenities. **Copper King** and **Clark Memorial** are free Forest Service campgrounds with no running water up Thompson River Road (catch this road five miles east of town). Copper King is four miles off Hwy. 200; Clark Memorial is another mile and a half up the road.

Recreation

The **Thompson Falls Golf Club** is a nine-hole public course just northwest of town near the state recreation area.

Several looped hiking trails lead to small lakes in the Lolo National Forest north of Thompson Falls. Reach the **Four Lakes Creek** trailhead by driving north of Thompson River Rd. (which intersects Hwy. 200 five miles east of town) about six miles, turn left onto the West Fork Thompson River Rd., and follow it, bearing left as it becomes Four Lakes Creek Rd. (Forest Service Rd. 7669), some eight miles to the trailhead. A Lolo National Forest map will detail the trails.

Fishing access to the Thompson River is easy; a road runs along it almost the entire way from Hwy. 200 north to Hwy. 2. Expect to pull mostly rainbow trout, and perhaps some brown trout, from the stretch near Hwy. 200.

Food and Drink

Ferk's, 809 Main St., tel. (406) 827-9994, has good burgers and is, in general, a pleasant place to dine in Thompson Falls. **La Roq's** is the kind of place you'd call an "honest bar," which means, in part, that some serious drinking has been known to occur here. The **Rimrock Lodge,** tel.

(406) 427-3536, serves breakfast, lunch, and dinner and has good river views.

NORTH OF THOMPSON FALLS ON HIGHWAY 200

Trout Creek

Trout Creek is west of Thompson Falls and 15 miles east of Noxon. It has a few motels, a recreation area with a small swimming beach, and a ranger station. The **Lakeside Motel,** tel. (406) 827-4458, has rooms for $30 s, $35 d. **North Shore Campground** is a National Forest campground on Noxon Reservoir about two miles west of Trout Creek.

If you're in the mood to drive back roads, **Vermillion Falls** is 12 miles from Trout Creek on Vermillion River Road. A couple of miles farther along the road, find **Willow Creek Campground,** a small, free, and primitive (no water) Forest Service campground.

Noxon

You wouldn't immediately assume that quiet, pleasant Noxon would warrant a byline in the *New York Times.* However, the chief spokesman for the Montana Militia, the antigovernment paramilitary operation, lives in the woods hereabouts.

There's a dam on the Clark Fork at Noxon, a small town on the west bank of the river. The 190-foot-high dam, which harnesses the Noxon rapids, was built in 1959 and has two viewpoints less than a mile from Hwy. 200. The **Noxon Motel,** tel. (406) 847-2600, just across the bridge from Hwy. 200, has clean and comfortable rooms, a hot tub, and a quiet, scenic location; $25 s, $29 d. For the best steak in this corner of the state, stop at **Toby's Bar.**

Heron

The Cabinet Gorge was named by David Thompson, who thought of the French word for a small room when he saw the high rock walls that formed the gorge. Of course, there's a dam here now, just over the state line into Idaho.

The **Wilderness Lodge,** Rte. 2, Box 41, Heron, MT 59844, tel. (406) 847-2277, is tucked away on Elk Creek in the northern Bitterroot Mountains. Motel rooms ($35) and cabins ($50) are rented by the day and the week; there's also a hot tub. The Wilderness Lodge also offers recreation, including guided horseback riding and fishing.

THE BITTERROOT VALLEY

Probably nowhere else in Montana provides such a diverse and satisfying unity of attractions as the Bitterroot Valley. First of all, let's make it clear that the Bitterroot is stunningly beautiful. The Bitterroot River, flanked by groves of cottonwood, winds through a wide fertile valley of farm- and pastureland. The heavily wooded humped arch of the Bitterroot Mountains rears back to reveal precipitous canyons and jagged peaks. Historic, quiet old towns slumber in a purposeful way: there are comings and goings, but no commotion.

Opportunities for recreation are almost limitless. The Bitterroot River provides great fishing; the Bitterroot National Forest offers thousands of acres of wilderness, with over 1,600 miles of maintained trails to dramatic peaks, pristine lakes, and wildlife viewing. Across the valley to the east, the Sapphire Range offers gem hunting and more wildlife habitat. Proximity to Missoula lends sophistication to the services in the Bitterroot, but suburban sprawl also engulfs the lower valley with residential subdivisions.

THE LAND

The Bitterroot River flows north in a wide valley between two mountain ranges. The Sapphire Range to the east is characterized by relatively low, forested peaks. To the west rise the deep canyons and jagged peaks of the Bitterroot Mountains, whose rugged watershed forms the Montana-Idaho border.

The Bitterroot Range was formed as the granite of the Idaho Batholith rose to the surface. As this piston of molten rock pushed upward, the existing surface layers of rock and soil were hoisted higher and higher, until they became unstable. Over the course of millions of years, these older

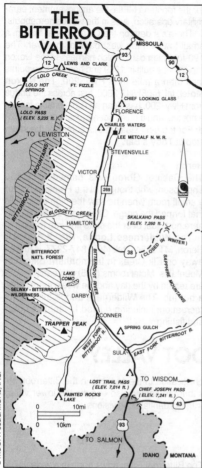

THE BITTERROOT VALLEY

MISSOULA

12 LEWIS AND CLARK

93

LOLO CREEK

90

12

LOLO HOT SPRINGS

FT. FIZZLE

LOLO

LOLO PASS (ELEV. 5,235 ft.)

CHIEF LOOKING GLASS

TO LEWISTON

FLORENCE

CHARLES WATERS

LEE METCALF N.W.R.

STEVENSVILLE

VICTOR

269

BLODGETT CREEK

HAMILTON

SKALKAHO PASS (ELEV. 7,260 ft.)

38

(CLOSED IN WINTER)

BITTERROOT NAT'L FOREST

LAKE COMO

SELWAY - BITTERROOT WILDERNESS

DARBY

CONNER

TRAPPER PEAK

SPRING GULCH

SULA

LOST TRAIL PASS (ELEV. 7,014 ft.)

TO WISDOM

CHIEF JOSEPH PASS (ELEV. 7,241 ft.)

43

PAINTED ROCKS LAKE

0   10mi

0   10km

93

TO SALMON

IDAHO   MONTANA

© MOON PUBLICATIONS, INC.

rocks were sloughed off the rising batholith, skidding eastward on the batholith's molten slopes.

These crumpled rock sheets came to rest east of the batholith and formed the Sapphire Range. The Bitterroot River now runs in the gulf formed between the rising and the displaced mountains.

The Bitterroot Range's odd, diagonally pitched eastern face lends the range a distinctive, evenly hunched edge. This skirt of rock is in fact the remains of the molten lubricant, called mylonite, which coated the batholith proper and on which the Sapphire Range skidded eastward. Behind

this thousand-foot-thick veneer of rock rear the heavily glaciated granite peaks of the Idaho Batholith, here called the Bitterroots.

While the streams that flow out of the Sapphires have better fishing, the Bitterroot drainages are more distinctive and better explored. Curiously evenly spaced down the length of the valley, these streams debouch from alpine lakes in rounded valleys scooped out by glaciers, then fall quickly through narrow canyons gashed through the resistant mylonite.

Flora and Fauna

The wildlands of the Selway-Bitterroot Wilderness and the Bitterroot National Forest protect many species of wildlife, though none are unique to the Bitterroots. Elk, bighorn sheep, and mountain goats are frequently encountered, as are smaller mammals like the pika and badger. Ospreys nest along the Bitterroot River, and bald eagles are frequent visitors to the valley.

Because the Bitterroot Range rises 5,000 feet from the valley floor to its highest peaks in three miles, a variety of ecosystems sustains a wide cross section of plantlife. These range from the sage and juniper of the valley floor to the fir and larch forests of the upper reaches, with ponderosa pine mediating the transition. The subalpine larch, a deciduous conifer, clings to rock faces high above the point where other trees cease to grow.

HISTORY

In 1805, Lewis and Clark passed down the Bitterroot Valley from the south, over Lost Trail Pass. The Corps of Discovery had already crossed the Continental Divide at Lemhi only to discover that, although the Salmon River in Idaho flowed into the Columbia drainage, it did so as the aptly named "River of No Return." The Salmon was hopelessly impassable. The corps climbed up into Montana again, this time to follow the Bitterroot down to Lolo Creek, where they established a favorite camping spot, called Traveler's Rest. From here, the corps followed Lolo Creek up and over Lolo Pass, and down more hospitable drainages to the Columbia. The following year, they retraced their trail to Traveler's Rest. Clark and half the corps returned up the Bitterroot to cross over Gibbon Pass into the Big Hole.

Lewis is responsible for the name of the plant that gives this valley its name. While local Indians found the roots of the bitterroot both tasty and fortifying, Lewis pronounced it bitter and nauseating. His name now identifies the plant in Latin *Lewisia rediviva*.

The Bitterroot Valley, with its fertile bottomland and protected climate, from the first attracted farmers. The discovery of gold in nearby valleys and the establishment of mining boomtowns created a demand for foodstuffs. As farmers moved into the area, they began to pressure the government to remove the Flathead from the valley, and in 1872 James Garfield, who later became the 20th U.S. president, was sent to transfer the Indians north to the Mission Valley.

Five years later, the Nez Perce passed through the Bitterroot on their tragic flight across the Northwest. Under the leadership of Chief Joseph, the band of about 700 Indians and nearly 2,000 horses traveled from Idaho down Lolo Creek and up the Bitterroot toward Crow country, fleeing the Army infantry. Chief Joseph vowed to the Army and the Bitterroot settlers to march peaceably through the settled areas of the Bitterroot in return for unmolested passage. The offer was not accepted officially, and the Nez Perce simply skirted a hastily constructed barricade at Fort Fizzle and proceeded up the Bitterroot. No shots were fired as they passed through the valley. Once over the Continental Divide in the Big Hole, however, Col. John Gibbon and 183 men ambushed the Nez Perce at the Battle of the Big Hole.

Agriculture

Farming really took hold in the Bitterroot after the Northern Pacific extended a spur line to Hamilton. One of the largest enterprises in the valley was Marcus Daly's Bitterroot Stock Farm. The copper magnate from Butte preferred the Bitterroot as a summer home, and he built a magnificent mansion on his 26,000-acre holding. Considering the fact that Daly modeled his farm on an Irish manor, it's no surprise that racehorses were the most noted of the farm's products.

In the early years of this century, the Bitterroot was home to an elaborate irrigation scheme that turned the valley into a huge apple orchard. The Big Ditch, as it was functionally named, provided water to the eastside bench land, which was divided into subdivisions of 10 acres each. At the height of apple euphoria, 22,000 acres of the Bitterroot were in fruit production. The soil and climate didn't quite live up to the exaggerated promises of the developers, and by the 1950s apple production ceased to be a significant element of the area's economy.

While agriculture remains important in the Bitterroot, much of the farmland in the lower valley has now been subdivided into small "ranchettes." This part of the valley has largely been converted into a bedroom community of Missoula.

RECREATION

The Bitterroot National Forest contains 1.6 million acres, with nearly 750,000 of these protected as wilderness. Forest Service roads provide entrance for mountain bikers or off-road vehicle enthusiasts, while 950 miles of maintained trails give hikers access to some of the most tortured geology and pristine landscapes in the Rockies.

Fishing

All the larger streams that feed into the Bitterroot River harbor rainbow, cutthroat, and brook trout, and some of the higher lakes in the Bitterroots, such as the Big Creek Lakes, are known for good fishing.

For the angler, though, the real news is the Bitterroot itself. The river seems largely untainted by the effect of a century's worth of foresting, farming, suburban sprawl, and irrigating. In fact, even in the busy heart of the valley, the cottonwoods and willows that line the shore shield the angler from the realities of Bitterroot development. The trout here are both numerous and large. Rainbows and browns fill up the majority of creels, but cutthroat and the elusive bull are also apprehended. The lower part of the river near Missoula is where the lunkers are most likely lurking (and rumor has it, largemouth bass), while farther south, up Connor way, is where the trout are thickest.

The state has established six fishing-access sites on the river, and there's also easy access from bridges. At no place is the Bitterroot far from the road, though remember to ask for permission before crossing private land. Boat rentals are available in Hamilton, and organized float and fishing trips are offered by the region's many outfitters.

THE LOWER BITTERROOT

From Hamilton (pop. 4,059, elev. 3,600 feet) north to Missoula, the Bitterroot is at its most genteel. Excluding lodges of typically nomadic Indians, this part of the valley is the oldest continuously inhabited area in Montana, and it shows. Interesting old Victorian farmhouses are scattered amongst the fields, and isolated apple trees from once substantial orchards can still be seen in meadows. Main streets have changed little since they were built. Despite the crags of the Bitterroot Range rising to the west, here the Bitterroot feels lived-in and comfortable.

The visitor should leave Hwy. 93 as soon as possible (at Florence at the Missoula end, and at Hamilton from the south) and instead take the East Side Highway, MT 269. While 93 is undeniably a faster road, it's also very busy (commuters' cars sport bumper stickers declaring "Pray for me. I drive Highway 93."). The East Side Highway affords the best views onto the Bitterroots and goes through the pretty towns of Corvallis and Stevensville. It also avoids the more obvious effects of the subdivisions in the lower valley, the part of the Bitterroot that is not so much Missoula's bedroom as its stable.

Try to pick up a copy of a handy brochure called *East Side Highway: Bitterroot Valley Scenic and Historic Drive* from a tourist bureau in Hamilton or Stevensville. As you drive through these old communities, you'll want to know more about the architecture and history.

History

Father Pierre Jean deSmet established St. Mary's Mission near Stevensville in 1841. It was abandoned in 1850, and the land was purchased by John Owen to build Fort Owen, a trading post and Indian agency. After gold was discovered in nearby valleys, Owen and the other frontiersmen living in the valley found a market for the agricultural riches of the Bitterroot in the mining boomtowns.

Hamilton is also known for the Rocky Mountain Research Laboratory, where research on Rocky Mountain spotted fever was conducted. The fever, which is spread by ticks and is debilitating if not fatal to humans and livestock, is endemic to parts of the Bitterroot. The discovery of a treatment opened infested and otherwise uninhabitable areas of the valley.

A BIT ABOUT THE BITTERROOT

While the bitterroot lily, Montana's state flower, throughout most of the western part of the state, the Bitterroot Valley is, unsurprisingly, a good place to plan a sighting.

Legend holds that the plant sprang from the tears of a Flathead mother whose family was starving. The sun, hearing the mother's sorrow, sent a bird as a messenger to turn her tears into a plant whose roots were nutritious (albeit as bitter as the mother's sorrow) but whose beauty would reflect the devotion of the grieving woman.

The roots of these beautiful, light pink flowers were a staple of the Indian diet. It was eaten fresh in season and also dried for use in the winter or when traveling. The Flathead boiled or steamed the roots, then mixed them with berries, marrow, or meat. Although the snow-white meat of the root can be bitter to the point of causing nausea, the Flathead found that if it was gathered prior to flowering, or dried sufficiently, the bitterness was much reduced.

Elaborate rituals accompanied the bitterroot's harvest. Among the Flatheads, one old woman led other female gatherers out in the search. When the party reached the first bitterroot, the leader would stick her elkhorn digger at the base of the plant. After the others planted their diggers, a prayer was offered, and the first plant was uprooted. Only after the prayer was offered was the season open—to dig *before* the ceremony was to invite a small harvest. The following day, the first root was given to the chief and a daylong feast ensued.

Sights

Hamilton is unique in the fact that it didn't just spring up as opportunity (or the railroad) allowed. Rather, it sprang fully formed from the brow of copper magnate Daly, who, after designing his model Irish manor, decided to establish a model town nearby. In 1890, Daly brought in planners who laid down a city complete with free plots for churches, ready-designed banks, shops, schools, and rather glorious homes. As a result, Hamilton wears its age very gracefully. Stop to picnic or let the kids loose in one of its parks. An easy stop for either one is a small playground only one block west of Hwy. 93 on Bedford, two blocks south of Main. There's a more substantial park where Madison Street bumps up against the Bitterroot River.

Daly's most famous racehorse was Tammany. In keeping with the Daly tradition, Tammany did not simply have a stable, but a brick edifice called Tammany Castle. To see what upscale horses lived in at the turn of the century go one mile east of Hamilton on MT 269. Look to the south about 100 yards. The stable is not open to the public.

Hamilton contains a number of handsome old homes and public buildings. The **Ravalli County Museum** is housed in the Old Ravalli County Court House, built in 1900. This stone and brick landmark bears a resemblance to the University of Montana's Main Hall. The museum has a good collection of Flathead Indian artifacts, pioneer-era memorabilia, and an exhibit on wood ticks. The museum is at the corner of Bedford and 3rd Streets. Summer hours are Mon.-Fri. 10 a.m.-4 p.m., Sunday 2:30-5 p.m.; winter hours are Monday, Wednesday, and Friday 1-4 p.m., Sunday 2:30-5 p.m. No admission fee. Like the courthouse, the **City Hall,** at 175 S. 3rd, is on the National Register of Historic Places.

Saint Mary's Mission at Stevensville was rebuilt in 1866 by Father Anthony Ravalli out of the original hewn logs of the 1841 structure. The one-room chapel with front belfry is open to the public Wed.-Sat. 10 a.m.-5 p.m., Sunday 10 a.m.-2 p.m.; $3 admission, tel. (406) 777-5734. The interior, with its wood-burning stove and wainscoting, is pretty much as Father Ravalli left it. Also on the grounds are the mission pharmacy and a graveyard. While Father Ravalli's grave is meant to be the draw here, more curious is the sign indicating Indian Graves before an open field. Saint Mary's Mission is on 4th St. two blocks west of Main.

What's left of **Fort Owen** is just east of Hwy. 93 on the Stevensville cutoff (follow signs for the Fort Owen Monument after the Forest Service office). The original 1850 structure evolved from the log palisade of a frontier trader into an adobe-brick fortress with turrets and walkways after Owen became the federal Indian agent to the Flathead. Of the original buildings, one barracks remains and serves as a museum with interpretive exhibits. The fort is on private land and is open during daylight hours.

Marcus Daly bought his Bitterroot Stock Farm in 1889 and built the **Marcus Daly Mansion** in 1897. After his death, the house was enlarged in

1910 to its present Georgian-revival splendor. Built primarily as a summer home for the Daly family, "Riverside," as the mansion was known, looks over the Bitterroot Valley to the rugged peaks in Blodgett Canyon and vies with the Bitterroots themselves for splendor. The house remained in private hands until 1987, when it was acquired by the state.

Riverside is probably the most beautiful estate in Montana. A tree-lined boulevard leads to 50 acres of grounds, which contain an arboretum of specimen trees, a swimming pool, a playhouse, and a tennis court. The 24,213-square-foot mansion contains 42 rooms, 24 of which are bedrooms and 15 of which are baths. Some of the original furniture and most of the old fixtures remain. The grounds alone are worth a strolling tour.

The mansion is located four miles south of Corvallis and two miles north of Hamilton on MT 269. After leaving the highway, follow a boulevard about a mile until you reach the grounds. Riverside is open daily April 15-October 15, 11 a.m.-4 p.m.; $5 adult, $3 children 5-14. Tours leave on the hour 11 a.m.-4 p.m. Admission is free; grounds are open 9 a.m.-5:30 p.m. For more information, call (406) 363-6004.

Hiking

Any creek worth mentioning in the Bitterroots has a trail up it, and all are worth considering for a hike. The Forest Service map of the Bitterroot National Forest will apprise the hiker of dozens of likely destinations. The traveler with some time to spend in the Bitterroots can ask locals for recommendations (every undergrad at the University of Montana has a favorite valley) or ask rangers for the inside scoop. But if you have only a day to spend in the lower Bitterroots, consider one of the following.

A largely overlooked long day-hike (or unstressful overnight trip) that's close to Missoula leads up the Sweeney Creek drainage to **Peterson Lake.** You'll need a vehicle, because the allure of the hike is how high the trailhead is. Forest Service roads (turn west on Forest Service Rd. 1315, two miles south of Florence) will take the hiker most of the way up the canyon wall to a trailhead. After a couple miles of easy traversing, the hiker drops onto alpine lakes, with the car having done most of the climbing.

Another popular ascent of intermediate challenge involves climbing **St. Mary's Peak.** Again,

Saint Mary's Mission, Stevensville

JUDY JEWELL

this hike boasts a trailhead midway up the mountain, and one of the great views that the peak affords is onto the local lookout tower. From Hwy. 93, go two miles south of the Stevensville turnoff. A brown sign promising St. Mary's Peak points up the switchbacks of Forest Service Rd. 739. The trailhead is about 10 miles from the highway, and it's a 4.5-mile hike to the lookout.

Between Victor and Hamilton, at the crossroads hamlet of Corvallis, turn west to reach the **Mill Creek** trail. It's about three miles in along a great trail to a waterfall; if you want to make a backpacking trip out of it, keep going for another 11 miles to a high mountain lake.

The **Blodgett Creek Canyon** just west of Hamilton is probably the most beautifully precipitous of the many valleys gashed in the side of the Bitterroots. Although the landscape is very rugged, the trail is relatively level and well maintained. There's no hidden reward at the trail's end, so hike in until lunch seems propitious, and come back out. Back roads out of Hamilton itself lead to Blodgett Creek trailhead, or you can turn west two miles north of Hamilton on Hwy. 93, just north of the Bitterroot River Bridge.

The **Lee Metcalf National Wildlife Refuge** is a good place for short hikes along the Bitterroot River. It's a good place too for adding the word "riparian" to your vocabulary. This riverside refuge is full of ospreys, eagles, and whatever migrating birds need a place to spend the night. White-tailed deer and coyotes also live here. In the summer, after nesting season, a two-mile loop trail is open through the refuge. Two

shorter trails are open year-round, and picnics are encouraged. From the East Side Hwy. (Hwy. 269), watch for the binocular signs indicating a sanctioned wildlife-viewing area, either just south of Florence or just north of Stevensville.

Other Recreation
Cross-country skiing is pretty much the order of the season after snowfall, and is as casual as just parking the car and putting on your skis. All of the Bitterroot canyons are good bets, and they are even more pleasant covered with snow, as they tend to be pretty rocky and rugged in summer. The real treasure for cross-country skiers, though, is Lolo Pass. Snow simply dumps along the pass all winter, but the Highway Department keeps the road open. Lolo Pass is 37 miles east of Lolo on Hwy. 12. It's very popular, but it's still possible to strike out and get away from the crowds.

Take a dip in the big outdoor pool at **Lolo Hot Springs,** on Hwy. 12 about 12 miles northeast of the state line, tel. (406) 273-2290. Adults pay $4 for a swim; it's $2 for children under 12.

Lolo Hot Springs also offers **horseback trail rides** for $15 an hour and, in the winter, **snowmobile rentals** for $95 a day.

There are **public golf courses** in Stevensville and Hamilton. The Stevensville course, just north of town on Wildfowl Ln., tel. (406) 777-3636, has nine holes; the Hamilton Golf Club, on Golf Course Rd. southeast of town, tel. (406) 363-4251, has an 18-hole course.

Outfitters

If the thought of all that nature in the Bitterroot makes you a little jumpy or just lonely, consider hiring an outfitter to ease that transition into the wilderness. After seeing the piles of fliers at the chamber of commerce, you'll wonder if there's anyone in the Bitterroot who is *not* an outfitter or who at least doesn't run a "guest ranch." The following are just highlights of what's available, but an inquiring letter to the chamber will be sure to result in cascades of mail.

Catch Montana offers wading and float fishing on the Bitterroot, Rock Creek, and Clark Fork April-November. Prices run $150-250 per day. Contact them at P.O. Box 428, Hamilton, MT 59840, tel. (406) 363-6253 or (800) 882-7844.

Bill Abbot and his guides at **Trout Fishing Only,** tel. (406) 363-2408, will row you into good fishing waters, then tell you what to do when you get there. They specialize in multiday trips on the Bitterroot, Beaverhead, and Big Hole Rivers, and will arrange lodging and lunches. Rates run about $200-250 per day.

Rocky Mountain Adventures, 765 Little Sleeping Child Rd., Hamilton, MT 59840, tel. (406) 363-0200, offers hunting and fishing trips and horse or rafting excursions. **Lone Tree Outfitting,** 1531 Iron Cap Rd., Stevensville, MT 59870, tel. (406) 777-3906, offers big-game hunting to both the able and the handicapped.

Highway 93 is fairly lined with fly shops, and store personnel will, in the way of cagey anglers, offer a few tips.

Accommodations

B&Bs: A well-run Bitterroot Valley B&B is **Deer Crossing B&B,** south of Hamilton at 396 Hayes Creek Rd., tel. (406) 363-2232 or (800) 763-2232. The large log house has rooms ranging in price from $70 (two twin beds) to $100 (a many-windowed upstairs suite); there's also a compact bunkhouse. There's also a hot tub, a pool table, and horses to ride. Children are welcome at this B&B, and it's a great place to bring teenagers. **Bavarian Farmhouse,** at 163 Bowman Rd. in Hamilton, tel. (406) 363-4063, is a renovated 1890s farmhouse that offers five guest rooms.

Motels: There's one motel in Stevensville, **St. Mary's Motel and RV Park,** along Hwy. 93. Singles are $40, doubles $45, tel. (406) 777-2838 or (800) 624-7015. Pets are okay here once they've gained approval from the management.

There are more motels to choose from in Hamilton. Economical lodging can be found at the **Sportsman,** $35 s, $43 d, 410 N. 1st St., tel. (406) 363-2411; and at the **Bitterroot Motel,** $31 s, $35 d, 408 S. 1st St., tel. (406) 363-1142. Both accept pets. Another budget motel is at **Deffy's,** 321 S. 1st St., tel. (406) 363-1244. The "1st Street" that these motels share as an address is actually busy Hwy. 93. The only motel not on 1st St. is the **City Center Motel,** at the quiet end of Main Street, 415 W. Main St., tel. (406) 363-1651. Rooms here are $36 s, $44 d, and some have full kitchens.

Somewhat more expensive rooms are offered at the **Comfort Inn,** 1115 N. 1st St., tel. (406) 363-6600 or (800) 442-4667, $51-62 s, $52-64 d. There's a casino attached to the motel, and an exercise room, sauna, and hot tub. Pets are okay for a $4 fee. The **Best Western Hamilton Inn** has rooms for $48 s, $63 d, 409 1st St., tel. (406) 363-2142 or (800) 426-4586. Amenities include an outdoor hot tub and some rooms with refrigerators and microwaves.

Hot Springs: For a slightly different twist in lodging, consider staying at one of the local hot springs resorts. Some of the best in the state are in the Bitterroot Valley. **Lolo Hot Springs Resort** is 30 miles up Hwy. 12 along Lolo Creek, 38500 Hwy. 12, Lolo, MT 59847, tel. (406) 273-2290. The mineral water is channeled into a large outdoor swimming pool and warmer indoor soaking pool, and there's a motel (perfectly nice budget rooms start at $41 s, $47 d), camping (tepees rent for $25 a night), a bar and restaurant. Lewis and Clark camped and bathed here. Nowadays, these hot springs are popular with skiers returning from a long day in cross-country heaven at Lolo Pass. Nonguests may swim all day for $4, $2 children.

Lodges: In Victor, **Bear Creek Lodge,** 1184 Bear Creek Trail, tel. (406) 642-3750 or (800) 270-5550, is on 115 acres adjacent to the Selway-Bitterroot Wilderness Area. The lodge was built in 1991 from huge logs salvaged from the Yellowstone fires of 1988, and it has attractive rooms and common areas, including a hot tub, sauna, and exercise room. The lodge is well situated for hikers and anglers, with a mile of private fishing access to Bear Creek. Rates, including all meals and beverages, run $210 s, $300 d. During the summer, there's a three-day minimum, and the lodge closes Jan.-February.

Camping

The U.S. Forest Service maintains a number of campsites in the Bitterroots. Most require a fair amount of determination to make use of: some are essentially trailheads into Bitterroot canyons, and others demand long dusty drives on county roads, but some are handy enough for the more casual traveler to consider.

Lewis and Clark Campground is 12 miles west of Lolo on Hwy. 12, and for the angler, right on Lolo Creek. An even more enticing fishing/camping site is the state's **Chief Looking Glass Fishing-Access Site,** which is a developed campsite as well. Look for the fishing-access sign on Hwy. 93 about midway between Lolo and Stevensville, at milepost 77. Then turn east one mile to the river.

Charles Waters is a developed site at the trailhead up Bass Creek, with access to hiking up the canyon and fishing in the stream. Watch for the Forest Service sign for Bass Creek Trail four miles south of Florence or four miles north of Stevensville on Hwy. 93. It's about three miles in to the campsite.

There's more luxury at some of the area's private campgrounds. If you're driving south from Missoula, the first you'll find north of Hamilton is **Rockford's Campground,** one mile south of Victor. As with motels, Hamilton is where the action is in campgrounds. **Bitterroot Family Campground** has a pool and showers and is eight miles south of Hamilton on Hwy. 93, tel. (406) 363-2430 or (800) 453-2430. **Angler's Roost,** three miles south of Hamilton, offers most facilities, tel. (406) 363-1268.

Food and Drink

The hungry traveler will not want for opportunities to fill up in the Bitterroot. There are so many cafes and restaurants along the road that one imagines that Bitterroot residents do little but journey from coffee klatch to lunch and back again. The traveler can't go far wrong with most Bitterroot eateries, and there are a few worth planning ahead for.

A little ways west of the Bitterroot Valley proper, the **Lumberjack Bar** is a mile north of Hwy. 12, west of Lolo. The bar itself is hewn from an enormous log, and the stools are also made from logs. If you're not intent on watching whatever sports event is on the bar TV, cozy up to the big fireplace and watch the ever-absorbing bar scene.

Glen's Mountain View Cafe, right on Hwy. 93 at Florence, tel. (406) 273-2534, is a little roadside cafe with extraordinary pastries. Not that the rest of the menu is lacking (Glen's raises its own beef), but the pies are reckoned to be the best in the area.

The Fort Owen Inn is near the site of old Fort Owen. It's a western kind of place well used by locals as a hangout and dance hall. The steaks are the news here. The supper club offers a selection of 10 cuts of well-marbled beef. The Fort Owen Inn is right off Hwy. 93 at Stevensville, tel. (406) 777-3483.

In Victor, eat your beef at the **Victor Steakhouse,** tel. (406) 642-3300. It's not long on atmosphere, but the steaks ($10-15) are delicious.

The Banque in Hamilton offers well-prepared food in a historic bank building, lending the dining enterprise a kind of ersatz Montana elegance. The savvy traveler will not be surprised to learn that steaks headline the menu. The Banque is at 225 W. Main St., tel. (406) 363-1955.

A couple of doors down from The Banque, in a converted office building at 217 W. Main St., the hip and convivial **Wild Oats Cafe and Coffeehouse,** tel. (406) 363-4567, serves delicious sandwiches for about $5, and a wide range of teas in addition to the expected espresso drinks. It's a good place to chat with a few locals.

The Bitterroot's best burgers are in Hamilton at **Nap's,** 220 N. 2nd St., tel. (406) 363-0136. Get a big burger, a basket of fries, and a coke for $6. At **The Spice of Life,** 163 S 2nd St., you'll find world cuisine in a homey bistro setting. If you're just looking for coffee and a snack, try **A Place to Ponder,** 162 S 2nd St., a bakery and coffeeshop. Another cool place to hang out is **Stone Pony Bakery and Café,** 310 S 1st St., tel. (406) 363-2411.

Shopping

The most obvious craft in the Bitterroot Valley is log-house construction. If you're not in the market for a new house, the Bitterroot offers local pottery at **Wild Rose Pottery,** in Victor at 2387 Meridian Rd. (just off Hwy. 93 behind the Sinclair station), tel. (406) 642-6514.

Mountain Outfitters Sporting Goods repairs bikes at 205 W. Main St., tel. (406) 363-1560.

Hamilton supports a good general bookstore, **Chapter One,** 252 Main St., tel. (406) 363-5220.

Services

The **Marcus Daly Memorial Hospital** is at 1200 Westwood Dr. in Hamilton, tel. (406) 363-2211. The Hamilton **sheriff** can be reached at (406) 363-3033.

Hamilton's **post office** is at 340 W. Main Street. There are also post offices on the main streets of Stevensville, Corvallis, and Victor.

The **Main Street Wash O Mat** is at 711 W. Main St. in Hamilton, tel. (406) 363-9969.

Information

The **Bitterroot Valley Chamber of Commerce** is just east of the stoplight in Hamilton, 105 E. Main St., tel. (406) 363-2400.

The **Bitterroot National Forest Headquarters** is in Hamilton at 316 N. 3rd, tel. (406) 363-3131. The **Stevensville Ranger District Office** is at 88 Main St., tel. (406) 777-5461.

The **Hamilton Public Library** is at 306 State St., tel. (406) 363-1670.

Read the *Ravalli Republic* to keep up on who's been arrested for what, and how big a fish they've caught lately.

Transportation

Rent-A-Wreck operates along Hwy. 93 north of Hamilton, tel. (406) 363-1430.

THE UPPER BITTERROOT

The Bitterroot Valley narrows upstream from Hamilton, and the character of the land changes. The river flows faster and the mountains encroach. With rocky ramparts closing in, the Bitterroot ceases to be a broad valley with farms and subdivisions and becomes a wooded canyon. Here, loggers and (for want of a better term) woodsmen predominate. Though the media has seized upon Darby as a hotbed of militia activity, such pursuits are not particularly noticeable to the visitor. For the traveler, recreation is the draw in the upper Bitterroot.

The Land

Darby marks the southern edge of old Lake Missoula, which existed in the bad old days when the entire Missoula Valley system was alternately underwater and drained as the ice age saw necessary. At Connor, just south of Darby,

the Bitterroot divides into the West Fork and the East Fork. The highway also divides. Highway 93 follows the East Fork up Lost Trail Pass over the Continental Divide into Idaho or into the Big Hole Valley. The West Fork proceeds up Hwy. 473 first along a paved road, then along an improved road to Painted Rocks Lake.

The West Fork remains mostly canyon country, but at Sula on Hwy. 93 the East Fork opens onto pastureland. All of a sudden it's cattle country, a last reprise of the Bitterroot Valley before it disappears into the heights of the Continental Divide.

History

Lewis and Clark straggled off Lost Trail Pass in September of 1805 after being foiled on their way to the Columbia by the chasms of the Salmon River. They crept back into Montana via the Bitterroot and almost immediately met a lodge of Flathead Indians. At present-day Sula, the Corps of Discovery found 400 Flathead and 500 horses encamped and quickly made friends. Remem-

The Medicine Tree is a Flathead Indian spiritual site.

JUDY JEWELL

ber the landscape. The enormous painting in the Montana House of Representatives in Helena depicts this meeting.

The valley at the junction of the East Fork and Camp Creek later became known as Ross's Hole. Alexander Ross was a Canadian trapper who nearly died of cold here with his family in 1824.

The Nez Perce passed through Ross's Hole in 1877 on their way to the Battle of the Big Hole, only minutes over the Continental Divide. While the tribal leaders felt they had escaped the pursuing Army, others, with "medicine powers," began to foresee the coming ambush. By this time, the Army, under the command of General Gibbon, had caught up with the fleeing Indians, who unwisely had taken a break from their flight from Idaho once they had reached Montana.

Sights

An inconspicuous turnout between mileposts 20 and 21 is at the base of the **Medicine Tree,** a sacred Flathead Indian site. In the 1800s, a bighorn sheep's horn was found embedded in the trunk of this ponderosa pine. (A vandal later sawed the horn out of the tree, and no trace of it remains.) When the Salish lived in the Bitterroot Valley, they would regularly leave gifts (many of which were stolen by whites) at the tree, and it is still a place where offerings are made. Traditionally, natural objects were left, and gifts of herbs and feathers are now joined by brightly colored cloth ribbons tossed high in the branches and cigarettes pressed into the bark. During the Gulf War, the number of yellow ribbons in the Medicine Tree gave an indication of how many tribal members serve in the armed forces. It is, of course, wrong to remove any object from the tree or to damage the tree in any way.

Recreation

The upper Bitterroot has reserved some of the best recreation for those willing to drive the extra miles to get there. You can grow hoarse talking about the hiking possibilities in the Bitterroot, whether the upper valley or the lower, but probably the most astonishing ascent of the entire range is the climb up **Trapper Peak.** At 10,157 feet, it's the highest mountain in the Bitterroots, but it's not even a particularly difficult day-hike. The trailhead is reached by following West Fork Rd., MT 473, at Connor. Once you pass the

Trapper Peak Civilian Jobs Corps Center, go almost seven miles to the signs pointing to the Trapper Peak trailhead. Switchbacks take you most of the way up the back of the mountain, though there's enough slogging left to satisfy more energetic hikers. If you do only one ascent in the Bitterroots, this should be it.

If a day on the mountain isn't possible for you, then enjoy the other end of Trapper Peak at **Lake Como.** This lake just west of Darby is nestled in a valley rimmed by the most unrestrained peaks in the Bitterroots. It should be no surprise that other people know of Lake Como (the Italian Lake Como is its namesake and chief rival in beauty), and don't expect to be the only camper at the lake. There's good trout fishing but too many speedboats to make it a bucolic getaway. There's an easy eight-mile loop trail around the lake. Watch for Lake Como signs five miles north of Darby.

Another good but slightly longer day-hike will take the curious to **Overwhich Falls,** which drops 200 feet along the wall of the Continental Divide near Lost Trail Pass. It's about six miles in, but after following the switchbacks up to the trailhead it's fairly easy going. From the Indian Trees Forest Service Campground follow the signs for Road 729 to Porcupine Saddle. From the trailhead, the trail follows Shields Creek to the falls.

Just across the road from Lost Trail Hot Springs, the **Nee-Me-Poo Trail** traces the route of the Nez Perce on their 1877 flight from the Army. The trail heads uphill through an open ponderosa pine forest past views down the Bitterroot Valley to Gibbons Pass, six miles from the road. It's a pleasant hike with a daypack filled with trail mix and water, but it's hard to hike this route without imagining what it would be like to walk it with family, friends, co-workers, and neighbors of all ages, pursued by the U.S. Army.

Another good West Fork hike starts from the Sam Billings campground and sticks pretty close to aptly named Boulder Creek for the four-mile trip to Boulder Lake.

Painted Rocks Lake is a reservoir on the West Fork of the Bitterroot that receives a lot less activity than Lake Como and offers better fishing, though irrigation usually draws it down during the late summer and fall. There are Indian pictographs on the rocks to the west of the lake. Painted Rocks Lake is 23 miles southwest of the junction of Hwys. 473 and 93. South of the lake, down

West Fork Rd., the still-standing Alta Ranger Station was the nation's first ranger station.

After a day of hiking, stop by **Lost Trail Hot Springs** for a swim. The resort, seven miles south of Sula, charges $4 for a swim ($3 children and seniors). The pool is large and pleasantly warm; inside there's a hot tub and sauna.

The Bitterroot south of Darby (upstream) becomes a stream with fast action. The river's never far out of sight, and access is easy if you maintain the courtesy of asking permission to cross private property. There's one fishing-access site that warrants mention. The **Hannon Memorial Fishing Access Site** at Connor allows the angler to fish both the East and the West forks of the Bitterroot as they converge. Camping is allowed.

Lost Trail Powder Mountain straddles the Idaho-Montana border on Hwy. 93, tel. (406) 821-3211. Though the vertical drop is only 1,200 feet, there's usually good snow here from December into April. Lift tickets go for $18 adult, with half-day rates available.

Motels and Cabins

Darby is a rough-hewn little town that seems only now beginning to change from its early logging days. The downtown storefronts have been spruced up over the past few years, and when it comes to in-town lodging, things are in the process of being boosted above the rustic level. Try the comfortable log cabins or motel rooms (from $35) at **Honey's Motel,** one mile north of town, tel. (406) 821-3111. Honey's also offers horse boarding. To stay in mini log cabins, go to the **Log Cabin Motel,** Hwy. 93 S, tel. (406) 821-3282; each cabin has a single and a double bed and goes for $45.

Resorts

A few miles outside Darby is one of Montana's most exclusive resorts. Perched above the Valley, the **Triple Creek Guest Ranch,** 5551 West Fork Rd., tel. (406) 821-4664, www.triplecreekranch .com, offers accommodations in 18 cabins, with amenities ranging from very comfortable to sumptuous. There are hot tubs aplenty, a well-kept heated swimming pool, tennis courts, horseback riding, fishing (all gear provided), and hiking trails heading out from the ranch property. Many guests come here to sample the various activities, rather than concentrate strictly on fishing or riding,

and an activities director helps them plan their days. Though no minimum stay is imposed, there's enough to keep most people busy for nearly a week. The Triple Creek is very much geared toward couples, but singles and small groups are welcome. It is an adults-only place; no children under 16. Rates run $510-995 per couple per night for extraordinarily comfortable "simple" cabins with a shared hot tub, to $850 for the luxury cabins, with a sitting room and a private hot tub. Two-bedroom cabins go for $595-995 a couple, with an extra $200 per person. This includes all meals, drinks (rooms come stocked with a wet bar), and on-ranch activities.

If those prices aren't in your budget but you hanker for a relaxing Montana mountain getaway, consider the **Nez Perce Ranch,** 7206 Nez Perce Rd., Darby, MT 59829, tel. (406) 349-2100. This comfortable resort offers self-catering accommodations (with daily maid service) along the Bitterroot River in three large log cabins. The ranch sits on 100 forested acres with half a mile of private fishing access. Each cabin has two bedrooms, full kitchen, and porch with barbecue. Prices are $1,120 per week, though if there are openings, you can reserve a cabin for a three-day minimum at $200 per night.

Another fun, midrange place to stay is the **Lost Trail Hot Springs Resort.** While hotsprings resorts can veer from the near-bizarre and seedy to the oversanitized and commercial, Lost Trail strikes a happy balance. It provides convention facilities (for very small conventions) and the clear, hot mineral water that you expect, but it also offers recreational opportunities like mountain biking, hiking, cross-country skiing, horseback riding, and fishing, plus the usual bar and restaurant facilities. Lost Trail Hot Springs is six miles south of Sula on Hwy. 93, and six miles north of Lost Trail Pass. Motel rooms are $55, cabins are $65. The address is 8321 Hwy. 93 S., Sula, MT 59871, tel. (406) 821-3574.

Camp Creek Inn, four miles south of Sula at 7674 Hwy. 93 S., tel. (406) 821-3508, has B&B lodgings in cabins and guest rooms on an old homestead ranch. Rates start at $60 d, $70 d for a housekeeping cabin. During the winter, a $60 per person package includes lodging, breakfast, and skiing at Lost Trail Powder Mountain. Horse boarding is available, and the inn keeps several horses for trail rides.

Camping

The Forest Service maintains a number of campgrounds in the upper Bitterroot, mostly off the beaten path. A couple are handy for casual campers who don't want to get too far off the highway. **Indian Trees** is six miles south of Sula, at a location where Flathead women once spiked ponderosa pines to extract sap, which was used as a sweetener. It's right next door to Lost Trail Hot Springs and costs $11 a night.

Lewis and Clark camped at **Spring Gulch,** and so can you. The campground is right on the East Fork River, five miles north of Sula on Hwy. 93. The **Sula Store** offers campsites at the beginning of the canyon leading from Ross's Hole.

There are several Forest Service campgrounds up the West Fork Rd.; **Sam Billings** is a lovely free spot (no water) near the Boulder

Creek trailhead, and there's another past Painted Rocks Lake at Alta ($7).

Food and Drink

The **Old West Restaurant** has brought good food to Darby, at 200 S Main St. **Triple Creek Restaurant,** about 13 miles south of Darby, tel. (406) 821-4665, is an elegant spot (though kids are not welcome) open Tues.-Sat. for dinner from late May through mid-October.

Information

The **Sula Ranger Station** is just south of Sula on Hwy. 93. The address is simply Sula, MT 59871, tel. (406) 821-3201. The **Darby Ranger Station** can be contacted at P.O. Box 266, Darby, MT 59829, tel. (406) 821-3913. The **sheriff** can be reached at (406) 363-3033.

MISSOULA

Missoula, tucked in a fertile valley and filled with students, loggers, and writers, is the hub of western Montana. The Missoula Valley has always been a crossroads, first for Indians, then for white settlers, nowadays for Montana's major highways. It remains a great focus and jumping-off point for the traveler.

The city (pop. 51,204) takes its sense of confluence seriously. Practically within city limits the Clark Fork is joined by the Blackfoot and Bitterroot Rivers and several smaller streams. As home to the University of Montana, Missoula is a center of learning and one of the state's major cultural centers. Missoula has preserved much of its historic architectural character, and offers good restaurants and a full-bodied nightlife. Missoula's nickname, the Garden City, is apt. As a locale, it's about as temperate, fertile, and hospitable as these things get in Montana.

But Missoula is more than a picturesque university town. The university and artistic population is notoriously Bohemian and political, while the working core of the city is, in Montana terms, decidedly blue collar. Depending on the perspective, Missoula is either a working-class town with a radical university imposed on it or a liberal-arts college town infiltrated by the proletariat. But the juxtaposition works: scratch a logger and find a poet.

For many visitors, Missoula, or something like it, is the very image of what they expect of all Montana. However, Montanans from the rest of the state mistrust Missoula. To them the town is Montana with an attitude. Much of the East vs. West dichotomy of Montana is really shorthand for ambivalence about Missoula and the progressive politics and lifestyles that emerge from it. Throughout the rest of Montana, the university is disdainfully referred to as "the dance school."

For a traveler, Missoula is an agreeable home base for excursions into the wonders of western Montana. However, for a visitor with a little time and a taste for artistic and political ferment, Missoula can become addictive. The city's saloons and salons are filled with testimonials of those who planned to pass through but have yet to leave.

THE LAND

Missoula (elev. 3,205 feet) is at the mouth of Hell Gate Canyon, the Clark Fork River's path between Mt. Jumbo (north, with the "L" for Lola, spelled out in white stone on the hills) and Mt. Sentinel (south, with an "M" for Missoula) on the eastern edge of town. This narrow valley immediately broadens, as four other sizable river val-

leys join it and open up the landscape. The Flathead-Jocko Valley comes in from the north, the Hell Gate and the Blackfoot from the east, the Bitterroot from the south, and the Missoula Valley from the west.

This bowl-like setting makes for both pleasingly temperate weather and the dreaded phenomenon of winter temperature inversion, in which warm, moist air is trapped and held in the valley by high pressure aloft. This stagnant air is apt to contain particulate pollution, largely from wood stoves.

HISTORY

With the five valleys nearly converging here, it's no surprise that the area has long been used as a thoroughfare. Salish Indians from the Bitterroot and Mission Valleys traveled through Hell Gate Canyon to reach buffalo-hunting grounds east of the mountains. They were regularly attacked by the Blackfeet as they entered the canyon, thus giving the passage a formidable reputation. In fact, "Missoula" is from a Salish word that has been variously translated as "by the cold chilling waters," "river of awe," or simply an exclamation of surprise and horror.

The first white settlers seemed to agree. As the story goes, French trappers were horrified when they came across the remains of all the Salish who never made it through the canyon and called it Porte de l'Enfer, which, anglicized, became Hell Gate. It's markedly different from the pleasant, seemingly benign city that Missoula has become.

The first whites on record to explore the Missoula area were Meriwether Lewis and a brigade of his men on their return trip from the Pacific. Lewis and his group camped at the confluence of the Rattlesnake and Clark Fork Rivers in July 1806, and headed through Hell Gate Canyon without incident.

White Settlement

The Hell Gate Treaty of 1855 opened Missoula and much of western Montana to white settlement. The treaty council took place about seven miles west of Missoula (on present-day Hwy. 263), where a state monument can now be found.

In 1860, C.P. Higgins and Frank Worden, the area's first white settlers, established a trading post, Hell Gate Ronde, four miles west of what is now downtown Missoula. Within the year, a log cabin was standing at the mouth of the Rattlesnake, and by 1863 the Mullan Road was running through Hell Gate Canyon (it's now Front Street in downtown Missoula). Once the road was open, Worden and Higgins built a sawmill, flour mill, and store at the intersection of the Mullan Road and Higgins Avenue, along the banks of the Clark Fork. Their enterprise, named Missoula Mills, quickly replaced Hell Gate Ronde as the hub of settlement action.

When Chief Joseph and the Nez Perce retreated across Montana in 1877, Missoula citizens asked the federal government for protection from the Indians, and Fort Missoula was hastily established just southwest of town.

Development

Missoula's growth was spurred on by the arrival in 1883 of the Northern Pacific Railway. The town was a division point and repair center for the line. In 1885, 300 Missoulians incorporated as a city, and by 1925 the population had climbed to 12,000.

Logs representing thousands of felled trees choke the Blackfoot River east of Missoula, circa 1900.

MONTANA HISTORICAL SOCIETY, HELENA

Timber was also important to Missoula's development. In 1886, A.B. Hammond built what was reputedly the world's largest lumber mill at Bonner (seven miles east of Missoula). It produced timbers for railroads and mines as well as construction lumber.

When other Montana cities vied for the state capital and prison, Missoula alone attempted to land the university. It was established (as Montana State University) in Missoula in 1895. Since then it has become a major cultural force, as well as one of the city's leading employers.

The wood-products industry is the main source of jobs in Missoula today. Another of Missoula's major employers is the U.S. Forest Service. The regional office was established here in 1908. As befits its history as a transportation corridor, Missoula is now home to a large number of truck drivers—trucking employs roughly as many Missoulians as the university.

The railroad, however, is no longer the force it once was in Missoula's development: both of the city's depots have served as restaurants, and the Burlington Northern pulled out of town in the late 1980s. But the purchase of rail lines by freeway builder and mining entrepreneur Denny Washington has brought some life back into the region's rail business, and his Montana Interlink cars are now riding the rails through Missoula and the West.

SIGHTS

Most of Missoula's historic downtown is located on the north side of the Clark Fork. The historic residential areas are across the river, near the university.

Downtown

The old business district was located near the river, along the Mullan Road (now Front St.), on which early settlers traveled west. However, most of the early buildings burned in 1884, and when the city rebuilt, the influence of the incoming Northern Pacific Railway attracted the downtown northward from the Clark Fork along Higgins Avenue.

Many of these early buildings remain. The **Missoula Mercantile building** (now the Bon), at the corner of Front and Higgins, was built between 1882 and 1891. The Merc (as it was known) was established in 1866 and was the city's primary mercantile establishment for over a century. Note the cast-iron facade facing Higgins Avenue.

North on Higgins is the **Higgins Block** (1889), containing well-preserved late-19th-century commercial architecture. On the corner, beneath a prominent cupola, is a gingerbread bank in the Queen Anne style. Farther along the same block are other old stores, now housing trendy businesses. One vintage interior worth visiting, **Butterfly Herbs,** has an espresso bar in the back.

The **County Courthouse,** 200 W. Broadway, was constructed in 1910. This large, three-story edifice is noteworthy for its murals. These scenes from Montana history were painted by Edgar Paxson, who was called Cot-lo-see, "He Who Sees Everything," by admiring Indians. Around the courthouse, pawnbrokers double as bail bondsmen, and the offices of lawyers and private investigators recall local author James Crumley's detective novels.

Missoula's two **train stations** are imposing and handsome. The Northern Pacific depot was built in 1889 at the north end of Higgins Ave., and the Spanish-style Milwaukee depot was built in 1910 under the Higgins Avenue Bridge on the south side of the Clark Fork. Neither is in operation as a rail depot. The square outside the NP depot, near the red X public art installations, hosts a farmers' market on summer Saturday mornings.

Missoula's newest addition to downtown, and a major source of civic pride is its **carousel,** which stands in Caras Park near the river just west of the Higgins Bridge. All the horses were hand-carved—making this the first hand-carved carousel assembled in the U.S. for over 60 years—and each of the horses has a highly personal, sometimes touching story associated with it. The fundraising, carving, and construction process really hit a community nerve, and almost any local will regale you with stories about the carousel and the meanings of each of the horses. The carousel is open daily for rides; there's also a gift shop. Call (406) 728-0447 for more information.

The **Missoula Museum of the Arts,** 335 N. Pattee, tel. (406) 728-4447, is in the city's old Carnegie library. It houses a small permanent collection and displays traveling art exhibits.

Trolley tours of the town are offered by Discover Missoula Montana, tel. (406) 721-0245.

The University

The **University of Montana** is located on the south side of the Clark Fork, at the mouth of the river's Hell Gate Canyon. A green and leafy campus built around a central oval, it's a pleasant place to explore, as is the university district, an area of grand and historic old homes.

For the youthful traveler, the campus is a good center for information about what's going on in Missoula. Flyers and posters abound and the campus paper, the *Kaimin,* is printed four times a week and has good listings. The university also offers the traveler easy access to cultural amenities in short supply elsewhere in Montana, and provides cheap eats and entertainment. The general **information** number for the campus is (406) 243-0211; the university's information line is (406) 243-4636.

The university, established by the Montana Legislature in 1895, has developed into an academically broad-based institution with a strong liberal-arts emphasis. Its schools of journalism and forestry are nationally recognized, as is its graduate program in creative writing. The university is proud of its ability to produce Rhodes scholars: only three public institutions in the U.S. have produced more.

The earliest remaining building on campus is the **University Hall,** built in 1899. Besides containing the university president's office, the building's central tower houses a carillon. At noon each day, students are serenaded by a quarter-hour recital of bell music.

Behind University Hall is **Mansfield Library,** named for Montana's former senator Mike Mansfield and his wife, Maureen. Across a grassy mall from the library is the **University Center** (UC), a modern three-story building constructed around a central atrium. It's a good place to hang out and watch student behavior. On the second floor, in the Copper Commons, quick and inexpensive food is available. On the ground floor is the UC Bookstore, a good all-purpose bookstore and art-supply source, tel. (406) 243-4921.

One of the university's newer additions is the **Montana Theatre,** which houses two stages for live theater. Call (406) 243-4581 for current listings.

For a bird's-eye, or rather a mountain-goat's-eye, view of the university and the city, climb up Mt. Sentinel to the university's "M." It's a 40-minute hike from the trailhead at the north end of the UC parking lot.

The University District

The university district is one of Missoula's most pleasant neighborhoods and contains some interesting architectural specimens. Some of the old homes have been turned into fraternity or sorority houses, but others remain private homes. None are open to the public, but a stroll or drive through the area is a pleasant way to learn that Missoula took its turn-of-the-century affluence seriously. The grandest homes face onto Gerald Avenue (parallel one block east of S. Higgins). See especially the neoclassical mansion at 1005 Gerald (built in 1902-03), once the home of John R. Toole, a prominent early Montana politician and industrialist, as well as the university president's house at 1325 Gerald, built around 1930. A good brochure, *Historic Missoula,* is available from the chamber of commerce.

Another landmark of sorts in the university district is **Freddy's Feed and Read,** a small cooperative grocery and alternative bookstore at 1221 Helen, tel. (406) 549-2127. It remains a very good bookstore and has fine whole foods, but its niche in history will be its reputation, from the early 1970s, as a focus of social and political change. Freddy's, as a "radical bookstore," became a catalyst for the sorts of liberation of thought that flourished during the period of the store's founding. Of course, that era seems as remote now as the era of the city's mansions, but Freddy's is a useful monument to what access to the written word once meant.

South of the university, Missoula's **Vietnam Veterans' Memorial** is in a rose garden at Brooks and Franklin.

Rocky Mountain Elk Foundation

Hunters and other wildlife enthusiasts will want to stop by the Rocky Mountain Elk Foundation, 2291 W. Broadway, tel. (406) 523-4545. Their visitor center is open daily 8:30 a.m.-8:30 p.m. during the summer; winter hours are Mon.-Fri. 8:30 a.m.-5 p.m., Sat.-Sun. 11 a.m.-4 p.m. The large display area has a mix of wildlife art and mounted animals, including some truly impressive elk. There's also a theater with wildlife films and a gift shop.

The elk foundation is a nonprofit organization, mostly composed of hunters concerned with wildlife habitat conservation. Along with their conservation work, they are strong proponents of responsible hunting and publish a good free brochure of tips for hunters.

Fort Missoula

Of the 1877 fort site, two original buildings (a stone powder magazine and an officers' quarters) remain and are now part of the **Fort Missoula Historical Museum,** which contains exhibits of local history. Other buildings of interest have been relocated to the fort, including an old church, a schoolhouse, and a Forest Service lookout tower. The rest of the fort now houses National Guard and Forest Service offices. The wide boulevards, green lawns, and white military buildings evoke a real sense of history, if not nostalgia.

During the summer, Fort Missoula is open Tues.-Sat. 10 a.m.-5 p.m., Sunday noon-5 p.m. Winter hours are Tues.-Sat. noon-5 p.m., tel. (406) 728-3476. To get there, take Hwy. 93 south to Reserve St., turn right, and follow signs at the junction with South Avenue.

Smokejumping Training Center

Undeniably unique to Missoula and a curious source of pride to natives is the Forest Service Smokejumping Training Center, tel. (406) 329-4934. Here, firefighters are trained in the science of fighting forest fires, as well as the art of parachuting into forest wildfires. The center is open to visitors and features exhibits, films, a diorama, and a tour of the parachuting base. The center is just past Johnson Bell Airport, on Hwy. 93

RECREATION

Hiking

Many of the in-town hikes are on paths shared by bicyclists. A casual walker can just wander down to the river and pick up the paths that run on either bank in the downtown area. Heading east, the **Kim Williams Trail** follows the south bank of the Clark Fork out of town.

For those who want more of a challenge, head over to the university and follow the zigzag trail up Mt. Sentinel to the "M." It takes about 40 minutes, and a little huffing and puffing, to get there, but on a clear day, there are great views of Missoula and Hell Gate Canyon.

Head out Van Buren to Rattlesnake Drive and the **Rattlesnake National Recreational Area and Wilderness** for as much of a wilderness hike as you're likely to find in any city. Missoula's outdoor stores sell trail maps.

For guided hikes and wildlife-viewing expeditions, contact **Beargrass Sallies** at the Grizzly Hackle fly-fishing shop, 215 W. Front, tel. (406) 721-8996. These tours include rambles to historical sites as well as mountain hikes.

Bicycling

Missoula has a reputation as a great bike town, and everybody seems to be on a mountain bike. Bicycle enthusiasts will do well to stop by the **Adventure Cycling Association** headquarters, 150 E. Pine, tel. (406) 721-1776. They publish a small bicycle-touring map of Missoula as well as a host of other maps for routes stretching across the nation. Two major bike routes cross in Missoula—the north-south Great Parks route and the west-east Transamerica route. Adventure Cycling also operates bicycle tours and is a clearinghouse for information on cycle touring. There's always a chance for casual or obsessive bike talk at their offices.

The **Rattlesnake National Recreation Area,** a corridor through the Rattlesnake Wilderness, is a mountain biker's dream, but be sure to avoid cycling in the adjacent wilderness area; maps are available at local outdoor stores.

THE UNUSUAL EVOLUTION OF FORT MISSOULA

Fort Missoula was built in 1877, in response to the movement of the Nez Perce and white settlers' fear of the increasingly recalcitrant Flathead Indians. However, the threat of Indian attack never really materialized, and troops at the fort saw real action only once, at the Battle of the Big Hole. There, troops from Fort Missoula attempted an ambush of Chief Joseph's retreating Nez Perce and were disastrously defeated.

Thereafter, the story of Fort Missoula ceases to sound much like that of an embattled frontier outpost and begins to take on more curious dimensions. In 1888, the Twenty-fifth Infantry Corps, an all-black regiment under the authority of white officers, was garrisoned at the fort. In 1896, bicycle enthusiast Lieutenant James Moss established the Twenty-fifth Infantry Bicycle Corps, which sought to test the potential of the bicycle as a military conveyance. The lieutenant, in comparing the bicycle to the horse, reasoned that the bike "doesn't require as much care. It needs no forage; it moves much faster over

fair roads, it is not as conspicuous . . . it is noiseless and raises but little dust."

In order to prove to General Nelson Miles that the bicycle was a viable means of troop transport, Moss and 20 men left Missoula on bicycles the following year, bound for St. Louis—1,900 miles overland. The trip, made on mud trails and sandy paths, took only 41 days. The Army higher-ups were not impressed, however, and the Bicycle Corps returned to Missoula by train.

During WW I, the fort served as an Army training center, and during the Depression it was the regional headquarters for the Civilian Conservation Corps (CCC). During WW II, 1,200 Italian seamen and 650 American men of Japanese descent were detained at the fort, and, following the war, it served as a prison for court-martialed military personnel.

Fort Missoula was closed as a military post in 1947. The fort presently houses government offices and a historical museum. Its grounds are used for such benign events as dog shows.

Mount Sentinel's summit can be reached by riding south out Pattee Canyon Dr. to the unmarked, gated Crazy Canyon Rd. and climbing to the top of the 5,158-foot peak. A less strenuous fat-tire ride is on the path along the Clark Fork, perhaps venturing east of downtown into the **Kim Williams Nature Area,** named for the late National Public Radio commentator whose voice represented all things Missoulian to many across the country. Pick up a copy of Bikecentennial's mountain-bike map of the Missoula area at their office, or see *Mountain Bike Adventures in the Northern Rockies* by Michael McCoy for details on these and other rides.

Mountain bikes can be rented at the **Open Road,** 517 S. Orange St., tel. (406) 549-2453, and **New Era,** 741 S. Higgins, tel. (406) 728-2080. Guests at the Birchwood Hostel can rent bikes from Ernie, the hostel's proprietor.

Fishing
Fishing in Missoula can be as unpremeditated as throwing a line into the Clark Fork from a bridge in the middle of town. The Clark Fork, which was horribly polluted until cleanup measures were taken in the 1970s, is now home to some trout.

Excellent fishing spots abound within an hour's drive of town. The **Clark Fork, Blackfoot,** and **Bitterroot Rivers** harbor rainbow, brown, cutthroat, and bull trout. Like the Clark Fork, the Blackfoot has had some environmental hurdles to overcome in recent years, but local anglers say it's on its way back. **Rock Creek** is reached by traveling 26 miles east of Missoula on I-90 to exit 126. Rock Creek has been designated a blue-ribbon trout stream, though it is not necessarily an *easy* stream to fish. Catch-and-release fishing is enforced along the middle stretch of the creek and fishing with bait is prohibited, except by children.

Campsites along Rock Creek range from **Ekstrom's Stage Station,** a full-service tent and RV campground (complete with flush toilets, hot showers, a store, and swimming pool) one-half mile from the freeway on Rock Creek Rd., tel. (406) 825-3183, to **Siria,** a small, bare-bones Forest Service campground with no drinking water, 29 bumpy miles up Rock Creek Road.

The **Montana Dept. of Fish, Wildlife, and Parks** has an office in Missoula at 3201 Spurgin Rd., tel. (406) 542-5500.

For fishing supplies, fly-casting and fly-fishing classes, or guided trips, stop by **Grizzly Hackle,** 215 W. Front, or call (406) 721-8996. They also rent rods and waders for $15-20 a day and can arrange accommodations on some of the area's rivers. Guided trips are available in all permutations—a basic daylong wading trip runs $185 for one or two people. **Western Waters** leads twice-daily fishing float trips on the Clark Fork west of Missoula for $150 per person. Call (406) 543-3203 to reserve a spot.

Kayaking
The many rivers of western Montana offer wonderful opportunities for kayak and raft trips. The fully insured and experienced **10,000 Waves Raft and Kayak Adventures,** tel. (406) 549-6670 or (800) 537-8315, P.O. Box 7924, Missoula, MT 59807, is the best of the local outfitters and offers trips on the Bitterroot, Blackfoot, and on the Clark Fork through both the Hell Gate Canyon and Alberton Gorge. Trips are available in regular inflatable rafts, hardshell or inflatable kayaks, or on the new "sit-on-tops." Raft trips are least expensive, starting as low as $39 for a half-day excursion; full-day trips, which include lunch, begin at $65. Guided kayak trips are $60 half-day, $95 full-day. 10,000 Waves also offers a variety of kayak lessons and clinics, beginning with half-day sessions at $80.

Skiing
There are two downhill ski areas just outside Missoula. **Montana Snowbowl** is the big one—it has over 30 runs, reaching up to three miles long, and a 2,600-foot vertical drop. It's about 12 miles out of town, reached by taking the Reserve St. exit from I-90 and driving north on Grant Creek Rd. to Snowbowl Rd., tel. (406) 549-9777. Lift tickets at Snowbowl are $26 for adults, $13 for children, with lessons and student, senior, and half-day rates available. Both skis and snowboards can be rented.

Marshall Mountain Ski Area, seven miles east of Missoula just off Hwy. 200, tel. (406) 258-6000, is smaller and several dollars less expensive than Snowbowl. Lift tickets cost $19 for adults, $17 for students, and $11 for children. Hourly rates are also available. Marshall Mountain is open Mon.-Sat. 9 a.m.-9 p.m., Sunday 9 a.m.-4 p.m.

There are a couple of popular cross-country ski areas in the Garnet Range east of Missoula. **Garnet Resource Area,** a BLM-operated ghost mining town, has 55 miles of ski and snowmobile trails. Follow Hwy. 200 east five miles to Garnet Range Rd., then turn south and follow signs along the Forest Service road. Or follow I-90 26 miles to Bearmouth and turn north five miles on Hwy. 10 to Bear Gulch Road. Follow signs for Garnet.

Skiers can rent cabins in and around the town of Garnet, but there's no driving in to them—food and gear must be packed in. Maps and rental information are available from the BLM office at 3255 Fort Missoula Rd., tel. (406) 329-3914.

The University of Montana School of Forestry, tel. (406) 243-0211, maintains the **Lubrecht Experimental Forest** and its half-dozen cross-country ski trails. From Missoula, take Hwy. 200 to Greenough. Turn right (east) one-half mile beyond the post office and go another quarter mile to Lubrecht Camp. A map of the trails can be picked up at the forest headquarters at Lubrecht Camp.

Closer to town, there's challenging cross-country skiing up Pattee Canyon, and the **Rattlesnake National Recreation Area and Wilderness** (RNRAW) has miles of trails; many are suited for skiing. Consult the RNRAW map, available at outdoor stores, for possibilities.

Golf
Nine-hole public golf courses include the **Highlands Golf Club** at 102 Ben Hogan Dr., featuring the historic Greenough Mansion as its clubhouse/restaurant, tel. (406) 721-4653, and the course on the **University of Montana** campus, tel. (406) 728-8629. **Larchmont Golf Course,** 3200 Old Fort Rd., tel. (406) 721-4416, has 18 holes.

Swimming
Missoula is a good place to get some exercise after a long car trip. The university's indoor **Grizzly Pool** has regularly scheduled public hours; adults pay $1.50 for a swim and sauna, children $1.25. Call (406) 243-2763 for the schedule. Outdoor pools are in **McCormick Park,** at the west end of the Orange St. Bridge, tel. (406) 721-PARK, and at **Playfair,** behind Sentinel High School (facing onto Bancroft St.), tel. (406) 721-PARK).

ACCOMMODATIONS

Because Missoula is a real crossroads, a great number and variety of lodgings are available. Unless there's a big football game, graduation, or some other major event going on at the university, you'll have little trouble finding something.

Hostels
The **Birchwood Hostel** is at 600 S. Orange, tel. (406) 728-9799. Take the Orange St. exit from I-90; go south about one mile, cross the river, and continue four blocks past the bridge to S. 4th Street. The hostel offers four bunkrooms (each holding four to eight people), a family room, showers, a fully equipped kitchen, and a laundry room. The very helpful proprietor maintains a good "what's happening in Missoula" bulletin board and library. Check-in time is from 5-10 p.m., and a dorm bed costs $10, there's one double bed for $25.

B&Bs
Once the home of the university's second president, **Goldsmith's Inn,** 809 E. Front, tel. (406) 721-6732, is Missoula's top-flight bed and breakfast. Relocated to the north bank of the Clark Fork and renovated to its original 1911 splendor, Goldsmith's boasts a total of seven rooms: four suites with private sitting areas—one suite has a private deck and a hot tub—and three queen rooms. All rooms have private bathrooms and range in cost $79-129 d, including breakfast. The dining room at Goldsmith's is open to the public; a summer breakfast on the deck overlooking the river is a Missoula tradition.

Another handsome home turned B&B is the **Greenough B&B,** 631 Stephens Ave., tel. (406) 728-3626 or (800) 718-3626. This refurbished National Registry-listed home offers three guest rooms (one a suite linked to the "maid's quarters" with two twin beds) all with private baths. Room rates range $70-95.

Hotels and Motels
Missoula has several motel strips with plenty of inexpensive options. Most convenient to downtown and the university are the older places along East and West Broadway. The Hwy. 93 strip south of town offers newer lodgings but is

farther from the center of things (unless your focus is the Bitterroot Valley).

The following are convenient to both downtown and the university. Most are very good values for comfortable rooms. The **Campus Inn** 744 E. Broadway, tel. (406) 549-5134 or (800) 232-8013, has rooms at $55 s, 65 d. Facilities include an outdoor pool, exercise room and hot tub, and a restaurant. There's a good free continental breakfast, and pets are okay with a $6 fee. The **Uptown Motel,** 329 Woody, tel. (406) 549-5141 or (800) 315-5141 $38 s, $48 d, offers movie channels, modem phones, and some kitchenettes, and is convenient to good dining at nearby restaurants. The **City Center Motel,** 338 E. Broadway, tel. (406) 543-3193, $72 s, $46 d, has movie channels and a burger restaurant adjoining. The **Downtown Motel,** 502 E. Broadway, tel. (406) 549-5191, has comfortable rooms at $37 s, $43 d, in a residential setting. **Bel Aire Motel,** 300 E. Broadway, tel. (406) 543-3183 or (800) 543-3184, offers rooms at $45-55 s, $55-65 d, with an indoor pool and hot tub, kitchenettes, guest laundry, and fitness room. Pets are okay with a $5 fee **Best Western Executive Motor Inn** is right downtown at 201 E Main, tel. (406) 543-7221 or (800) 528-1234. Rooms are $50 s, $60 d, and there's a pool. Rooms have coffeemakers, some have refrigerators.

The university/downtown also has some of Missoula's nicest and most expensive lodgings. The **DoubleTree Hotel Missoula/Edgewater** is right on the Clark Fork across from the university at 100 Madison, tel. (406) 728-3100 or, outside Montana, (800) 547-8010. Rooms are $94-109 s or d, depending on view. Facilities include a pool and hot tub, and some rooms accessible to guests with disabilities. This is a quiet and sophisticated place to stay, with a good restaurant and a classy gift shop. Right downtown and on the river, the **Holiday Inn Missoula Parkside,** 2005 S. Pattee, tel. (406) 721-8550 or (800) 399-0408, has rooms at $92 s/d. The hotel offers an indoor pool, hot tub, sauna, and fitness center. Rooms come with irons and ironing boards, coffeemakers, and free movie channels.

West of downtown are several more lodging options. **Brownie's Plus Motel,** 1540 W. Broadway, tel. (406) 543-6614 or (800) 543-6614, $37 s, $48 d, is a clean and friendly spot and an excellent value. All rooms have air-conditioning, TVs, and new queen beds. Dogs okay with $5

fee. The **Red Lion Inn,** 700 W. Broadway, tel. (406) 728-3300 or (800) 547-8010, has rooms at $84 s, $99 d. The large complex houses two pools, a spa, a restaurant, and a meeting room. Rates include a good continental breakfast. **Orange Street Budget Motor Inn,** 801 N. Orange St., tel. (406) 721-3610 or (800) 328-0801, is convenient to downtown and I-90 exit 104. There's a free continental breakfast and exercise room.

South of Missoula's older center is the Hwy. 93 strip, the booming new commercial zone that best exemplifies the city's rapid growth and lack of meaningful land-use planning. These lodgings are recommended if you're coming in from the Bitterroot valley or on Hwy. 12 from Lolo Pass. Brooks Street in the address is actually Hwy. 93. **4-Bs Inn South and Conference Center,** 3803 Brooks, tel. (406) 251-2665 or (800) 272-9500, has rooms at $60 s, $70 d; there's a hot tub, and pets okay. **Super 8 Brooks Street,** 3901 Brooks, tel. (406) 251-2255, offers rooms at $45 s, 56 d.

If you're just passing through Missoula and don't want to deal with the city, you can opt for something at the newish complex of motels, casinos, and restaurants that has sprung up at I-90 exit 101, seven miles west of Missoula. These aren't particularly convenient for activities in Missoula itself, however, and there's no bus access to downtown or the university. Most of these places belong to the national chains; for a quality local product, try the **4Bs Inn North,** 4953 N. Reserve St., tel. (406) 542-7500 or (800) 272-9500.

Campgrounds

There are three private campgrounds in Missoula. The **Missoula KOA,** complete with swimming pool, hot tub, and cabins, is open all year at 3695 Tina Ave. (exit 101 off I-90), tel. (406) 549-0881 or (800) 562-5366. **Out Post Campground,** on Hwy. 93 two miles north of I-90, tel. (406) 549-2016,is also open year-round and has a few freeway-side tent sites among the RVs and trailers. **Jim and Mary's Adult RV Park,** Hwy. 93, one mile north of I-90, tel. (406) 549-4416, is an adults-only campground with no tent sites. It's open April 1-Oct. 30.

The Dept. of Fish, Wildlife, and Parks operates a couple of campgrounds a little farther from town. **Chief Looking Glass** is on the Bitterroot River 14 miles south of Missoula on Hwy. 93 (to milepost 77), then one mile east on the county road; open May 27-Sept. 15. **Beavertail Hill,** open May 20-Sept. 15, is a quarter mile south of the Beavertail Hill exit off I-90 (milepost 130, 26 miles southeast of Missoula).

FOOD AND DRINK

There are reasons to linger over Missoula's abundance of good restaurants. For the traveler coming to Missoula from the east, this may be the first ethnic food seen in days. For the traveler heading into eastern Montana, Missoula may be the last place to enjoy a choice beyond fast food and steaks. Every franchise imaginable is to be found along the Hwy. 93 Strip. However, for those with a hankering for something local, Missoula shouldn't disappoint.

Casual Meals

On campus, eating cheap is easy at the University Center, where the **Copper Commons** cafeteria is open 7 a.m.-10 p.m. during the week and 9 a.m.-9 p.m. on weekends.

If it's juice and coffee that you're after, **Butterfly Herbs** houses a juice and espresso bar at 232 N. Higgins, tel. (406) 728-8780. Over on the other side of the Clark Fork, try breakfast or lunch at **Food for Thought,** across from the university at the corner of Arthur and Daly, 504 Daly, tel. (406) 721-6033. This low-key sandwich-and-salad place has spawned **Second Thought,** a coffee spot, deli, and newsstand with a good selection of high-quality literary remainder books, at 529 S Higgins, tel. (406) 549-2790.

Healthy breakfast pastries and lunches can also be had at **Mammyth Bakery,** 131 W. Main, tel. (406) 549-5542. One of Missoula's best-loved breakfast joints is the **Old Town Cafe,** 127 W. Alder, tel. (406) 542-3188. Breakfasts are huge and the atmosphere decidedly Missoulan: half logger, half granola-head.

The **Shack,** tel. (406) 549-9903, 222 West Main, has been one of Missoula's favorite breakfast and lunch stops since the 1950s. It's going stronger than ever and is now open for dinner.

The old Union Club Bar used to be a mandatory stop on election nights. Now, as the **Hob Nob Cafe,** 208 E Main St., tel. (406) 542-3188, it's one of Missoula's most hip eateries. Grilled fish, pasta, homemade soups, and spicy vegetarian dishes, along with the now mandatory pool table, make this a popular hangout. The menu changes weekly.

Tories's, tel. (406) 721-2510, in front of the Holiday Village Shopping Mall at 1916 Brooks, is one of Missoula's original health food restaurants. You can count on good vegetarian cooking here. Downtown, the place to go for vegetarian food is the **Black Dog,** tel. (406) 542-1138, 138 W Broadway, where the food (including vegan dishes) is tasty and inexpensive. The **Mustard Seed** offers good Chinese-inspired food in a pleasant environment at 419 W. Front, tel. (406) 728-7825.

Good Mexican food is available at **Casa Pablo's,** 147 W. Broadway, tel. (406) 721-3854. It's a good place to go if you're really hungry since portions are huge, and there's plenty of atmosphere in the well-preserved turn-of-the-century dining room (formerly a bar). The waiting area is a gem of an art deco cocktail lounge.

Missoula's favorite pizza-of-the-moment is found at **McKenzie River Pizza,** tel. (406) 721-0077, 137 W. Front Street. Nontraditional pizzas are the specialty here; try the Buffalo chicken wing pie.

Goldsmith's, on the banks of the Clark Fork at 809 E. Front, tel. (406) 721-6732, is part B&B, part restaurant, and part ice cream shop. On a hot afternoon, the back deck overlooking the river is a good place to relax with a huckleberry cone. It's also a popular place for breakfast, lunch, dinner, and Sunday brunch.

For good fast food, pass up the national chains and try **93-Stop-and-Go,** a burger joint at 2205 Brooks. There are those who swear by their Duper Sauce. Here, as elsewhere in the state, **4-Bs** restaurants are dependable purveyors of inexpensive standard American fare in pleasant-enough surroundings. The chain began in Missoula (before spreading across the state and region), and the city is blessed with five different locations. Most 4-Bs are open 24 hours, making them popular with a late-night student crowd.

Other all-night hangouts are associated with downtown bars. Open for food and gambling is the **Oxford Club,** at North Higgins and Pine. Although not for the faint of heart or the easily appalled, the Ox is a Missoula fixture. Late at night, this is local color at its most opaque. The Oxford's brains and eggs is considered a rite of passage of sorts. The server calls the order by shouting, "He needs 'em."

Fine Dining

The **Depot** at 201 W. Railroad, tel. (406) 728-7007, offers steaks, fresh fish, and seafood in conjunction with a vaunted salad bar. The city's best view is found at **Shadow's Keep,** at the end of Whitaker Drive, overlooking the Missoula valley, tel. (406) 728-5132. The menu tends to grilled steaks, chops, and pasta.

If you're looking for a break from steaks, **Perugia,** 1106 W Broadway, tel. (406) 543-3757, serves a mix of Mediterranean-influenced dishes, including some Middle-Eastern specialties, in addition to Italian pastas and grilled meats. Open for dinner only.

Drink

Nowhere does Missoula's unique mix of population become more apparent than in its many and bustling watering holes. Some bars are of interest because of their historic character, others because of the characters they attract. Re-

JUDY JEWELL

The Oxford Club is renowned for its 24-hour cafe and its gambling.

member that bar life in Montana is primarily social in nature. Bars are where people meet up. There is no stigma attached to not drinking alcohol. Even if you don't care for a drink, go along for the friendly welcome. Be prepared, however, for lots of unrepentant gambling and a certain loss of ambience to the chattering of electronic gaming devices.

The downtown area is chockablock with curious old bars. The **Missoula Club,** 139 W. Main, is a peanut-shells-on-the-floor, grill-in-the-back sports bar, with fixtures unchanged since the 1940s. The Mo Club can get pretty busy at night, but it's a great place to hole up late in the afternoon. Don't attempt to resist their grilled hamburgers. They are, in their simplicity, the stuff of legend.

Also legendary, but for different reasons, is the **Oxford Club** at Pine and N. Higgins. Although not always edifying, it has character by the bottleful and a certain attraction for writers. Watch the creative-writing students who eye the bar's sullen denizens, waiting for epiphanies. Another bar with an edge to it is the **Stockman's,** 125 W. Front, popular with poker players. Its motto, "Liquor up front, Poker in the rear," has had habitués chortling for decades.

More standard youthful hangouts are the **Rhino,** 158 Ryman, and the **Top Hat,** at 134 W. Front. The latter offers live music (blues and swing, mostly) in an atmosphere heavy with Missoula's peculiar, indolent funkiness. Missoula's music club scene is found at the **Pine Street Tavern,** 130 W. Pine, where there's jazz, blues, and a bit of everything, and at **Jay's Upstairs,** 121 W. Main, Missoula's post-grunge club, where snowboarders hang out and listen to bands like the Honky Sausage or the Velcro Sheep. **Buck's Club,** 1805 Regent St., is another popular club where the music ranges from country to reggae to acid jazz.

If you're searching for the gay bar in town, descend the steps at 225 Ryman Ave. to the **AmVets** (yes, the AmVets) **Bar.**

Red's White Sox Bar, at 217 Ryman, is a safe haven for Chisox fans and others willing to stand up for a favorite team. (Missoula has a rookie-league baseball team—the Mustangs.) Another old-time bar that's a comfortable place to play pool and mingle in a comfortably mixed locals/students atmosphere is the **Silver Dollar,** 307 W. Railroad Street.

If you want to go out and sample Missoula night life but aren't into the bar scene, go to **Break Espresso,** 432 N Higgins, tel. (406) 728-7300, a coffee shop that stays open late and is a magnet for caffeine propelled studying and hanging out.

EVENTS

Early each April, the university plays host to an international **wildlife film festival.** Call the university's information line at (406) 243-4636 for schedules.

A Native American **powwow** is held annually, usually in May, in the university field house. The chamber of commerce, tel. (406) 543-6623, can provide exact dates and times.

The 221-mile bicycle **Tour of Swan River Valley** is an annual springtime event. Register well in advance for the TOSRV ride; it's sponsored by the Missoula Bike Club, tel. (406) 728-7984.

Missoula's Mendelssohn Club sponsors a midsummer choral festival, drawing choirs from all over the world for a series of free concerts. Contact the **International Choral Festival,** 131 S Higgins, Missoula, MT 59802, tel. (406) 721-7985, for specifics.

The **Western Montana Fair** is held in Missoula during the third week of August. It's time to take in a rodeo, a delectable Montalado (a Montana-style enchilada), the llama pavilion, and coin-operated animal tricks that will send chills up the spine of any animal-rights activist.

SHOPPING

For many travelers, Missoula will either be one of the first or one of the last places visited in Montana. Missoula's shops offer the visitor either a last chance to stock up on vital comestibles and to drink that final espresso, or the first opportunity in days to assuage deprivations incurred farther inland.

Butterfly Herbs, 232 N. Higgins, tel. (406) 728-8780, offers tea, coffee, herbs, spices, soaps, and in fact a little of everything. The store itself is a well-preserved specimen from the turn of the century. The back of the store is a good espresso bar and cafe.

Local artist Monte Dollack's whimsical posters and cards have gained a wide following. Visit the **Monte Dollack Gallery** at 139 W. Front, tel. (406) 549-3248.

The **Good Food Store,** 920 Kensington, tel. (406) 728-5823, is Missoula's best source for natural and health foods.

Freddy's Feed and Read, near the university at 1221 Helen, tel. (406) 549-2127, is the place for good literature and alternative books (it's also a natural-foods grocery). The **Bird's Nest,** 219 N. Higgins, tel. (406) 721-1125, is a center for new and secondhand regional books, and **Fact and Fiction,** at 216 W. Main, tel. (406) 721-2881, is a good general bookstore. Most periodicals are available at **Garden City News,** 329 N. Higgins, tel. (406) 543-3470. Out-of-state newspapers are a specialty.

Because of Missoula's access to the outdoors, recreation stores are important to the visitor. A good source of equipment, for both sale and rent, is the **Trail Head,** at N. Higgins and Pine, tel. (406) 543-6966. The staff are usually able to offer good advice on local trails and conditions. **Rent-a-Sport,** 2600 Industry Rd., tel. (406) 549-8225, rents almost everything associated with sports and recreation.

SERVICES

For emergency, police, fire, and ambulance, dial 911. The **police station** is at 435 Ryman, tel. (406) 523-4777.

The main Missoula **post office** is at 1100 W. Kent, tel. (406) 329-2200, but the downtown Hell Gate Station, 200 E. Broadway, tel. (406) 329-3105, may prove to be more convenient.

The city's two major hospitals are **Community Hospital,** 2827 Fort Missoula Rd., tel. (406) 728-4100, and **St. Patrick's,** located right downtown at 500 W. Broadway, tel. (406) 543-7271. The **Blue Mountain Clinic,** recently moved after it was bombed by anti-abortion terrorists, is now open at 610 N. California, tel. (406) 721-1646, offer health services for both women and men.

The **First Interstate Bank** at 101 E. Front, tel. (406) 721-4200, is the main bank in town and the place to go to exchange foreign currency.

If you become truly enchanted with Missoula, you may find yourself at 539 S. 3rd Ave. W, tel.

(406) 720-7060. This is where the **Job Service** is located.

Are dirty clothes taking over your suitcase? Well, positively snappy laundromats abound in Missoula. The following are particularly conveniently located: **Dud's-n-Sud's,** 1502 Toole Ave., tel. (406) 549-1223, is near a strip of inexpensive motels. Toward the university, a couple of places cater to students: the **Dry Cleaning and Laundry Shoppe,** at 700 S.W. Higgins, tel. (406) 728-7245, has a pleasant-enough "study area" complete with an aquarium and a TV. **Sparkle Laundry,** 812 S. Higgins, tel. (406) 721-5146, is outfitted with a TV, video games, and a frozen-yogurt concession. **Grimebusters,** 1202 W. Kent (near Brooks), tel. (406) 721-3429, has the ultimately pragmatic sideline—a used-clothing store. They also do dry cleaning.

INFORMATION

The Missoula **Chamber of Commerce,** 825 E. Front, Missoula, MT 59807, tel. (406) 543-6623 or (800) 526-3456, has racks brimming with brochures on Missoula and the surrounding area. They range from the strictly commercial to a well-done brochure on Missoula's historic buildings. The chamber of commerce will also keep you abreast of "What's Up in Missoula," with their weekly updated telephone recording, tel. (406) 728-INFO (4636).

The regional **U.S. Forest Service** office, at 340 N. Pattee, tel. (406) 329-3511, sells national forest maps. This also is a good place for general information on hiking and camping in national forests.

The **Dept. of Fish, Wildlife, and Parks** has a regional office at 3201 Spurgin Rd., tel. (406) 542-5500. They'll offer advice on fishing and hunting, and can provide a list of public campgrounds.

The **public library,** always a good source of information, is at 301 E. Main, tel. (406) 721-2810. What you don't find on their shelves may well be in the stacks of the **university library,** tel. (406) 243-6860. Of particular interest there is the Mansfield collection, located on the third level down. United States Senator Mike Mansfield left his papers to the University of Montana, and they're housed down here along with a great collection of regional history.

TRANSPORTATION

Air
Johnson Bell Airport is on Hwy. 93 just north of town, tel. (406) 728-4381. Delta, Horizon, Sky West, Big Sky, and Northwest airlines fly into Missoula, but don't expect to find bargain airfares. Shuttle service is available from the airport.

Automobile
All roads lead to Missoula. I-90 will get you there. So will Hwys. 93 and 200. Highway 12 jogs north to join with I-90 in Missoula. Bicycle touring notwithstanding, a car provides you with the most opportunities to get to the really great places. Auto rentals are available at the airport—Hertz, Budget, National, and Avis all have headquarters there. In town, some of the cheaper places include **Rent-A-Wreck,** 2401 W. Broadway, tel. (406) 721-3833 or (800) 421-7253 (their prices shoot up if you drive over 50 miles); **Payless,** at the Holiday Inn, 200 S. Pattee, tel. (406) 728-5475 or (800) 237-2804 (airport shuttle available); and **U-Save,** 3605 Reserve St., tel. (406) 251-5745 or (800) 426-5299. Be sure to ask about restrictions and additional fees.

Bus
The **Greyhound** station is at 1660 W. Broadway, tel. (406) 549-2339. Greyhound buses run three times daily along the interstate. Several smaller bus lines operate out of the same terminal (same telephone number, too). **Intermountain Transportation** goes between Hamilton and Kalispell, and to Great Falls via Lincoln. **Rimrock Stage** goes to Helena and Bozeman, and **Missouri Valley Trails** goes to Helena.

Mountain Line Transit operates the city buses. Buses run Mon.-Saturday. Most buses leave the downtown from Main between Pattee and Higgins; others run along Main and can be boarded at the corner of Broadway. Mountain Line's main office is at 1221 Shakespeare, tel. (406) 721-3333. Call them or stop by for schedules, which are also available at several locations around town, including the University Center, the library, and the Birchwood Hostel.

Taxi
Taxi service is provided by **Yellow Cab,** tel. (406) 543-6644.

THE FLATHEAD RESERVATION

The Flathead Reservation measures about 65 by 35 miles east to west. The reservation is managed by the Confederated Salish and Kootenai Tribes, with headquarters at Pablo. A council of 10 elected members, each representing a district of the reservation, governs the tribes. Of about 6,500 tribal members, some 3,800 live on the reservation. The Flathead population is centered at Arlee; most of the Kootenai tribal members live near Elmo.

The Culture Committee of the Confederated Salish and Kootenai Tribes works to keep traditions alive on the reservation. A longhouse in St. Ignatius, for example, is used for spiritual ceremonies and storage of herbs and medicinal plants, and a summer camp immerses tribal youngsters in native language and traditions. Along with the preservation of traditional ways comes preservation of natural resources, and the Confederated Tribes have earned a reputation as environmental stewards. Several businesses are run by the tribes, including S and K Electronics, a high-tech firm north of Pablo.

The Mission Mountains Tribal Wilderness is the first place in the United States where an Indian nation has designated tribal lands as a wilderness preserve. It covers the west side of the range's peaks; to the east, it's the Flathead National Forest, with access from Hwy. 83 in the Swan Valley. Any hiking or camping in the Mission Mountains Tribal Wilderness requires a tribal conservation permit, available at many local stores. A three-day conservation permit costs $6; in order to fish on tribal land, which includes the southern half of Flathead Lake, an $18 conservation and fishing permit is required. Proceeds from the permits are used to maintain and improve the reservation's recreational resources.

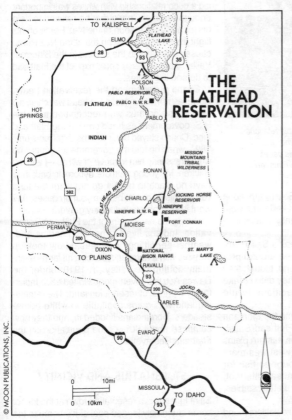

HISTORY

Salish-speaking Indians originally lived near the Pacific coast. Legend has it that an argument developed as to whether flying ducks quacked with their wings or with their bills. The ones who voted for the wings ended up moving to the Bitterroot Valley. Most Salish-speaking tribes still live near the coast. When the wing-quacker group, which be-

MONTANA HISTORICAL SOCIETY, HELENA

Chief Charlo maintained amicable relations with white settlers but resisted the U.S. government's efforts to move his people from the Bitterroot Valley to the Flathead Reservation

came known as the Flathead Salish, arrived in the Bitterroot Valley, the Pend d'Oreille who were living there moved north, apparently as a gesture of friendliness.

The Pend d'Oreille also speak a Salish language. Their base was the area around present-day Paradise and Plains and, though they hunted in western Montana, they didn't make regular buffalo-hunting expeditions to the plains.

Until the Blackfeet moved onto the Montana plains in the mid-1700s, the Flathead Salish spent a great deal of time on the eastern plains hunting buffalo. Travel to the west was more limited, generally just far enough to fish for salmon west of Lolo Pass. Camas, bitterroot, and serviceberries were other dietary staples; the Flathead still gather them.

Lewis and Clark and early white settlers found the Flathead to be friendly and helpful. The Flat-

head continued good relations with white settlers, with many intermarriages. They also got along well with Iroquois and other East Coast Native Americans who moved out west with fur trappers and traders in the early 1800s.

The 1855 Hell Gate Treaty formed the Flathead Reservation, but Victor, head chief of the Salish, refused to move his people from their home in the Bitterroot Valley. By the 1870s, the influx of white settlers into the valley made the government attempt to foist a new treaty onto the Flathead. Charlo, Victor's son and the new head chief of the tribe, held firm against moving to the reservation in the Jocko-Mission Valley, but he and his people did what they could to accommodate the white homesteaders. Maintaining a good relationship with whites was important enough to Chief Charlo that he refused to help his friend Chief Joseph of the Nez Perce on his flight east. He told Joseph that if the Nez Perce caused any harm to the settlers in the Bitterroot Valley, the Nez Perce could expect the Flathead to defend the whites.

Charlo never signed the reservation treaty. However, in 1872, Arlee, a Flathead war chief, did sign it, and he thus won recognition from the U.S. government as head chief of the Flathead tribe. Charlo stayed behind in the Bitterroots until 1891, when he told the government agents who were pressuring him to move, "I will go—I and my children. My young men are becoming bad; they have no place to hunt. I do not want the land you promise. I do not believe your promises. All I want is enough ground for my grave."

During the early years of the Flathead Reservation, Indians lived in both log cabins and, weather permitting, in tepees. Many took up farming, with a number of successful farms eventually dotting the valley. In 1910, under the Dawes Act, the government allotted each Indian family a parcel of reservation land. The remaining land was made available to white homesteaders. Non-Indians flooded in, and they now comprise about 80% of the population on the Flathead Reservation.

ST. IGNATIUS AND VICINITY

Saint Ignatius is a reservation town at the feet of some stunningly jagged peaks. It's home to the Salish Cultural Committee, tel. (406) 745-4572, and a longhouse, located near the St. Ignatius Mission, used for spiritual and ceremonial events. There's a full day's worth of sightseeing in the vicinity of St. Ignatius.

National Bison Range

It may sound a little boring, driving around in your car for two hours on a one-way road, staring out the window for a glimpse of shaggy critters. But it's not. The National Bison Range has two driving tours, and it's worth taking a couple of hours to go on the long one. Stop in at the visitor center and find out where the herds have been spotted recently. Bison are the main attraction, but expect to see bighorn sheep, pronghorn, elk, mule deer, white-tailed deer, and mountain goats as well. Even if all the animals are in hiding, the land, the sky, and the light are beautiful here. As with most wildlife viewing, it's best to visit early in the morning or around dusk.

The National Bison Range was established in 1908, in response to concern that the buffalo had been slaughtered to the point of extinction. Part of the original herd was purchased from the Conrad family of Kalispell, who were early buffalo ranchers. A bison roundup is held in early October at the Bison Range.

The Bison Range is on a parcel of land carved from the Flathead Reservation by Hwy. 212 near Moiese. If you're approaching from Hwy. 93, catch Hwy. 212 between St. Ignatius and Ronan. If you're on Hwy. 200, there's a turnoff to Hwy. 212 near Dixon. From the north, turn off Hwy. 93 at St. Ignatius. The visitor center, tel. (406) 644-2211, at the entrance of the range collects a $4 fee and dispenses brochures.

If there's no time for a tour, at least be sure to keep your eyes peeled as you drive Hwy. 93 north of Ravalli. Sometimes the bison come down off their mountain to water just a hundred yards or so from the highway.

Fort Connah

In 1846-47, Angus McDonald (a Canadian fur trader who, like David Thompson, had a good reputation with the local Indians) built Fort Connah as a Hudson's Bay Company trading post six miles north of St. Ignatius on Post Creek. It was the last of the company's trading posts in the United States and was situated near an Indian trail in hopes that such a location would give the Canadian traders an edge on the increasingly competitive American fur traders. Fort Connah operated until 1871. The one building that remains is on private land.

St. Ignatius Mission

Saint Ignatius became, in 1854, the site of the second Catholic mission in Montana. Father Adrian Hoecken, a Jesuit priest, originally established the mission in Idaho, but it was moved to the Mission Valley at the behest of the Pend d'Oreille Indians. A boys' school, a mill, and a press (which printed a dictionary of the Pend d'Oreille language) eventually grew up around the mission.

One of the Jesuits' original log buildings (a chapel that doubled as living quarters for the priests) still stands beside the brick church, which was built in 1891. The church deserves as much of a look as the wooden chapel; there are striking murals inside, painted by Brother Joseph Carignano, the mission cook. While these murals may not initially impress those who hold them up against those at St. Paul's Cathedral or Chartres, they clearly succeeded in illustrating the life of Jesus and in imparting biblical stories to the Indians. Sunday mass is still held weekly at 9:30 a.m. Good Friday and Easter services at the mission church have developed into a uniquely Flathead Catholic ceremony.

St. Ignatius Mission, second Catholic mission in Montana

HAYES FOUNDATION COLLECTION/MONTANA HISTORICAL SOCIETY, HELENA

Ninepipe National Wildlife Refuge

This wetland waterfowl refuge is north of the bison range between Hwy. 93 and Hwy. 212. The large reservoir and many smaller lakes are rimmed with marshlands, making it difficult to hike from many of the roadside viewing points. The best views are generally from the road that goes along the northern edge of the reservoir off of Hwy. 212. The many "pothole" lakes around the refuge were dug out as glaciers moved across the land some 12,000 years ago.

Ninepipe is in the path of a major migratory flyway in the Rocky Mountain Trench. Prime birdwatching occurs in September. Canada geese, mergansers, mallards, redheads, great blue herons, grebes, double-crested cormorants, American wigeons, pintails, whistling swans, California gulls, ring-billed gulls, pheasants, bald eagles, and American avocets are some of the birds you might spot here.

Check at the headquarters of the National Bison Range for information on the birds and regulations. (There are information sites at the various roadside viewing areas, but they seem to be perpetually out of brochures.) Since the refuge is on tribal land, a tribal fishing permit is required before throwing a line into the reservoir. Permits are available at local sporting-goods stores and at the tribal headquarters in Pablo. No hunting is permitted on the refuge, and it is closed during both waterfowl-hunting season (in the fall) and nesting season (March through mid-July).

Kicking Horse Reservoir

Kicking Horse Reservoir is just east of Hwy. 93 across from the turnoff to Hwy. 212. It's the site of a Job Corps program run by the Confederated Salish and Kootenai Tribes. A tribal cultural center, tel. (406) 675-0160, opened east of the Job Corps center in 1995.

Sqelix'u AqtÀmak nik Cultural Center

Also known as "The People's Center," this tribal gallery and gift shop also runs tours and educational programs. It's in Pablo, tel. (406) 675-0160, and is open April through Sept. daily 9 a.m.-9 p.m., Oct. through March Mon.-Fri., 9 a.m.-5 p.m.

Recreation

To explore the **Mission Mountains Tribal Wilderness,** first pick up a tribal recreation permit ($6 permit available at Allard's Trading Post

and other local stores). And, unless you know the area, a map of the Flathead National Forest or the Flathead Reservation is another essential.

Saint Mary's Lake is less than 10 miles from St. Ignatius on St. Mary's Lake Road. (Find the road just southeast of the mission and follow it as it turns to a fairly bumpy, dusty gravel road, turns left, and heads into the hills.) There are several places to pitch a tent around the lake, and it's worth taking along fishing gear and a tribal fishing permit—there are some lunker trout around here. Just over a mile up the road is the first of the **Twin Lakes,** which are a little more isolated and quieter than St. Mary's. (No motorboats are allowed on the Twin Lakes; St. Mary's does permit them.)

Accommodations

Doug Allard's Lodgepole Motel ($44 s or d) on Hwy. 93 in St. Ignatius, tel. (406) 745-2951, is part of a complex that includes a free museum, a small grocery store, a huckleberry jam factory, and a trading post with a good selection of beadwork done by tribal members. There's also a chance for a close view of some buffalo here; Allard has a small herd paddocked near the trading post.

Hostel & Campgrounds: Established with cyclists and backpackers in mind, **Hostel of the Rockies,** tel. (406) 745-3959, is a friendly place on the northern outskirts of St. Ignatius. Lodging is bunk-style ($10) in the "earthship," an environmentally friendly, passive solar heated building constructed of recycled materials. Showers and toilets are in a separate bathhouse, where visitors can use a laundry. There's also a pleasant camping area, open both to tenters and RVs (full hook-ups).

Free camping behind the senior center in Charlo is provided by the Lions Club. It's a convenient place to stay if you want to get an early jump on bird- and animal watching. For a post-bison beer, stop in to the **Branding Iron Bar** in Charlo.

Guest Ranch: Up against the Mission Mountains, **Cheff's Guest Ranch,** 4274 Eagle Pass Rd., Charlo, MT 59824, tel. (406) 644-2557, offers accommodations on a working cattle and horse ranch. They also run pack trips and short horseback rides. B&B rates are $100 per couple per night. Three-day ($270) and seven-day ($550) per person rates include all meals, lodging, and horseback riding.

Food and Drink

A number of cafes in the Mission Valley, especially those near the National Bison Range, feature buffalo burgers. This low-cholesterol meat is reported to taste something like venison. It comes from bison raised on ranches, not from the tourist attractions roaming the bison range. The **Bison Inn**, on Hwy. 93 in Ravalli, is a good local stop for buffalo burgers as well as more standard diner breakfasts, lunches, and dinners.

Shopping

Doug Allard's Trading Post (in the same complex as the motel, museum, and bison herd) has a wide selection of beadwork done on the Flathead Reservation. Expect to find some great beaded earrings and hair ornaments, as well as less apparently traditional beaded cigarette-lighter covers. A couple of miles north of Allard's, the **Four Winds Trading Post**, tel. (406) 745-4336, specializes in moccasins, Indian artifacts, and toy trains. Preston Miller, proprietor of Four Winds, also collects historic buildings from around the Mission Valley and has moved several to the trading post.

Events

Arlee, 15 miles south of St. Ignatius on Hwy. 93, is the site of the **Fourth of July Powwow**, held annually by the Confederated Salish and Kootenai Tribes. It's a major event, not to be missed if you're anywhere in the area. Expect to see both traditional and fancy dancing to the accompaniment of amazing drumming. Groups of drummers, as well as individual dancers, compete for prize money. In another area of the powwow, the sounds of hand drums signal stick games, which are ritualistic and high-stake gambling competitions. For those not up to the complications and $100 ante of a stick game, poker and blackjack games are set up in small shacks.

Jewelry, crafts, and cassette tapes of popular drum groups are for sale at a number of booths. There's also plenty of food, including fry bread and "Indian tacos." The powwow grounds are the site of an encampment during this long weekend. Tepees, tents, and campers crowd into the dusty field and the celebration goes on late into the night. The powwow grounds are right in Arlee, just east of Hwy. 93.

There is no admission fee, non-Indians are welcome, and drugs and alcohol are strictly prohibited.

RONAN AND VICINITY

Ronan was named for Peter Ronan, an Indian agent. The area around Ronan was part of the Flathead Reservation until 1910.

The **"Garden of the Rockies"** pioneer museum is on Round Butte Rd., five blocks west of Hwy. 93. There are mock-ups of a doctor's office, barbershop, schoolroom, kitchen, bedroom, and living room. Expect a friendly volunteer to give you a personalized tour; perhaps you'll get a demonstration of a favorite object, such as a hand-pumped vacuum cleaner.

Pablo, five miles north of Ronan, is the headquarters of the Confederated Salish and Kootenai Tribes and home of **Salish-Kootenai College**, which offers programs in general studies, Native American studies, nursing, and a range of human services and vocational fields. The college library is a good place to read up on the Salish and Kootenai tribes. Both traditional and modern Native American art are represented in the college's collection.

Pablo National Wildlife Refuge, off Hwy. 93 about a dozen miles north of the Ninepipe Refuge (see above), is a similar waterfowl sanctuary and is governed by similar regulations.

Accommodations

The **Allentown Motel** is five miles south of Ronan and connected with a good restaurant, tel. (406) 644-2588.

B&Bs: For a beautiful view, friendly welcoming people, and top-notch accommodations, go to the **Timbers B&B**, tel. (406) 676-4373 or (800) 775-4373. The home is located on 21 acres with a magnificent view of the Mission Mountains. This B&B is perfect for a family or friends traveling together, as the lodging is a private two-bedroom suite with one shared bath. The suite is air-conditioned and has a phone and TV.

Food and Drink

Allentown Restaurant is five miles south of Ronan on Hwy. 93, just across from one of the pullouts for Ninepipe National Wildlife Refuge. The menu departs a bit from the fancy steak and seafood fare, though that's still a major focus, and there's been some attention given to the wine list. Dinners run around $15; breakfast and lunch are also served. The Allentown attracts travelers who marvel at the views of the Mission Mountains and locals who, at night, may happen upon its bar midway along journeys elsewhere.

Events and Recreation

Ronan celebrates **Pioneer Days** during the second week of August, complete with the obligatory rodeo. Call the chamber of commerce at (406) 676-8300 for more information.

Ronan's nine-hole **golf course** is three miles west of Hwy. 93 on Round Butte Rd., tel. (406) 676-4653. Greens fee is $9 for nine holes, $14 for 18.

Information

Write to the **chamber of commerce** at P.O. Box 254, Ronan, MT 59864, or call them at (406) 676-8300.

Ronan has a small **library** on the corner of Main and 2nd Streets, tel. (406) 676-3682. There's also a library on the campus of Salish-Kootenai College, tel. (406) 675-4800.

HOT SPRINGS AND VICINITY

The western part of the Flathead Reservation has a couple of commercial hot springs in and around the town of Hot Springs, and a large grant has been procured to develop the area as a healing resort.

Locals mix with day-trippers up from Missoula at the free, informal, outdoor hot pool back behind the old bathhouse in Hot Springs. When you hit the T-intersection in town, take a right, follow on up the hill, and bear right. There is some talk of plans to renovate the old bathhouse and return it to its previous status as a tourist destination.

Wild Horse Hot Springs, six miles off Hwy. 28 from Hot Springs, tel. (406) 741-3777 or (800) 204-1677, is a place to relax in a private room with a "plunge," a steam room, a shower, and a toilet. The plunge is like a cement baby pool, with hot water. It's not a posh place, but it somehow has the feeling of a refuge, a place where chills and bone weariness melt away and you're left with your pores open to the rolling hills and golden light of the surrounding reservation.

The bathhouse is open year-round 8 a.m.-9 p.m. An hourlong soak costs $5. There are a couple of apartments with kitchens available for rent by the night here ($55-65), but most people just come for a soak.

If you do want to spend the night within an easy sniff of the waters, **Symes Hot Springs Hotel & Mineral Baths,** 104 Wall St. in Hot Springs, tel. (406) 741-2361, has rooms with bathtubs plumbed with the local sulfurous brew; there are also outdoor pools. Under new ownership, the imposing spa is being restored to its original beauty, and the rooms are newly updated. The hotel has the air of an old-fashioned therapeutic spa (you may feel it's improper to speak above a whisper), but the rooms are clean, comfortable, and newly renovated; some have kitchens. Cabins are also available. If you're here for the real treatment, there's a massage therapist and chiropractic physician on site. Lodging prices start at $24 s, $35d in the hotel; cabins are $60.

Another Hot Springs original is the **Hot Springs Spa,** tel. (406) 741-2283, 308 N. Springs St. The spa has hot tubs, massages ($35), and rooms starting at $24; some of the rooms are plumbed with hot mineral water and have individual mineral water-jet tubs.

Free camping is provided by the Lions Club on Hwy. 28 between Plains and Hot Springs. It's an informal, indeed bare-bones, place up on a bluff.

There's good food at **Mary's** and an open seat at any of the town's three bars.

Perma

Perma is on the bank of the Flathead River, which flows into the Clark Fork near the junction of Hwys. 135 and 200. Salish and Kootenai Indians made annual trips to this area to dig camas roots.

This was Pend d'Oreille country, and traces of their vision quests remain near Perma. Just across the bridge to Hot Springs, a dirt road turns off abruptly to the left, then follows the river a mile and a half down to a clearing near the bend. It takes a little looking, but several red ocher animal figures and a number of hatch marks (which may count the days a young Pend d'Oreille spent on a vision quest) are visible on a cliff by the clearing. This is reservation land, so get a tribal permit before poking around or fishing.

Dixon

Dixon, a small town on Hwy. 200 between Perma and Ravalli, is noted for its bar. The **Dixon Bar** has the longest standing liquor license in the state of Montana, and also has had the distinction of having three poems about it appear on one page of the *New Yorker* magazine. Stop by and ask the bartender to let you read them.

FLATHEAD LAKE

When western Montanans go away for a weekend, there's a pretty good chance they're headed to Flathead Lake. At 28 miles long, seven to eight miles wide, and over 300 feet deep, it's the largest natural freshwater lake west of the Mississippi. The lakeshore is dotted with campgrounds and summer cabins, many owned by the same families for years.

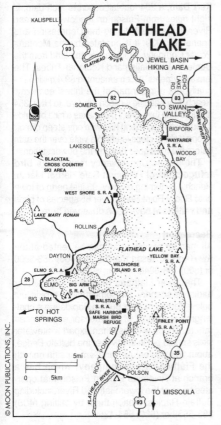

Flathead Lake fills a trench carved by glaciers during the Pleistocene epoch. A terminal moraine at the foot of the lake divides the Flathead Valley from the Mission Valley to the south. Until glacial ice receded, Flathead Lake drained to the west in the area of Big Arm. The outlet is now via the lower Flathead River, which exits the lake at Polson and flows into the Clark Fork around Paradise. Kerr Dam, just southwest of Polson, controls the water level of the lake and the lower Flathead River.

Three upper forks of the Flathead River join above Kalispell to pour into Flathead Lake. The North Fork originates in southeastern British Columbia, the Middle Fork rises in the northern part of the Bob Marshall Wilderness (near the southern edge of Glacier National Park), and the South Fork flows from the southeastern region of the Bob Marshall Wilderness, via Hungry Horse Reservoir.

HISTORY

David Thompson was the first white in the area (1808). While he was residing at his Saleesh House, a trading enterprise near present-day Thompson Falls, his Indian neighbors told him of Salish (Flathead) Lake and guided him there in 1809. Jocko Finley, a Scot-Indian, assisted Thompson and became a major fur trader in the southern Flathead Valley. Fur trappers worked the Flathead Lake area from about 1810 through the middle part of the century. Fort Connah, south of Flathead Lake in the Mission Valley, was the main trading post for the region.

Steamboats ran on Flathead Lake in the late 1800s and early 1900s. Their route was from Demersville (a now-defunct town on the Flathead River, halfway between Kalispell and Flathead Lake) down to Polson.

The first white settlers on the eastern banks of the lake arrived in 1891 and quickly lit upon the idea of growing cherries there. Homesteading started in earnest around 1910, when reservation land became available to non-Indians under the Dawes Act. Fruit orchards grew up all along the eastern shore of the lake. They've been subject to periodic killing frosts, most recently in 1989.

POLSON

Polson (pop. 4,316, elev. 2,949 feet) is tucked into a glacial moraine at the foot of Flathead Lake where the lower Flathead River drains from the lake. Highway 93 takes a turn here and becomes an east-west road for its run through Polson. It's the seat of Lake County and the business center of Flathead Lake and the upper Mission Valley.

History
Ferry service across the lower Flathead River began in the mid-1800s, and in 1880 a store was built at the foot of the lake. By 1898, there was enough of a town to warrant a post office, and it took its name from David Polson, who'd been ranching about five miles northwest of town since 1870.

Sights
People come to Polson for the lake. There's plenty of public shoreline, and several parks make appealing sitting, swimming, fishing, or boat-launching spots. **Boettcher Park** is toward the eastern edge of town, **Sacajawea Park** is right downtown off Kootenai Ave., and **Riverside Park** is on the east end of the bridge over the river.

Lake cruises on the *Port of Polson Princess* run several times daily during the summer, leaving from the KwaTaqNuk Resort marina. A three-hour tour departs daily at 1:30 p.m. and makes a loop around Wildhorse Island. The fare is $16 for adults, $8 for children. Ninety-minute sunset cruises depart at 7:30 p.m.; $10 for adults, $5 for children. Family rates and senior-citizen discounts are offered. Call (406) 883-2448 for reservations.

Polson is a treasure trove for small-museum aficionados. The **Polson-Flathead Historical Museum** at 704 Main St., tel. (406) 883-3049, is a dark, jumbled place that houses a stuffed steer named Rudolf and a 7.5-foot sturgeon caught in Flathead Lake in 1955 and reputed to have been the Flathead Monster. Summer hours are Mon.-Fri. 9 a.m.-6 p.m., Sunday noon-6 p.m., $2 donation requested.

The **Miracle of America Museum** on Hwy. 93, just below Hwy. 35 junction ($2.50 admission, open Mon.-Sat. 8 a.m.-5 p.m., Sunday 2-6 p.m. in the summer; the rest of the year open till dark), is marked by a large log towboat in the parking lot. Inside this "Smithsonian of the West," the intrepid museum-goer will find a unique homage to cleanliness: a collection of antique vacuum cleaners. Music lovers will thrill to the sound of the violano, a coin-operated violin-piano combination; the State Fiddlers' Hall of Fame is also housed here. There's simply a *lot* of everything here, from old motorcycles to vintage tractor seats. For information, call (406) 883-6804.

If it's not too much of a letdown to visit a dam after steeping oneself in our nation's heritage, the **Kerr Dam,** a 204-foot-tall concrete arch dam, is eight miles from Polson on the lower Flathead River. It was built during the Depression and opened in 1939. It is operated by the Montana Power Company, which leases the land from the Confederated Salish and Kootenai Tribes. The lease payments, which amount to $9.4 million annually, are a major part of the tribes' economy. Reach it by heading west on 7th Ave. to Hwy. 354 and following the signs. (This makes a nice bike ride if you don't mind rolling hills with one steep climb.) A long flight of steps leads to a vista over the dam before the road goes down to the power station.

The Nature Conservancy maintains a **bird refuge** north of Polson at Safe Harbor Marsh. Reach it by turning off Hwy. 93 just north of town onto Rocky Point Road. Over 65 species of birds and waterfowl have been observed here.

Recreation
All manner of watercraft can be rented at the KwaTaqNuk Resort marina, tel. (406) 383-3900 or (800) 358-8046.

The lower Flathead River has spectacular badlands scenery and some thrilling rapids just below Kerr Dam. The Buffalo Rapids are a challenging stretch of whitewater for experienced rafters. Those with less than expert whitewater skills should put in the river at the Buffalo Bridge, about 10 miles below Kerr Dam, or sign on with the **Flathead Raft Company,** which has a branch at Riverside Park in Polson that operates tours of the lower Flathead River, including Buffalo Rapids. Reach them by calling (406) 883-5838 or (800) 654-4359.

THE FLATHEAD MONSTER

Is there a monster lurking deep in Flathead Lake? Sightings have been reported for well over 100 years. And in 1955 it was even reported to have been caught. Although the creature in question turned out to be a 7.5-foot, 181-pound white sturgeon, it is still preserved in the Polson-Flathead Historical Museum.

Polson's 18-hole **golf course** is east of downtown on the lake side of Hwy. 93. Call (406) 883-2440 for a tee time or more information.

There's a good **swimming** beach right near the golf course in Boettcher Park.

Since the southern half of Flathead Lake is on the Flathead Reservation, **anglers** need a tribal permit, which can be purchased at tribal headquarters in Pablo or at many stores in Polson. Although there's been a sharp decrease in the number of kokanee salmon in the lake in recent years, there are still lake trout, whitefish, and some cutthroat trout throughout the lake, as well as largemouth bass and perch in warm, shallow spots, such as Polson Bay. Fishing Flathead Lake requires some thought about water depth and temperature. Michael S. Sample's *Angler's Guide to Montana* (see **Booklist**) has tips about which fish live where and when.

Although the lower Flathead River doesn't have much in the way of trout, there are plenty of big pike.

There are **cross-country ski trails** about five miles north of Polson, east of Hwy. 93.

Accommodations

Polson's premier accommodations are at the **Best Western KwaTaqNuk Resort,** a large lakeside hotel owned by the Confederated Salish and Kootenai Tribes. During the summer, lakeside rooms start at $109 s, $119 d; rooms with a view of Polson are $88 s, $98 d. Spring, fall, and winter rates are $20-30 lower for all types of rooms. The KwaTaqNuk has both indoor and outdoor pools; a marina with canoe, boat, jet-ski, and sailboard rentals as well as lake cruises; an art gallery; restaurants; and convention facilities. Call (406) 883-3636 or (800) 882-6363 for reservations.

There are several other attractive motels along Hwy. 93 just east of Polson's city center. **Port Polson Inn** on Hwy. 93 across the road from the lake, tel. (406) 883-5385 or (800) 654-0682, has both indoor and outdoor hot tubs, an exercise room and sauna, kichenettes, and free continental breakfast. During the summer, rooms are $69 s and $84 d; winter rates run $40 s, $53 d. Slightly less expensive, the **Cherry Hill Motel** at 1810 Hwy. 93 has duplex units on a bluff overlooking the lake, tel. (406) 883-2737. There's also a **Days Inn,** tel. (406) 883-3120 or (800) 329-7466, with great views of Flathead Lake and the Mission Mountains and rooms at $62 s, $67 d during the summer, $36 s and $38 d during the offseason.

B&Bs: Just north of Polson on Kings Point, is **Swan Hill B&B,** tel. (406) 883-5292 or (800) 537-9489, 460 Kings Point. This excellent B&B is in a modern redwood home perched above the lake in 10 acres of pine forest. The inn is completely handicapped accessible, has an indoor pool and sauna, and vast deck areas from which to watch the glimmering of the lake and the deer sauntering through the yard. There are four guest rooms, all with private baths; rooms are $75-85. From the B&B, hikers can easily walk to the Nature Conservancy refuge.

Campgrounds: Just west of the city center and east of the bridge, **Riverside Park** has camping for both tents ($8) and RVs ($15). It's not the most lovely campground on Flathead Lake, but it's convenient to breakfast or dinner in town.

Food and Drink

The place to eat lunch in Polson is **Watusi Cafe,** tel. (406) 883-6200, 318 Main Street. The owner-chef was formerly the private cook for a couple of health-conscious celebrity ranchers before deciding to open a cafe in Polson. The menu offers great, nutritious soups and sandwiches (made with homemade breads), as well as home-fried potato chips.

Several lively bars on Polson's Main St. may lure some travelers away from the lake. Also on Main, **Bogi's Sa'm'ich House and '50s Restaurant** at 224 Main is a fun place for lunch. (Note the old records decorating the outside wall.) **The Old Mill Place,** 501 Main, tel. (406) 892-1490, is an old-fashioned ice cream parlor and coffee shop, with light meals and deli sandwiches.

Locals favor the **Rancho Deluxe Supper Club,** 602 6th St. W, tel. (406) 883-2300, for good steak, chops, and fish dinners overlooking Flathead River. The **4-Bs,** at the intersection of Hwys. 93 and 35, tel. (406) 883-6100, has the basic but satisfying fare that Montana travelers have come to expect.

Entertainment and Events

The former golf course clubhouse is now the **Polson Performing Arts Center,** home to the Port Polson Players, a summer theater. The season starts in July, with plays Wed.-Sun. evenings at 8 p.m. For information about what's on and reservations, call (406) 883-9212.

Fiddle players flock to Polson the fourth weekend of July for the **Montana State Fiddlers' Contest.** Call (406) 883-5969 for details.

Services

St. Joseph Hospital, Skyline Drive, tel. (406) 883-5377, has 24-hour emergency service. The local **laundromat** is on the corner of 1st St. and Hwy. 93, by the stoplight. The **post office** is at 219 1st St. East.

Information

Contact the **Polson Chamber of Commerce** at P.O. Box 677, Polson, MT 59860, tel. (406) 883-5969.

The public **library,** near the lake at 1st St. E and 1st Ave. W, tel. (406) 883-4003, has several cases of books on Montana, a good variety of magazines, and lovely views onto Flathead Lake. Across the hall in the same building, find **Sandpiper Gallery,** 2 1st Ave. E., tel. (406) 883-5956, with its displays of regional arts and crafts.

WEST SIDE OF FLATHEAD LAKE

Driving along the west side of Flathead Lake, you get a good view across the water to the Mission Mountains. There's more of an open feeling to this side of the lake than to the east side-off to the west the rolling Salish Mountains gentle the light and lend a glow to the surrounding land and sky.

Wildhorse Island

There are indeed wild horses on this island near the Big Arm of Flathead Lake. There's also a thriving herd of bighorn sheep and a wealth of birdlife, including ospreys, bald eagles, red-tailed hawks, and Canada geese. The island exists because its rock base resisted the plowing action of the glacier that scooped out Flathead Lake. It was used as a sort of safehouse for the local Flathead and Pend d'Oreille horses when Blackfeet came on raids.

Private concerns took over the island for many years, but it became a state park in 1977 and in 1983 the BLM began turning horses loose there. In 1940, two bighorn sheep were transplanted there as a tourist attraction. The herd grew to beyond what the island could support, and many sheep died of starvation before the Montana Dept. of Fish, Wildlife, and Parks began moving Wildhorse Island bighorns to other areas of the state.

Wildhorse Island is a day-use park; camping and fires (including campstoves) are prohibited,

---

THE DECLINE OF THE KOKANEE

The prized kokanee salmon once made up 90% of the fish population in Flathead Lake, but in recent years they've virtually disappeared. The kokanee (the freshwater version of the sockeye) is not native to the Flathead River system—it has been introduced, along with other species including lake, rainbow, and brook trout and northern pike. Species native to the system include wests-

kokanee salmon

lope cutthroat trout, bull trout, and mountain whitefish, and it's the whitefish that are now the dominant species.

Mysis shrimp, another introduced species, may be to blame for the kokanee's demise in Flathead Lake. Apparently, the tiny shrimp, introduced as fish food, beats the salmon to food sources deep in the lake and wins the competition for habitat.

and there are still some private land holdings to avoid. You'll need a boat to get here. Boats can be rented in Big Arm for the trip to the island. Motorboats are recommended; they go for around $30 a day at the Big Arm Resort and Marina. The *Port of Polson Princess* cruises from Polson around Wildhorse Island every day of the summer at 1:30 p.m., but it doesn't dock.

Angel Point, north of Wildhorse Island near Rollins, is the site of several pictographs. The red drawings, which have suffered from vandalism, are only visible from a boat on the lake.

Camping

Big Arm State Recreation Area, just north of milepost 74 on Hwy. 93, has camping for $11 per night (includes the $4 day-use fee). It's a good spot if you want to swim or boat, but the campsites are packed close together, making it a little uncomfortable for just plain camping. Don't expect to find peace and solitude here, but it's a lovely lakeside spot, and it's understandable that families flock here. **Elmo State Recreation Area,** on Hwy. 93 right near the turnoff for Hwy. 28 (to Hot Springs and Plains), is an open lakeside site, with a tenters' area right down by the water. This campground has showers, a rarity in the public campgrounds of Montana.

Between Dayton and Lakeside on Hwy. 93, **West Shore State Recreation Area** is yet another state campground on Flathead Lake. The $11 fee includes both day use ($4) and camping.

Elmo

Elmo, hub of the Flathead Reservation's Kootenai population, is the site of the **Standing Arrow Powwow** during the third weekend of July. Though not as large as the powwow held in Arlee, it's a good opportunity to see dancing, drumming, and stick games. The **Kootenai Cultural Committee,** tel. (406) 849-5541, the powwow's sponsor, has its headquarters in Elmo.

Dayton

The **Mission Mountain Winery** has some vineyards, a winery, and a tasting room in Dayton. They produce mostly Johannesburg Riesling and a blush wine called "Sundowner," but they also have a dry chardonnay and a cabernet sauvignon for those who are willing to pay more than $8 per bottle.

Lake Mary Ronan

Lake Mary Ronan is six miles off Hwy. 93 near Dayton. It's a popular place to fish, especially for kokanee salmon, which flourish here as they used to in Flathead Lake. Since the lake is not on reservation land, only a state fishing permit is needed. There are several resorts on the lake, all with cabins, tent and RV camping, and restaurants.

Lake Mary Ronan Resort, tel. (406) 849-5454, has cabins with bedding (but no cooking gear) ranging $45-90 per night, and campsites from $10. They also have a restaurant and a lounge with country music on the weekends. Boat rentals start at $10 per day, and showers are $2.50 if you're not staying at the resort. A friendly attitude is both preached and practiced here.

Camp Tuffit, tel. (406) 849-5220, has the venerable feel of your aunt's backyard—very pretty, well manicured, with green grass and Adirondack chairs. Cabins start at $25-39 a night and go to $75 for a multiroom cabin with a pool table. Boats go for $15-30 per day. There isn't really any tent camping here, but RV spaces are $15 per night.

Lambeth State Park has a $4 day-use admission fee, with an additional $7 for camping.

"SWIMMER'S ITCH"

There are swimming beaches at almost every park on Flathead Lake, and by midsummer the water is warm enough for enjoyable swimming. There is one special caveat here, though. Once the water warms up, it is home to a parasite that causes a condition known as "swimmer's itch." Adults and strong swimmers are less prone to the affliction—apparently, the parasite lives in the warmer shallow water, where children are more likely to play.

It's easy enough to figure that this is something to avoid, and there are a number of ideas about how to do that. Repeated ins and outs of the water seem to encourage the parasite to cling to one's skin. Local wisdom also has it that coating your body with suntan lotion or another oily substance will protect you from swimmer's itch.

Should precautions fail, calamine lotion and cortisone creams are the usual remedy.

Rollins

Okay, so you picked up a bottle of wine in Dayton. Now stop at **M & S Meats** in Rollins, tel. (406) 844-3414, for some buffalo jerky to add to your Montana gift basket. If you'd rather not tote M & S's renowned buffalo meat and sausage, stop at the cafe next door for an exceptionally tasty buffalo burger.

Rollins is also the base for **sea kayak tours** of Flathead Lake. Glacier Sea Kayaking runs full day instruction and exploration trips, as well as customized tours, overnight and full moon trips as well as sunset dinner cruises. Call (408) 862-9010 for reservations and more information.

Lakeside

There are several motels in Lakeside, all with essentially the same name. The **Lake Shore Motel,** tel. (406) 844-2433, has small cottages from $60 s to $70 d and rents boats and canoes. The Lake Shore also has a 1,600-square foot house for rent.

The **Bayshore Resort Motel,** tel. (406) 844-3131 or (800) 844-3132, 616 Lakeside Blvd., is one of two motels in central Lakeside that share access to the lake. In addition to lodging, the resort offers charter fishing. Rooms are available from May through October and start at $65 s, $84 d. Immediately across the drive is the **Lakeside Resort Motel,** tel. (406) 844-3570 or (800) 348-4822, with a number of lodging choices. In addition to the motel units (some with kitchenettes), there are one-, two- and three-bedroom cottages, all with complete kitchens and barbecues, on the lake. The motel also rents boats. Lodging prices range $60-105 a night.

For something more private and exclusive, consider staying at **Angel Point Guest Suites,** tel. (406) 844-2204 or (800) 214-2204, 829 Angel Point Road. Located on a peninsula jutting out into Flathead Lake, with 322 feet of shoreline, the Angel Point Guest Suites are two large suites (actually the ground floor of an enormous private home) with complete kitchen, dining and sitting area, and large two-room baths. Both suites have private entrances. Guests have full run of the extensive property, including a dock, fishing platform, patio, barbecue area, beach pavillion, and gazebo. The suites are available either on a self-catering basis, or as B&B. There's a three-day minimum stay, $100-115 a night; free use of canoe and rowboat.

Located at the Lakeside Marina, **Rosario's,** tel. (406) 844-2888, is the restaurant of choice in the area. Rosario's developed considerable fame and allegiance when it was located in Townsend, south of Helena, and it didn't take the locals along the Flathead to welcome another good restaurant to the lake. Diners get a choice of excellent pizzas or full Italian meals, including veal, chicken, and pasta dishes. The views over the marina and lake are spectacular.

The **Blacktail Inn,** 105 Blacktail Rd., tel. (406) 844-3055, is a good bet for American-style food and drink in Lakeside. They are open for breakfast, lunch, and dinner and serve a dinner buffet in addition to some fairly standard menu selections.

Blacktail Cross Country Ski Area is about eight miles from Lakeside. Pick up a trail map and brochure at the ranger station in Bigfork, the Forest Service office in Kalispell, or at the Lakeside Grocery and Deli. The trails, which range from easy to difficult, are at about a 5,500-foot elevation, which means a fairly long skiing season and a chance to get above the clouds. If you have two vehicles, park one at the lower parking lot and use it to shuttle back to the upper lot at the end of your ski tour. Only upper lot parking is necessary if you plan to ski the easiest (and the only groomed) trail of the network. Do not ski on the road. There is log-truck traffic on it, even in winter.

Somers

You'll have a hard time finding a lodging closer to Flathead Lake than the **Osprey Inn Bed and Breakfast** at 5557 Hwy. 93 S, tel. (406) 857-2042 or (800) 258-2042, located about a mile south of Somers proper. This comfortable inn faces directly onto Flathead, where there's a gravel beach, a small dock (guests can use the canoe or rowing shell), and at night a lakeside campfire. From the second floor deck (where you can eat breakfast in good weather), there are tremendous views of the Mission Mountains rising above the lake's eastern shore. Guests have the choice of three rooms in the main house (one is a two-bedroom suite ideal for a family) or an adjacent log cabin. There's a downstairs common room, with fireplace and TV, which gives out onto a lakefront patio. The hosts are a model of helpful but not intrusive hospitality. There's a hot tub for everyone's use; rooms range $90-120.

As if you need another reason to stay at the Osprey Inn: the **Montana Grill,** tel. (406) 857-3889, is an easy stroll away. One of the very best places to eat along Flathead Lake, this massive, three-story log lodge serves up mesquite-grilled fresh fish flown in from the Pacific, great steaks and prime rib, and a wide selection of stir-fries, pasta, and continental-influenced dishes (dinners run $15-20; also open for lunch and Sunday brunch). Service is very prompt and professional while retaining a Montana friendliness; the wine list is quite good and well priced. Views from the dining room are stunning; there's a lively bar on the main floor.

Another good place to eat or have a drink is **Tiebecker's Pub & Eatery,** tel. (406) 857-3335, 75 Somers Rd., located in the historic office building of the Somers Lumber Company, the mill that built the town at the turn-of-the-century. In addition to the pub, which offers a number of Montana microbrews, there is a dining room specializing in Italian grilled and barbecued meats, as well as fresh fish and steaks. Dinners are in the $8-12 range.

Lake cruises depart from a dock across from the Montana Grill. To reserve a daytime or sunset cruise on the 65-foot *Far West,* call (408) 857-3203; you can also arrange a sailboat cruise at the same number. Aspiring anglers can call **Flathead Lake Charter Service** at (408) 857-3439 to arrange fishing trips.

Somers Bay is a good place to paddle a canoe. The water here is relatively shallow and warmer than the rest of the lake, and the lakeshore is dotted with old wharves and buildings, islands, and birds (keep an eye out for ospreys diving into the lake).

Vacation Home Rentals

If you're looking to rent a private home on this part of Flathead Lake, contact **Flathead Lake Beach Homes,** tel. (406) 857-2079, 290 Sunny Slope, Somers, MT 59932. Prices for a week's house rental begin at around $1,000. If you don't need a whole house, this company also offers lake-front room rentals in private homes, where you share the rest of the house with other guests. You can also contact Flathead Lake Beach Homes for activities bookings in the area: fishing charters, rafting, parasailing, sailboat charters, and so on.

EAST SIDE OF FLATHEAD LAKE

Sights

Cherry orchards are both a business and an attraction around Flathead Lake. Cherries are usually harvested beginning around the third week of July.

The University of Montana runs a biological station at Yellow Bay. Limnology, the study of the life of lakes, ponds, and streams, is a major research focus here. The biological station has conducted most of its research on water quality and plankton, but the recent acquisition of a research boat will enable them to study the lake's fish. Summer classes in freshwater biology and ecology are offered for credit and for audit. The summer term runs for eight weeks, with housing available in cabins or dorm rooms.

For more information, call (408) 982-3301. If your interest is more casual, drop by the station. Students are often pleased to discuss their research, and there are newsletters and bulletin boards to browse.

Accommodations

Schiefelbein Haus, tel. (406) 887-2431, is a small motel and RV park near the Finley Point cherry orchards. Rooms are $38, $48-60 with kitchens. The adjacent restaurant is well-loved and serves German-style food, as well as barbecued meats cooked over local cherry wood coals. There's also a *bier garten,* which gets very convivial once the high-spirited RVers start to raise their tackards. **Jorgensen's Cabins,** tel. (406) 887-2724, and **Pineglen Resort,** tel. (406) 887-2455, are in the same Finley Point neighborhood.

The campgrounds off Hwy. 35 can be quite pleasant during off-peak times, and crowded and noisy during summer weekends. **Finley Point State Recreation Area** is four miles off Hwy. 35 on cherry-tree-studded Finley Point. It has a boat launch ($4 for day use, plus an additional $7 to camp). Just above the Finley Point turnoff on Hwy. 35 is the **Rocky G Campground,** a Good Sam Park trailer campground. It has a restaurant with Mexican food. The **Yellow Bay State Recreation Area** and campground is right next to the University of Montana's Biological Study and Research Station.

At Woods Bay (between Yellow Bay and Bigfork), **Deer Trail Cottages** is on a private beach, tel. (406) 837-4542.

BIGFORK

Bigfork is situated on a bay where the Swan River empties into Flathead Lake. It's an exceptionally lovely site that's turned into the kind of upscale resort community that was once foreign to the state. Certainly no other town in northwestern Montana is so devoted to art galleries, fine restaurants, high-end boutiques—and real estate offices.

The year-round population of about 1,500 can rise exponentially during the summer. High summer is theater season in Bigfork, with its accompanying tour buses and crowds. If the prospect of crowded sidewalks seems a little daunting, consider visiting Bigfork in the offseason, when it's a pleasant place to wander through the galleries and bookshops.

Tourism is obviously the mainstay of Bigfork's economy, but agriculture, especially fruit growing, is also of some importance. A number of artists have taken up residence in Bigfork, adding a cultural depth that represents Bigfork at its best. Noted chefs have also moved here to practice their own kind of artistry. Bigfork could with ample reason claim to be the culinary capital of Montana.

History
Bigfork was founded in 1902, about the time the hydroelectric plant at the mouth of the Swan River was built to supply electricity for Kalispell. The electric company is still here, and the bridge is the best place to stand and ponder how it works. (Water from the Swan River is diverted to a higher level, then dropped through turbines to generate power.)

Recreation
In keeping with its role as a resort village, Bigfork has one of the best 18-hole public golf courses in the West. The **Eagle Bend Golf Club** is on Holt Dr. west of Hwy. 35, tel. (406) 837-3700. It's gotten high ratings from *Golf Digest* magazine and from Montana golfers. Eagle Bend also houses the **Bigfork Athletic Club,** which includes racquetball, squash, aerobics, and a weight room, tel. (406) 837-2582.

To arrange a **sailboat tour** of Flathead Lake, call (406) 837-5569. Parasailing trips are also available from Marina Cay, tel. (406) 837-2161. For a seaplane tour of Flathead Lake or Glacier Park, call (408) 837-4048. Flights leave from Bigfork harbor.

Jewel Basin Hiking Area was set aside as an easily reached wilderness-like area. There are 35 miles of trails that make day-hike loops or longer backpack trips. To get there from Bigfork, take Echo Lake Rd. off Hwy. 83. (It can also be reached from the west side of Hungry Horse Reservoir.) An extremely helpful map costs $1 at the Forest Service offices in Bigfork, Hungry Horse, or Kalispell.

Hikes take you through wildflower meadows and thickets of subalpine fir. Climbing in from the west, you'll first have expansive views of the Flathead Valley and Lake, then pass over a ridge and realize that Jewel Basin is indeed a basin. It's hard to say which are the jewels—the lakes that stud the basin or the Indian paintbrush, bear grass, fire-

---

OSPREYS

osprey,
Pandion haliaetus

Several ospreys maintain nests along the north shore of Flathead Lake. As you drive along Hwy. 82 between Bigfork and Somers, notice, perched atop telephone poles, the large nests made of cow dung and sticks.

Fledgling birdwatchers may initially confuse an osprey with another fish-eating bird, the bald eagle. An osprey is smaller than an eagle and has a white belly (an eagle's belly is dark). A feet-first plunge into water is the osprey's distinctive fishing style.

Ospreys winter in Mexico, from about late September to mid-April. It's thought that mates winter separately but reunite at the site of the previous year's nest. Eggs hatch in late May or early June. Canada geese may compete for osprey nests.

weed, and showy daisies strewn through the meadows. Some of the lakes are stocked with trout.

Some of the state's wildest water is found in the mile or so of the Swan River immediately before the Bigfork dam. Kayakers love it, but it's not for the inexperienced.

Accommodations

For as popular a destination as Bigfork, there aren't a lot of places to stay. For an attractive motel, go to the **Timbers Motel,** located slightly out of Bigfork proper, above Bigfork Bay and Hwy. 35, tel. (406) 837-6200 or (800) 821-4546. Rooms here start at $58 s, $68 d, with winter rates running about $20 less. There's a pool, a sauna, and an outdoor hot tub; pets are welcome with a $5 fee. The setting, back off the highway among trees, is rather snug and comfortable. The Timbers also has an RV park.

Marina Cay, tel. (406) 837-5861 or (800) 433-6516, 180 Vista Lane, is a large, attractive resort complex right on the bay that contains the majority of the rooms available in Bigfork. Facilities include a number of good restaurants and bars, a marina with boat rentals and other recreational outings, lounge-side pool and a couple of hot tubs. The basic rooms start at $65 and go to $105 in high season. Condominiums are also available, starting at $175; substantially lower off-season rates can make Marina Cay a very good value.

B&Bs: At $35 s and $45 d, **Schwartz's Bed and Breakfast,** 890 McCaffery Rd., tel. (406) 837-5463, is the least expensive of Bigfork's several B&Bs. It's located on a private lake, and guests have free use of the communal canoe. If you want access to Bigfork and its amenities but also want a rural setting, then consider **Burggraf's Countrylane B&B,** tel. (406) 837-4608 or (800) 525-3344, a beautiful modern log home located on seven shoreline acres of Swan Lake, the next lake over from Bigfork. All rooms have private baths, and the rates ($90-125) include a full breakfast, hors d'oeuvres, a bottle of wine, fresh fruit, and the use of a canoe. Burggraf's is seven miles from Bigfork off Rainbow Rd. **O'Duachain Country Inn Bed and Breakfast,** 675 Ferndale Dr., tel. (406) 837-6851, has rooms for $95 s, $110 d. Reduced winter rates are available, and they have a hot tub.

Somewhere between a B&B and a private lodge, the **Coyote Roadhouse Inn,** tel. (406) 837-4250, 602 Three Eagle Lane, Ferndale, MT 59911, is a beautiful restaurant and inn located on the Swan River a few miles east of Bigfork. Accommodations in the lodge consist of six master suites; four of the suites have private baths (two have Jacuzzis), while two suites share a bath. During the evenings, in the inn's great room, the Roadhouse Inn serves refined Northern Italian cuisine, while across the meadow is the Coyote Riverhouse, another fabulous restaurant that features the "cuisines of the sun." Rooms at the inn range $90-135.

Guest Ranches: One of Montana's most famous and exclusive, **Flathead Lake Lodge** is a well-established, full-service dude ranch that runs close to $1,792 per week, per adult (includes all meals and activities). The ranch is located right on the shores of Flathead Lake, just south of Bigfork, so if you're looking for a family ranch vacation that mixes swimming, fishing, tennis, and windsurfing with the traditional horseback riding and campfire sing-alongs, then this is it. Check out the web page at www.averills.com, or write to P.O. Box 248, Bigfork, MT 59911, tel. (406) 837-4391.

Camping: There are several RV campgrounds near Bigfork: **CJ's RV Resort** is west of Bigfork on Sylvan Drive, **Bigwoods Campground** is a half mile south of Bigfork on Hwy. 35. **Wayfarer State Recreation Area** is a campground just across Hwy. 35 from the main road into Bigfork. It's open mid-May to mid-Sept. and charges $11 per night.

Food and Drink

You can eat very well in Bigfork; people drive for miles to dine here. Reservations are mandatory at most restaurants. Many are closed in the winter.

Casual Meals: If you're just looking for a snack and a place to hang in Bigfork, try **Brookie's Cookies,** 191 Mill St., tel. (406) 837-2447, with espresso and fresh baked goods. For an inexpensive Mexican lunch or dinner, stop by **Del Norte,** at 355 Grande Ave., tel. (406) 837-0076. On the next block down, the **Harbor,** tel. (406) 837-5550, 425 Grand Ave., has a comfortable, easy-going bar and restaurant. The **Garden Bar,** 451 Electric Ave., tel. (406) 837-9914, is a casual place to drop in for a beer. The bar itself is chatty and friendly, and the tables out back provide a quiet place to sit and read in the afternoon. Another friendly, light and airy bar downtown is **Sabo's,** tel. (406) 837-

5251, which features quite a number of Montana microbrews, burgers, and pizza.

Fine Dining: The **Bigfork Inn**, tel. (406) 837-6680, 604 Electric Ave., is one of Bigfork's originals, the place that put Bigfork on the culinary map several decades ago. Open for dinner only, the menu is eclectic, with steaks, pasta, schnitzel, and a showcase duck with local bing cherry and blackcurrent sauce ($16). Overlooking Bigfork Harbor is **Swan River Cafe**, tel. (406) 837-2220, 360 Grand Avenue. The specialty here is pasta or sandwiches for lunch, or steaks, lamb, chicken, and more pasta for dinner ($12-17). On pleasant afternoons, the bayside deck is a great place to relax and have a leisurely meal.

Another well-regarded dinner restaurant in downtown Bigfork is **Showthyme!**, tel. (406) 837-0707, 548 Electric Ave., located in an old brick bank building next door to the Bigfork Playhouse. Food here is subtle, refined, and often innovative. A chicken breast stuffed with a chile rellino is $14, steaks are served with fresh porcini mushrooms and blue cheese. Vegetarian and pasta dishes are also featured; there's outside seating in good weather.

Located in a rambling, art-filled building shaded by trees, the **Bridge Street Gallery Restaurant**, tel. (406) 837-5825, 408 Bridge St., is one of Bigfork's most unique restaurants. The food is excellent, with continental-influenced dishes like wild mushroom- and zucchini-filled streudel and roast chicken stuffed with artichokes and gorgonzola for $12-19. As pleasing is the setting: diners can choose to sit in the gallery or outdoors on a series of garden-like verandahs.

Located in a cozy renovated home near the river is **Tuscany's Ristorante**, tel. (406) 837-6065, 331 Bridge St., with classic Italian cuisine. The **Grill at Eagle Bend**, tel. (406) 837-7305, is located west of Bigfork, and overlooks the Eagle Bend Golf Course. Grilled Pacific seafood, steaks, pasta, and stir-fries ($11-20) are the specialties here.

The establishment that is often considered Montana's best restaurant is in fact two restaurants. The **Coyote Roadhouse Inn**, tel. (406) 837-4250, 602 Three Eagle Ln., and the **Coyote Riverhouse**, tel. (406) 837-1233, 600 Three Eagles Ln., are located across a meadow from each other a few miles west of Bigfork, in Ferndale. The Roadhouse is part of an inn that features six B&B suites and serves fine Northern

Italian cuisine ($15-20) in the dining room, while the Riverhouse, which overlooks the Swan River, is a rustic log structure that features an extensive menu of Cajun, Sicilian, and Mayan dishes, as well as fresh fish specialties. Reservations are required at both restaurants.

A bit farther afield, the **Echo Lake Cafe**, tel. (406) 837-4920, 1195 Hwy. 83, is located near Echo Lake, north of Big Fork. Although the restaurant serves many kinds of food (it's open for all three meals) the specialties here are Dutch and German dishes, prepared by a native-born Netherlander.

Entertainment

Bigfork is known throughout the state for its summer theater productions; the **Bigfork Summer Playhouse** mounts classic Broadway musicals Mon.-Sat. evenings all summer. A brochure and schedule of upcoming plays is available from P.O. Box 456, Bigfork, MT 59911, tel. (406) 837-4886. Recently produced plays include *Follie's, Cabaret,* and *Grease.* The theater is right in the heart of Bigfork, on Electric Avenue.

Bigfork makes a big deal of holidays. Christmas brings lots of lights and conifer boughs, then there's Easter, cherry blossoms in early May, a whitewater festival in mid-May, the playhouse's opening night on the Fourth of July, and the Festival of the Arts in early August . . . it's hard to arrive in Bigfork when there's not *something* going on.

Shopping

Several arts and crafts galleries are in downtown Bigfork. The **Bigfork Art and Cultural Center,** 525 Electric Ave., tel. (406) 837-6927, shares a building with the public library. The **Bridge Street Gallery Restaurant,** 408 Bridge St., tel. (406) 837-5825 (open only during the summer) sells wine by the glass, bottle, or case alongside the art exhibits. **Gary Riecke's studio,** tel. (406) 837-5335, across from the Bigfork Inn at 452 Electric Ave., features western and wildlife art. Sculptor **Bob Stayton** has his studio at 470 Electric Ave., tel. (406) 837-3790, which also displays the work of some 20 other artists. Also on Electric Ave. find the **Kootenai Galleries and Cultural Center,** 573 Electric Ave., tel. (406) 837-4848

Electric Avenue Books, 490 Electric Ave., tel. (406) 837-6072, is a good general bookstore with a congenial atmosphere. It's a pleasant place for a bookstore lover to pass an hour or so on an inclement day; open in summer daily 9 a.m.-10 p.m. **Bay Books and Prints,** on Grand Ave., tel. (406) 837-4646, specializes in books on Montana. Charley Russell and Lewis and Clark buffs will find it especially hard to leave without a book or two. Most of the books are used, with a good selection of rare and out-of-print titles. The place closes up during the winter, when the owner heads to Arizona.

Information
The **chamber of commerce** is at 645 Electric Ave., tel. (406) 837-5888, or write to P.O. Box 237, Bigfork, MT 59911. The **library** is at 525 Electric Ave., with the Art and Cultural Center.

THE SWAN AND BLACKFOOT VALLEYS

The Swan Valley is not as large and broad as the valleys to the west of it, but with two rivers and many lakes, the Swan Range shooting out to the east, and the Mission Mountains stacking up high in the southwest, it is quite beautiful. This valley between the Bob Marshall and Mission Mountains Wilderness Areas is a popular vacation spot for Montanans, but it doesn't draw the crowds that you'll find around Flathead Lake, Bigfork, or Glacier National Park.

Even the amateur geologist can pick out the signs of the glaciers that formed the Swan Valley. Drive down Hwy. 83 and look up at the jagged peaks and high cirques of the Mission and Swan Ranges. Visit the Mt. Morrell Lookout and see some of the glaciers that remain on the Mission Range. Notice the distinctive pothole lakes southeast of Salmon Lake. And the big lakes—Seeley, Salmon, Alva, Placid, and Inez—all were formed when glaciers melted 10,000 years ago.

Wildlife viewing is a special attraction of the Swan Valley and its many lakes. While a canoe is probably the best vehicle for nature watching around the lakes and rivers here, keep your eyes open while you're driving or biking Hwy. 83; there are several designated wildlife-viewing areas, mostly featuring water birds.

Toward the southern end of the valley, Salmon Lake, Seeley Lake, and Lake Alva are nesting sites for loons. These large, white-necklaced, solid-boned birds are known for their eerie wails and their diving abilities. (Loons have been reported to dive up to 200 feet, though usual dives are much more shallow.) During the loons' nesting period (May through mid-June), it is important to stay well away from the nests, especially while fishing on the lakes. The presence of humans can cause the loons to abandon their nests.

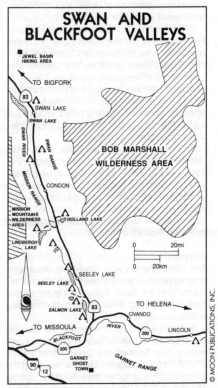

SWAN AND BLACKFOOT VALLEYS

The Timber Industry in the Swan Valley

Highway 83 is Swan Valley Highway. It's a lovely road to drive, but to venture far off it often means an eyeful of clearcuts.

The railroad received land grants here, the checkerboarded square miles that, in many places, were sold or leased to homesteaders. Timber companies bought some of this land in northwestern Montana, but the railroad held onto a lot of it. In 1968, Burlington Northern bought a small Montana timber company called Plum Creek and proceeded to have it harvest the old-growth timber on its land-grant land. The clearcuts here were a mile square—larger than most. Increasing environmental awareness over the past decade has led to smaller clearcuts, and in 1993 Plum Creek began running big ads in western Montana newspapers touting its new environmental guidelines, which avoid such large clearcuts.

With land in Washington, Idaho, and Montana, Plum Creek has become one of the largest timber companies in the Northwest. In Washington, much of its timber harvest is sold as "raw" unmilled logs to foreign countries, especially Japan. The profits from these raw log exports have been sunk into Plum Creek's operations in Idaho and Montana, where the company is able to outbid smaller local outfits. Needless to say, this has put a fatal pressure on many smaller mills.

The large clearcuts in the Swan Valley have threatened watersheds and grizzly habitats. Because of the scope of the logging on private lands, the Flathead National Forest has taken the uncommon precaution of withholding timber sales on national forest tracts adjacent to private lands that have been grossly overcut, even by Forest Service standards.

Recreation

The lakes and the easy access to mountains and wilderness are the main recreational attractions of the Swan Valley, but there's more here than boating, fishing, hiking, hunting, and horseback riding.

Highway 83 through the Swan River Valley is the stage for a popular bicycle tour held every spring. The **Tour of the Swan River Valley** (TOSRV West) starts in Missoula, heads up the Swan Valley, and comes back down through the Mission Valley. Even with summer traffic, Hwy. 83 is a good cycling road with plenty of rest stops and campsites.

The Swan Valley has surprisingly good cross-country skiing in the winter. It's high enough to have snow when it's raining in nearby Missoula.

Anglers stand a chance of hooking bull trout and kokanee salmon in Swan Lake, and Lindbergh and Holland Lakes are also worth fishing for these two species as well as cutthroat and rainbow trout.

SWAN LAKE

The **Swan River National Wildlife Refuge** is a nesting area for bald eagles, blue herons, and other birds. Canada geese, whistling swans, and mallards winter here. Other animals that can be spotted in this marsh, grassland, and river habitat include elk, moose, deer, beaver, river otter, muskrat, and both grizzly and black bear. The refuge is on the Swan River in the northern part of the Swan Valley, near the town of Swan Lake.

Accommodations

At the north end of Swan Lake, the **Swan Lake Recreation Area** includes a Forest Service campground ($7 per night) on the east side of the highway and a day-use area with a swimming beach and a boat launch on the west side. **Point Pleasant State Forest Campground** is a small, free campground seven miles south of Swan Lake.

Burggraf's Countrylane Bed and Breakfast, Rainbow Dr., tel. (406) 837-4608 or (800) 525-3344, is an attractive log B&B with rooms for $75-85. It's on the west side of Swan Lake and has canoes for guests to use.

HOLLAND LAKE AND CONDON

All of the Seeley-Swan valley is lovely, but perhaps no single spot captures the essence of this narrow, lake-filled valley flanked by saw-toothed peaks as Holland Lake. In addition, the lake is graced with a charming old-fashioned resort that has played home to three generations of visitors.

Recreation

Holland Lake is the trailhead for a popular trail into the **Bob Marshall Wilderness Area.** It's about 10 miles from road's end to the wilderness boundary, and most people entering this way go around Upper Holland Lake and up over

JAMES McQUILLEN

a landmark you truly can't miss, at the junction of Highways 200 and 83

Gordon Pass toward the South Fork of the Flathead River.

Across Hwy. 83 from Holland Lake, several roads lead west from Condon toward the **Mission Mountains Wilderness Area.** The Lindbergh Lake road leads to a campground (free, no water) and several trailheads. Lindbergh Lake is, indeed, named for Charles Lindbergh, who camped here not long after his trans-Atlantic flight. Hikers should pick up either a Flathead National Forest map (south half) or a more detailed Mission Mountains Wilderness map. Both are available at the ranger station in Bigfork. Be aware that the Mission Mountains are home to some grizzly bears.

Accommodations
Holland Lake Lodge is at the end of Holland Lake Rd., tel. (406) 754-2282 or (800) 648-8859. It's a downhome, woodsy kind of place, with rooms in the main lodge (bathrooms down the hall) or else in cabins scattered along the lakefront. The Holland Lake Lodge can't compete with the luxury of the new guest ranches that new money is bringing into Montana; however, there's a veneer of charm and rustic comfort at this long-established lodge that only 70 years of history can produce. Meals in the restaurant are very good, especially in high season when the French-born chef is in attendence. You'll want to kill some time in the friendly bar and lounging area. Cabins and lodge rooms range $70-155; the lodge also has canoes for rent ($5 an hour) and offers guided horseback rides as well as longer pack trips into the Bob Marshall Wilderness.

During the winter, the lodge maintains cross-country ski trails and rents skis and snowmobiles. If you visit in the middle of February, you may have the opportunity to rub up against the unique sub-culture of dogsled racing. This is the turnaround point in a 500-mile dogsled race that starts and finishes in Helena. A week or so after the dogsled race there's a big snow dance at the lodge.

The **33—Bar Ranch B&B** is a log lodge on 90 acres in Condon, tel. (406) 754-2820. Lodge rooms run $65-95 d, and a separate housekeeping log chalet is $115 d. If you need corral and pasture for a horse, that, too, is available with a little advance notice.

If you like the beauty of the area but aren't so sure about rustic accommodations, then the **Swan Valley Super 8,** tel. (406) 745-2688, on Hwy. 83 near mile post 46, is a good choice. When you see it, you won't believe that it's a Super 8; chain motels aren't often as attractive as this.

Camping
Holland Lake is the site of one of the prettiest, and sometimes one of the most crowded, Forest Service campgrounds in the area ($11 per night). It's south of Condon and east of Hwy. 83 on Holland Lake Road. The lake contains cutthroat, bull, and rainbow trout and kokanee salmon.

Holland Lake is a popular departure point for horse trips into the Bob Marshall Wilderness Area and, in addition to the traditional Forest Service campground, there's a horse-packers' campground a little farther down the road from the Holland Lake campground. **Owl Creek Packers' Camp** charges a few dollars for a corral fee. At the road's end there are short hiking trails for the casual day-hiker as well as trails leading into the Bob Marshall Wilderness Area. The hike in to Holland Falls is not difficult (three miles for the roundtrip).

Food and Drink

The dining room at **Holland Lake Lodge** is open to the public, and it's well worth a visit. During the summer, when a professional French chef is in residence, the dinners ($10-15) are particularly inspired and feature both steaks and more continental fare like roast duck. But even the simpler lunch menu and winter fare have some treats; the "Gut Bomb" is a locally renowned burger.

The **Hungry Bear Restaurant** south of Condon, tel. (406) 754-2240, is basically a steakhouse, though they do serve pizza and huckleberry daiquiris.

BOB MARSHALL WILDERNESS AREA

The Bob Marshall Wilderness Area was formed in 1964, when 950,000 acres were set aside to remain forever wild. In 1978, the Scapegoat Wilderness was added to the south, and the Great Bear Wilderness to the north of the Bob Marshall. The three contiguous areas include a million and a half acres, falling roughly east of the Swan Valley. The designated wilderness areas receive heavy use during the summer and fall. Backpacking and horse packing are the main summer activities, while hunting predominates in the fall, starting mid-September.

Great Northern Mountain (8,705 feet) is the highest spot in the Great Bear Wilderness. The Middle Fork of the Flathead runs through the Great Bear. The South Fork of the Flathead River starts as Danaher Creek deep in the Bob and flows toward the southern tip of Hungry Horse Reservoir.

The Chinese Wall is an impressive and popular destination. To the west, the earth's crust has thrust upward and forced the eastern part to slide underneath it for a distance of about 20 miles. Haystack Mountain provides a good view of the Chinese Wall from the west.

Access to the Wilderness

Napa Point Road starts near the headquarters of the Swan River State Forest and provides ac-

cess to the **Inspiration Pass** trailhead. It's a challenging but fairly lightly used trail. Sup Creek Campground near the trailhead is a good place to spend the night before embarking on the full-day's hike to Sunburst Lake.

Smith Creek Pass also receives less traffic than many of the other trails that lead into the wilderness. To reach the trailhead, take Falls Creek Rd. (across from the Condon Work Center on Hwy. 83) four miles to Smith Creek Road. Make a sharp right and drive another mile to the trailhead. The climb up the west side of the pass is not easy, and coming down the east side can be even tougher.

Gordon Pass, starting from Holland Lake, is well maintained and heavily used by horse packers and hikers. Big Salmon Lake is a popular destination. Trails come at it from every direction, but the shortest route is from Holland Lake.

Pyramid Pass, with a trailhead near Seeley Lake, leads to the headwaters of the South Fork of the Flathead River. Reach the trailhead by taking Cottonwood Lakes Rd. (just north of the town of Seeley Lake) to Morrell Rd. (No. 467). Turn left on Morrell Rd. and travel for six miles to Pyramid Pass Rd. (No. 4381, a.k.a. Upper Trail Creek Road). Turn right and drive six miles to the trailhead. Pyramid Pass is a steep climb and receives medium to heavy use by both backpackers and horse packers.

From the south, reach the **North Fork of the Blackfoot** trailhead by taking Hwy. 200 to five miles east of Ovando and turning up the North Fork of Blackfoot Road. Drive four miles to North Fork Trailhead Road, and take it seven miles to the trailhead. It's a fairly heavily used trail, with both foot and horse traffic.

Many outfitters run trips into the Bob; the **Seven Lazy P's** guides, based in Choteau, tel. (406) 466-2044, have excellent reputations.

SEELEY LAKE AND VICINITY

Seeley Lake is a town with all services, the only place in the Swan Valley that can really boast that. J.B. Seeley was the first white resident, and the lake and the town that now bear his name support a community of summer homes and dude ranches. The timber industry is a major employer of the year-round residents.

Because of the many moderately priced motels and comfortable, long-established lodges and resorts, Seeley Lake has a long tradition of hosting summer family reunions and weddings. With the lake's water recreation and access to hiking, good restaurants, golf, and just plain relaxation, there's something for everyone to do here.

Recreation

The **Clearwater Canoe Trail** is really a floating and hiking loop trail. There's a three-mile canoe segment from an access point off Hwy. 83 four miles north of the town of Seeley Lake, then a one-mile hike back to the put-in spot. The meandering Clearwater River is a good place to watch birds. Keep a special eye out for loons.

Morrell Lake and **Morrell Falls** are on a national recreation trail north of Seeley Lake via Cottonwood Lakes Rd. to the east of Hwy. 83. It's an easy two-mile hike in to the falls (actually a 100-foot-long lower fall topped by a series of smaller falls and cascades). **Morrell Mountain Lookout** is about 18 miles from the highway via Cottonwood Lakes Rd. (follow it for nine miles) and Road 4365 (follow it for another nine miles). It's a rough drive in a passenger car, and it's wise to check with the ranger station (tel. (406) 677-2233) for current road conditions. The lookout has views of the Mission Mountains, the Swan Range, and the Blackfoot and Clearwater Valleys.

The **Mission Mountains Wilderness Area** falls on the eastern part of the mountains' divide; the western part is the Mission Mountains Tribal Wilderness and is managed by the Confederated Kootenai and Salish Tribes. The wilderness managed by the Forest Service has about 45 miles of trails. While some people do take horses into the Missions, the steep terrain makes hiking more practical and popular. There are a number of trails into the Mission Mountains Wilderness Area. They include Glacier Creek, Cold Lakes, Piper Creek, Fatty Creek, Beaver Creek, Lindbergh Lake, Jim Lakes, Hemlock Creek, Meadow Lake, and Elk Point. Maps of the Mission Mountains Wilderness or the southern half of the Flathead National Forest are available at the ranger station in Bigfork.

Seeley Lake is a good place to **fish** for bass, and it's also stocked with rainbow trout. To the south, Salmon Lake has rainbow and cutthroat trout and kokanee salmon.

Seeley Lake gets pretty snowy in the winter. Most local lodgings are proud to point out that you can ski or snowmobile from your door into a million acres of wilderness. Groomed cross-country ski trails are located one mile northeast of Seeley Lake; the Double Arrow Lodge maintains trails on its property.

The **Double Arrow Lodge** runs an outfitting service, tel. (406) 677-2411 or 677-2317.

Accommodations

Motels: The **Duck Inn Motel,** on Hwy. 83, tel. (406) 677-2335 or (800) 237-9978, is one of the better deals on Seeley Lake, located convenient to services in the little town center. Rates run $31 s, $40 d. **Wilderness Gateway Inn,** tel. (406) 677-2095 or (800) 355-5588, at the south end of town, is a spiffier place than the typical Swan Valley motel, with a hot tub and AAA approval. Rooms are $48 s, $54 d, with a wide range of discounts offered. Pets are okay. About halfway up the lake, the new, log-fronted **Elk Horn Motel and Cafe,** tel. (406) 677-2278, has rooms for $45 s, $50 d. The Elk Horn has access to the lake and to hiking trails.

B&Bs: The **Emily A. Bed & Breakfast,** tel. (406) 677-FISH or (800) 977-4639, at mile marker 20 on Hwy. 83 north of Seeley Lake, is easily one of the most attractive and enjoyable B&Bs in this part of the state. The 11,000-square-foot log home overlooks the Clearwater River and its own tiny lake, and it offers a stunning view of the Mission and Swan peaks. The house sits on 158 acres, which allows opportunities for hiking, fishing, and birdwatching; you can also borrow the family canoe and go for a paddle. In winter there are dogsled rides available and you can explore the cross-country ski trails. The beautiful home is flanked by wide porches, perfect for settling in with a novel or a cup of coffee; guests can also cozy up to the enormous two-story stone fireplace that dominates the central foyer.

There are five guest rooms, two with private bath ($95 a night). There's also a two-bedroom family suite with kitchen facilities ($150). All rooms are nicely decorated and furnished with period furniture. There's also a homestead-era cabin that sleeps six, for rent with advance reservations only ($100), or you can opt to stay in the tepee.

Lodges & Resorts: The most attractive and upscale resort in the Seeley-Swan is **Double Arrow Resort,** P.O. Box 747, Seeley Lake, MT 59868, tel. (406) 677-2777 or (800) 468-0777, a gem of a Swan Valley hideout. The lodge and cabins sit on a bluff overlooking a stream and a meadow filled alternately with golfers and browsing deer; the old lodge and dining room, built in the 1930s, are extremely welcoming and idyllic; you'll want to curl up with a book or watch the sun set from the verandah. The food here is also top-notch.

In high season, rooms in the lodge start at $95 a night, homey cabin rooms at $95 a night and up, and larger log lodges rent for $250-500 a night, and sleep up to 10 people. During the off season, lodge rooms and cabins start at $65, and the larger lodges are discounted accordingly. Breakfast (with the best coffee for miles around) and use of a large indoor pool, jacuzzi, and tennis courts are included.

The Double Arrow is also a good base for recreation. The nine-hole course is a real beauty, shaded by ponderosa pines and cleft by a chattering stream. It offers a full range of horseback activities, as well as mountain bike, canoe, and fishing gear rentals. In winter, the Double Arrow is the center of a series of cross-country trails and also rents snowmobiles; you can even arrange horse-drawn sleigh rides.

North of the town of Seeley Lake, immediately behind the Elkhorn Motel (with which it is associated) but on the lake itself, the **Wapiti Resort,** tel. (406) 677-2775 or (800) 867-5678, is an out-of-the-ordinary cabin resort built on the original town site of Seeley. Besides the newly remodeled guest cabins, there are RV sites—or go western and rent one of the tepees for the night. The restaurant at the Elkhorn is only a quarter mile away. In addition to food and lodging, the Wapiti offers diversion in the form of a rebuilt Old Town, which re-creates a late 19th-century village, and Camp Nine, the re-creation of an old-time logging camp (complete with bunkhouses for rent). Wapiti Resort caters to groups of any size and is a favorite for business getaways and reunions. Cabins rent for $90-130 a night in high season. Hostel-like bunk rooms are $15 per person, and rustic cabins (shower in the showerhouse) are $40 per couple.

On the north shores of Seeley Lakes is **Tamaracks Resort,,** tel. (406) 677-2433 or (800) 447-7216. The resort consists of a central lodge and lakefront cabins with kitchens for $75-95 a night. The resort is right on Seeley Lake, and canoes, fishing boats, and mountain bikes are available for rent. There's also an area for RV and tent campers.

The **Lodges on Seeley Lake** (formerly the Leisure Lodge), on Boy Scout Rd. just west of Seeley Lake townsite, tel. (406) 677-2376, was one of local writer Norman Maclean's favorite spots. Rooms are in rustic cabins, though there's a central lodge with games and easy chairs. Cabins all have bathroom facilities, are all set up for full housekeeping, and come with either propane or wood stoves plus electric baseboards. Rates range $75-145.

Campgrounds: There are three national forest campgrounds around Seeley Lake: **Big Larch** is closest to the highway on the east side of the lake; **River Point** and **Seeley Lake** are farther around the southern and western sides of the lake. Just south of Seeley Lake, the campground at **Placid Lake** is usually less crowded than its northern counterparts.

Food and Drink
In these parts, the **Seasons Restaurant at Double Arrow Resort,** two miles south of Seeley Lake, tel. (406) 677-2777, is the best place to eat. The menu specializes in continental-style cuisine, with dishes like pork tenderloin with black current and port wine sauce or chicken piccatta; there's also fresh seafood, plus a few pasta dishes. Entrees range $12-23; there's also a popular Sunday brunch. It's a pleasure to eat here, and not just because the food is good; the dining room, overlooking the Seeley valley, is beautiful and the service top-notch.

For a good steak without the European sauces, go to **Lindey's Prime Steak House,** tel. (406) 677-9229, located on the lake in the townsite.

Information
The **Seeley Lake Ranger Station** is about three miles north of town, at the northern end of Seeley Lake. Besides the expected Forest Service brochures and maps, a good selection of field guides is sold here.

Services
Seeley Lake has a **clinic** at the north end of town with a nurse on call 24 hours at (408) 627-2277. For **emergency** services, call 911.

With showers as well as a laundromat, **Cher's Wash House,** back behind the mercantile, is a godsend to backpackers just coming out of the Bob Marshall or Mission Mountains Wilderness Areas.

BLACKFOOT VALLEY

The Blackfoot River is well known to local anglers and floaters. It's a lovely, undammed river noted for its variety of fish habitats and its 30 miles of "recreation corridor," which allow easy public access to the river.

Meriwether Lewis traveled along the Blackfoot River after he and William Clark split up on their return trip across Montana. Lewis noted two swans near the mouth of the Clearwater River. You're unlikely to find swans here nowadays, but there is some attractive countryside near the ranching towns of Greenough and Ovando. Read Norman Maclean's classic, *A River Runs Through It,* to get a feel for the place.

Sights
The **Blackfoot-Clearwater Wildlife Management Area,** east of Hwy. 83 and north of Hwy. 200, includes the southern part of Salmon Lake as well as the lower Clearwater River. Near the junction of the two highways the land is prairie, but the northeastern corner of the area rises into forested mountains. The entire area is closed Dec. 1-May 15, but open to hunters and anglers at other times of the year (within the restrictions of hunting season, of course). There are plenty of deer and elk here, and black bear, grouse, and waterfowl.

Garnet Ghost Town is run by the BLM, tel. (406) 329-3914. To reach it, take Hwy. 200 about 24 miles east of Missoula and turn south at Greenough Hill. The rough Garnet access road is 11 miles from the turnoff.

Recreation
Fishing, especially for brown trout, has long been a major preoccupation in the Blackfoot Valley, but past mining and ongoing heavy logging have deteriorated conditions. Rehabilitation efforts are underway and, according to local anglers, beginning to pay off. On the Blackfoot and its tributaries, catch-and-release is required for cutthroat and bull trout. For the more preva-

lent brown and rainbow trout, check current regulations.

The **Clearwater Bridge** is a fishing-access site on Sunset Hill Rd. (which intersects Hwy. 200 just east of Greenough Hill). Farther down Sunset Hill Rd. is another fishing-access site. To reach the **Scotty Brown Bridge,** turn down the gravel road seven miles east of Clearwater Junction on Hwy. 200. It's marked with a fishing-access-site sign, and the road leads to several fishing and camping sites.

Blackfoot River Road has two junctions with Hwy. 200, one just north of the McNamara Bridge (14 miles east of Missoula) and the other at the Roundup Bridge (28 miles east of Missoula). There are a number of fishing-access sites along this road, most with undeveloped campsites nearby.

During the winter, the recreational focus shifts to **snowmobiling.** There are over 200 miles of groomed trails, many of them springing from a hub in Lincoln.

Guest Ranches
The **Lake Upsata Guest Ranch,** tel. (406) 793-5894, (800) 594-7687, or e-mail mail@upsata.com, P.O. Box 6, Ovando MT 59854, is a beautifully located guest ranch that offers more than the usual horseback rides and campfires, although these traditional activities are by no means neglected. The lodge and the eight guest units (each individual log cabin comes with two beds, private baths, and stocked refrigerator) share a great view of a small, private lake backed up against the Swan Mountains. Swimming, canoeing, kayaking, and fishing in Lake Upsata are each right outside your cabin door, and the ranch also sponsors a number of naturalist activities that include discussions of local wildlife and ecology; field trips are planned to local ghost towns, nature reserves, and areas of natural historic interest. And of course there are the horses: trail rides take place daily. Other activities include free use of mountain bikes, tubing down the Blackfoot River, and hanging out in the tree house or tepee. Whitewater raft trips or guided fishing expeditions on area rivers can be arranged with local outfitters (separate charge).

At Lake Upsata Guest Ranch children and families aren't simply tolerated, they are catered to. Many activities are planned expressly with kids in mind; after a week on the lake, your kids won't want to go back home.

During the high season, the ranch asks for one-week minimum stay; during the fall and spring, three-day minimums are possible. Prices are $220 a day adult, $190 for children, which includes all meals, activities, and lodging.

For food in this stretch of the Blackfoot, there's a collection of truck stops at Clearwater Junction, where Hwys. 83 and 200 join, though the restaurants at Seeley Lake are just 15 miles north. In Ovando, **Trixie's Antler Bar** has a far-reaching reputation as a *real* Montana bar, the kind that posts a sign bidding customers to leave their guns outside.

Outfitters

The Ovando area offers good west-side access to the Scapegoat and Bob Marshall Wilderness Areas. For an outfitted packtrip into these stunningly beautiful areas, contact the **White Tail Ranch Outfitters,** tel. (406) 793-5666 or (800) 987-5666, Ovando, MT, 59854. During the summer, a number of different trips are offered to different destinations in the wilderness areas; these book up fast, so contact the outfitters as early as possible. Two-to four-day trips are $210 a day, while longer trips are $190 a day. White Tail Ranch also offers guest ranch accommodations with horseback riding for $120.

Lincoln

There was a gold strike here, at roughly the same time in 1865 that President Lincoln was assassinated—hence the name of the gold-laced Lincoln Gulch and of the valley's major town. There's not too much to Lincoln today, but you'll be happy to see the town's motels and cafes if you're caught in bad weather or grow weary on the Hwy. 200 slog between Missoula and Great Falls.

If you find yourself in Lincoln in the winter, and you're looking for something to do, try dogsledding. **Montana Mush,** tel. (406) 362-4988 or 362-4004, offers a chance to ride through the southern edge of the Scapegoat Wilderness on a dogsled. Rates are $30 an hour.

Accommodations and Food

Lincoln has several motels, and while none of them are fancy or expensive, most are serviceable and have charming names and friendly proprietors. **Lincoln Lodge Hotel, Restaurant, Bar, and Casino** is off the highway on Sleepy Hollow Ln., tel. (406) 362-4396. The name sort of says it all. Two people can share a room for $30 here. **Leeper's Motel,** tel. (406) 362-4333, has separate units in a grove of trees just back from Hwy. 200. The **Three Bears,** tel. (406) 362-4355, has log cabins, and pets are okay. Both Leeper's and Three Bears charge around $45 d. Every room in the similarly priced brick **Blue Sky Motel,** tel. (406) 362-4450, boasts a fireplace.

There's not much in the way of restaurants, but Lincoln has a sprinkling of cafes plus the old and venerable **Lambkin's,** tel. (406) 362-4271, a good place for such standard fare as chicken-fried steak. The **Seven Up Supper Club,** east of town on Hwy. 200, tel. (406) 362-4255, is a good log-lodge western steakhouse, open Tues.-Sat. 5-10 p.m., Sunday 2-10 p.m.

NORTH OF FLATHEAD LAKE

KALISPELL

There's something that makes Kalispell more likeable than the sum of its parts. Perhaps the synergy starts with the name. It rolls off the tongue in just the right way, and it *means* something . . . it's the Kalispel Indian word for "Prairie above the Lake."

Drive around northwestern Montana for a while, and by the time you pull into Kalispell you'll feel that you're in a real city. Indeed, Kalispell, the seat of Flathead County with a population of roughly 16,000 and growing fast, is the metropolitan center of northwestern Montana. On a summer afternoon, the intersection of Highways 2 and 93 has the closest thing to a traffic jam you'll ever find in the whole state.

Kalispell is the commercial center for the booming "resort-ification" of northwestern Montana, though like too many other Montana towns, the locals seem to measure success by the length and relentlessness of suburban commercial strips. Kalispell once had a pleasant, hippy back-to-the-earth nonchalance, but it's now about real estate, decor, and New West art galleries.

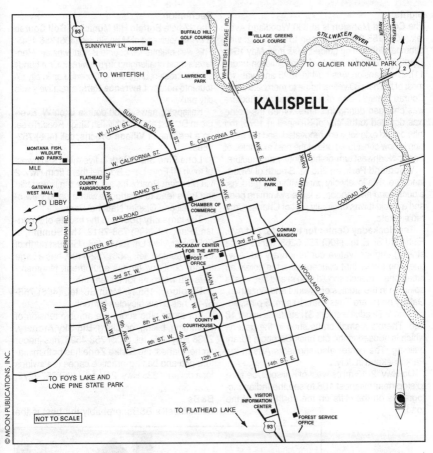

KALISPELL

The Land

Kalispell is on the Flathead River near where the Stillwater and Whitefish Rivers converge with it (elev. 2,930 feet), about seven miles above Flathead Lake. It's at the upper end of the Flathead Valley, and the mountains visible to the north are part of the Whitefish Range; to the east, the Swan Range rises. Between Kalispell and Flathead Lake, the Flathead River is as convoluted as the folds of a brain.

History

In the days before the railroad, Flathead Lake steamers made it up as far as Demersville, a now nonexistent town four miles southeast of Kalispell.

When transcontinental railroad building was underway, Charles Conrad, a Fort Benton freight kingpin, got a hot tip from the head of the Great Northern Railway, Jim Hill, to move west to the Flathead area. Conrad did, and in 1891 the Great Northern arrived. The existing towns of Demersville and Ashley (half a mile west of present-day Kalispell) picked up and moved to form a new town, Kalispell. Conrad prospered and became a uniquely Montanan model citizen, keeping his own buffalo herd (on what is now known as Buffalo Hill, just north of downtown).

Sights

The **Conrad Mansion** is at 330 Woodland Ave., tel. (406) 755-2166. It's open to the public with genuinely interesting guided tours from May 15 to October 15 ($7 for adults, $1 for children under 11). The mansion was built in 1895 and was, for most of the next 80 years, home to members of the Conrad family. None of the original architecture was changed during this time. When the home was donated to the city of Kalispell in 1975, the interior and exterior were renovated, and the mansion is now considered one of the best examples of Pacific Northwest turn-of-the-century architecture.

Woodland Park, on 2nd St. E north of Woodland Ave., is a lovely city park, with rose gardens, a duck pond and lagoon, a large swimming pool, and a track. It was originally part of Charles Conrad's estate.

The **Hockaday Center for the Arts**, 2nd Ave. E and 3rd St. E, tel. (406) 755-5268, hangs some striking and innovative contemporary art. Anyone who thinks that conceptual art is solely an urban phenomenon should stop in and see what's going on in the studios of Twodot and Bozeman. Gallery hours are Tues.-Sat. 10 a.m.-5 p.m.; admission is $2 adult, seniors $1, students under 18 free. There's a small crafts shop in the gallery, which is housed in the old brick Carnegie library building. The center also sponsors Arts in the Park weekend in July.

On Hwy. 2, 13 miles west of Kalispell, be sure to stop near milepost 108 to see the Indian pictographs on the cliffs on the north side of the road.

Recreation

The 27-hole **Buffalo Hill Municipal Golf Course** is at the north end of Main St., tel. (406) 756-4545. This well-maintained course is northwestern Montana's most challenging. In the winter, it's a handy spot for cross-country skiing. Continue an in-city ski tour into nearby **Lawrence Park,** a relatively wild city park.

Kalispell's newest golf course is on W. Evergreen Dr., just east of Whitefish Stage Road. To set up a tee time at **Village Greens,** call (406) 752-4666.

Lone Pine State Park is five miles southwest of town off Foys Lake Rd. (get there from Hwy. 2 via Meridian Road). It's set up on a hill, and hiking trails lead to overlooks with a good view of Kalispell and Glacier National Park.

The large **city pool** is in the middle of Woodland Park, tel. (406) 758-7812. **The Summit,** at 205 Sunnyview Ln. (on Buffalo Hill just north of the city center), tel. (406) 752-4100, has a large indoor pool and fitness equipment. Nonmembers are welcome for a small fee.

Bikology, 155 N. Main St., tel. (406) 755-6748, has a few bicycles for rent.

For those who scorn the aerobic tension of swimming, biking, or hiking, **Big Sky Archery,** 2333 Hwy. 2 E, tel. (406) 752-4526, has indoor archery lanes; the **Strike Zone** has both miniature golf and batting-practice cages (24 swings for a dollar), 1335 Hwy. 2 W, tel. (406) 257-7272.

B&Bs

Of Kalispell's B&Bs, probably the best is the

The Conrad Mansion, built in 1895, is considered one of the best examples of Pacific Northwest turn-of-the-century architecture

FRANK JEWELL

Keith House Inn, 538 5th Ave. E., tel. (406) 752-7913, a brick mansion built in 1911, with six guest rooms, all with private baths. The entire house has been meticulously restored and is filled with antiques and art. Rooms are $85-165.

Located east of Kalispell in the farming community of Creston, **Creston Inn,** tel. (406) 755-7517 or (800) 257-7517, 70 Creston Rd., offers four guest rooms in a renovated 1920s farmhouse. Each of the rooms ($80-95) has a private bath; the setting, with the Rockies looming above a stream-fed meadow, is spectacular.

Hotels and Motels

During the summer, Kalispell's lodgings fill up quickly with people on their way to and from Glacier National Park. It's wise to reserve in advance. In winter, expect much lower rates—sometimes as much as half the summer rate listed here.

Kalispell's lodgings are generally of good quality, though most rooms are found in large motel complexes that flank the busy highway intersections. There is one noteworthy exception. The **Kalispell Grand Hotel,** tel. (406) 755-8100 or (800) 858-7422, 100 Main St., is a beautifully renovated hotel right in downtown Kalispell. While the lobby and sitting areas preserve a comfortable turn-of-the-century glamour, the guest rooms are very nicely furnished and fully modern, with gleaming and large bathrooms. Pets are okay and there's free parking. The Grand is also convenient to downtown dining, shopping, and gaming. Double rooms start at $75.

There are a couple of inexpensive older motels with perfectly comfortable rooms in the $45 d range; small dogs are okay at both. The **Vacationer Motel** is at 285 7th Ave. NE, tel. (406) 755-7144 or (800) 833-0328. The **White Birch Motel,** 17 Shady Ln., tel. (406) 752-4008, has kitchenettes available. The motel sits on seven acres just east of Kalispell. Also a good value is the **Kalispell Super 8,** 1341 1st Ave. E, tel. (406) 755-1888 or (800) 800-8000, with rooms at $50 s, $60 d. **Motel 6,** 1540 Hwy. 93 S., tel. (406) 752-6355, rates are $42 s, $48 d.

You'll find more extras at the following. The **Aero Inn,** 1830 Hwy. 93 S., tel. (406) 755-3798 or (800) 843-6114, $63 s, $72 d, has an indoor pool, hot tub, and sauna. Kitchenettes are available, pets are okay in smoking rooms, and there's a free continental breakfast.

Glacier Gateway Motel, 264 N. Main St., tel. (406) 755-3330, has rooms beginning at $70 d; kitchenettes available. **Best Western Outlaw Inn,** 1701 Hwy. 93 S., tel. (406) 755-6100 or (800) 237-7445, with rooms at $69-109 s/d, has indoor pools, a casino and restaurant adjoining, health club, and small convention facilities. Another high quality convention-style hotel is **Cavanaugh's at Kalispell Center,** 20 N. Main St., tel. (406) 752-6660 or (800) 843-4667. Rooms are $95 s, $105 d, and facilities include an indoor pool, sauna, and hot tub. Cavanaugh's is also connected to a large downtown shopping mall.

The **DoubleTree Inn,** 1330 Hwy. 2. W, tel. (406) 755-6700 or (800) 547-8010, $69 s/d and up, is a large motel complex with heated pool, hot tub, irons and ironing boards in all rooms, casino and restaurant, free continental breakfast and in-room coffee makers. Both a motel and an entertainment center, **Diamond Lil Inn,** 1680 Hwy. 93 S., tel. (406) 752-3467 or (800) 843-7301, offers rooms at $70 s, $74 d. There's a large casino and restaurant on site, as well as a heated outdoor pool, outdoor hot tubs, and laundry facilities; dogs are okay, and children under 12 are free.

Equally all-encompassing, the **Ramada Klondike Inn,** 4834 Hwy. 93 S, tel. (406) 857-2200, offers rooms at $79 s, $89 d. This huge complex is south of Kalispell near Flathead Lake and Somers, and includes a casino, pool, and restaurant.

Kalispell's newest hotel is the **Hampton Inn,** 1140 US 2 W., tel. (406) 755-7900 or (800) 426-7866. Facilities include pool and hot tub, and rates (starting at $83 s/d) include a continental breakfast.

Guest Ranches: One of the most popular guest ranches in this part of the state is the **Hargrave Cattle & Guest Ranch,** tel. (406) 858-2284 or (800) 933-0696, 300 Thompson River Rd., Marion, MT 59925. Located 20 miles west of Kalispell, this is an old-fashioned cattle ranch that takes guests in on the side, so don't expect the Hargrave's ranch to have the sophisticated burnish of some of the new resort guest ranches. But this is the real thing: 350 cattle live here, there's ranch work to do, and you're welcome to join in on the branding, calving, and livestock trailing. You're also welcome to use the ranch as a base for exploring the area, planning fishing trips, hiking and the like. It's a little bit country at the Hargraves, and this is a very friendly, welcoming place to come if you'd like to spend time at a real ranch with special civilized touches.

During the summer season, weeklong minimums are required; rates are $1,050 a week, which includes all horseback riding and lessons, an overnight campout, all meals, lodging, and use of the ranch facilities. From October 15 to May 1, the ranch is open to B&B guests on a daily basis ($80 per couple). Lodging is either in log cabins or in the ranch "headquarters" building.

Camping

There's not much in the way of peaceful tent camping in Kalispell, but there are a handful of RV-style campgrounds right in town. **Greenwood Trailer Village,** on Hwy. 2 just east of its intersection with Hwy. 93, tel. (406) 257-7719, has some tent sites. The tent fee is $10.50 per night and the campground is open April through October. **Glacier Pine RV Campground** (with 75 tent sites) is one mile east of Kalispell on Hwy. 35, tel. (406) 752-2760. Their season parallels Greenwood's, with a fee of $10 per night. **Rocky Mountain Hi** costs $8 per night and is open year-round. Go four miles east of Kalispell on Hwy. 2, then follow the signs, tel. (406) 755-9573. **Lake Blaine Resort** is nearby, at the junction of Hwys. 2 and 35.

There are some less developed campgrounds a little farther from town. One option is Whitefish Lake State Park. To get to **Ashley Lake State Recreation Area,** go 16 miles west of Kalispell on Hwy. 2, then 13 miles north on the county road that starts around milepost 105. It's $11 a night for a relatively peaceful campground with running water, pit toilets, and fishing for cutthroat and kokanee. The campground is officially open from mid-May to mid-September. Still farther west of Kalispell (32 miles) is the **McGregor Lake** Forest Service campground. Even though it's on the edge of a burn, it's not a bad spot, and it has a few relatively isolated tent sites. Lake trout are the big fish here, but kokanee salmon, cutthroat and brook trout, and yellow perch are also caught.

Food and Drink

If a full breakfast isn't necessary, head to the **Montana Coffee Traders,** tel. (406) 756-2326, 326 W. Center St., for espresso drinks.

If you're staying downtown, **Trattoria on Main,** at 34 Main St., tel. (406) 7555-5000, is a good place to know about. Formerly the well-loved Norm's, a combination of newsstand and soda fountain, the Trattoria thankfully didn't change many of the restaurant's physical elements when the menu changed. The newsstand is still in place, as is the soda fountain, although now the restaurant is in the business of turning out good quality pasta and pizza. Another good downtown bet for a pasta dinner is **Café Vinny's,** 120 Main St., tel. (406) 756-3061, located in the front of a pasta-making shop. Kalispell's crown jewel of fun, **Moose's Saloon,** 173 N. Main St., tel. (406) 755-2338, is a place to spend an evening throwing peanut shells on the floor while drinking beer and listening to local musicians. Legend has it that this is where Evel Knievel came up with the idea to blast across Hells Canyon on his motorcycle. Pizza is the food of choice at the Moose.

Dos Amigos offers dishes beyond the usual Mexican standards, with a wide selection of more inventive Southwestern-style dishes. The menu is large, ranging from paella to cajun curried ribs to grilled red snapper with cilentro pesto; most dishes are around $10. It's open for lunch and dinner right downtown at 25 2nd Ave. W, tel. (406) 752-2711.

The **Alley Connection,** next door to the Kalispell Grand Hotel on 1st St. W, is a cozily elegant steakhouse for lunch or dinner.

For serious fine dining, Kalispell's best restaurant is **Café Max,** 121 Main St., tel. (406) 755-7687. The changing menu is very cosmopolitan, and filled with the kinds of dishes—duck breast, veal, fresh seafood, as well as game—that you don't often associate with Montana restaurants. Service is very professional, and desserts are a wonder. Entrees range $15-22. Reservations are recommended, and when you call make sure to ask if the place has received its liquor license yet; otherwise, inquire about bringing in your own wine in a brown paper bag. Montana's archaic liquor laws make it difficult for small independently owned restaurants to get licenses (even to sell just wine and beer). Additionally, the powerful Tavern Owners Association, sees to it that all available liquor licenses go to casinos, not restaurants.

Shopping

Kalispell's a big enough city to do some serious stocking up in; indeed it's the commercial center for this part of the state. There's also some fairly interesting recreational shopping to be done here.

For high-quality local crafts, **Hockaday Center for the Arts** at 2nd Ave. E. and 3rd St., tel. (406) 755-5268, has a small crafts shop tucked into its gallery space. **Montana Expressions,** 17 Main St., tel. (406) 756-8555, is a furniture and interior design store steeped in western rusticity—look here for hewn-log beds and ethnic textiles. There's even more next door at **Ciao,** tel. (406) 755-7373, a furniture gallery and design center that features that "Northern Rockies Rustic" look that's prevalent in design magazines.

Sportsman and Ski Haus, tel. (406) 755-6484, is a large store at 40 E. Idaho St. (right by the intersection of Hwys. 2 and 93). It's open every day and has a good selection of sporting, skiing, and camping goods. You can rent just about any kind of sporting equipment imaginable, from wetsuits to mountain bikes to tennis racquets. **Rocky Mountain Outfitters,** 135 Main St., tel. (406) 752-2446, has high-quality camping and rock-climbing equipment. Both Sportsman and Rocky Mountain stock well-made clothing by such companies as Patagonia and Woolrich.

If your taste runs more to traditional western wear, buy the real goods at **Western Outdoor Store,** 48 Main St., tel. (406) 756-5818.

Books West, at First and Main downtown, tel. (406) 752-6900, is a good general bookstore with a great selection of nature guides, fiction by Montana and regional authors, and USGS maps.

Events

For almost two weeks in mid-July, the entire Flathead region hosts the **Flathead Festival,** a music festival that emphasizes jazz but usually includes folk and country musicians.

The **Northwest Montana Fair** is held at the fairgrounds in Kalispell in mid-August every year. Call (406) 752-6166 for exact dates.

Information

The **chamber of commerce** is downtown at 15 Depot Loop, tel. (406) 758-2800, Kalispell, MT 59901. During the summer, a **visitor information center** is headquartered on Hwy. 93 at the south end of town. They have more of a spectrum of information than the chamber of commerce does, plus they're located right next door to the **Flathead National Forest Headquarters,** tel. (406) 755-5401. The Forest Service office has a variety of pamphlets and fliers, plus some books for sale from the Glacier Natural History Association.

The regional office of the **Montana Dept. of Fish, Wildlife, and Parks** is at 490 N. Meridian Rd., tel. (406) 752-5501 or, for a 24-hour recording, (406) 257-4630.

The Flathead Chapter of the **Montana Wilderness Association** can be reached at P.O. Box 543, Kalispell, MT 59903, tel. (406) 755-6304. The **public library** is at 247 1st Ave. East.

Services

Dial 911 for fire, police, or medical emergency help. **Kalispell Regional Hospital,** tel. (406) 752-5111, is the biggest and most complete hospital until you get to Missoula. It's on Sunnyview Ln., off Hwy. 93 just north of downtown.

The **post office** is on the corner of 1st Ave. W and 3rd Street.

The **Washing Well Laundry,** 710 W. Idaho St. (Hwy. 2 W), tel. (406) 257-0561, is one conveniently located laundromat. There's also a laundromat in the Fred Meyer store on Hwy. 2 E, tel. (406) 755-2002.

Transportation

Glacier International Airport, eight miles northeast of Kalispell on Hwy. 2, is served by Delta, Northwest, and Horizon.

Rental Cars: At the airport, you'll find **Avis,** tel. (406) 257-2727; **Budget,** tel. (406) 755-7500; **Hertz,** tel. (406) 756-8686 or (800) 654-3131; and **National,** tel. (406) 257-7144 or (800) 227-7368. **U-Save,** 1010 E. Idaho St. (at Balding's Cars and Trucks) has service to the airport, tel. (406) 257-1900 or (800) 262-1958. **Sears** is downtown at 191 7th Ave. NE, tel. (406) 755-7507.

Intermountain Transport is at 1301 Hwy. 93 in Kalispell. A bus leaves for Missoula (where it connects with the I-90 Greyhound) each morning at 10:30; the bus from Missoula comes in at 1:30 p.m.

WHITEFISH AND VICINITY

Whitefish (pop. 5,793) calls itself the "recreation capital of Montana." It's a likely enough claim, what with the town's 3,033-foot setting at the base of a major ski mountain some 40 miles from Glacier National Park. To orient yourself in Whitefish, it may help to realize that Hwy. 93,

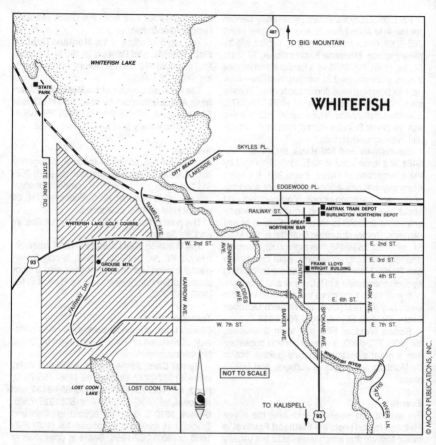

WHITEFISH

usually a north-south road, turns to the west as it heads up from Whitefish.

Success as a tourist destination has brought a number of changes to this once sleepy hamlet. Big Mountain is developing into one of the West's major ski areas, and this area of northwestern Montana now attracts a lot of wealth and celebrities.

History

Fur trading and logging brought the first white settlers to this area, but it took the railroad to bring about permanent and stable settlements. In 1893 Whitefish became a division point for the Great Northern Railway. Railroad workers flooded into town, and the bars followed. In 1904 Whitefish supported 14 saloons. Central Avenue was a muddy rut then; the Cadillac Hotel, at the corner of Central and Railway, had a wooden boardwalk built on stilts to avoid the mud.

Whitefish was originally densely forested. It took six years to clear land for the city, and for many years tree stumps poked up in the middle of streets, giving the town the nickname of Stumptown.

The railroad activity helped loggers to prosper but thwarted the trapping trade, although trapping for beaver, mink, and muskrat continued around Whitefish until the 1960s.

Sights

Most people come here for the proximity to Big Mountain and Glacier National Park. In fact, that's why most of the local people ended up here. It's the sort of place a skier or avid outdoorsperson moves to.

Surprisingly enough, Whitefish has a **Frank Lloyd Wright building,** but only the most fervid architectural buff would find it particularly interesting. It's on Central Avenue between 3rd and 4th streets, and looks like any old one-story modern office building, currently housing insurance offices and opticians.

The old **Great Northern depot** is styled along the same lines as the Glacier Park chalet hotels. It is currently used by Burlington Northern and Amtrak, and also houses the Whitefish Chamber of Commerce, Museum, and an espresso bar. It's definitely worth a stop for visitor information and a cup of coffee.

Big Mountain Ski and Summer Resort

With about 300 inches of snow a year, 64 runs (the longest of which is 2.5 miles), and the pleasant, Amtrak-accessible town of Whitefish at the bottom of the hill, it's easy to see why people come from all over to ski Big Mountain. The elevation at the summit of Big Mountain is 7,000 feet, the base is at 4,600 feet, and the vertical drop is 2,300 feet. The season runs from Thanksgiving through Easter, and there are lights for night skiing. Lift tickets cost $40 for adults, $27 for ages seven to 18 and seniors, $20 for children 12 and under. Night skiing is cheaper: $12 for all ages. If you haven't been to Big Mountain for a while, you'll be surprised to see how it's expanded. An entire resort community has built up around the ski area, with several hotels and condominiums, a handful of restaurants, a grocery store, a day-care center, and ski shops. For information on the ski area and ski passes, call (406) 862-1900, or write Big Mountain, Box 1400, Whitefish, MT 59937. For information on lodging at Big Mountain call (800) 858-5439. The web address is www.bigmtn.com.

The **Big Mountain Nordic Center** is just below the main parking lot. Its 15-km (10-mile) trail network is rather challenging for both winter skiing (including skating) and summer mountain biking.

In summer, several of the lodges remain open and provide relatively inexpensive lodging to visitors. Mountain bikes are available for rent, and there are 7.5 miles of dirt trails in the village area. The resort's tennis courts are free to overnight guests. The Glacier Chaser chairlift remains in operation and takes people to the top of Big Mountain for $10 adult, $8 senior or youth (six and under are free). Lunch is available at the cafeteria at the top. Old West Adventures offers a variety of horseback trail rides, wagon rides, and overnight camp trips; some trips include meals. Contact the information center for details, tel. (406) 862-2900.

Other Recreation

The Forest Service (irregularly) maintains cross-country ski trails at **Round Meadows,** about 10 miles northwest of town. Take Hwy. 93 north to Star Meadows Road. A trail map is available from the ranger station in Whitefish or the Forest Service office in Kalispell. The elevation here is relatively low (approximately 3,300 feet), and good skiing is generally limited to late December through early March. Once the snow melts, mountain bikers take to the trails here.

Dogsledding is another winter sport to consider if you want a day away from the skis. **Dog Sled Adventures,** tel. (406) 881-2275, operates out of Olney about 20 miles north of Whitefish. A good day trip is the 12-mile loop through the Stillwater State Forest.

Even during the summer, there's plenty of reason to make the steep, tortuous drive (or bike ride, for the ambitious and low-geared) to Big Mountain. The **Danny On Trail** leads from the main parking lot 3.8 miles up to the summit. There are plenty of huckleberries on the trail late in the summer, and spur trails offer wildflower meadows and vistas of the Flathead Valley. For $9 ($7 for children and seniors) you can buy a ride up on the chairlift (and eat lunch at the mountain-top cafeteria) and either hike or ride back down. The thrifty will appreciate the free ride down on the chairlift that's available to those who make the hike up. The entire trail is usually clear of snow from July through mid-September.

The Forest Service has an information center in the basement of the Summit House and, on Tuesday afternoons in the summer, hosts an environmental-lecture series.

Glacier Cyclery, 336 2nd St., tel. (406) 862-6446, has a good-looking fleet of mountain bikes for rent at $23 per day, $16 for a half day. Hours are Mon.-Fri. 9 a.m.-6 p.m., Saturday 9 a.m.-

5 p.m. The staff will provide you with a hand-drawn bike map of the area and suggest rides; they also sell Flathead National Forest maps with good mountain-bike roads highlighted. During the summer, Glacier Cyclery stables a fleet of mountain bikes on Big Mountain.

Whitefish Stage Road, about a mile east of Hwy. 93 (via Hwy. 40), is a good bicycle route to Kalispell. Even though there's not much of a shoulder, it doesn't have a lot of traffic if you avoid the rush hours.

The best bets for summer **swimming** in Whitefish are **City Beach** or the beach at **Whitefish Lake State Recreation Area** ($4 for day use). Boat tours of the lake start at City Beach.

As befits the recreational capital of Montana, Whitefish has two golf courses. If you're a duffer, or just want a casual, inexpensive round of golf, you'll probably be most comfortable at the nine-hole **Par 3 on 93,** tel. (406) 862-7273. If you've got a good swing and the right clothes, the **Whitefish Lake Golf Course** is one of the best in the state. This country club-like 36-hole course is on Hwy. 93 W, across from the Grouse Mountain Lodge, tel. (406) 862-4000.

Drive north to fish in **Upper Stillwater Lake,** off Hwy. 93 just north of Olney. The lake reportedly has bull, cutthroat, rainbow, and brook trout; perch; and northern pike in it. There's a small undeveloped lakeside campground.

For guided fishing trips, call or stop by **Lakestream Flyshop,** 15 Central Ave., tel. (406) 862-1298. Fish Whitefish Lake with outfitter Jim Crumal, tel. (406) 862-5313, on his 24-foot boat. He also runs two-hour boat tours of Whitefish Lake ($75 for up to eight people).

Whitefish B&Bs

Most of Whitefish's accommodations are either along the long Hwy. 93 strip south of town, or up at Big Mountain Ski Resort. Quality is quite high, as are prices, and be sure to reserve early. Ask motels if they have ski packages, which include lift tickets.

The **Good Medicine Lodge,** at 537 Wisconsin Ave., tel. (406) 862-5488 or (800) 860-5488, is especially attractive, a cross between a small inn and a B&B. While a bid breakfast buffet is provided and there are pleasant common rooms, the atmosphere is low-key and you don't feel as if you need to whisper as you pad around. The nine rooms, with vaulted wood ceilings, upscale-rustic

decor, and great views, run $85-95 s, $95-115 d ($10 less in the winter). There's also a Master Suite ($145) and a Family Suite ($195). Some rooms are handicapped accessible, all rooms have telephones, and there's a hot tub and a guest laundry. The lodge has adopted a "green" policy, and recycles and conserves water. Although the Good Medicine Lodge was recently built, it is located in an older residential neighborhood on the way to Big Mountain.

For comfort in a historic, beautifully restored home, the **Garden Wall Bed and Breakfast,** tel. (406) 862-3440 or (888) 530-1700, conveniently located at 504 Spokane Ave., is a good choice. The home was built in the 1920s, with strong Arts-&-Crafts influences; fabrics, tiles, wall coverings, and art have been carefully selected to evoke the era. Most of the furniture is native to 1920s Montana, which lends a specifically regional atmosphere to the graciously decorated rooms. Modern considerations haven't been neglected, however, and all rooms have private baths. Both the owner and the innkeeper have trained as professional chefs, and the breakfasts are renowned. Double rooms go for $85-105, a suite for four is available for $175. The innkeepers are avid outdoorspeople and are happy to help plan excursions.

South of Whitefish, along Hwy. 40, is another excellent B&B. **LaVilla Montana,** P.O. Box 4390, Whitefish, MT 59937, tel. (406) 892-0689 or (800) 652-8455, is a spacious and beautifully decorated home with outgoing and gracious hosts. The four guest rooms are subtly decorated in a western style: the common areas, which include a fireplace-dominated kitchen, a library, and two-story great room (leading to a large redwood deck and hot tub), are equally filled with fine art and top-notch furniture. There's a two-bedroom suite with a full kitchen that sleeps up to four; the entire establishment is air-conditioned. The innkeepers are great cooks and their sense of hospitality extends from daily fresh towels and linen to impromptu chats with fresh squeezed lime rickies and locally brewed beers on the back deck. The inn sits on 10 acres of meadow between Columbia Falls and Whitefish. Rates begin at $80 a night.

Whitefish Hotels, Motels, and Cabins

Don't be confused: in the following addresses, Spokane Ave. is the same as Hwy. 93, which can be a nightmarishly busy street. Unfortunately, almost all the lodgings in Whitefish are located here. Following are summer high season rates; there's usually a slight reduction in the winter rates.

The **Super 8,** 828 Spokane Ave., tel. (406) 862-8255 or (800) 800-8000, $75 s 79 d, has a hot tub, and small pets are okay. **Quality Inn Pine Lodge,** 920 Spokane St., tel. (406) 862-7600 or (800) 305-7463, $95 s, 100 d, is an attractive motel with an indoor/outdoor pool, jacuzzi, exercise room, and some rooms with kitchenettes and fireplaces. **Lazy Bear Lodge,** 6390 Hwy. 93 S., tel. (406) 862-4020 or (800) 888-4479, $99 s, $109 d, has an indoor pool with a 90-foot water slide and two hot tubs.

Chalet Motel, 6430 Hwy. 93 S, tel. (406) 862-5581 or (800) 462-3266, $60 s, $75 d offers an indoor pool, sauna, and hot tub. **Best Western Rocky Mountain Lodge,** 6510 Hwy. 93 S, tel. (406) 862-2569 or (800) 862-2569, has rates from $109 s or d. This is one of the newest Whitefish accommodations, with a grand lobby, continental breakfast, pool, hot tub, exercise room, and guest laundry. Available are attractive mini-suites with fireplace, jacuzzi tub, microwave, refrigerator and wet bar.

Mountain Holiday Motel, 6595 Hwy. 93 S, tel. (406) 862-2548 or (800) 543-8064, $55 s $65 d, is a relatively good deal with indoor and outdoor pools, sauna, and hot tub. The **Duck Inn,** 1305 Columbia Ave., tel. (406) 862-3825 or (800) 344-2377, $49-109 s/d, is a small intimate inn overlooking the river, with fireplaces, theme rooms, complimentary breakfast, and an intimate and friendly ambiance.

If you're heading to Montana hoping to stay in your own log cabin, then consider the **North Forty Resort,** tel. (406) 862-7740 or (800) 775-1740, 3765 Hwy. 4 W, between Whitefish and Columbia Falls. The recently constructed deluxe cabins (there are nearly 30 of them) are located in a quiet, pine-shaded grove, and all have full kitchens, baths, and fireplaces; the furniture is handcrafted in Montana. All cabins sleep at least five, and others sleep up to eight. Hot tubs and a sauna are also available; children under 13 free. Rates are $79-125 d in summer and Christmas holidays, dropping to $59-89 in the off season.

Whitefish Condos and Home Rentals
To rent a condo on Whitefish Lake, call **Bay Point on the Lake,** (406) 862-2331 or (800) 327-2108.

Rates for these comfortable and quiet lodgings vary seasonally, and there are eight different room configurations with three different luxury levels available, so it's best to call and discuss your needs. Condos begin at $109-169 double in summer high season. For a vacation home rental, call **Five Star Rentals & Property Management,** at (406) 862-5994.

Resorts: The Grouse Mountain Lodge, across from the golf course at 1205 Hwy. 93 W, is a large recreation, convention, lodging, and restaurant complex, and is the deluxe place to stay in Whitefish. Summer and winter rates are $125 s/d; spring and fall, rates drop to $84. For this, you get access to a pool, a sauna, three hot tubs, tennis courts, and pleasant rooms that look out onto a golf course rather than onto a highway strip; tel. (406) 862-3000 or (800) 321-8822. The restaurant in the lodge is good, and it's an easy stroll across to the excellent steakhouse in the club house.

Staying on the Slopes at Big Mountain
If you plan to stay at Big Mountain, you'll generally pay for the convenience of skiing to and from your door, but there are frequent deals, especially for groups. The easiest way to arrange for lodgings here is to call Big Mountain's central reservation number, (800) 858-5439, and discuss your lodging needs with the reservations clerk. The lodges at Big Mountain are also open in summer, and rates are generally about 25% lower than the high season winter prices given below.

Following is information on the individual lodging units available on Big Mountain. *All* of the following prices are per person, based on double occupancy. Additionally, there are always promotional packages, and prices vary from day to day during the week. It's really easier just to call central reservations and let them help you iron out the rather confusing range of options. **Hibernation House,** 3808 Big Mountain Rd., tel. (406) 862-1960 or (800) 858-5439, is the "economy" bed and breakfast hotel, with rooms starting at $32 per person. **Alpinglow Inn,** 3900 Big Mountain Rd., tel. (406) 862-6966 or (800) 754-6760, is just across from lifts and adjacent to the cross-country trails. Facilities include two outdoor hot tubs and two saunas. Rooms are recently remodeled, and a variety of bed configurations are available, as are handicaped accessible rooms. Per person room prices begin at $58.

Kandahar Lodge 3824 Big Mountain Rd., tel. (406) 862-6098 or (800) 862-6094, with rooms starting at $69 per person, is Big Mountain's fanciest, with an excellent restaurant and alpine lodge decor; suites with kitchens are available.

Edelweiss Condominiums, 3898 Big Mountain Rd., tel. (406) 862-5252 or (800) 228-8260, has one-bedroom units from $105; all units have kitchens and fireplaces. **Anapurna Properties,** tel. (406) 862-3687 or (800) 243-7547, offers condos and private homes, with indoor pool and hot tubs. Call for prices.

Just down the hill from Big Mountain is **Ptarmigan Village,** 3000 Big Mountain Rd., tel. (406) 862-3594 or (800) 552-3952, a condominium development three miles from the ski lifts with condos starting at $90.

Camping

Whitefish Lake State Park is about two miles west of town off Hwy. 93. Pick this as your place to stay if you're after convenience, if you want to spend some time near civilization, if you want to eat out or shop in Whitefish, or if you want a handy launching-off spot for a trip to Glacier National Park. It's a crowded place, even for a state park campground, and trains rattle and toot their way through all night long, but it's a good place to meet friendly people (including the campground hosts). There's a boat launch and a swimming beach popular with local kids (there's a $4 day-use fee, $11 for camping). The campground has running water and flush toilets, and it's open mid-May through mid-September.

Out of town, **Tally Lake** (U.S. Forest Service) campground is open Memorial Day through Labor Day, $7 per night. It's six miles west of Whitefish on Hwy. 93, then 15 miles west on Forest Service Road 113. Several trails originate from various points around Tally Lake. From the campground, the **Tally Lake Overlook** is a 1.2-mile hike. The **Boney Gulch Trail** is a steep three-mile trail. Its trailhead is on Road 913 about three miles from the campground.

If you have a backpacking trip in mind, the **Reed Divide Tally Mountain Bill Creek Trail** begins at the junction of Road 913, some two miles from the campground, and runs nearly the length of its name, some 20 miles. For the less

driven hiker, the **Stove Pipe Canyon Trail** is just one mile long and goes into a canyon that is true to its name. This trail starts off Road 2924 on the west side of the lake.

Food and Drink

Casual Meals: Whitefish is a great place to eat breakfast. **Buffalo Cafe,** 516 3rd St. E., tel. (406) 862-2833, is populated with an easy mix of locals and tourists. The breakfast menu features about half a dozen variations on huevos rancheros and at least as many omelettes. They're open for breakfast and lunch. The egg-fest continues at the **Whitefish Grille,** tel. (406) 862-3354, 235 Central Ave., which serves breakfast all day and wraps and sandwiches. At dinner, fine dining prevails, with steak, chicken, duck, and pasta leading the menu.

The **Great Northern Bar and Grill,** 27 Central Ave., tel. (406) 862-2816, is a friendly, low-key bar with sports on the TV in the front and sandwiches and spaghetti served up at the tables in the back. It's open for lunch and dinner, and usually has live music in the bar on weekend nights. The local brew, Black Star, is served on tap.

For a fancier dinner, walk down a block to **Truby's,** 115 Central Ave., tel. (406) 862-4979. The specialty here is wood-fired pizza, but you'll also find a pleasant selection of steaks, pasta, salads, and burgers. There's a pleasant outdoor patio where, during the summer, lunches and drinks are served.

The **Bulldog Grill,** 144 Central Ave., tel. (406) 862-5601, is known as a good bar to hang out in and maybe munch a burger. **Casey's,** a casino bar at 101 Central Ave., tel. (406) 862-8150, is housed in Whitefish's oldest building. It was built in 1903, when Whitefish was a rollicking railroad town.

Kitchen Connection, 242 Central Ave., tel. (406) 862-2722, bills itself as a gourmet food shop. It's open Mon.-Sat. 9 a.m.-5 p.m. and offers sandwiches, salads, and pastries.

Stageline Pizza, one of four in the northwest Montana chain, at 901 Wisconsin Ave., tel. (406) 862-4441, has free delivery and reasonably priced pizzas with all the standard add-ons, and even sauerkraut. **Jimmy Lee's,** 6550 Hwy. 93 S, tel. (406) 862-5303, is a popular local spot for typical Chinese fare. It opens at 5 p.m. for dinner; meals run $5-8. "Jimmy's lunch" is a particularly tasty noodle dish. **Dos Amigos,** Wisconsin Ave.

(on the road to Big Mountain), tel. (406) 862-9994, has good Mexican food. This is the original Dos Amigos; the one in Kalispell followed after this place proved such a hit.

Fine Dining: Tupelo Grille, tel. (406) 862-6136, 17 Central Ave., has an eclectic menu that ranges from Cajun food to beef stroganoff and homemade ravioli. Most entrees are under $12.

For years the best place to eat in Whitefish has been the clubhouse at the golf course, called **Whitefish Lake Restaurant,** tel. (406) 862-5285. It's still a very good place to eat, especially if you're hankering for a steak, fresh seafood, and prime rib, all in the $17-20 range. For upscale dining with a bit more modern flair, go to **Logans,** tel. (406) 862-3000 at the Grouse Mountain Lodge. Dishes here include duck, pork, salmon, as well as steaks and pasta; $14-18.

If you're staying on Big Mountain, or feel like a steep drive, the ski lodges at the base of the slopes have quite good food. The best dining is at **Kandahar Lodge,** tel. (406) 862-6098, for serious French and Italian cuisine in the $16-19 range; or check out the **Hell Roaring Saloon & Eatery,** tel. (406) 862-6364, in the Chalet, for good Southwestern-influenced food.

Entertainment
Though it may seem that Whitefish is wholly devoted to outdoor recreation, there are a number of artists and other culture mavens in town. The **Whitefish Theatre Company,** tel. (406) 862-5371, draws enough support to produce plays almost year-round.

Shopping
The streets of downtown Whitefish are lined with shops and galleries. One of the nicest places to shop is **Montana Territory,** 239 Central Ave., tel. (406) 296-2769, with handcrafted leather goods and designer clothes, art and decorative objects made by Montana-born or -dwelling artistans. **Artistic Touch,** 209 Central Ave., tel. (406) 862-4813, has an excellent selection of high-quality crafts. At 3706 Hwy. 93 W., tel. (406) 862-9043, **O'Keef's** has attractive, though pricey, jewelry and crafts. **Tomahawk Trading Company,** 131 Central Ave., tel. (406) 862-9199, features Indian jewelry.

Bookworks, at 110 Central Ave., tel. (406) 862-4980, is an excellent place to pick up regional literature and field guides.

If you're traveling Montana with your campstove and espresso pot, a stop at **Montana Coffee Traders,** tel. (406) 862-7633, is almost imperative. It's south of town at 5810 Hwy. 93 S, about a quarter mile south of the Hwy. 40 intersection. Besides a variety of home-roasted coffee beans, there's a selection of coffee-drinking paraphernalia, locally made and imported gifts, and a little garden center that springs up in the front yard during the spring and summer.

Third St. Market, at the corner of 3rd and Spokane, tel. (406) 862-5054, is the local health-food store. Many of the towns in this part of Montana have small health-food stores, but this one is more of a complete food store and community rendezvous than most.

Sportsman and Ski Haus has a branch at the Whitefish Mall, tel. (406) 862-3111. It's open every day and stocks all sorts of sporting and skiing equipment.

Information
The **Whitefish Chamber of Commerce,** P.O. Box 1120, Whitefish MT 59937, tel. (406) 862-3501, has its offices in the train depot and dispenses an array of brochures and maps. There's also a small historical museum in the depot.

The **Whitefish Ranger Station,** tel. (406) 863-5400, is on Hwy. 93 near the turnoff for the Whitefish Lake State Recreation Area (and next door to Grouse Mountain Lodge).

Whitefish magazine comes out twice a year and is well worth reading for a look at how Whitefish residents view their town and the surrounding area.

Services
The **post office** is at 424 Baker Avenue.

Martin's Laundromat, at the corner of 3rd and Baker, tel. (406) 862-4646, is as convenient as any in western Montana. It's no chore to toss a load into the washer and wander through the shops and galleries while it's spinning.

Transportation
Amtrak stops at the N. Central Ave. depot, tel. (406) 862-2268, on its way across the top of the country. The Empire Builder runs between Chicago and Seattle or Portland, and stops in Whitefish four times a week. The eastbound train comes through around 6:30 a.m., the westbound at approximately 11:30 p.m.

Styled similarly to the lodges in Glacier Park, the Whitefish train depot serves Amtrak and also houses the Whitefish Chamber of Commerce, a museum, and an espresso bar.

Intermountain Transport uses Stumps Pumps, a gas station at 403 2nd St. E, tel. (406) 862-6700, as its Whitefish terminal.

The **Duck Inn,** 1305 Columbia Ave., tel. (406) 862-3825 or (800) 344-2377, doubles as a rental car agency. Rentals are also available from **Hertz,** tel. (406) 862-1210 or (800) 654-3131; and **Budget Rent-a-Car,** tel. (406) 862-8170 or (800) 527-0700.

COLUMBIA FALLS

There are no falls in Columbia Falls (pop. 3,922, elev. 2,960 feet). When it was time to name the town, Columbia was the initial choice. Since that name had already been taken, "Falls" was tacked on for the euphony it lent.

When Columbia Falls was established in the 1890s, it was supposed to have become a division point for the Great Northern Railway. Kalispell, then Whitefish, became the actual division points, leaving Columbia Falls built to a rather grander scale than its activity would warrant.

Today, Columbia Falls is the industrial center of the Flathead Valley. Aluminum smelting is big business (Anaconda Aluminum is based here). Timber is also important—Plum Creek, the timber giant, has a big mill here.

For the traveler, Columbia Falls is a handy jumping-off point for both Hungry Horse Reservoir and Glacier National Park. There are several motels and enough stores to do some last-minute stocking-up before heading into the mountains.

Recreation
Test the nine slides and hot tub at **Big Sky Waterslide,** tel. (406) 892-5025, any day between Memorial Day and Labor Day.

The **Meadow Lake Resort** at 1415 Tamarack Ln., tel. (406) 892-2111, has an 18-hole golf course open to the public. Greens fees are $32, with reduced fees for resort guests.

If you're looking for a guided hiking vacation in northwestern Montana, call **Great Northern Llama Co.,** tel. (406) 755-9044, 600 Blackmer Lane, Columbia Falls, MT 59912. This outfitter offers two- to four-day trips into the Flathead National Forest featuring ridgetop hiking in the company of pack llamas. Prices for a fully outfitted trip (includes tents, food, and camping gear) cost $165 per adult, per day, and $140 per child.

Accommodations
B&Bs: One of the finest B&Bs in Montana is **Bad Rock Country Bed & Breakfast,** tel. (406) 892-2829 or (800) 422-3666, www.badrock.com, just south of Columbia Falls off Hwy. 206. In addition to the rooms in the main house (including a two room family suite), behind the house are four modern, stylishly simple log cabin suites (no kitchens), constructed with squared logs and each furnished with rustic pine furniture and fitted with a gas fireplace. All rooms have private baths and queen or king beds, breakfast is ample and delicious, and the hospitality is top-notch. The B&B is located in a 30-acre meadow, with views onto the mountains leading to Glacier Park; from the hot tub, the lighted runs of Big Mountain are visible at night. Rooms in the main house are $115-135, while the cabins are $140-155.

Motels: The newly remodeled **Glacier Mountain Shadows Resort,** at the junction of Hwys. 2 and 206, tel. (406) 892-2181 or (800) 766-1137, has rooms starting at $62, an indoor pool, a casino, and live music in the lounge. There'a an RV camp at the resort as well, and you can also opt to sleep in one of the tepees (bring your own sleeping bag) for $20 a night. The local **Super 8,** 7336 US 2 E, tel. (406) 892-0888, has rooms at $57-72 s, $70-77 d.

Resorts: At **Meadow Lake Resort,** a small hotel and condominiums border an 18-hole championship golf course. There are tennis courts, a fitness center, an outdoor swimming pool, and a year-round outdoor hot tub on the grounds. During the winter, the resort runs a shuttle to and from the Big Mountain ski area. The restaurant here is one of the area's best. During the summer, condos rent for $129-244 a night; single rooms in the hotel run $129. Find Meadow Lakes at 100 St. Andrews Dr., tel. (406) 892-7601 or (800) 321-4653.

Camping: The Forest Service's **Big Creek Campground** is 21 miles north of Columbia Falls on Road 210, where Big Creek runs into the North Fork of the Flathead River. During the summer it's one of the quieter spots around, as well as one of the least expensive.

Food and Drink
The **Pines Cafe** is a handy stop along Hwy. 2, tel. (406) 892-2053, featuring inexpensive breakfasts, mounted fish, and a museum. An excellent addition to the dining options in Columbia Falls is the **Cimarron Deli,** 420 Nucleus Ave., tel. (406) 892-1490, with a full-service deli, plus a bistro dining room open daily for three meals a day. At night, the menu expands to include Italian dishes and steaks. The **Nite Owl** and the **Back Room** is a casual bar/cafe/dinnerhouse complex that serves really good pizza, chicken, and ribs at 522 9th St. W, tel. (406) 892-3131 or 892-9944. It doesn't look like much, but ponder the always full parking lot and rest assured that this is the best inexpensive food in Columbia Falls.

For upscale dining, head to **Tracy's,** tel. (406) 892-7601, at Meadow Lake Resort. The dining room looks over the golf course and features a number of game dishes (pheasant, or venison loin with bourbon and juniper berries for $16) along with the salmon, steaks, and fresh seafood.

Perhaps the most fun place on the road between Kalispell and Glacier Park is the **Blue Moon,** just west of Columbia Falls where Hwy. 2 makes a sharp turn to the right and picks up Hwy. 40. There's live music here almost every night in the summer, and Wednesday nights bring free dancing lessons.

Services and Information
For **emergency** services, call 911. The **post office** is at 530 1st Ave. West. Lovers of cleanliness will want to stop by **Falls Coin Laundry and Car Wash** on Hwy. 2 W, tel. (406) 892-4200.

The Columbia Falls **Chamber of Commerce** is at 233 13th St. E, tel. (406) 892-2072. Write them at P.O. Box 312, Columbia Falls, MT 59912. The **Flathead County Library** has a branch at 130 6th St. W in Columbia Falls.

HUNGRY HORSE

There's pretty obviously a story surrounding the name of Hungry Horse, the next town down the road from Columbia Falls. During the severe winter of 1900, two draft horses, Tex and Jerry, used for logging the area wandered off. When they were found, about a month later, they were all scraggly and hungry.

Though there'd been settlements in the area since the turn of the century, the Hungry Horse post office wasn't established until 1948, when the federal government began planning to dam the South Fork of the Flathead River. The dam was completed in 1952.

Sights
Fans of dam technology will want to tour the visitor information center at the **Hungry Horse Dam,** tel. (406) 387-5241, four miles south of town. The 564-foot-high concrete dam holds back the 34-mile-long Hungry Horse Reservoir. Guided tours of the dam are offered during the summer months.

A road circles the reservoir and provides access to a number of trails into the surrounding national forest and wilderness areas. Jewel Basin Hiking Area lies to the west of the reservoir, the Great Bear Wilderness is to the east, and the Bob Marshall Wilderness is to the south. Great

Northern Mountain, east of the reservoir, rises to an elevation of 8,720 feet. The South Fork of the Flathead River flows into the southern end of the reservoir. You'll see a number of guest ranches around the reservoir, and there's no dearth of public campgrounds.

Hungry Horse Reservoir is a good place to fish for cutthroat and bull trout; most people fish from boats, and the best fishing is during the late summer and fall.

Accommodations
The **Diamond R Guest Ranch,** tel. (406) 756-1573 or (800) 597-9465, open May-Nov., is 50 miles south of Hungry Horse Dam. Some of the wood-heated cabins date from 1926; there's also a restaurant and a guide service here. In addition to trail rides, the Diamond R offers fishing and floating trips on the South Fork Flathead River. Cabins are $40 s, $70 double; full board is available for $35 a person a day.

Camping
There are eight Forest Service campgrounds around Hungry Horse Reservoir. It's necessary to bring your own drinking water to all of them; even those that once had piped water have had their services cut back. Because of these cutbacks, all the public campgrounds around the reservoir are now free.

Doris Point Campground is eight miles down Road 895 from Hungry Horse; **Lost Johnny Point** is a mile farther. **Lid Creek** is 15 miles from Hungry Horse; **Lakeview** is 24 miles; **Handkerchief Lake** is 35 miles from Hungry Horse on Road 895, then another two miles on Road 897. There's a trail from Handkerchief Lake up to the Jewel Basin Hiking Area. **Spotted Bear** is at the south end of the reservoir, 55 miles from Martin City on Road 38 (and about equal distance from Hungry Horse). **Elk Island** (accessible only by boat), **Murray Bay,** and **Emery Bay** are along the east side of the reservoir. Emery Bay is the closest spot to Martin City; it's seven miles down Road 38.

Food
The huckleberry is the culinary specialty of Hungry Horse. The **Huckleberry Patch** at 8858 Hwy. 2 E, tel. (406) 387-5000, is a convenient place to load up on gifts of huckleberry preserves and to toss down a slice of huckleberry pie or a huckleberry milkshake in the cafe. (They also offer all-you-can-eat spaghetti for less than $5.) It is, of course, easy enough to pick your own berries. They start ripening around mid-July, and almost any trip off Hwy. 2 into the hills will lead to good picking—but watch out for bears; they feast on berries to prepare for hibernation.

Great Bear Wilderness Area
The Great Bear Wilderness Area comprises 285,771 acres just south of Glacier National Park, north of the Bob Marshall, on the west side of the Continental Divide. A small airstrip at Schafer Meadows is an unusual feature of this wilderness area. It's possible to fly in: **Strand Aviation,** tel. (406) 247-7678, and **Eagle Aviation,** tel. (406) 755-2376, will fly in three to five people for between $130 and $145, with extra fees for heavy or bulky equipment.

Trailheads from the Spotted Bear Ranger Station lead to Lodgepole Creek and the Spotted Bear River. Just about every trail in the wilderness complex will go into the valley of the South Fork of the Flathead River. The headwaters of the Middle Fork of the Flathead River are in the Great Bear Wilderness.

Information
The *Hungry Horse News* is the newspaper of record in these parts, definitely worth picking up if you want to read a weekly paper loaded with stories of mountain lions in the streets, bear maulings and bee stings in Glacier Park, and numerous DUI violations.

The Forest Service has two **ranger stations** in the area. One is in Hungry Horse, tel. (406) 387-5243, and the other, which is staffed May through October only, is at Spotted Bear, at the southern end of Hungry Horse Reservoir.

THE NORTHWESTERN CORNER

This is big timber country. Logging and the wood-products industry pervades just about everyone's life in one way or another. There's a swagger in the calk boots and a pride in hauling logs.

But the forests are disappearing, and it's on everybody's mind. The old growth has been depleted to the point where mills have found it necessary to retool their equipment to accept smaller logs.

For years, Champion International was one of the region's biggest employers, and they owned large tracts of timberland as well as plywood mills and sawmills. They were known for, to put it gently, a vigorous harvest. Their cut was, in fact, unsustainable. In 1993, Champion became a champ in the "cut and run" game. Having extracted as much as they profitably could from the forest, they sold 867,000 acres to Plum Creek and their mills to Stimson Lumber, an Oregon company. This was not done without loss of logging and mill jobs.

THE LAND

The Kootenai (KOOT-nee) National Forest is the defining physical feature of this far corner of the state. It has a Pacific quality, and its lush hillsides are drained by the Kootenai, the Clark Fork, and a host of smaller rivers and streams.

Trees are everywhere, and where they aren't, their absence is more than conspicuous—it's almost an affront to those who don't depend on logging for a living.

Western red cedar, western hemlock, western white pine, whitebark pine, lodgepole pine, ponderosa pine, alpine larch, western larch, mountain hemlock, grand fir, subalpine fir, Douglas fir, Engelmann spruce, juniper, cottonwood, quaking aspen, alder, and paper birch are all native to northwestern Montana. Years of forest management, however, have changed the composition of the new-growth forests to increase their timber yields. Timber managers often replant only a single, fast-growing tree species, changing the forest from a diverse system with literally dozens of different species to a "monocrop" similar in composition to a potato patch.

Logging increases erosion and decreases water quality, threatening fish habitats, but logged areas do support both plant and animal life. Wildflowers bloom in clearcuts, huckleberries and elderberries invade, and deer and elk populations flourish in open areas created by timber cutting. There are also moose in the forested areas here, and some bighorn sheep and mountain goats on the hillsides.

Experienced mushroom hunters might try collecting morels in old burn areas and beneath Douglas fir and ponderosa pine trees. Moist

JUDY JEWELL

the Kootenai River

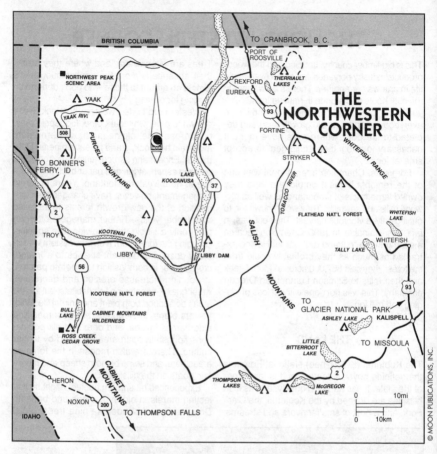

spring weather can bring about a veritable fungal bloom in open areas.

HISTORY

The Kootenai

The Kootenai Indians moved from the north to the Tobacco Plains area around present-day Eureka and along the Kootenai River around the 1500s. The Upper and Lower Kootenai had different cultural traditions and lived in different areas, but they thought of themselves as one people. The Upper Kootenai lived closer to the Rocky Mountains and had more of a plains tradition than did the Lower Kootenai, who used canoes more than horses and caught more salmon than buffalo. After the Blackfeet arrived on the plains in the 1700s, the Kootenai largely restricted their travel to the west side of the Rockies.

Though many of the Kootenai people in Montana now live on the Flathead Reservation (mostly around Elmo), the name, "Kootenai," whose origin is uncertain, still brings to mind the mountains, tall trees, and rushing waters of the northwest corner of the state. (Some sources say their name means "Deer Robes" and alludes to their skill as deer hunters and tanners, but this is not certain because "Kootenai" is not even a word in the Kootenai language.)

Whites Arrive

David Thompson was the first white man in the area. He explored the Kootenai River in 1808 and portaged around Kootenai Falls. He sent Finan McDonald to the area near Libby to establish a trading post for the North West Company. Trappers and fur traders followed in the wake of Thompson and McDonald, but it took gold and silver to bring a significant number of white settlers to the region. Placer mining started in 1869 and continued for about 20 years.

Even with trapping and mining activity, this corner of Montana was an isolated place until the Great Northern Railway came through in 1893. The railroad truly opened the north to development. Not only was there an easy way to get into the area, there was a way to haul away abundant natural resources, particularly the trees. The growth of the timber industry was thus linked to the railroad.

Though much of the focus today is on the forests, mines still operate around Libby and Troy. Improved methods of extracting minerals and rising prices fuel interest in both small and large operations. In fact, there are prospectors who want to build tunnels under the Cabinet Mountains Wilderness area to extract the silver and copper deposits there.

This area, which for years was so remote and hard to penetrate because of its densely forested mountains, now has an abundance of roads. More than 7,000 miles of roads have been built in the Kootenai National Forest, with another 50-75 miles added each year.

BULL RIVER ROAD
AND THE CABINET MOUNTAINS
WILDERNESS

Bull River Road (Hwy. 56) runs from Hwy. 200 (just west of Noxon) to Troy. The Bull River and several lakes are along the road, and the Cabinet Mountain Wilderness is just to the east. Fishing is good in the river (but not spectacular in Bull Lake, which does not feed the river). There's a good chance that wildlife will be somewhere along this road almost anytime you drive it. You'll

probably see deer, and there are also plenty of elk and moose in the area.

Highway 56 was an Indian trail; it was also used by smugglers bringing Chinese laborers down from Canada to work on the construction of the Northern Pacific Railroad.

Ross Creek Cedar Grove

Ross Creek Cedar Grove is about four miles off Hwy. 56 just south of Bull Lake (17 miles north of Hwy. 200). The gravel road has a steep section and isn't suitable for large RVs. The western red cedar forest here is a Pacific rainforest, a little unusual for Montana. It gets 50 inches of rain a year, so don't be surprised if you take the mile-long nature hike in a shower. The raised boardwalk trail on the interpretive hike protects the forest floor and makes it easy to hike in the rain. There are trails up the Middle Fork and the South Fork of Ross Creek starting from the parking lot of the cedar grove. Bring your cross-country skis here in the winter for a lovely, easy tour through the big trees.

Indian history records that Bull Lake was formed when a landslide blocked a stream and destroyed a camp. There is still some evidence of such a slide at the foot of the lake.

Cabinet Mountains Wilderness

The Cabinet Mountains Wilderness comprises nearly 95,000 acres in the Kootenai National Forest. It can be reached from Hwy. 56 or Hwy. 200. Snowshoe Peak is the high point in the wilderness, at 8,738 feet. There is good hiking here, and some rock-climbing on the peaks.

To reach the trail to **St. Paul Lake,** a 4,715-foot-high lake in a cirque beneath St. Paul Peak, go up East Fork Rd. off Bull River Road. About a mile up East Fork Rd. is a Forest Service sign noting directions and distances to several trailheads. The St. Paul Lake trailhead is four miles from this point, up a gravel road that's easy to drive in a passenger car until the final short descent to the trailhead, which requires some caution. The hike in to the lake is four miles each way; the roundtrip is a good day's walk for the average hiker. The trail, which is shown on the Kootenai National Forest map, passes through some old-growth western red cedar and western hemlock before it reaches the lake. Even if you don't want to take the hike up to the lake, consider fishing the East Fork of the Bull River for trout.

Accommodations

The **Bull River Forest Service Campground** is by the Cabinet Mountains where Bull River runs into the Clark Fork. Dirty campers can wander just west of the campground to a private RV campground with showers for rent.

There's also camping on the road to the Ross Creek Cedar Grove. **Bad Medicine Forest Service Campground** is two miles off Hwy. 56 overlooking Bull Lake. There is a boat launch at this cedar-scented site.

The **Bull Lake Guest Ranch,** tel. (406) 295-4228 or (800) 995-4228, 15303 Bull Lake Rd., offers both B&B accommodations ($36 s, $54 d) and full board lodging ($120 per couple per day) at their ranch near Bull Lake. Although the ranch no longer offers horseback riding (other nearby outfitters do, however), the area is noted for its

---

THE WESTERN LARCH

A northwestern Montana hillside strewn with yellowing "evergreen" trees does not necessarily mean blight. It may be a stand of larch, or tamarack, trees.

Western and alpine larch, both found in northwestern Montana, are the only conifers that shed their needles each fall. Around mid-September, the trees respond to the shortening days with yellowed needles, which drop before winter hits.

The needles usually collect in piles beneath the trees, but enough of them end up in streams to form a regional collectible—larch balls. These wads of needles, sometimes the size of a grapefruit, have been packed together by river currents and eddies.

The larger western larch is more common. The trees grow at lower elevations than their alpine relatives. North-facing slopes provide good habitat for the hardy western larch, which can withstand fires and temperature extremes that thwart other species.

Larch wood is dense and durable—good for hot fires and for structural support. Because of a funny incompatibility with concrete (the wood secretes a sugar that weakens the concrete), it's not used as much for construction as you might expect. Some larch extracts are used pharmaceutically and in baking powder.

---

excellent fishing, hiking, mountain biking, and climbing. The lodge is open all winter, making this a good option for a cross-country or snowmobile getaway. Accommodations are in a six-bedroom lodge (there's also a primitive cabin available that sleeps six), and facilities include two common rooms and a game room with pool and table tennis. All rooms have queen beds, and two also have a twin bed.

TROY AND VICINITY

At 1,892 feet, Troy is the lowest point in Montana. It's a town of about 1,000 on the west bank of the Kootenai River, which flows northwest from Troy into Idaho. The Purcell Mountains are to the north of Troy, the Cabinet Mountains to the south. Ice-age glaciers covered the Purcells and ground them down to softer peaks. To the south, glaciers carved valleys and cirques in the Cabinet Mountains, but did not cover them so completely as to smooth them out.

The Yaak River drains the Purcell Mountains in the far northwest corner of the state and flows into the Kootenai river just west of Troy. The Yaak has gained a certain literary fame since writer Rick Bass moved to the area and wrote *Winter Notes* about snow, woodcutting, and isolation. The road between Yaak and Rexford has both densely forested areas and massive clearcuts. It's illustrative of the Northwest timber industry.

Though the timber industry provides the basis for Troy's economy today, both the railroad and mining have been important to the town's development. Mining still plays a major role. The ASARCO mine began processing copper and silver in 1981.

The high school team is, of course, the Trojans.

Sights

Troy's **historical museum** is housed in an old railroad building on Hwy. 2. Old railroad and logging equipment figures prominently in the collection, but one special prize is a cigar lighter. There's a short nature trail behind the museum.

Troy's as good a place as any to stock up on groceries, and the IGA (across the street from the museum) has the special attraction of mounted animal heads all over the walls.

Recreation

Pulpit Mountain Trail, a national recreation trail, is a five-mile (one-way) hike just north of Troy. It passes an old fire lookout on Pulpit Mountain and has good views of the Cabinet Mountains. The easiest way to walk the trail is to start from the trailhead on Lynx Creek Rd. and hike to where the trail comes out on Rabbit Creek Road.

To reach the **Northwest Peak Scenic Area,** turn up Pete Creek Rd. just west of Yaak. This is an isolated area of the state, and it's rare to see many other hikers on the trails. One of the more popular trails leads to Northwest Peak. It's a two-mile hike to the peak, which has grand views and a deserted lookout. Call (406) 295-4693 for trail information.

Cross-country ski the four-and-a-half mile Hellroaring Creek trail, 29 miles northwest of Troy on the Yaak River Road.

Accommodations

There are a couple of inexpensive motels along Hwy. 2 in Troy. At the **Holiday Motel,** on Hwy. 2 at 218 E. Missoula, tel. (406) 295-4117, you won't spend over $40 for a double; small pets are okay. The **Ranch Motel,** 914 E. Missoula, tel. (406) 295-4332, charges $32 for a single, $38 for a double. There are some two-bedroom units, and some units have kitchenettes ($40-50). A picnicking area is adjacent.

Yaak River Campground (U.S. Forest Service), seven miles west of Troy on Hwy. 2, is a good entrance or exit campground to the state. There are plenty of paths down to the river. Head up the Yaak to **Yaak Falls Campground,** set by a cascade eight miles up from Hwy. 2.

Whitetail Campground is on a quiet stretch of the Yaak River; it's not a bad place for a swim. **Pete Creek** is an exceptionally pretty campground set on a bluff above Pete Creek, just west of the town of Yaak.

Bill and Judy McAffee operate an outfitting service and the **Tamarack Lodge,** on the Yaak River Rd. near Yaak, tel. (406) 295-4880, which caters largely to hunters and anglers.

Food and Drink

The **Silver Spur Restaurant,** on Hwy. 2 W, tel. (406) 295-9937, is a popular family place, but the sort of popular family place that's got a log cabin motif and a bar. Also worth a stop is the

Gold Rush, on the highway at the east end of town, tel. (406) 295-4914.

Though the Trojan Lanes does serve pizza, a less intimidating bet is the **Gold Nugget,** a cubbyhole of a pizza place on the east edge of town. **R Place** is a tiny, inexpensive burger joint across from the museum. They also serve sandwiches, fish, and Mexican food.

If you're hankering for a lively bar, wander down by the railroad tracks, where the **Home Bar** and several others accommodate locals and the occasional passerby.

Information

The **ranger station** is on the west edge of town; visitor information is dispensed at the historical museum, and the **public library** is at the corner of 3rd and Spokane, tel. (406) 295-4040.

LIBBY

Libby's a timber town, through and through. It's at 2,066 feet and the population is approximately 2,700. It must also be the longest town in Montana, as it spills along the Kootenai River valley, with the Cabinet Mountains to the south, the Purcell Mountains to the northwest, and the Salish Mountains to the northeast. Though it's not an obvious tourist town, it's easy to spend a day or two in the area.

History

David Thompson's reconnoitering in 1808 resulted in a small influx of fur traders during the first half of the 1800s, but little development occurred until gold was found in 1865. A mining town was thrown up by Libby Creek in the 1880s, and it moved to wherever the gold seemed to be. Sometimes the development was called New Town; other times Old Town seemed the more appropriate name. The name of a prospector's daughter ultimately won out. Libby ended up in its present location when the railroad came through in 1892.

Trees were initially harvested for mine timbers, then for railroad bridges and ties. Ultimately, the timber industry eclipsed both mining and the railroad, and has become Libby's increasingly unreliable mainstay.

Mining, however, still figures in the local economy. Perhaps it's not the sort of mining that one thinks of immediately, but W.R. Grace and Co.

has a vermiculite mining and processing operation in Libby. Vermiculite, used as an insulation material and as a potting-soil additive, is a type of mica that becomes light and puffy when it's heated.

Sights

The **Heritage Museum** on Hwy. 2 is a large polygonal log building. The dark interior is full of display cases brimming with Libby's old musical instruments (including two ukelins, one pianoette, two mandolin harps, and the sheet music for "Let Me Call You Sweetheart"), household implements, and logging equipment. There are special displays on the region's wildlife, logging, and mining. Open daily and admission is free.

Of the several historical buildings in downtown Libby, the oldest is what is now the dentist's office at 209 W. 2nd Street. It was built in 1899 and was originally the Libby hospital. The ballpark across the street was once the site of an Indian camp. One place that's changed a bit over the years is the white-and-red apartment building on E. 1st St. across from the train depot. It was once known as Helen Hunter's Place and, in 1906, was Libby's first brothel.

Montana City Old Town is south of Hwy. 2 on Main St., then right at the radio station, tel. (406) 293-8426. In addition to false-fronted stores, there's a theater company that puts on vaudeville acts and dramas in the Opera House.

If you're out to relive Libby's history, it may be more profitable to pan for gold on Libby Creek than to watch vaudeville or go glassy-eyed over displays of old kitchenware. Gold was discovered in Libby Creek in 1865 and was mined fairly intensively around the turn of the century. There's still some gold there, though. The original dredging equipment got only 85-90% of what gold was in the creek. What's left is most likely to be found near the bottom of gravel piles left by early miners. The Forest Service has an area set aside for gold panning on Libby Creek; it's important not to search outside the designated area, as there are a number of mining claims staked close by.

To reach the **Libby Creek Gold Panning Area,** turn from Hwy. 2 onto Bear Creek Rd. (seven miles south of Libby) and drive 18 miles to the small parking area beside Libby Creek. (Or take Libby Creek Rd., 12 miles down Hwy. 2 from Libby, and follow it just over 10 miles to the panning zone.) Howard Lake Campground is a mile south of the gold-panning area. If you tire of prospecting, follow Libby Creek Rd. (the road that goes west at the Howard Lake junction) to its end and take an easy two-mile roundtrip hike along Libby Creek past an old miner's cabin.

Hikes and Walks

For a look at the cascading, 200-foot-high **Kootenai Falls** from the highway, there's a turnout on Hwy. 2 about five miles west of Libby. This is one of the few waterfalls on a major Northwest river that hasn't had its power harnessed to elec-

cascading 200-foot
Kootenai Falls

W. C. McRAE

trical generators. A trail leads from the casual campground by the highway pullout, across a bridge over the railroad tracks, and down to viewpoints of the cascades. Continue west on the trail to a swinging footbridge downstream from the falls. Bighorn sheep are often seen just east of here grazing on the cliffs across the river.

Kootenai River Road runs west along the north side of the river, starting at Hwy. 37 just over the bridge from downtown Libby. The road is closed to motor vehicles about seven miles from there, and it makes an enjoyable walk. Before white men came to the area, this was an Indian trail. The WPA *Montana, A State Guide Book* speaks of ceremonial sweat baths used by the Kootenai Indians along this trail where Pipe Creek flows into the Kootenai about five miles west of Libby.

This stretch is now pretty developed, and you can't see the broken rocks anymore, but, if you walk down the closed part of the road, you'll get a feeling for why this spot was used for ceremonial sweat baths.

Walk far enough along this trail and you'll reach Kootenai Falls. Actually, this is a good mountain-bike ride–hike combination. The first couple of miles are along an old road dotted with abandoned cabins. When the road runs out, leave your bike and take to foot. The trail isn't always apparent, but if you keep to the ridge just above the river you'll be okay. Near the head of the falls the trail traverses rock slides. This is a good place to turn back. Even if you can see the swinging bridge below the falls, don't try to hike there. It gets dangerous quickly, and you'll understand why the Kootenai Indians built rock cairns to ensure safe passage around the gorges and cataracts.

Other Recreation

The Kootenai River is popular with rafters and canoeists, as anyone who has seen the Meryl Streep thriller *The River Wild* can aver—parts of the film were shot along the Kootenai. The Canoe Gulch Ranger Station on Hwy. 37 is a good put-in spot, and boats can be taken out in town just below the California Ave. Bridge. The trip is a little too challenging for inexperienced river runners, and it's important to remember that Kootenai Falls, five miles downstream from Libby, are not passable.

Cabinet Mountain Adventures, tel. (406) 295-1301 or (800) 201-7238, P.O. Box H, Troy, MT. 59935, offers guided raft trips down the Kootenai River. Rafters have a choice of four different runs, ranging from one hour ($12) to all-day trips ($70). Depending on the river flow, you may get to pass through some of the canyons filmed in the movie (though not the really scary rapids).

There are large rainbow trout living below Libby Dam, but those who fish this part of the Kootenai River should pay close attention to the water level; release of water from the dam can cause quick rises. Fishing is best when the water level drops. For water-release schedules, call Libby Dam's River Discharge Information at (406) 293-3421.

The 23-mile **Skyline National Recreation Trail** starts at the west fork of Quartz Creek, northwest of Libby, and ends in the Yaak Valley.

The downhill ski area at 5,952-foot **Turner Mountain,** 22 miles up Pipe Creek Rd. from Libby, has a 2,400-foot vertical drop.

There are groomed **cross-country ski trails** at Bear Creek and Flatiron Mountain near Libby. Few of the logging roads around Libby are plowed in the winter. Stop by the ranger station to find out which roads have been set aside for skiers. Snowmobilers should check with the Forest Service to see which roads are designated for snowmobile use.

Cabinet View Golf Course, tel. (406) 293-7332, is a nine-hole course (with plans to expand to a full 18 holes).

There's bowling at **Lincoln Lanes,** 138 Commerce Way, tel. (406) 293-3123.

Accommodations

Perhaps the most interesting accommodation in the Libby area is the **Big Creek Baldy Mountain Fire Lookout,** available for $25 per night. It's about 26 miles from Libby via Pipe Creek Road. The cabin is equipped with everything but sleeping bags and food. Reservations and the key to the lookout are available from the Libby Ranger Station, one mile northeast of Libby on Hwy. 37, tel. (406) 293-8861.

There is a host of inexpensive motels along and around Hwy. 2 in Libby. **Sandman Motel,** tel. (406) 293-8831, is set back off Hwy. 2 just a bit. It rents doubles for $42 and has an outdoor hot tub. Some rooms have microwaves and refrigerators, and all are air-conditioned. Pets are okay with a $5 fee. There's also a newly refurbished and comfortable **Super 8,** 448 Hwy. 2 W, tel. (406) 293-2771 or (800) 800-8000; all rooms have recliners, there's a swimming pool, and it's conveniently located next to a restaurant and near Libby's largest casino; $45 s, $54 d. **Venture Motor Inn,** 443 Hwy. 2 W, tel. (406) 293-7711 or (800) 221-0166, is the deluxe place to stay in Libby. It has a heated pool, hot tub, and restaurant, with rooms starting at $54 s, $69 d.

There's a **free campground** behind the Libby Chamber of Commerce building. It's a bit too much in the thick of things for tent camping, but the convenience and the price are enticing. **Scholl's Conoco** on Hwy. 2 has RV camping and, important for tent campers, showers. Between Libby and Troy, the **Lions Club** maintains a free primitive campground at the Kootenai Falls viewpoint. A trail leads down to the falls. **Carrigan,** yet another free campground 12 miles up Pipe Creek Rd., is isolated, with no running water, and is run by Champion.

Food and Drink

The best meal in town is served at a converted church now known as **Hidden Chapel,** 1207 Utah Ave., tel. (406) 293-3129. Open for both lunch and dinner, it serves steaks, seafood, and continental entrees for $12-20. Pleasant atmosphere, and in summer there's outdoor seating.

La Casa de Amigos serves up Mexican and American lunches and dinners downtown at 316 California Ave., tel. (406) 293-8676. There's a **4-Bs** at 442 Hwy. 2, tel. (406) 293-8751. **Beck's Montana Cafe,** 2425 Hwy. 2 W, tel. (406) 293-6687, is a good, locally owned family restaurant.

If it's a good steak you're after, **M-K Steak House** on Hwy. 2, tel. (406) 293-5686, is the place to eat in Libby. For a bar with live music on the weekends, try the **Pastime,** 216 Mineral Ave., tel. (406) 293-9925. The Pastime has been around since 1916, when it was known as the Pastime Pool Hall. Note the original carvings behind the bar.

Espresso has come 'round the mountain to Libby. Pull off Hwy. 2 at **Hava Java** to satisfy your coffee needs.

The **Red Dog Saloon** is seven miles up Pipe Creek Rd. in Libby, on the way to Turner Mountain. It's a little ways off the main drag, but haven't you been craving a pizza with whole-wheat crust? It's a friendly local hangout for both food and drinks.

Events

Logger Days are held in mid-July every year. Libby's **Nordicfest,** held the third weekend of September, features Scandinavian food, crafts, music, and dancing.

Shopping

Little Bear Tipi Pole Company, 22983 Hwy. 2 S, about 20 miles from Libby, tel. (406) 293-9880, is a genuine old hippie enterprise, replete with tepees for sale and for rent.

Cabinet Books and Music, in the Libby Shopping Center, has a selection of regional books along with mainstream paperbacks.

Information

Visitor information is proffered on Hwy. 2 at Fireman's Park, tel. (406) 293-4167; contact the chamber of commerce at P.O. Box 704, Libby MT 59923. The **Libby Ranger Station** is across the river, a half mile north on Hwy. 37, tel. (406) 293-8861. Another ranger station is at **Canoe Gulch,** 13 miles north of Libby on Hwy. 37, near Libby Dam.

Services

For **police or ambulance service** in Libby, call (406) 293-4112. The **fire department** answers at 911. **Saint John's Lutheran Hopital** is at 350 Louisiana Ave., tel. (406) 293-7761.

Two of the laundromats in Libby are **Janet's,** 221 W. 9th, and **A & J Suds and Scrub,** 1770 Hwy. 2 West.

Transportation

Amtrak stops ever so briefly in Libby; the eastbound train comes through at 4:30 a.m., the westbound at 11:30 p.m. Call Amtrak at (800) 872-7245 for reservations. **Libby Cab** operates 24 hours a day in Libby and Troy, tel. (406) 293-7349.

LAKE KOOCANUSA

Ninety-mile-long Lake Koocanusa, framed by the Purcell and Salish Mountains, was formed in 1972 when the Libby Dam backed up the Kootenai River from just above Libby all the way north into Canada.

Libby Dam now provides hydroelectric power, via the Bonneville Power Administration, to much of the Northwest and stores water in Lake Koocanusa to prevent flooding downstream. Water is released from the dam to supply the 17 dams downstream on the Columbia River. The dam itself is a straight axis, concrete gravity dam: it holds back Lake Koocanusa by its own weight.

The Libby Dam has an attractive **visitor center,** tel. (406) 293-5577, 17 miles north of Libby. The center is open late May through early Sept., 9:30 a.m.-6 p.m., for guided tours of the dam and powerhouse. There's a boat launch and picnic area.

Paved roads circle a good portion of Lake Koocanusa. Highway 37 runs along the east side; Forest Service Road 228 follows the western shore. There are only a couple of places to cross the lake. Libby Dam has a bridge, and Montana's highest and longest bridge spans the lake just south of Rexford.

The name "Koocanusa," derived from "Kootenai," "Canada," and "U.S.A.," was coined by residents of Rexford, a town largely flooded by the lake. Part of the town simply picked up and moved to higher ground, a grand tradition among dam-flooded sites. Actually, Rexford had already moved once before that; it was originally built right along the banks of the Kootenai River and was relocated alongside the railroad tracks in the early 1890s.

Recreation

There is good fishing around Libby Dam, most notably for kokanee salmon. Bald eagles are onto this one, too, and can be spotted here in the fall, swooping down for spawning kokanee. Late Oct. through mid-Nov. is the peak season for eagle viewing. Arrive early in the morning and you may see 40 or 50 eagles just downstream from the dam.

Just up the road from the visitor center is a trail (approximately two miles) to Alexander Mountain, continuing on another mile and a half to Fleetwood Point.

The short trail to Little North Falls (off Road 228) is handicapped-accessible.

Camping

Campsites are abundant around Lake Koocanusa. On the west side, six miles above Libby Dam, is **McGillivray,** a large Forest Service campground and recreation area ($12 per night). There's a boat launch and a swimming area on the lake at McGillivray, but they can only be used when the lake is filled with water, generally any time after early July. If McGillivray is too crowded, check the sign at the entrance for smaller and less developed campgrounds in the area.

Rexford Beach Campground is one of the few national forest campgrounds where reservations can be made with a toll-free phone call. It will cost $6, in addition to the usual $12 camping fee, but to gain that peace of mind that reservations lend, call (800) 283-CAMP (2267). **Tetrault Lake** and **Sophie Lake,** north of Rexford near Lake Koocanusa, both have Forest Service campgrounds by them.

Rocky Gorge and **Peak Gulch** are Forest Service campgrounds on Lake Koocanusa on Hwy. 37 south of the Lake Koocanusa Bridge. **Mariners' Haven,** tel. (406) 296-3252, is a private campground near Rexford with tepee rentals, a grocery store, and marina.

Information

The **Canoe Gulch Ranger Station,** on Hwy. 37 just south of its junction with Road 228, tel. (406) 293-7773, or 293-5758 for a recording, has information on recreation around Lake Koocanusa.

EUREKA

Eureka (pop. 1,108, elev. 2,577 feet) is located on the Tobacco River in the Tobacco Valley, so named because that was a crop grown by the area's Kootenai Indians (though some sources contend that missionaries attempted to grow tobacco here, and the name comes from their failed efforts). The Tobacco Valley was formed by glacial action, and it joins Plains and the Paradise Valley in the hotly contested battle over who gets the title of "banana belt of Montana." The mountains off to the east are part of the Whitefish Range.

History

The Tobacco Plains were home base to the Kootenai Indians, who hunted, fished, and gathered in the Kootenai River basin. The northern part of Hwy. 93 was originally an Indian trail and was used later by fur traders and pack trains traveling between Missoula and Vancouver, British Columbia. David Thompson was in the area in 1808; he was the first white to see it.

Trappers, traders, prospectors, and home-steaders began to settle the valley in the early 1880s. The first homesteaders were stockmen who established ranches in the town of Eureka.

Eureka, like the rest of northwestern Montana, has a timber-based economy. There's a little twist on it here, though; Eureka calls itself the "Christmas tree capital of the world." Farming supplements timber around Eureka; in fact, coming in to Eureka from the big timber country to the west, it looks strikingly agricultural.

Sights

Eureka doesn't just have the standard small-town historical museum; rather, it has a full-blown **historical village** near the south end of downtown. Most of the buildings there were salvaged from the town of Rexford. The old Rexford general store now houses a museum, which boasts, among the old books and papers, an ancient permanent-wave machine. Be sure to take your camera and flash attachment in with you, as you'll want to get the caretaker's permission to drag a chair over by the machine and have your picture taken with the wicked-looking clamps and wires dangling around your head. Another oddity here are larch balls, which can be had for a quarter each. Larch balls form when larch trees drop their needles into a stream and the currents and eddies form the needles into a ball.

There's an Amish community centered in West Kootenai and Rexford, on the west side of Lake Koocanusa about 14 miles north of the Koocanusa Bridge. The **Kootenai General Store** is a good place to stop to get the feel for the community, which formed in the 1970s when about 20 families moved here from the Midwest. They hold an annual auction of quilts, furniture, and prefabricated log homes in mid-June. For the exact date, contact Kootenai Log Homes, 5388 West Kootenai, Rexford, MT 59930, tel. (406) 889-3258.

When Libby Dam flooded the Kootenai River to form the lake, fish habitats were destroyed. **Murray Springs Fish Hatchery,** seven miles northwest of Eureka, near the north end of Lake Koocanusa, was built in 1978 in an attempt to restore cutthroat trout to the area.

Murphy Lake, 14 miles southeast of Eureka on Hwy. 93, is home to a loon population as well as a host of other animals, including horned grebes, bald eagles, herons, ospreys, white-tailed and mule deer, and beavers. Be sure to respect the privacy of nesting loons, which is protected during nesting season by boating restrictions on the southern end of the lake.

Recreation

Ten Lakes Scenic Area is adjacent to the Canadian border near Eureka and has been nominated for wilderness-area designation. To reach the Ten Lakes area, turn off Hwy. 93 at Grave Creek (about 10 miles south of Eureka) and follow the road for 30 miles, almost to its end. Several hiking trails start at the end of the road (just beyond Little Therriault Lake) and lead to many of the lakes in the area.

loon, Gavia immer

Paradise and Bluebird Lakes are the closest, about two miles in, with about a 1,000-foot elevation gain. A pamphlet with a rough trail map is available at the Murphy Lake Ranger Station south of Eureka. Pick up a map of the Kootenai National Forest for clearer detail.

In the winter, Grave Creek Rd. and several spur roads are groomed for cross-country skiing and snowmobiling. To access 4.5 miles of easy, snowmobile-free cross-country skiing, park at the Birch Creek Recreation Area adjacent to the Murphy Lake ranger station.

Accommodations

It's not expensive to stay the night in Eureka. The newly remodeled **Creek Side Motel,** 1333 Hwy. 93 N, tel. (406) 296-2361, has rooms for $32 s or $42 d per night. They also have a campground with sites for both RVs and tents, plus shower and laundry facilities. **Ksanka Inn,** Hwy. 93 and Hwy. 37, tel. (406) 296-3127, is a 24-hour store, deli, and bakery as well as a motel. Rates here run $31 s, $36 d.

Crystal Lakes Condominiums, northeast of Fortine on Hwy. 93, tel. (406) 882-4586, face onto the Whitefish Range. This resort area includes a pool, hot tub, tennis courts, and cross-country ski trails. There's a public nine-hole, par-three golf course across the highway from Crystal Lakes.

B&Bs: Located on 50 acres and bordering a trout stream, **Huckleberry Hannah's Montana Bed & Breakfast,** 3100 Sophie Lake Rd., tel. (406) 889-3381 or (800) 889-3381, offers a variety of lodging options. There are bedrooms and suites (all with private baths) in the 5,000-square-foot log lodge ($55-90 for a double), and also a lakeside cottage with a kitchen that sleeps up to six ($100 for a double and $25 a person thereafter).

Resorts: Southeast of Eureka, near Stryker, **Loon's Echo Resort,** tel. (406) 882-4676 or (800) 956-6632, is one of Montana's most unique and secluded resorts. Established as a fish farm on Fish Lake at the turn of the century, a 65-acre homestead (which included the 40-acre lake) was carved out of the Stillwater State Forest. The land passed through a number of hands, each owner building his own home or cabin on the lake, until the present owners bought the property and developed it into a recreational resort. There are basically two choices for lodging. Five freestanding cabins and houses ($140-325 double per day) have been updated and remodeled into secluded housekeeping units that sleep from two to 10 people. Additionally, a new log lodge has just been completed that features two suites ($145) and three standard guest rooms ($100), as well as a very good restaurant, 40-foot lap pool and exercise area, billiard room and hot tub. Fishing is great in Fish Lake, or the private stocked pond, and yes, there are two pairs of nesting loons on the lake. The lodge is open year-round, and offers cross-country and snowmobiling packages, as well as discounted packages to Big Mountain Ski Area in Whitefish, only 30 minutes away.

Camping: North of Eureka, the Ten Lakes Scenic Area has two campgrounds, **Big Therriault Lake** and **Little Therriault Lake.** To the south, **Murphy Lake, North Dickey Lake,** and **South Dickey Lake** all have campgrounds.

Food and Drink

Dewey Street Diner, on Dewey St. (Hwy. 93), tel. (406) 296-2197, draws a big local crowd. It has a salad bar. The sporting visitor will undoubtedly venture into **TJ's Restaurant and Lounge,** which houses a card room and a pawnbroker on Hwy. 93 next to the Big Sky Lanes, tel. (406) 296-3174. The obligatory **Stockman's Bar** is a good bet if you want a beer with your burger.

For fine dining, it's hard to beat the restaurant at **Loon's Echo Resort,** tel. (406) 882-4676. For this part of Montana, the menu has an international feel, with fresh fish, steak, pork, and chicken served with imaginative sauces, as well as a selection of salads and pasta.

Information and Services

The **Eureka Ranger Station** is on the north edge of town, at 1299 Hwy. 93, tel. (406) 296-2536 or 296-2769 for recorded information. There's also a ranger station at Murphy Lake, south of Eureka, tel. (406) 882-4451.

For **police, fire, and ambulance emergencies** in Eureka call 911. **Eureka Laundry and Lockers** is at 308 Dewey St., tel. (406) 296-2204.

DOVER PUBLICATIONS, INC.

GLACIER NATIONAL PARK

Glacier National Park contains over 1,500 square miles of extraordinarily scenic wilderness. Towering, glacier-pocked summits bend over mirrorlike lakes. Wildlife, from wolves to bald eagles, from moose to ptarmigans, inhabits the park's thick forests, streamsides, and rocky promontories; over 60 species of mammals and 200 species of birds make their homes in Glacier. Easily one of the most spectacular drives in the country is Going-to-the-Sun Road, which climbs from lakes and forest, up the sheer face of the Rockies, to a fragile,

alpine meadow almost 7,000 feet above sea level.

Glacier is a park for the outdoor-minded: you'll want to leave the car behind. Over 700 miles of hiking trails link backcountry peaks and lakes. In winter the park's roads double as cross-country ski trails.

Sometimes called the "Crown of the Continent" for its staggeringly rugged skyline, Glacier, and its Canadian cousin Waterton Lakes National Park, forms one of the crown jewels of the National Park system.

INTRODUCTION

THE LAND

Peak for peak, and valley for valley, Glacier National Park contains some of the most astonishing geology in the country. Three geologic stages have successively acted on the land, each leaving distinctive and unique features.

Belt Sedimentary Rock
The rocks that form the mountains of Glacier National Park were laid down when the area was resting under primordial seas. The profusion of primitive algae and limestone indicates that the oldest formation in the park, the **Altyn Formation,** developed under a shallow sea perhaps 1.5 billion years ago. Altyn Formation, stark

white, is the bottom tier of the immense layer cake that is Glacier National Park.

In response to ancient geologic forces, the seafloor fell; plantlife here ended, but fine gray silt began to accumulate. Almost 2,700 feet of this barren clay, called the **Appekunny Formation,** sits on top of the fossil-rich Altyn. About 900 million years ago, the **Grinnell Formation** began layering on top of the Appekunny Formation in the increasingly shallow seas. These two formations, together over 5,500 feet thick, comprise the most evident and colorful of the geologic layers in the park. Iron traces in the Grinnell Formation, which formed in oxygen-rich shallow seas, were transformed by pressure and heat into hematite, a barn-red mineral. Similar sediments from the Appekunny Formation, which formed deep in the sea where there was little oxygen for the iron to

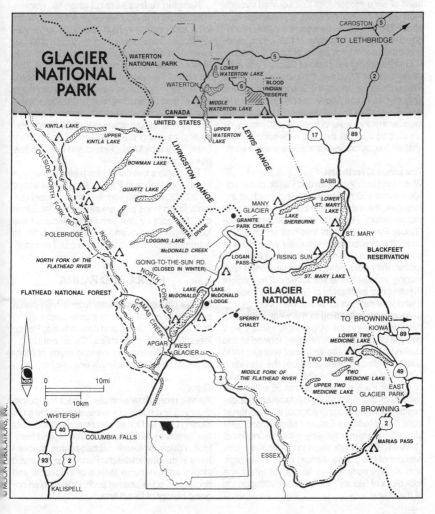

bond with, instead reacted with silicate minerals to form a dull green chlorite. At their juncture, red and green layers overlap, indicating an interregnum of shifting sea levels.

In time, the shallow seas again supported life. The resulting sedimentary limestone, called the **Helena** or **Siyeh Formation,** contains rich deposits of primitive algae. This 3,500-foot-thick deposit is shot through with a volcanic sill, a thin band of once-molten rock that squirted through the Helena Formation along a horizontal fault about 750 million years ago. It's easily recognized as the resistant layer of black rock sandwiched between thick bands of white limestone.

On the very highest peaks of Glacier Park, at elevations above 7,000 feet, the two youngest of the Precambrian formations, the **Snowslip** and **Shepard,** rise as horns above deeply glaciered valleys. To capture the full mystery of the park, remember that the peaks of these 10,000 mountains are capped with rock that was once sediment in a shallow sea, before vertebrate life began on earth.

The Lewis Overthrust

When the North American and Pacific plates collided some 150 million years ago, much of the rock near the old seacoast buckled and warped into mountains. However, the 18,000 feet of proto-Glacier Park sediments that had accumulated under the Precambrian seawater were durable enough that, instead of fracturing into a bulldozed rubble, they split along a deep horizontal fault roughly parallel to the soil surface. The ancient Precambrian sediments of Glacier Park became a wedge of rock cut loose from its moorings.

As mountain building to the west continued, this free-floating bit of geologic history was gouged up out of the bowl it was formed in and pushed eastward onto the top of younger rock. Under continued pressure from the elevating bulwark of the new Rocky Mountains, the rocks of Glacier Park slid east almost 35 miles over the top of much younger Cretaceous-era deposits. View the leading edge of the overthrust from Two Medicine Lake or other sharp cliffs along the eastern front, where the mountains of Glacier National Park seem to rise up like a rock wall out of the prairie. Almost three miles high, with ancient sedimentary layers still intact, the rock block of Glacier Park is literally sitting on top of the plains.

Glaciation

During the last ice age, glaciers filled the park. Like a scoop pulled through a block of ice cream, these glaciers deepened, rounded, and straightened the park's valleys. The largest glaciers scoured out St. Mary and McDonald Valleys. Dammed by moraines, these now hold lakes with expansive views up to narrow peaks, also carved by glaciers.

Hanging valleys were cut when two glaciers intercepted one another—the smaller glacier left a scooped valley high above the larger valley floor. Sometimes two or more glaciers formed on different sides of a peak; when they finished carving out **cirques** on each side, little was left of the original peak but a craggy **horn.** Other glaciers formed along a mountain ridge and edged downstream in a parallel movement. The peaks that divide these U-shaped valleys are finlike: when marshaled into regiments, as along Lake McDonald or St. Mary Lake, they look like upside-down boats, keels pointed skyward.

The glaciers that carved the peaks and valleys in Glacier National Park disappeared about 10,000-12,000 years ago; the small glaciers currently found in the park are much younger. Since the 19th century, the remaining glaciers have lost almost three-quarters of their mass due to warmer temperatures and decreased snowfall.

FLORA AND FAUNA

Glacier National Park rises from a high-plains ecosystem on the east to alpine tundra along the Continental Divide and back down to Pacific forests, all within 25 miles. It's an amazingly concentrated venue for viewing many of Montana's wide-ranging animals and plants.

Flora

Plants, more than animals, reflect the quick-changing and numerous ecosystems in the park. Skirting Lake McDonald and other westside lakes are forests of red cedar, Douglas fir, and hemlock. Watch for skunk cabbages and bracken ferns in marshy lowlands. Farther up mountain slopes are extensive stands of lodgepole and deciduous, cone-bearing larch, indicating an ongoing history of forest fires.

Along the Continental Divide are expanses of alpine tundra. The midsummer wildflower display, including lemon-yellow glacier lilies, dark blue gentians, pink heathers, and the greenish white spires of bear grass, is spectacular. Examine rocky outcrops for colorful lichens.

The east side of the park is much drier, with aspen commingling with the dominating conifers. Wildflowers include red and white geraniums, Indian paintbrush, gaillardia, and pasqueflowers.

Fauna

Although grizzly bears are the most talked about animal in the park, they are much less numerous than the smaller black bears. Both species deserve respect. Recognize grizzly bears by the hypertrophied shoulder muscles, which form a substantial hump just behind the neck. Generally a mottled brown color, grizzlies also have a dish-shaped face. Black bears aren't always black, but are often brown or cinnamon colored. And, at 200 pounds, they are a third the size of their grizzly brethren.

Mountain goats haunt the peaks and escarpments of Glacier Park. Near Logan Pass, they gather at natural salt licks in the cliffs above the road. Bighorn sheep, a few wolves, white-tailed deer, and moose are other large residents. Near streams, watch for beavers and river otters. Hoary marmots abound along hiking trails, and ground squirrels nose into pant legs and lunch bags at every picnic area.

Ospreys and bald eagles are the park's principal birds of prey. Watch for water ouzels (a.k.a. "dippers") near streams; they're not drowning themselves, they're diving and bouncing around underwater looking for food. A hatch of ptarmigans sauntering across the road often brings traffic to a halt.

HISTORY

Salish tribes west of the Continental Divide traditionally traveled over Marias Pass on yearly trips to hunt buffalo. After the Blackfeet Indians moved to prairies east of the park in the late 1700s, they consolidated their hold over the entire area; Marias Pass became the scene of bloody battles when Salish hunting parties encountered Blackfeet warriors.

BEAR GRASS

Bear grass covers the slopes of Glacier in July and August. Not every summer brings a bumper crop, however, and that has less to do with the weather than it does with the plant's life cycle. An individual bear grass plant blooms only once every seven years. Some years, the torchlike stalks are abundant; other years they're a mere scattering.

Native Americans used the long, tough leaves of the plant (a member of the lily family) for trading, especially with Pacific coast tribes, who wove the leaves into clothing and watertight baskets. Some tribes also roasted and ate the root.

Though bears don't eat bear grass, elk and mountain goats do.

JUDY JEWELL

Bear grass is the highlight of the summer wildflower display.

Early frontiersmen who explored the Glacier Park area also had to be wary of the Blackfeet. Peter Fidler, an agent of the Hudson's Bay Company and in 1792 the first white to tour the Glacier Park area, did so in the company of Blackfeet warriors. Twenty years later, trapper Finan McDonald crossed Marias Pass with a group of

Flathead Indians and was immediately ambushed by the Blackfeet landlords.

Under pressure from the railroads, miners, and settlers, the Blackfeet sold the eastern slope of the park in 1895 for $1.5 million, thus opening the area up for business. Copper mining was a bust, as was oil exploration. Tourism—amply advertised by the Great Northern Railroad, which in 1891 completed its service through Marias Pass just south of the park—was left as the area's economic mainstay. Conservationists, leagued with powerful railroad interests, sought to establish the area as a national park. In 1910, President W.H. Taft signed the bill creating Glacier National Park.

Between 1910 and 1917, the Great Northern spent $1.5 million developing tourist facilities. It built a series of huge lodges, chalets, and tent camps, each a day's horseback ride away. The Great Northern's recommended itinerary of hikes, fishing, and trail rides required a full week to "do" the park.

This leisurely, genteel, and recreation-oriented era was challenged in 1933 when the CCC finished the Going-to-the-Sun Road, thus introducing the automobile to Glacier Park's backcountry.

The volume and pace of traffic in the park quickened; in 1925, only 40,000 people visited Glacier; in 1936, 210,000 visitors traveled through, many simply to experience the Going-to-the-Sun Road. The old Great Northern facilities fell into disuse, and strip towns grew up on the outskirts of the park to service the needs of motorists. Fragile ecosystems in the park began to deteriorate under the weight of increased traffic. Tourism in Glacier reached a nadir during the late 1960s, when a survey found that the average tourist spent only 25 hours in the park.

Glacier Park's backcountry is still not on the typical tourist's itinerary, and many people still zoom over Going-to-the-Sun Road on a cross-country road-trip blitz. But increased environmental awareness since the 1970s has multiplied the number of people who linger amongst Glacier's unique topography and wildlife haunts.

ACCOMMODATIONS

The enormous lodges built by the Great Northern Railroad still stand at East Glacier, Waterton,

GLACIER'S BACKCOUNTRY CHALETS

For many hikers, backcountry chalets were a big part of Glacier's charm. Sperry and Granite Park chalets, remnants of the Great Northern's heyday in the park, are each a day's hike from Logan Pass. These chalets traditionally offered an evening meal, dormitory-style lodging, breakfast, and a pack lunch, and were booked up months in advance.

Granite Park Chalet, built in 1914, is perched on an igneous outcropping at the north end of the Garden Wall. Four trails lead to the chalet; the most popular is the seven-mile-long, stunningly beautiful, nearly level Highline Trail, which follows the base of the Garden Wall from Logan Pass. Other trails come in from the loop on Going-to-the-Sun Road (four miles), over Swiftcurrent Pass from Many Glacier (eight miles), and from Goat Haunt at the head of Waterton Lake (an approximately 23-mile backpacking trip via the northern extension of the Highline Trail).

Sperry Chalet is midway on a trail between Lake McDonald Lodge and Logan Pass, perched on a rocky ledge 6,560 feet above sea level.

In 1993, the Park Service was forced to close Granite Park and Sperry Chalets because their

crude sewage-treatment systems did not comply with legal standards. Bringing the toilets up to code would require a substantial investment of federal money, and several alternatives have been considered. It is likely that composting pit toilets will replace the existing flush toilets, which allowed waste to drain over rock outcroppings, attracting grizzly bears and creating generally unsanitary conditions. However, because of the cold, high-elevation setting, composting toilets already in place at Granite Park have not completely processed feces.

In order to cut back on the amount of sewage, a reduction in the chalets' services has been proposed, making them primitive overnight shelters rather than full-service backcountry lodges. Such proposals have drawn criticism from many devoted chalet lovers, who think it is important that the historically significant chalets continue to be used to the fullest.

Granite Park Chalet has now reopened as a self-service hiking shelter, but Sperry Chalet is still closed. Call the **Glacier National Park Information Line** at, tel. (406) 888-7800, to check on the status of the chalets and, if possible, to reserve a bunk.

and Many Glacier, and they have become near trademarks for the park itself. These old lodges are tremendously evocative and charming, but rooms aren't cheap, and for the money the amenities aren't great. That said, you simply must stay in at least one of these old landmarks. (But don't try to bring a dog along; no pets are allowed in Glacier Park lodgings.) See specific areas, following, for accommodations details; see below for central reservations numbers.

Campers are in luck. There are good campsites at each entry to the park and at lakeside recreation areas. Motels abound just outside of the park boundaries, particularly near the west entrance.

Unfortunately, Sperry Chalet is still closed, but Granite Park is now open again.

INFORMATION

A seven-day entrance pass to Glacier National Park is $10 per vehicle. Bicyclists, motorcyclists, and foot travelers pay $5. Admission to Waterton Lakes Park is an additional C$4 per day per person, or C$8 for a family group.

Contact the **Superintendent, Glacier National Park,** West Glacier, MT 59936, tel. (406) 888-7800, for more information, or visit the website at www.nps.gov/glac. To contact Waterton National Park, call (403) 859-2224.

For reservations at any of Glacier & Waterton Park's lodges or motels, call (602) 207-6000, or visit the website of Glacier Park Inc. (or GPI, the official concessionaire in charge of lodging and transportation in the park) at www.glacierparkinc .com. Canadians can call (800) 215-2395 year-round for lodging information.

Classes

The **Glacier Park Institute,** tel. (406) 755-1211, P.O. Box 7457, Kalispell, MT 59904, offers a number of classes and seminars, Elderhostel programs (academic college classes for seniors), and day-long explorations—some available for university credit. This private nonprofit corporation offers course work that examines the Glacier Park's cultural and natural resources while increasing public awareness of ecosystem management and sustainability issues. Classes are held in June, July, and August in Glacier National Park, and from April through October at facilities at Big Creek in the Flathead National Forest.

Websites and Publications

The park service distributes a free *Summer Vacation Planner* at the park gates and neighboring tourist centers. It contains a good overview of current information on rates, programs, recreation, and services. Much of the same information is available from the official website, www.nps.gov/glac.

Another very helpful website is the commercial site at http://www.americanparknetwork.com /parkinfo/gl/. There is a ton of up-to-date information here amongst the ads for decongestants and banks. The photos are nice as well. GPI's website (see above) provides current rates on park accommodations.

GETTING THERE

Kalispell offers the closest airline service to the park. **Amtrak** stops at East Glacier and Belton (a.k.a. West Glacier) four times weekly when the park is open, May 15-Sept. 15. Amtrak stops at Essex, near the southern tip of the park, year-round.

Independent bus lines associated with Greyhound, tel. (800) 231-2222, can get you as close as Whitefish on the west and Great Falls on the east.

GPI operate shuttles from both Kalispell and Great Falls to the park for those travelers who want to stick to public transportation in the park. For information, call (406) 226-9311 or, in the off-season, (602) 207-6000. Reservations are required. From Kalispell, you can also arrange a shuttle to the park by contacting Flathead Glacier Transportation, tel. (800) 829-7039, or Kalispell Taxi and Airport Shuttle, tel. (406) 752-2842.

GETTING AROUND

Red roll-top **park buses** operate out of the lodges at East Glacier, Many Glacier, Waterton, and Lake McDonald and offer guided tours of the park and a shuttle service from one lodge to another. The "hiker's shuttle" is the most direct option; it drops off hikers and recreationalists at trailheads and also offers lodge-to-lodge transportation. Unfortunately, these shuttles operate only after a minimum number of people have signed up, and can't be counted on if you have a tight schedule. The tour buses run to a schedule, but have mandated stops at beauty spots and nature paths, and might not be exactly what you're looking for if you just want to get from point A to B. Fares for these buses are relatively inexpensive. It costs just $20 to go from St. Mary's clear over to Lake McDonald Lodge. It's definitely possible to leave the car behind and see the park by public transportation, but be prepared to spend some time doing it.

Package tours of the park linked by the shuttle buses are also available through Amtrak, tel. (800) 872-7245. A five-day bus tour of the park makes a circuit of the park's most popular areas, with accommodations in the lodges. For a person traveling alone, such a junket costs $600-750; sharing a room with one other person cuts the cost about in half.

From East Glacier, **Sun Tours,** tel. (406) 226-9220 or (800) 786-9220, offers interpretive tours of Glacier Park from a Native American perspective. Tours highlight Blackfeet culture and history, and how that culture and history relate to the park's natural features.

Since the Going-to-the-Sun Road is narrow and tortuous by modern standards, there is a limit on the size of vehicles allowed between Avalanche Campground on the western side of the divide and Sun Point to the east. All vehicles (including towed campers) must measure in at less than 24 feet in length and less than eight feet in width (including mirrors).

Bicycles are not allowed on Going-to-the-Sun Road during the middle of the day between June 15 and Labor Day. Before planning a trip, contact the NPS for other cycling restrictions before planning a trip.

WEST GLACIER PARK AND THE MIDDLE FORK OF THE FLATHEAD RIVER

The Middle Fork of the Flathead River runs out of the Bob Marshall and Great Bear Wilderness Areas and along the southwest border of the park to West Glacier. West Glacier, while more restrained than its Yellowstone counterpart, certainly exudes the last-chance-to-buy aura of a town on the brink of a national park.

SIGHTS

Save your money up for a **helicopter ride** over the park. Several heli-tour outfitters work out of the West Glacier area, and short flights start at about $65 per person. Call the **Vista Motel,** tel. (406) 888-5311; **Glacier Heli-Tours,** tel. (406) 387-4141 or (800) 879-9310; or **Kruger Heli-copters,** tel. (406) 387-4565.

For those who wish to remain more firmly planted, amble over to the Belton Chalets and dream of spending a night there, preparing to take the train back east, after a week of horseback chalet-hopping through the park. Until the Going-to-the-Sun Road was built in the 1930s, this is how most people toured the park. Romantic as it seems, it was obviously a vacation

for the wealthy. For better or worse, the paved road opened the park to middle-class tourists.

It's amazing how gravity has gone awry just outside the park entrance. The **House of Mystery,** tel. (406) 892-4550, bends all the rules on Hwy. 2 west of West Glacier. Another local roadside attraction, the **Glacier Park Maze,** tel. (406) 387-5902, is a two-story, mile-long science fair experiment. Both these places are open May-September.

Head about 35 miles southeast on Hwy. 2 to visit the **goat lick,** a mineral-laden cliff that provides goats with salt. A parking area near milepost 182 vents onto a short trail to the overlook. Spring is the big mineral-licking season; evenings in early June are certain to keep visitors entranced with billy, nanny, and kid goats. Binoculars help.

RECREATION

Hiking
Most of the hikes in this part of Glacier are long backpacking trips on little-used trails into wild country. Animals, including bears, abound in these woods and stream bottoms. Glacier Park

maps show trails along every creek. Those planning to hike in the area should seek up-to-date trail information from the Walton Ranger Station on Hwy. 2 near Essex, tel. (406) 888-5628. They can also provide backcountry permits, which are required for overnight hikes; in this section of the park, there is no constraint but good sense concerning where to camp.

A couple of shorter hikes do originate at the Walton Station. Hike to **Ole Creek** and follow the trail as far as you like. The same trailhead provides access to the **Scalplock Lookout,** four unrelentingly steep miles to great views.

Leave the highway about two miles east of the goat lick to find a trail into the Great Bear Wilderness Area.

For a guided expedition into the park, contact **Glacier Wilderness Guides,** P.O. Box 535, West Glacier, MT 59936, tel. (406) 387-5335, or in Montana (800) 521-RAFT.

Rafting

Several whitewater companies are based in West Glacier. Float trips on the Middle Fork of the Flathead comprise most of their scheduled outings, though arrangements can be made to float the South Fork (in the Bob Marshall Wilderness Area) or the North Fork (in the northwest corner of Glacier Park). Actress Meryl Streep rowed parts of the Flathead in *The River Wild,* but not every stretch of the river is as harrowing as it looks in that film. Half-day and full-day trips along the lower stretch of the Middle Fork are good family floats, with great scenery and some whitewater. The river's upper stetch is a wild four- to six-day trip (around $900).

Glacier Raft Co., tel. (406) 888-5454 or (800) 235-6781 gets good recommendations from local folks. It and other operators offer similar trips and prices: **Glacier Wilderness Guides,** tel. (406) 888-5466; **Great Northern Float Trips,** tel. (406) 387-5340 or (800) 535-0303; **Wild River Adventures,** tel. (406) 387-9453 or (800) 826-2724. Day-long floats run about $70, and half days are about $36. Each of these companies will provide longer trips, with the option of adding hikes and horseback rides to the river-running.

The Middle Fork is a Wild and Scenic River, and this official designation is particularly apt in its upper reaches in the Bob Marshall and Great Bear Wilderness Areas. It's possible to fly in to float this wilderness river; the Schaeffer Meadows airstrip is near the river in the Bob Marshall.

The wilderness stretches of the river are not easy; indeed they can be dangerous for novice rafters. Even the lower reaches are better floated in a raft or kayak than a canoe, and anyone with questionable skills should sign on with an outfitter. Early summer is the best time to float the Middle Fork; water levels are high, but not at flood stage, and some of the chill has gone out of the air.

Fishing

The stretch of the Middle Fork of the Flathead paralleling Hwy. 2 isn't a particularly noteworthy fishing stream, but its upper reaches in the Great Bear Wilderness are loaded with trout. These aren't official fishing waters of the national park, so a Montana fishing license is required. The raft companies listed above do double duty as fishing outfitters.

Bicycling

Rent bikes at **Grizzly Mountain Bike Rentals,** tel. (406) 888-5787. It's right by the park entrance and charges $8 an hour, or $23 a day.

During the summer, the Forest Service roads and ski trails around Essex are suitable for mountain biking, and the Izaak Walton Inn in Essex has bikes for rent, tel. (406) 888-5700.

Cross-Country Skiing

Ski trails around the **Izaak Walton Inn** in Essex are free to hotel guests; nonguests can pay a few dollars for a day pass. Over 30 km (19 miles) of trails are groomed regularly, and though most of them are geared toward novice or intermediate skiers, a few runs are studded with faceplant opportunities, even for good skiers. There's usually enough snow for skiing from Thanksgiving through mid-April.

Trail networks are also maintained by the Glacier Wilderness Resort and the Glacier Highland Motel. The Glacier Highland's seven miles (11 km) of trails start right behind this West Glacier motel; stop in the office to get a map.

The 13 miles of trails near the Glacier Wilderness Resort are between West Glacier and Essex. Skiers follow old sections of Hwy. 2 and climb to Garry Lookout.

More than 19 miles (30 km) of groomed trails and worthy snow from Thanksgiving to mid-April invite cross-country skiers to the grounds of the Izaak Walton Inn.

JUDY JEWELL

Golf

Glacier View Golf Club, tel. (406) 888-5471 or (406) 888-9917, is just north of Hwy. 2 on the way into the park. It's a public 18-hole course looking onto the mountains.

ACCOMMODATIONS

West Glacier Area

Remember that there are more accommodations in Apgar, just inside the park entrance.

The **Great Northern Chalets,** tel. (406) 387-5340 or (800) 735-7897, offers 12 chalets, each of which will sleep four to six people. Each chalet contains a kitchenette, fireplace, and barbecue; there's also an indoor pool and spa. The owners also operate a whitewater raft outfitting service, and can arrange horseback riding and fishing trips. Chalets rent for $165-225 in high season.

The view from the **Vista Motel,** tel. (406) 888-5311 or (800) 837-7101, is indeed grand. Perched on a bluff overlooking Hwy. 2 and the peaks of Glacier, with a helicopter in the front yard, this is a hard one to miss on the drive in from Kalispell. The view *is* the best thing about this place, and that, plus convenience, friendliness, and a heated pool, makes it a good bet for rooms in the $65 range. Though operations scale down in the winter, the Vista is open all year.

The **River Bend Motel,** 200 Going-to-the-Sun Road, tel. (406) 888-5662, is just off Hwy. 2 toward the park entrance. Its location on the

Flathead River makes for easy access to fishing and float trips, which can be arranged by the management. Rooms run about $70, cottages a few dollars more. The motel season is mid-May through mid-Septmber.

Izaak Walton Inn

Those who aren't bent on barreling right down Going-to-the-Sun Road after spending a night near the park entrance would be wise to look 30 miles southeast to the Izaak Walton Inn in Essex. The hotel was built by the Great Northern in 1939 to house railroad workers. (Essex was, and is still, an important railroad post; it's where extra engines are added to help trains over Marias Pass.) It's now popular with park visitors and has gained a cultlike standing among railroad buffs and cross-country skiers.

And well it should. The Izaak Walton is truly one of Montana's best getaways. Amtrak's Empire Builder stops a stone's throw from the half-timbered hotel, and groomed ski trails run for miles. Energetic skiers can take a guided tour in the park, or can drive themselves to the unplowed Going-to-the-Sun Road or to East Glacier for a ski trip to Two Medicine Lake. Cross-country skis and snowshoes are available for rent. In summer, the lodge is open to hikers, anglers (this isn't called the Izaak Walton for nothing), and mountain bikers (bikes also for rent).

Even if you don't have time or the inclination to head into the wilderness, the Izaak Walton has atmosphere to spare; you'll love curling up in the lobby by the fireplace or having a drink in the friendly downstairs bar.

Rooms in the lodge are $98 (all rooms now have private baths). The Izaak Walton has also renovated some cabooses and plunked them down on a hillside across the tracks. The cabooses have kitchenettes, sleep four, and cost $475 for a three-night stay, $850 for seven nights. None of the rooms have TV, radio, or telephones, but there is a Finnish sauna. Call (406) 888-5700 for reservations. If you arrive via Amtrak, the Izaak Walton also has a number of cars for rent.

If you're intrigued by the Izaak Walton, check out the website at www.vtown.com/izaakw.

Campgrounds

All of West Glacier's campgrounds are private RV enterprises ($12-20 a night), though there is a Forest Service campground, **Big Creek,** at the north end of Camas Creek Rd. about 20 miles northwest of West Glacier, and there are many coveted campsites in Glacier Park itself.

Lake Five Resort is on Belton Stage Rd. a little ways north of Hwy. 2. It's a pleasant Montana-style lakeside resort complete with boat rentals and lake swimming. The season runs mid-May through mid-Sept., tel. (406) 387-5601.

Tent campers and RVers alike will be glad for the **West Glacier KOA,** tel. (406) 387-5341, and will find it handy (two miles west of the park entrance), well-equipped, and large. Even bigger and closer to the park, **Glacier Campground** is noted for its evening barbecues and a generally high activity level on the sprawling, forested campground. The season for both the KOA and Glacier Campground runs mid-May through Sept., tel. (406) 387-5689.

FOOD AND DRINK

The **West Glacier Restaurant** at the River Bend Motel, tel. (406) 888-5403, is open May through Sept. for breakfast, lunch, and dinner. This is not an expensive (or fancy) place—it's easy to eat dinner for less than $10—and, as befits a place on the Flathead River, the house specialty is trout.

Casual barbecue dinners are served at the **Glacier Campground,** tel. (406) 387-5689. Steak, chicken, or ribs come with an assortment of picnic-style side dishes. It's a fun place to eat with a family or a group—dinners are about $12, with children's prices available.

The **Dew Drop Inn** is a roadside bar as classic as its name. It's in Coram, just west of West Glacier, tel. (406) 387-5445.

The food at the **Izaak Walton Inn** tastes sublime after a day of cross-country skiing, and it has just enough of a healthy edge to keep you eating more. Lunchtime teriyaki chicken is served on a whole-wheat roll at this Essex hotel . . . But there's really more of an emphasis on railroading than on food groups here. Rather than ordering oatmeal, ask for the "Caboose"; the chicken sandwich is a "Brakeman." The dining room looks right out on the tracks, and railroad workers mix with Essex neighbors, railroad buffs, and cross-country skiers in the dining room. It's a great place to stop for a meal, and it'll make most diners want to sign up for a hotel room. Lunches are $5-6; dinners are roughly twice that.

INFORMATION

Rangers at the **Walton Station** on Hwy. 2 near Essex, tel. (406) 888-5628, will offer advice on local hiking trails and dispense information sheets on mountain goats (the goat lick is just up the road).

TRANSPORTATION

Amtrak stops seasonally at West Glacier's Belton Station daily at 9:30 p.m. (westbound) and 7 a.m. (eastbound). The stop at Essex is year-round.

Park buses shuttle rail passengers from the train station to various destinations within the park: it's $5 to Lake McDonald Lodge, $15 to Logan Pass, and $25 to St. Mary.

Car rentals are available at Glacier Highland Motel, just across from the depot, tel. (406) 888-5427 or (800) 766-0811.

THE NORTH FORK
OF THE FLATHEAD RIVER

The North Fork of the Flathead River forms the northwestern border of Glacier National Park. Roads both inside and outside the park run up the valley to the small settlement of Polebridge. Since early in the park's history, the hamlet of Polebridge has been a quiet neighbor just outside Glacier's boundary. Many residents of Polebridge have fought development that would bring them fully into the tourist hubbub. The North Fork Road is still not paved all the way to town, and there's no electricity running up the North Fork, though both of these "improvements" are persistently rumored to be in the offing.

Don't look for naturalist-led day-hikes or bus tours of this northwest corner of Glacier—it's the park's least developed vally—though perhaps also its most threatened. Curiously, the Inside North Fork Road is the park's oldest, built in 1901 when oil was struck near Kintla Lake.

Threats of road building, logging, dams, mineral exploration, and general development continue in the non-national park areas of the North Fork. In the late 1980s, environmental groups successfully squelched plans to dig an open-pit coal mine just over the border into Canada. Now, logging and the attendant road networks threaten the area's habitats, and there are fears that Polebridge is all too ripe for development.

SIGHTS

Five miles up Camas Creek Rd. from Apgar, **McGee Meadows** is a marshy magnet for wildlife. Moose are particularly fond of such boggy areas, and may be spotted by quiet evening visitors. The road, relatively high and exposed here, yields good views of the park's mountains. To the west there are a couple of hiking trails from Camas Creek Rd. into the Apgar Mountains. Howe Ridge is to the east, and ridge runners need to hike up from the Inside North Fork Road—the trail past shallow Howe Lake crosses moose and beaver habitat.

Bowman Lake is one of the park's prettiest. Long and thin and surrounded by mountains, this is a good spot for photography and reflection.

Spend a night up the North Fork and look at the stars. With no electric lights to compete, they're particularly bright. The local cafe and saloon in Polebridge is called the Northern Lights, which are, indeed, commonly visible.

RECREATION

Hiking

A flat, seven-mile trail edges Bowman Lake's northwest shore and is a good up-and-back walk for a family. Extend the trip by continuing past the lake on a relatively gentle creekside climb to Brown Pass. (It's another seven miles between the backcountry campground at the head of Bowman Lake and the Brown Pass campground.) From the pass, hikers can cross the divide and continue east to Goat Haunt, on Waterton Lake, or take the high road back west to Kintla Lake.

Or, try this variation: start at **Kintla Lake,** hike 32 miles east to Goat Haunt, and then head south to a terminus at Logan Pass. Cut this trip shorter by taking the boat from Goat Haunt up to Waterton. The country between Upper Kintla Lake and Brown Pass is phenomenal, one of the places a hiker is most likely to see black bears or grizzlies. The Hole-in-the-Wall Campground, a mile west of the Continental Divide along this trail, may be the park's finest, and is certainly one of the most remote.

The **Numa Lookout** trail, five uphill miles to Numa Ridge, is a good place to walk slowly with an eye out for wildlife and good views of Bowman Lake and the Livingston Range. Catch the trail at Bowman Lake Campground.

Also starting at the foot of Bowman Lake, a trail skirts Numa Ridge and runs almost six miles to tiny **Akokala Lake.**

Fishing and Boating

Fish the lakes up the North Fork for magnificent scenery and an occasional cutthroat trout. Most anglers take to boats on Bowman Lake, which is open to motorboats with less than 10-horse-power engines; no motorized boats are allowed in Kintla Lake. Canoeists will go nuts over both these lakes—they're long, with miles of animal-sheltering shoreline to explore.

Skiing

The broad North Fork Valley is just as beautiful, and even more isolated, when it's covered with snow. Skiing is generally good here—cold temperatures keep the snow powdery. And it can get *cold*—a 35°-below-zero morning at the North Fork Hostel may sharply reduce outhouse visits, and early-morning ski tours may not start quite so early.

Two ski trails start at the Polebridge Ranger Station: one, suitable for beginners, heads three miles north to Big Prairie; the other follows the six-mile-long unplowed road to Bowman Lake. Stop in at the ranger station before heading out—they'll tell you whether it's safe to ski onto Bowman Lake.

ACCOMMODATIONS AND FOOD

There isn't much to say about lodgings in the North Fork, except that Polebridge's **North Fork Hostel and Square Peg Ranch** is a great place for a budget traveler, or anyone with a relaxed sense of sociability. Lights and kitchen appliances are powered by propane, wood stoves provide the heat, guests come prepared with sleeping bags and food, and the outhouse is plastered with reading material. The hostel's owner is one of the North Fork's leading environmentalists, and he has done much to keep prospectors out of town. Reservations are a good idea at the North Fork—call (406) 888-5241. It's open year-round, and beds go for $12 a night for the first two nights, $10 a night thereafter. Two cabins near the hostel rent for $25 a night, and two larger log homes sleep six and go for $250 a week. The hostel offers free use of mountain bikes, canoes, skis, and snowshoes. The hostel may close for the month of March, and it's wise to call ahead during the winter months. The **Northern Lights Saloon and Café** is part of the complex and offers light meals and drinks.

The other place to stay in Polebridge is not much more expensive, and no fancier than the hostel. **Polebridge Mercantile,** tel. (406) 888-5105, rents one-room cabins for $30 a night. Anyplace else, these propane-powered cabins would be the really *cool* place in town to stay, but

here they've got strong competition from the hostel. Either way, bring a sleeping bag or bedding, and don't even bother with a blow-dryer or travel iron. The **bakery** in the Mercatile is a great place for specialty breads, pastries, sandwiches, and coffee.

During the summer, the cafe next to the mercantile is worth a stop for its conviviality as well as its good food. The **Northern Lights** pours beer as well as coffee and is a comfortable Polebridge hangout. Indeed, it's the only restaurant for miles around.

Campgrounds

Bowman Lake Campground is the largest and most popular in the North Fork. Hiking trails wander off in all directions, including an easy one along the lakeshore. The campground at **Kintla Lake** is smaller, with fewer trails to choose from, but equally desirable. Both these campgrounds are fairly developed, though not to the parking-lot degree of those in the more traveled areas of Glacier.

Other roadside campgrounds a notch down in development are **Big Creek,** a Forest Service campground on the Outside North Fork Road near the Camas Creek entrance to the park; **Logging Creek** and **Quartz Creek,** on Inside North Fork Road between Apgar and Polebridge; **Bowman Creek,** near Polebridge; and **River,** on the North Fork River north of Polebridge. These are primitive campgrounds; bring your own water.

PRACTICALITIES

Information

The **Polebridge Ranger Station,** tel. (406) 888-5416, is right near the no-longer-pole-constructed bridge over the North Fork. Stop here for backcountry permits, trail information, or a chat about the local wolf packs.

Transportation

Drive in from the park on Camas Creek or Inside North Fork Roads; the Inside North Fork is rougher, but there are some campgrounds along it. From Columbia Falls, the Outside North Fork Rd., with good views of the Livingston Range, leads to Polebridge. Blankenship Road connects the Outside North Fork Road with West Glacier. In the winter, Outside North Fork Road and Blankenship Road are plowed.

LAKE McDONALD VALLEY AND GOING-TO-THE-SUN ROAD

THE LAND

The forests surrounding Lake McDonald are Glacier Park at its most Pacific. Western red cedar and western hemlock form the climax forest; Douglas fir, larch, pine, and spruce add diversity.

The oldest rocks on the west side of the park are around the head of Lake McDonald. These slatelike rocks were laid down under sea water. Up the Going-to-the-Sun Road, greenish mudstones of the Appekunny Formation developed in shallower water. Farther east, and higher on the slopes, the rocks of the Grinnell Formation were originally mudflats. They turned red when exposure to the air oxidized their ferrous minerals.

Once the road begins climbing, it moves into the Empire Formation, grayish-green rocks deposited underwater, and then to the Helena (Siyeh) limestones, which come into view near the Loop. The Helena Formation is dotted with stromatolites, cabbagelike fossil traces of blue-green algae.

Lake McDonald Valley has all the earmarks of glacial action—it's long, straight, and U-shaped. The lake itself is 10 miles long, a mile wide, and over 400 feet deep. Dozens of hiking trails take in everything from damp old-growth forests to alpine meadows.

SIGHTS

Apgar

Just inside the park entrance at West Glacier, Apgar Village greets visitors with an information center, gift shops (the **Montana House** is actually worth a stop for good-quality crafts), motels, a campground, cafes, and lovely Lake McDonald. The National Park Service purchased much of the town in 1930, but part of it is still privately owned.

Going-to-the-Sun Road

It took practically 20 years to build this road; when it opened for travel in 1933, it was an instant hit. The road, which starts its 52-mile run over the spine of the Rockies at Apgar, is one spectacular drive, even when clogged with traffic. Glacier may be a hiker's park at heart, but for those without the capacity or the time for trail walking, the Going-to-the-Sun Road provides a good view of the park's muscles and bones.

From Lake McDonald, the road follows McDonald Creek to the east and slightly uphill. The grade increases after Logan Creek, and it becomes genuinely steep as it approaches the Loop, a big switchback that brings the road under the Garden Wall, which it follows to the Continental Divide at Logan Pass. Approaching the pass from the west, it's easy to follow the changes in vegetation and geology: the lush coniferous forests near Lake McDonald give way to shrubs and scattered pines, and distinctive green and red mudstones and buff-colored limestones replace the dark shalelike rocks near the lake.

For those who prefer a chauffeured drive, tour buses operated by GPI, tel. (406) 226-9311, leave Lake McDonald Lodge for loop tours of the park each morning at 9.

Lake McDonald Area

An early homesteader, George Snyder, built a small hotel by Lake McDonald in 1895, 15 years before the area became a national park. John Lewis, a Columbia Falls furrier, took over Snyder's hotel, built the present lodge in 1914, and decorated it with hunting trophies (most of which still stare down from timbered beams and balconies). Charley Russell had a cabin nearby, and it has long been rumored that the pictographs around the lodge's fireplace are his work.

One needn't be a hotel guest to lounge in the **Lake McDonald Lodge** lobby or in the chairs overlooking the lake, and it's a comfortable stop after a day of hiking.

Lake McDonald has long been the territory of tourist cruise boats, and a boat is launched daily at 10 a.m., 1:30, 3:30, and 7 p.m. for a rather mundane hourlong tour. The boat dock is behind the lodge; adults pay $7, children

Going-to-the-Sun Road follows McDonald Creek on the west side of the park.

JUDY JEWELL

$3.50. The evening tour is especially popular—sunsets can be phenomenal.

Evening programs by park naturalists are scheduled nightly at Lake McDonald Lodge, Apgar Campground, and Fish Creek Campground.

In years past, bald eagles would flock to Lake McDonald to feed on spawning kokanee salmon. Since salmon populations have dwindled, the eagles have found better meals near Libby Dam, in the far northwest corner of Montana, and only a few show up in October to snatch fish from Lake McDonald.

RECREATION

Hiking
One of the park's easiest and most popular hikes takes in the western red cedar and hemlock forest near Avalanche Campground. The mile-long, wheelchair-accessible **Trail of the Cedars** follows a boardwalk over the floor of the old-growth

forest, past Avalanche Gorge, and returns via the campground. It's a splendid trail, even with crowds; solitude seekers will like it even better in the winter, when cross-country skiers may share the trail with moose.

Another cedar-hemlock hike starts at the Lake McDonald Ranger Station road, 1.2 miles north of Lake McDonald Lodge, and passes a bog lake and the **Sacred Dancing Cascades.** A park naturalist leads this hike several times a week (check at the Apgar information center for the schedule).

A forested trail starts at Fish Creek Campground and follows a ridge along the **west bank of Lake McDonald,** eventually looping around the muddy head of the lake and ending up at the lodge. It's 6.7 miles from the campground to the lodge; a short walk from the campground goes to **Rocky Point,** yielding good views of the lake and the mountains.

The trail to **Avalanche Lake** starts near the Trail of the Cedars and follows Avalanche Creek two miles through forest to the lake. Waterfalls draining Sperry Glacier tumble over the 1,500-foot wall, which encloses a cirque, and pour the glacial water into Avalanche Lake.

Hike from the Lake McDonald Lodge up to **Sperry Chalet** (6.2 miles one-way) or three steep miles farther to **Lake Ellen Wilson** or, on another spur, to **Sperry Glacier.** The trail continues on another 10 miles from Lake Ellen Wilson (which has a campground) over Gunsight Pass and returns to Going-to-the-Sun Road at the Jackson Glacier viewpoint, five miles east of Logan Pass. From this point, it's another long day's hike over Piegan Pass and down the other side of the Continental Divide to the Many Glacier Hotel.

From the same trailhead near the lodge, paths branch off to shallow **Fish Lake** (six miles roundtrip), the **Mt. Brown Lookout** (a steep, arduous 10-mile roundtrip), and Snyder Lake (4.5 miles in to a campground beside an emerald lake nestled in the mountains).

Bicycling
Because of heavy traffic and slim shoulders, bicycle travel along **Going-to-the-Sun Road** is restricted during the busy summer months. From June 15 to Labor Day, bikes are prohibited on the road between Apgar and Sprague Creek Camp-

ground, and between Logan Creek and Logan Pass, 11 a.m.-4 p.m. Logan Creek, at the base of the Loop, is about 10 miles from Sprague Creek Campground and about six miles from Avalanche Campground. Between Apgar and Logan Creek, the road stays in the McDonald Creek Valley, climbing some, but not dramatically. Shortly after it crosses Logan Creek, the road really takes off uphill. Expect the ride between Logan Creek and Logan Pass to take three hours, and expect to feel more exhilarated than exhausted upon reaching the summit.

Cyclists who'd rather not dodge the cars on Going-to-the-Sun Road can bike the paved trail between Apgar and the park entrance. Also starting in Apgar, Camas Creek Rd. heads up toward the North Fork area, and it is paved for the first 12 miles.

Boating and Fishing
Rent boats at the Apgar dock. Canoes and rowboats are $5 an hour, motorboats are $15. There's fishing tackle for rent at the boat dock, but the savvy angler won't bother with the few planted cutthoat or the lake trout that migrated over to Lake McDonald from Flathead Lake.

Horseback Riding
Apgar Corral, (406) 888-5522 (between the village and the park entrance), and **Lake McDonald Corral,** tel. (406) 888-5670 (across the road from the lodge), offer rides ranging from a $15 one-hour amble to a $50 daylong ride. Call for specific destinations and departure times.

Cross-Country Skiing
In the winter, Going-to-the-Sun Road is plowed to the head of Lake McDonald. From the parking area there, it's possible to ski as far up the road as stamina permits. The skiing is technically easy, and there's usually some wildlife around. Pull off the main drag and follow the **Sacred Dancing Cascade** hiking trail or ski up to the **Trail of the Cedars.**

For a longer trip (about 12 miles), ski up Camas Creek Rd., take a right at McGee Meadow, and return on the **Inside North Fork Road.** A final detour through the Fish Creek Campground to **Rocky Point** adds a couple of miles and a good view of Lake McDonald.

ACCOMMODATIONS

Lake McDonald Lodge is perhaps the most charming of the Glacier Park lodges. It retains rugged, hunting-lodge touches, such as grizzly bear hides draped over the balcony railings, animal heads posted on massive timbered columns above the lobby, and a walk-in fireplace bordered by pictographs (rumored to have been drawn by Charley Russell). The rooms aren't as comfortable as the lobby, however, and, at $124 d, they're no bargain. An adjoining motel costs

spectacular Lake
McDonald

$85 d, and cabins are $78. The lodge's season run's from early June through late September. Reservations are essential: call (602) 207-6000.

In Apgar Village, the **Village Inn** is also operated by Glacier Park, Inc. (a.k.a. Greyhound-Dial). The lakeside motel rooms are adequate, though nowhere near as charming as the Lake McDonald Lodge. Rooms start at $87 d; kitchenette suites run $120. The motel is open mid-May through late September. Reservations are handled by the same telephone operators listed above for Lake McDonald Lodge.

Less expensive rooms are a stone's throw away at **Apgar Village Lodge,** (406) 888-5484. It's open May through mid-Oct., with motel rooms for around $65 and cabins for $70-100.

Campgrounds

The **Apgar Campground** is the park's largest and most bustling. Depending on how you look at it, it's either conveniently or annoyingly close to Apgar Village. Most campers enjoy the proximity to Lake McDonald. Sites are $12.

Just slightly off the beaten path, **Fish Creek Campground** is a tri-looped jumble of trailers. It's off Camas Creek Rd. on the northwestern shore of Lake McDonald. Fish Creek is a handy base for day-trips around the Lake McDonald area and up the North Fork of the Flathead River. Get up early and there's seclusion enough for a bracing, naked plunge into the lake. Sites are $15.

Sprague Creek Campground, on Going-to-the-Sun Road just west of Lake McDonald Lodge, gains some cachet by not permitting towed RVs, but it's really no more private or secluded than Apgar or Fish Creek. It is, however, a handy jumping-off point for bicyclists heading up the Going-to-the-Sun Road—two campsites are reserved until 7 p.m. for cyclists. Up to 12 people can be accommodated in these $4 per person spots. Motorists pay $12 a night.

FOOD AND DRINK

Lake McDonald Lodge serves reasonably good $10-15 dinners in a well-detailed dining room. The faux-hunting-lodge theme strongly influences the dinner menu (though there's no venison or elk-meat sausage). Though the lodge dining room entrees can be pricey for a budget traveler, it's possible to order chili or a salad and enjoy the ambience. A breakfast buffet and lunch are also served.

There's a coffee shop, replete with high 1960s-era architectural touches, across from the lodge. Food is tolerable and less expensive than the lodge dining room, but, remember, in a national park you'll always pay more for food, good or bad.

In Apgar, visitors can make the tough choices at **Eddie's Cafe**—ice cream or soup o' the day, which'll it be? Eddie's also serves full dinners with beer or wine; expect to pay at least $10.

Camp stores at both Apgar and the Lake McDonald Lodge complex stock essential groceries.

INFORMATION

The **Apgar Visitor Center** has park rangers on duty 8 a.m.-8 p.m. (shorter hours during the spring and fall, weekends during the winter) to answer questions, suggest hikes, and issue backcountry permits. The **Lake McDonald Ranger Station** is on a spur road at the head of the lake, about a mile past the lodge.

TRANSPORTATION

Red roll-top **park buses** depart from the Village Inn to the Lake McDonald Lodge twice each morning, and continue on to The Loop East Glacier and Many Glacier.

LOGAN PASS TO ST. MARY

From the Highline Trail at Logan Pass to Two Dog Flats around St. Mary Lake, the scenery on the east face of Glacier National Park is just as spectacular as, and more exposed than, that on the west side of the Divide. Geology is suddenly lucid as red Grinnell rocks and the green rocks of the Appekunny Formation glow in the morning light bouncing off St. Mary Lake. Westbound travelers will do well to stop in the St. Mary information center and purchase a copy of *Geology Along Going-to-the-Sun Road,* a book explaining roadside geology markers.

East of the pass, drying winds blow across stands of aspen and cottonwoods to the plains, which suddenly replace the mountains a few miles east of St. Mary.

SIGHTS

Logan Pass

Logan Pass, at 6,680 feet, is an alpine-arctic tundra environment. Even though the landscape here is shaped by a harsh climate, it's not able to withstand flower picking or trampling by hordes of hikers. To learn more about alpine ecology, stop in for a naturalist's talk at the Logan Pass visitor center. Talks are usually scheduled for 11 a.m., noon, and 1 p.m. daily from early June through Labor Day. The visitor center stays open as long as the road is passable—usually from June through October.

Glaciers started on either side of the Continental Divide at Logan Pass and eventually ran backwards into each other. Rather than leaving a spiky arête like the Garden Wall, chiseled away on both sides, the wall was entirely eroded.

St. Mary Lake

Even nonhikers will want to stop at the **Sun Point** trailhead and walk a few yards to the "peak-finder." Of the nine peaks visible from Sun Point, **Going-to-the-Sun Mountain** stands out at 9,942 feet. The mountain, whose name was taken for the road, recalls Napi, the Blackfoot

Old Man, who left his home in the sun to help the Blackfeet. Once he had finished his work on earth, he returned home via this mountain.

Boat tours of St. Mary Lake set out several times a day from the dock across from the Rising Sun complex. The 7 p.m. sunset cruise is popular but, unlike the daytime rides, it's not accompanied by a park naturalist. The one-hour ride costs $7 for adults, $3.50 for children.

For those who stick to the road, there's an official photography turnout overlooking **Wild Goose Island.** A real snob will pass this up, but it *is* a great cliche of a place to stop and put the Instamatic to work.

RECREATION

Hikes around Logan Pass

Glacier Park's most popular trail is the boardwalk from Logan Pass to **Hidden Lake Overlook,** a three-mile roundtrip hike through delicate alpine meadows, home to marmots, ptarmigan, and mountain goats. The weather can be blustery up here, even in midsummer, and the 500-foot climb to over 7,000 feet above sea level can be surprisingly fatiguing.

For a fairly level trail that goes on for miles, the **Highline Trail** can't be beat. It's the main route to Granite Park chalet, and it can be frustratingly crowded, but the above-timberline views, bear grass meadows, and chattering marmots are absorbing enough to eclipse the other hikers.

Glacier Park's mandatory photo stop at Wild Goose Island rarely disappoints.

JUDY JEWELL

Hikes around St. Mary Lake

Walk out to **Sun Point** for a view of St. Mary Lake and the surrounding mountains. This was the site of the most elaborate of the Glacier Park chalets; fell into disuse once the Going-to-the-Sun Road became the focus of a trip to the park and was dismantled in the late 1940s. From Sun Point, the trail skirts the lakeshore for less than a mile to **Baring Falls.**

Sunrift Gorge is on Baring Creek just above the falls—cap off the Sun Point walk by taking the spur trail and climbing to the gorge. Or, follow the lead of most gorge-viewers and park in the Sunrift Gorge pullout and walk 50 yards up the path to the narrow chasm, formed not by erosion but by a vertical slip of the rock.

Those in search of a *real* hike will want to continue past Sunrift Gorge to **Siyeh Pass** and **Preston Park.** This is no easy amble—the trail shoots up once it leaves Baring Creek, and Siyeh is Glacier's highest pass. As one would expect, persevering hikers are rewarded with great views and a delicate alpine environment. After passing alpine larch trees at Preston Park, the Siyeh Bend cutoff trail heads back to Going-to-the-Sun Road, making this a 12-mile hike. (Actually, most people do this hike in the opposite direction—it's an easier uphill, but yields less-spectacular views.) Park naturalists set out daily at 9 a.m. from Siyeh Bend on Going-to-the-Sun Road, marshaling hikers along on one of the park's best naturalist-led hikes.

An eight-mile hike to **Gunsight Lake** starts at either Sun Point or, more commonly, at the Jackson Glacier Overlook west of St. Mary Lake on Going-to-the-Sun Road. There's a campground at Gunsight Lake; Gunsight Pass is another *steep* two miles up the trail. From the pass, the trail drops down to Lake Ellen Wilson, and Sperry Chalet, and ultimately reaches the road again at Lake McDonald Lodge. The whole Gunsight Pass route takes two or three days to hike. Besides the inevitable switchbacks and vistas, expect to see mountain goats along this trail.

Boating and Fishing

Though boats are permitted on St. Mary Lake, there's no place to rent them. Anglers generally prefer boat fishing to bank fishing on St. Mary Lake, which is not really known for good fishing but does have some whitefish, rainbow, and brook trout. Hikers are rewarded by better fishing

at Red Eagle Lake, south of the park entrance, or at Gunsight Lake.

Cross-Country Skiing

Loop trails around **Red Eagle Valley,** near the park entrance, offers several miles of skiing for beginning and intermediate skiers. For those who want more of a challenge, the trail to Red Eagle Lake is a 14-mile roundtrip along Red Eagle Creek.

ACCOMMODATIONS

Rising Sun Motor Inn is operated by the Glacier Park concessionaire, Greyhound-Dial, near St. Mary Lake. Uninspiring motel rooms and cabins have the familiar steep tariffs of the other park lodging—$85 for a double motel room, $78 for a cottage (really just a cabin). For reservations, call (602) 207-6000.

At the St. Mary crossroads, the **St. Mary Lodge & Resort,** tel. (406) 732-4431 or (800) 732-9265 in Montana, is (some would say thankfully) *not* a Glacier Park, Inc. enterprise. The views don't suffer for being just outside the park boundaries, and the accommodations are every bit as comfortable as, and a touch cheaper than, those inside the park. None of the rooms either here or in the park lodges have TVs or radios, but who needs them when there's Singleshot Mountain out there?

A new addition to the St. Mary Lodge are the **Pinnacle Cottages,** two-bedroom cabins with full kitchens and kitchenettes.

Campgrounds

The **Rising Sun Campground** isn't particularly appealing in itself—83 shrubby, often hot sites ($12)—but it's just across the road from St. Mary Lake; there's a hiking trail heading up Rose Creek to Otokomi Lake, and there are pay showers in the nearby cabins complex.

Just inside the park boundary, the rather drab **St. Mary Campground** is about twice as large as Rising Sun and costs $15 a night, but is not so well-positioned for boaters and hikers. It is open for primitive camping in the off-season, $6 (Sept.-May).

Chewing Blackbones KOA, north of St. Mary on Hwy. 89, tel. (406) 732-4452, is a large Blackfeet-owned campground on Lower St. Mary Lake. It's a good bet when the park campgrounds are full. There's another KOA in St. Mary, tel. (406) 732-4422.

FOOD AND DRINK

Hungry travelers should note that between Lake McDonald and St. Mary, Rising Sun is the only place to buy food. The **Rising Sun** coffee shop serves Indian tacos as well as all the most predictable cafe breakfasts, lunches, and dinners. Like the motel, the coffee shop is open mid-June through late September. A camp store with a small grocery section is the alternative to the coffee shop.

There's a better meal waiting in St. Mary. The best bet is the **Park Cafe,** which serves up good vegetarian and Mexican food and delicious pies at the junction of Hwy. 89 and Going-to-the-Sun Road. The **Snowgoose Grille** at St. Mary Lodge features whitefish from St. Mary Lake and other entrees that occasionally transcend the expected steak, trout, and chicken dishes. Try the homemade sourdough scones or one of the huckleberry concoctions. The Snowgoose is open for breakfast, lunch, and dinner mid-May through Sept., tel. (406) 732-4431. Also part of the lodge is **Glacier Perk,** a coffeehouse with espresso and smoothies.

Also in St. Mary, **Johnson's,** at the north end of town, tel. (406) 732-5565, takes pride in home cooking and large portions—refuel after a long hike with their pie and cinnamon rolls.

INFORMATION

Rangers at the **Logan Pass Visitor Center** keep the fireplace stoked on chilly days and dispense maps, backcountry permits, and advice. More detailed maps and books on the park's trails, geology, and history are available from the **Glacier Natural History Association** here. The setup is much the same at the **St. Mary Visitor Center,** just inside the eastern park entrance

TRANSPORTATION

Red **park buses** leave from the St. Mary Visitor Center to Logan Pass, and Lake McDonald, Many Glacier, and East Glacier.

EAST GLACIER AND VICINITY

While East Glacier is not the best base for a several-day tour of the park, it is a handy entrance point for travelers from the east. Camp or hike at nearby Two Medicine lakes, with all the scenery and far less company than you'll find at Many Glacier or Lake McDonald.

There's more of a Native American presence here than in many other areas of the park. Even though most of East Glacier is controlled by non-Indians, it is within the Blackfeet Reservation boundaries and is part of an area historically and culturally important to the Blackfeet.

For the Native American angle on the park, consider joining one of Sun Tour's interpretive tours of the park—van tours featuring Blackfoot guides. For more information call tel. (406) 226-9220 or (800) 786 9220.

THE LAND

The Lewis Overthrust came to a halt just west of present-day East Glacier, and its leading edge is

visible at Running Eagle Falls near Lower Two Medicine Lake. The hard Precambrian rock of the Lewis Formation rolled on top of a younger, softer shale, which has worn away to form the gentler, hilly landscapes east of the overthrust.

Glaciers dug out the bottoms of the three Two Medicine Lakes (upper, middle, and lower). Moraines formed dams, allowing water to fill the troughs. Two Medicine Valley is surrounded by peaks, many adorned with waterfalls and hanging valleys.

Floodwaters coursed the Two Medicine area in 1964 and 1975, uprooting trees and boulders. There's still flotsam and jetsam along the stream banks, and boulders prematurely rounded by torrents of sandy floodwater.

HISTORY

Blackfeet camped in the Two Medicine Valley and gathered by the middle lake to make medicine. The name "Two Medicine" may harken to a time when, because of a dispute, one group camped on the upper lake, another group on the lower, or it may refer to the two different waterfalls manifested at Running Eagle Falls. When white prospectors exhibited interest in the northern Rockies, the Blackfeet were forced onto a reservation and ceded their mountain territories—the land that now composes the eastern half of Glacier National Park.

Rising Wolf Mountain, just north of Lower Two Medicine Lake, was named for the first white man in the area—Hugh Monroe, a Hudson's Bay trapper who came to the area in 1815 and married a Blackfeet woman.

When James J. Hill was planning the route of the Great Northern Railway, he heard rumors of a "lost" pass over the Continental Divide. In the winter of 1889, railroad surveyor John J. Stevens found Marias Pass and deemed it navigable by rail.

Early national park visitors typically pulled in on the train from the east, disembarking at East Glacier and spending a night at Glacier Park Lodge before saddling up to ride the circuit of backcountry chalets and tent camps in the company of a guide. For a hearty evocation of such a trip, read Mary Roberts Rinehart's *Through Glacier Park in 1915.* Once Going-to-the-Sun Road was built, auto travel supplanted both the train and the horse, and the spotlight was off the massive lodge.

SIGHTS

East Glacier

Stop by Glacier Park Lodge to sit in the lobby and write postcards or wander through the gardens. Blackfeet culture is the focus of twice-weekly evening talks in the hotel lobby; one need not be a hotel guest to listen in. Check the lecture schedule at the information desk in the lobby.

The **John L. Clarke Western Art Gallery** displays the work of western artists, including the eponymous Clarke, a part-Blackfeet, part-Scottish wildlife sculptor who lived in East Glacier from the early 1900s until his death in 1970.

Park Tours

Red roll-top **park buses** depart from Glacier Park Lodge for loop tours of the park every day at 10 a.m. Half-day excursions to Two Medicine Lake leave at 9:30 a.m. and 1:30 p.m. For fares

and information, call GPI at (406) 226-9311 or (602) 207-6000. Buses also link Glacier Park Lodge with other Glacier Park destinations, including Waterton Lakes Park.

Two Medicine

Two Medicine has some of the park's most spectacular scenery, but it's a ways from the Going-to-the-Sun Road drag strip and is often overlooked.

A glacier gouged Lower Two Medicine Lake at the foot of purplish red Rising Wolf Mountain (elev. 9,505 feet). Backcountry chalets built by the Great Northern were the first stop on a horseback circuit popular in the pre-automobile days. One wood chalet remains as the Two Medicine camp store.

Boat tours of Two Medicine Lake leave the dock at 10:30 a.m. and 1, 2:30, and 3:30 p.m. daily. The 45-minute tour costs $7 for adults, $4.50 children.

RECREATION

Hikes near Two Medicine Lakes

It's a short walk from the well-marked bridge over Two Medicine Creek through some conifers and across a rocky creekside to **Running Eagle Falls** (a.k.a. Trick Falls). When there's plenty of water, it appears to be like any other waterfall. The "trick" comes when water volume decreases late in the summer and water spouts from a hole beneath the main shelf of the falls. Look at the rim of the falls for the fault line marking the eastern edge of the Lewis Overthrust. Running Eagle, or Pitamakan, was a Blackfeet woman who reportedly led warriors over Cut Bank Pass on raids against Flathead and Kootenai tribes to the west.

Combine a hike to the fork-topped **Twin Falls** with a boat ride across Two Medicine Lake. Naturalist-led trips leave the Two Medicine boat dock at 1 and 2:30 p.m. daily for the cruise and two-mile hike.

For a full day's hike, **Upper Two Medicine Lake** is five miles from the Two Medicine Campground. The trail runs along the south shore of Lower Two Medicine Lake. To shorten the hike, catch the tour boat to the head of the lake.

Triple Divide Peak

Hike eight miles up the valley of Cut Bank Creek to Triple Divide Pass. The trail starts at the campground and, after a hike and a final scramble

JUDY JEWELL

*Running Eagle Falls in June, when it's all
treat and no trick*

from cairn to cairn, reaches the spot where Atlantic, Pacific, and Hudson Bay Creeks issue
from the Continental Divide.

Boating
Canoes, rowboats, and motorboats are rented for
$5-10 an hour at the boat dock on Lower Two
Medicine Lake. Though motorboats are permit-
ted, speed is limited to 10 mph.

Fishing
Pick up a tribal permit at the lodge or Two Medicine camp store to fish the Two Medicine River
or Lower Two Medicine Lake. Once inside the
park boundaries, stop by any visitor center or
ranger station and get park fishing regulations
(no license is necessary). Brook and rainbow
trout lurk in Lower Two Medicine Lake and Cut
Bank Creek.

Horseback Riding
Horseback rides are offered by East Glacier's

Great Bear Outfitters, tel. (406) 226-9220.
Short, inexpensive pony rides are offered in addition to hourly horse rentals. Great Bear also
has guides for big-game hunting in the fall.

Golf
The nine holes of the **Glacier Golf Course** span
Hwy. 49 just north of the lodge. Since the course is
run by Glacier Park, Inc., it keeps the same season
as the lodge. Call (406) 226-4411 for tee times.

Cross-Country Skiing
Once the snow starts piling up (late December),
it's easy to strap on skis at East Glacier and glide
to Two Medicine Lake. On nice days, it's an easy
day-trip.

ACCOMMODATIONS

Step upstairs from **Brownie's Market** to find a
charming youth hostel with sloping linoleum floors
and lots of old photos and books in the sleeping
rooms. Dorm-room beds go for $12 a night for
HI/AYH members, $15 for nonmembers. A pri-
vate room is $17 s ($20 nonmember) or $24 d
($30 nonmember). Brownie's is closed Oct. 15-
May 1, tel. (406) 226-4426. **Backpackers Inn,**
tel. (406) 226-9392, also offers even cheaper hostel accommodations in East Glacier.

Glacier Park Lodge charges $99-187 s, $105-
187 d; tel. (406) 226-5551 (during the summer
months) or (602) 207-6000 (offseason). It's a spectacular building, with huge Douglas fir timbers
forming the Ionic columns in the Grecian-revival
lobby, meticulously groomed gardens out front,
and a heated pool out the back door. The lodge is
open Memorial Day through early Sept. and is big
enough to house conventions. Even if you stay
elsewhere, plan to check out its impressive lobby
and common rooms.

Between the hostels and the lodge fall several
small motels, most of which house guests in detached, cabin-like units. All these places are comfortable; none are fancy. **East Glacier Motel,** tel.
(406) 226-5593, has cheery motel rooms and cottages (some with kitchens) at $55-65; open sum-
mer season only. At **Jacobson's Cottages,** tel.
(406) 226-4422 or (888) 226-4422, convention-
ally shaped units ($48 s, $55-59 d) are tucked
behind the A-frame office, and the proprietor will

pick you up at the Amtrak stop. Cabins at **Sears Motel,** tel. (406) 226-4432, are $45-54, and have color cable TV. The friendly folks here also have a tent and RV campground and also operate Rent-A-Wreck. Ask in advance and they'll pick you up at the train depot. Surely you'll meet Foozie, the Old English sheepdog, whose favorite trick is sneezing. Rooms at the **Mountain Pine Motel** are nice, $50 s, $60 d, tel. (406) 226-4403.

There's a more secluded feeling to the cabins at **Bison Creek Ranch,** two miles west of town on Hwy. 2, tel. (406) 226-4482 or (888) 226-4482. Two-person cabins run $35-55; some have kitchens. There's also a family-style restaurant, and the cabins are available B&B style.

Pretty much all of East Glacier packs up and heads somewhere with less snow and howling wind from October through April. Off-season travelers should look to **Porter's Alpine Motel,** off Hwy. 2, tel. (406) 226-4402. Double rooms are $65 from mid-June through mid-Sept., $45 the rest of the year.

Bear Creek Guest Ranch is 17 miles west of East Glacier via Hwy. 2, tel. (406) 226-4489 or (800) 445-7379. It's a long-established guest ranch with cabin and lodge accommodations, full meal service ("no vegetarians, we eat beef"), and horseback riding.

Camping

For RV campers, the **Y Lazy R** RV park is behind Porter's Motel near the intersection of Hwys.

2 and 49. The Sears Motel, tel. (406) 226-4432, also has a campground.

Camp on **Two Medicine Lake,** 12 miles from East Glacier via Hwy. 49. The national park campground here is open from the second weekend in June through Labor Day. Campfire presentations by park naturalists and Blackfeet tribal members are held every evening at 8 p.m. at the amphitheater in Loop B.

Head west of East Glacier on Hwy. 2 to reach Forest Service campgrounds. **Summit Campground,** near the rest area at Marias Pass, is 10 miles from East Glacier. Historical cachet and convenience are the most this campground has to offer, but it's got plenty of both, and there are often empty spaces when the national park campgrounds are full. **Devil's Creek Campground** is another six miles southwest on Hwy. 2.

FOOD AND DRINK

Serrano's has good Mexican food at 29 Dawson Ave., tel. (406) 226-9392. The **Glacier Village Restaurant and Villager Dining Room,** at the junction of Hwys. 49 and 2, tel. (406) 226-4464, puts out some tasty dinners ($6-15)—even the chicken salad makes you notice that it's good food, and special care is lavished on desserts. The adjoining cafe slings breakfast eggs and hash browns for $3. On the same block, **PJ's Diner** is a cubbyhole cafe with similar $3 breakfasts and huckleberry shakes.

Josephine Lake is a short walk or canoe ride from Many Glacier Hotel.

JUDY JEWELL

Right in the cabin-motel heart of East Glacier, the **Thimbleberry** serves good, American-style food for breakfast, lunch, and dinner, tel. (406) 226-5523. Next door to Brownie's Grocery and the hostel is the **Whistle Stop Restaurant,** with a bakery, great breakfasts (huckleberry French toast), and evening meals.

Not to forget the **Great Northern Steak and Rib House,** the western-theme Glacier Park Lodge dining room, with steak and barbecue specialties. Dinners here run $12-18; breakfast is a buffet.

A **camp store** at the Two Medicine Campground sells groceries and camping provisions during the campground's season. The store is housed in the one remaining Two Medicine chalet.

West of East Glacier, at Marias Pass, is **Summit Station,** a bar and restaurant with a prime-rib special on the weekends, tel. (406) 226-4428.

INFORMATION AND SERVICES

There's no Glacier National Park visitor center in East Glacier, but the **information desk** at the lodge is staffed by generally helpful people. The **ranger station** at Two Medicine Lake has more specific information on nearby hiking trails.

The **post office** is east of Hwy. 2, behind the Glacier Park Trading Company. A **laundromat** and **showers** are two blocks south at the Y Lazy R RV park behind the Exxon station.

TRANSPORTATION

Amtrak stops at the East Glacier Park station during the summer. The westbound train comes through around 7:30 p.m.; eastbound service is around 9 a.m. daily. From Sept. through May, the train stops in Browning rather than East Glacier; check exact dates with Amtrak, tel. (800) 872-7245.

If you're getting around the park on red roll-top **park buses,** you can catch a ride from Glacier Park Lodge to St. Mary, Many Glacier, Waterton, or Lake McDonald (via Hwy. 2).

Car rentals are available from **Rent-A-Wreck** at the Sears Motel, tel. (406) 226-9293.

MANY GLACIER

Aside from the Going-to-the-Sun Road, this is the most popular and the most spectacular area of Glacier National Park. The mountains are *right there,* with the knife-edge-thin Garden Wall as a backdrop to the southwest, and a glacier but a day-hike away. Many Glacier is spectacular enough to warrant a quick detour just for a snooze on the hotel veranda, but it also makes a good base for several days' worth of hiking, canoeing, and bicycle or horseback riding.

THE LAND

Head up any of the numerous valleys converging on the hotel and, on the way to high cirques and glaciers, observe all four of Glacier's geologic formations. Tan Altyn limestone is exposed in the hotel parking lot. Climb through the green layers of Appekunny mudstone, look for mud cracks and ripple marks in the red Grinnell muds, then scale the buff-colored Helena (or Siyeh)

Formation, where large stromatolites abound. High on the Garden Wall, the Purcell diabase is a dark, 100-foot-tall layer of igneous rock that shot up through the muds and limes until it spread into a yielding gap in the sedimentary layers. The molten intrusion seared the adjacent limestone layers, turning them to marble.

Just east of Many Glacier is the edge of the Lewis Overthrust. Chief Mountain, visible from the road between Babb and Waterton Lakes National Park, is the far eastern outpost of the overthrust of Precambrian rock and the leading edge of the Rocky Mountains. Younger Cretaceous shales, buried by older rocks in most of Glacier Park, take over the valley floor just east of the mountains.

Glaciers filled Swiftcurrent Valley and left their trademark U-shaped valleys running down from the peaks and converging in Many Glacier Valley. Valley floors here are striped with moraines and dotted with glacial lakes, which get colder and more milky-blue as they near their glacial sources. Cirques tucked into the face of the Gar-

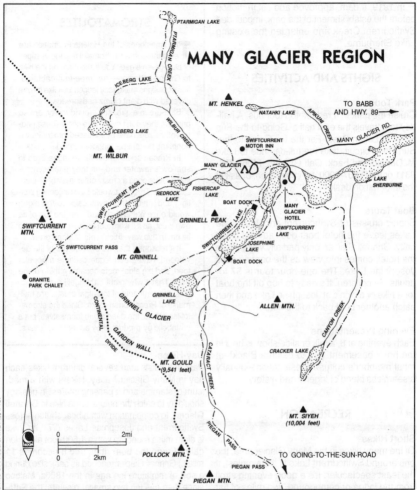

MANY GLACIER REGION

PTARMIGAN LAKE

ICEBERG LAKE

PTARMIGAN CREEK

WILBUR CREEK

ICEBERG LAKE

MT. HENKEL

NATAHKI LAKE

APIKUNI CREEK

TO BABB
AND HWY. 89

MANY GLACIER RD.

MT. WILBUR

SWIFTCURRENT
MOTOR INN

MANY GLACIER

LAKE
SHERBURNE

SWIFTCURRENT PASS

REDROCK
LAKE

FISHERCAP
LAKE

BOAT DOCK

MANY
GLACIER
HOTEL

SWIFTCURRENT
MTN.

BULLHEAD LAKE

GRINNELL PEAK

SWIFTCURRENT
LAKE

SWIFTCURRENT PASS

MT. GRINNELL

JOSEPHINE
LAKE

BOAT DOCK

GRANITE
PARK CHALET

GRINNELL
LAKE

ALLEN MTN.

CONTINENTAL DIVIDE

GRINNELL GLACIER

GARDEN WALL

CRACKER LAKE

CANYON CREEK

MT. GOULD
(9,541 feet)

CATARACT CREEK

MT. SIYEH
(10,004 feet)

PIEGAN PASS

POLLOCK MTN.

PIEGAN CREEK

TO GOING-TO-THE-SUN-ROAD

PIEGAN PASS

PIEGAN MTN.

0   2mi

0   2km

© MOON PUBLICATIONS, INC.

den Wall were the starting points for many glaciers, and the Grinnell and Gem Glaciers still creep across the shady flank of the *arête*.

HISTORY

Copper was discovered in the Altyn Formation in 1892. Within a few years, the Blackfeet were forced to sell much of their reservation land, allowing prospectors free reign over the east face of the mountains. A mining town was erected near Lake Sherburne, but it proved hardly worth digging for the small amounts of copper embedded in the limestone. Even though the first oil ever found in Montana came from a local copper mine, the town of Altyn didn't live long enough to see the national park established in 1910.

In 1919, a dam, approved and set in motion before the establishment of the park, impounded Swiftcurrent Creek and enlarged the existing Lake Sherburne.

SIGHTS AND ACTIVITIES

Park Tours
Cruise the park in a red roll-top tour bus. A half-day tour travels the east half of Going-to-the-Sun Road to Logan Pass. For the full Going-to-the-Sun Road circuit, take the full-day ride to Lake McDonald and back. Call GPI, tel. (406) 226-9311 or (602) 207-6000, for information, or ask at the information desk.

Boat Tours
Scenic cruises of Swiftcurrent and Josephine Lakes leave the hotel boat dock several times daily. Grinnell Glacier, only partially visible from the hotel, comes into view as the boat crosses Josephine Lake. The one-hour tour is $7 for adults, $4 children. It's easy to hop off the boat for a hike or a picnic at Josephine Lake and then catch another boat back to the hotel.

Evening Presentations
Each evening at 8, a talk or slide show is held in the hotel basement. Try to catch a Blackfeet tribal member's cultural presentation—usually a seamless blend of legend and history.

RECREATION

Short Hikes
Of the many hikes in the Many Glacier area, the one around Swiftcurrent Lake is the simplest, if the least spectacular. It's a good evening stroll from the lodge or campgound, two miles of flat lakeside terrain. The trail occasionally breaks out of the trees for views of the Garden Wall and nearby mountains. Pick up a nature guide at the official trailhead, the picnic area halfway between the lodge and the campground.

Another easy walk combines a $7 boat trip to the far end of Josephine Lake with a two-mile roundtrip hike to **Grinnell Lake**, a milky aqua lake full of icy water and glacial flour from Grinnell Glacier.

STROMATOLITES

The limestones of the Helena Formation are shot through with stromatolites, the vestiges of blue-green algae. You'll see them on the hike to Grinnell Glacier—the three-foot cabbage-flower designs make rock ledges look like they're covered with giant chintz bedspreads.

Blue-green algae, still around today, are so primitive they don't even have cells. These photosynthesizers have been tossed into their own nonplant, nonanimal kingdom called Protista.

In Precambrian times, these algae lived in shallow seawater and, as they photosynthesized, developed a crusty outer layer of calcium carbonate. This crust would block incoming sunlight and inhibit photosynthesis, so the algae would ooze out and spread over the top of its own crust, as if it were just another sunny rock to lie on. In this way, thick reefs of algae grew.

It's reckoned that, as other forms of life developed, blue-green algae became a popular food, and big algal reefs became a thing of the past. That's why giant cabbagelike stromatolites, the remnants of the algal crusts, are hallmarks of Precambrian rocks. Since the stromatolites are not the dead algae themselves, but a metabolic by-product, they are not true fossils.

Day-Hikes
Park naturalists lead several different hikes each day in Many Glacier Valley. Hikers with a modicum of stamina and a passing interest in geology should try to catch the naturalist-led hike to **Grinnell Glacier**. In combination with a boat shuttle across Swiftcurrent and Josephine Lakes ($7), the hike is eight miles roundtrip with a 1,600-foot elevation gain. (Forgo the boat rides and it becomes 11 miles.) Grinnell Glacier reached its peak size during a sort of miniature ice age in the 1800s. Melting since then has left two smaller glaciers: the **Salamander** clings high on the Garden Wall; **Grinnell Glacier** proper is below and to the left. A warming trend starting in the 1980s has enlarged the iceberg-laden lake beneath the glacier, making it particularly hazardous to walk onto the glacial ice.

Watch out for bears on the trail to **Iceberg Lake**, an aptly named glacial lake 4.7 miles from the trailhead in the Swiftcurrent parking lot. The trail crosses alpine meadows before dropping into a cirque holding the milky blue lake. Mountain goats, marmots, and an occasional bear share this path with a myriad of hikers.

Take the same initial stretch of trail to reach **Ptarmigan Falls** (two miles) and **Ptarmigan Lake** (4.3 miles). The waterfalls and flower-strewn meadows make up for the steepness of the trail. Hikers reaching the lake with unbounded energy should go another mile to the 183-foot-long **Ptarmigan Tunnel,** which emerges onto the north face of the Ptarmigan Wall, looking out to the Belly River country.

Longer Hikes
For an extended jaunt, start at the camp store parking lot and head up Swiftcurrent Creek past **Red Rock Falls,** cross the Continental Divide at **Swiftcurrent Pass,** and join up with the **Highline Trail** on the other side. It's eight miles from the trailhead in the camp store parking lot to the **Granite Park** chalet (and campground), and an-other eight miles from the chalet to Logan Pass.

Start at the hotel, pass Josephine and Grinnell Lakes, and skirt Mt. Siyeh and Going-to-the-Sun Mountain on the 12-mile route across **Piegan Pass** to **Going-to-the-Sun Road.** Geology, wild-flower meadows, waterfalls, mountain goats, and big views are highlights of this hike. There are no backcountry campgrounds along this trail.

Boating
Rent a canoe or rowboat at the boat dock behind the hotel. Determined canoeists will heft their boats a quarter mile over the moraine separating Swiftcurrent and Josephine Lakes. The isola-tion and views from Josephine Lake are worth the portage.

Motorboats, except for the "scenic cruise boats," are prohibited on Swiftcurrent and Josephine Lakes but are allowed on larger Lake Sherburne.

Horseback Riding
The corral behind the Many Glacier Hotel parking lot is the starting point for a number of regularly scheduled guided horseback rides. An all-day ride over Swiftcurrent Pass to Granite Park chalet leaves each morning at 8:45 ($55). Other day-long rides go to Poia Lake ($47) and Cracker Lake ($42).

Shorter rides are $20-25 and leave several times a day for Grinnell Lake, Josephine Lake, or Cracker Flats. If horses and guides are available, private trail rides cost $15 an hour. Call (406) 732-5597 to register for all rides in advance.

Fishing
There are trout in Swiftcurrent Lake, but they're not always eager to swallow a hook. Both Josephine and Grinnell Lakes are home to brook trout—it's worth the extra hike to Grinnell Lake for both the beautiful turquoise lake and the fish. For a change from the trout, head down to Sher-burne Lake for northern pike.

ACCOMMODATIONS

The **Many Glacier Hotel,** a 200-room Swiss-style chalet in an isolated valley on Swiftcurrent Lake, is currently managed by the huge Grey-hound-Dial Soap corporation, which seems to be letting it run down a bit. The tacky early-'70s dorm decor is only ameliorated by the perfect setting and the stunning views from the lobby windows. Geology comes right down to meet you here, and wildlife is often spotted on the slopes across the lake. The hotel is open from the second week of June through the first week in Sept.; rooms run $99-124 d.

The **Swiftcurrent Cottages** are especially popular with families; at $40 and up, they're not expensive, and, though they lack toilets and kitchens, they evoke pleasant hazy memories of some idealized summer camp or the perfect 1962 family vacation.

Less appealing than the lodge or cabins, but sometimes available on short notice, are motel rooms in the **Swiftcurrent Motor Inn.** At $73-85 d, they cost considerably more than similar ac-commodations anywhere else in the state, but you don't really have a choice. Both the motel and the cabins have short seasons—late June through Labor Day.

Make reservations for any of these places by calling (602) 207-6000. From Canada, call (403) 236-3400 year-round.

No reservations are accepted for the **Many Glacier Campground,** so campers need to grab a spot early in the day—it's often full shortly after noon. The campground's season runs from mid-June through the third week in September. Campsites cost $12 a night.

FOOD AND DRINK

The dining room at the **Many Glacier Hotel** has a continental, Swiss-inspired theme. It's the same meat and fish dispensed to other Glacier Park hotels, but here it's sauced and stuffed, rather than grilled or breaded and fried. In the hotel basement, **Heidi's** serves ice cream and hot dogs.

In the **Swiftcurrent Motor Inn** you'll find the **Italian Gardens Cafe** and a camp store.

INFORMATION AND SERVICES

Rangers dispense trail information and backcountry permits from their station near the campground.

Glean general trail information and specifics on bus tours and hotel activities from the information desk in the **Many Glacier Hotel** lobby.

The most coveted of all camper services—**showers** and a **laundromat**—are in the Swiftcurrent cabin complex. Purchase shower tokens at the camp store.

Transportation

Many Glacier is 12 miles west of Babb, a crossroads town on the Blackfeet Reservation nine miles north of St. Mary. Travelers relying on public transportation can catch a red **park bus** from any Glacier Park lodge to the Many Glacier Hotel and vice versa. Early-rising hikers can catch a special morning bus to their favorite trailheads at Siyeh Bend, Logan Pass, or The Loop.

WATERTON LAKES NATIONAL PARK

Waterton Lakes National Park is just across the Canadian border from Glacier. Though a much smaller park (it covers only 203 square miles), it's worth visiting for spectacular scenery and a distinctly Canadian flavor.

The two parks are known collectively as the Waterton-Glacier International Peace Park, but they are managed separately with separate entry fees. A 24-hour pass to Waterton costs C$4 per person, or C$8 per group in one vehicle.

There's actually a town in Waterton Park, with a handful of year-round residents, a number of private summer cottages, and a small tourist strip on the Cameron Creek delta. Development has been kept pretty well in check, though; there are no soaring condominium towers and no McDonald's.

All prices quoted for Waterton are in Canadian dollars. The exchange rate is approximately US$1 = C$1.35. Alberta's **area code** is 403.

THE LAND

Waterton Valley was filled by an enormous glacier during the ice age ending 10,000 years ago. It advanced down the valley until it met resistance from the hard-rock protrusion now called the Bear's Hump (the high ridge overlooking the townsite). The glacier piled up behind the Bear's Paw and Vimy Ridge, digging deep into the ground, and eventually slipped over the top and cut a channel. This Bosporus Channel now links Upper and Middle Waterton Lakes. The bowl dug out behind the resisting ridge now contains the nearly 500-foot-deep Upper Waterton Lake.

Once the valley glacier reached the present-day prairies, it began to melt. As ice melted and the glacier shrunk back, piles of debris were dropped, forming long chains of moraines. A huge piece of ice left behind by the retreating glacier formed Middle and Lower Waterton Lakes.

Waterton crosses half a dozen ecological zones as it ascends from wetlands through prairie, parkland, montane, subalpine, and alpine zones.

The views from Waterton are outstanding—both the look down Waterton Lake and the view of the prairies meeting the mountains.

As over most of the east slope of the Rockies, the wind can be persistent and strong in Waterton.

HISTORY

Native people camped in the Waterton Valley some 8,500 years ago. By 500 B.C. a plains culture based on buffalo hunting was firmly established. By A.D. 500 the locals picked up and moved to the western slopes of the Rockies, and became known as the Kootenai (or, in Canada, the Kootenay). Kootenai hunters continued to travel

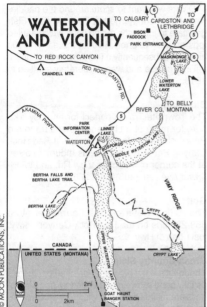

WATERTON AND VICINITY

TO CALGARY
TO CARDSTON AND LETHBRIDGE
BISON PADDOCK
PARK ENTRANCE
TO RED ROCK CANYON
CRANDELL MTN.
RED ROCK CANYON RD.
MASKINONGE LAKE
LOWER WATERTON LAKE
AKAMINA PKWY.
PARK INFORMATION CENTER
LINNET LAKE
WATERTON
TO BELLY RIVER CG, MONTANA
BOSPORUS
MIDDLE WATERTON LAKE
BERTHA FALLS AND BERTHA LAKE TRAIL
BERTHA LAKE
VIMY RIDGE
CRYPT LAKE TRAIL
CANADA
UNITED STATES (MONTANA)
UPPER WATERTON LAKE
CRYPT LAKE
0   2mi
0   2km
GOAT HAUNT RANGER STATION

© MOON PUBLICATIONS, INC.

regularly to the Waterton area for bison until forced from the plains by the Blackfeet, who controlled the southern Alberta plains from the early 1700s until the buffalo disappeared a century later.

Thomas Blakiston, a British military man, was sent to the Canadian West in 1857 to pave the way for settlers. He named Waterton Lakes for an eccentric British naturalist.

Oil seepages had been noticed by Indians and early white settlers, and in the early 1900s modest oil strikes were accompanied by major machinery and ruckus. This disruption, and the formation of Glacier National Park in 1910, led to the establishment of Waterton Lakes Dominion Park in 1911. Although hunting and commercial fishing were prohibited within park boundaries, building was not, and a community soon developed on the north shore of Upper Waterton Lake. Kootenai Brown, a well-educated mountain man who'd settled near the lakes, was named the park's first superintendent.

The Prince of Wales Hotel was built by the Great Northern Railway in 1926 as a stopover for tour buses shuttling between Glacier National Park and Jasper, Alberta.

In 1932, the Canadian and U.S. governments agreed to form the Waterton-Glacier International Peace Park as a symbol of friendship between the two countries. Both parks are now designated "biosphere reserves."

SIGHTS

The MV *International* has cruised Upper Waterton Lake since the Prince of Wales Hotel opened in 1927. The two-hour roundtrip boat ride from the Waterton marina to Goat Haunt, Montana, at the southern end of the lake costs $13 and departs several times daily from mid-May to mid-Sept., tel. (403) 859-2362. Backpackers and Crypt Lake hikers should let the cruise personnel know of their plans before boarding the boat.

Cameron Falls drops from a hanging valley, where a small glacier came in from the side and was swallowed up by the large Waterton Valley glacier.

A paddle-wheeled boat submerged in Emerald Bay beneath the Prince of Wales Hotel can be seen through the clear water. It holds a particular fascination for divers.

Take the nine-mile-long **Red Rock Canyon Parkway** from town to the canyon. At road's end, there's a short, self-guided walk around the canyon and a picnic area; it's a 20-minute amble to Blakiston Falls.

A **bison paddock** north of the park entrance corrals a small herd of buffalo. There's a quite pretty driving tour through the paddock, which is more interesting than it sounds.

WHITE SETTLEMENT AND INDIAN WARS

Hiking
Walkers and bicyclists share the **Townsite Trail,** a two-mile tour along the lakefront to Cameron Falls.

Take off from the park information center and follow the trail up the **Bear's Hump** for a great view of the lakes and town below. It's less than a mile to the top of the ridge, but the climb is steep and views are often accompanied by stiff winds.

The **Bertha Lake Trail** is a three-mile tromp through montane and subalpine forests to a high cirque lake. Waterton is known for its variety of wildflowers, and they're particularly well displayed along this trail. For hikers not up to the seven-mile roundtrip, **Bertha Falls** is just under two miles up the same trail.

Take the boat to **Goat Haunt** at the south end of Upper Waterton Lake and from there hike a mile to Rainbow Falls and back, or take off on foot back to Waterton town site. There's an eight-mile trail up the west side of the lake, though the trail passes mostly through lodgepole pine, Engelmann spruce, and some aspen and birch trees with only a few views over the lake.

Debark the tour boat at Crypt Landing for the five-mile hike to **Crypt Lake.** On the way to the lake, hikers pass several waterfalls, sidle along steep trails, creep through a natural tunnel, and climb 3,000 feet. This is a hike to challenge both muscles and nerves. It's rather scarier than most day-hikes, but when you get to the lake, you're up there with the mountain goats.

For a longer backpack, try the **Tamarack Tour** toward the northwestern end of the park. Start on the Rowes Lake trail from the trailhead on the Akamina Parkway, and follow it north and west past tiny Lone Lake, Twin Lakes, and Lost Lake to Avion Ridge and Goat Lake. (For the best views and a hike through an alpine larch forest, forgo the Bauerman Trail, a.k.a. Snowshoe Trail, and take to the more difficult, less well maintained, Avion Ridge.) The last three miles to Red Rock Canyon are on the Bauerman Trail, rounding out an approximately 27-mile trip.

Before setting out on an overnight trek, get a free backcountry permit and trail information from the park information center or administrative office.

Fishing
There's a C$5 fee for a four-day Canadian National Park fishing permit. Purchase one at the park information center or administrative office if you plan to go after the trout, northern pike, or whitefish of the Waterton lakes.

Swimming
The lakes are a little too chilly for most swimmers, but there's a public outdoor pool on Cameron Falls Dr., tel. (403) 859-2333, open mid-June through Labor Day.

Divers will want to scout around the paddlewheel boat submerged in Emerald Bay. Fish gravitate to the rusty, rotting boat, which hauled logs on the Waterton River in the early 1900s and was subsequently a floating tearoom, until it fell into disuse and was deliberately scuttled in 1918.

Bicycling
The Townsite Trail is perfect for an easy bike ride; for more of a challenge, pedal up to the Prince of Wales Hotel for tea or out Red Rock Canyon Parkway. **Pat's** rents mountain bikes at the corner of Mountain View Rd. and Windflower Ave., tel. (403) 859-2266.

Golf
The 18-hole **Waterton Golf Course,** tel. (403) 859-2383, is on the Red Rock Canyon Pkwy. just north of Hwy. 5.

Cross-Country Skiing
Though it's not a big winter destination, there's usually good snow around Waterton, and several trails are maintained each winter for cross-country skiing. Check at the park administrative office for current trail conditions.

ACCOMMODATIONS

Waterton Park has a new toll-free reservation number, (888) 859-8669, which makes finding and booking a room much easier.

The **Prince of Wales Hotel** is perched on a bluff over town. It's run as part of the Glacier Park, Inc. hotel system and has a Laura Ashley–British Isles theme overlaid on the Glacier Park hotel chassis. Big wing-backed chairs look out from the lobby over Upper Waterton Lake, and the Garden Court dining room looks out onto neither a garden nor a court. Rooms run C$189-245 d—the top-end fees buy an awe-inspiring view onto the lake. The hotel is open Memorial Day weekend through early Sept.; call (403) 236-3400 or the GPI reservation line (602) 207-6000 for reservations.

A congenial alternative to the Prince of Wales is the **Kilmorey Lodge** at the base of the hill, just on the edge of town, tel. (403) 859-2334. It's like an overgrown log-cabin B&B, with a homey

view of Waterton Lake from the lobby of the Prince of Wales

lounge complete with an oversized atlas of Canada on the coffee table, a tiny bar, and a dining room. Rooms run C$86-100 d. During the winter, cross-country ski packages are offered; two nights' lodging and several meals are included for C$90 per person, double-occupancy fee.

Downtown, the **Bayshore Inn,** tel. (403) 859-2211 or (800) 661-8080, is a nice lakeside motel, with lake views and a hot tub. Double rooms run C$119-129; again, the extra $10 buys the view. The **Aspen Village Inn,** tel. (403) 859-2255, isn't right on the lake, but it's a very pleasant place, with room rates at C$122.

Crandell Mountain Lodge, tel. (403) 859-2288, is open April 1-Oct. 31 and has 13 country inn-style rooms from C$84-179 d.

Campgrounds

The wind-tossed **Townsite Campground** is of the parking-lot variety, but many of the 238 sites are close to the lake, and there are showers. It's immediately south of downtown, near the Bertha Lake trailhead and the Falls Theatre on Windflower Drive. No reservations are taken, so get there early in the day, especially on summer weekends. Camping fees are C$15 (C$21 with hookups), and the camping season runs mid-May to early October.

Belly River Campground is a cheaper (C$10) but not necessarily more appealing alternative off Chief Mountain International Highway just north of the international border. It's away from the lakes, can be hot, and is open mid-May through mid-September. The **Crandell Mountain Campground** is a pleasant, though sometimes crowded, spot five miles from town on the Red Rock Canyon Parkway. It's open mid-May through Labor Day, and it charges C$13 to camp.

FOOD AND DRINK

Pearl's, on Windflower Ave., tel. (403) 859-2284, has soup, salad, and sandwiches (all under C$10) with a healthy touch and patio seating that recalls school desks. **Zummmm's,** on the corner of Waterton Ave. and Cameron Falls Dr., tel. (403) 859-2388, is just a shade more expensive, and also has a deck, good sandwiches, and berry pie.

Things get fancier as you head toward the Prince of Wales Hotel. Midway between downtown and the hilltop hotel, the **Lamp Post,** Kilmorey Lodge's dining room, strikes a happy medium for a good dinner in comfortable, attractive surroundings. Lunches are about C$10, and dinners are C$15-20; call (406) 859-2334. For a drink, try the intimate bar inside the Kilmorey. After a few dinners in Glacier Park hotels, this may provide a welcome fresh touch. Tucked behind the Kilmorey Lodge, the outdoor **Gazebo Cafe** is informal and reasonably priced for pasta or salads.

The dining room at the **Prince of Wales,** tel. (403) 859-2231, puts a British Isles twist on the standard Glacier Park hotel menu: they serve shepherd's pie for C$9 at lunch; dinners thankfully include British Columbia salmon. Prices at dinner range from C$18-25. There's also a quite charming tea room here, serving up delicious scones and other pastries from 2 to 5 p.m.

If you prefer to focus on eclecticism and economy, try the **New Frank Restaurant,** 106 Waterton Ave., tel. (403) 859-2240, where a Chinese-Western six-course evening buffet costs C$13 ($7 for

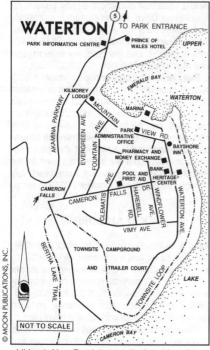

The **Waterton Natural History Association** runs summer classes, including a one-day "Vision Quest" class, based on Native American spiritual quests. Contact the Waterton Natural History Association, P.O. Box 145, Waterton Park, Alberta T0K 2M0, tel. (403) 859-2624 for schedules.

Free interpretive programs are presented each evening in the **Falls Theatre** across from Cameron Falls, and in the theater at **Crandell Campground.** Programs focus on both history and nature studies, and usually include slides or a movie.

First aid is proffered at the swimming pool on Cameron Falls Dr., tel. (403) 859-2333. For **emergency services,** call (403) 859-2636. The **police station** is at the corner of Waterton Ave. and Cameron Falls Dr., tel. (403) 859-2244 or Zenith 5000.

There is a **treasury branch authority** upstairs from Caribou Clothing on Waterton Ave., but it closes at 1 p.m. If you need money changed at other times, the pharmacy on Waterton Ave. offers a fair exchange rate. Most businesses will accept U.S. dollars at the current exchange rate, but dispensing foreign currency in change is restricted.

The **Itussiststukiopi Coin-Op Laundrette** is on Windflower Ave., tel. (403) 859-2460.

children). New Frank is open for breakfast, lunch, and dinner.

INFORMATION AND SERVICES

Just across from the Prince of Wales Hotel, the **Park Information Centre** is open mid-May through Labor Day, tel. (403) 859-2445. The **park administration office** is open year-round on Mountain View Rd., tel. (403) 859-2224. The in-town **Heritage Centre** is run by the Waterton Natural History Association, tel. (403) 859-2267. The friendly staff will help plan hikes, meals, and motel stays. A small historical museum and a bookshop operate out of the same Waterton Ave. building.

TRANSPORTATION

The Chief Mountain International Highway (Hwy. 17) connects Glacier and Waterton national parks, but both the highway and the customs stations along it close down mid-Sept. to mid-May, forcing drivers to head north from Montana on Hwy. 89 to Cardston, then west on Hwy. 5 to Waterton.

Citizens of Canada and the U.S. will generally find the border crossing expeditious. Remember not to bring firearms into Canada, or citrus fruits into the States, and you probably won't have any trouble.

Red park buses leave from the Prince of Wales Hotel at 2 p.m. daily for Many Glacier and East Glacier.

BOOKLIST

DESCRIPTION AND TRAVEL

Alwin, John A. *Eastern Montana: A Portrait of the Land and Its People.* Montana Geographic Series, no. 2. Helena: *Montana* magazine 1982. A broad overview of the people, sights, and regions of eastern Montana, in text and photos.

Federal Writers' Project of the Work Projects Administration for the State of Montana. *Montana: A State Guide Book.* State of Montana: Department of Agriculture, Labor and Industry, 1939. New York: Hastings House, 1949. Long out of print, but it's worth snaring a copy at a used-book store.

Gildart, R.C., ed. *Glacier Country: Montana's Glacier National Park.* Montana Geographic Series, no. 4. Helena: *Montana* magazine, 1990. An introduction to Glacier Park and its natural history, with ample illustrations and intelligent text.

Gildart, R.C. *Montana's Flathead Country.* Montana Geographic Series, no. 14. Helena: *Montana* magazine, 1986. Colorful histories, a look at the environment, and splendid photos define the area around Flathead Lake.

Gildart, R.C. *Montana's Missouri River.* Montana Geographic Series, no. 8. Helena: *Montana* magazine, 1985. Text and photographs celebrate the Wild and Scenic Missouri.

Meloy, Mark. *Islands on the Prairie: The Mountain Ranges of Eastern Montana.* Montana Geographic Series, no. 13. Helena: *Montana* magazine, 1986. Pictures and text about the often-ignored mountains in eastern Montana.

Moore, Rae Ellen. *Just West of Yellowstone.* Laclede, ID: Great Blue Graphics, 1987. Charming illustrations and handwritten text give a real picture of West Yellowstone and surrounding areas.

Mullan, John. *Miners and Travelers' Guide to Oregon, Washington, Idaho, Montana, Wyoming, and Colorado via the Missouri and Columbia Rivers.* 1865. New York: Arno Press, reprinted 1973.

Pringle, Heather. *Waterton Lakes National Park.* Vancouver, B.C.: Douglas and McIntyre, 1986. A comprehensive guide to history, nature, and hikes in Waterton.

Schneider, Bill. *Montana's Yellowstone River.* Montana Geographic Series, no. 10. Helena: *Montana* magazine, 1985. An enthusiastic portrait of the Yellowstone River, with a strong conservationist cast.

Tirrell, Norma. *Montana.* Oakland, CA: Compass American Guides, 1991. An easy-reading and attractive guide.

Wetzel, Betty. *Missoula: The Town and the People.* Helena: *Montana* magazine, 1987. What makes Missoula tick.

HISTORY

Bradshaw, Glenda Clay. *Montana's Historical Highway Markers.* Helena: Montana Historical Society Press, 1989. A complete reference to the roadside historical signs in the state, with special notice taken of early illustrators who conceived the markers.

Brown, Mark H., and W.R. Felton. *Before Barbed Wire.* New York: Bramhall House, 1956. A commemoration of the life of L.A. Huffman, the frontier photographer who captured on film the era of the Indians and the open range.

Cheney, Roberta Carkeek. *Names on the Face of Montana.* Missoula: Mountain Press, 1983. When you must know how Twodot and Ubet got their names, check this book.

Chesarek, Frank, and Jim Brabeck, eds. *Montana: Two Lane Highway in a Four Lane World.* Missoula: Mountain Press, 1978. A western Montana eighth-grade class dedicated themselves to writing a one-volume history of Montana; now out of print, it may be the single best overview of the colorful history of the state, told with energy and insight.

Connell, Evan S. *Son of the Morning Star.* New York: Harper Collins, 1984. Story of the Battle of Little Bighorn.

Garcia, Andrew. *Tough Trip through Paradise.* Sausalito, CA: Comstock Editions, 1967. Maybe it's true, maybe only half so, but it's a whale of a story about mountain men and Indian life in 1878.

Howard, Joseph Kinsey. *Montana: High, Wide, and Handsome.* Lincoln: University of Nebraska Press, 1943. A lively and opinionated history.

Lopach, James, ed. *We the People of Montana.* Missoula: Mountain Press, 1983. A historical analysis of the Montana governmental system.

Malone, Michael P., and Richard B. Roeder. *Montana: A History of Two Centuries.* Seattle: University of Washington, 1976. Now the accepted text on Montana's history, it is authoritative, rich in vignettes, almost punchy.

Rinehart, Mary Roberts. *Through Glacier Park in 1915.* Niwot, CO: Roberts Rinehart Publishers, 1983. An early account of horsepacking through the park.

Thompson, Larry. *Montana's Explorers.* Montana Geographic Series, no. 9. Helena: *Montana* magazine, 1985. It's not *all* explorers; the focus is on naturalists, including Lewis and Clark and Prince Maximilian of Weid.

Vichorek, Daniel N. *Montana's Homestead Era.* Montana Geographic Series, no. 15. Helena: *Montana* magazine, 1987. A mix of reminiscence and history, regarding the huge influx of homesteaders during the early 20th century.

West, Carroll Van. *A Traveler's Companion to Montana History.* Helena: Montana Historical Society Press, 1986. An excellent roadside historical companion.

Wilson, Gary. *Honky-Tonk Town: Havre's Bootlegging Days.* Havre: High-Line Books, 1986. Most Montana towns have had *somebody* chronicle their history, and a few of the resulting books are actually pretty good reads. Pick up *Honky-Tonk Town* if you want old-time Havre to come to life.

NATIVE AMERICANS

Bryan, William L., Jr. *Montana's Indians.* Montana Geographic Series, no. 11. Helena: *Montana* magazine, 1985. Historical and contemporary sketches.

Eagle/Walking Turtle. *Indian America.* Santa Fe: John Muir Press, 1991. Tribal histories and cultural information for visitors.

Ewers, John C. *The Blackfeet: Raiders on the Northwestern Plains.* Norman: University of Oklahoma Press, 1958. An anthropological study of the Blackfeet, this is fascinating reading for non-anthropologists, too.

Hungry Wolf, Adolf and Beverly, compilers. *Indian Tribes of the Northern Rockies.* Skookumchuck, B.C.: Good Medicine Books, 1989. Tribal histories from Indian and non-Indian sources.

Lowie, Robert H. *Indians of the Plains.* Lincoln: University of Nebraska Press, 1954. An anthropological look at all the Plains tribes.

Miller, David Humphreys. *Custer's Fall: The Indian Side of the Story.* Lincoln: University of Nebraska, 1957. An enthralling retelling of the familiar Custer story based on Indian documentation.

Wilfong, Cheryl. *Following the Nez Perce Trail.* Corvallis, OR: Oregon State University Press, 1990. An absolutely wonderful, well-thought-out, and moving book that will enhance any trip intersecting with the Nez Perce Trail.

LEWIS AND CLARK

Ambrose, Stephen. *Undaunted Courage.* New York: Simon & Schuster, 1996. Scholarly, readable account of Corps of Discovery, focusing on Lewis.

Cutright, Paul Russell. *Lewis and Clark: Pioneering Naturalists.* Lincoln: University of Nebraska Press, 1969. Lewis and, to a lesser extent, Clark were the first to write of Montana's flora and fauna. Cutright's narrative draws the reader into the observations of prairie dogs and candlefish.

De Voto, Bernard, ed. *The Journals of Lewis and Clark.* Boston: Houghton Mifflin, 1953. Of the one-volume versions of the journals, this is the best.

Duncan, Dayton. *Out West.* New York: Viking Penguin, 1987. Along the Lewis and Clark Trail in the 1980s.

Lavender, David. *The Way to the Western Sea.* New York: Harper and Row, 1988. One of the West's most noted historians gives the fascinating details of the Lewis and Clark story.

Olmstead, Gerald. *Fielding's Lewis and Clark Trail.* New York: William Morrow and Co., 1986. How to do what Dayton Duncan did.

NATURAL SCIENCES AND THE ENVIRONMENT

Alt, David, and Donald W. Hyndman, *Roadside Geology of Montana.* Missoula: Mountain Press, 1986. A comprehensive road-by-road guide to Montana's unique geology. For those willing to read slowly, there's a wealth of information.

Anderson, Bob. *Beartooth Country.* Montana Geographic Series, no. 7. Helena: *Montana* magazine, 1984. An environmentally conscious look at Montana's highest country.

Bass, Rick. *The Ninemile Wolves.* Livingston: Clark City Press, 1992. Passionate book-length essay chronicling wolves' return to northwestern Montana.

Chronic, Halka. *Pages of Stone: Geology of Western National Parks and Monuments,* Vol. 1: Rocky Mountains and Western Great Plains. Seattle: The Mountaineers, 1984. A clearly written and untechnical geology to the West, including Yellowstone and Glacier parks.

Ferguson, Gary. *Montana National Forests.* Billings and Helena: Falcon Press, 1990. A guide to Montana's 10 national forests, amply illustrated.

Fischer, Carol and Hank. *Montana Wildlife Viewing Guide.* Billings and Helena: Falcon Press, 1990. A guide to 113 designated refuges and habitats where Montana wildlife is most easily viewed.

Gildart, Robert C., and Jan Wassink. *Montana Wildlife.* Montana Geographic Series, no. 3. Helena: *Montana* magazine, 1982. An illustrated study of Montana's wildlife heritage and its many ecosystems and species.

Hart, Jeff. *Montana: Native Plants and Early Peoples.* Helena: Montana Historical Society, 1976. Well-illustrated and engagingly written, this is the best book on ceremonial and medicinal plant usage by native Montanans.

Horner, Jack, and James Gorman. *Digging Dinosaurs.* New York: Harper Collins, 1990. Read this before visiting Choteau or the Museum of the Rockies and you'll be able to keep up with the seven-year-olds.

Manning, Richard. *Last Stand.* Salt Lake City: Gibbs Smith, 1991. Manning went after the story of logging in Montana and lost his position as the *Missoulian*'s environmental reporter.

McEneaney, Terry. *Birders' Guide to Montana.* Helena: Falcon Press, 1993. Montana's best birding sites and tips on planning a birding trip.

McMillion, Scott. *Mark of the Grizzly.* Helena: Falcon Press, 1998. Well-told stories of grizzly attacks on humans. Dare you to read it in the tent.

McPhee, John. *Rising From the Plains.* New York: Farrar, Straus, Giroux, 1986. Okay, so it's about Wyoming. It's still a good read, and the most lucid account of Rocky Mountain geology in print.

Reese, Rick. *Greater Yellowstone.* Montana Geographic Series, no. 6. Helena: *Montana* magazine, 1984. One of the best of this series, with a strong focus on environmental issues.

Van Bruggen, Theodore. *Wildflowers, Grasses and Other Plants of the Northern Plains and Black Hills.* Interior, SD: Badlands Natural History Association, 1971. A good guide to the plant life of Montana's arid plains, with photographs.

RECREATION

Bach, Orville. *Hiking the Yellowstone Backcountry.* San Francisco: Sierra Club Books, 1973. Pick a trail and leave the crowded roads of Yellowstone National Park.

Cogswell, Ted. *Montana Golf Guide.* Great Falls: Art Craft, 1985. A complete listing.

Feldman, Robert. *The Rockhound's Guide to Montana.* Billings and Helena: Falcon Press, 1985. Feldman breaks the state into over 50 rock-hunting regions, complete with maps.

Fischer, Hank. *Floater's Guide to Montana.* Billings and Helena: Falcon Press, 1986. A comprehensive guide to floating 26 Montana rivers.

Fothergill, Chuck, and Bob Sterling. *The Montana Angling Guide.* Woody Creek, Colorado: Stream Stalker, 1988. Comprehensive guide with river maps and fishing tips.

Glacier Natural History Association. *Hiker's Guide to Glacier National Park.* West Glacier: Glacier Natural History Association, 1978. Glacier's greatest hits—details on day-hikes and overnight trips.

Glacier Natural History Association. *Short Hikes and Strolls in Glacier National Park.* West Glacier: Glacier Natural History Association, 1978. For those not up to the stiffer hikes in the above book, try these easy jaunts.

Green, Stewart M. *Back Country Byways.* Billings and Helena: Falcon Press, 1991. A guide to BLM-designated scenic back roads throughout the West.

Henkel, Mark. *The Hunter's Guide to Montana.* Billings and Helena: Falcon Press, 1985. A sensitive guide to hunting in Montana, with a focus on the process of becoming acquainted with wildlife.

Holt, John. *Knee Deep in Montana's Trout Streams.* Boulder: Pruett Publishing Company, 1991. Holt's books (he also authored *Waist Deep in Montana's Lakes* and *Reel Deep in Montana's Rivers*) include frank discussions of environmental and cultural issues affecting Montanans; they're also chock-full of fishing advice.

Kilgore, Gene. *Ranch Vacations.* Sante Fe: John Muir Press, 1994. A comprehensive guide to guest and dude ranches throughout the West.

McCoy, Michael. *Mountain Bike Adventures in the Northern Rockies.* Seattle: The Mountaineers, 1989. Some of the West's best trails for the mountain biker.

Rudner, Ruth. *Bitterroot to Beartooth.* San Francisco: Sierra Club Books, 1985. Indispensable for serious hikers in southwestern Montana, and good environmental reference for casual hikers or readers.

Sample, Michael S. *Angler's Guide to Montana.* Billings and Helena: Falcon Press, 1984.

Schneider, Bill. *Hiker's Guide to Montana.* Billings and Helena: Falcon Press, 1990. Descriptions and maps of 100 hikes, mostly in western Montana.

Stienstra, Tom. *Rocky Mountain Camping.* San Francisco: Fog Horn Press, 1993. An exhaustive listing of public and private campgrounds in Montana, Wyoming, and Colorado.

Thompson, Curt. *Floating and Recreation on Montana Rivers.* Lakeside, Montana: Curt Thompson, 1993. Thorough and up-to-date milepost guide to the state's 81 rivers.

Williams, Rebecca, ed. *Roads and Trails of Waterton-Glacier International Peace Park: The Ruhle Handbook.* Billings and Helena: Falcon Press, 1986. An update of George Ruhle's noteworthy logbook of the park.

LITERATURE

Bass, Rick. *Winter: Notes from Montana.* Boston: Houghton Mifflin Company, 1992. Journals of the author's first winter in far northwestern Montana.

Bevis, William W. *Ten Tough Trips: Montana Writers and the West.* Seattle: University of Washington Press, 1990. One of the first works of literary criticism solely on Montana writers.

Blew, Mary Clearman. *All But the Waltz.* New York: Viking Penguin, 1991. Blew's family came to Montana in 1882. These affecting essays trace their lives in the Judith Basin country. Also look for her collections of short stories, *Runaway* and *Lambing Out.*

Cannon, Hal, ed. *Cowboy Poetry: A Gathering.* Salt Lake City: Peregrine Smith, 1985. A historical overview of cowboy poetry.

Cannon, Hal, ed. *New Cowboy Poetry: A Contemporary Gathering.* Salt Lake City: Peregrine Smith, 1990. An anthology of the best of today's cowboy poets.

Crumley, James. *The Last Good Kiss.* New York: Random House, 1978. Follow hard-boiled Montana detectives around the seedy sides of the West in this book—and in *Dancing Bear* and *The Wrong Case.*

Ford, Richard. *Wildlife.* New York: Atlantic Monthly Press, 1990. A Great Falls teenager watches his father go off to fight fires and his mother take up with another man.

Frazier, Ian. *Great Plains.* New York: Farrar, Straus, Giroux, 1989. A wonderful conglomeration of Frazier's rambles across the historical and contemporary plains.

Fromm, Pete. *Indian Creek Chronicles: A Winter in the Bitterroot.* New York: Lyons and Burford, 1993. Good book to read in front of a toasty fireplace.

Garcia, Andrew. *Tough Trip through Paradise.* Sausalito, CA: Comstock Editions, 1967. Discovered in 1948, this is the powerfully written chronicle of the 1878 Montana frontier penned by a white man who lived with Native Americans.

Guthrie, A.B., Jr. *The Big Sky.* Boston: Houghton Mifflin Company, 1947. Classic, unvarnished tale of a young man living the western life.

Hugo, Richard. *Making Certain It Goes On.* New York: W.W. Norton, 1984. Hugo's collected poems. For a change of pace, try Hugo's detective novel, *Death and the Good Life,* which hopscotches between the lower Flathead River and Portland, Oregon.

Kittredge, William, ed. *Montana Spaces.* New York: Nick Lyons Books, 1988. Evocative essays by the likes of Thomas McGuane and Gretel Ehrlich with perfect black-and-white photos by John Smart.

Kittredge, William, and Annick Smith, eds. *The Last Best Place.* Helena: Montana Historical Society Press, 1988. This 1,158-page compendium anchors down every Montanan's bedside table. From Native American myths to Paul Zarzyski's modern cowboy poems, it's all here.

Krakel, Dean. *Downriver: A Yellowstone Journey.* San Francisco: Sierra Club Press, 1987. The eclectic chronicle of a float trip down the full length of the Yellowstone River.

Maclean, Norman. *A River Runs through It.* Chicago: University of Chicago Press, 1976. The classic novella of fly-fishing and two brothers' love and doomed relationship.

McGuane, Thomas. *Keep the Change.* Boston: Houghton Mifflin, 1989. In this, as in the earlier *Something to Be Desired* and *Nobody's Angel,* tough, sensitive guys try to set their lives straight in Deadrock, Montana (which is a lot like Livingston).

McMurtry, Larry. *Lonesome Dove.* New York: Pocket Books, 1985. A masterfully written epic of the last days of the great Texas cattle drives, told from the point of view of faded but wise-cracking cowboys. Also from McMurtry, *Buffalo Girls* is an engaging saga of Calamity Jane and her gang.

Raban, Jonathan. *Badlands.* New York: Vintage Books, 1996. Rambling narrative that examines the homesteading movement on the eastern Montana plains.

Stegner, Wallace. *Wolf Willow.* New York: Viking Press, 1962. Stegner spent his youth on a homestead *just* north of Montana, in Saskatchewan.

Stockton, Bill. *Today I Baled Some Hay to Feed the Sheep the Coyotes Eat.* Billings and Helena: Falcon Press, 1983. Vignettes by a Montana-raised, Paris-educated writer and illustrator on the vicissitudes of sheep ranching.

Van Cleve, Spike. *A Day Late and a Dollar Short.* Kansas City: Lowell Press, 1982. The full-spirited reminiscences of one of Montana's foremost dude ranchers and storytellers.

Welch, James. *The Indian Lawyer.* New York: W.W. Norton, 1990. A Blackfeet lawyer in Helena finds his life suddenly very complicated . . . it's a page-turner with good insights. Welch's other novels include *Fools Crow, Winter in the Blood,* and *The Death of Jim Loney.*

MAGAZINES

Montana magazine is published in Helena, and is a good collage of history, photography, travel information, discussion of current issues, and whatnot. You're warned: it can become addictive reading. Call (800) 821-3874 in Montana, or (800) 654-1105 out of state for subscription information.

Montana Outdoors is published by the Montana Dept. of Fish, Wildlife, and Parks, and contains the latest information on fishing, hunting, and recreation, and of course, great photography. Call (800) 678-6668 for subscription information.

Montana Atlas & Gazetteer. Freeport, ME: De-Lorme Mapping Co., 1994. A handy collection of topographic maps covering the entire state.

INDEX

CONSERVATION/WILDERNESS AREAS

events: see festivals and events
Eyer Park: 86

F

Fairmont Hot Springs: 265-266
Fairview: 135
Fairweather, Bill: 290, 292
farming: general discussion 20, 22; Bitterroot
  Valley 325; drought, effect of 6, 20; erosion

143-144; land use issues 11; see also
  homesteaders/immigrants; specific place
fauna: 7-10, 61, 116-117, 199, 201, 246, 254,
  256, 315, 324, 338, 399; see also specific
  fauna; place
fax machines: 55
Fergus County Courthouse: 175
ferries: 156-157
Fidler, Peter: 399-400

FESTIVALS/EVENTS

general discussion: 33
Balloon Roundup: 80
Bannack Days: 286
Bigfork Festival of Arts: 362
Big Sky Arts Festival: 212
Charles M. Russell Western Art Auction:
  33, 149
Choteau Rodeo: 169
Chouteau County Fair: 154
College National Finals Rodeo: 33, 222
Crow Fair: 33, 101
Ennis Rodeo: 208
Federation of Fly Fishers Conclave: 250
Festival of Nations: 241
Flathead Festival: 375
Fort Benton Summer Celebration: 154
Fort Union Rendezvous: 134
Fourth of July Powwow: 351
Havre Festival Days: 159
Hays Mission Canyon Dance: 118
Hill County Fair: 159
Intermountain Opera: 222
International Choral Festival: 345
Iron Ring Celebration: 129
Jaycee Bucking Horse Sale: 80
John Colter Run: 206
Lewis and Clark Expedition Festival (Cut
  Bank): 164
Lewis and Clark Festival (Great Falls): 149-
  150
Lewis and Clark Pageant (Three Forks): 206
Little Bighorn Days: 98-99
Livingston Roundup Rodeo: 228
Logger Days: 392
Midland Empire Fair: 70
Milk River Indian Days: 118
Missoula Powwow: 345
Montana Cowboy Poetry Gathering: 33,
  179

Montana Governor's Cup: 125
Montana State Fair: 150
Montana State Fiddlers' Contest: 356
Montana Winter Fair: 222
Mountain Men Rendezvous: 241
National Ski-Joring Finals: 241
Nordicfest: 392
North American Indian Days: 33, 165
Northern International Livestock Exposition:
  33, 70
Northwest Montana Fair: 375
Oil Discovery Celebration: 129
Park County Fair: 228
Pioneer Days (Ennis): 208
Pioneer Days (Ronan): 352
Red Bottom Day: 128
Red Lodge Music Festival: 241
Red Lodge Rodeo: 241
Reenactment of Custer's Last Stand: 33,
  98-99
Rendezvous Cross Country Ski Race: 33,
  250
Rocky Boy Powwow: 159
Standing Arrow Powwow: 357
St. Patrick's Day Parade: 264
Sweet Pea Festival: 33, 222
Taste of Bozeman: 222
Three Forks Rodeo: 206
Tour of Swan River Valley: 345, 364
Two Moons Annual World Peace
  Gathering: 106
Western Montana Fair: 345
Wild Game Cookoff: 208
Wildlife Film Festival: 345
Winter Carnival: 241
Winternational Sports Festival: 264-265
Wolf Point Wild Horse Stampede: 31, 128
World's Champion Pack Horse Race: 236
Yellowstone Boat Float: 28

GUEST RANCHES

MUSEUMS

(continues on next page)

MUSEUMS
(continued)

Museum of the National Park Ranger: 251
Museum of the Northern Great Plains: 153
Museum of the Plains Indian: 164-165
Museum of the Rockies: 217
Museum of the Upper Missouri: 153
Museum of the Yellowstone: 247
Musselshell Valley Historical Museum: 190-191
Nevada City Music Hall: 293
O'Fallon Historical Museum: 90
Old Trail Museum: 166
Paris Gibson Square Museum of Art: 146
Park County Museum: 225
Peter Yegen, Jr. Museum: 67
Phillips County Museum: 121
Pioneer Town: 130
Polson-Flathead Historical Museum: 354
Poplar Museum: 129
Powder River Historical Museum: 96
Powell County Museum: 267
Prairie County Museum: 83
Range Riders Museum: 31, 78

Ravalli County Museum: 327
Richey Historical Museum: 137
Robber's Roost: 293-294
Rosebud County Pioneer Museum: 76
Schoolhouse History & Art Center: 75
Sheridan County Museum: 131
Teton Trail Village: 166
Thompson Falls Historical Museum: 321
Towe Ford Collection: 267
Troy Historical Museum: 388
Upper Musselshell Historical Society Museum: 191
Utica Museum: 197
Valley County Pioneer Museum: 123
Virginia City: 291-292
Western Heritage Center: 65-66
Wibaux County Museum: 89
Wolf Point Area Historical Society Museum: 128
World Museum of Mining: 260
Yellowstone Art Museum: 66
Yesterday's Playthings: 267
see also battlefields/monuments

Montana, Joe: 90
Montana Law Enforcement Museum: 267
Montana Post Building: 291
Montana Rockies Rail Tours: 45
Montana Snowbowl: 340
Montana State Fair: 33, 150
Montana State Fiddlers' Contest: 356
Montana State University: 64, 158, 217, 336
Montana Theatre: 338
Montana Winter Fair: 33, 222
moose: 9, 53; *see also specific place*
Morrell Falls/Lake: 367
Moss Mansion: 66
Mother Lode Theater: 261-262
mountain biking: *see* bicycling/mountain bikes
mountain goats: 9, 256, 399; *see also specific place*
mountain lions: 9, 53, 315; *see also specific place*
Mountain Men Rendezvous: 241
Mountain Sky Guest Ranch: 232

movies: *see* theater/cinema/performing arts
Mt. Baldy: 225
Mt. Brown Lookout: 409
Mt. Haggin Wildlife Management Area: 271
Mt. Helena: 306
Mt. Sentinel: 340
mule deer: 9, 65; *see also specific place*
Mule Ranch Vista: 271
Mullan, John: 317
Mumma, John: 10
Murphy Lake: 394
Murray Hotel: 227
Murray Springs Fish Hatchery: 394
Musselshell: 190
Musselshell River: 180-181, 188, 192
Musselshell Valley Historical Museum: 190-191
Mussigbrod Lake: 279
MV *International*: 423
Myers Ranch Wagon Trains: 92
Myrna Loy Center for the Performing Arts: 305

WEB SITES

ABOUT THE AUTHORS

William McRae

Bill McRae was born in eastern Montana and grew up on his family's ranch. He used his college years as an excuse to travel, attending universities in the U.S., Canada, Scotland, England, and France. He has taught English at several universities, worked as a waiter and bartender, was features editor for a community newspaper, and ran a catering company. In his free time, he enjoys gardening, playing bridge, restoring houses, and buying bargain airline tickets. Other books by Bill include guides to Canada, the Pacific Northwest, Utah, and Seattle. He lives in Portland, Oregon, where he works as a full-time writer.

Judy Jewell

Judy Jewell grew up in Baltimore and retains an affection for both the Orioles and crab cakes. Since moving west in 1977, she's been a biology student, a pizza cook, a bartender, a crayfish-eyestalk plucker, a Forest Service grunt, a health worker, a calligrapher, and a bookseller. She is also author of the Compass American guide to Oregon, and co-author (with Bill McRae) of Lonely Planet's *Pacific Northwest: A Travel Survival Kit*.

MOON TRAVEL HANDBOOKS

LOSE YOURSELF IN THE EXPERIENCE, NOT THE CROWD

For 25 years, Moon Travel Handbooks have been the guidebooks of choice for adventurous travelers. Our award-winning Handbook series provides focused, comprehensive coverage of distinct destinations all over the world. Each Handbook is like an entire bookcase of cultural insight and introductory information in one portable volume. Our goal at Moon is to give travelers all the background and practical information they'll need for an extraordinary travel experience.

The following pages include a complete list of Handbooks, covering North America and Hawaii, Mexico, Latin America and the Caribbean, and Asia and the Pacific. To purchase Moon Travel Handbooks, check your local bookstore or order by phone: (800) 345-5473 M-F 8 am.-5 p.m. PST or outside the U.S. phone: (530) 345-5473.

"An in-depth dunk into the land, the people and their history, arts, and politics."
—*Student Travels*

"I consider these books to be superior to Lonely Planet. When Moon produces a book it is more humorous, incisive, and off-beat."
—*Toronto Sun*

"Outdoor enthusiasts gravitate to the well-written Moon Travel Handbooks. In addition to politically correct historic and cultural features, the series focuses on flora, fauna and outdoor recreation. Maps and meticulous directions also are a trademark of Moon guides."
—*Houston Chronicle*

"Moon [Travel Handbooks] . . . bring a healthy respect to the places they investigate. Best of all, they provide a host of odd nuggets that give a place texture and prod the wary traveler from the beaten path. The finest are written with such care and insight they deserve listing as literature."
—*American Geographical Society*

"Moon Travel Handbooks offer in-depth historical essays and useful maps, enhanced by a sense of humor and a neat, compact format."
—*Swing*

"Perfect for the more adventurous, these are long on history, sightseeing and nitty-gritty information and very price-specific."
—*Columbus Dispatch*

"Moon guides manage to be comprehensive and countercultural at the same time . . . Handbooks are packed with maps, photographs, drawings, and sidebars that constitute a college-level introduction to each country's history, culture, people, and crafts."
—*National Geographic Traveler*

"Few travel guides do a better job helping travelers create their own itineraries than the Moon Travel Handbook series. The authors have a knack for homing in on the essentials."
—**Colorado Springs** *Gazette Telegraph*

MEXICO

"These books will delight the armchair traveler, aid the undecided person in selecting a destination, and guide the seasoned road warrior looking for lesser-known hideaways."

—*Mexican Meanderings* Newsletter

"From tourist traps to off-the-beaten track hideaways, these guides offer consistent, accurate details without pretension."

—*Foreign Service Journal*

Archaeological Mexico	**$19.95**
Andrew Coe	420 pages, 27 maps
Baja Handbook	**$16.95**
Joe Cummings	540 pages, 46 maps
Cabo Handbook	**$14.95**
Joe Cummings	270 pages, 17 maps
Cancún Handbook	**$14.95**
Chicki Mallan	240 pages, 25 maps
Colonial Mexico	**$18.95**
Chicki Mallan	400 pages, 38 maps
Mexico Handbook	**$21.95**
Joe Cummings and Chicki Mallan	1,200 pages, 201 maps
Northern Mexico Handbook	**$17.95**
Joe Cummings	610 pages, 69 maps
Pacific Mexico Handbook	**$17.95**
Bruce Whipperman	580 pages, 68 maps
Puerto Vallarta Handbook	**$14.95**
Bruce Whipperman	330 pages, 36 maps
Yucatán Handbook	**$16.95**
Chicki Mallan	400 pages, 52 maps

LATIN AMERICA AND THE CARIBBEAN

"Solidly packed with practical information and full of significant cultural asides that will enlighten you on the whys and wherefores of things you might easily see but not easily grasp."

—*Boston Globe*

Belize Handbook	**$15.95**
Chicki Mallan and Patti Lange	390 pages, 45 maps
Caribbean Vacations	**$18.95**
Karl Luntta	910 pages, 64 maps
Costa Rica Handbook	**$19.95**
Christopher P. Baker	780 pages, 73 maps
Cuba Handbook	**$19.95**
Christopher P. Baker	740 pages, 70 maps
Dominican Republic Handbook	**$15.95**
Gaylord Dold	420 pages, 24 maps
Ecuador Handbook	**$16.95**
Julian Smith	450 pages, 43 maps
Honduras Handbook	**$15.95**
Chris Humphrey	330 pages, 40 maps
Jamaica Handbook	**$15.95**
Karl Luntta	330 pages, 17 maps
Virgin Islands Handbook	**$13.95**
Karl Luntta	220 pages, 19 maps

NORTH AMERICA AND HAWAII

"These domestic guides convey the same sense of exoticism that their foreign counterparts do, making home-country travel seem like far-flung adventure."

—*Sierra Magazine*

Alaska-Yukon Handbook	**$17.95**
Deke Castleman and Don Pitcher	530 pages, 92 maps
Alberta and the Northwest Territories Handbook	**$17.95**
Andrew Hempstead and Nadina Purdon	530 pages, 72 maps,
Arizona Traveler's Handbook	**$17.95**
Bill Weir and Robert Blake	512 pages, 54 maps
Atlantic Canada Handbook	**$17.95**
Nan Drosdick and Mark Morris	460 pages, 61 maps
Big Island of Hawaii Handbook	**$15.95**
J.D. Bisignani	390 pages, 23 maps

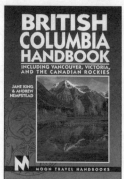

Boston Handbook	**$13.95**
Jeff Perk	200 pages, 20 maps
British Columbia Handbook	**$16.95**
Jane King and Andrew Hempstead	430 pages, 69 maps
Colorado Handbook	**$18.95**
Stephen Metzger	480 pages, 59 maps
Georgia Handbook	**$17.95**
Kap Stann	370 pages, 50 maps
Hawaii Handbook	**$19.95**
J.D. Bisignani	1,030 pages, 90 maps
Honolulu-Waikiki Handbook	**$14.95**
J.D. Bisignani	400 pages, 20 maps
Idaho Handbook	**$18.95**
Don Root	610 pages, 42 maps
Kauai Handbook	**$15.95**
J.D. Bisignani	320 pages, 23 maps
Maine Handbook	**$18.95**
Kathleen M. Brandes	660 pages, 27 maps
Massachusetts Handbook	**$18.95**
Jeff Perk	600 pages, 23 maps
Maui Handbook	**$15.95**
J.D. Bisignani	420 pages, 35 maps
Michigan Handbook	**$15.95**
Tina Lassen	300 pages, 30 maps
Montana Handbook	**$17.95**
Judy Jewell and W.C. McRae	480 pages, 52 maps
Nevada Handbook	**$18.95**
Deke Castleman	530 pages, 40 maps
New Hampshire Handbook	**$18.95**
Steve Lantos	500 pages, 18 maps
New Mexico Handbook	**$15.95**
Stephen Metzger	360 pages, 47 maps
New York Handbook	**$19.95**
Christiane Bird	780 pages, 95 maps
New York City Handbook	**$13.95**
Christiane Bird	300 pages, 20 maps
North Carolina Handbook	**$14.95**
Rob Hirtz and Jenny Daughtry Hirtz	275 pages, 25 maps
Northern California Handbook	**$19.95**
Kim Weir	800 pages, 50 maps
Oregon Handbook	**$17.95**
Stuart Warren and Ted Long Ishikawa	588 pages, 34 maps
Pennsylvania Handbook	**$18.95**
Joanne Miller	448 pages, 40 maps

Road Trip USA	$22.50
Jamie Jensen	800 pages, 165 maps
Santa Fe-Taos Handbook	**$13.95**
Stephen Metzger	160 pages, 13 maps
Southern California Handbook	**$19.95**
Kim Weir	720 pages, 26 maps
Tennessee Handbook	**$17.95**
Jeff Bradley	530 pages, 44 maps
Texas Handbook	**$18.95**
Joe Cummings	690 pages, 70 maps
Utah Handbook	**$17.95**
Bill Weir and W.C. McRae	490 pages, 40 maps
Virginia Handbook	**$15.95**
Julian Smith	340 pages, 30 maps
Washington Handbook	**$19.95**
Don Pitcher	870 pages, 113 maps
Wisconsin Handbook	**$18.95**
Thomas Huhti	590 pages, 69 maps
Wyoming Handbook	**$17.95**
Don Pitcher	610 pages, 80 maps

ASIA AND THE PACIFIC

"Scores of maps, detailed practical info down to business hours of small-town libraries. You can't beat the Asian titles for sheer heft. (The) series is sort of an American Lonely Planet, with better writing but fewer titles. (The) individual voice of researchers comes through."

—Travel & Leisure

Australia Handbook	**$21.95**
Marael Johnson, Andrew Hempstead, and Nadina Purdon	940 pages, 141 maps
Bali Handbook	**$19.95**
Bill Dalton	750 pages, 54 maps
Bangkok Handbook	**$13.95**
Michael Buckley	244 pages, 30 maps
Fiji Islands Handbook	**$14.95**
David Stanley	300 pages, 38 maps
Hong Kong Handbook	**$16.95**
Kerry Moran	378 pages, 49 maps
Indonesia Handbook	**$25.00**
Bill Dalton	1,380 pages, 249 maps

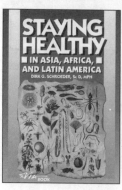

Micronesia Handbook	**$14.95**
Neil M. Levy	340 pages, 70 maps
Nepal Handbook	**$18.95**
Kerry Moran	490 pages, 51 maps
New Zealand Handbook	**$19.95**
Jane King	620 pages, 81 maps
Outback Australia Handbook	**$18.95**
Marael Johnson	450 pages, 57 maps
Philippines Handbook	**$17.95**
Peter Harper and Laurie Fullerton	670 pages, 116 maps
Singapore Handbook	**$15.95**
Carl Parkes	350 pages, 29 maps
South Korea Handbook	**$19.95**
Robert Nilsen	820 pages, 141 maps
South Pacific Handbook	**$22.95**
David Stanley	920 pages, 147 maps
Southeast Asia Handbook	**$21.95**
Carl Parkes	1,080 pages, 204 maps
Tahiti-Polynesia Handbook	**$15.95**
David Stanley	380 pages, 35 maps
Thailand Handbook	**$19.95**
Carl Parkes	860 pages, 142 maps
Vietnam, Cambodia & Laos Handbook	**$18.95**
Michael Buckley	760 pages, 116 maps

OTHER GREAT TITLES FROM MOON

"For hardy wanderers, few guides come more highly recommended than the Handbooks. They include good maps, steer clear of fluff and flackery, and offer plenty of money-saving tips. They also give you the kind of information that visitors to strange lands—on any budget—need to survive."

—*US News & World Report*

Moon Handbook	**$10.00**
Carl Koppeschaar	141 pages, 8 maps
The Practical Nomad: How to Travel Around the World	**$17.95**
Edward Hasbrouck	575 pages
Staying Healthy in Asia, Africa, and Latin America	**$11.95**
Dirk Schroeder	230 pages, 4 maps

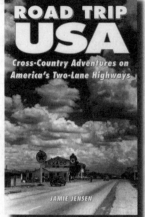

WHERE TO BUY MOON TRAVEL HANDBOOKS

BOOKSTORES AND LIBRARIES: Moon Travel Handbooks are distributed worldwide. Please contact our sales manager for a list of wholesalers and distributors in your area.

TRAVELERS: We would like to have Moon Travel Handbooks available throughout the world. Please ask your bookstore to write or call us for ordering information. If your bookstore will not order our guides for you, please contact us for a free catalog.

> **Moon Travel Handbooks**
> **P.O. Box 3040**
> **Chico, CA 95927-3040 U.S.A.**
> **tel.: (800) 345-5473, outside the U.S. (530) 345-5473**
> **fax: (530) 345-6751**
> **e-mail: travel@moon.com**

IMPORTANT ORDERING INFORMATION

PRICES: All prices are subject to change. We always ship the most current edition. We will let you know if there is a price increase on the book you order.

SHIPPING AND HANDLING OPTIONS: Domestic UPS or USPS first class (allow 10 working days for delivery): $4.50 for the first item, $1.00 for each additional item.

Moonbelt shipping is $1.50 for one, 50 cents for each additional belt.

UPS 2nd Day Air or Printed Airmail requires a special quote.

International Surface Bookrate 8-12 weeks delivery: $4.00 for the first item, $1.00 for each additional item. Note: We cannot guarantee international surface bookrate shipping. We recommend sending international orders via air mail, which requires a special quote.

FOREIGN ORDERS: Orders that originate outside the U.S.A. must be paid for with an international money order, a check in U.S. currency drawn on a major U.S. bank based in the U.S.A., or Visa, MasterCard, or Discover.

TELEPHONE ORDERS: We accept Visa, MasterCard, or Discover payments. Call in your order: (800) 345-5473, 8 a.m.-5 p.m. Pacific standard time. Outside the U.S. the number is (530) 345-5473.

INTERNET ORDERS: Visit our site at: www.moon.com

NOTES

ORDER FORM

Prices are subject to change without notice. Be sure to call (800) 345-5473,
or (530) 345-5473 from outside the U.S. 8 a.m.–5 p.m. PST for current prices and editions.
(See important ordering information on preceding page.)

Name: _____ Date: _____

Street: _____

City: _____ Daytime Phone: _____

State or Country: _____ Zip Code: _____

QUANTITY	TITLE	PRICE

Taxable Total_____

Sales Tax (7.25%) for California Residents_____

Shipping & Handling_____

TOTAL_____

Ship: ☐ UPS (no P.O. Boxes)   ☐ 1st class   ☐ International surface mail
Ship to: ☐ address above   ☐ other _____

_____

Make checks payable to: **MOON TRAVEL HANDBOOKS**, P.O. Box 3040, Chico, CA 95927-3040
U.S.A. We accept Visa, MasterCard, or Discover. **To Order**: Call in your Visa, MasterCard, or Discover number,
or send a written order with your Visa, MasterCard, or Discover number and expiration date clearly written.

Card Number: ☐ **Visa**   ☐ **MasterCard**   ☐ **Discover**

☐ ☐ ☐ ☐   ☐ ☐ ☐ ☐   ☐ ☐ ☐ ☐   ☐ ☐ ☐ ☐

Exact Name on Card: _____

Expiration date:_____

Signature: _____

U.S.~METRIC CONVERSION

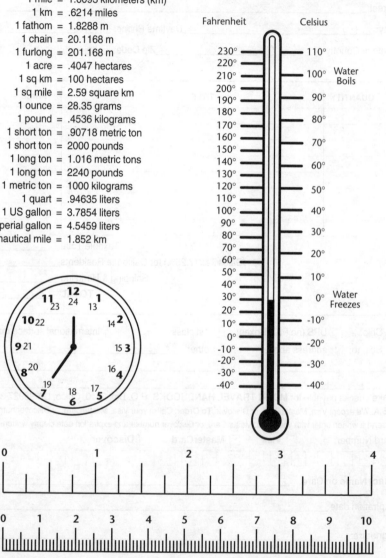

1 inch = 2.54 centimeters (cm)
1 foot = .304 meters (m)
1 yard = 0.914 meters
1 mile = 1.6093 kilometers (km)
1 km = .6214 miles
1 fathom = 1.8288 m
1 chain = 20.1168 m
1 furlong = 201.168 m
1 acre = .4047 hectares
1 sq km = 100 hectares
1 sq mile = 2.59 square km
1 ounce = 28.35 grams
1 pound = .4536 kilograms
1 short ton = .90718 metric ton
1 short ton = 2000 pounds
1 long ton = 1.016 metric tons
1 long ton = 2240 pounds
1 metric ton = 1000 kilograms
1 quart = .94635 liters
1 US gallon = 3.7854 liters
1 Imperial gallon = 4.5459 liters
1 nautical mile = 1.852 km

To compute celsius temperatures, subtract 32 from Fahrenheit and divide by 1.8. To go the other way, multiply celsius by 1.8 and add 32.

Fahrenheit   Celsius

230°   110°
220°
210°   100° Water Boils
200°
190°   90°
180°
170°   80°
160°
150°   70°
140°   60°
130°
120°   50°
110°
100°   40°
90°
80°   30°
70°
60°   20°
50°
40°   10°
30°   0°   Water Freezes
20°
10°   -10°
0°
-10°   -20°
-20°   -30°
-30°
-40°   -40°

inch 0   1   2   3   4

cm 0 1 2 3 4 5 6 7 8 9 10